NORTHERN
CALIFORNIA

Welcome to Northern California

It's easy to tap into the good life in Northern California. Indulge in rounds of golf at Pebble Beach, and then follow scenic trails through Yosemite National Park. Sip wine at picturesque Napa and Sonoma vineyards, and then dine in stellar locavore restaurants. Urban pleasures await, too. San Francisco's cable cars zip you through vibrant neighborhoods filled with chic boutiques and cutting-edge museums. Note, though, that this book was produced in the middle of the COVID-19 pandemic. As you plan your upcoming travels, please confirm that places are still open and let us know when we need to make updates at editors@ fodors.com.

TOP REASONS TO GO

★ **San Francisco:** This diverse city beguiles with natural beauty and contagious energy.

★ **Wine Country:** Top-notch whites and reds in Napa, Sonoma, and beyond.

★ **Feasts:** Cutting-edge cuisine, food trucks, fusion flavors, farmers' markets.

★ **Stunning Scenery:** Picture-perfect backdrops from the Golden Gate Bridge to redwood forests.

★ **Outdoor Adventures:** National park excursions, hiking, and golfing are all excellent.

★ **Road Trips:** The Pacific Coast Highway offers spectacular views and thrills aplenty.

Contents

Fodor's Features

MAPS

Chapter 1

EXPERIENCE NORTHERN CALIFORNIA

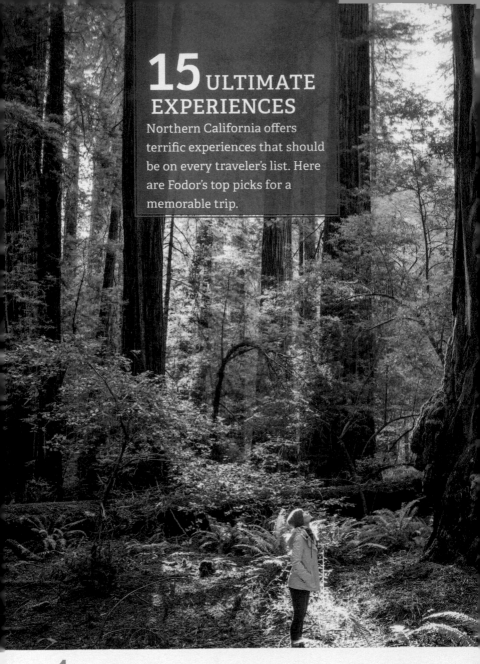

15 ULTIMATE EXPERIENCES

Northern California offers terrific experiences that should be on every traveler's list. Here are Fodor's top picks for a memorable trip.

1 Crane Your Neck at Redwood National and State Parks

Redwood National and State Parks have the tallest trees on Earth (300–400 feet) and hug 40 miles of California coastline. There are countless things to see and do including camping, hiking, fishing, and kayaking. *(Ch. 14)*

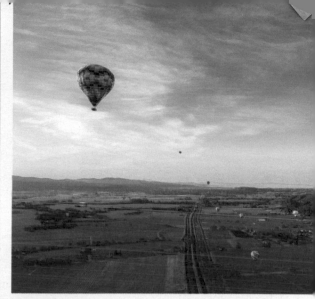

2 Enjoy the View from a Hot-Air Balloon

It's worth rising early for a balloon ride at dawn over vineyards in either Napa or Sonoma. *(Ch. 12)*

3 Ogle General Sherman

Sequoia National Park's General Sherman tree is the largest living tree in the world, at 275 feet tall and 36 feet in diameter at its roots. *(Ch. 5)*

4 Hike the Pacific Crest Trail

The Pacific Crest Trail stretches 2,659 miles along the U.S. coast from Mexico to Canada. It peaks at Forester Pass in Kings Canyon National Park, at 13,153 feet. *(Ch. 5)*

5 Commune with Nature at Yosemite National Park

Nestled in the Sierra Nevada, Yosemite National Park is known for its giant sequoia trees, epic waterfalls, and abundant wildlife. *(Ch. 6)*

6 Witness Greatness in Sport

Sports fans have their pick of great Northern California teams, including the Giants or '49ers in San Francisco and the Golden State Warriors in Oakland. *(Chs.10 and 11).*

7 Spot Whales in Monterey

Depending on the season, you can charter boats to view migrating gray, humpback, and blue whales. Monterey is also prime territory for killer whales, bottlenose dolphins, and more. *(Ch. 4)*

8 Get an Adrenaline Rush at Lake Tahoe

Straddling California and Nevada, Lake Tahoe is a wonderland for adventure enthusiasts year-round, with world-class skiing in winter and lake sports in summer. *(Ch. 9)*

9 Drink all the Wine

Don't tell the French, but the best wine is from Napa and Sonoma counties. Both are flush with world-class wineries. *(Ch. 12)*

10 Dive into History in San Francisco's Chinatown

San Francisco's Chinatown is the largest outside of Asia and the oldest in the U.S. Don't miss the Dragon Gate, Golden Gate Fortune Cookie Factory, and the Old Telephone Exchange. *(Ch. 10)*

11 Take the Scenic 17-Mile Drive

This stretch of road in Pebble Beach takes you past enchanting sights, like Fanshell Beach, Point Joe, the Lone Cypress, and more. (Ch. 4)

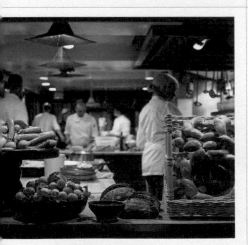

12 Eat Your Way Through Berkeley

Explore Berkeley's campus, and then dine in the nearby Gourmet Ghetto (Shattuck Avenue), where chef Alice Waters got her start. (Ch. 11)

13 Play Arcade Games at Musée Mécanique

This quirky "museum" at Fisherman's Wharf in San Francisco has more than 200 antique arcade games, including coin-operated fortune tellers, moving dioramas, and stereoscopes. *(Ch. 10)*

14 Ski at Mammoth

Mammoth Mountain (a dormant volcano) is the largest ski resort in California; its 3,500 acres of skiable area hosts millions of skiers and snowboarders each year. *(Ch. 7)*

15 Cross the Golden Gate Bridge

Opened in 1937, the Golden Gate Bridge is one of the most iconic symbols of San Francisco. Visitors can cross the mile-long suspension bridge by foot, bicycle, or car. *(Ch. 10)*

California Today

"Has the Golden State Lost Its Luster?" "Is the California Dream Dead?" So read the rueful headlines upon the early-2021 announcement of California's first-ever population decline (in 2020) and, based on recent census data, the loss of a congressional seat. These articles and similar pieces detailed the supposedly insurmountable obstacles—most notably the high cost of living (especially housing), but also wildfires, drought, crime, traffic congestion, homelessness, COVID-19, and high taxes—fueling out-of-state migration.

So dire were some of the assessments that one might have assumed there was no reason to stay (or come for a visit). This was despite the fact that everything that has lured settlers and tourists from the get-go—among them breathtaking scenery, abundant natural resources, agricultural bounty, and a hospitable climate—remains well in evidence.

Although California, like the rest of the nation and world, faces daunting challenges, the same gloomy predictions (often bearing precisely the same "lost its luster" and "dream dead" headlines) have appeared before: in the middle of the Great Recession (2009), after the first dot-com implosion (2000), all the way back to the gold and silver busts of the 19th century. And guess what? In every instance, the state bounced back, sometimes brilliantly.

Each allegedly ruinous calamity required reinvention, and each time residents rose to the occasion. Based on the past, there's no reason to think that the Golden State won't regain its luster—if it's even been lost.

POPULATION, POTENTIAL

California's birth rate and the pace of migration may have slowed, but they're hardly stagnant. For perspective, consider that the current population of just under 40 million (an eighth of the U.S. total) represents a 2.2 million increase between 2010 and 2020, the third-highest after Texas and Florida. While many residents departing California cite the high cost of living, recent transplants tend to perceive the same potential in the state as previous settlers.

HISTORICAL CONTEXT

By most accounts, the ancestors of California's indigenous peoples migrated from Asia, traversing a land bridge across the Bering Strait that formerly joined what's now Russia and Alaska. Some of these trailblazers continued south to California, flourishing for centuries off the fertile land. Many famous place names—Malibu, Napa, Ojai, Shasta, and Sonoma among them—reflect this heritage.

Millennia later, Spanish explorers ventured north from Mexico searching for gold, with converts to Christianity the quest of 18th-century missionaries. Nineteenth-century miners rushed here from the world over also seeking gold—the state achieved statehood two years after the precious metal's 1848 discovery.

During the 20th century, successive, sometimes overlapping, waves of newcomers followed in their footsteps: real-estate speculators, would-be motion-picture actors and producers, Dust Bowl farmers and migrant workers, Asians fleeing poverty or chasing opportunity, sexual and gender pioneers, artists, dot-commers, and venture capitalists.

POLITICS

The result is a population that leans toward idealism (some say utopianism)—without necessarily being as liberal as voter-registration statistics might lead one to think. (Democrats hold a 2–1 registration advantage over Republicans, the latter essentially tied with "no party preference.") This is Ronald Reagan's old stomping ground after all, and Herbert Hoover's, and Richard Nixon was born here. If you wander into some inland counties, you may see signs proposing a breakaway, more conservative 51st State of Jefferson. Many residents in these areas supported 2021 efforts to recall Governor Gavin Newsom, a liberal Democrat. (Early summer polls indicated the special-election race might be tight, but the governor prevailed by a substantial margin.)

DEMOGRAPHICS

As with politics, despite the stereotype of the blue-eyed, blond surfer, California's population isn't homogeneous either. Latino residents outnumber Whites 39%–36%, with Asians (15%) and African Americans (6%) the next-largest groups. Residents here speak more than 220 languages, making California by far the nation's most linguistically diverse state.

ECONOMICS

Back to California's supposedly desperate situation: keep in mind that, in 2021, the Golden State reported a $75 billion budget *surplus*, hardly numbers to prompt despair and proving the Great Recession doomsayers predicting economic catastrophe way off the mark. California, responsible for 14% of gross domestic product, leads all other states in terms of the income generated by agriculture, tourism, entertainment, and industrial activity. With a gross state product of approximately $3 trillion (median household income about $75,000), by many estimates, California would have the world's fifth-largest economy were it an independent nation.

STILL DREAMIN'

In mid-2021, dueling state-of-the-state analyses appeared within days of each other. A historian's *New York Times* opinion piece described the 2020 census numbers and the loss of the seat in Congress as among recent negative "firsts" for California that had "sapped the collective sense of zealous optimism." The historian also predicted "decades of pain" if politicians don't quickly produce solutions to California's pressing problems.

Two days before the *Times* piece ran, the University of California published a study suggesting pretty much the opposite: that the rate of residents moving out of state is not unusual and isn't something to fret over; that residents, by a 2–1 majority, still believe in the California Dream; and that the state attracts more than half the nation's venture-capital investments, a sign that favorable economic conditions persist.

The naysayers may well be right about California's demise, but if history is any indication, the populace will likely shift gears as necessary. And again the next time it's required.

WHAT'S WHERE

1 Monterey Bay Area. Postcard-perfect Monterey, Victorian-flavored Pacific Grove, and exclusive Carmel all share this stretch of California coast. To the north, Santa Cruz boasts a boardwalk, a UC campus, and plenty of surfers.

2 Sequoia and Kings Canyon National Parks. Breathtaking—with towering redwoods and jagged mountains.

3 Yosemite National Park. Immortalized by photographer Ansel Adams, the granite monoliths, verdant valleys, and lofty waterfalls are still camera ready.

4 Eastern Sierra. In the Mammoth Lakes region, sawtooth mountains and deep powdery snowdrifts beckon winter-sport enthusiasts.

5 Sacramento and the Gold Country. The 1849 gold rush began here, and the former mining camps along 185 miles of Highway 49 replay the past.

6 Lake Tahoe. High Sierra peaks reflected in crystalline waters make the perfect setting for year-round outdoor activities.

7 San Francisco. To see why many have left their hearts here, you need only explore the city's iconic neighborhoods.

8 The Bay Area. The area that rings San Francisco is home to some of the nation's great universities, fabulous water views, Silicon Valley, and Alice Waters's Chez Panisse.

9 Napa and Sonoma. Acclaimed vintages, luxe lodgings, and epicurean eats—these counties still comprise *the* California Wine Country.

10 The North Coast. Secluded beaches, wave-battered bluffs, and towering redwood forests are among the attractions here.

11 Redwood National and State Parks. More than 200 miles of trails, ranging from easy to strenuous, travel amid the redwoods.

12 The Far North. Snowcapped Mt. Shasta, pristine wilderness, and abundant backwoods character are highlights here.

What to Eat and Drink in Northern California

Oysters

SOURDOUGH BREAD
In California, sourdough history is tied to the Gold Rush, when French bakers set up shop in San Francisco to feed the miners. For the perfect loaf, head to Boudin Bakery in San Francisco where they've been perfecting their sourdough recipe since 1849.

WINE
You could throw a rock and hit a world-class wine up and down the coast of California. Monterey, Napa, and Sonoma all have some of the best vintages on the planet.

FRESH PACIFIC SEAFOOD
You don't have to go far to find seafood, most of it freshly sourced from the waters off California. Always check out the day's catch—shucked and placed on ice or served in a sandwich, salad, or other dish.

IRISH COFFEE

Inspired by a drink in Ireland, the owner of the Buena Vista in San Francisco set out to re-create the concoction and stumbled upon what we now know as an Irish Coffee. The mixture of coffee, whiskey, and floating cream can still be enjoyed out of a chalice at the same Buena Vista location since its humble beginnings.

BURGERS

If there's any debate about the home of the burger, just ask Fat Burger, Carl's Jr, McDonald's, In-N-Out, Umami Burger, The Habit Burger Grill, Hamburger Mary's, Johnny Rockets, The Counter, Original Tommy's, and Jack in the Box, which all started in the Golden State.

SUSHI

Outside of Japan, there is no better place to eat raw fish than in California. At Akiko in San Francisco, you can find the freshest, most savory cuts of fish that rivals any place in the world.

CHEESE

Wisconsin? Please. The best cheese is clearly from California. Have you heard of Humboldt Fog? That comes from Cypress Grove in Humboldt County. How about Red Hawk, that gooey triple-crème that melts in your mouth? Marin County. And cheddar? Sorry Wisconsin, but Fiscalini Bandaged Cheddar from Modesto has you beat any day of the week.

VEGETARIAN FOOD

Californians are known to be health conscious, eating lots of fresh local produce (including adding avocado to everything). There are plentiful vegetarian and vegan options throughout the state.

BEER

California is a hotbed of beer-making, and craft brewers are dominating the beer scene like never before. Check out 21st Amendment in San Francisco.

MAI TAIS

White rum, dark rum, Curaçao liqueur, orgeat syrup, and lime juice makes the perfect Mai Tai. The drink was invented (allegedly) by Victor Bergeron in 1944 of the famed restaurant Trader Vic's in Oakland, California, though Donn Beach (of Don the Beachcomber fame) claims he invented it in the 1930s in Hollywood.

10 Best Photo Ops in San Francisco

THE PALACE OF FINE ARTS

This stirringly lovely, terracotta-color, domed structure on a lagoon near the Marina's yacht harbor has an otherworldly quality about it. Built in 1915 for an exposition, the palace is a San Francisco architect's version of a Roman ruin, and it's been eliciting gasps ever since. It's a popular wedding spot, which is good if you like happy couples in your photos.

THE PAINTED LADIES

Familiar to fans of the 1990s' TV show *Full House*, the so-called Painted Ladies or Seven Sisters are a row of seven colorful and beautifully maintained Queen Anne–style houses just off Alamo Square Park. Take photos at midday for clear city views.

TWIN PEAKS

These two adjacent peaks near Noe Valley are at the near geographic center of San Francisco, with an elevation of 925 feet. Especially pretty (and popular, but chilly) at sunrise and sunset, the peaks provide sweeping 180-degree views of the Bay Area, with a great perspective on downtown San Francisco, the Bay Bridge, and the tips of the Golden Gate Bridge.

LANDS END COASTAL TRAIL

This 4-mile trail winds and twists along the rugged cliffs of San Francisco Bay, offering stunning views of the Golden Gate Bridge and surprisingly woodsy forest. At the 1.3-mile mark, turn left at the wooden staircase to explore Mile Rock Beach and the Lands End Labyrinth. On a clear day, you can see the Golden Gate Bridge in the distance.

THE PRESIDIO

As the gateway to the Golden Gate Bridge, San Francisco's 1,500-acre Presidio is part of the National Park System and offers incredible views of the bridge and the sprawling landscape that surrounds it. The Presidio also abuts Baker Beach, a stretch of sand with an alternative perspective.

MUIR WOODS NATIONAL MONUMENT

Naturalist John Muir wrote, "Most people are on the world, not in it—have no conscious sympathy or relationship to anything about them ..." It's hard not to feel connected as you walk the shaded paths of Muir Woods amid the towering majesty of the redwood groves.

UNION SQUARE

This lively and central location is a great spot to capture cable cars as they rumble by. Also, the towering Dewey Monument pillar, topped triumphantly by Nike, the Greek goddess of victory, is a legitimately beautiful sculpture. Relax on the steps and soak in or photograph the city.

Treasure Island

TREASURE ISLAND

Tiny, man-made Treasure Island is generally off the tourist track, so your photos won't be crowded with selfie-takers. Sitting right in the middle of San Francisco Bay, it offers gorgeous views of the San Francisco skyline, especially at night when everything is lit up.

HAWK HILL

At a high point on the south-facing Marin Headlands, Hawk Hill lies opposite the city with vistas of the Pacific and of the Golden Gate Bridge as it enters San Francisco. True to its name, it's also a great spot for nature watching. Hawk Hill is the site of the autumnal raptor migration and also serves as a habitat for the Mission Blue Butterfly.

BERNAL HEIGHTS

This somewhat stumpy-looking mound rises unenthusiastically above the houses of the surrounding neighborhood. But, pictures taken *from* Bernal Heights Hill offer 360-degree panoramic views. Take a sunset stroll here for stunning San Fran shots.

What to Read and Watch

WINE COUNTRY WOMEN OF NAPA VALLEY BY MICHELLE MANDRO AND DONA KOPOL BONIK

Winemakers, chefs, executives, and other women holding key positions share insights and recipes in this large-format volume filled with photography.

THE MALTESE FALCON BY DASHIELL HAMMETT

There was a time when San Francisco's most notorious antiheroes weren't billionaires in T-shirts, but rather chain-smoking, hard-boiled detectives. In *The Maltese Falcon,* detective Sam Spade criss-crosses an atmospheric 1930s San Francisco to locate a jeweled statue. Dashiell Hammett's novel is a legendary piece of noir fiction, but the film, which starred an in-his-prime Humphrey Bogart, is also a classic.

THE GIRLS BY EMMA CLINE

In this nuanced coming-of-age story set in the Sonoma County town of Petaluma, the 14-year-old narrator yearns for excitement, attention, and beauty—and falls into the violent, psychological mind-trip of a Charles Manson–like cult. Beautiful and gripping, Cline's novel shares a gritty, late 1960s Sonoma County—one that couldn't be further from today's world of Cabernets and Pinots.

GUN, WITH OCCASIONAL MUSIC BY JONATHAN LETHEM

Lethem started his career with a captivating but decidedly weird novel set in San Francisco and Oakland. In this sci-fi noir detective story, people rub elbows with talking, man-sized, genetically engineered animals, and everyone lives under a monetized "karma" system like that used in modern-day China to track and influence its citizens.

BURMA SUPERSTAR BY DESMOND TAN AND KATE LEAHY

Burmese food is increasingly popular in San Francisco, where the Burma Superstar restaurant is a hit. This cookbook offers a look into the flavor-packed southeast Asian cuisine.

THE MAYOR OF CASTRO STREET BY RANDY SHILTS

Randy Shilts's biography of gay civil rights icon Harvey Milk is perhaps the most well-regarded and authoritative reckoning of his life to date. Milk was a bombastic, iconic figure whose advocacy and brutal murder permanently shaped the political landscape of not just San Francisco, but the entire country.

MR. PENUMBRA'S 24-HOUR BOOKSTORE BY ROBIN SLOAN

This novel about a quirky used-book store in San Francisco does double duty. Not only is it a story of mystery, love, code-breaking, secret societies, and adopted and inherited culture, but it's also a narrative about the dangers of rapid technological advancement (and of rejecting technology), tribalism, and other timely issues.

NOSE: A NOVEL BY JAMES CONAWAY

A fictitious Northern California wine-making region—couldn't be Napa or Sonoma, could it?—is the setting for a mystery.

THE BIRDS

Alfred Hitchcock's 1963 *The Birds* centers around a small Northern Californian town under attack by swarming, possessed birds. Although, you'll never again look at a crow in quite the same way after watching this graphic thriller, it also showcases the beauty of Sonoma County's coast and the charm of Bodega Bay, the town where most of the movie was filmed.

Chapter 2

TRAVEL SMART

Updated by
Daniel Mangin

★ **CAPITAL:**
Sacramento

👥 **POPULATION:**
39.5 million

💬 **LANGUAGE:**
English

$ **CURRENCY:**
U.S. dollar

📞 **COUNTRY CODE:**
1

⚠ **EMERGENCIES:**
911

🚗 **DRIVING:**
On the right

⚡ **ELECTRICITY:**
120–240 v/60 cycles;
plugs have two or three
rectangular prongs

🕐 **TIME:**
Three hours behind New
York

🌐 **WEB RESOURCES:**
www.visitcalifornia.com,
www.parks.ca.gov, dot.
ca.gov/travel, travel.state.
gov

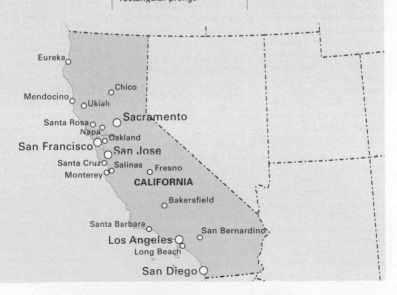

Know Before You Go

To help you prepare for a visit to the vast, diverse, unique state of California, below are tips about driving, destinations, the weather, saving money at restaurants and hotels, wildlife, cannabis tourism, and things to see and do that may save you time or money or increase peace of mind.

ROAD TRIPS TAKE TIME

California has some of the most scenic drives in the world. It's also the third-largest state behind Alaska and Texas and, in square miles, is similar in size to Sweden, Japan, or Paraguay. So, if you want to see all its beaches, deserts, mountains, and forests, you'll need a car—and, perhaps, a bit of patience.

A road trip through even half of the state takes several hours in the best of traffic (frequently not the case), and this doesn't count contending with winding, mountainous terrain or coastal fog. Rule of thumb: factor in an extra 20% or 25% more time than the GPS driving estimate to reduce the chance you'll miss events or connections. Who knows? You might be pleasantly surprised and arrive early—or at least on time.

DON'T LET GPS LEAD YOU ASTRAY

"Your GPS is Wrong: Turn Around," warns a sign on a steep dead-end road that some smartphone mapping apps mistake for a small mountain town's main drag below. Although GPS is generally reliable in cities and suburbs, it's less so in coastal, mountain, and desert areas, including some national and state parks. In addition to referencing the maps in this book, back yourself up with old-school atlases or fold-out paper maps.

If you plot out a trip and begin navigation while your smartphone reception is good, you should still receive turning directions even if you move out of cell range. If you're already out of range when initiating a destination search, however, you won't be able to access route information.

THE COAST CAN BE FOGGY IN SUNNY CA

California rightfully earns its sunny reputation: on average, the sun shines more than two-thirds of the year in most regions, but with deserts, beaches, mountains, and forests, you should prepare for wide variations in both temperature and conditions. This is especially true along the coast and at higher altitudes, where it's best to dress in layers year-round. On a day when it's 85 or 95 degrees inland, the temperature along the coast can be 55 and windy.

In July and August, hot inland temperatures often cause cooler Pacific Ocean air—in the form of fog—to blanket areas nearest the shore. As a rule along the coast: the farther south you go, the drier and hotter the weather tends to be. The farther north, the cooler and wetter you're likely to find it.

"WINE COUNTRY" IS MORE THAN NAPA AND SONOMA

Modern California winemaking got its start in Sonoma County, and Napa Valley wines raised the state's profile worldwide, but with about 4,000 wineries from the Oregon border to San Diego County producing nearly ¾ billion gallons—80-plus percent of the U.S. total—the whole state's pretty much "Wine Country." Tasting rooms abound, even in unlikely places.

The top red-wine grapes include Cabernet Sauvignon, Pinot Noir, Zinfandel, and Merlot. Among the whites, Chardonnay is by far the most planted, with French Colombard, Sauvignon Blanc, and Pinot Gris the runners-up.

NO NEED TO BREAK THE BANK

Away from coastal California or the eastern mountains on summer weekends or during ski season, much of California is affordable. In some cases, it's even a bargain. Tasting fees in lesser-known wine regions, for example, are at least half the price of those in high-profile ones, and some wineries even provide sips for free. In many inland areas, except for the fanciest bed-and-break-fasts, room rates trend way lower than by the shore.

AVOIDING STICKER SHOCK AT RESTAURANTS
Even if you're not dining at temples of haute cuisine, eating out in California can induce sticker shock. There are several ways to avoid this. Have the day's fancy meal at brunch or lunch, when prices tend to be lower. Happy hour, when a restaurant might serve a signature appetizer or smaller version of a famous plate at a lower price, is another option. Even small towns in the interior are likely to have a purveyor or two of gourmet food to go, making picnicking in a park or eating back at your lodging a viable strategy.

AVOIDING STICKER SHOCK AT HOTELS
California's hotels, inns, and resorts are the most expensive from late spring to early fall. The easiest way to avoid sticker shock is to come during winter when, except at ski resorts and a few desert hot spots, prices are the least expensive. Year-round you can save money by traveling midweek, when rates tend to drop. Visiting during the shoulder seasons of mid-to-late spring and mid-to-late fall, when the weather can be nice and the crowds less formidable, can also save you money.

Many travelers cut costs by booking a big-city business hotel on the weekend, when rates trend lower (with Sunday often the cheapest night of the week at such places). Conversely, weekend prices at beach or countryside resorts are generally high but sometimes drop midweek.

MAKERS AND MUSEUMS
The state's early-21st-century DIY types birthed what's come to be known as the maker movement, and throughout California you'll see evidence of this artisanal activity. Blue jeans, lasers, Apple computers, sourdough bread, Popsicles, McDonald's, Barbie Dolls, Hollywood movie glamour, and television all emerged from California. Nearly 3,000 museums (more than any other state) honor such accomplishments and more—if you can think of it, there's probably a museum here that celebrates it.

PLAY BALL
The weather is great year-round, so there's a dynamic sports culture in the Golden State. Spectacular (and often free) recreation areas and parks offer opportunities for surfing, skiing, hiking, and biking, among other activities.

If you're more into spectating, California supports more professional sports teams than any other state, including five MLB, four NBA (plus one WNBA), three NFL and NHL franchises, and several (men's and women's) soccer squads. Any day of the week, you can witness athletic greatness at the highest levels.

CALL OF THE WILDLIFE
Off the coast, creatures from gray and humpback whales to blue whales and orcas might come into view, along with sea lions, elephant seals, dolphins, and the occasional shark. Inland forests contain black bears, mountain lions, bobcats, beavers, and foxes. The desert supplies no end of reptiles, and the entire state is a birder's paradise.

Wild animals generally avoid interacting with humans, but contact is not unheard of. Most state and national parks post advice about steering clear of potentially dangerous encounters and what to do if you find yourself in one.

POT IS LEGAL, BUT...
Marijuana is legal in California for medical and recreational purposes. If you're 21 (or 18 with a doctor's order) and have proof of age or medical status, you can acquire and use marijuana, albeit not always in public. The California Cannabis Portal website maintains a searchable database (⊕ search. cannabis.ca.gov/retailers) of licensed dispensaries, where cannabis might come as flowers, edibles, and concentrates, among other things. The Cannabis Travel Association (⊕ www. cannabistravelassociation. org) promotes "safe and responsible cannabis tourism," and provides general information.

Getting Here and Around

From San Francisco To:	By Air	By Car
San Jose	No flights	1 hr
Monterey	N/A (no nonstops)	2 hrs
Los Angeles	1 hr 30 mins	5 hrs 40 mins
Portland, OR	1 hr 50 mins	10 hrs
Mendocino	No flights	3 hrs
Yosemite NP/ Fresno	1 hr	3 hrs
Lake Tahoe/ Reno	1 hr	3 hrs 30 mins

From San Francisco to:	Route	Distance
San Jose	U.S. 101	50 miles
Monterey	U.S. 101 to Hwy. 156 to Hwy. 1	120 miles
Los Angeles	I–80 to I–580 to I–5	382 miles
Portland, OR	I–80 to I–505 to I–5	635 miles
Mendocino	U.S. 101 to Hwy. 128 to Hwy. 1	174 miles
Yosemite NP	I–80 to I–580 to I–205 to Hwy. 120 east	184 miles
Lake Tahoe/ Reno	I–80	220 miles

 ## Air

Most national and many international airlines fly to California. Flying time to the state is about 6½ hours from New York and 4¾ hours from Chicago. Travel from London to either Los Angeles or San Francisco is 11½ hours and from Sydney approximately 14 hours. Flying between San Francisco and Los Angeles takes about 90 minutes.

 ## Bus

Greyhound is the primary bus carrier in California. Regional bus service is available in metropolitan areas.

🚗 Car

A car is essential in most of California, the exceptions being parts of its largest cities, where it can be more convenient to use public transportation, taxis, or ride-sharing services. Two main north–south routes run through California: I–5 through the middle of the state, and U.S. 101, a parallel route closer to the coast. Slower but more scenic is Highway 1, which winds along much of the coast.

The state's main east–west routes are I–8, I–10, and I–15 (in the south) and I–80 (in the north). Much of California is mountainous, and you may encounter winding roads and steep mountain grades.

CAR RENTAL

When you reserve a car, ask about cancellation penalties, taxes, drop-off charges (to drop off in another city), and surcharges (for age, additional drivers, or driving across state or country borders).

ROAD CONDITIONS

View current road conditions online or download the easier-to-use Caltrans QuickMap smartphone app. Rainy weather can make driving along the coast or in the mountains treacherous. Some smaller routes over mountain ranges and in the deserts are prone to flash flooding. Many smaller roads over the Sierra Nevada are closed in winter, and if it's snowing, tire chains may be required on routes that are open. Note, though, that most rental-car companies prohibit chain installation on their vehicles. If you disregard this rule, your insurance likely won't cover chains-related damage.

Chains or cables generally cost $30–$75. ■TIP→ It's less expensive to purchase chains before you get to the mountains. On some highways and freeways, uniformed chain installers will apply chains for a fee (around $30), though these installers are not allowed to sell or rent chains. On lesser roads, you're on your own.

RULES OF THE ROAD

All passengers must wear a seat belt at all times. A child must be secured in a federally approved child passenger restraint system and ride in the back seat until at least eight years of age or until the child is at least 4 feet 9 inches tall. Unless indicated, right turns are allowed at red lights after you've come to a full stop. Drivers with a blood-alcohol level higher than 0.08 are subject to arrest.

You must turn on your headlights whenever weather conditions require the use of windshield wipers. Texting on a wireless device is illegal. If using a mobile phone while driving, it must be hands-free and mounted (i.e., it's not legal having it loose on the seat or your lap). For more driving rules, refer to the Department of Motor Vehicles driver's handbook at ⊕ *www.dmv.ca.gov.*

 Train

Amtrak provides rail service within California. On some trips, passengers board motor coaches part of the way.

Essentials

Activities

Athletic Californians often boast that it's possible to surf in the morning and ski in the afternoon (or vice versa) in the Golden State. With thousands of hiking, biking, and horse-riding trails and hundreds of lakes, rivers, and streams for fishing, swimming, and boating—not to mention sandy coastal strands for sunning and surfing and other beaches with dunes or rocks to explore—there's no shortage of outdoor fun to be had. One challenge on many a hiker's bucket list is the Pacific Crest Trail, which travels the length of the state. The National Park Service operates numerous parks and sites in California, and the state park system is robust.

Dining

California has led the pack in bringing natural and organic foods to the forefront of American dining. Though rooted in European cuisine, California cooking sometimes has strong Asian and Latin influences. Wherever you go, you're likely to find that dishes are made with fresh produce and other local ingredients.

The restaurants we list are the cream of the crop in each price category. *Restaurant reviews have been shortened. For full information, visit Fodors.com. For price information, see the Planning sections in each chapter.*

DISCOUNTS AND DEALS
The better grocery and specialty-food stores have grab-and-go sections, with prepared foods on a par with restaurant cooking, perfect for picnicking.

MEALS AND MEALTIMES
Lunch is typically served from 11 or 11:30 to 2:30 or 3, with dinner service starting at 5 or 5:30 and lasting until 9 or later. Restaurants that serve breakfast usually open by 7, sometimes earlier, with some serving breakfast through the lunch hour. Most weekend brunches start at 10 or 11 and go at least until 2.

PAYING
In 2020, most restaurants began taking only credit cards and not cash, though some still don't accept one or the other. In most establishments tipping is the norm, but some include the service in the menu price or add it to the bill. *For guidelines on tipping see the Tipping chart, below.*

RESERVATIONS AND DRESS
It's a good idea to make a reservation when possible. Where reservations are indicated as essential, book a week or more ahead in summer and early fall. Large parties should always call ahead to check the reservations policy. Except as noted in individual listings, dress is informal.

Health/Safety

If you have a medical condition that may require emergency treatment, be aware that many rural and mountain communities have only daytime clinics, not hospitals with 24-hour emergency rooms. Take the usual precautions to protect your person and belongings. In large cities, ask at your lodging about areas to avoid, and lock valuables in a hotel safe when not using them. Car break-ins are common in some larger cities, but it's always a good idea to remove valuables from your car or at least keep them out of sight.

COVID-19
Although COVID-19 brought travel to a virtual standstill for most of 2020 and into 2021, vaccinations have made travel possible and safe again. Remaining requirements and restrictions—including those for non-vaccinated travelers—can,

however, vary from one place (or even business) to the next. Check out the websites of the CDC and the U.S. Department of State, both of which have destination-specific, COVID-19 guidance. Also, in case travel is curtailed abruptly again, consider buying trip insurance. Just be sure to read the fine print: not all travel-insurance policies cover pandemic-related cancellations.

THE OUTDOORS

At beaches, heed warnings about high surf and deadly rogue waves, and don't fly within 24 hours of scuba diving. When hiking, stay on trails, and heed all warning signs about loose cliffs, predatory animals, and poison ivy or oak.

Before heading out into remote areas, let someone know your trip route, destination, and estimated time and date of return. Make sure your vehicle is in good condition and equipped with a first-aid kit, snacks, extra water, jack, spare tire, tools, and a towrope or chain. Mind your gas gauge, keeping the needle at above half if possible and stopping to top off the tank whenever you can.

In arid regions, stay on main roads, and watch out for wildlife, horses, and cattle. Don't enter mine tunnels or shafts. Not only can such structures be unstable, but they might also have hidden dangers such as pockets of bad air. Be mindful of sudden rainstorms, when floodwaters can cover or wash away roads and quickly fill up dry riverbeds and canyons. Never place your hands or feet where you can't see them: rattlesnakes, scorpions, and black widow spiders may be hiding there.

Sunscreen and hats are musts, and layered clothing is best as desert temperatures can fluctuate greatly between dawn and dusk. Drink at least a gallon of water a day (three gallons if you're hiking or otherwise exerting yourself). If you have

a headache or feel dizzy or nauseous, you could be suffering from dehydration. Get out of the sun immediately, dampen your clothing to lower your body temperature, and drink plenty of water.

Although you might not feel thirsty in cooler, mountain climes, it's important to stay hydrated (drinking at least a quart of water during activities) at high altitudes, where the air is thinner, causing you to breathe more heavily. Always bring a fold-up rain poncho to keep you dry and prevent hypothermia. Wear long pants, a hat, and sturdy, closed-toe hiking boots with soles that grip rock. If you're going into the backcountry, bring a signaling device (such as a mirror), emergency whistle, compass, map, energy bars, and water purifier.

🖥 Lodging

With just under 5,600 lodgings, California has inns, motels, hotels, and specialty accommodations to suit every traveler's fancy and finances. Retro motels recalling 1950s roadside culture but with 21st-century amenities are a recent popular trend, but you'll also see traditional motels and hotels, along with luxury resorts and boutique properties. Reservations are a good idea throughout the year but especially so in the summer. On weekends at smaller lodgings, minimum-stay requirements of two or three nights are common, though some places are flexible about this in winter. Some accommodations aren't suitable for children, so ask before you book.

The lodgings we review are the top choices in each price category. *Hotels reviews have been shortened. For full information, visit Fodors.com.* We don't specify whether the facilities cost extra; when pricing accommodations, ask

Essentials

what's included and what costs extra. *For price information, see the Planning sections in each chapter.*

APARTMENT AND HOUSE RENTALS

You'll find listings for Airbnb and similar rentals throughout California.

BED-AND-BREAKFASTS

California has more than 1,000 bed-and-breakfasts. You'll find everything from simple homestays to lavish luxury lodgings, many in historic hotels and homes. The California Association of Boutique and Breakfast Inns represents 200 member properties you can locate and book through its website.

HOTELS

Some properties allow you to cancel without a penalty—even if you prepaid to secure a discounted rate—if you cancel at least 24 hours in advance. Others require you to cancel a week in advance or penalize you the cost of one night. Small inns and B&Bs are most likely to require you to cancel far in advance. Most hotels allow children under a certain age to stay in their parents' room at no extra charge, but others charge for them as additional adults; find out the cutoff age for discounts.

$ Money

On the coast, you'll pay top dollar for everything from gas and food to lodging and attractions. Aside from desert and ski resorts, inland prices tend to be lower.

TAXES

The base state sales tax is 7.25%, but local taxes can add as much as 3.25%. Exceptions include grocery-store food items and some takeout. Hotel taxes vary from about 8% to 15%.

Tipping Guidelines for California

Role	Tip
Bartender	$1–$3 per drink, or 15%–20% per round
Bellhop	$2–$5 per bag, depending on the level of the hotel
Hotel Concierge	$5–$10 for advice and reservations, more for difficult tasks
Hotel Doorman	$3–$5 for hailing a cab
Valet Parking Attendant	$3–$5 when you get your car
Hotel Maid	$4–$6 per day (either daily or at the end of your stay, in cash)
Waiter	18%–22% (20%–25% is standard in upscale restaurants); nothing additional if a service charge is added to the bill
Skycap at Airport	$2 per bag
Hotel Room-Service Waiter	15%–20% per delivery, even if a service charge was added since that fee goes to the hotel, not the waiter
Tasting-room server	$5–$10 per couple basic tasting, $5–$10 per person hosted seated tasting
Taxi Driver	15%–20%, but round up the fare to the next dollar amount
Tour Guide	15% of the cost of the tour, more depending on quality

ⓨ Nightlife

The good life in California extends to the evening with skilled mixologists serving up farm-to-bar cocktails in big-city night spots, some of them modeled on speakeasies of yore. Regular ole bartenders provide an additional layer of atmosphere to dives in towns large and small.

Packing

The California lifestyle emphasizes casual wear, and with the generally mild climate you needn't worry about packing cold-weather clothing unless you're going into mountainous areas. Jeans, walking shorts, and T-shirts are acceptable in most situations. Few restaurants require men to wear a jacket or tie, though a collared shirt is the norm at upscale establishments.

Summer evenings can be cool, especially near the coast, where fog often rolls in. Always pack a sweater or light jacket. If you're headed to state or national parks, packing binoculars, clothes that layer, long pants and long-sleeve shirts, sunglasses, and a wide-brimmed hat is wise. Pick up insect repellant, sunscreen, and a first-aid kit once in-state.

🎭 Performing Arts

With about 40 million residents, California supplies a built-in audience for touring and homegrown companies from the worlds of dance, opera, theater, comedy, and music of all types. A-list performers appear at venues large and intimate, and numerous cultural festivals fill the calendar. In all the major cities and some smaller ones you'll find a former movie palace or two (or more) converted into a performance venue. Look also for events sponsored by top-tier museums. Wineries throughout the state host concerts during the summer.

Shopping

California is home to world-class shopping in its big cities, where you'll find major designer labels and fine-jewelry establishments represented. The state was the birthplace of the maker movement, and artisans throughout California craft beautiful soaps, clothing from organic cotton, fashion jewelry from recycled products, and other handmade items.

📅 When to Go

Expect high summer heat in the desert areas and low winter temperatures in the Sierra Nevada and other inland mountain ranges.

HIGH SEASON $$$–$$$$

High season lasts from late May through early September (a little later in wine regions and well into winter in desert resorts and ski areas). Expect higher hotel occupancy rates and prices.

LOW SEASON $$

From December to March, tourist activity slows. Except in the mountainous areas, which may see snowfall and an influx of skiers, winters here are mild and hotels are cheaper.

VALUE SEASON $$–$$$

From April to late May and from late September to mid-November the weather is pleasant and hotel prices are reasonable.

Contacts

Air

AIRLINE SECURITY ISSUES
CONTACTS Transportation Security Administration. (*TSA*). ☎ *866/289–9673* ⊕ *www.tsa.gov.*

AIRLINES
CONTACTS Air Canada. ☎ *888/247–2262* ⊕ *www. aircanada.com.* **Alaska Airlines/Horizon Air.** ☎ *800/252–7522* ⊕ *www. alaskaair.com.* **American Airlines.** ☎ *800/433–7300* ⊕ *www.aa.com.* **Delta Airlines.** ☎ *800/221–1212 for U.S. reservations, 800/241–4141 for international reservations* ⊕ *www.delta.com.* **Frontier Airlines.** ☎ *801/401–9000* ⊕ *www.flyfrontier.com.* **JetBlue.** ☎ *800/538–2583* ⊕ *www.jetblue.com.* **Southwest Airlines.** ☎ *800/435–9792* ⊕ *www. southwest.com.* **United Airlines.** ☎ *800/864–8331* ⊕ *www.united.com.*

AIRPORTS
Oakland International Airport. ☎ *510/563–3300* ⊕ *www.oaklandairport.com.* **Sacramento International Airport.** ☎ *916/929–5411* ⊕ *www. sacramento.aero/smf.* **San Francisco International Airport.** ☎ *650/821–8211, 800/435–9736* ⊕ *www. flysfo.com.* **San Jose International Airport.** ☎ *408/392–3600* ⊕ *www. flysanjose.com.*

Bus

CONTACTS Greyhound. ☎ *800/231–2222* ⊕ *www. greyhound.com.*

Car

INFORMATION Caltrans Current Highway Conditions. ☎ *800/427–7623* ⊕ *quickmap.dot.ca.gov.* **511 Traffic/Transit Alerts.** ☎ *511.*

MAJOR RENTAL AGENCIES Alamo. ☎ *800/462–5266* ⊕ *www.alamo.com.* **Avis.** ☎ *800/633–3469* ⊕ *www.avis.com.* **Budget.** ☎ *800/218–7992* ⊕ *www. budget.com.* **Hertz.** ☎ *800/654–3131* ⊕ *www. hertz.com.* **National Car Rental.** ☎ *844/382–6875* ⊕ *www.nationalcar.com.*

ROADSIDE ASSISTANCE American Automobile Association. (*AAA*). ☎ *800/222–4357* ⊕ *www.aaa.com.*

SPECIALTY CAR AGENCIES Enterprise Exotic Car Rentals. ☎ *866/458–9227* ⊕ *exoticcars.enterprise. com.*

✚ Health/Safety

EMERGENCIES Ambulance, fire, police. ☎ *911 emergency.*

🍴 Reservation Service

CONTACTS California Association of Boutique and Breakfast Inns. (*CABBI*). ☎ *800/373–9251* ⊕ *www. cabbi.com.*

🚆 Train

CONTACTS Amtrak. ☎ *800/872–7245* ⊕ *www. amtrak.com.*

NORTHERN CALIFORNIA'S BEST ROAD TRIPS

Updated by
Daniel Mangin

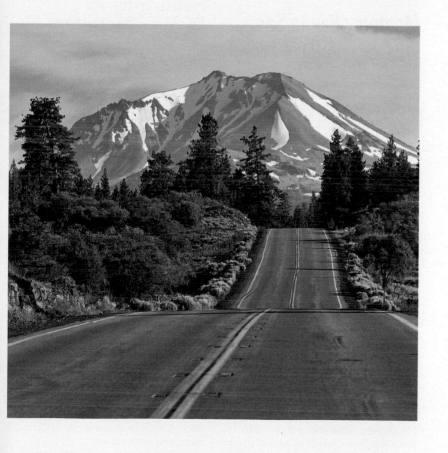

A California visit wouldn't be complete without taking a spin through the state's spectacular scenery.

However, adding a road trip to your itinerary is not just a romantic idea: it's often a practical one, too—perhaps linking one urban area with another, say, or sampling some of this massive state's remote areas. Whether you have just a few days or longer to spare, these itineraries will help you hit the road.

Monterey Bay to San Francisco, 4 Days

Another glorious section of Highway 1 stretches north from Monterey Bay to San Francisco. The drive to San Francisco only takes three hours, but there's enough history and scenery to fill three leisurely days. Book two nights at a Monterey or Carmel-by-the-Sea hotel or inn, arriving the evening before to maximize your time here. In the former, the tony **Monterey Plaza** is the gateway to Cannery Row, with the less-expensive **Casa Munras** winning bonus points for its tapas restaurant. Head to inland Carmel Valley to splurge at **Bernardus Lodge** or the **Quail Lodge & Golf Club**; Carmel's **Pine Inn** and **Tally Ho Inn** are less showy but well located.

DAY 1: MONTEREY
15 mins by car, less than an hour by foot.

Monterey is the perfect spot to kick off a coastal tour. Start with a visit to the enthralling **Monterey Bay Aquarium.** Exhibits such as the dramatic three-story kelp forest near the entrance give you a true sense of the local marine environment, much of it federally protected. For an even closer encounter, take to the water on a kayak or whale-watching

tour. While undoubtedly touristy, the shops and galleries of **Cannery Row** still make for an interesting diversion, and it's fun to watch the colony of sea lions at **Fisherman's Wharf.** Enjoy a seafood dinner downtown and an evening stroll before hitting the road the following day.

DAY 2: 17-MILE DRIVE AND CARMEL-BY-THE-SEA
The 17-Mile Drive's Pacific Grove entrance gate is 20 mins by car from Monterey.

Begin your drive with a spin along the shoreline in the charming Victorian town of **Pacific Grove.** Pick up Ocean View Boulevard near the aquarium and head north. If your visit falls between October and March, stop to see the migrating monarch butterflies at the **Monarch Grove Sanctuary.**

Enter the **17-Mile Drive** through the tollgate ($10.50 per car) off Sunset Drive in Pacific Grove. This scenic road winds its way along the coast through a hushed and refined landscape of stunning homes and the celebrated golf links at **Pebble Beach.** Perhaps the most famous (and photographed) resident is the **Lone Cypress,** which has come to symbolize the coast's solitude and natural beauty. Even though the drive is only 17 miles, take your time. If you stop for lunch or souvenir shopping, inquire about a refund on the entry toll.

Upon exiting the drive, continue south to **Carmel-by-the-Sea.** Spend the afternoon browsing its boutiques and galleries before walking to **Carmel Beach** for sunset, followed by dinner at one of Carmel's many fine restaurants.

DAY 3: SANTA CRUZ

A little less than 1 hr by car from Monterey or Carmel-by-the-Sea.

Depart your hotel midmorning, and pick up Highway 1, following its curve around Monterey Bay north toward Santa Cruz. For a magical experience, book an excursion with the naturalists at **Elkhorn Slough Safari Nature Boat Tours** to see otters and other creatures up close. In Aptos, **Seacliff State Beach,** a strand known for its tall sandstone bluffs, is one of two beaches of note beyond **Moss Landing.** The visitor center at the other, Capitola's surfing spot **New Brighton State Beach,** has exhibits about the Chinese village that once existed here.

From the beaches, continue to Santa Cruz, and check into your hotel. If it fits your budget, the **Dream Inn Santa Cruz,** the city's only lodging directly on the beach, is the most convenient choice, with the **Hotel Paradox** another good option. Once settled in, stroll the **Santa Cruz Boardwalk,** and catch the sunset over cocktails, dinner, or both. If time permits, walk or drive a bit of **West Cliff Drive,** which winds around to a lighthouse.

DAY 4: SANTA CRUZ TO SAN FRANCISCO

90 mins by car in light traffic, not counting stops.

Highway 1 darts up the coast 77 miles to San Francisco, occasionally so close to the Pacific that a section collapses into the sea and must be rebuilt. Although not as dramatic as Big Sur to the south or Mendocino to the north, the landscape still is fetching.

Let your desire to arrive in San Francisco control your pace. As you drive north, you can stop to check out the art galleries in small **Davenport** or ogle the ocean from the cliffs above. Farther along, at **Año Nuevo State Park,** you can hike a short way to the dunes to observe the resident elephant seals.

If you're getting hungry, knotty-pine-paneled **Duarte's Tavern,** in business in **Pescadero** since 1894, delivers a blast from the past along with stick-to-your-ribs American standards like deep-fried calamari and pork chops with old-school applesauce. To reach the restaurant, head east 2 miles on Pescadero Creek Road. **Half Moon Bay,** 17 miles north, has more updated fare. Suburban encroachment becomes more evident as you approach San Francisco. If pressed for time, head east on Highway 92 to I–280 north to get to San Francisco more quickly.

San Francisco's Greatest Hits, 3 Days

DAY 1: UNION SQUARE, CHINATOWN, NORTH BEACH
30–45 mins on public transport.

Straight from the airport, drop your bags at the lighthearted **Hotel Zetta,** south of Market Street (SoMa). A walk north to **Union Square** packs a wallop of people-watching, window-shopping, and architecture viewing. **Chinatown—** chock-full of dim sum shops, storefront temples, and open-air markets—promises authentic bites for lunch. Catch a Powell Street **cable car** to the end of the line, and get off to see the bay views and the antique arcade games at **Musée Mécanique,** the hidden gem of otherwise mindless **Fisherman's Wharf.** No need to go any farther than cosmopolitan **North Beach** for cocktail hour, dinner, and live music.

DAY 2: GOLDEN GATE PARK
5 mins by car or taxi, 45 mins by public transport from Union Square.

In **Golden Gate Park,** linger amid the flora of the **Conservatory of Flowers** and the **San Francisco Botanical Garden at Strybing Arboretum,** soak up some art at the **de Young Museum,** and find serene refreshment at the **San Francisco Japanese Tea Garden.** The Pacific surf pounds the cliffs below the **Legion of Honor** art museum, which has an exquisite view of the **Golden Gate Bridge**—when the fog stays away. A late-afternoon cocktail at the **Beach Chalet** will whet your appetite for dinner back in SoMa.

DAY 3: ROAMIN' AROUND
About 1 hr of driving total, not counting traffic.

Begin the day with a dose of culture at the **San Francisco Museum of Modern Art,** visiting one or two of the other nearby downtown museums on a day when SFMOMA is closed. Walk, drive, rideshare, or hop on a public bus heading less than a mile east to the **Ferry Building,** browsing the bodegas and lunching here before walking some of the **Embarcadero.** Afterward, if you haven't ridden a cable car yet, catch one on California Street up to Nob Hill. If you've been driving, retrieve your vehicle, and proceed to **Japantown.** Otherwise, rideshare or switch to public transit (on Sacramento Street); if on the bus, alight at Webster Street and walk south a few blocks. From Japantown, head to the gay **Castro** before bidding the City by the Bay adieu at a downtown hotel's plush lounge or trendy bar.

Sierra Riches: Yosemite, Gold Country, and Tahoe, 7 Days

This tour of some of California's most inspiring terrain serves up gold-rush-era history and offers a chance to hike a trail or two. Particularly in summer, book a room within Yosemite National Park (the Ahwahnee Hotel and the Wawona Hotel being the two historic choices) well ahead of your visit. Gateway towns such as Oakhurst and Mariposa can be less expensive, but you'll have to drive more.

DAY 1: INTO THE HIGH SIERRA
4–5 hrs by car from San Francisco.

First thing in the morning, head for the hills. Arriving in **Yosemite National Park, Bridalveil Fall,** and **El Capitan,** the 350-story granite monolith, greet you on your way to **Yosemite Village.** Ditch the car, and pick up information and refreshment before hopping on the shuttle to explore. Justly famous sights cram Yosemite Valley: massive **Half Dome** and **Sentinel Dome,** thundering **Yosemite Falls,** and wispy **Ribbon Fall** and **Nevada Fall.** Invigorating short hikes off the shuttle route lead to numerous vantage points. Even if you're not staying at the **Ahwahnee Hotel,** celebrate your arrival with a cocktail at the bar here.

DAY 2: YOSEMITE NATIONAL PARK
Yosemite shuttles run every 10–30 mins.

Ardent hikers consider **John Muir Trail to Half Dome** a must-do, tackling the rigorous 12-hour round-trip to the top of Half Dome. Mere mortals hike downhill from Glacier Point on Four-Mile Trail or **Panorama Trail,** the latter an all-day trek past waterfalls. Less demanding still is a drive to Wawona to the **Mariposa Grove of Big Trees** followed by lunch at the 19th-century **Wawona Hotel Dining Room.** In bad weather, take shelter in the **Ansel Adams Gallery** and **Yosemite Museum.** If conditions permit, head to **Glacier Point** for a breathtaking sunset view.

DAY 3: GOLD COUNTRY SOUTH
2½–3 hrs by car from Yosemite Valley to Plymouth.

Get an early start driving west from Yosemite to Highway 49, which traces the mother lode that yielded many fortunes in gold (and plenty of heartaches) in the 1800s. In the living-history town at **Columbia State Historic Park** you can ride a stagecoach and pan for riches. About 46

miles north, **Sutter Creek's** well-preserved downtown bursts with shopping opportunities, or you can explore history at the outdoor **Miner's Bend** park and **Knight Foundry.** Switch focus in the **Shenandoah Valley,** the heart of the Sierra Foothills Wine Country. Taste your way through Zinfandels at **Turley Wine Cellars,** that varietal plus Cabernets and Rhône-style wines at **Terra Rouge and Easton Wines,** or award-winning Barbera and much more at jolly **Jeff Renquist Wines.** Retire in modest boutique comfort at **Rest Hotel Plymouth,** whose owners also operate nearby **Taste** restaurant.

DAY 4: GOLD COUNTRY NORTH
1½–2 hrs by car from Plymouth to Nevada City, not counting stops.

From Plymouth, drive north on Highway 49. Once in El Dorado County, either detour east on U.S. 50 to learn about **Placerville**-area wines at **Starfield Vineyards** or **Lava Cap Winery,** or continue north on Highway 49 to **Marshall Gold Discovery State Historic Park.** Encompassing most of **Coloma,** the park preserves the spot where James Marshall's 1848 find set off the California gold rush.

If you went to the winery, backtrack to Highway 49, continuing north past

Coloma, with the goal in all cases to stop in Old Town **Auburn** for lunch. The **Auburn Ale House** is open daily, but there are other choices in the historic district. After lunch, continue north to Grass Valley's **Empire Mine State Historic Park,** among the gold-rush's most productive mines. The park closes at 5 pm, so try to arrive by 3. The drive to the mine, which is off Highway 20, takes 35 minutes in light traffic.

The same company has transformed the mid-19th-century **Holbrooke Hotel** in Grass Valley and its Nevada City contemporary, the **National Exchange Hotel,** into boutique gems. Stay overnight at either lodging but have dinner at the latter's **Lola** restaurant. Grass Valley's more affordable **Gold Mine Inn** is also well-run.

DAYS 5–7: LAKE TAHOE

About 1 hr by car from Nevada City or Grass Valley.

If you didn't have time to stroll through Nevada City's historic district on Day 4, do so for an hour before heading east on Highway 20 and then I–80 toward Lake Tahoe. Stop in **Truckee** for lunch and a spin through its historic downtown. From there, continue south on Highway 89 to **Tahoe City,** on the northern shore of jewel-like **Lake Tahoe.**

Where you stay and the time of year will determine the order in which you explore the 72-mile shoreline of Lake Tahoe, bisected north–south by the California–Nevada border. No matter how much you plan, some backtracking is inevitable. Two lodgings worth considering in North Lake Tahoe are the **Sunnyside Steakhouse and Lodge** (Tahoe City, California side) and the **Hyatt Regency Incline Village** (Nevada side). **The Landing Tahoe Resort & Spa** and **Black Bear Lodge** are good South Lake Tahoe (California) choices; **The Lodge at Edgewood Tahoe** provides the classiest, albeit expensive, stay in Stateline (Nevada).

Clockwise from South Lake Tahoe, the top sights and activities include riding

> ## Tip
>
> If possible, time your Sierras trip between late spring and early fall to avoid the summer crowds and road-closing winter snowfalls in Yosemite and around Lake Tahoe. Yosemite's waterfalls peak in spring and early summer, while autumn brings the grape harvest and farm-related festivals.

the **Heavenly Gondola** to see the lake from up high; hopping aboard a vintage **Tahoe Tastings** boat to (seasonally) sip wines; and visiting the three magnificent estates in **Pope-Baldwin Recreation Area.** Farther along, the lake views from **Emerald Bay State Park** inspire year-round; season and stamina permitting, hike down to the **Vikingsholm** Scandinavian-style castle.

Continuing clockwise, **North Lake Tahoe**'s pleasures include more boat rides from **Tahoe City** (also more history and ample dining); outdoor sports in **Incline Village** plus tours of **Thunderbird Lodge;** and Tahoe cruises aboard the stern-wheeler MS *Dixie II* departing from **Zephyr Cove.** Continue south to **Stateline,** to try your luck at the largest casinos, or head to the beaches and bays of **Lake Tahoe–Nevada State Park** to bask in the sun or go mountain biking.

Ultimate Napa and Sonoma Wine Trip, 4 Days

On this four-day loop north from San Francisco into the Wine Country, you'll taste well-known and under-the-radar wines, bed down in plush hotels, and dine at restaurants operated by celebrity chefs. Reservations are required for most tasting-room visits and recommended for dinner.

DAY 1: SOUTHERN SONOMA
About 90 mins total by car from San Francisco.

Head north from San Francisco to **Sonoma.** Less than an hour after crossing the Golden Gate Bridge, you'll be holding a glass of Chardonnay at **Sangiacomo Family Wines** (also known for Pinot Noir). The outdoor tasting areas here overlook land the Sangiacomos have farmed since 1927. For wines whose vines date from the 1800s, head straight downtown to visit **Bedrock Wine Co.** (with Zinfandel and other "heritage" wines that have great backstories).

Your initial tasting complete, explore the shops bordering or near Sonoma Plaza; if you're dying to taste more before lunch, many opportunities await. Have lunch just off the plaza at **Taub Family Outpost,** then head north to **Glen Ellen,** a town whose famous writer-residents have included M.F.K. Fisher, Hunter S. Thompson, and, most notably, Jack London. Visit **Jack London State Historic Park,** the memorabilia-filled estate of the famous writer, or enjoy a tasting at **Benziger Family Winery** or **Lasseter Family Winery.** Dine at **Glen Ellen Star,** and stay at the **Gaige House + Ryokan** or the **Olea Hotel.**

DAY 2: NORTHERN SONOMA
About 75 mins total by car.

From Glen Ellen, drive 40 minutes northwest on Highway 12 and north on U.S. 101 to **Healdsburg.** Start your tasting outside town amid rolling vineyards at **Ridge Vineyards** (Zinfandel, Cabernet, Petite Sirah) or **MacRostie Estate House** (Chardonnay and Pinot Noir). Have an informal lunch at **Dry Creek General Store,** in business since 1881.

After lunch, drive to the French-style château at **Jordan Vineyard & Winery** to taste Chardonnay and Cabernet Sauvignon. If you're staying at the luxurious, 250-acre **Montage Healdsburg** (with dinner at the resort's **Hazel Hill** restaurant), you're just minutes away. Two in-town lodgings, the

Harmon Guest House and the **River Belle Inn,** are highly recommended. Have dinner at **Bravas Bar de Tapas** or **Valette,** both near the plaza. For a splurge, reserve a table (well ahead) at **SingleThread Farms Restaurant.**

DAY 3: NORTHERN NAPA VALLEY
About 75 mins total by car.

Head into the northern Napa Valley via Alexander Valley Road and Highway 128, which winds east to **Calistoga** through dairy pasture and the vineyards of the Knights Valley appellation. **Chateau Montelena** made history in the 1970s when its Chardonnay took top honors at a famous Paris tasting; the winery also makes Cabernet Sauvignon. After a tasting here or at nearby **Tamber Bey** (Cabernet and other Bordeaux-style reds), continue south 15 minutes on Highway 29 to St. Helena.

Much Napa Valley history unfolded at **Charles Krug Winery,** which began operations in 1861. Taste Cabernets and other Bordeaux-style reds here, then have lunch downtown at **Cook St. Helena** or **Market,**, afterward poking through Main Street shops before continuing south on Highway 29 to **Hall St. Helena** (high-scoring Cabernets, impressive art collection) or its homey neighbor **Prager Winery & Port Works.**

Backtrack to Calistoga to stay at **Embrace Calistoga,** a small inn known for superb hospitality, or **Solage,** a full-service, upscale-casual, luxury resort. The latter's **Solbar** restaurant ranks high among Calistoga restaurants, with **Evangeline** or **Sam's Social Club** two other fine options.

DAY 4: SOUTHERN NAPA VALLEY
45 mins driving in Napa Valley, 1 hr back to San Francisco

After breakfast at your lodging, head south on Highway 29 to Oakville, where sipping wine at **Nickel & Nickel** or **Silver Oak** makes clear why collectors covet Oakville Cabernet Sauvignons. Nickel & Nickel is on Highway 29; Silver Oak is east of it on Oakville Cross Road. After tasting, have lunch in **Yountville** at Thomas Keller's **Bouchon Bistro** or more casual **La Calenda.** Lunch completed, walk south on Washington Street, whose intriguing shops include **The Conservatory,** for "considered luxury," and **Montecristi Panama Hats. Heron House Yountville,** which pours the Cabernets of nine small producers, carries upscale fashion, art, and household items.

From Yountville, pop back on Highway 29, and head south to Highway 121. Turn west (right) to reach the Carneros District's **Domaine Carneros,** world-famous for its sparkling wines. There's hardly a more elegant way to bid a Wine Country adieu than on the vineyard-view terrace of this winery's splendid château.

If you can't tear yourself away from the Wine Country, extend your stay at the **Archer Hotel Napa** or the **Inn on First** in downtown Napa or the sprawling **Carneros Resort & Spa,** a few-minutes' drive east of Domaine Carneros.

Best of the Northern Coast, 5 Days

Hit coastal Northern California's highlights in one Highway 1 itinerary: scenic coastal drives, windswept towns, wine tasting, culinary delights, redwood forests. Make this route part of a longer trip north to the Oregon border, or loop back to San Francisco.

DAY 1: MARIN COUNTY AND POINT REYES NATIONAL SEASHORE
Without stops, Point Reyes National Seashore is about 1½ hrs by car from San Francisco on Hwy 1. Point Reyes Lighthouse is 45 mins by car from the visitor center.

As you head out of San Francisco on the Golden Gate Bridge, pull over at the **scenic lookout** on the north side, and take in the classic views of the city's skyline. If you haven't yet checked out the picturesque harbor community of **Sausalito,** just north of the bridge, now is your chance. It will be hard not to linger, but there is much to see today. Bidding San Francisco farewell, you will quickly find yourself immersed in the natural splendor of Marin County. Exit U.S. 101 onto Highway 1 at **Mill Valley** and head to **Muir Woods National Monument.** Walking among the tall coastal redwoods, you may forget that San Francisco lies less than a dozen miles away. However, the proximity to the city means that Muir Woods attracts throngs; accessing it can be difficult if you don't make a parking or shuttle reservation a day or two ahead (more in summer).

NEVADA

Lake
Tahoe

Eureka
Ferndale
**The Avenue of
the Giants**
Garberville
**Humboldt
Redwoods State Park**
Fort Bragg
Mendocino
Little River   Philo
Anderson Valley   Boonville
Healdsburg
Bodega Bay
Point Reyes Station   **Marin County**
Point Reyes National Seashore
Bolinas   Mill Valley
Stinson Beach   Sausalito
San Francisco

From Muir Woods, continue on Highway 1 past the laid-back beach towns of **Stinson Beach** and **Bolinas** to **Point Reyes National Seashore.** Spend the remainder of the day at the park tide pooling, kayaking, hiking one of the many trails, or exploring the **Point Reyes Lighthouse.** In the winter and early spring, be on the lookout for migrating gray whales.

Point Reyes Station offers a selection of shops and dining options, including **Tomales Bay Foods,** a foodies' favorite. Spend a quiet evening in town and stay overnight at one of the small inns nearby.

DAY 2: HEALDSBURG
Point Reyes Station to Healdsburg, via Jenner, is 2 hrs by car.

Continue north on Highway 1 past the town of **Bodega Bay,** which starred in the 1963 Alfred Hitchcock movie *The Birds.* At Jenner, known for its resident harbor seals, turn east on Highway 116 and follow the Russian River inland, taking time to stop at a winery or two along the way.

Not only is **Healdsburg** home to many acclaimed restaurants and luxurious hotels—making it an excellent place

to stop for the night—but the town's compact layout and quality offerings also make it a favorite Wine Country destination. Ditch the car here, and stroll through the town's appealing square, with its many tasting rooms and boutiques.

DAYS 3–4: ANDERSON VALLEY AND MENDOCINO
Mendocino is 2 hrs by car from Healdsburg. Budget plenty of time for stops in Anderson Valley, and start early enough to ensure you end this scenic drive before sunset.

Driving north on U.S. 101 from Healdsburg, pick up Highway 128 at Cloverdale and head into the **Anderson Valley.** This wine region is famous for Pinot Noir and Chardonnay (also Gewürztraminer and other Alsace white varietals), and the laid-back atmosphere of its tasting rooms make them refreshing alternatives to those in Napa Valley. **Pennyroyal Farm, Roederer Estate,** and **Phillips Hill Winery** are all recommended. The small towns of **Boonville** and **Philo** have high-quality restaurants.

Highway 128 follows the Navarro River through several miles of dense and breathtaking redwood forest ending at the ocean. From here you meet up again with Highway 1 as it winds along a portion of the coast bestrewn with immense rock formations.

With their sophisticated restaurants and lodgings, the towns of **Mendocino** and **Little River,** just to the south, are great choices for your overnight stay, though Elk's **Harbor House Inn** wins the dining prize for its prix-fixe multicourse extravaganzas. **Fort Bragg** has reasonably priced motels and inns, some with full ocean views.

Spend the next day and a half exploring the area. Opportunities for stunning coastal walks abound, including the **Mendocino Headlands, Van Damme State Park,** and the **Fort Bragg Coastal Trail.** Save time to explore Mendocino itself with its New England–style architecture and art galleries and boutiques.

DAY 5: HUMBOLDT REDWOODS STATE PARK AND THE AVENUE OF THE GIANTS

Mendocino to Eureka via The Avenue of the Giants is 3 hrs by car.

Driving north on Highway 1, the road eventually curves inland and meets up with U.S. 101 near Leggett. Head north on U.S. 101 to reach the redwoods.

A drive through **The Avenue of the Giants** will take your breath away. The 32-mile stretch of road, also signed as Highway 254, runs alongside some of the planet's tallest trees as it weaves through a portion of **Humboldt Redwoods State Park.** Even if in a hurry, make time for a short hike through **Founders Grove** or **Rockefeller Forest.**

From here, you can continue your way up the coast through the **Redwood National and State Parks** and on to the Oregon border. Alternatively, you can head south on U.S. 101 and either return to **San Francisco** or combine this itinerary with a trip to the **Napa Valley** and inland **Sonoma County.**

Chapter 4

MONTEREY BAY AREA

FROM CARMEL TO SANTA CRUZ

Updated by
Cheryl Crabtree

4

⊙ Sights	🍴 Restaurants	🛏 Hotels	🛍 Shopping	🍸 Nightlife
★★★★★	★★★★☆	★★★★★	★★☆☆☆	★☆☆☆☆

WELCOME TO MONTEREY BAY AREA

TOP REASONS TO GO

★ **Marine life:** Monterey Bay is the location of the world's third-largest marine sanctuary, home to whales, otters, and other underwater creatures.

★ **Getaway central:** For more than a century, urbanites have come to the Monterey Bay area to unwind, relax, and have fun. It's a great place to browse unique shops and galleries, ride a giant roller coaster, or play a round of golf on a world-class course.

★ **Nature preserves:** More than the sea is protected here: the region boasts nearly 30 state parks, beaches, and preserves—fantastic places for walking, jogging, hiking, and biking.

★ **Wine and dine:** The area's rich agricultural bounty translates into abundant fresh produce, great wines, and fabulous dining. It's no wonder more than 300 culinary events take place here every year.

★ **Small-town vibes:** Even the cities here are friendly, walkable places where you'll feel like a local.

1 Carmel-by-the-Sea. Galleries and cobblestone streets are among its charms.

2 Carmel Valley. An esteemed wine region marks this celebrity enclave.

3 Pebble Beach. This world-class golf destination also has the stunning 17-Mile Drive.

4 Pacific Grove. A picturesque city known for its migrating butterflies.

5 Monterey. The state's first capital is rich in history and marine life.

6 Salinas. The heart of Steinbeck country is also known for its fruits and veggies.

7 Pinnacles National Park. A volcano with jagged spires and caves.

8 Moss Landing. This tiny fishing port is near marine preserves.

9 Aptos. A charming village that edges redwood forests and stellar beaches.

10 Capitola and Soquel. Seaside gateways to mountain wine country.

11 Santa Cruz. World-famous surf and a university are among its draws.

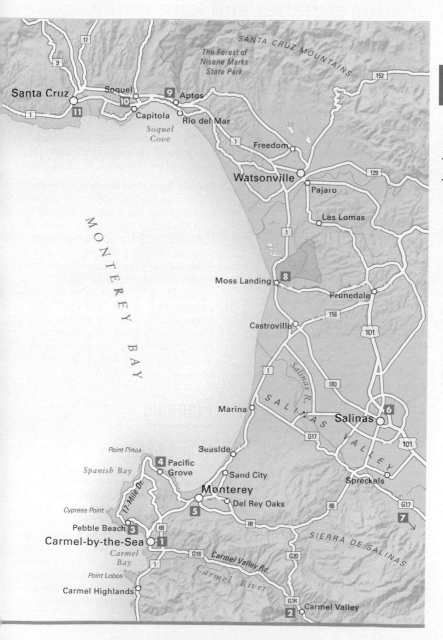

North of Big Sur, the coastline softens into lower bluffs, windswept dunes, pristine estuaries, and long, sandy beaches bordering one of the world's most amazing marine environments— Monterey Bay.

The bay itself is protected by the Monterey Bay National Marine Sanctuary, which holds the nation's largest undersea canyon—bigger and deeper than the Grand Canyon. Sunny coastal communities such as Aptos, Capitola, Soquel, and Santa Cruz offer miles of sand and surf. On-the-water activities abound, from whale-watching and kayaking to sailing and surfing. Bay cruises from Monterey and Moss Landing almost always encounter other enchanting sea creatures, among them sea otters, sea lions, and porpoises.

Land-based activities include hiking, ziplining in the redwood canopy, and wine tasting along urban and rural trails. Golf has been an integral part of the Monterey Peninsula's social and recreational scene since the Del Monte Golf Course opened in 1897. Today, Pebble Beach's championship courses host prestigious tournaments. Quaint, walkable towns such as Carmel-by-the-Sea and Carmel Valley Village are dotted with smart restaurants and galleries that encourage culinary and cultural immersion. Monterey's well-preserved waterfront invites historical exploration. Of course, whatever activity you pursue, natural splendor appears at every turn.

MAJOR REGIONS

The Monterey Peninsula. On the peninsula at the bay's southern end are Carmel-by-the-Sea—a good jumping-off point for the Carmel Valley wine region—Pebble Beach, Pacific Grove, and Monterey itself, home to a world-famous aquarium.

East and North of the Monterey Peninsula. Inland from the bay, amid a rich agricultural area that many refer to as Steinbeck Country, is Salinas, with Pinnacles National Park farther to the southeast. North of Monterey, Highway 1 cruises along the bay's curving coastline, passing windswept beaches piled high with dunes, as well as wetlands and artichoke and strawberry fields. Here you'll find Moss Landing, where otters and seals play; classic seaside villages such as Aptos, Soquel, and Capitola; and Santa Cruz, home of surf legends, a historic boardwalk, and UC Santa Cruz.

Planning

When to Go

Summer is peak season; mild weather brings in big crowds. In this coastal region a cool breeze generally blows and fog often rolls in from offshore; you will frequently need a sweater or windbreaker. Off-season, from November through April, fewer people visit and the mood is mellower. Rainfall is heaviest in January and February. Fall and spring days are often clearer than those in summer.

FESTIVALS AND EVENTS

Carmel Bach Festival. This three-week, mid-July festival has presented the works of Johann Sebastian Bach and his contemporaries since 1935. ⊕ *bachfestival.org*

Jazz Bash by the Bay. Bands play early jazz, big band, swing, ragtime, blues, zydeco, and gypsy jazz at waterfront venues during this festival, held on the first full weekend of March. ⊕ *jazzbashmonterey.com.*

Monterey International Blues Festival. This event on the last weekend in June draws blues fans to the Monterey Fairgrounds. ⊕ *montereyinternationalbluesfestival.com.*

Monterey Jazz Festival. The world's oldest jazz festival, held the third full weekend in September, attracts top-name performers and their fans to the Monterey Fairgrounds. ⊕ *montereyjazzfestival.org.*

Getting Here and Around

AIR

Monterey Regional Airport, 3 miles east of downtown Monterey off Highway 68, is served by Alaska, Allegiant, American, Avelo, JSX, and United. Taxi service costs from $14 to $16 to downtown, and from $23 to $25 to Carmel. Monterey Airbus service between the region and the San Jose and San Francisco airports starts at $42; the Early Bird Airport Shuttle costs from $100 to $235 ($250 from Oakland).

AIRPORT CONTACTS Monterey Regional Airport. (*MRY*) ✉ *200 Fred Kane Dr., at Olmsted Rd., off Hwy. 68, Monterey* ☎ *831/648–7000* ⊕ *www.montereyairport.com.*

GROUND TRANSPORTATION Central Coast Cab Company. ☎ *831/626–3333* ⊕ *www.centralcoastcabcompany.com.* **Early Bird Airport Shuttle.** ☎ *831/462–3933* ⊕ *www.earlybirdairportshuttle.com.* **Monterey Airbus.** ☎ *831/373–7777* ⊕ *www.montereyairbus.com.* **Yellow Cab.** ☎ *831/333–1234* ⊕ *www.yellowcab1234.com.*

BUS

Greyhound serves Santa Cruz and Salinas from San Francisco (3 hours) and San Jose (4½ hours). Monterey-Salinas Transit (MST) provides frequent service in Monterey County (from $2.50 to $3.50; day pass $10), and Santa Cruz METRO ($2; day pass from $6 to $14) buses operate throughout Santa Cruz County. You can switch between the lines in Watsonville.

BUS CONTACTS Monterey-Salinas Transit. ☎ *888/678–2871* ⊕ *mst.org.* **Santa Cruz METRO.** ☎ *831/425–8600* ⊕ *scmtd.com.*

CAR

Highway 1 runs south–north along the coast, linking the towns of Carmel-by-the-Sea, Monterey, and Santa Cruz; some sections have only two lanes. The freeway, U.S. 101, lies to the east, roughly parallel to Highway 1. The two roads are connected by Highway 68 from Pacific Grove to Salinas; Highway 156 from Castroville to Prunedale; Highway 152 from Watsonville to Gilroy; and Highway 17 from Santa Cruz to San Jose.

■TIP→ **Traffic near Santa Cruz can crawl to a standstill during commuter hours. Avoid traveling between 7 and 9 am and between 4 and 7 pm.**

The drive south from San Francisco to Monterey can be made comfortably in three hours or less. The most scenic way is to follow Highway 1 down the coast. A generally faster route is I–280 south to Highway 85 to Highway 17 to Highway 1. The drive from the Los Angeles area takes five or six hours. Take U.S. 101 to Salinas, and head west on Highway 68. You can also follow Highway 1 up the coast.

TRAIN

Amtrak's *Coast Starlight* runs between Los Angeles, Oakland, and Seattle. You can also take the *Pacific Surfliner* to San Luis Obispo and connect to Amtrak buses to Salinas or San Jose. From the train station in Salinas you can connect with buses serving Carmel and Monterey, and from the train station in San Jose with buses to Santa Cruz.

Restaurants

The Monterey Bay area is a culinary paradise. The surrounding waters are full of fish, wild game roams the foothills, and the inland valleys are some of the most fertile in the country—local chefs draw on this bounty for their fresh, truly Californian cuisine. Except at beachside stands and inexpensive eateries, where anything goes, casual but neat dress is the norm.

Hotels

Accommodations in the Monterey area range from no-frills motels to luxurious hotels. Pacific Grove, amply endowed with ornate Victorian houses, is the region's bed-and-breakfast capital; Carmel also has charming inns. Lavish resorts cluster in exclusive Pebble Beach and pastoral Carmel Valley.

High season runs from May through October. Rates in winter, especially at the larger hotels, may drop by 50% or more, and smaller inns often offer midweek specials. Whatever the month, some properties require a two-night stay on weekends. ■TIP→ **Many of the fancier accommodations aren't suitable for children; if you're traveling with kids, ask before you book.**

Restaurant and hotel reviews have been shortened. For full information, visit Fodors.com. Restaurant prices are the average cost of a main course at dinner, or if dinner is not served, at lunch. Hotel prices are the lowest cost of a standard double room in high season

What It Costs			
$	$$	$$$	$$$$
RESTAURANTS			
under $17	$17–$26	$27–$36	over $36
HOTELS			
under $150	$150–$250	$251–$350	over $350

Tours

Ag Venture Tours & Consulting
GUIDED TOURS | Crowd-pleasing half- and full-day wine tasting, sightseeing, walking, and agricultural tours are Ag Venture's specialty. Tastings are at Monterey and Santa Cruz Mountains wineries; sightseeing opportunities include the Monterey Peninsula, Big Sur, and Santa Cruz; and the agricultural forays take in the Salinas and Pajaro valleys. Customized itineraries can be arranged. ☎ 831/761–8463 ⊕ agventuretours.com ▱ From $55 (half-day) and $110 (full day).

Monterey Guided Wine Tours
SPECIAL-INTEREST | The company's guides lead customized wine tours in Monterey, Carmel, and Carmel Valley, along with the Santa Lucia Highlands, the Santa Cruz Mountains, and the Paso Robles area. Tours, which typically last from four to six hours, take place in a town car, a stretch limo, or a party bus. ☎ 831/920–2792 ⊕ montereyguidedwinetours.com ▱ From $175.

Visitor Information

CONTACTS Monterey County Convention & Visitors Bureau. ☎ 888/221–1010 ⊕ www.seemonterey.com. **Monterey Wine Country.** ☎ 831/375–9400 ⊕ www.montereywines.org. **Santa Cruz Mountains Winegrowers Association.** ✉ 335 Spreckels Dr., #B, Aptos ☎ 831/685–8463 ⊕ winesofthesantacruzmountains.com. **Visit Santa Cruz County.** ✉ 303 Water St.,

No. 100, Santa Cruz ☎ 831/425–1234, 800/833–3494 ⊕ visitsantacruz.org.

Carmel-by-the-Sea

26 miles north of Big Sur.

Even when its population quadruples with tourists on weekends and in summer, Carmel-by-the-Sea, commonly referred to as Carmel, retains its identity as a quaint village. Self-consciously charming, the town is populated by many celebrities, major and minor, and has its share of quirky ordinances. For instance, women wearing high heels do not have the right to pursue legal action if they trip and fall on the cobblestone streets, and drivers who hit a tree and leave the scene are charged with hit-and-run.

Buildings have no street numbers—street names are written on discreet white posts—and consequently no mail delivery. One way to commune with the locals: head to the post office. Artists started this community, and their legacy is evident in the numerous galleries.

GETTING HERE AND AROUND
From north or south follow Highway 1 to Carmel. Head west at Ocean Avenue to reach the main village hub.

TOURS
Carmel Food Tours
WALKING TOURS | Taste your way through Carmel-by-the-Sea culinary delights on this guided walking tour to restaurants and shops that serve small portions of standout offerings, from empanadas and ribs to honey and chocolate. Along the way, guides share colorful tales about local culture, history, and architecture. The Classic Tour (which departs from the Sunset Cultural Center) includes seven tasting stops and lasts three hours. The five-hour Bikes, Bites, & Bevs Tour combines a morning e-bike tour through Carmel to Point Lobos with four food and wine/cocktail destinations in the

afternoon. Tickets must be purchased in advance. ⊠ *Sunset Cultural Center, 9th Ave. at San Carlos St., Carmel* ☎ *831/256–3007, 831/216–8533 tickets* ⊕ *www.carmelfoodtour.com* ⊡ *From $94.*

Carmel Walks
WALKING TOURS | For insight into Carmel's history and culture, join one of these guided two-hour ambles through hidden courtyards, gardens, and pathways. Tours depart from the Pine Inn courtyard, on Lincoln Street. Call to reserve a spot. ⊠ *Lincoln St. at 6th Ave., Carmel* ☎ *831/223–4399* ⊕ *carmelwalks.com* ⊡ *From $30.*

ESSENTIALS
VISITOR INFORMATION Carmel Chamber of Commerce. ⊠ *Visitor center, in Carmel Plaza, Ocean Ave. between Junipero and Mission Sts., Carmel* ☎ *831/624–2522, 800/550–4333* ⊕ *carmelchamber.org.*

 Sights

Carmel Mission
RELIGIOUS SITE | Long before it became a shopping and browsing destination, Carmel was an important religious center during the establishment of Spanish California. That heritage is preserved in the Mission San Carlos Borroméo del Rio Carmelo, more commonly known as the Carmel Mission. Founded in 1771, it served as headquarters for the mission system in California under Father Junípero Serra. Adjoining the stone church is a tranquil garden planted with California poppies. Museum rooms at the mission include an early kitchen, Serra's spartan sleeping quarters and burial shrine, and the first college library in California. ⊠ *3080 Rio Rd., at Lasuen Dr., Carmel* ☎ *831/624–1271* ⊕ *carmelmission.org* ⊡ *$10* ⊘ *Closed Mon. and Tues.*

★ Ocean Avenue
NEIGHBORHOOD | Downtown Carmel's chief lure is shopping, especially along its main street, Ocean Avenue, between

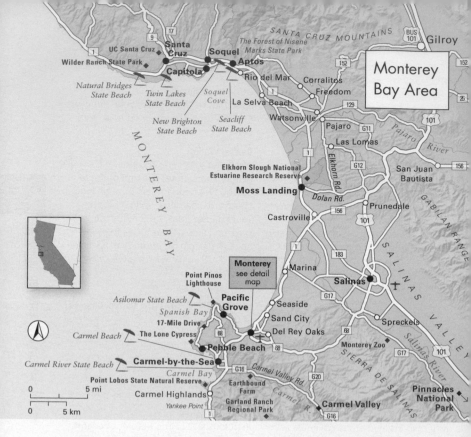

Junipero Avenue and Camino Real. The architecture here is a mishmash of ersatz Tudor, Mediterranean, and other styles. ⊠ *Carmel*.

★ Point Lobos State Natural Reserve

NATIONAL/STATE PARK | A 350-acre headland harboring a wealth of marine life, the reserve lies a few miles south of Carmel. The best way to explore here is to walk along one of the many trails. The Cypress Grove Trail leads through a forest of Monterey cypress (one of only two natural groves remaining) that clings to the rocks above an emerald-green cove. Sea Lion Point Trail is a good place to view sea lions. From those and other trails, you might also spot otters, harbor seals, and (in winter and spring) migrating whales. An additional 750 acres of the reserve is an undersea marine park open to qualified scuba divers. No pets

are allowed. ■**TIP➔** Arrive early (or in late afternoon) to avoid crowds; the parking lots fill up. ⊠ *Hwy. 1, Carmel* ☎ *831/624–4909* ⊕ *www.pointlobos.org* ⊡ *$10 per vehicle.*

Tor House

HOUSE | Scattered throughout the pines of Carmel-by-the-Sea are houses and cottages originally built for the writers, artists, and photographers who discovered the area decades ago. Among the most impressive dwellings is Tor House, a stone cottage built in 1919 by poet Robinson Jeffers on a craggy knoll overlooking the sea. Portraits, books, and unusual art objects fill the low-ceilinged rooms. The highlight of the small estate is Hawk Tower, a detached edifice set with stones from the Carmel coastline—as well as one from the Great Wall of China. The docents who lead tours (six people maximum) are well informed about the poet's work and life. Reservations are required. Call the reservation line or click on the reservation link on the website. ✉ *26304 Ocean View Ave., Carmel* ☎ *831/624–1813 direct docent office line, Mon., Tues., and Thurs. only* ⊕ *www.torhouse.org* ⚏ *$12* ⚐ *No children under 12.*

Beaches

Carmel Beach
BEACH—SIGHT | Carmel-by-the-Sea's greatest attraction is its rugged coastline, with pine and cypress forests and countless inlets. Carmel Beach, an easy walk from downtown shops, has sparkling white sands and magnificent sunsets. ■**TIP→ Dogs are allowed to romp off-leash here. Amenities:** parking (no fee); toilets. **Best for:** sunset; surfing; walking. ✉ *End of Ocean Ave., Carmel.*

Carmel River State Beach
NATURE PRESERVE | This sugar-white beach, stretching 106 acres along Carmel Bay, is adjacent to a bird sanctuary, where you might spot pelicans, kingfishers, hawks, and sandpipers. Dogs are allowed on leash. **Amenities:** parking (no fee); toilets. **Best for:** sunrise; sunset; walking. ✉ *Off Scenic Rd., south of Carmel Beach, Carmel* ☎ *831/649–2836* ⊕ *www.parks. ca.gov* ⚏ *Free.*

🍴 Restaurants

Anton and Michel
$$$ | AMERICAN | Carefully prepared California cuisine is the draw at this airy restaurant. The rack of lamb is carved at the table, the grilled halloumi cheese and tomatoes are meticulously stacked and served with basil and Kalamata olive tapenade, and the desserts are set aflame before your eyes. **Known for:** romantic courtyard with fountain; elegant interior with fireplace lounge; flambé desserts. ⑤ *Average main: $35* ✉ *Mission St. and 7th Ave., Carmel* ☎ *831/624–2406* ⊕ *antonandmichel.com.*

★ Aubergine
$$$$ | AMERICAN | To eat and sleep at luxe L'Auberge Carmel is an experience in itself, but even those staying elsewhere can splurge at the inn's intimate restaurant, which was awarded a Michelin star in 2019. Chef Justin Cogley's nine-course prix-fixe tasting menu (your only option at dinner, $205 per person) is a gastronomical experience unrivaled in the region. **Known for:** exceptional chef's choice tasting menu; expert wine pairings; intimate nine-table dining room. ⑤ *Average main: $185* ✉ *Monte Verde at 7th Ave., Carmel* ☎ *831/624–8578* ⊕ *auberginecarmel.com* ☾ *No lunch.*

★ Basil
$$ | MODERN AMERICAN | Eco-friendly Basil was Monterey County's first restaurant to achieve a green-dining certification, recognition of its commitment to using organic, sustainably cultivated ingredients in creative dishes such as black squid linguine with sea urchin sauce, charred octopus, and smoked venison and other house-made charcuterie. **Known for:** organic ingredients; creative cocktails; year-round patio dining. ⑤ *Average main: $25* ✉ *Paseo Square, San Carlos St., between Ocean Ave. and 7th Ave., Carmel* ☎ *831/626–8226* ⊕ *basilcarmel.com.*

Casanova
$$$ | MEDITERRANEAN | This restaurant inspires European-style celebration and romance in an intimate French-country setting. Feast on authentic dishes from southern France and northern Italy— think beef tartare and escargot. **Known for:** house-made pastas and gnocchi; private dining at antique Van Gogh's table; romantic candlelight dining room and outdoor patio. ⑤ *Average main: $34* ✉ *5th Ave., between San Carlos and Mission Sts., Carmel* ☎ *831/625–0501* ⊕ *www. casanovacarmel.com.*

The Cottage Restaurant
$$ | AMERICAN | This family-friendly spot serves sandwiches, pizzas, and homemade soups at lunch, but the best meal

Point Lobos State Natural Reserve offers stunning vistas of sea and sky.

is breakfast (good thing it's served all day). The menu offers six variations on eggs Benedict and all kinds of sweet and savory crepes. **Known for:** artichoke soup; eggs Benedict and crepes; daily specials. $ *Average main: $17* ✉ *Lincoln St. between Ocean and 7th Aves., Carmel* ☎ *831/625–6260* ⊕ *cottagerestaurant. com* ☯ *No dinner.*

Flying Fish Grill

$$$ | SEAFOOD | Simple in appearance yet bold with its flavors, this Japanese–California seafood restaurant is one of Carmel's most inventive eateries. The warm, wood-lined dining room is broken up into very private booths. **Known for:** almond-crusted sea bass served with Chinese cabbage and rock shrimp stir-fry; clay pot dinners for two cooked at the table; authentic Asian decor. $ *Average main: $30* ✉ *Carmel Plaza, Mission St. between Ocean and 7th Aves., Carmel* ☎ *831/625–1962* ⊕ *flyingfishgrill.com* ☯ *No lunch.*

Grasing's Coastal Cuisine

$$$$ | AMERICAN | Chef Kurt Grasing draws from fresh Carmel Coast and Central Valley ingredients to whip up contemporary adaptations of European-provincial and American dishes. Longtime menu favorites include duck with fresh cherries in a red wine sauce, a savory sausage and seafood paella, and grilled steaks and chops. **Known for:** artichoke-heart lasagna; grilled steaks; bar, patio lounge, and rooftop deck. $ *Average main: $39* ✉ *6th Ave. and Mission St., Carmel* ☎ *831/624–6562* ⊕ *grasings.com.*

L'Escargot

$$$ | FRENCH | Chef-owner Kericos Loutas personally sees to each plate of food served at this romantic, unpretentious French restaurant. Order the pan-roasted duck breast or the veal medallions with wild mushrooms or white wine sauce; or, if you can't decide, choose the three-course prix-fixe dinner. **Known for:** authentic French-country dishes; prix-fixe dinner option; locally sourced ingredients. $ *Average main: $36* ✉ *Mission*

and 4th Ave., Carmel ☎ 831/620–1942 ⊕ escargot-carmel.com ⊙ Closed Mon. and Tues.

★ The Pocket

$$ | **MODERN ITALIAN** | In surf lingo, "the pocket" is a perfect riding spot within a barrel-shape wave, and this Italian–Californian restaurant is likewise a perfect (casual and unfussy) gathering spot for those who seek first-rate food, wine, and cocktails. The co-owners—a chef and sommelier with years of experience running restaurants in Pebble Beach and around the world—craft seasonal menus that focus on seafood, fresh pastas, curries, steaks, and braised meats. **Known for:** sleek marble, wood, and slate dining room and bar; spacious garden seating; full bar, extensive list of more than 400 wines; lively atmosphere, especially during the daily happy hour. ⑤ Average main: $32 ⊠ Lincoln St., between 5th and 6th Ave., Carmel ☎ 831/626–8000 ⊕ www. thepocketcarmel.com.

Vesuvio

$$$ | **ITALIAN** | Chef and restaurateur Rich Pèpe heats up the night with this lively trattoria downstairs and swinging rooftop terrace, the Starlight Lounge 65°. Pèpe's elegant take on traditional Italian cuisine yields dishes such as wild-boar Bolognese pappardelle, lobster ravioli, and velvety limoncello mousse cake. **Known for:** traditional cuisine of Campania, Italy; two bars with pizzas and small plates; live music on rooftop terrace in summer. ⑤ Average main: $30 ⊠ 6th and Junipero Aves., Carmel ☎ 831/625–1766 ⊕ vesuviocarmel.com ⊙ No lunch.

Hotels

Cypress Inn

$$$ | **B&B/INN** | This luxurious inn has a fresh, Mediterranean ambience with Moroccan touches. **Pros:** luxury without snobbery; popular lounge and restaurant; British-style afternoon tea on Saturdays. **Cons:** not for the pet-phobic; some

rooms and baths are tiny; basic amenities. ⑤ Rooms from: $279 ⊠ Lincoln St. and 7th Ave., Carmel ☎ 831/624–3871, 800/443–7443 ⊕ cypress-inn.com ⇌ 44 rooms ⦿ Free breakfast.

The Hideaway

$$$ | **HOTEL** | On a quiet street with a residential vibe, The Hideaway is a peaceful haven for those seeking stylish comfort in the heart of town. **Pros:** easy walk to shops, restaurants, galleries; short walk to Carmel Beach; pet-friendly amenities. **Cons:** street parking only; no pool or hot tub; some rooms are tiny. ⑤ Rooms from: $295 ⊠ Junipero St. at 8th Ave., Carmel ☎ 888/565–1420 ⊕ hideawaycarmel.com ⇌ 24 rooms ⦿ Free breakfast.

Hyatt Carmel Highlands

$$$$ | **HOTEL** | High on a hill overlooking the Pacific, this place has superb views and accommodations that include king rooms with fireplaces, suites with personal Jacuzzis, and full town houses with many perks. **Pros:** killer views; romantic getaway; great food. **Cons:** thin walls; must drive to the center of town; some rooms and buildings need update. ⑤ Rooms from: $499 ⊠ 120 Highlands Dr., Carmel ☎ 831/620–1234 ⊕ www. hyatt.com ⇌ 48 rooms ⦿ No meals.

La Playa Carmel

$$$$ | **HOTEL** | A historic complex of lush gardens and Mediterranean-style buildings, La Playa has light and airy interiors done in Carmel Bay beach-cottage style. **Pros:** historic restaurant and bar; manicured gardens; two blocks from the beach. **Cons:** four stories (no elevator); busy lobby; some rooms are on the small side. ⑤ Rooms from: $449 ⊠ Camino Real at 8th Ave., Carmel ☎ 800/582–8900, 831/293–6100 ⊕ laplayahotel.com ⇌ 75 rooms ⦿ Free breakfast.

★ L'Auberge Carmel

$$$$ | **B&B/INN** | Stepping through the doors of this elegant inn is like being transported to a little European village. **Pros:** in town but off the main drag; four blocks from the beach; full-service luxury. **Cons:** touristy area; not a good choice for families; no a/c. ⑤ *Rooms from: $485 ✉ Monte Verde at 7th Ave., Carmel* ☎ *831/624–8578* ⊕ *www.laubergecarmel.com* ⤳ *20 rooms* ◯| *Free breakfast.*

Mission Ranch

$$ | HOTEL | Movie star Clint Eastwood owns this sprawling property whose accommodations include rooms in a converted barn, and several cottages, some with fireplaces. **Pros:** farm setting; pastoral views; great for tennis buffs. **Cons:** busy parking lot; must drive to the heart of town; old buildings. ⑤ *Rooms from: $175 ✉ 26270 Dolores St., Carmel* ☎ *831/624–6436, 800/538–8221, 831/625–9040 restaurant* ⊕ *www. missionranchcarmel.com* ⤳ *31 rooms* ◯| *Free breakfast.*

Pine Inn

$$ | HOTEL | A favorite with generations of visitors, the Pine Inn is four blocks from the beach and has Victorian-style furnishings, complete with a grandfather clock, padded fabric wall panels, antique tapestries, and marble tabletops. **Pros:** elegant; close to shopping and dining; full breakfast included weekdays. **Cons:** on the town's busiest street; public areas a bit dark; limited parking. ⑤ *Rooms from: $189 ✉ Ocean Ave. and Monte Verde St., Carmel* ☎ *831/624–3851, 800/228–3851* ⊕ *pineinn.com* ⤳ *49 rooms* ◯| *Free breakfast.*

Tally Ho Inn

$$ | B&B/INN | This inn is nearly all suites, many of which have fireplaces and floor-to-ceiling glass walls that open onto ocean-view patios. **Pros:** within walking distance of shops, restaurants, beach; free parking; spacious rooms. **Cons:** small property; busy area; basic breakfast. ⑤ *Rooms from: $229 ✉ Monte Verde St. and 6th Ave., Carmel* ☎ *831/624–2232, 800/652–2632* ⊕ *tallyho-inn.com* ⤳ *12 rooms* ◯| *Free breakfast.*

Tickle Pink Inn

$$$$ | B&B/INN | Atop a towering cliff, this inn has views of the Big Sur coastline, which you can contemplate from your private balcony. **Pros:** close to great hiking; intimate; dramatic views. **Cons:** close to a big hotel; lots of traffic during the day; basic breakfast. ⑤ *Rooms from: $389 ✉ 155 Highland Dr., Carmel* ☎ *831/624–1244, 800/635–4774* ⊕ *ticklepink.com* ⤳ *34 units* ◯| *Free breakfast.*

 Nightlife

BARS AND PUBS

Barmel

BARS/PUBS | Al Capone and other Prohibition-era legends once sidled up to this hip nightspot's carved wooden bar. Rock to DJ music and sit indoors, or head out to the pet-friendly patio. Some menu items pay homage to California's early days, and you can order Baja-style dishes from the adjacent Pescadero restaurant, which is under the same ownership. ✉ *San Carlos St., between Ocean and 7th Aves., Carmel* ☎ *831/626–2095* ⊕ *www.facebook.com/BarmelByTheSea.*

Mulligan Public House

BARS/PUBS | A sports bar with seven TV screens, 12 beers on tap, and extensive menu packed with hearty American pub food, Mulligan usually stays open until midnight. ✉ *5 Dolores St., at Ocean* ☎ *831/250–5910* ⊕ *mulliganspublichouse. com.*

 Shopping

ART GALLERIES

Carmel Art Association

ART GALLERIES | Carmel's oldest gallery, established in 1927, exhibits original paintings and sculptures by local artists. ✉ *Dolores St., between 5th and 6th Aves., Carmel* ☎ *831/624–6176* ⊕ *carmelart.org* ◷ *Closed Tues. and Wed.*

Dawson Cole Fine Art

ART GALLERIES | Amazing images of dancers, athletes, and other humans in motion come to life in this gallery that is devoted to the artworks of Monterey Bay resident Richard MacDonald, one of the most famed figurative sculptors of our time. ⊠ *Lincoln St., at 6th Ave., Carmel* ☎ *831/624–8200* ⊕ *dawsoncolefineart. com* ☑ *Free.*

Galerie Plein Aire

ART GALLERIES | The gallery showcases the oil paintings (mostly large-format seascapes and landscapes) of local artists Cyndra Bradford and Jeff Daniel Smith. ⊠ *3663 The Barnyard, Carmel* ☎ *831/277–6165* ⊕ *galeriepleinaire.com* ☾ *Closed Tues. and Wed.*

Gallery Sur

ART GALLERIES | Fine art photography of the Big Sur Coast and the Monterey Peninsula, including scenic shots and golf images, is the focus here. ⊠ *6th Ave., between Dolores and Lincoln Sts., Carmel* ☎ *831/626–2015* ⊕ *gallerysur.com.*

★ Weston Gallery

ART GALLERIES | Run by the family of the late Edward Weston, this is hands down the best photography gallery around, with contemporary color photography and classic black-and-whites. ⊠ *6th Ave., between Dolores and Lincoln Sts., Carmel* ☎ *831/624–4453* ⊕ *westongallery. com.*

MALLS

Carmel Plaza

SHOPPING CENTERS/MALLS | Tiffany & Co. and Anthropologie are among the name brands doing business at this mall on Carmel's east side, but what makes it worth a stop are homegrown enterprises such as Carmel Honey Company for local honey; Madrigal for women's fashion; and J. Lawrence Khaki's for debonair menswear. Flying Fish Grill and several other restaurants are here, along with the Wrath Wines tasting room (Chardonnay and Pinot Noir). The Carmel Chamber of Commerce Visitor Center (open daily) is on the second floor. ⊠ *Ocean Ave. and Mission St., Carmel* ☎ *831/624–1385* ⊕ *carmelplaza.com.*

SPECIALTY SHOPS

Bittner

SPECIALTY STORES | The shop carries collectible and vintage pens from around the world. ⊠ *Ocean Ave., between Mission and San Carlos Sts., Carmel* ☎ *831/626–8828* ⊕ *bittner.com.*

elizabethW

GIFTS/SOUVENIRS | Named after the designer and owner's pioneering great-grandmother, elizabethW handcrafts fragrances, essential oils, candles, silk eye pillows, and other soul-soothing goods for bath, body, and home. ⊠ *Ocean Ave., between Monte Verde and Lincoln, Carmel* ☎ *831/626–3892* ⊕ *elizabethw.com.*

Foxy Couture

CLOTHING | Shop for one-of-a-kind treasures at this curated collection of gently used luxury couture and vintage clothes and accessories—think Chanel, Hermes, and Gucci—without paying a hefty price tag. ⊠ *San Carlos St., in Vanervort Court, between Ocean and 7th Aves., Carmel* ☎ *831/625–9995* ⊕ *foxycouturecarmel. com* ☾ *Closed Tues. and Wed.*

Intima

SPECIALTY STORES | The European lingerie ranges from lacy to racy. ⊠ *San Carlos St., between Ocean and 6th Aves., Carmel* ☎ *831/625–0599* ⊕ *www.intimacarmel.com.*

Jan de Luz

SPECIALTY STORES | This shop monograms and embroiders fine linens (including bathrobes) while you wait. ⊠ *Dolores St., at 6th Ave. NE, Carmel* ☎ *831/622–7621* ⊕ *jandeluzlinens.com.*

Carmel Valley

10 miles east of Carmel.

Carmel Valley Road, which heads inland from Highway 1 south of Carmel, is the main thoroughfare through this valley, a secluded enclave of horse ranchers and other well-heeled residents who prefer the area's sunny climate to coastal fog and wind. Once thick with dairy farms, the valley has evolved into an esteemed wine appellation. Carmel Valley Village has crafts shops, art galleries, and the tasting rooms of numerous local wineries.

GETTING HERE AND AROUND

From U.S. 101 north or south, exit at Highway 68 and head west toward the coast. Scenic, two-lane Laureles Grade winds west over the mountains to Carmel Valley Road north of the village.

TOURS

Carmel Valley Grapevine Express

BUS TOURS | An incredible bargain, the express—aka MST's Bus 24—travels between downtown Monterey and Carmel Valley Village, with stops near wineries, restaurants, and shopping centers. ☎ 888/678–2871 ⊕ mst.org ☞ $10 all-day pass.

 Sights

Bernardus Tasting Room

WINERY/DISTILLERY | At the tasting room of Bernardus, known for its Bordeaux-style red blend, called Marinus, and Chardonnays, you can sample current releases and library and reserve wines. ⊠ 5 W. Carmel Valley Rd., at El Caminito Rd. ☎ 831/298–8021, 800/223–2533 ⊕ bernardus.com ☞ Tastings from $15.

Cowgirl Winery

WINERY/DISTILLERY | Cowgirl chic prevails in the main tasting building here, and it's just plain rustic at the outdoor tables, set amid chickens, a tractor, and a flatbed truck. The wines include Chardonnay,

Cabernet Sauvignon, Malbec, Pinot Noir, Rosé, and some blends. ⊠ 25 Pilot Rd., off W. Carmel Valley Rd. ☎ 831/298–7030 ⊕ cowgirlwinery.com ☞ Tastings from $20.

Earthbound Farm

FARM/RANCH | **FAMILY** | Pick up fresh vegetables, ready-to-eat meals, gourmet groceries, flowers, and gifts at Earthbound Farm, the world's largest grower of organic produce. You can also take a romp in the kids' garden, cut your own herbs, and stroll through the chamomile aromatherapy labyrinth. Special events, on Saturday from April through December, include bug walks and garlic-braiding workshops. ⊠ 7250 Carmel Valley Rd., Carmel ☎ 831/625–6219 ⊕ www.ebfarm.com ☞ Free.

★ Folktale Winery & Vineyards

WINERY/DISTILLERY | The expansive winery on a 15-acre estate (formerly Chateau Julienne) offers daily tastings, live music on weekends (plus Friday in summer and fall), and special events and programs such as Saturday yoga in the vineyard. Best-known wines include the estate Pinot Noir, Sparkling Rosé, and Le Mistral Joseph's Blend. Chefs in the on-site restaurant cook up small plates with wine pairing suggestions. Tours of the winery and organically farmed vineyards are available by appointment. ⊠ 8940 Carmel Valley Rd. ✤ At Schetter Rd. ☎ 831/293–7500 ⊕ folktalewinery.com ☞ Tastings from $20; tours $40 (includes tasting) ⊗ Closed Mon.–Wed.

Garland Ranch Regional Park

NATIONAL/STATE PARK | Hiking trails stretch across much of this park's 4,500 acres of meadows, forested hillsides, and creeks. ⊠ 700 W. Carmel Valley Rd., 9 miles east of Carmel-by-the-Sea ☎ 831/372–3196 ⊕ www.mprpd.org.

★ Holman Ranch Vineyards Tasting Room

WINERY/DISTILLERY | Estate-grown Chardonnay and Pinot Noir are among the standout wines made by Holman Ranch, which pours samples in its chic tasting room and on two patios in the historic Will's Fargo tavern building. The 15-acre ranch itself is just up the road, set amid rolling hills that were once part of the Carmel mission's land grant. You can book winery and vineyard tours by appointment ⊠ *18 W. Carmel Valley Rd.* ☎ *831/601–8761* ⊕ *holmanranch.com* ☙ *Tastings from $35* ☉ *Closed Tues. and Wed.*

Restaurants

Café Rustica

$$ | EUROPEAN | European country cooking is the focus at this lively roadhouse, where specialties include roasted meats, seafood, pastas, and thin-crust pizzas from the wood-fired oven. It can get noisy inside; for a quieter meal, request a table outside. **Known for:** Tuscan-flavored dishes from Alsace; open kitchen with wood-fired oven; outdoor patio seating. ⑤ *Average main: $26* ⊠ *10 Delfino Pl., at Pilot Rd., off Carmel Valley Rd.* ☎ *831/659–4444* ⊕ *caferusticavillage.com* ☉ *Closed Mon. No lunch Tues. and Wed.*

Corkscrew Café

$$ | MODERN AMERICAN | Farm-fresh food is the specialty of this casual, Old Monterey–style bistro. Herbs and seasonal produce come from the Corkscrew's own organic gardens, the catch of the day comes from local waters, and the meats are hormone-free. **Known for:** wood-fired pizzas; fantastic regional wine list; garden patio. ⑤ *Average main: $22* ⊠ *55 W. Carmel Valley Rd.* ☎ *831/659–8888* ⊕ *www.corkscrewcafe.com* ☉ *Closed Jan.*

Roux

$$$ | MODERN FRENCH | Chef Fabrice Roux, who hails from France, worked at lauded Parisian restaurants for more than a decade before coming to Carmel Valley to wow diners with his contemporary takes on traditional French-Mediterranean cuisine. The eclectic menu, with mostly small and large plates meant for sharing, focuses on local ingredients procured

that week: perhaps crispy duck leg confit, tuna tartare, or braised wild-boar bourguignon. **Known for:** expert food and wine pairings; European-style cottage with private room for dining and tastings; extensive wine list with more than 400 labels. ⑤ *Average main: $33* ⊠ *6 Pilot Rd.* ☎ *831/659–5020* ⊕ *rouxcarmel.com* ☉ *Closed Tues. No lunch Wed. and Thurs.* ⊟ *No credit cards.*

Wagon Wheel Coffee Shop

$ | AMERICAN | This local hangout—decorated with wagon wheels, cowboy hats, and lassos—serves terrific hearty breakfasts, including oatmeal and banana pancakes, eggs Benedict, and biscuits and gravy. The lunch menu includes a dozen different burgers and other sandwiches. **Known for:** traditional American breakfast; cowboy-theme setting; lively local clientele. ⑤ *Average main: $15* ⊠ *Valley Hill Center, 7156 Carmel Valley Rd., next to Quail Lodge, Carmel* ☎ *831/624–8878* ⊟ *No credit cards* ☉ *No dinner.*

Hotels

★ Bernardus Lodge & Spa

$$$$ | RESORT | The spacious guest rooms at this luxury spa resort have vaulted ceilings, French oak floors, featherbeds, fireplaces, patios, and bathrooms with heated-tile floors and soaking tubs for two. **Pros:** exceptional personal service; outstanding food and wine; serene, cushy full-service spa. **Cons:** hefty rates; can feel a little snooty; resort fee. ⑤ *Rooms from: $445* ⊠ *415 W. Carmel Valley Rd.* ☎ *831/658–3400* ⊕ *www.bernarduslodge.com* ⇨ *73 rooms* ⎪⎪ *No meals*

★ Carmel Valley Ranch

$$$$ | RESORT | The activity options at this luxury ranch are so varied that the resort provides a program director to guide you through them. **Pros:** stunning natural setting; tons of activities; River Ranch center with a pool, splash zone, boccie courts, and fitness center. **Cons:** must

drive several miles to shops and nightlife; high rates; footsteps from neighboring rooms easy to hear in some buildings. ⑤ *Rooms from: $699* ⊠ *1 Old Ranch Rd., Carmel* ☎ *831/625–9500, 855/687–7262 toll-free reservations* ⊕ *carmelvalleyranch.com* ⤳ *181 suites* ⊙l *No meals.*

Quail Lodge & Golf Club

$$$$ | **HOTEL** | **FAMILY** | A sprawling collection of ranch-style buildings on 850 acres of meadows, fairways, and lakes, Quail Lodge offers luxury rooms and outdoor activities at surprisingly affordable rates. **Pros:** on the golf course; on-site restaurant; spacious rooms. **Cons:** service sometimes spotty; 5 miles from the beach and Carmel Valley Village; basic amenities. ⑤ *Rooms from: $395* ⊠ *8205 Valley Greens Dr., Carmel* ☎ *866/675– 1101 reservations, 831/624–2888* ⊕ *www.quaillodge.com* ⤳ *93 rooms* ⊙l *No meals.*

★ Stonepine Estate

$$$$ | **RESORT** | Set on 330 pastoral acres, the former estate of the Crocker banking family has been converted to a luxurious inn. **Pros:** supremely exclusive; close to Carmel Valley Village; attentive, personalized service. **Cons:** difficult to get a reservation; far from the coast; expensive rates. ⑤ *Rooms from: $500* ⊠ *150 E. Carmel Valley Rd.* ☎ *831/659–2245* ⊕ *www.stonepineestate.com* ⤳ *13 units* ⊙l *No meals.*

 Activities

GOLF
Quail Lodge & Golf Club

GOLF | Robert Muir Graves designed this championship semiprivate 18-hole course next to Quail Lodge that provides challenging play for golfers of all skill levels. The scenic course, which incorporates five lakes and edges the Carmel River, was completely renovated in 2015 by golf architect Todd Eckenrode to add extra challenge to the golf experience, white sand bunkers, and other enhancements. For the most part flat, the walkable

course is well maintained, with stunning views, lush fairways, and ultrasmooth greens. ⊠ *8000 Valley Greens Dr., Carmel* ☎ *831/620–8808 golf shop, 831/620–8866 club concierge* ⊕ *www.quaillodge.com* 🖃 *$196* ⅀. *18 holes, 6500 yards, par 71.*

SPAS
★ Refuge

FITNESS/HEALTH CLUBS | At this co-ed, European-style center on 2 serene acres you can recharge without breaking the bank. Heat up in the eucalyptus steam room or cedar sauna, plunge into cold pools, and relax indoors in zero-gravity chairs or outdoors in Adirondack chairs around firepits. Repeat the cycle a few times, then lounge around the thermal waterfall pools. Talk is not allowed, and bathing suits are required. ⊠ *27300 Rancho San Carlos Rd., south off Carmel Valley Rd., Carmel* ☎ *831/620–7360* ⊕ *refuge.com* 🖃 *$44* ☞ *$52 admission; $155 50-min massage (includes Refuge admission), $12 robe rental, hot tubs (outdoor), sauna, steam room. Services: aromatherapy, hydrotherapy, massage.*

Pebble Beach

Off North San Antonio Ave. in Carmel-by-the-Sea or off Sunset Dr. in Pacific Grove.

In 1919 the Pacific Improvement Company acquired 18,000 acres of prime land on the Monterey Peninsula, including the entire Pebble Beach coastal region and much of Pacific Grove. Pebble Beach Golf Links and The Lodge at Pebble Beach opened the same year, and the private enclave evolved into a world-class golf destination with three posh lodges, five golf courses, hiking and riding trails, and some of the West Coast's ritziest homes. Pebble Beach has hosted major international golf tournaments, including the U.S. Open in 2019. The annual Pebble Beach Food & Wine, a four-day event in late April with 100 celebrity chefs, is one of the West Coast's premier culinary festivals.

GETTING HERE AND AROUND

If you drive south from Monterey on Highway 1, exit at 17-Mile Drive/Sunset Drive in Pacific Grove to find the northern entrance gate. Coming from Carmel, exit at Ocean Avenue and follow the road almost to the beach; turn right on North San Antonio Avenue to the Carmel Gate. You can also enter through the Highway 1 Gate off Highway 68. Monterey–Salinas Transit buses provide regular service in and around Pebble Beach.

Sights

★ The Lone Cypress

FOREST | The most-photographed tree along 17-Mile Drive is the weather-sculpted Lone Cypress, which grows out of a precipitous outcropping above the waves about 1½ miles up the road from Pebble Beach Golf Links. You can't walk out to the tree, but you can stop for a view of it at a small parking area off the road.

★ 17-Mile Drive

SCENIC DRIVE | Primordial nature resides in quiet harmony with palatial, mostly Spanish Mission–style estates along 17-Mile Drive, which winds through an 8,400-acre microcosm of the Pebble Beach coastal landscape. Dotting the drive are rare Monterey cypresses, trees so gnarled and twisted that Robert Louis Stevenson described them as "ghosts fleeing before the wind." The most famous of these is the **Lone Cypress**. Other highlights include **Bird Rock** and **Seal Rock,** home to harbor seals, sea lions, cormorants, and pelicans and other sea creatures and birds, and the **Crocker Marble Palace,** inspired by a Byzantine castle and easily identifiable by its dozens of marble arches.

■ TIP➔ **If you spend $35 or more on dining in Pebble Beach and show a receipt upon exiting, you'll receive a refund off the drive's $10.75 per-car fee.** ⊠ *Hwy. 1 Gate, 17-Mile Dr., at Hwy. 68* 🖃 *$11 per car, free for bicyclists.*

Hotels

★ Casa Palmero

$$$$ | RESORT | This exclusive boutique hotel evokes a stately Mediterranean villa. **Pros:** ultimate in pampering; sumptuous decor; more private than sister resorts. **Cons:** rates out of reach for most visitors; not the best views compared to sister lodges; some showers on the small side. ⑤ *Rooms from: $1150* ⊠ *1518 Cypress Dr.* ☎ *831/622–6650, 800/877–0597 reservations* ⊕ *www.pebblebeach.com* ↪ *24 rooms* �‖ *Free breakfast.*

The Inn at Spanish Bay

$$$$ | RESORT | This resort sprawls along a breathtaking stretch of shoreline and has plush, 600-square-foot rooms. **Pros:** attentive service; many amenities; spectacular views. **Cons:** huge hotel; 4 miles from other Pebble Beach Resorts facilities; atmosphere too snobbish for some. ⑤ *Rooms from: $870* ⊠ *2700 17-Mile Dr.* ☎ *831/647–7500, 800/877–0597* ⊕ *www.pebblebeach.com* ↪ *269 rooms* �‖ *No meals.*

The Lodge at Pebble Beach

$$$$ | RESORT | Most rooms have wood-burning fireplaces and many have wonderful ocean views at this circa-1919 resort, which was expanded to include the 38-room Fairway One complex in 2017. **Pros:** world-class golf; borders the ocean and fairways; fabulous facilities. **Cons:** some rooms are on the small side; very pricey; not many activities if you don't golf. ⑤ *Rooms from: $990* ⊠ *1700 17-Mile Dr.* ☎ *831/624–3811, 800/877–0597* ⊕ *www.pebblebeach.com* ↪ *199 rooms* �‖ *No meals.*

Activities

GOLF
The Hay

GOLF | The only 9-hole, par-3 course on the Monterey Peninsula open to the public, Peter Hay attracts golfers of all skill levels. It's an ideal place for warm-ups, practicing short games, and for those

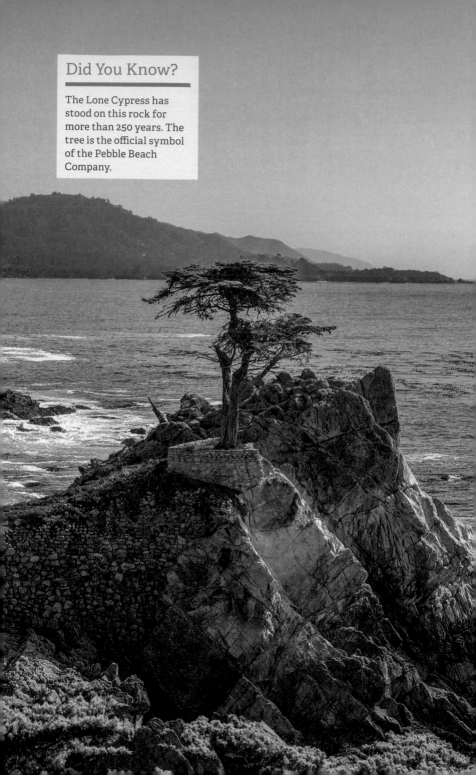

Did You Know?

The Lone Cypress has stood on this rock for more than 250 years. The tree is the official symbol of the Pebble Beach Company.

who don't have time to play 18 holes. ✉ *17-Mile Dr. and Portola Rd.* ☎ *800/877-0597* ⊕ *www.pebblebeach.com* ✉ *$65* ⛳ *. 9 holes, 725 yards, par 27.*

Links at Spanish Bay

GOLF | This course, which hugs a choice stretch of shoreline, was designed by Robert Trent Jones Jr., Tom Watson, and Sandy Tatum in the rugged manner of traditional Scottish links, with sand dunes and coastal marshes interspersed among the greens. A bagpiper signals the course's closing each day. ■TIP→ **Nonguests of the Pebble Beach Resorts can reserve tee times up to two months in advance.** ✉ *17-Mile Dr., north end* ☎ *800/877-0597* ⊕ *www.pebblebeach.com* ✉ *$295* ⛳ *. 18 holes, 6821 yards, par 72.*

★ Pebble Beach Golf Links

GOLF | Each February, show-business celebrities and golf pros team up at this course, the main site of the glamorous AT&T Pebble Beach National Pro-Am tournament. On most days the rest of the year, tee times are available to guests of the Pebble Beach Resorts who book a minimum two-night stay. Nonguests can reserve a tee time only one day in advance on a space-available basis; resort guests can reserve up to 18 months in advance. ✉ *17-Mile Dr., near The Lodge at Pebble Beach* ☎ *800/877-0597* ⊕ *www.pebblebeach.com* ✉ *$575* ⛳ *. 18 holes, 6828 yards, par 72.*

Poppy Hills

GOLF | An 10-hole course designed in 1986 by Robert Trent Jones Jr., Poppy Hills reopened in 2014 after a yearlong renovation that Jones supervised. Each hole has been restored to its natural elevation along the forest floor, and all 18 greens have been rebuilt with bent grass. Individuals may reserve up to a month in advance. ■TIP→ **Poppy Hills, owned by a golfing nonprofit, represents good value for this area.** ✉ *3200 Lopez Rd., at 17-Mile Dr.* ☎ *831/622-8239* ⊕ *poppyhillsgolf.com* ✉ *$250* ⛳ *. 18 holes, 7002 yards, par 73.5.*

Spyglass Hill

GOLF | With three holes rated among the toughest on the PGA tour, Spyglass Hill, designed by Robert Trent Jones Sr. and Jr., challenges golfers with its varied terrain but rewards them with glorious views. The first 5 holes border the Pacific, and the other 13 reach deep into the Del Monte Forest. Reservations are essential and may be made up to one month in advance (18 months for resort guests). ✉ *Stevenson Dr. and Spyglass Hill Rd.* ☎ *800/877-0597* ⊕ *www.pebblebeach.com* ✉ *$415* ⛳ *. 18 holes, 6960 yards, par 72.*

Pacific Grove

3 miles north of Carmel-by-the-Sea.

This picturesque town, which began as a summer retreat for church groups more than a century ago, recalls its prim and proper Victorian heritage in its host of tiny board-and-batten cottages and stately mansions. However, long before the church groups flocked here the area received thousands of annual pilgrims—in the form of bright orange-and-black monarch butterflies. They still come, migrating south from Canada and the Pacific Northwest to take residence in pine and eucalyptus groves from October through March. In Butterfly Town USA, as Pacific Grove is known, the sight of a mass of butterflies hanging from the branches like a long, fluttering veil is unforgettable.

A prime way to enjoy Pacific Grove is to walk or bicycle the 3 miles of city-owned shoreline along Ocean View Boulevard, a cliff-top area landscaped with native plants and dotted with benches meant for sitting and gazing at the sea. You can spot many types of birds here, including the web-footed cormorants that crowd the massive rocks rising out of the surf. Two Victorians of note along Ocean View are the Queen Anne–style Green Gables, at No. 301—erected in 1888, it's now an inn—and the 1909 Pryor House, at No. 429, a massive, shingled, private residence with a leaded- and beveled-glass doorway.

GETTING HERE AND AROUND
Reach Pacific Grove via Highway 68 off Highway 1, just south of Monterey. From Cannery Row in Monterey, head north until the road merges with Ocean Boulevard and follow it along the coast. MST buses travel within Pacific Grove and surrounding towns.

Sights

Lovers Point Park
CITY PARK | FAMILY | The coastal views are gorgeous from this waterfront park whose sheltered beach has a children's pool and a picnic area. The main lawn has a volleyball court and a snack bar. ⊠ *Ocean View Blvd. northwest of Forest Ave.* ⊕ *www.cityofpacificgrove.org/living/recreation/parks/lovers-point-park.*

Monarch Grove Sanctuary
NATURE PRESERVE | FAMILY | The sanctuary is a reliable spot for viewing monarch butterflies between November and February. ■TIP➜ **The best time to visit is between noon and 3 pm.** ⊠ *250 Ridge Rd., off Lighthouse Ave.* ⊕ *www.pgmuseum. org/monarch-viewing.*

Pacific Grove Museum of Natural History
MUSEUM | The museum, a good source for the latest information about monarch butterflies, has permanent exhibitions about the butterflies, birds of Monterey County, biodiversity, and plants. There's a native plant garden, and a display documents life in Pacific Grove's 19th-century Chinese fishing village. ⊠ *165 Forest Ave., at Central Ave.* ☎ *831/648–5716* ⊕ *pgmuseum.org* ☜ *$9* ☉ *Closed Mon.*

Point Pinos Lighthouse
LIGHTHOUSE | FAMILY | At this 1855 structure, the West Coast's oldest continuously operating lighthouse, you can learn about the lighting and foghorn operations and wander through a small museum containing U.S. Coast Guard memorabilia. ⊠ *Asilomar Ave., between Lighthouse Ave. and Del Monte Blvd.* ☎ *831/648–5722* ⊕ *cityofpg.org/lighthouse* ☜ *$5* ☉ *Closed weekdays some months; visit website for current schedule.*

Beaches

Asilomar State Beach
BEACH—SIGHT | A beautiful coastal area, Asilomar State Beach stretches between Point Pinos and the Del Monte Forest. The 100 acres of dunes, tidal pools, and pocket-size beaches form one of the region's richest areas for marine life—including surfers, who migrate here most winter mornings. Leashed dogs are allowed on the beach. **Amenities:** none. **Best for:** sunrise; sunset; surfing; walking. ⊠ *Sunset Dr. and Asilomar Ave.* ☎ *831/646–6440* ⊕ *www.parks.ca.gov.*

🍽 Restaurants

Beach House
$$$ | MODERN AMERICAN | Patrons of this bluff-top perch sip classic cocktails, sample California fare, and watch the otters frolic on Lovers Point Beach below. The sunset discounts between 4 and 5:30 (reservations recommended) are a great value. **Known for:** sweeping bluff-top views; heated patio; seafood and organic pastas. ⑤ *Average main: $28* ⊠ *620 Ocean View Blvd.* ☎ *831/375–2345* ⊕ *beachhousepg.com* ☉ *No lunch.*

★ Fandango
$$$ | MEDITERRANEAN | The menu here is mostly Mediterranean and southern French, with such dishes as osso buco and paella. The decor follows suit: stone walls and country furniture lend the restaurant the earthy feel of a European farmhouse. **Known for:** wood-fire-grilled rack of lamb, seafood, and beef; convivial residential vibe; traditional European flavors. ⑤ *Average main: $36* ⊠ *223 17th*

St., south of Lighthouse Ave. ☎ *831/372–3456* ⊕ *fandangorestaurant.com.*

Fishwife

$$ | **SEAFOOD** | Fresh fish with a Latin accent makes this a favorite of locals for lunch or a casual dinner. Standards are the sea garden salads—topped with your choice of fish—and the fried seafood plates. **Known for:** fisherman's bowls with fresh local seafood; house-made desserts; crab cakes and New Zealand mussels. ⑤ *Average main: $22* ⊠ *1996½ Sunset Dr., at Asilomar Blvd.* ☎ *831/375–7107* ⊕ *fishwife.com.*

Jennini Kitchen + Wine Bar

$$ | **MEDITERRANEAN** | Sommelier Thamin Saleh, who named his lively restaurant and wine bar after his hometown in Palestine, designed a seasonally changing menu of small plates and entrées that showcases the cuisine of the eastern Mediterranean and southern Spain. Dishes might include chicken and merguez tagine, crispy lamb shanks, hummus and baba ghanoush, and filone bread with goat butter. **Known for:** Sunday night paella (order 24 hours in advance other nights); eclectic, value-driven wine list with 180 selections; creative twists on classic dishes. ⑤ *Average main: $25* ⊠ *542 Lighthouse Ave.* ☎ *831/920–2662* ⊕ *www.jeninni.com* ☯ *No lunch. Closed Tues. and Wed.*

★ Passionfish

$$$ | **MODERN AMERICAN** | South American artwork and artifacts decorate Passionfish, and Latin and Asian flavors infuse the dishes. The chef shops at local farmers' markets several times a week to find the best produce, fish, and meat available, then pairs it with creative sauces like a caper, raisin, and walnut relish. **Known for:** sustainably sourced seafood and organic ingredients; reasonably priced wine list that supports small producers; slow-cooked meats. ⑤ *Average main: $28* ⊠ *701 Lighthouse Ave.* ☎ *831/655–3311* ⊕ *www.passionfish.net* ☯ *No lunch.*

Peppers Mexicali Cafe

$$ | **MEXICAN** | This cheerful, white-walled storefront serves traditional dishes from Mexico and Latin America, with an emphasis on fresh seafood. Excellent red and green salsas are made throughout the day, and there's a large selection of beers, along with fresh lime margaritas. **Known for:** traditional Latin American dishes; fresh lime margaritas; daily specials. ⑤ *Average main: $20* ⊠ *170 Forest Ave., between Lighthouse and Central Aves.* ☎ *831/373–6892* ⊕ *peppersmexicalicafe. com* ☯ *Closed Tues. No lunch Sun.*

Red House Café

$$ | **AMERICAN** | When it's nice out, sun pours through the big windows of this cozy restaurant and across tables on the porch; when fog rolls in, the fireplace is lit. The American menu changes with the seasons, but grilled lamb chops atop mashed potatoes are often on offer for dinner, and a grilled calamari steak might be served for lunch, either in a salad or as part of a sandwich. **Known for:** cozy homelike dining areas; comfort food; stellar breakfast and brunch. ⑤ *Average main: $22* ⊠ *662 Lighthouse Ave., at 19th St.* ☎ *831/643–1060* ⊕ *redhousecafe.com* ☯ *No dinner Mon.*

 ## Hotels

Gosby House Inn

$$ | **B&B/INN** | Though in the town center, this turreted butter-yellow Queen Anne Victorian has an informal feel. **Pros:** peaceful; homey; within walking distance of shops and restaurants. **Cons:** too frilly for some; area is busy during the day; limited parking. ⑤ *Rooms from: $165* ⊠ *643 Lighthouse Ave.* ☎ *831/375–1287* ⊕ *gosbyhouseinn.com* ⇥ *22 rooms* ⑩ *Free breakfast.*

★ Green Gables Inn

$$ | **B&B/INN** | Stained-glass windows and ornate interior details compete with spectacular ocean views at this Queen Anne–style mansion. **Pros:** exceptional views; impeccable attention to historic detail; afternoon wine and cheese served in the parlor. **Cons:** some rooms are small; thin walls; breakfast room can be crowded. $ *Rooms from: $179* ✉ *301 Ocean View Blvd.* ☎ *831/375–2095* ⊕ *www.greengablesinnpg.com* ⌨ *11 rooms* ⎮○⎮ *Free breakfast.*

Martine Inn

$$$ | **B&B/INN** | The glassed-in parlor and many guest rooms at this 1899 Mediterranean-style villa have stunning ocean views. **Pros:** romantic; exquisite antiques; ocean views. **Cons:** not child-friendly; sits on a busy thoroughfare; inconvenient parking. $ *Rooms from: $259* ✉ *255 Ocean View Blvd.* ☎ *831/373–3388* ⊕ *martineinn.com* ⌨ *25 rooms* ⎮○⎮ *Free breakfast.*

Monterey

2 miles southeast of Pacific Grove, 2 miles north of Carmel.

Monterey is a scenic city filled with early California history: adobe buildings from the 1700s, Colton Hall, where California's first constitution was drafted in 1849, and Cannery Row, made famous by author John Steinbeck. Thousands of visitors come each year to mingle with otters and other sea creatures at the world-famous Monterey Bay Aquarium and in the protected waters of the national marine sanctuary that hugs the shoreline.

GETTING HERE AND AROUND

From San Jose or San Francisco, take U.S. 101 south to Highway 156 West at Prunedale. Head west about 8 miles to Highway 1 and follow it about 15 miles south. From San Luis Obispo, take U.S. 101 north to Salinas and drive west on Highway 68 about 20 miles.

Many MST bus lines connect at the Monterey Transit Center, at Pearl Street and Munras Avenue. In summer (daily from 10 until at least 7) and on weekends and holidays the rest of the year, the free MST Monterey Trolley travels from downtown Monterey along Cannery Row to the Aquarium and back.

TOURS

Old Monterey Walking Tour

WALKING TOURS | Learn all about Monterey's storied past by joining a guided walking tour through the historic district. Tours begin at the Custom House in Custom House Plaza, across from Fisherman's Wharf and are typically offered Thursday through Sunday at 11, 1, and 3. ■**TIP→ Tours are free for everyone on the last Sunday of the month.** ✉ *Monterey* ⊕ *www.parks.ca.gov/?page_id=951* ⌨ *Tours $10.*

The Original Monterey Walking Tours

WALKING TOURS | Learn more about Monterey's past, primarily the Mexican period until California statehood, on a guided tour through downtown Monterey. You can also join a guided walking tour of Cannery Row in the morning. Tours last 1½ to 2 hours and are offered Thursday–Sunday at 10 am and 2. Reservations are essential. ✉ *Monterey* ☎ *831/521–4884* ⊕ *www.walkmonterey.com* ⌨ *From $25.*

ESSENTIALS

VISITOR INFORMATION Visit Monterey. ✉ *401 Camino El Estero* ☎ *888/221–1010* ⊕ *www.seemonterey.com.*

Sights

A Taste of Monterey

WINERY/DISTILLERY | Without driving the back roads, you can taste the wines of nearly 100 area vintners (craft beers, too) while taking in fantastic bay views. Bottles are available for purchase, and food is served from 11:30 until closing. ✉ *700 Cannery Row, Suite KK* ☎ *831/646–5446* ⊕ *atasteofmonterey.com* ⌨ *Tastings $20.*

Cannery Row

NEIGHBORHOOD | When John Steinbeck published the novel *Cannery Row* in 1945, he immortalized a place of rough-edged working people. The waterfront street, edging a mile of gorgeous coastline, once was crowded with sardine canneries processing, at their peak, nearly 200,000 tons of the smelly silver fish a year. During the mid-1940s, however, the sardines disappeared from the bay, causing the canneries to close. Through the years the old tin-roof canneries have been converted into restaurants, art galleries, and malls with shops selling T-shirts, fudge, and plastic sea otters. Recent tourist development along the row has been more tasteful, however, and includes stylish inns and hotels, wine tasting rooms, and upscale specialty shops. ⊠ *Cannery Row, between Reeside and David Aves.* ⊕ *canneryrow.com.*

Colton Hall

MUSEUM | A convention of delegates met here in 1849 to draft the first state constitution. The stone building, which has served as a school, a courthouse, and the county seat, is a city-run museum furnished as it was during the constitutional convention. The extensive grounds outside the hall surround the Old Monterey Jail. ⊠ *570 Pacific St., between Madison and Jefferson Sts.* ☎ *831/646–3933* ⊕ *www.monterey.org/museums* ⌖ *Free.*

Fisherman's Wharf

PEDESTRIAN MALL | FAMILY | The mournful barking of sea lions provides a steady soundtrack all along Monterey's waterfront, but the best way to actually view the whiskered marine mammals is to walk along one of the two piers across from Custom House Plaza. Lined with souvenir shops, the wharf is undeniably touristy, but it's lively and entertaining. At Wharf No. 2, a working municipal pier, you can see the day's catch being unloaded from fishing boats on one side and fishermen casting their lines into the water on the other. The pier has a couple of low-key restaurants, from whose seats lucky customers might spot otters and

harbor seals. ⊠ *At end of Calle Principal* ⊕ *www.montereywharf.com.*

Fort Ord National Monument

NATIONAL/STATE PARK | Scenic beauty, biodiversity, and miles of trails make this former U.S. Army training grounds a haven for nature lovers and outdoor enthusiasts. The 7,200-acre park, which stretches east over the hills between Monterey and Salinas, is also protected habitat for 35 species of rare and endangered plants and animals. There are 86 miles of single-track, dirt, and paved trails for hiking, biking, and horseback riding. The main trailheads are the Creekside, off Creekside Terrace near Portola Road, and Badger Hills, off Highway 68 in Salinas. Maps are available at the various trail-access points and on the park's website. ■ TIP→ **Dogs are permitted on trails, but should be leashed when other people are nearby.** ⊠ *Bordered by Hwy. 68 and Gen. Jim Moore and Reservation Rds.* ☎ *831/582–2200* ⊕ *www.blm.gov/programs/national-conservation lands/california/fort-ord-national-monument* ⌖ *Free.*

★ Monterey Bay Aquarium

ZOO | FAMILY | Playful otters and other sea creatures surround you the minute you enter this extraordinary facility, where all the exhibits convey what it's like to be in the water with the animals. Leopard sharks swim in a three-story, sunlit kelp forest exhibit; sardines swim around your head in a circular tank; and jellyfish drift in and out of view in dramatically lighted spaces that suggest the ocean depths. A petting pool puts you literally in touch with bat rays, and the million-gallon Open Seas exhibit illustrates the variety of creatures—from hammerhead sharks to placid-looking turtles—that live in the eastern Pacific. Splash Zone's 45, interactive, bilingual exhibits let kids commune with African penguins, clownfish, and other marine life. The only drawback to the aquarium experience is that it must be shared with the throngs that congregate

Monterey

Sights ▼

1. A Taste of Monterey.................C2
2. Cannery Row.........................C3
3. Colton Hall............................C7
4. Fisherman's Wharf D5
5. Fort Ord National Monument......J8
6. Monterey Bay Aquarium.......... B2
7. Monterey County
   Youth Museum D7
8. Monterey History and
   Art Association Salvador Dali
   Exposition.......................... D6
9. Monterey Museum of Art at
   Pacific Street C7
10. Monterey State Historic Park D6
11. Presidio of Monterey
    Museum C5

Restaurants ▼

1. Estéban Restaurant D8
2. Monterey's Fish House............. J6
3. Old Fishermen's Grotto............ D6
4. Old Monterey Café D7
5. Tarpy's Roadhouse J9

Hotels ▼

1. Casa Munras Garden
   Hotel & Spa........................ D8
2. Hyatt Regency Monterey H9
3. InterContinental the
   Clement Monterey................. B2
4. Monterey Plaza Hotel & Spa C4
5. Monterey Tides J7
6. Portola Hotel & Spa at
   Monterey Bay...................... D6
7. The Sanctuary
   Beach Resort J7
8. Spindrift Inn C3

KEY

1 Exploring Sights

1 Restaurants

1 Hotels

i Tourist information

Monterey
Municipal Beach

Del Monte Avenue

Del Monte Avenue

Helvic Ave.

Portola Ave.

Bald Verde Ave.

Encina Ave.

Lake Drive

1st St.
2nd St.
3rd Street
4th Street
5th Street
6th Street
7th Street
8th Street

Cunningham Dr.

Stone Road

Park Avenue

East Road

University Way
Cabrillo Highway

Fairground Road

Monterey Salinas Hwy

Mark Thomas Dr.

daily, but most visitors think it's worth it. ⊠ *886 Cannery Row* ☎ *831/648–4800 info, 866/963–9645 for advance tickets* ⊕ *www.montereybayaquarium.org* ☐ *$50.*

Monterey County Youth Museum (MY Museum)

MUSEUM | FAMILY | Monterey Bay comes to life from a child's perspective in this fun-filled, interactive indoor exploration center. The seven exhibit galleries showcase the science and nature of the Big Sur coast, theater arts, Pebble Beach golf, and beaches. Also here are a live performance theater, a creation station, a hospital emergency room, and an agriculture corner where kids follow artichokes, strawberries, and other fruits and veggies on their evolution from sprout to harvest to farmers' markets. ⊠ *425 Washington St., between E. Franklin St. and Bonifacio Pl.* ☎ *831/649–6444* ⊕ *mymuseum.org* ☐ *$8* ⊙ *Closed Mon.*

Monterey History and Art Association Salvador Dali Exposition

MUSEUM | Whether you're a fan of surrealist art or not, come to The Dali Expo to gain rare insight into the life and work of famed Spanish artist Salvador Dali, who lived in Monterey in the 1940s. The permanent exhibition houses nearly 600 artworks in various media, including 400 Dali originals. The museum's name reflects Dali's ties to nearby 17-Mile Drive, where he lived, worked, and hosted parties that included Andy Warhol, Walt Disney, Bob Hope, and other celebrities. ⊠ *5 Custom House Plaza* ☎ *831/372–2608* ⊕ *www.mhaadali.com* ☐ *$20.*

Monterey Museum of Art at Pacific Street

MUSEUM | Photographs by Ansel Adams and Edward Weston and works by other artists who have spent time on the peninsula are on display here, along with international folk art, from Kentucky hearth brooms to Tibetan prayer wheels. ⊠ *559 Pacific St., across from Colton*

Steinbeck's Cannery Row

"Cannery Row in Monterey in California is a poem, a stink, a grating noise, a quality of light, a tone, a habit, a nostalgia, a dream. Cannery Row is the gathered and scattered, tin and iron and rust and splintered wood, chipped pavement and weedy lots and junk heaps, sardine canneries of corrugated iron, honky tonks, restaurants and whore houses, and little crowded groceries, and laboratories and flophouses." —John Steinbeck, *Cannery Row*

Hall ☎ *831/372–5477* ⊕ *montereyart.org* ☐ *$15* ⊙ *Closed Sun.–Wed.*

★ Monterey State Historic Park

NATIONAL/STATE PARK | You can glimpse Monterey's early history in several well-preserved adobe buildings in Custom House Plaza and the downtown area. Although most are only open via guided tours (check ahead for details), some also have beautiful gardens to explore. Set in what was once a hotel and saloon, the **Pacific House Museum** now houses a visitor center and exhibits of gold-rush relics; photographs of old Monterey; and Native American baskets, pottery, and other artifacts. The adjacent **Custom House,** built by the Mexican government in 1827 and now California's oldest standing public building, was the first stop for sea traders whose goods were subject to duties. (In 1846 Commodore John Sloat raised the American flag over this adobe structure and claimed California for the United States.)

Exhibits at **Casa Soberanes** (1842), once a customs-house guard's residence, survey Monterey life from Mexican rule to the present. A veranda encircles the second

California sea lions are intelligent, social animals that live (and sleep) close together in groups.

floor of **Larkin House** (1835), whose namesake, an early California statesman, brought many of the antique furnishings inside from New Hampshire. **Stevenson House** was named in honor of author Robert Louis Stevenson, who boarded here briefly in a tiny upstairs room that's now furnished with items from his family's estate. Other rooms include a gallery of memorabilia and a children's nursery with Victorian toys. ■TIP→ **If the buildings are closed, you can access a cell-phone tour 24/7 (831/998–9458) or download an app.** ⊠ *Pacific House Museum visitor center, 10 Custom House Plaza* ☎ *831/649 2007* ⊕ *www.parks.ca.gov/mshp* ☎ *Free–$5, 1-hr history walk $10.*

Presidio of Monterey Museum
MUSEUM | This spot has been significant for centuries. Its first incarnation was as a Native American village for the Rumsien tribe. The Spanish explorer Sebastián Vizcaíno landed here in 1602, and Father Junípero Serra arrived in 1770. Notable battles fought here include the 1818 skirmish in which the corsair Hipólito Bruchard conquered the Spanish garrison that stood on this site and claimed part of California for Argentina. The indoor museum tells the stories; plaques mark the outdoor sites. ⊠ *Presidio of Monterey, Corporal Ewing Rd., off Lighthouse Ave.* ☎ *831/646–3456* ⊕ *www.monterey. org/museums* ☎ *Free* ⊗ *Closed Tues. and Wed.*

🍴 Restaurants

Estéban Restaurant
$$$ | SPANISH | In a festive fireplace dining room at Casa Munras hotel, Estéban serves modern and classic versions of Spanish cuisine: empanadas, Moorish chickpea stew, and three types of paella. Midweek specials abound: on Tuesday nights, feast on a four-course prix-fixe paella dinner ($38 per person), bottles of wine are half off on Monday, and Wednesday wine flights are just $16 for three tastes. **Known for:** daily tapas happy hour from 4:30 to 6; patio with firepit; special menus for kids and pups. ⑤ *Average main: $30* ⊠ *700 Munras Ave.*

🖷 831/375–0176 ⊕ www.estebanrestaurant.com ☾ No lunch.

Monterey's Fish House

$$ | **SEAFOOD** | Casual yet stylish and always packed, this seafood restaurant is removed from the hubbub of the wharf. The bartenders and waitstaff will gladly advise you on the perfect wine to go with your poached, blackened, or oak-grilled seafood. **Known for:** seafood, steaks, house-made pasta; festive atmosphere; oyster bar. ⑤ *Average main: $22* ⊠ *2114 Del Monte Ave., at Dela Vina Ave.* 🖷 *831/373–4647* ⊕ *montereyfishhouse. com* ☾ *No lunch weekends.*

Old Fisherman's Grotto

$$$ | **SEAFOOD** | Otters and seals frolic in the water just below this nautical-theme Fisherman's Wharf restaurant famous for its creamy clam chowder. Seafood paella, sand dabs, filet mignon, teriyaki chicken, and several pastas are among the many entrée options. **Known for:** Monterey-style clam chowder and calamari; bay views; full bar and carefully curated wine list. ⑤ *Average main: $29* ⊠ *39 Fisherman's Wharf* 🖷 *831/375–4604* ⊕ *oldfishermansgrotto.com.*

Old Monterey Café

$ | **AMERICAN** | Breakfast here gets constant local raves—its fame rests on familiar favorites: a dozen kinds of omelets, and pancakes from blueberry to cinnamon-raisin-pecan. For lunch are good soups, salads, and sandwiches. **Known for:** seven types of eggs Benedict; upbeat, team-style service; all meals cooked to order. ⑤ *Average main: $15* ⊠ *489 Alvarado St., at Munras Ave.* 🖷 *831/646–1021* ⊕ *oldmontereycafeca. com* ☾ *No dinner.*

Tarpy's Roadhouse

$$$ | **AMERICAN** | Fun, dressed-up American favorites—a little something for everyone— are served in this renovated early-1900s stone farmhouse several miles east of town. The kitchen cranks out everything from Cajun-spiced prawns to meat loaf with marsala–mushroom gravy to grilled ribs and steaks. **Known for:** American comfort food with a California twist; rustic dining: indoor fireplace or garden courtyard; generous portions. ⑤ *Average main: $29* ⊠ *2999 Monterey–Salinas Hwy., Hwy. 68* 🖷 *831/647–1444* ⊕ *tarpys.com.*

 Hotels

Casa Munras Garden Hotel & Spa

$$ | **HOTEL** | **FAMILY** | A cluster of Spanish-themed buildings in the heart of downtown, Casa Munras pays homage to Monterey's roots and the legacy of Spanish diplomat Don Estéban Munras, who built a residence on the site in 1824. **Pros:** full-service spa, heated swimming pool, hot tub, and fitness room; excellent on-site tapas restaurant; walk to downtown sights and restaurants. **Cons:** $15 parking fee; pool area can get noisy; thin walls. ⑤ *Rooms from: $199* ⊠ *700 Munras Ave.* 🖷 *831/375–2411, 800/222–2446* ⊕ *www.hotelcasamunras.com* ⇄ *163 rooms* ¶◯¶ *No meals.*

Hyatt Regency Monterey

$$ | **RESORT** | **FAMILY** | A 22-acre resort amid cypress forests on the Del Monte Golf Course, the Hyatt Regency Monterey is a good choice for business travelers and families (especially those with pets) seeking relatively affordable lodgings with numerous on-site services. **Pros:** half the rooms overlook the golf course; six tennis courts, firepits, two pools and hot tubs, hammocks, swings on property; on-site restaurant with live weekend entertainment. **Cons:** not in heart of downtown; sprawling resort that can seem packed during busy seasons; not ideal for pet-phobic guests. ⑤ *Rooms from: $179* ⊠ *1 Old Golf Course Rd.* 🖷 *831/372–1234* ⊕ *www.hyatt.com* ⇄ *560 rooms* ¶◯¶ *No meals.*

InterContinental the Clement Monterey

$$$ | **HOTEL** | **FAMILY** | Spectacular bay views, upscale amenities, assiduous service, and a superb location next to the

The Monterey Bay National Marine Sanctuary

Although Monterey's coastal landscapes are stunning, their beauty is more than equaled by the wonders that lie offshore. The Monterey Bay National Marine Sanctuary—which stretches 276 miles, from north of San Francisco almost down to Santa Barbara—teems with abundant life, and has topography as diverse as that aboveground.

The preserve's 5,322 square miles include vast submarine canyons, which reach down 10,663 feet at their deepest point. They also encompass dense forests of giant kelp—a kind of seaweed that can grow more than a hundred feet from its roots on the ocean floor. These kelp forests are especially robust off Monterey.

The sanctuary was established in 1992 to protect the habitat of the many species that thrive in the bay. Some animals can be seen quite easily from land. In summer and winter you might glimpse the offshore spray of gray whales as they migrate between their summer feeding grounds in Alaska and their breeding grounds in Baja. Clouds of marine birds—including white-faced ibis, three types of albatross, and more than 15 types of gull—skim the waves, or roost in the rock islands along 17-Mile Drive. Sea otters dart and gambol in the calmer waters of the bay; and of course, you can watch the sea lions—and hear their round-the-clock barking—on the wharves in Santa Cruz and Monterey.

The sanctuary supports many other creatures, however, that remain unseen by most on-land visitors. Some of these are enormous, such as the giant blue whales that arrive to feed on plankton in summer; others, like the more than 22 species of red algae in these waters, are microscopic. So whether you choose to visit the Monterey Bay Aquarium, take a whale-watch trip, or look out to sea with your binoculars, remember you're seeing just a small part of a vibrant underwater kingdom.

aquarium propelled this luxury hotel to immediate stardom. **Pros:** a block from the aquarium; fantastic waterfront views from some rooms; great for families. **Cons:** a tad formal; not budget; Cannery Row crowds everywhere on busy weekends and holidays. $ *Rooms from: $305* ✉ *750 Cannery Row* ☎ *831/375–4500* ⊕ *www.ictheclementmonterey.com* ⤶ *208 rooms* ⅼ◎ⅼ *No meals.*

Monterey Plaza Hotel & Spa

$$$ | **HOTEL** | Guests at this Cannery Row hotel can see frolicking sea otters from its wide outdoor patio and many room balconies. **Pros:** on the ocean; many amenities; attentive service. **Cons:** touristy area; heavy traffic; resort fee. $ *Rooms from: $306* ✉ *400 Cannery Row* ☎ *831/920–6710* ⊕ *www.montereyplaza-hotel.com* ⤶ *290 rooms* ⅼ◎ⅼ *No meals.*

Monterey Tides

$$ | **RESORT** | One of the area's best values, this hotel has a great waterfront location—2 miles north of Monterey, with views of the bay and the city skyline—and offers a surprising array of amenities. **Pros:** on the beach; great value; family-friendly. **Cons:** several miles from major attractions; big-box mall neighborhood; most rooms on the small side. $ *Rooms from: $206* ✉ *2600 Sand Dunes Dr.* ☎ *831/394–3321, 800/242–8627* ⊕ *montereytides.com* ⤶ *196 rooms* ⅼ◎ⅼ *No meals.*

Portola Hotel & Spa at Monterey Bay

$$$ | HOTEL | One of Monterey's largest hotels, and locally owned and operated for more than 40 years, the coastal-themed Portola anchors a prime city block between Custom House Plaza and the Monterey Conference Center. **Pros:** walk to sights and downtown restaurants and shops; three on-site restaurants and coffee shop; pet- and family-friendly. **Cons:** crowded when conferences convene; no limit on dog size; parking fee. ⑤ *Rooms from: $269* ✉ *2 Portola Plaza* ☏ *831/649–4511, 888/222–5851* ⊕ *www.portolahotel.com* ⇌ *379 rooms* ⦿ *No meals.*

The Sanctuary Beach Resort

$$$$ | HOTEL | FAMILY | Walk to the sand from spacious, luxurious bungalows furnished in contemporary, ocean-themed style at this 19-acre, wellness-centered resort next to Marina Dunes Preserve and a secluded stretch of Marina State Beach. **Pros:** easy access to hiking and biking trails; heated pool; on-site spa services; each bungalow has two rooms that can combine for families and groups. **Cons:** not in the heart of town; parking lot relatively far from rooms; area weather is often cooler than other parts of the bay. ⑤ *Rooms from: $399* ✉ *3295 Dunes Dr., Seaside* ☏ *855/693–6583* ⊕ *www.the-sanctuarybeachresort.com* ⇌ *60 rooms* ⦿ *No meals.*

Spindrift Inn

$$$ | HOTEL | This boutique hotel on Cannery Row has beach access and a rooftop garden that overlooks the water. **Pros:** close to aquarium; steps from the beach; friendly staff. **Cons:** throngs of visitors outside; can be noisy; not good for families. ⑤ *Rooms from: $279* ✉ *652 Cannery Row* ☏ *831/646–8900, 800/841–1879* ⊕ *www.spindriftinn.com* ⇌ *45 rooms* ⦿ *Free breakfast.*

Former Capital of California

In 1602 Spanish explorer Sebastián Vizcaíno stepped ashore on a remote California peninsula. He named it after the viceroy of New Spain—Count de Monte Rey. Soon the Spanish built a military outpost, and the site was the capital of California until the state came under American rule.

ⓨ Nightlife

BARS

Alvarado Street Brewery & Grill

BREWPUBS/BEER GARDENS | Housed in an historic Beaux Arts building that dates back to 1916, this craft brewery lures locals and visitors alike with a full bar and 20 craft beers on tap, decent gastropub menu, beer garden, and shaded sidewalk patio. The company also has a brewery, bistro, and wine bar in Carmel Plaza in Carmel-by-the-Sea. ✉ *426 Alvarado St.* ☏ *831/655–2337* ⊕ *www.alvaradostreetbrewery.com.*

Cibo

MUSIC CLUBS | An Italian restaurant and event venue with a big bar area, Cibo brings live jazz and other music to downtown from Tuesday through Sunday. ✉ *301 Alvarado St., at Del Monte Ave.* ☏ *831/649–8151* ⊕ *cibo.com.*

Crown & Anchor

BARS/PUBS | An authentic British pub, downtown Crown & Anchor has 20 beers on tap, classic cocktails, and a full menu, including 18 daily specials available in the restaurant and heated patio until midnight. ✉ *150 W. Franklin St.* ☏ *831/649–6496* ⊕ *crownandanchor.net.*

Peter B's Brewpub

BREWPUBS/BEER GARDENS | House-made beers, 18 HDTVs, a decent pub menu, and a pet-friendly patio ensure lively crowds at this craft brewery in back of the Portola Hotel & Spa. ⊠ *2 Portola Plaza* ☎ *831/649–2699* ⊕ *www.peterbsbrew-pub.com.*

Turn 12 Bar & Grill

BARS/PUBS | The motorcycles and vintage photographs at this downtown watering hole pay homage to nearby 11-turn Laguna Seca Raceway. The large-screen TVs, heated outdoor patio, happy-hour specials, and live entertainment keep the place jumpin' into the wee hours. ⊠ *400 Tyler St., at E. Franklin St.* ☎ *831/372–8876* ⊕ *turn12barandgrill.com.*

Shopping

Alvarado and nearby downtown streets are good places to start a Monterey shopping spree, especially if you're interested in antiques and collectibles.

Cannery Row Antique Mall

ANTIQUES/COLLECTIBLES | Bargain hunters can sometimes find little treasures at the mall, which houses more than 100 local vendors under one roof. ⊠ *471 Wave St.* ☎ *831/655–0264* ⊕ *canneryrowantique-mall.com.*

The Custom House Gift Shop

SPECIALTY STORES | This store sells 1800s-theme items such as toys, as well as books related to Monterey and California heritage. ⊠ *Custom House Plaza, in the Custom House bldg.* ☎ *831/649–7111.*

Old Monterey Book Co.

BOOKS/STATIONERY | Antiquarian books and prints are this shop's specialties. ⊠ *136 Bonifacio Pl., off Alvarado St.* ☎ *831/372–3111* ⊗ *Closed Mon.*

Activities

Monterey Bay waters never warm to the temperatures of their Southern California counterparts—the warmest they get is the low 60s. That's one reason why the marine life here is so diverse, which in turn brings out the fishers, kayakers, and whale-watchers. During the rainy winter, the waves grow larger, and surfers flock to the water. On land pretty much year-round, bikers find opportunities to ride, and walkers have plenty of waterfront to stroll.

BIKING

Adventures by the Sea

BICYCLING | You can rent surreys plus tandem, standard, and electric bicycles from this outfit that also conducts bike and kayak tours, and rents kayaks and stand-up paddleboards. There are multiple locations along Cannery Row and Custom House Plaza as well as branches at Lovers Point in Pacific Grove and 17-Mile Drive in Pebble Beach. ⊠ *299 Cannery Row* ☎ *831/372–1807, 800/979–3370 reservations* ⊕ *adventuresbythesea.com.*

FISHING

J&M Sport Fishing

FISHING | This outfit takes beginning and experienced fishers out to sea to catch rock cod, ling cod, sand dabs, mackerel, halibut, salmon (in season), albacore, squid, Dungeness crab, and other species. ⊠ *66 Fisherman's Wharf* ☎ *831/372–7440* ⊕ *jmsportfishing.com.*

HIKING

Monterey Bay Coastal Recreation Trail

HIKING/WALKING | From Custom House Plaza, you can walk along the coast in either direction on this 29-mile-long trail and take in spectacular views of the sea. The trail runs from north of Monterey in Castroville south to Pacific Grove, with sections continuing around Pebble Beach. Much of the path follows an old Southern Pacific Railroad route. ☎ *888/221–1010* ⊕ *seemonterey.com/things-to-do/parks/coastal-trail.*

KAYAKING
★ Monterey Bay Kayaks
KAYAKING | For many visitors the best way to see the bay is by kayak. This company rents equipment and conducts classes and natural-history tours. ✉ *693 Del Monte Ave.* ☎ *831/373–5357* ⊕ *www.montereybaykayaks.com.*

WHALE-WATCHING
Thousands of gray whales pass close by the Monterey Coast on their annual migration between the Bering Sea and Baja California, and a whale-watching cruise is the best way to see these magnificent mammals close up. The migration south takes place from December through March; January is prime viewing time. The whales migrate north from March through June. Blue whales and humpbacks also pass the coast; they're most easily spotted in late summer and early fall.

Fast Raft Ocean Safaris
TOUR—SPORTS | Naturalists lead whale-watching and sightseeing tours of Monterey Bay aboard the 33-foot *Ranger,* a six-passenger, rigid-hull, inflatable boat. The speedy craft slips into coves inaccessible to larger vessels, and its quiet engines enable intimate marine experiences without disturbing wildlife. Children ages eight and older are welcome to participate. From April to November, the boat departs from Moss Landing Harbor North Boat Launching Ramp. ✉ *32 Cannery Row, Suite F2* ☎ *408/659–3900* ⊕ *www.fastraft.com* ✉ *From $185.*

Monterey Bay Whale Watch
WHALE-WATCHING | The marine biologists here lead three- to five-hour whale-watching tours. ✉ *84 Fisherman's Wharf* ☎ *831/375–4658* ⊕ *montereybaywhalewatch.com.*

Princess Monterey Whale Watching
WHALE-WATCHING | Tours are offered daily on a 100-passenger high-speed cruiser and a large 100-foot boat. ✉ *96 Fisherman's Wharf* ☎ *831/372–2203* ⊕ *montereywhalewatching.com.*

Salinas

17 miles east of Monterey on Hwy. 68.

Salinas, a hardworking city surrounded by vineyards and fruit and vegetable fields, honors the memory and literary legacy of John Steinbeck, its most famous native, with the National Steinbeck Center. The facility is in Old Town Salinas, where renovated turn-of-the-20th-century stone buildings house shops and restaurants.

ESSENTIALS
VISITOR INFORMATION California Welcome Center. ✉ *1213 N. Davis Rd.* ☎ *831/757–8687* ⊕ *www.visitcalifornia.com.*

Sights

Monterey Zoo
ZOO | **FAMILY** | Exotic animals, many of them retired from film, television, and live production work or rescued from less-than-ideal environments, find sanctuary here. The zoo offers daily tours (1 pm and 3 pm June–August, 1 pm September–May), but for an in-depth experience, stay in a safari bungalow on-site at Vision Quest Safari B&B, where guests can join the elephants in their enclosures for breakfast. The inn's room rate includes a complimentary zoo tour. ✉ *400 River Rd.* ☎ *831/455–1901* ⊕ *www.montereyzoo.com* ✉ *$35.*

★ National Steinbeck Center
MUSEUM | The center's exhibits document the life of Pulitzer- and Nobel-prize winner John Steinbeck and the history of the nearby communities that inspired novels such as *East of Eden*. Highlights include reproductions of the green pickup-camper from *Travels with Charley* and the bunk room from *Of Mice and Men*. **Steinbeck House,** the author's Victorian birthplace, at 132 Central Avenue, is two blocks from the center. Now a popular (lunch-only) restaurant and gift shop with docent-led tours, it displays memorabilia.

✉ *1 Main St.* ☎ *831/775–4721* ⊕ *www. steinbeck.org* ☞ *$15.*

San Juan Bautista State Historic Park

HISTORIC SITE | With the low-slung, colonnaded **Mission San Juan Bautista** as its drawing card, this park 20 miles northeast of Salinas is about as close to early-19th-century California as you can get. Historic buildings ring the wide green plaza, among them an adobe home furnished with Spanish-colonial antiques, a hotel frozen in the 1860s, a blacksmith shop, a pioneer cabin, and a jailhouse. The mission's cemetery contains the unmarked graves of more than 4,300 Native American converts. ■**TIP➜ On the first Saturday of the month, costumed volunteers engage in quilting bees, tortilla making, and other frontier activities, and sarsaparilla and other nonalcoholic drinks are served in the saloon.** ✉ *19 Franklin St., San Juan Bautista* ☎ *831/623–4881* ⊕ *www.parks.ca.gov* ☞ *$3 park, $4 mission.*

Pinnacles National Park

38 miles southeast of Salinas.

It was Teddy Roosevelt who recognized the uniqueness of this ancient volcano—its jagged spires and monoliths thrusting upward from chaparral-covered mountains—when he made it a national monument in 1908. Though only about two hours from the bustling Bay Area, the outside world seems to recede even before you reach the park's gates.

GETTING HERE AND AROUND

One of the first things you need to decide when visiting Pinnacles is which entrance—east or west—you'll use, because there's no road connecting the two rugged peaks separating them. Entering from Highway 25 on the east is straightforward. The gate is only a mile or so from the turnoff. From the west, once you head east out of Soledad on Highway 146, the road quickly becomes narrow and hilly, with many blind curves. Drive slowly and cautiously along the 10 miles or so before you reach the west entrance.

ESSENTIALS
Pinnacles Visitor Center

INFO CENTER | At the park's main visitor center, near the eastern entrance, you'll find a helpful selection of maps, books, and gifts. The adjacent campground store sells light snacks. ✉ *5000 Hwy. 146, Paicines* ☎ *831/389–4485* ⊕ *www.nps. gov/pinn.*

West Pinnacles Visitor Contact Station

INFO CENTER | This small ranger station is just past the park's western entrance, about 10 miles east of Soledad. Here you can get maps and information, watch a 13-minute film about Pinnacles, and view interpretive exhibits. No food or drink is available here. ✉ *Hwy. 146, Soledad* ☎ *831/389–4427* ⊕ *www.nps.gov/pinn.*

◉ Sights

Pinnacles National Park

NATIONAL/STATE PARK | **FAMILY** | The many attractions at Pinnacles include talus caves, 30 miles of hiking trails, and hundreds of rock-climbing routes. A mosaic of diverse habitats supports an amazing variety of wildlife species: 160 birds, 48 mammals, 70 butterflies, and nearly 400 bees. The park is also home to some of the world's remaining few hundred condors in captivity and release areas. Fourteen of California's 25 bat species live in caves and other habitats in the park. President Theodore Roosevelt declared this remarkable 26,000-acre geologic and wildlife preserve a national monument in 1908. President Barack Obama officially designated it a national park in 2013.

The pinnacles are believed to have been created when two major tectonic plates collided and pushed a smaller plate down beneath the earth's crust, spawning volcanoes in what's now called the Gabilan Mountains, southeast of Salinas and

Monterey. After the eruptions ceased, the San Andreas Fault split the volcanic field in two, carrying part of it northward to what is now Pinnacles National Park. Millions of years of erosion left a rugged landscape of rocky spires and crags, or pinnacles. Boulders fell into canyons and valleys, creating talus caves and a paradise for modern-day rock climbers. Spring is the most popular time to visit, when colorful wildflowers blanket the meadows; the light and scenery can be striking in fall and winter; the summer heat is often brutal. The park has two entrances—east and west—but they are not connected. The Pinnacles Visitor Center, Bear Gulch Nature Center, Park Headquarters, the Pinnacles Campground, and the Bear Gulch Cave and Reservoir are on the east side. The Chaparral Parking Area is on the west side, where you can feast on fantastic views of the Pinnacles High Peaks from the parking area. Dogs are not allowed on hiking trails. ■TIP➜ **The east entrance is 32 miles southeast of Hollister via Highway 25. The west entrance is about 12 miles east of Soledad via Highway 146.** ✉ *5000 Hwy. 146, Paicines* ☎ *831/389–4486* ⊕ *www. nps.gov/pinn* ✎ *$30 per vehicle, $15 per visitor if biking or walking.*

 Activities

HIKING

Hiking is the most popular activity at Pinnacles, with more than 30 miles of trails for every interest and level of fitness. Because there isn't a road through the park, hiking is also the only way to experience its interior, including the High Peaks, the talus caves, and the reservoir.

★ Balconies Cliffs–Cave Loop

TRAIL | FAMILY | Grab your flashlight before heading out from the Chaparral Trailhead parking lot for this 2.4-mile loop that takes you through the Balconies Caves. This trail is especially beautiful in spring, when wildflowers carpet the canyon floor. About 0.6 mile from the start of the

trail, turn left to begin ascending the Balconies Cliffs Trail, where you'll be rewarded with close-up views of Machete Ridge and other steep, vertical formations; you may run across rock climbers testing their skills before rounding the loop and descending back through the cave. *Easy–Moderate.* ✉ *Pinnacles National Park* ⊹ *Trailhead: Chaparral Parking Area.*

★ Bear Gulch Cave–Moses Spring–Rim Trail Loop

TRAIL | FAMILY | Perhaps the most popular hike at Pinnacles, this relatively short (2.2-mile) loop trail is fun for kids and adults. It leads to the Bear Gulch cave system, and if your timing is right, you'll pass by several seasonal waterfalls inside the caves (flashlights are required). If it's been raining, check with a ranger, as the caves can flood. The upper side of the cave is usually closed in spring and early summer to protect the Townsend's big-ear bats and their pups. *Easy.* ⊹ *Trailhead: Bear Gulch Day Use Area.*

Moss Landing

12 miles north of Salinas.

Moss Landing is not much more than a couple of blocks of cafés and restaurants, art galleries, and studios, plus a busy fishing port, but therein lies its charm. It's a fine place to overnight or stop for a meal and get a dose of nature.

GETTING HERE AND AROUND

From Highway 1 north or south, exit at Moss Landing Road on the ocean side. MST buses serve Moss Landing.

TOURS

Elkhorn Slough Safari Nature Boat Tours

BOAT TOURS | This outfit's naturalists lead two-hour tours of Elkhorn Sough aboard a 27-foot pontoon boat. Reservations are required. ✉ *Moss Landing Harbor* ☎ *831/633–5555* ⊕ *elkhornslough.com* ✎ *$43.*

ESSENTIALS
VISITOR INFORMATION Moss Landing Chamber of Commerce. ☎ *831/633–4501* ⊕ *mosslandingchamber.com.*

 Sights

Elkhorn Slough National Estuarine Research Reserve
NATURE PRESERVE | The reserve's 1,700 acres of tidal flats and salt marshes form a complex environment that supports some 300 species of birds. A walk along the meandering waterways and wetlands can reveal hawks, white-tailed kites, owls, herons, and egrets. Also living or visiting here are sea otters, sharks, rays, and many other animals. ✉ *1700 Elkhorn Rd., Watsonville* ☎ *831/728–2822* ⊕ *elkhornslough.org* ⏱ *Closed Mon. and Tues.*

 Restaurants

Haute Enchilada
$$ | SOUTH AMERICAN | Part of a complex that includes art galleries and an events venue, the Haute adds bohemian character to the seafaring village of Moss Landing. The inventive Latin American–inspired dishes include shrimp and black corn enchiladas topped with a citrus cilantro cream sauce, and roasted *pasilla* chilies stuffed with mashed plantains and caramelized onions. **Known for:** extensive cocktail and wine list; many vegan and gluten-free options; artsy atmosphere. ⑤ *Average main: $26* ✉ *7902 Moss Landing Rd.* ☎ *831/633–5843* ⊕ *hauteenchilada.com* ⏱ *Closed Tues. and Wed.*

Phil's Fish Market & Eatery
$$ | SEAFOOD | Exquisitely fresh, simply prepared seafood (try the cioppino) is on the menu at this warehouselike restaurant on the harbor; all kinds of glistening fish are for sale at the market in the front. **Known for:** cioppino; clam chowder; myriad artichoke dishes. ⑤ *Average main: $22* ✉ *7600 Sandholdt Rd.* ☎ *831/633–2152* ⊕ *philsfishmarket.com.*

 Hotels

Captain's Inn
$$ | B&B/INN | Commune with nature and pamper yourself with upscale creature comforts at this green-certified complex in the heart of town. **Pros:** walk to restaurants and shops; tranquil natural setting; closest Monterey Bay hotel to Pinnacles National Park. **Cons:** rooms in historic building don't have water views; far from urban amenities; not appropriate for young children. ⑤ *Rooms from: $189* ✉ *8122 Moss Landing Rd.* ☎ *831/633–5550* ⊕ *www.captainsinn.com* ⇆ *10 rooms* ❍ *Free breakfast.*

 Activities

KAYAKING
Monterey Bay Kayaks
KAYAKING | Rent a kayak to paddle out into Elkhorn Slough for up-close wildlife encounters. ✉ *2390 Hwy. 1, at North Harbor* ☎ *831/373–5357* ⊕ *montereybaykayaks.com.*

Aptos

17 miles north of Moss Landing.

Backed by a redwood forest and facing the sea, downtown Aptos—known as Aptos Village—is a place of wooden walkways and false-fronted shops. Antiques dealers cluster along Trout Gulch Road, off Soquel Drive east of Highway 1.

GETTING HERE AND AROUND
Use Highway 1 to reach Aptos from Santa Cruz or Monterey. Exit at State Park Drive to reach the main shopping hub and Aptos Village. You can also exit at Freedom Boulevard or Rio del Mar. Soquel Drive is the main artery through town.

ESSENTIALS
VISITOR INFORMATION Aptos Chamber of Commerce. ✉ *7605–A Old Dominion Ct.* ☎ *831/688–1467* ⊕ *aptoschamber.com.*

4

Monterey Bay Area APTOS

Beaches

★ Seacliff State Beach

BEACH—SIGHT | FAMILY | Sandstone bluffs tower above this popular beach with a long fishing pier. The 1.5-mile walk north to adjacent New Brighton State Beach in Capitola is one of the nicest on the bay. Leashed dogs are allowed on the beach. **Amenities:** food and drink; lifeguards; parking (fee); showers; toilets. **Best for:** sunset; swimming; walking. ✉ *201 State Park Dr.* ☎ *831/685–6500* ⊕ *www.parks. ca.gov* 🚗 *$10 per vehicle.*

Restaurants

Bittersweet Bistro

$$$ | MEDITERRANEAN | A large old tavern with cathedral ceilings houses this popular bistro, where the Mediterranean–California menu changes seasonally, but regular highlights include paella, seafood puttanesca, and pepper-crusted rib-eye steak with Cabernet demi-glace. **Known for:** value-laden happy hour; seafood specials; house-made desserts. ⑤ *Average main: $29* ✉ *787 Rio Del Mar Blvd., off Hwy. 1* ☎ *831/662–9799* ⊕ *www.bittersweetbistro.com* ⊗ *Closed Mon. and Tues.*

Hotels

Seascape Beach Resort

$$$$ | RESORT | FAMILY | It's easy to unwind at this full-fledged resort on a bluff overlooking Monterey Bay. The spacious suites sleep from two to eight people. **Pros:** time share–style apartments; access to miles of beachfront; superb views. **Cons:** far from city life; most bathrooms are small; some rooms need updating. ⑤ *Rooms from: $387* ✉ *1 Seascape Resort Dr.* ☎ *831/662–7171, 866/867–0976* ⊕ *seascaperesort.com* 🛏 *285 suites* 🍽 *No meals.*

Capitola and Soquel

4 miles northwest of Aptos.

On the National Register of Historic places as California's first seaside resort town, the village of Capitola has been in a holiday mood since the late 1800s. Casual eateries, surf shops, and ice cream parlors pack its walkable downtown. Inland, across Highway 1, antiques shops line Soquel Drive in the town of Soquel. Wineries dot the Santa Cruz Mountains beyond.

GETTING HERE AND AROUND

From Santa Cruz or Monterey, follow Highway 1 to the Capitola/Soquel (Bay Avenue) exit about 7 miles south of Santa Cruz and head west to reach Capitola and east to access Soquel Village. On summer weekends, park for free in the lot behind the Crossroads Center, a block west of the freeway, and hop aboard the free Capitola Shuttle to the village.

ESSENTIALS

VISITOR INFORMATION Capitola-Soquel Chamber of Commerce. ✉ *716-G Capitola Ave., Capitola* ☎ *831/475–6522* ⊕ *capitolachamber.com.*

Beaches

★ New Brighton State Beach

BEACH—SIGHT | FAMILY | Once the site of a Chinese fishing village, New Brighton is now a popular surfing and camping spot. Its Pacific Migrations Visitor Center traces the history of the Chinese and other peoples who settled around Monterey Bay. It also documents the migratory patterns of the area's wildlife, such as monarch butterflies and gray whales. Leashed dogs are allowed in the park. New Brighton connects with Seacliff Beach, and at low tide you can walk or run along this scenic stretch of sand for nearly 16 miles south (though you might have to wade through a few creeks). ■ **TIP→** The 1½-mile stroll from

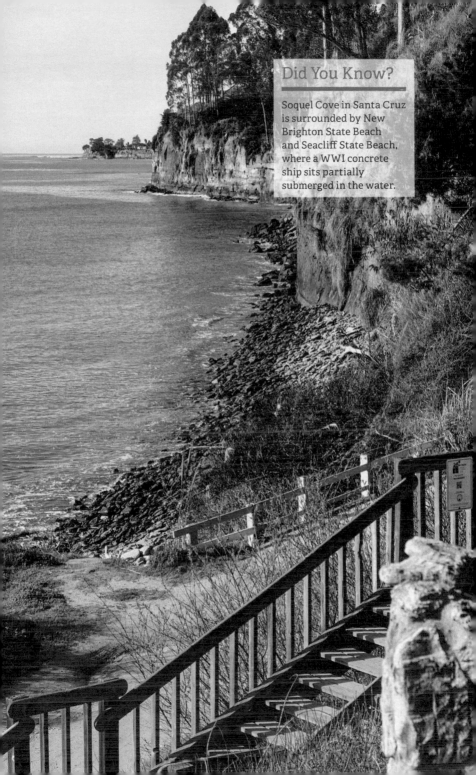

Did You Know?

Soquel Cove in Santa Cruz is surrounded by New Brighton State Beach and Seacliff State Beach, where a WWI concrete ship sits partially submerged in the water.

New Brighton to Seacliff's concrete ship is a local favorite. **Amenities:** parking (fee); showers; toilets. **Best for:** sunset; swimming; walking. ⊠ *1500 State Park Dr., off Hwy. 1, Capitola* ☎ *831/464–6329* ⊕ *www.parks.ca.gov* ⊡ *$10 per vehicle.*

Restaurants

Carpo's

$ | **SEAFOOD** | **FAMILY** | Locals love this casual counter where seafood predominates, but you can also order burgers, salads, and steaks. Baskets of battered snapper are among the favorites, along with calamari, prawns, seafood kebabs, fish-and-chips, and homemade olallieberry pie. **Known for:** large portions of healthy comfort food; lots of options under $12; soup and salad bar. ⑤ *Average main: $14* ⊠ *2400 Porter St., at Hwy. 1, Soquel* ☎ *831/476–6260* ⊕ *carposrestaurant. com.*

Gayle's Bakery & Rosticceria

$$ | **CAFÉ** | **FAMILY** | Whether you're in the mood for an orange-olallieberry muffin, a wild rice and chicken salad, or tri-tip on garlic toast, this bakery-deli's varied menu is likely to satisfy. Munch on your lemon meringue tartlet or chocolate brownie on the shady patio, or dig into the daily blue-plate dinner—teriyaki grilled skirt steak with edamame–shiitake sticky rice, perhaps, or roast turkey breast with Chardonnay gravy—amid the whirl of activity inside. **Known for:** prepared meals to go; on-site bakery and rosticceria; deli and espresso bar. ⑤ *Average main: $17* ⊠ *504 Bay Ave., Capitola* ☎ *831/462–1200* ⊕ *www.gaylesbakery. com.*

Shadowbrook

$$$$ | **EUROPEAN** | To get to this romantic spot overlooking Soquel Creek, you can take a cable car or walk the stairs down a steep, fern-lined bank beside a running waterfall. Dining room options include the rooftop Redwood Room, the wood-paneled Wine Cellar, the creekside, glass-enclosed Greenhouse, the Fireplace Room, and the airy Garden Room. **Known for:** romantic creek-side setting; prime rib and grilled seafood; local special-occasion favorite for nearly 70 years. ⑤ *Average main: $36* ⊠ *1750 Wharf Rd., at Lincoln Ave., Capitola* ☎ *831/475–1511* ⊕ *www.shadowbrook-capitola.com.*

🛏 Hotels

Inn at Depot Hill

$$$ | **B&B/INN** | This inventively designed B&B in a former rail depot views itself as a link to the era of luxury train travel. **Pros:** short walk to beach and village; historic charm; excellent service. **Cons:** fills quickly; hot-tub conversation audible in some rooms; rooms need updating. ⑤ *Rooms from: $309* ⊠ *250 Monterey Ave., Capitola* ☎ *831/462–3376, 800/572–2632* ⊕ *www.innatdepothill.com* ⤴ *13 rooms* ⊓⊙⊦ *Free breakfast.*

Santa Cruz

5 miles west of Capitola, 48 miles north of Monterey.

The big city on this stretch of the California coast, Santa Cruz (pop. 63,364) is less manicured than Carmel or Monterey. Long known for its surfing and its amusement-filled beach boardwalk, the town is an eclectic mix of grand Victorian-era homes, beachside inns, and multimillion dollar compounds owned by tech gurus. The opening of the University of California campus in the 1960s swung the town sharply to the left politically, and the counterculture more or less lives on here. At the same time, a revitalized downtown and an insane real-estate market reflect the city's proximity to Silicon Valley, which is just a 30-minute drive to the north, and to a growing wine region in the surrounding mountains.

Amble around downtown's Santa Cruz Farmers' Market (Wednesday afternoons year-round) to experience the local culture, which derives much of its character from close connections to food and farming. The market covers a city block and includes not just the expected organic produce, but also live music and booths with local crafts and prepared food.

GETTING HERE AND AROUND

From the San Francisco Bay area, take Highway 17 south over the mountains to Santa Cruz, where it merges with Highway 1. Use Highway 1 to get around the area. The Santa Cruz Transit Center is at 920 Pacific Avenue, at Front Street, a short walk from the wharf and boardwalk, with connections to public transit throughout the Monterey Bay and San Francisco Bay areas. You can purchase day passes for Santa Cruz METRO buses here.

ESSENTIALS

VISITOR INFORMATION Visit Santa Cruz County. ⊠ *303 Water St., Suite 100* ☎ *831/425–1234, 800/833–3494* ⊕ *www.visitsantacruz.org.*

Sights

Monterey Bay National Marine Sanctuary Exploration Center

INFO CENTER | FAMILY | The interactive and multimedia exhibits at this fascinating interpretive center reveal and explain the treasures of the nation's largest marine sanctuary. The two-story building, across from the main beach and municipal wharf, has films and exhibits about migratory species, watersheds, underwater canyons, kelp forests, and intertidal zones. The second-floor deck has stellar ocean views and an interactive station that provides real-time weather, surf, and buoy reports. ⊠ *35 Pacific Ave., near Beach St.* ☎ *831/421–9993* ⊕ *montereybay.noaa.gov/vc/sec* ⊠ *Free* ⊗ *Closed Mon. and Tues.*

Mystery Spot

LOCAL INTEREST | Hokey tourist trap or genuine scientific enigma? Since 1940, curious throngs baffled by the Mystery Spot have made it one of the most visited attractions in Santa Cruz. The laws of gravity and physics don't appear to apply in this tiny patch of redwood forest, where balls roll uphill and people stand on a slant. ■**TIP→ On weekends and holidays, it's wise to purchase tickets online in advance.** ⊠ *465 Mystery Spot Rd., off Branciforte Dr. (north off Hwy. 1)* ☎ *831/423–8897* ⊕ *mysteryspot.com* ⊠ *$8, parking $5.*

Pacific Avenue

NEIGHBORHOOD | When you've had your fill of the city's beaches and waters, take a stroll in downtown Santa Cruz, especially on Pacific Avenue between Laurel and Water streets. Vintage boutiques and mountain-sports stores, sushi bars, and Mexican restaurants, day spas, and nightclubs keep the main drag and the surrounding streets hopping from midmorning until late evening.

★ Santa Cruz Beach Boardwalk

CAROUSEL | FAMILY | Santa Cruz has been a seaside resort since the mid-19th century. Along one end of the broad, south-facing beach, the boardwalk has entertained holidaymakers for more than a century. Its Looff carousel and classic wooden Giant Dipper roller coaster, both dating from the early 1900s, are surrounded by high-tech thrill rides and easygoing kiddie rides with ocean views. Video and arcade games, a minigolf course, and a laser-tag arena pack one gigantic building, which is open daily even if the rides aren't running. You have to pay to play, but you can wander the entire boardwalk for free while sampling carnival fare such as corn dogs and garlic fries. ⊠ Along Beach St. ☎ 831/423–5590 info line ⊕ beachboardwalk.com ⊠ $40 day pass for unlimited rides, or pay per ride ⊙ Some rides closed Sept.–May.

Santa Cruz Municipal Wharf

MARINA | FAMILY | Jutting half a mile into the ocean near one end of the boardwalk, the century-old Municipal Wharf is lined with seafood restaurants, a wine bar, souvenir shops, and outfitters offering bay cruises, fishing trips, and boat rentals. A salty soundtrack drifts up from under the wharf, where barking sea lions lounge in heaps on the crossbeams. ⊠ Beach St. and Pacific Ave. ☎ 831/459–3800 ⊕ www.santacruzwharf.com.

Santa Cruz Surfing Museum

MUSEUM | This museum inside the Mark Abbott Memorial Lighthouse chronicles local surfing history. Photographs show old-time surfers, and a display of boards includes rarities such as a heavy redwood plank predating the fiberglass era and the remains of a modern board chomped by a great white shark. Surfer docents reminisce about the good old days. ⊠ Lighthouse Point Park, 701 W. Cliff Dr. near Pelton Ave. ☎ 831/420–6289 ⊠ $2 suggested donation ⊙ Closed Tues. and Wed. except open Tues. July–early Sept.

Seymour Marine Discovery Center

ZOO | FAMILY | Part of the Long Marine Laboratory at the University of California Santa Cruz's Institute of Marine Sciences, the center looks more like a research facility than a slick aquarium. Interactive exhibits demonstrate how scientists study the ocean, and the aquarium displays creatures of interest to marine biologists. The 87-foot blue whale skeleton is one of the world's largest. ∎TIP➔ General tours take place in the afternoon, and there's an abbreviated tour at 11 am for families with small children. ⊠ 100 Shaffer Rd., end of Delaware Ave., west of Natural Bridges State Beach ☎ 831/459–3800 ⊕ seymourcenter.ucsc.edu ⊠ $10 ⊙ Closed Mon.

Surf City Vintners

WINERY/DISTILLERY | A dozen tasting rooms of limited-production wineries occupy renovated warehouse spaces west of the beach. MJA, Sones Cellars, Santa Cruz Mountain Vineyard, and Equinox are good places to start. Also here are the Santa Cruz Mountain Brewing Company and El Salchichero, popular for its homemade sausages, jams, and pickled and candied vegetables. ⊠ Swift Street Courtyard, 334 Ingalls St., at Swift St., off Hwy. 1 (Mission St.) ⊕ surfcityvintners.com.

UC Santa Cruz

COLLEGE | The 2,000-acre University of California Santa Cruz campus nestles in the forested hills above town. Its sylvan setting, ocean vistas, and redwood architecture make the university worth a visit, as does its arboretum ($5, open daily from 9 to 5), whose walking path leads through areas dedicated to the plants of California, Australia, New Zealand, and South Africa. ∎TIP➔ Free shuttles help students and visitors get around campus, and you can join a guided tour (online reservation required). ⊠ Main entrance at Bay and High Sts. (turn left on High for arboretum) ☎ 831/459–0111 ⊕ www.ucsc.edu/visit.

★ West Cliff Drive

SCENIC DRIVE | The road that winds along an oceanfront bluff from the municipal wharf to Natural Bridges State Beach makes for a spectacular drive, but it's even more fun to walk or bike the paved path that parallels the road. Surfers bob and swoosh in Monterey Bay at several points near the foot of the bluff, especially at a break known as **Steamer Lane.** Named for a surfer who died here in 1965, the nearby Mark Abbott Memorial Lighthouse stands at Point Santa Cruz, the cliff's major promontory. From here you can watch pinnipeds hang out, sunbathe, and frolic on Seal Rock. ⊠ *Santa Cruz.*

Wilder Ranch State Park

NATIONAL/STATE PARK | In this park's Cultural Preserve you can visit the homes, barns, workshops, and bunkhouse of a 19th-century dairy farm. Nature has reclaimed most of the ranch land, and native plants and wildlife have returned to the 7,000 acres of forest, grassland, canyons, estuaries, and beaches. Hike, bike, or ride horseback on miles of ocean-view trails. Dogs aren't allowed at Wilder Ranch. ⊠ *Hwy. 1, 1 mile north of Santa Cruz* ☎ *831/426–0505 Interpretive Center, 831/423–9703 trail information* ⊕ *www.parks.ca.gov* ⊠ *$10 per car* ☉ *Interpretive center closed Mon.–Wed.*

Beaches

Natural Bridges State Beach

BEACH—SIGHT | **FAMILY** | At the end of West Cliff Drive lies this stretch of soft sand edged with tide pools and sea-sculpted rock bridges. ■**TIP→ From September to early January a colony of monarch butterflies roosts in the eucalyptus grove. Amenities:** lifeguards; parking (fee); toilets. **Best for:** sunrise; sunset; surfing; swimming. ⊠ *2531 W. Cliff Dr.* ☎ *831/423–4609* ⊕ *www.parks.ca.gov* ⊠ *Beach tree, parking $10.*

Twin Lakes State Beach

BEACH—SIGHT | **FAMILY** | Stretching a half mile along the coast on both sides of the small-craft jetties, Twin Lakes is one of Monterey Bay's sunniest beaches. It encompasses Seabright State Beach (with access in a residential neighborhood on the upcoast side) and Black's Beach on the downcoast side. Families often come here to sunbathe, picnic, and hike the nature trail around adjacent Schwann Lake. Parking is tricky from May through September—you need to pay for an $8 day-use permit at a kiosk and the lot fills quickly—but you can park all day in the harbor pay lot and walk here. Leashed dogs are allowed. **Amenities:** food and drink; lifeguards (seasonal); parking; showers; toilets; water sports (seasonal). **Best for:** sunset; surfing; swimming; walking. ⊠ *7th Ave., at East Cliff Dr.* ☎ *831/427–4868* ⊕ *www. parks.ca.gov.*

🍴 Restaurants

Crow's Nest

$$$ | **SEAFOOD** | **FAMILY** | Vintage surfboards and local surf photography line the walls and nearly every table overlooks sand and surf at this restaurant on the Santa Cruz Harbor. For sweeping ocean views and fish tacos, burgers, and other casual fare, head upstairs to the Breakwater Bar & Grill. **Known for:** house-smoked salmon and calamari apps; crab-cake eggs Benedict and olallieberry pancakes; on-site market with pizzas, sandwiches, soups, and salads. ⑤ *Average main: $27* ⊠ *2218 E. Cliff Dr., west of 7th Ave.* ☎ *831/476–4560* ⊕ *crowsnest-santacruz.com.*

★ Laili Restaurant

$$ | **MEDITERRANEAN** | Exotic Mediterranean flavors with an Afghan twist take center stage at this artsy, stylish space with soaring ceilings. In the evening, locals come to relax over wine and soft jazz at the blue-concrete bar, on the heated patio with twinkly lights, or at a communal table near the open kitchen.

Known for: house-made pastas and numerous vegetarian and vegan options; fresh naan, chutneys, and dips with every meal; traditional dishes like pomegranate eggplant and maushawa soup. $ *Average main: $24 ✉ 101–B Cooper St., near Pacific Ave.* ☎ *831/423–4545* ⊕ *lailirestaurant.com.*

La Posta Via

$$ | ITALIAN | Authentic Italian fare made with fresh local produce lures diners into cozy, modern-rustic La Posta. Nearly everything is made in-house, from the pizzas and breads baked in the brick oven to the pasta and the vanilla-bean gelato. **Known for:** seasonal wild-nettle lasagna; braised lamb shank; in the heart of the Seabright neighborhood. $ *Average main: $24 ✉ 538 Seabright Ave., at Logan St.* ☎ *831/457–2782* ⊕ *lapostarestaurant. com* ⊗ *Closed Mon. No lunch.*

Oswald

$$$$ | EUROPEAN | Sophisticated yet unpretentious European-inspired California cooking is the order of the day at this intimate and stylish bistro with a seasonal menu, which might include such items as seafood risotto or crispy duck breast in a pomegranate reduction sauce. The creative concoctions poured at the slick marble bar include whiskey mixed with apple and lemon juice, and tequila with celery juice and lime. **Known for:** house-made pork sausage; craft cocktails; local art displays that change monthly. $ *Average main: $34 ✉ 121 Soquel Ave., at Front St.* ☎ *831/423–7427* ⊕ *oswaldrestaurant.com* ⊗ *Closed Sun.–Tues.*

★ Soif

$$$ | MEDITERRANEAN | Wine reigns at this sleek bistro and wineshop that takes its name from the French word for thirst— the selections come from near and far, and you can order many of them by the taste or glass. Mediterranean-inspired small plates and entrées are served at the copper-top bar, the big communal table, and private tables. **Known for:** Mediterranean-style dishes; diverse, interesting wine selection; jazz combo or solo pianist plays on some evenings. $ *Average main: $27 ✉ 105 Walnut Ave.* ☎ *831/423–2020* ⊕ *www.soifwine.com* ⊗ *Closed Mon. and Tues. No lunch.*

Zachary's

$ | AMERICAN | This noisy café filled with students and families defines the funky essence of Santa Cruz. It also dishes up great breakfasts: stay simple with sourdough pancakes, or go for Mike's Mess— eggs scrambled with bacon, mushrooms, and home fries, then topped with sour cream, melted cheese, and fresh tomatoes. **Known for:** nearly everything made in-house; "Mike's Mess" egg dishes; local organic ingredients. $ *Average main: $15 ✉ 819 Pacific Ave.* ☎ *831/427–0646* ⊕ *www.zacharyssantacruz.com* ⊗ *Closed Mon. No dinner.*

Hotels

Babbling Brook Inn

$$$ | B&B/INN | Though it's in the middle of Santa Cruz, this B&B has lush gardens, a running stream, and tall trees that make you feel like you're in a secluded wood. **Pros:** close to UCSC; within walking distance of downtown shops; woodsy feel. **Cons:** near a high school; some rooms close to a busy street; many stairs and no elevator. $ *Rooms from: $280 ✉ 1025 Laurel St.* ☎ *831/427–2437, 800/866–1131* ⊕ *babblingbrookinn.com* ⊅ *13 rooms* ⦿ *Free breakfast.*

Carousel Beach Inn

$$ | HOTEL | This basic but comfy motel, decorated in bold, retro, seaside style and across the street from the boardwalk, is ideal for travelers who want easy access to the sand and the amusement park rides without spending a fortune. **Pros:** steps from Santa Cruz Main Beach; affordable lodging rates and ride packages; free parking and Wi-Fi. **Cons:** no pool or spa; no exercise room; not pet-friendly. $ *Rooms from: $159 ✉ 110 Riverside Ave.* ☎ *831/425–7090*

⊕ *carousel-beach-inn.com* ⇄ *34 rooms* ꜟ⊙ꜟ *Free breakfast.*

★ Chaminade Resort & Spa

$$$ | **RESORT** | **FAMILY** | Secluded on 300 hilltop acres of redwood and eucalyptus forest laced with hiking trails, this Mission-style complex also features a lovely terrace restaurant with expansive views of Monterey Bay. Guest rooms are furnished in an eclectic, bohemian style that pays homage to the artsy local community and the city's industrial past. **Pros:** peaceful, verdant setting; full-service spa and large pool; ideal spot for romance and rejuvenation. **Cons:** not within walking distance of downtown; not near the ocean; resort fee. $ *Rooms from: $279* ⊠ *1 Chaminade La.* ☎ *800/283–6569, 831/475–5600* ⊕ *www.chaminade.com* ⇄ *156 rooms* ꜟ⊙ꜟ *No meals.*

Dream Inn Santa Cruz

$$$$ | **HOTEL** | A short stroll from the boardwalk and wharf, this full-service luxury hotel is the only lodging in Santa Cruz directly on the beach, and its rooms all have private balconies or patios overlooking Monterey Bay. Accommodations have contemporary furnishings, bold colors, and upscale linens, but the main draw here is having the ocean at your doorstep. **Pros:** restaurant with sweeping views of Monterey Bay; cool mid-century modern design; walk to boardwalk and downtown. **Cons:** expensive; area gets congested on summer weekends; pool area and hallways can be noisy. $ *Rooms from: $324* ⊠ *175 W. Cliff Dr.* ☎ *831/740–8069* ⊕ *www.dreaminnsantacruz.com* ⇄ *165 rooms* ꜟ⊙ꜟ *No meals.*

Hotel Paradox

$$$ | **HOTEL** | About a mile from the ocean and two blocks from Pacific Avenue, this stylish, forest-theme complex (part of the Marriott Autograph Collection) is among the few full-service hotels in town. **Pros:** close to downtown and main beach; spacious pool area with cabanas, firepits, hot tub, and dining and cocktail service; on-site farm-to-table restaurant.

Cons: pool area can get crowded on warm-weather days; some rooms on the small side; thin walls. $ *Rooms from: $279* ⊠ *611 Ocean St.* ☎ *831/425–7100, 855/425–7200* ⊕ *hotelparadox.com* ⇄ *172 rooms* ꜟ⊙ꜟ *No meals.*

Hyatt Place Santa Cruz

$$ | **HOTEL** | Vintage surfboards and local art grace the walls of the spacious, ocean-theme lobby at this downtown hotel. **Pros:** close to restaurants and shops; outdoor pool and hot tub and 24-hour fitness center; on-site restaurant and bar. **Cons:** not on the beach; valet parking only; fronts busy road. $ *Rooms from: $219* ⊠ *407 Broadway* ☎ *831/226–2304* ⊕ *hyattplace.com* ⇄ *106 rooms* ꜟ⊙ꜟ *No meals.*

Pacific Blue Inn

$$ | **B&B/INN** | Green themes predominate in this three-story, eco-friendly inn on a sliver of prime downtown real estate. **Pros:** free parking; free bicycles; downtown location. **Cons:** tiny property; not suitable for children; parking lot is a block away. $ *Rooms from: $189* ⊠ *636 Pacific Ave.* ☎ *831/600–8880* ⊕ *pacificblueinn. com* ⇄ *9 rooms* ꜟ⊙ꜟ *No meals.*

Sea & Sand Inn

$$ | **HOTEL** | Location is the main appeal of this motel atop a waterfront bluff, where all rooms have an ocean view and the boardwalk is just down the street. **Pros:** beach is steps away; friendly staff; tidy landscaping. **Cons:** tight parking lot; fronts a busy road; can be noisy. $ *Rooms from: $249* ⊠ *201 W. Cliff Dr.* ☎ *831/427–3400* ⊕ *seaandsandinn.com* ⇄ *22 units* ꜟ⊙ꜟ *Free breakfast.*

★ West Cliff Inn

$$$ | **B&B/INN** | On bluffs across from Cowell Beach, this three-story, Italianate property, built in 1877, exudes classic California beach style. **Pros:** killer bay and boardwalk views; walking distance of the beach; close to downtown. **Cons:** boardwalk noise; street traffic. $ *Rooms from: $299* ⊠ *174 West Cliff Dr.*

☎ 831/457–2200 ⊕ www.westcliffinn. com ⊅ 9 units ⦿I Free breakfast.

Nightlife

Catalyst

DANCE CLUBS | This huge, grimy, and fun club books rock, indie rock, punk, death-metal, reggae, and other acts. ☒ 1011 Pacific Ave. ☎ 877/987–6487 ⊕ catalystclub.com.

Kuumbwa Jazz Center

MUSIC CLUBS | The center draws top performers such as Lee Ritenour, Chris Potter, and the Dave Holland Trio. A café serves meals an hour before most shows. ☒ 320–2 Cedar St. ☎ 831/427–2227 ⊕ kuumbwajazz.org.

Moe's Alley

MUSIC CLUBS | Blues, salsa, reggae, funk: delightfully casual Moe's presents it all (and more). ☒ 1535 Commercial Way ☎ 831/479–1854 ⊕ moesalley.com ⊘ Closed Mon.

Performing Arts

Tannery Arts Center

ARTS CENTERS | The former Salz Tannery now contains nearly 30 studios and live-work spaces for artists whose disciplines range from ceramics and glass to film and digital media; most have public hours of operation. Performances also take place at the on-site Colligan Theater, and the center hosts assorted arts events on weekends and, occasionally, on weekdays. ☒ 1060 River St., at intersection of Hwys. 1 and 9 ⊕ tanneryartscenter.org.

Shopping

Bookshop Santa Cruz

BOOKS/STATIONERY | In 2021, the town's best and most beloved independent bookstore celebrated its 55th anniversary of selling new, used, and remaindered titles. The children's section is especially comprehensive, and the shop's special events calendar is packed with readings, social mixers, book signings, and discussions. ☒ 1520 Pacific Ave. ☎ 831/423–0900 ⊕ bookshopsantacruz.com.

O'Neill Surf Shop

SPORTING GOODS | Local surfers get their wetties (wet suits) and other gear at this O'Neill store or the one in Capitola, at 1115 41st Avenue. There's also a satellite shop on the Santa Cruz Boardwalk. ☒ 110 Cooper St. ☎ 831/469–4377 ⊕ www.oneill.com.

Santa Cruz Downtown Farmers' Market

OUTDOOR/FLEA/GREEN MARKETS | **FAMILY** | Santa Cruz is famous for its long tradition of organic growing and sustainable living, and its downtown market (one of five countywide) reflects the incredible diversity and quality of local agriculture and the synergistic daily life of community-minded residents. The busy market, which always has live music, happens every Wednesday from 1 to 6, rain or shine. The stalls cover much of an entire city block near Pacific Avenue and include fresh produce plus everything from oysters, beer, bread, and charcuterie to arts and crafts to prepared foods made from ingredients sourced from on-site vendors. ☒ Cedar St. at Lincoln St. ☎ 831/454–0566 ⊕ www.santacruzfarmersmarket.org.

Activities

BICYCLING
Another Bike Shop

BICYCLING | Mountain bikers should head here for tips on the best area trails and to browse cutting-edge gear made and tested locally. ☒ 2361 Mission St., at King St. ☎ 831/427–2232 ⊕ www.anotherbikeshop.com.

BOATS AND CHARTERS
Chardonnay II Sailing Charters

BOATING | The 70-foot Chardonnay II departs year-round from Santa Cruz yacht harbor on whale-watching, sunset, and other cruises around Monterey Bay. Most

O'Neill: A Santa Cruz Icon

O'Neill wet suits and beachwear weren't exactly born in Santa Cruz, but as far as most of the world is concerned, the O'Neill brand is synonymous with Santa Cruz and surfing legend.

The O'Neill wet-suit story began in 1952, when Jack O'Neill and his brother, Robert, opened their first surf shop in a garage across from San Francisco's Ocean Beach. While shaping balsa surfboards and selling accessories, the O'Neills experimented with solutions to a common surfer problem: frigid waters. Tired of being forced back to shore, blue-lipped and shivering after just 20 or 30 minutes riding the waves, they played with various materials and eventually designed a neoprene vest.

In 1959, Jack moved his shop 90 miles south to Cowell's Beach in Santa Cruz. It quickly became a popular surf hangout, and O'Neill's new wet suits began to sell like hotcakes. In the early 1960s, the company opened a warehouse for manufacturing on a larger scale. Santa Cruz soon became a major surf city, attracting wave riders to prime breaks at Steamer Lane, Pleasure Point, and the Hook. In 1965, O'Neill pioneered the first wet-suit boots, and, in 1971, Jack's son invented the surf leash. By 1980, O'Neill stood at the top of the world wet-suit market. On June 2, 2017, Jack O'Neill passed away at the age of 94, in his longtime Pleasure Point residence overlooking the surf.

regularly scheduled excursions cost $70; food and drink are served on many of them. Reservations are essential. ⊠ *Santa Cruz West Harbor, 790 Mariner Park Way* 🕾 *831/423–1213* ⊕ *chardonnay.com.*

Stagnaro Sport Fishing, Charters & Whale Watching Cruises

BOATING | Stagnaro (aka Santa Cruz Whale Watching) offers salmon, albacore, and rock-cod fishing expeditions (fees include bait) as well as whale-watching, dolphin, and sea-life cruises year-round. ⊠ *1718 Brommer St., near Santa Cruz Harbor* 🕾 *831/427–0230* ⊕ *stagnaros.com* 🕾 *From $61.*

GOLF
DeLaveaga Golf Course

GOLF | Woodsy DeLaveaga, a public course set in a hilly park, overlooks Santa Cruz and the bay. With its canyons, tree-lined fairways, and notoriously difficult par-5, dogleg 10th hole, the course

challenges novices and seasoned golfers. ⊠ *401 Upper Park Rd.* 🕾 *831/423–7214* ⊕ *www.delaveagagolf.com* 🕾 *$60 weekdays, $80 weekends/holidays* 🏌 *18 holes, 5700 yards, par 70.*

Pasatiempo Golf Club

GOLF | Designed by famed golf architect Dr. Alister MacKenzie in 1929, this semiprivate course, set amid undulating hills just above the city, is among the nation's top championship courses. Golfers rave about the spectacular views and challenging terrain. According to the club, MacKenzie, who designed Pebble Beach's exclusive Cypress Point course and Augusta National in Georgia, the home of the Masters Golf Tournament, declared this his favorite layout. ⊠ *20 Clubhouse Rd.* 🕾 *831/459–9155* ⊕ *www.pasatiempo.com* 🕾 *From $325* 🏌 *18 holes, 6125 yards, par 72.*

KAYAKING
Kayak Connection

KAYAKING | From March through May, participants in this outfit's tours mingle with gray whales and their calves on their northward journey to Alaska. Throughout the year, the company rents kayaks and paddleboards and conducts tours of Natural Bridges State Beach, Capitola, and Elkhorn Slough. ✉ *Santa Cruz Harbor, 413 Lake Ave., No. 3* ☎ *831/479–1121* ⊕ *kayakconnection.com* ✍ *From $65 for scheduled tours.*

Venture Quest Kayaking

KAYAKING | Explore hidden coves and kelp forests on guided two-hour kayak tours that depart from Santa Cruz Wharf. The tours include a kayaking lesson. Venture Quest also rents kayaks (and wet suits and gear), and arranges tours at other Monterey Bay destinations, including Elkhorn Slough. ✉ *2 Santa Cruz Wharf* ☎ *831/427–2267 kayak hotline, 831/425–8445 rental office* ⊕ *kayaksantacruz.com* ✍ *From $35 for rentals, $60 for tours.*

SURFING
Club-Ed Surf School and Camps

SURFING | Find out what all the fun is about at Club-Ed. Your first private or group lesson ($100 and up) includes all equipment. ✉ *Cowell's Beach, at Dream Inn Santa Cruz* ☎ *831/464–0177* ⊕ *club-ed.com.*

Cowell's Surf Shop

SURFING | This shop sells gear, clothing, and swimwear; rents surfboards, stand-up paddleboards, and wet suits; and offers lessons. ✉ *30 Front St.* ☎ *831/427–2355* ⊕ *www.facebook.com/cowellssurfshop.*

Richard Schmidt Surf School

SURFING | Since 1978, Richard Schmidt has shared the stoke of surfing and the importance of ocean awareness and conservation with legions of students of all ages. Today, the outfit offers surfing and stand-up paddleboard lessons (equipment provided) as well as marine adventure tours in Santa Cruz and elsewhere on the bay. Locations depend on where the waves are breaking or the wind's a'blowing, but outings typically convene at Cowell's Beach or Pleasure Point. ✉ *Santa Cruz* ☎ *831/423–0928* ⊕ *www.richardschmidt.com* ✍ *From $100.*

ZIPLINING
Mount Hermon Adventures

TOUR—SPORTS | Zipline through the redwoods at this adventure center in the Santa Cruz Mountains. On some summer weekends there's an aerial adventure course with obstacles and challenges in the redwoods. ■TIP→ **To participate (reservations essential), you must be at least 10 years old and at least 54 inches tall, and weigh between 75 and 250 pounds.** ✉ *17 Conference Dr., 9 miles north of downtown Santa Cruz near Felton, Mount Hermon* ☎ *831/430–4357* ⊕ *mounthermonadventures.com* ✍ *From $79.*

SEQUOIA AND KINGS CANYON NATIONAL PARKS

Updated by
Cheryl Crabtree

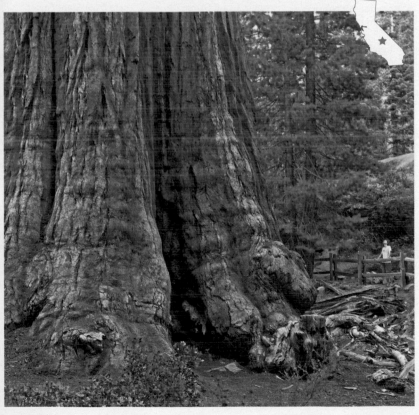

🏕 Camping	🛏 Hotels	🏃 Activities	👁 Scenery	👥 Crowds
★★★★☆	★★★★☆	★★★★☆	★★★★★	★★★☆☆

WELCOME TO SEQUOIA AND KINGS CANYON NATIONAL PARKS

TOP REASONS TO GO

★ **Gentle giants:** You'll feel small—in a good way—walking among some of the world's largest living things in Sequoia's Giant Forest and Kings Canyon's Grant Grove.

★ **Because it's there:** You can't even glimpse it from the main part of Sequoia, but the sight of majestic Mt. Whitney is worth the trip to the eastern face of the High Sierra.

★ **Underground exploration:** Far older even than the giant sequoias, the gleaming limestone formations in Crystal Cave will draw you along dark, marble passages.

★ **A grander-than-Grand Canyon:** Drive the twisting Kings Canyon Scenic Byway down into the jagged, granite Kings River canyon, deeper in parts than the Grand Canyon.

★ **Regal solitude:** To spend a day or two hiking in a subalpine world of your own, pick one of the many trailheads at Mineral King.

1 Giant Forest–Lodgepole Village. One of Sequoia's most visited areas has major sights such as Giant Forest, General Sherman Tree, Crystal Cave, and Moro Rock.

2 Grant Grove Village–Redwood Canyon. The "thumb" of Kings Canyon is its busiest section, where Grant Grove, General Grant Tree, Panoramic Point, and Big Stump are the main draws.

3 Cedar Grove. The drive through the high-country of Kings Canyon to Cedar Grove Village, on the canyon floor, reveals magnificent granite formations of varied hues. Rock meets river in breathtaking fashion at Zumwalt Meadow.

4 Mineral King. In Sequoia's southeast section, the highest road-accessible part of the park is a good place to hike, camp, and soak up the grandeur of the Sierra Nevada.

5 Mt. Whitney. The highest peak in the Lower 48 stands on the eastern edge of Sequoia; to get there from Giant Forest you must either backpack eight days through the mountains or drive nearly 300 miles around the park to its other side.

The word "exceptional" best describes these two parks, which offer some of the nation's greatest escapes. Drives along their byways deliver stunning vistas at nearly every turn. Varied ecosystems provide opportunities for repeat adventures, among them hikes to groves of giant sequoias—some of the planet's largest, and oldest, living organisms.

This rare species of tree grows only at certain elevations and in particular environments on the Central Sierra's western slopes. Their monstrously thick trunks and branches, remarkably shallow root systems, and neck-craning heights really are almost impossible to believe, as is the fact they can live for more than 2,500 years. Several Native American groups lived among these magnificent trees for thousands of years before modern visitors arrived. By the late 1800s, word of the giant sequoias (*Sequoiadendron giganteum*) had spread, attracting logging enterprises and mobilizing those who wanted to protect these living treasures.

Sequoia National Park—the nation's second oldest after Yellowstone—was established in 1890, officially preserving the world's largest sequoia groves in the Giant Forest and other areas of the park. At first, visitors traveled along a pack road to view the towering marvels. In 1903, a road into the Giant Forest allowed access by wagon. It wasn't until 1926, with the opening of the General's Highway, that autos could chug up the mountain. Kings Canyon National Park, which included the General Grant National Park formed a week after Sequoia, was established in 1940.

Today, the two parks, which share a boundary and have been administered jointly since World War II, encompass 865,964 wild and scenic acres between the foothills of California's Central Valley and its eastern borders along the craggy ridgeline of the Sierra's highest peaks. Next to or a few miles off the 46-mile Generals Highway are most of Sequoia National Park's main attractions, as well as Grant Grove Village, the orientation hub for Kings Canyon National Park.

Sequoia includes Mt. Whitney, the highest point in the lower 48 states (although it is impossible to see from the western part of the park and is a chore to ascend from either side). Kings Canyon has two portions: the smaller is shaped like a bent finger and encompasses Grant Grove Village and Redwood Mountain Grove (both with many sequoias), and the larger is home to stunning Kings River Canyon, where unspoiled peaks and valleys are a backpacker's dream.

AVERAGE HIGH/LOW TEMPERATURES (MID-LEVEL ELEVATIONS)					
JAN.	FEB.	MAR.	APR.	MAY	JUNE
42/24	44/25	46/26	51/30	58/36	68/44
JULY	AUG.	SEPT.	OCT.	NOV.	DEC.
76/51	76/50	71/45	61/38	50/31	44/27

Planning

When to Go

The best times to visit are spring and fall, when temperatures are moderate and crowds thin. Summertime can draw hordes of tourists to see the giant sequoias, and the few, narrow roads mean congestion at peak holiday times. If you must visit in summer, go during the week. By contrast, in wintertime you may feel as though you have the parks all to yourself. But because of heavy snows, sections of the main park roads can be closed without warning, and low-hanging clouds can move in and obscure mountains and valleys for days. From early October to late April, check road and weather conditions before venturing out.
■TIP→ **Even in summer, you can escape hordes of people just walking ¼ to ½ mile off the beaten path on a less-used trail.**

Getting Here and Around

AIR
The closest airport to Sequoia and Kings Canyon national parks is Fresno Yosemite International Airport (FAT).

AIRPORT CONTACTS Fresno Yosemite International Airport. (FAT) ✉ 5175 E. Clinton Way, Fresno ☎ 800/244–2359 automated info, 559/621–4500 ⊕ www. flyfresno.com.

CAR
Sequoia is 36 miles east of Visalia on Route 198; Grant Grove Village in Kings Canyon is 56 miles east of Fresno on

Route 180. There is no automobile entrance on the eastern side of the Sierra. Routes 198 and 180 are connected by Generals Highway, a paved two-lane road (also signed as Highway 198) that sometimes sees delays at peak times due to ongoing improvements. The road is extremely narrow and steep from Route 198 to Giant Forest, so keep an eye on your engine temperature gauge, as the incline and congestion can cause vehicles to overheat; to avoid overheated brakes, use low gears on downgrades.

If you are traveling in an RV or with a trailer, study the restrictions on these vehicles. Do not travel beyond Potwisha Campground on Generals Highway (Route 198) with an RV longer than 22 feet; take straighter, easier Route 180 through the Kings Canyon park entrance instead. Maximum vehicle length on Generals Highway is 40 feet, or 50 feet combined length for vehicles with trailers. For current road and weather conditions, call ☎ 559/565–3341 or visit the park website: ⊕ www.nps.gov/seki.

Park Essentials

ACCESSIBILITY
All the visitor centers, the Giant Forest Museum, and Big Trees Trail are wheelchair accessible, as are some short ranger-led walks and talks. General Sherman Tree can be reached via a paved, level trail near a parking area. None of the caves is accessible, and wilderness areas must be reached by horseback or on foot. Some picnic tables are extended to accommodate wheelchairs. Many of the major sites are in the 6,000-foot

Seeing the Parks in One Day

Sequoia National Park in One Day

After overnighting in Visalia or Three Rivers, take off early on Route 198 to the **Sequoia National Park entrance.** Pull over at the **Hospital Rock** picnic area to gaze up at the imposing granite Moro Rock, which you later will climb. Heed signs that advise "10 mph" around tight turns as you climb 3,500 feet on **Generals Highway** to the **Giant Forest Museum.** Spend a half hour here, then examine trees firsthand by circling the lovely **Round Meadow** on the **Big Trees Trail**, to which you must walk from the museum or its parking lot across the road.

Get back in your car, and continue a few miles north on Generals Highway to see the jaw-dropping **General Sherman Tree.** Then set off on the **Congress Trail** so that you can be further awed by the Senate and House big-tree clusters. Buy lunch at the **Lodgepole** complex, 2 miles to the north, and eat at the nearby **Pinewood** picnic area. Now you're ready to climb **Moro Rock.**

You can drive there or, if it is summer, park at the museum lot and take the free shuttle. Count on spending at least an hour for the 350-step ascent and descent, with a pause on top to appreciate the 360-degree view. Next, proceed past the **Tunnel Log** to **Crescent Meadow.** Spend a relaxing hour or two strolling on the trails that pass by, among other things, **Tharp's Log.** By now you've probably renewed your appetite; head to **Lodgepole Grill & Market** or the restaurant at **Wuksachi Lodge.**

Kings Canyon National Park in One Day

Enter the park via the **Kings Canyon Scenic Byway** (Route 180), having spent the night in Fresno or Visalia. Or wake up already in **Grant Grove Village**, perhaps in the **John Muir Lodge.** Stock up for a picnic with takeout from the **Grant Grove Restaurant** or with food from the nearby market. Drive east a mile to see the **General Grant Tree** and compact **Grant Grove's** other sequoias. If it's no later than mid-morning, walk up the short trail at **Panoramic Point**, for a view of Hume Lake and the High Sierra. Either way, return to Route 180, and continue east. Stop at Junction View to take in several peaks towering over Kings Canyon. From here, visit **Boyden Cavern** or continue to **Cedar Grove Village**, pausing along the way at **Grizzly Falls.** Eat at a table by the **South Fork of the Kings River** or on the Cedar Grove Snack Bar's deck. Now you are ready for the day's highlight: strolling **Zumwalt Meadow**, which lies a few miles past the village.

After you have enjoyed that short trail and its views of **Grand Sentinel** and **North Dome**, head to **Roads End**, where backpackers embark for the High Sierra wilderness. Make the return trip—with a stop at **Roaring River Falls**—past Grant Grove and briefly onto southbound **Generals Highway.** Stop at **Redwood Mountain Overlook**, and use binoculars to look down upon the world's largest sequoia grove. Drive another couple of miles to the **Kings Canyon Overlook** to survey some of what you have done today. Make reservations for a late dinner at **Wuksachi Lodge.**

range, and thin air at high elevations can cause respiratory distress for people with breathing difficulties. Carry oxygen if necessary. Contact the park's main number for more information.

PARK FEES AND PERMITS

The admission fee is $35 per vehicle, $30 per motorcycle, and $20 per person for those who enter by bus, on foot, bicycle, horse, or any other mode of transportation; it is valid for seven days in both parks. U.S. residents over the age of 62 pay $80 for a lifetime pass, and permanently disabled U.S. residents are admitted free.

If you plan to camp in the backcountry, you need a permit, which costs $15 for hikers or $30 for stock users (e.g., horseback riders). One permit covers the group. Availability of permits depends upon trailhead quotas. Reservations are accepted by mail or email for a $15 processing fee, beginning March 1, and must be made at least 14 days in advance (☎ 559/565–3766). Without a reservation, you may still get a permit on a first-come, first-served basis starting at 1 pm the day before you plan to hike. For more information on backcountry camping or travel with pack animals (horses, mules, burros, or llamas), contact the Wilderness Permit Office (☎ 530/565–3766).

PARK HOURS

The parks are open 24/7 year-round. They are in the Pacific time zone.

CELL PHONE RECEPTION

Cell phone reception is poor to nonexistent in the higher elevations and spotty even on portions of Generals Highway, where you can (on rare clear days) see the Central Valley. Public telephones may be found at the visitor centers, ranger stations, some trailheads, and at all restaurants and lodging facilities in the park.

Hotels

Hotel accommodations in Sequoia and Kings Canyon are limited, and, although they are clean and comfortable, they tend to lack much in-room character. Keep in mind, however, that the extra money you spend on lodging here is offset by the time you'll save by being inside the parks. You won't be faced with a 60- to 90-minute commute from the less-expensive motels in Three Rivers (by far the most charming option), Visalia, or Fresno. Reserve as far in advance as you can, especially for summertime stays.

Restaurants

In Sequoia and Kings Canyon national parks, you can treat yourself (and the family) to a high-quality meal in a wonderful setting in the Peaks restaurant at Wuksachi Lodge, but otherwise you should keep your expectations modest. You can grab bread, spreads, drinks, and fresh produce at one of several small grocery stores for a picnic, or get takeout food from the Grant Grove Restaurant, the Cedar Grove Grill, or one of the two small Lodgepole eateries.

Hotel and restaurant reviews have been shortened. For full information visit Fodors.com. Hotel prices are the lowest cost of a standard double room in high season. Restaurant prices are the average cost of a main course at dinner, or if dinner is not served, at lunch.

What It Costs			
$	$$	$$$	$$$$
RESTAURANTS			
under $17	$17–$26	$27–$36	over $36
HOTELS			
under $150	$150–$250	$251–$350	over $350

Tours

★ Sequoia Parks Conservancy Field Institute
SPECIAL-INTEREST | The Sequoia Parks Conservancy's highly regarded educational division conducts half-, single-, and multiday tours that include backpacking hikes, natural-history walks, astronomy programs, snowshoe treks, and custom adventures. ✉ *47050 Generals Hwy., Unit 10, Three Rivers* ☎ *559/565–4251* ⊕ *www.sequoiaparksconservancy.org* 🎟 *From $150 for 2-hr guided tour.*

Sequoia Sightseeing Tours
GUIDED TOURS | This locally owned operator's friendly, knowledgeable guides conduct daily interpretive sightseeing tours in Sequoia and Kings Canyon. Reservations are essential. The company also offers private tours. ✉ *Three Rivers* ☎ *559/561–4189* ⊕ *www.sequoiatours. com* 🎟 *From $79 tour of Sequoia; from $169 tour of Kings Canyon.*

Visitor Information

NATIONAL PARK SERVICE Foothills Visitor Center. ✉ *47050 Generals Hwy., Rte. 198, 1 mile north of Ash Mountain entrance, Sequoia National Park* ☎ *559/565–3341.* **Sequoia and Kings Canyon National Parks.** ✉ *47050 Generals Hwy. (Rte. 198), Three Rivers* ☎ *559/565–3341* ⊕ *nps.gov/seki.*

Sequoia National Park

Sequoia National Park is all about the trees, and to understand the scale of these giants you must walk among them. If you do nothing else, get out of the car for a short stroll through one of the groves. But there is much more to the park than the trees. Try to access one of the vista points that provide a panoramic view over the forested mountains. Generals Highway (which connects Routes 198 and 180) will be your route to most of the park's sights. A few short spur roads lead from the highway to some sights, and Mineral King Road branches off Route 198 to enter the park at Lookout Point, winding east from there to the park's southernmost section.

Giant Forest— Lodgepole Village

Giant Forest is 16 miles from the Sequoia National Park Visitor Center.

The Sequoia National Park entrance at Ash Mountain is the main gateway to the Giant Forest and many of the park's major sights. From there, the narrow, twisty General's Highway snakes up the mountain from a 1,700-foot elevation through the Giant Forest (a 45-minute drive from the entrance) up to 6,720 feet at Lodgepole Village.

◉ Sights

HISTORIC SIGHTS
Giant Forest Museum
MUSEUM | Well-imagined and interactive displays at this worthwhile stop provide the basics about sequoias, of which there are 2,161 with diameters exceeding 10 feet in the approximately 2,000-acre Giant Forest. ✉ *Sequoia National Park* ✛ *Generals Hwy., 4 miles south of Lodgepole Visitor Center* ☎ *559/565–4436* 🎟 *Free* ✆ *Shuttle: Giant Forest or Moro Rock–Crescent Meadow.*

SCENIC DRIVES
★ Generals Highway
SCENIC DRIVE | One of California's most scenic drives, this 46-mile road (also signed as Route 198) is the main asphalt artery between Sequoia and Kings Canyon national parks. Named after the landmark Grant and Sherman trees that leave so many visitors awestruck, Generals Highway runs from Sequoia's Foothills Visitor Center north to Kings Canyon's Grant Grove Village. Along the way, it

passes the turnoff to Crystal Cave, the Giant Forest Museum, Lodgepole Village, and other popular attractions. The lower portion, from Hospital Rock to the Giant Forest, is especially steep and winding. If your vehicle is 22 feet or longer, avoid that stretch by entering the parks via Route 180 (from Fresno) rather than Route 198 (from Visalia or Three Rivers). Take your time on this road—there's a lot to see, and wildlife can scamper across at any time. ⊠ *Sequoia National Park.*

SCENIC STOPS
Auto Log
FOREST | Before its wood showed signs of severe rot, cars drove right on top of this giant fallen sequoia. Now it's a great place to pose for pictures or shoot a video. ⊠ *Sequoia National Park ⊕ Moro Rock–Crescent Meadow Rd., 1 mile south of Giant Forest.*

Crescent Meadow
TRAIL | A sea of ferns signals your arrival at what John Muir called the "gem of the Sierra." Walk around for an hour or two, and you might decide that the Scotland-born naturalist was exaggerating a bit, but the verdant meadow is quite pleasant, and you just might see a bear. Wildflowers bloom here throughout the summer. ⊠ *Sequoia National Park ⊕ End of Moro Rock–Crescent Meadow Rd., 2.6 miles east off Generals Hwy. ☞ Shuttle: Moro Rock–Crescent Meadow.*

★ Crystal Cave
CAVE | One of more than 200 caves in Sequoia and Kings Canyon, Crystal Cave is composed largely of marble, the result of limestone being hardened under heat and pressure. It contains several eye-popping formations. There used to be more, but some were damaged or obliterated by early-20th-century dynamite blasting. You can see the cave only on a tour. The Daily Tour ($17), a great overview, takes about 50 minutes. To immerse yourself in the cave experience—at times you'll be crawling on your belly—book the exhilarating Wild Cave Tour ($140). Availability is limited—reserve tickets at least 48 hours in advance at ⊕ *www.recreation.gov* or stop by either the Foothills or Lodgepole visitor center first thing in the morning to try to nab a same-day ticket; they're not sold at the cave itself. ⊠ *Crystal Cave Rd., off Generals Hwy.* ☎ *877/444–6777* ⊕ *www.sequoiaparksconservancy.org/ crystalcave.html* ⊠ *$17* ⊗ *Closed Oct.– late May.*

★ General Sherman Tree
LOCAL INTEREST | The 274.9-foot-tall General Sherman is one of the world's tallest and oldest sequoias, and it ranks No. 1 in volume, adding the equivalent of a 60-foot-tall tree every year to its approximately 52,500 cubic feet of mass. The tree doesn't grow taller, though—it's dead at the top. A short, wheelchair-accessible trail leads to the tree from Generals Highway, but the main trail (½ mile) winds down from a parking lot off Wolverton Road. The walk back up the main trail is steep, but benches along the way provide rest for the short of breath. ⊠ *Sequoia National Park ⊕ Main trail Wolverton Rd. off Generals Hwy. (Rte. 198) ☞ Shuttle: Giant Forest or Wolverton–Sherman Tree.*

★ Moro Rock
NATURE SITE | This sight offers panoramic views to those fit and determined enough to mount its 350 or so steps. In a case where the journey rivals the destination, Moro's stone stairway is so impressive in its twisty inventiveness that it's on the National Register of Historic Places. The rock's 6,725-foot summit overlooks the Middle Fork Canyon, sculpted by the Kaweah River and approaching the depth of Arizona's Grand Canyon, although smoggy, hazy air often compromises the view. ⊠ *Sequoia National Park ⊕ Moro Rock–Crescent Meadow Rd., 2 miles east off Generals Hwy. (Rte. 198) to parking area ☞ Shuttle: Moro Rock–Crescent Meadow.*

Tunnel Log

LOCAL INTEREST | This 275-foot tree fell in 1937, and soon a 17-foot-wide, 8-foot-high hole was cut through it for vehicular passage (not to mention the irresistible photograph) that continues today. Large vehicles take the nearby bypass. ⊠ *Sequoia National Park* ✛ *Moro Rock–Crescent Meadow Rd., 2 miles east of Generals Hwy. (Rte. 198)* ☞ *Shuttle: Moro Rock–Crescent Meadow.*

TRAILS

★ Big Trees Trail

TRAIL | The 0.7-mile, wheelchair-accessible portion of this path is a must, as it does not take long, and the setting is spectacular: beautiful Round Meadow, surrounded by many mature sequoias. Well-thought-out interpretive signs along the way explain the ecology on display. Parking at the trailhead lot off Generals Highway is for cars with handicap placards only. The full, round-trip loop from the Giant Forest Museum is about a mile long. *Easy.* ⊠ *Sequoia National Park* ✛ *Trailhead: Off Generals Hwy. (Rte. 198), near the Giant Forest Museum* ☞ *Shuttle: Giant Forest.*

★ Congress Trail

TRAIL | This 2-mile trail, arguably the best hike in the parks in terms of natural beauty, is a paved loop that begins near General Sherman Tree. You'll get close-up views of more big trees here than on any other Sequoia hike. Watch for the clusters known as the House and Senate. The President Tree, also on the trail, supplanted the General Grant Tree in 2012 as the world's second largest in volume (behind the General Sherman). An offshoot of the Congress Trail leads to Crescent Meadow, where, in summer, you can catch a free shuttle back to the Sherman parking lot. *Easy.* ⊠ *Sequoia National Park* ✛ *Trailhead: Off Generals Hwy. (Rte. 198), 2 miles north of Giant Forest* ☞ *Shuttle: Giant Forest.*

Crescent Meadow Trails

TRAIL | A 1-mile trail loops around lush Crescent Meadow to Tharp's Log, a cabin built from a fire-hollowed sequoia. From there you can embark on a 60-mile trek to Mt. Whitney, if you're prepared and have the time. Brilliant wildflowers bloom here in midsummer. *Easy.* ⊠ *Sequoia National Park* ✛ *Trailhead: The end of Moro Rock–Crescent Meadow Rd., 2.6 miles east off Generals Hwy. (Rte. 198)* ☞ *Shuttle: Moro Rock–Crescent Meadow.*

Little Baldy Trail

TRAIL | Climbing 700 vertical feet in 1¾ miles of switchbacking, this trail ends at a granite dome with a great view of the peaks of the Mineral King area and the Great Western Divide. The walk to the summit and back takes about four hours. *Moderate.* ⊠ *Sequoia National Park* ✛ *Trailhead: Little Baldy Saddle, Generals Hwy. (Rte. 198), 9 miles north of General Sherman Tree* ☞ *Shuttle: Lodgepole-Wuksachi-Dorst.*

Marble Falls Trail

TRAIL | The 3.7-mile trail to Marble Falls crosses through the rugged foothills before reaching the cascading water. Plan on three to four hours one-way. *Moderate.* ⊠ *Sequoia National Park* ✛ *Trailhead: Off dirt road across from concrete ditch near site 17 at Potwisha Campground, off Generals Hwy. (Rte. 198).*

Muir Grove Trail

TRAIL | You will attain solitude and possibly see a bear or two on this unheralded gem of a hike, a 4-mile round-trip from the Dorst Creek Campground. The remote grove is small but lovely, its soundtrack provided solely by nature. The trailhead is subtly marked. In summer, park in the amphitheater lot and walk down toward the group campsite area. *Easy.* ⊠ *Sequoia National Park* ✛ *Trailhead: Dorst Creek Campground, Generals Hwy. (Rte. 198), 8 miles north of Lodgepole Visitor Center* ☞ *Shuttle: Lodgepole-Wuksachi-Dorst.*

Tokopah Falls Trail

TRAIL | This trail with a 500-foot elevation gain follows the Marble Fork of the Kaweah River for 1¾ miles one-way and dead-ends below the impressive granite cliffs and cascading waterfall of Tokopah Canyon. The trail passes through a mixed-conifer forest. It takes 2½ to 4 hours to make the round-trip journey. *Moderate.* ✉ *Sequoia National Park* ⊹ *Trailhead: Off Generals Hwy. (Rte. 198), ¼ mile north of Lodgepole Campground* ⌁ *Shuttle: Lodgepole-Wuksachi-Dorst.*

VISITOR CENTERS

Lodgepole Visitor Center

INFO CENTER | Along with exhibits on the area's history, geology, and wildlife, the center screens an outstanding 22-minute film about bears. You can buy books, maps, wilderness permits, and tickets to cave tours here. ✉ *Sequoia National Park* ⊹ *Generals Hwy. (Rte. 198), 21 miles north of Ash Mountain entrance* ☎ *559/565–3341* ⊙ *Closed Oct.–Apr.* ⌁ *Shuttle: Giant Forest or Wuksachi-Lodgepole-Dorst.*

Restaurants

Lodgepole Market and Café

$ | **CAFÉ** | The choices here run the gamut from simple to very simple, with several counters only a few strides apart in a central eating complex. The café also sells fresh and prepackaged salads, sandwiches, and wraps. **Known for:** quick and convenient dining; many healthful options; grab-and-go items for picnics. ⑤ *Average main: $12* ✉ *Next to Lodgepole Visitor Center* ☎ *559/565–3301* ⊕ *www.visitsequoia.com/dine/lodgepole-dining.*

The Peaks

$$$ | **MODERN AMERICAN** | Huge windows run the length of the Wuksachi Lodge's high-ceilinged dining room, and a large fireplace on the far wall warms both body and soul. The diverse dinner menu—by far the best at both parks—reflects a commitment to locally sourced and sustainable products. **Known for:** seasonal menus with fresh local ingredients; great views of sequoia grove; box lunches. ⑤ *Average main: $28* ✉ *Wuksachi Lodge, 64740 Wuksachi Way, Wuksachi Village* ☎ *559/625–7700* ⊕ *www.visitsequoia.com/dine/the-peaks-restaurant.*

Hotels

★ Wuksachi Lodge

$$ | **HOTEL** | The striking cedar-and-stone main building is a fine example of how a structure can blend effectively with lovely mountain scenery. **Pros:** best place to stay in the parks; lots of wildlife; easy access to hiking and snowshoe/ski trails. **Cons:** rooms can be small; main lodge is a few-minutes' walk from guest rooms; slow Wi-Fi. ⑤ *Rooms from: $229* ✉ *64740 Wuksachi Way, Wuksachi Village* ☎ *559/625–7700, 888/252–5757 reservations* ⊕ *www.visitsequoia.com/lodging/wuksachi-lodge* ⇆ *102 rooms* ⍾ *No meals.*

Mineral King

25 miles east of Generals Hwy. (Rte. 198) via Mineral King Rd.

A subalpine valley of fir, pine, and sequoia trees with myriad lakes and hiking trails, Mineral King sits at 7,500 feet at the end of a steep, winding road. This is the highest point to which you can drive in the park. It is open only from Memorial Day through late October.

Sights

SCENIC DRIVES

Mineral King Road

SCENIC DRIVE | Vehicles longer than 22 feet are prohibited on this side road into southern Sequoia National Park, and for good reason: it's smaller than a regular two-lane road, some sections are unpaved, and it contains 589 twists and turns. Anticipating an average speed of 20 mph is optimistic. The scenery is splendid as you climb nearly 6,000 feet from Three Rivers to the Mineral King Area. In addition to maneuvering the blind curves and narrow stretches, you might find yourself sharing the pavement with bears, rattlesnakes, and even soft-ball-size spiders. Allow 90 minutes each way. ⊠ *Sequoia National Forest ✛ East off Sierra Dr. (Rte. 198), 3 ½ miles northeast of Three Rivers* ☉ *Road typically closed Nov.–late May.*

TRAILS
Mineral King Trails

TRAIL | Many trails to the high country begin at Mineral King. Two popular day hikes are Eagle Lake (6.8 miles round-trip) and Timber Gap (4.4 miles round-trip). At the Mineral King Ranger Station (☎ *559/565–3768*) you can pick up maps and check about conditions from late May to late September. *Difficult.* ⊠ *Sequoia National Park ✛ Trailheads: At end of Mineral King Rd., 25 miles east of Generals Hwy. (Rte. 198).*

VISITOR CENTERS
Mineral King Ranger Station

INFO CENTER | The station's small visitor center has exhibits on area history. Wilderness permits and some books and maps are available. ⊠ *Sequoia National Park ✛ Mineral King Rd., 24 miles east of Rte. 198* ☎ *559/565–3341* ☞ *Typically closed mid-Sept.–mid-May.*

 Hotels

Silver City Mountain Resort

$$$ | RESORT | High on Mineral King Road, this privately owned resort has rustic cabins and deluxe chalets—all with a stove, refrigerator, and sink—plus three hotel rooms with private baths. **Pros:** rustic setting; friendly staff; great location for hikers. **Cons:** long, winding road is not for everybody; not much entertainment except hiking; some units have shared baths. ⑤ *Rooms from: $170* ⊠ *Sequoia National Park ✛ Mineral King Rd., 21 miles southeast of Rte. 198* ☎ *559/242–3510, 559/561–1322 reservations* ⊕ *www.silvercityresort.com* ☉ *Closed Nov.–late May* ⇄ *16 units* ⍥*No meals.*

Mt. Whitney

276 miles by car from Sequoia National Park/Foothills Visitor Center (looping around the Sierra Nevada) on U.S. 395, 60 miles on foot (an 8-day trek) along Mt. Whitney Trail.

At 14,494 feet, Mt. Whitney is the highest point in the contiguous United States and the crown jewel of Sequoia National Park's wild eastern side. The peak looms high above the tiny, high-mountain desert community of Lone Pine, where numerous Hollywood Westerns have been filmed. The high mountain ranges, arid landscape, and scrubby brush of the eastern Sierra are beautiful in their vastness and austerity.

Despite the mountain's scale, you can't see it from the more traveled west side of the park because it is hidden behind the Great Western Divide. The only way to access Mt. Whitney from the main part of the park is to circumnavigate the Sierra Nevada via a 10-hour, nearly 400-mile drive outside the park. No road ascends the peak; the best vantage point from which to catch a glimpse of the mountain is at the end of Whitney Portal Road. The 13 miles of winding road leads from U.S. 395 at Lone Pine to the trailhead for the hiking route to the top of the mountain. Whitney Portal Road is closed in winter.

Sights

TRAILS

Mt. Whitney Trail

TRAIL | The most popular route to the summit, the Mt. Whitney Trail can be conquered by very fit and experienced hikers. If there's snow on the mountain, this is a challenge for expert mountaineers only. All overnighters must have a permit, as must day hikers on the trail beyond Lone Pine Lake, about 2½ miles from the trailhead. From May through October, permits are distributed via a lottery run each February by ⊕ *recreation.gov.* The Eastern Sierra Interagency Visitor Center (☎ *760/876–6200*), on Route 136 at U.S. 395 about a mile south of Lone Pine, is a good resource for information about permits and hiking. ⊠ *Kings Canyon National Park* ☎ *760/873–2483 trail reservations* ⊕ *www.fs.usda.gov/inyo.*

Activities

BIRD-WATCHING

More than 200 species of birds inhabit Sequoia and Kings Canyon national parks. Not seen in most parts of the United States, the white-headed woodpecker and the pileated woodpecker are common in most mid-elevation areas here. There are also many hawks and owls, including the renowned spotted owl. Due to the changes in elevation, both parks have diverse species ranging from warblers, kingbirds, thrushes, and sparrows in the foothills to goshawk, blue grouse, red-breasted nuthatch, and brown creeper at the highest elevations. The Sequoia Parks Conservancy (☎ *559/565–4251* ⊕ *www.sequoiaparksconservancy.org*) has information about bird-watching in the southern Sierra.

CAMPING

Some campgrounds are open year-round, others only seasonally. Except for Bearpaw (around $350 a night including meals), fees at the campgrounds range from $22 to $45, depending on location and size. There are no RV hookups at any of the campgrounds. Expect a table and a fire ring with a grill at standard sites. You can make reservations (book as far ahead as possible) at Bearpaw, Dorst Creek, Lodgepole, and Potwisha. The rest are first-come, first-served. The Lodgepole and Dorst Creek campgrounds can be quite busy in the summer and are popular with families. Black bears are prevalent in these areas; carefully follow all posted instructions about food storage. Bear-proof metal containers are provided at many campgrounds.

Atwell Mill Campground. At 6,650 feet, this peaceful, tent-only campground is just south of the Western Divide. ⊠ *Mineral King Rd., 20 miles east of Rte. 198* ☎ *559/565–3341.*

Bearpaw High Sierra Camp. Classy camping is the order of the day at this tent hotel and restaurant. Make reservations starting on January 2. ⊠ *High Sierra Trail, 11.5 miles from Lodgepole Village* ☎ *866/807–3598* ⊕ *www.visitsequoia.com.*

Buckeye Flat Campground. This tents-only campground at the southern end of Sequoia National Park is smaller—and consequently quieter—than campgrounds elsewhere in the park. Because of its low elevation (2,800 feet), it's hot in summer. ⊠ *Generals Hwy., 6 miles north of Foothills Visitor Center* ☎ *559/784–1500.*

Dorst Creek Campground. Wildlife sightings are common at this large campground at elevation 6,700 feet. ⊠ *Generals Hwy., 8 miles north of Lodgepole Visitor Center* ☎ *559/565–3341, 877/444–6777.*

Lodgepole Campground. The largest Lodgepole-area campground is also the noisiest, though things quiet down at night. ⊠ *Off Generals Hwy. beyond Lodgepole Village* ☎ *559/565–3341, 877/444–6777.*

Potwisha Campground. On the Marble Fork of the Kaweah River, this midsize, year-round campground at an elevation of 2,100 feet gets no snow in winter and can be hot in summer. ⊠ *Generals Hwy., 4 miles north of Foothills Visitor Center* ☎ *559/565–3341, 877/444–6777.*

CROSS-COUNTRY SKIING
Alta Market and Ski Shop
SKIING/SNOWBOARDING | Rent cross-country skis and snowshoes here. Depending on snowfall amounts, instruction may also be available. Reservations are recommended. Marked trails cut through Giant Forest, about 5 miles south of Wuksachi Lodge. ⊠ *Sequoia National Park* ⚡ *At Lodgepole, off Generals Hwy. (Rte. 198)* ☎ *559/565–3301* ☞ *Shuttle: Wuksachi-Lodgepole-Dorst.*

EDUCATIONAL PROGRAMS
Free Nature Programs
WILDLIFE-WATCHING | Almost any summer day, ½-hour to 1½-hour ranger talks and walks explore subjects such as the life of the sequoia, the geology of the park, and the habits of bears. Giant Forest Museum, Lodgepole Visitor Center, and Wuksachi Village are frequent starting points. Look for less frequent tours in the winter from Grant Grove. Check bulletin boards throughout the park for the week's offerings. ⊕ *www.sequoiaparks-conservancy.org.*

Junior Ranger Program
HIKING/WALKING | **FAMILY** | Children over age five can earn a patch upon completion of a fun set of age-appropriate tasks outlined in the Junior Ranger booklet. Pick one up at any visitor center. ☎ *559/565–3341.*

Sequoia Parks Conservancy Evening Programs
HIKING/WALKING | The Sequoia Parks Conservancy offers hikes and evening lectures during the summer and winter. The popular Wonders of the Night Sky programs celebrate the often stunning views of the heavens experienced at both parks year-round. ⊠ *Sequoia National Park* ☎ *559/565–4251* ⊕ *www.sequoiaparksconservancy.org.*

Sequoia Parks Conservancy Seminars
WILDLIFE-WATCHING | Expert naturalists lead seminars on a range of topics, including birds, wildflowers, geology, botany, photography, park history, backpacking, and pathfinding. Reservations are required. Information about times and prices is available at the visitor centers or through the Sequoia Parks Conservancy. ⊠ *Sequoia National Park* ☎ *559/565–4251* ⊕ *www.sequoiaparksconservancy.org.*

FISHING
There's limited trout fishing in the creeks and rivers from late April to mid-November. The Kaweah River is a popular spot; check at visitor centers for open and closed waters. Some of the park's secluded backcountry lakes have good fishing. A California fishing license, required for persons 16 and older, costs about $10 for one day, $24 for two days, and $48 for 10 days (discounts are available for state residents and others). For park regulations, closures, and restrictions, call the parks at ☎ *559/565–3341* or stop at a visitor center. Licenses and fishing tackle are usually available at Hume Lake.

California Department of Fish and Game
FISHING | The department supplies fishing licenses and provides a full listing of regulations. ☎ *916/928–5805* ⊕ *www.wildlife.ca.gov.*

HORSEBACK RIDING
Grant Grove Stables
HORSEBACK RIDING | Grant Grove Stables isn't too far from parts of Sequoia National Park and is perfect for short rides from June to September. Reservations are recommended. ☎ *559/335–9292 summer* ⊕ *www.nps.gov/seki/planyourvisit/horseride.htm* 🎫 *From $50.*

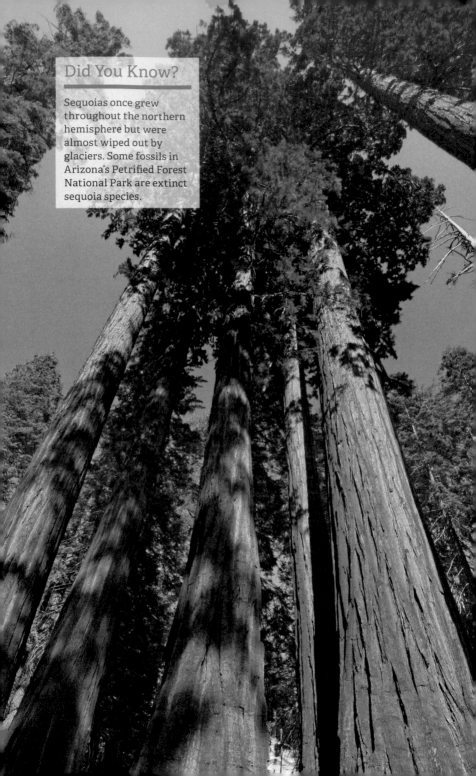

Did You Know?

Sequoias once grew
throughout the northern
hemisphere but were
almost wiped out by
glaciers. Some fossils in
Arizona's Petrified Forest
National Park are extinct
sequoia species.

Horse Corral Packers

HORSEBACK RIDING | One- and two-hour trips through Sequoia are available for beginning and advanced riders. ⊠ *Big Meadow Rd., 12 miles east of Generals Hwy. (Rte. 198) between Sequoia and Kings Canyon national parks* ☎ *559/565–3404 summer, 559/565–6429 off-season,* ⊕ *hcpacker.com* ⊠ *From $50.*

Kings Canyon National Park

Kings Canyon National Park consists of two sections that adjoin the northern boundary of Sequoia National Park. The western portion, covered with sequoia and pine forest, contains the park's most visited sights, such as Grant Grove. The vast eastern portion is remote high country, slashed across half its southern breadth by the deep, rugged Kings River canyon. Separating the two is Sequoia National Forest, which encompasses Giant Sequoia National Monument. The Kings Canyon Scenic Byway (Route 180) links the major sights within and between the park's two sections.

Grant Grove Village— Redwood Canyon

56 miles east of Fresno on Rte. 180, 26 miles north of Lodgepole Village in Sequoia National Park.

Grant Grove Village, home to the Kings Canyon Visitor Center, Grant Grove Cabins, John Muir Lodge, a market, and two restaurants, anchors the northwestern section of the park. Nearby attractions include the General Grant Tree and Redwood Canyon sequia grove. The Kings Canyon Scenic Byway begins here and travels 30 miles down to the Kings River Canyon and Cedar Grove.

◉ Sights

HISTORIC SIGHTS
Fallen Monarch

TOUR—SIGHT | This toppled sequoia's hollow base was used in the second half of the 19th century as a home for settlers, a saloon, and even a U.S. Cavalry stable. As you walk through it (assuming entry is permitted, which is not always the case), notice how little the wood has decayed, and imagine yourself tucked safely inside, sheltered from a storm or protected from the searing heat. ⊠ *Kings Canyon National Park* ✛ *Grant Grove Trail, 1 mile north of Kings Canyon Park Visitor Center.*

Gamlin Cabin

BUILDING | Despite being listed on the National Register of Historic Places, this replica of a modest 1872 pioneer cabin is only borderline historical. The structure, which was moved and rebuilt several times over the years, once served as U.S. Cavalry storage space and, in the early 20th century, a ranger station. ⊠ *Grant Grove Trail.*

SCENIC DRIVES
★ **Kings Canyon Scenic Byway**

SCENIC DRIVE | The 30-mile stretch of Route 180 between Grant Grove Village and Zumwalt Meadow delivers eye-popping scenery—granite cliffs, a roaring river, waterfalls, and Kings River canyon itself—much of which you can experience at vista points or on easy walks. The canyon comes into view about 10 miles east of the village at **Junction View.** Five miles beyond, at **Yucca Point,** the canyon is thousands of feet deeper than the more famous Grand Canyon. **Canyon View,** a special spot 1 mile east of the Cedar Grove Village turnoff, showcases evidence of the area's glacial history. Here, perhaps more than anywhere else, you'll understand why John Muir compared Kings Canyon vistas with those in Yosemite. ∎TIP➔ **Note that this byway is a dead-end road—you have to turn around and head back the way you came.**

The drive takes about an hour each way without stops. ✉ *Kings Canyon National Park* ✛ *Rte. 180 north and east of Grant Grove village.*

SCENIC STOPS
Boyden Cavern
NATURE SITE | The Kings River has carved out hundreds of caverns, including Boyden, which brims with stalagmite, stalactite, drapery, flowstone, and other formations. In summer, the Bat Grotto shelters a slew of bats. If you can't make it to Crystal Cave in Sequoia, Boyden is a reasonable substitute. Regular tours take about 45 minutes and start with a steep walk uphill. ✉ *Sequoia National Forest, 74101 E. Kings Canyon Rd. (Rte. 180), between Grant Grove and Cedar Grove* ☎ *888/965–8243* ⊕ *boydencavern.com* ☜ *$16.*

General Grant Tree
LOCAL INTEREST | President Coolidge proclaimed this to be the "nation's Christmas tree," and, 30 years later, President Eisenhower designated it as a living shrine to all Americans who have died in wars. Bigger at its base than the General Sherman Tree, it tapers more quickly. It's estimated to be the world's third-largest sequoia by volume. A spur trail winds behind the tree, where scars from a long-ago fire remain visible. ✉ *Kings Canyon National Park* ✛ *Trailhead: 1 mile north of Grant Grove Visitor Center.*

Project Survival's Cat Haven
ZOO | Take the rare opportunity to glimpse a Siberian lynx, a clouded leopard, a Bengal tiger, and other endangered wild cats at this conservation facility that shelters more than 30 big cats. A guided hour-long tour along a ¼-mile walkway leads to fenced habitat areas shaded by trees and overlooking the Central Valley. ✉ *38257 E. Kings Canyon Rd. (Rte. 180), 15 miles west of Kings Canyon National Park, Dunlap* ☎ *559/338–3216* ⊕ *cathaven.com* ☜ *$15* ⊘ *Closed Tues. May–Sept. Closed Tues. and Wed. Oct.–Apr.*

Redwood Mountain Sequoia Grove
FOREST | One of the world's largest sequoia groves, Redwood contains within its 2,078 acres nearly 2,200 specimens whose diameters exceed 10 feet. You can view the grove from afar at an overlook or hike 6 to 10 miles via moderate loop trails down into the richest regions, which include two of the world's 25 heaviest trees. ✉ *Kings Canyon National Park* ✛ *Drive 6 miles south of Grant Grove on Generals Hwy. (Rte. 198), then turn right at Quail Flat; follow it 2 miles to the Redwood Canyon trailhead.*

TRAILS
Big Baldy Trail
TRAIL | This hike climbs 600 feet and 2 miles up to the 8,209-foot summit of Big Baldy. Your reward is the view of Redwood Canyon. Round-trip, the hike is 4 miles. *Moderate.* ✉ *Kings Canyon National Park* ✛ *Trailhead: 8 miles south of Grant Grove on Generals Hwy. (Rte. 198).*

Big Stump Trail
TRAIL | From 1883 until 1890, logging was done here, complete with a mill. The 1-mile loop trail, whose unmarked beginning is a few yards west of the Big Stump entrance, passes by many enormous stumps. *Easy.* ✉ *Kings Canyon National Park* ✛ *Trailhead: Near Big Stump Entrance, Generals Hwy. (Rte. 180).*

★ Grant Grove Trail
TRAIL | Grant Grove is only 128 acres, but it's a big deal. More than 120 sequoias here have a base diameter that exceeds 10 feet, and the **General Grant Tree** is the world's third-largest sequoia by volume. Nearby, the Confederacy is represented by the **Robert E. Lee Tree,** recognized as the world's 11th-largest sequoia. Also along the easy-to-walk trail are the **Fallen Monarch** and the **Gamlin Cabin,** built by 19th-century pioneers. *Easy.* ✉ *Kings Canyon National Park* ✛ *Trailhead: Off Generals Hwy. (Rte. 180), 1 mile north of Kings Canyon Park Visitor Center.*

Panoramic Point Trail

TRAIL | You'll get a nice view of whale-shape Hume Lake from the top of this Grant Grove path, which is paved and only 300 feet long. It's fairly steep—strollers might work here, but not wheelchairs. Trailers and RVs are not permitted on the steep and narrow road that leads to the trailhead parking lot. *Moderate.* ⊠ *Kings Canyon National Park* ⊹ *Trailhead: At end of Panoramic Point Rd., 2.3 miles from Grant Grove Village.*

Redwood Canyon Trails

TRAIL | Two main trails lead into Redwood Canyon grove, the world's largest sequoia grove. The 6.5-mile **Hart Tree and Fallen Goliath Loop** passes by a 19th-century logging site, pristine Hart Meadow, and the hollowed-out Tunnel Tree before accessing a side trail to the grove's largest sequoia, the 277.9-foot-tall Hart Tree. The 6.4-mile **Sugar Bowl Loop** provides views of Redwood Mountain and Big Baldy before winding down into its namesake, a thick grove of mature and young sequoias. *Moderate.* ⊠ *Kings Canyon National Park* ⊹ *Trailhead: Off Quail Flat. Drive 5 miles south of Grant Grove on Generals Hwy. (Rte. 198), turn right at Quail Flat and proceed 1½ miles to trailhead.*

VISITOR CENTERS

Kings Canyon Visitor Center

INFO CENTER | The center's 15-minute film and various exhibits provide an overview of the park's canyon, sequoias, and human history. Books, maps, and weather advice are dispensed here, as are (if available) $15 wilderness permits. ⊠ *Kings Canyon National Park* ⊹ *Grant Grove Village, Generals Hwy. (Rte. 198), 3 miles northeast of Rte. 180, Kings Canyon National Park entrance at Big Stump* ☎ *559/565–3341.*

Restaurants

Grant Grove Restaurant

$ | **AMERICAN** | Gaze at giant sequoias and a verdant meadow while enjoying a meal in this eco-friendly restaurant's spacious dining room with a fireplace or on its expansive deck. The menu centers around locally sourced natural and organic ingredients and offers standard American fare. **Known for:** takeout service year-round; walk-up window for pizza, sandwiches, coffee, ice cream; picnic tables on outdoor deck. ⑤ *Average main: $16* ⊠ *Grant Grove Village* ☎ *559/335–5500.*

Hotels

Grant Grove Cabins

$ | **HOTEL** | Some of the wood-panel cabins here have heaters, electric lights, and private baths, but most have woodstoves, battery lamps, and shared baths. **Pros:** warm, woodsy feel; clean; walk to Grant Grove Restaurant. **Cons:** can be difficult to walk up to if you're not in decent physical shape; costly for what you get; only basic amenities. ⑤ *Rooms from: $135* ⊠ *Kings Canyon Scenic Byway in Grant Grove Village* ☎ *866/807–3598* ⊕ *www.visitsequoia.com/Grant-Grove-Cabins.aspx* ⇆ *50 units* ⑩ *No meals.*

John Muir Lodge

$$ | **HOTEL** | In a wooded area in the hills above Grant Grove Village, this modern, timber-sided lodge has rooms and suites with queen- or king-size beds and private baths. **Pros:** open year-round; common room stays warm; quiet. **Cons:** check-in is down in the village; spotty Wi-Fi, remote location. ⑤ *Rooms from: $210* ⊠ *Kings Canyon Scenic Byway, ¼ mile north of Grant Grove Village, 86728 Hwy. 180* ☎ *866/807–3598* ⊕ *www.visitsequoia.com/john-muir-lodge.aspx* ⇆ *36 rooms* ⑩ *No meals.*

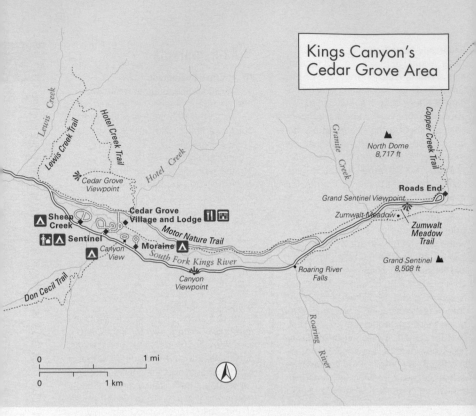

Copper Creek Trail

Granite Creek

North Dome
8,717 ft

Lewis Creek

Hotel Creek Trail

Lewis Creek Trail

Hotel Creek

Cedar Grove
Viewpoint

Roads End

Grand Sentinel Viewpoint

Cedar Grove
Village and Lodge

Zumwalt Meadow

Sheep
Creek

Zumwalt
Meadow
Trail

Motor Nature Trail

Sentinel

Canyon
View

Moraine

South Fork Kings River

Grand Sentinel
8,508 ft

Canyon
Viewpoint

Roaring River
Falls

Don Cecil Trail

Roaring River

0   1 mi

0   1 km

Montecito-Sequoia Lodge

$$ | **HOTEL** | **FAMILY** | Outdoor activities are
what this year-round family resort is all
about, including many that are geared
toward teenagers and small children.
Pros: friendly staff; great for kids; lots
of fresh air and planned activities. **Cons:**
can be noisy with all the activity; no
TVs or phones in rooms; not within
national park. ⑤ *Rooms from: $229*
✉ *63410 Generals Hwy., 11 miles south
of Grant Grove, Sequoia National Forest*
☎ *559/565–3388, 800/227–9900* ⊕ *www.
mslodge.com* ⊘ *Closed 1st 2 wks of
Dec.* ⇥ *52 rooms* ⑩ *All meals.*

Cedar Grove

35 miles east of Grant Grove Village.

The Cedar Grove section of Kings Canyon
National Park bears many similarities to
Yosemite Valley: a mighty river flowing through a verdant valley, ringed by
massive glacier-hewn granite cliffs that
loom several thousand feet above. Drive
along the Kings Canyon Scenic Byway to
access this relatively uncrowded wonderland, where you can hike excellent
backcountry trails, stroll around lush
Zumwalt Meadows, and take a break in
Cedar Grove Village.

Sights

HISTORIC SIGHTS
Knapp's Cabin

BUILDING | Stop here not so much for the cabin itself, but as an excuse to ogle the scenery. George Knapp, a Santa Barbara businessman, stored gear in this small wooden structure when he commissioned fishing trips into the canyon in the 1920s. *Kings Canyon National Park ✛ Kings Canyon Scenic Byway, 2 miles east of Cedar Grove Village turnoff.*

TRAILS
Don Cecil Trail

TRAIL | This trail climbs 4,000 feet up the cool north-facing slope of the Kings River canyon, passing Sheep Creek Cascade and providing several fine glimpses of the canyon and the 11,000-foot Monarch Divide. The trail leads to Lookout Peak, which affords a panorama of the park's backcountry. This strenuous, all-day hike covers 13 miles round-trip. *Difficult.* *Kings Canyon National Park ✛ Trailhead: At Sentinel Campground, Cedar Grove Village.*

Hotel Creek Trail

TRAIL | For gorgeous canyon views, take this trail from Cedar Grove up a series of switchbacks until it splits. Follow the route left through chaparral to the forested ridge and rocky outcrop known as Cedar Grove Overlook, where you can see the Kings River canyon stretching below. This strenuous, 5-mile round-trip hike gains 1,200 feet and takes three to four hours to complete. *Difficult.* *Kings Canyon National Park ✛ Trailhead: At Cedar Grove Pack Station, 1 mile east of Cedar Grove Village.*

Mist Falls Trail

TRAIL | This sandy trail follows the glaciated South Fork Canyon through forest and chaparral, past several rapids and cascades, to one of the largest waterfalls in the two parks. Nine miles round-trip, the hike is relatively flat, but climbs 600 feet in the last 2 miles. It takes from four to five hours to complete. *Moderate.* *Kings Canyon National Park ✛ Trailhead: At end of Kings Canyon Scenic Byway, 5½ miles east of Cedar Grove Village.*

Roaring River Falls Walk

TRAIL | Take a shady five-minute walk to this forceful waterfall that rushes through a narrow granite chute. The trail is paved and mostly accessible. *Easy.* *Kings Canyon National Park ✛ Trailhead: 3 miles east of Cedar Grove Village turnoff from Kings Canyon Scenic Byway.*

★ Zumwalt Meadow Trail

TRAIL | Rangers say this is the best (and most popular) day hike in the Cedar Grove area. Just 1½ miles long, it offers three visual treats: the South Fork of the Kings River, the lush meadow, and the high granite walls above, including those of Grand Sentinel and North Dome. *Easy.* *Kings Canyon National Park ✛ Trailhead: 4½ miles east of Cedar Grove Village turnoff from Kings Canyon Scenic Byway.*

VISITOR CENTERS
Cedar Grove Visitor Center

INFO CENTER | Off the main road and behind the Sentinel Campground, this small ranger station has books and maps, plus information about hikes and other activities. *Kings Canyon National Park ✛ Kings Canyon Scenic Byway, 30 miles east of Rte. 180/198 junction ☎ 559/565–3341 ☉ Closed mid-Sept.–mid-May.*

Restaurants

Cedar Grove Grill

$ | **AMERICAN** | The menu here is surprisingly extensive, with dinner entrées such as pasta, pork chops, trout, and steak. For breakfast, try the egg burrito, French toast, or pancakes; sandwiches, wraps, burgers (including vegetarian patties) and hot dogs dominate the lunch choices. **Known for:** scenic river views; extensive options; alfresco dining on balcony overlooking the Kings River. **$** *Average main:*

$16 ⊠ Cedar Grove Village ☎ 886/807–3598 ⊕ www.visitsequoia.com/dine/cedar-grove-grill ⊗ Closed Oct.–May.

 Hotels

Cedar Grove Lodge

$ | HOTEL | Backpackers like to stay here on the eve of long treks into the High Sierra wilderness, so bedtimes tend to be early. **Pros:** a definite step up from camping in terms of comfort; great base camp for outdoor adventures; on-site snack bar. **Cons:** impersonal; not everybody agrees it's clean enough; remote location. ⓢ Rooms from: $147 ⊠ Kings Canyon Scenic Byway ☎ 866/807–3598 ⊕ www.visitsequoia.com/lodging/cedar-grove-lodge ⊗ Closed mid-Oct.–mid-May ⊅ 21 rooms ⊙ No meals.

Activities

CAMPING

Azalea Campground. Of the three campgrounds in the Grant Grove area, Azalea is the only one open year-round. It sits at 6,500 feet amid giant sequoias. ⊠ Kings Canyon Scenic Byway, ¼ mile north of Grant Grove Village ☎ 559/565–3341.

Canyon View Campground. The smallest and most primitive of four campgrounds near Cedar Grove, this one is near the start of the Don Cecil Trail, which leads to Lookout Point. The elevation of the camp is 4,600 feet along the Kings River. There are no wheelchair-accessible sites. ⊠ Off Kings Canyon Scenic Byway, ½-mile east of Cedar Grove Village ☎ No phone.

Crystal Springs Campground. Near the Grant Grove Village and the towering sequoias, this camp is at 6,500 feet. There are accessible sites here. ⊠ Off Generals Hwy. (Rte. 198), ¼ mile north of Grant Grove Visitor Center ☎ No phone.

Sentinel Campground. At 4,600 feet and within walking distance of Cedar Grove Village, Sentinel fills up fast in summer. ⊠ Kings Canyon Scenic Byway, ¼ mile west of Cedar Grove Village ☎ 559/565–3341.

Sheep Creek Campground. Of the overflow campgrounds, this is one of the prettiest. ⊠ Off Kings Canyon Scenic Byway, 1 mile west of Cedar Grove Village ☎ No phone.

Sunset Campground. Many of the easiest trails through Grant Grove are adjacent to this large camp, near the giant sequoias at 6,500 feet. ⊠ Off Generals Hwy., near Grant Grove Visitor Center ☎ No phone.

CROSS-COUNTRY SKIING

Grant Grove Ski Touring Center

SKIING/SNOWBOARDING | The Grant Grove Market doubles as the ski-touring center, where you can rent cross-country skis or snowshoes in winter. This is a good starting point for a number of marked trails, including the Panoramic Point Trail and the General Grant Tree Trail. ⊠ Grant Grove Market, Generals Hwy. (Rte. 198), 3 miles northeast of Rte. 180, Big Stump entrance ☎ 559/335–5500 ⊕ www.visitsequoia.com/cross-country-skiing.aspx ⊠ From $15.

FISHING

There is limited trout fishing in the park from late April to mid-November, and catches are minor. Still, Kings River is a popular spot. Some of the park's secluded backcountry lakes have good fishing. Licenses are available, along with fishing tackle, in Grant Grove and Cedar Grove. See Activities, in Sequoia National Park for more information about licenses.

HIKING

Roads End Permit Station

INFO CENTER | You can obtain wilderness permits, maps, and information about the backcountry at this station, where bear canisters, a must for campers, can be rented or purchased. When the station is closed (typically October–mid-May), complete a self-service permit form. ⊠ Kings Canyon National Park ✛ Eastern end of Kings Canyon Scenic Byway, 6 miles east of Cedar Grove Visitor Center.

HORSEBACK RIDING
Cedar Grove Pack Station
HORSEBACK RIDING | Take a day ride or plan a multiday adventure along the Kings River canyon with Cedar Grove Pack Station. Popular routes include the Rae Lakes Loop and Monarch Divide. Closed early September–late May. ⊠ *Kings Canyon National Park* ⊹ *Kings Canyon Scenic Byway, 1 mile east of Cedar Grove Village* ☎ *559/565–3464 summer, 559/337–2413 off-season* ⊕ *www.nps.gov/seki/plan-yourvisit/horseride.htm* 🖼 *From $50 per hr or $90 per day.*

Grant Grove Stables
HORSEBACK RIDING | A one- or two-hour trip through Grant Grove leaving from the stables provides a taste of horseback riding in Kings Canyon. The stables are closed October–early June. ⊠ *Kings Canyon National Park* ⊹ *Rte. 180, ½ mile north of Grant Grove Visitor Center* ☎ *559/335–9292* ⊕ *www.nps.gov/seki/planyourvisit/horseride.htm* 🖼 *From $50 per hr, $90 for 2 hrs.*

What's Nearby

Three Rivers

7 miles south of Sequoia National Park's Foothills Visitor Center.

Three Rivers is a good spot to find a room when park lodgings are full. Either because residents here appreciate their idyllic setting or because they know that tourists are their bread and butter, you'll find them eager to share tips about the best spots for "Sierra surfing" the Kaweah's smooth, moss-covered rocks or where to find the best cell reception (it's off to the cemetery for Verizon customers).

GETTING HERE AND AROUND
Driving is the easiest way to get to and around Three Rivers, which straddles a stretch of Highway 198. In summer, the Sequoia Shuttle connects Three Rivers to Visalia and Sequoia National Park.

CONTACTS Sequoia Shuttle. ☎ *877/287–4453* ⊕ *www.sequoiashuttle.com.*

Sights

Sequoia National Forest and Giant Sequoia National Monument
FOREST | Delicate spring wildflowers, cool summer campgrounds, and varied winter-sports opportunities—not to mention more than half of the world's giant sequoia groves—draw outdoorsy types year-round to this sprawling district surrounding the national parks. Together, the forest and monument cover nearly 1,700 square miles, south from the Kings River and east from the foothills along the San Joaquin Valley. The monument's groves are both north and south of Sequoia National Park. One of the most popular is the **Converse Basin Grove,** home of the Boole Tree, the forest's largest sequoia. The grove is accessible by car on an unpaved road.

The Hume Lake Forest Service District Office, at 35860 Kings Canyon Scenic Byway (Route 180), has information about the groves, along with details about recreational activities. In springtime, diversions include hiking among the wildflowers that brighten the foothills. The floral display rises with the heat as the mountain elevations warm up in summer, when hikers, campers, and picnickers become more plentiful. The abundant trout supply attracts anglers to area waters, including 87-acre **Hume Lake,** which is also ideal for swimming and nonmotorized boating. By fall, the turning leaves provide the visual delights, particularly in the Western Divide, Indian Basin, and the Kern Plateau. Winter activities include downhill and cross-country skiing, snowshoeing, and snowmobiling. ⊠ *Sequoia National Park* ⊹ *Northern Entrances: Generals Hwy. (Rte. 198), 7* miles southeast of Grant Grove; Hume Lake Rd. between Generals Hwy. (Rte. 198) and Kings Canyon Scenic Byway (Rte. 180); Kings Canyon Scenic Byway (Rte. 180) between Grant Grove and Cedar Grove. Southern Entrances: Rte. 190 east of Springville; Rte. 178 east of Bakersfield ☎ 559/784–1500 forest and monument, 559/338–2251 Hume Lake ⊕ www.fs.usda.gov/sequoia.

🍴 Restaurants

Gateway Restaurant and Lodge
$$$ | **AMERICAN** | The view's the draw at this roadhouse that overlooks the Kaweah River as it plunges out of the high country. The Gateway serves everything from osso buco and steaks to shrimp in Thai chili sauce; dinner reservations are essential on summer weekends. **Known for:** scenic riverside setting; fine dining in otherwise casual town; popular bar. ⑤ Average main: $30 ⊠ 45978 Sierra Dr. ☎ 559/561–4133 ⊕ www.gateway-sequoia.com.

Sierra Subs and Salads
$ | **AMERICAN** | This well-run sandwich joint satisfies carnivores and vegetarians alike with crispy-fresh ingredients prepared with panache. Depending on your preference, the centerpiece of the Bull's Eye sandwich, for instance, will be roast beef or a portobello mushroom; whichever you choose, the accompanying flavors—of ciabatta bread, horseradish-and-garlic mayonnaise, roasted red peppers, Havarti cheese, and spinach—will delight your palate. **Known for:** many vegetarian, vegan, and gluten-free options; weekly specials; Wi-Fi. ⑤ Average main: $12 ⊠ 41651 Sierra Dr. ☎ 559/561–4810 ⊕ www.sierrasubsandsalads.com ⊙ Closed Sun. and Mon. No dinner.

Hotels

Buckeye Tree Lodge
$$ | **B&B/INN** | Every room at this two-story motel has a patio facing a sun-dappled grassy lawn, right on the banks of the Kaweah River; individually decorated cottages and cabins across the river have private outdoor spaces with barbecue grills. **Pros:** near the park entrance; fantastic river views; kitchenette in some rooms. **Cons:** can fill up quickly in the summer; could use a little updating; some rooms are tiny. ⑤ Rooms from: $200 ⊠ 46000 Sierra Dr., Hwy. 198 ☎ 559/561–5900 ⊕ www.buckeye-tree.com ⋗ 22 units ⓄⒷ Free breakfast ⌖ 2-night minimum on summer weekends.

Lazy J Ranch Motel
$$ | **B&B/INN** | Surrounded by 12 acres of green lawns and a split-rail fence, the Lazy J is a modest compound of one-story motel buildings and freestanding cottages near the banks of the Kaweah River. **Pros:** pleasant landscaping; quiet rooms; friendly staff. **Cons:** on the far edge of town; can't see the river from most rooms; dated style and fixtures. ⑤ Rooms from: $150 ⊠ 39625 Sierra Dr., Hwy. 198 ☎ 559/561–4449 ⊕ www.lazyjranchmotel.com ⋗ 18 units ⓄⒷ Free breakfast.

★ Rio Sierra Riverhouse
$$$ | **B&B/INN** | Guests at Rio Sierra come for the river views, the sandy beach, and the proximity to Sequoia National Park (6 miles away), but invariably end up raving equally about the warm, laid-back hospitality of proprietress Mars Roberts. **Pros:** seductive beach; river views from all rooms; contemporary ambience. **Cons:** books up quickly in summer; some road noise audible in rooms; long walk or drive to restaurants. ⑤ Rooms from: $275 ⊠ 41997 Sierra Dr., Hwy. 198 ☎ 559/561–4720 ⊕ www.rio-sierra.com ⋗ 3 rooms ⓄⒷ No meals ⌖ 2-night min stay on summer weekends. Closed Jan.–mid-Mar.

⊛ Activities

HORSEBACK RIDING
Wood 'n' Horse Training Stables
HORSEBACK RIDING | For hourly horseback rides, riding lessons, or trail rides in the foothills, contact this outfit. Rates start at $50 for lessons and $70 for trail rides. ✉ *42846 N. Fork Dr.* ☎ *559/561–4268* ⊕ *www.wdnhorse.com.*

RAFTING
Kaweah White Water Adventures
BOATING | Kaweah's trips include a two-hour excursion (good for families) through Class III rapids, a longer paddle through Class IV rapids, and an extended trip (typically Class IV and V rapids). ✉ *40443 Sierra Dr.* ☎ *559/740–8251* ⊕ *www.kaweah-whitewater.com* ☞ *From $50 per person.*

Visalia

35 miles west of the Sequoia National Park entrance.

Visalia's combination of a reliable agricultural economy and civic pride has produced the Central Valley's most vibrant downtown, with numerous restaurants, craft breweries, and cafés. If you're into history, drop by the visitor center and pick up a free map of a self-guided historic downtown walking tour. A clear day's view of the Sierra from Main Street is spectacular, and even Sunday night can find the streets bustling with pedestrians. Visalia provides easy access to grand Sequoia National Park and the serene Kaweah Oaks Preserve.

GETTING HERE AND AROUND
Highway 198, just east of its exit from Highway 99, cuts through town (and proceeds up the hill to Sequoia National Park). Greyhound stops here, but not Amtrak. KART buses serve the locals, and, in summer, the Sequoia Shuttle ($20) travels among Visalia, Three Rivers, and Sequoia National Park with a stop in Three Rivers.

VISITOR INFORMATION
CONTACTS **Visalia Convention & Visitors Bureau (Visit Visalia).** ✉ *112 E. Main St.* ☎ *559/334–0141, 800/524–0303* ⊕ *www.visitvisalia.com.*

◉ Sights

Bravo Farms Traver
FACTORY | FAMILY | For one-stop truck-stop entertainment, pull off the highway in Traver, where at Bravo Farms you can try your luck at an arcade shooting gallery, watch cheese being made, munch on barbecue and ice cream, play a round of mini golf, peruse funky antiques, buy produce, visit a petting zoo, and climb a multistory tree house. Taste a few "squeekers" (fresh cheese curds, so named because chewing them makes your teeth squeak), and then be on your way. ✉ *36005 Hwy. 99, 9 miles north of Hwy. 198 and Visalia, Traver* ☎ *559/897–5762* ⊕ *www.bravofarms.com* ☞ *Free.*

★ Colonel Allensworth State Historic Park
HISTORIC SITE | It's worth the slight detour off Highway 99 to learn about and pay homage to the dream of Allen Allensworth and other Black pioneers who in 1908 founded Allensworth, the only California town settled, governed, and financed by African Americans. At its height, the town prospered as a key railroad transfer point, but after cars and trucks reduced railroad traffic and water was diverted for Central Valley agriculture, the town declined and was eventually deserted. Today, the restored and rebuilt schoolhouse, library, and other structures commemorate Allensworth's heyday, as do festivities that take place each October. ✉ *4129 Palmer Ave., 48 miles south of Visalia, Allensworth* ✢ *From Visalia, take Hwy. 99 south to Earlimart, and then turn west toward Allensworth* ☎ *661/849–3433* ⊕ *www.parks.ca.gov* ☞ *$6 per car.*

Exeter Murals

PUBLIC ART | More than two dozen murals in the Central Valley city of Exeter's cute-as-a-button downtown make it worth a quick detour if you're traveling on Route 198. Several of the murals, which depict the area's agricultural and social history, are quite good. All adorn buildings within a few blocks of the intersection of Pine and E streets. If you're hungry, the **Wildflower Cafe,** at 121 South E Street, serves inventive salads and sandwiches. Shortly after entering Exeter, head west on Pine Street (it's just before the water tower) to reach downtown. ✉ *204 E. Pine St., Exeter ✚ Rte. 65, 2 miles south of Rte. 198, about 11 miles east of Visalia* ⊕ *cityofexeter.com/galleries/exeter-murals.*

Kaweah Oaks Preserve

NATURE PRESERVE | Trails at this 344-acre wildlife sanctuary off the main road to Sequoia National Park lead past majestic valley oak, sycamore, cottonwood, and willow trees. Among the 134 bird species you might spot are hawks, hummingbirds, and great blue herons. Bobcats, lizards, coyotes, and cottontails also live here. The Sycamore Trail has digital signage with QR codes you can scan with your smartphone to access plant and animal information. ✉ *Follow Hwy. 198 for 7 miles east of Visalia, turn north on Rd. 182, and proceed ½ mile to gate on left side* ☎ *559/738–0211* ⊕ *www. sequoiariverlands.org* 🎟 *Free.*

Lake Kaweah

BODY OF WATER | The Kaweah River rushes out of the Sierra from high above Mineral King in Sequoia National Park. When it reaches the hills above the Central Valley, the water collects in Lake Kaweah, a reservoir operated by the Army Corps of Engineers. You can swim, sail, kayak, water ski, hike, camp, fish, and picnic here. The visitor center at Lemon Hill has interesting exhibits about the dam that created the lake. ✉ *34443 Sierra Dr. (Rte. 198), about 20 miles east of Visalia* ☎ *559/597–2301, 877/444–6777*

campground reservations, 559/597–2005 Lemon Hill visitor center 🎟 *$5 day use.*

★ McKellar Family Farms

FARM/RANCH | **FAMILY** | Taste, touch, and feel your way through orange and mandarin groves on a guided tour of this 180-acre working citrus farm. Tours last 60 minutes; tractor-pulled wagon tours are also available. Kids and adults love the challenge of navigating the nation's only orange-grove maze, answering questions at a series of checkpoints to earn a prize at the end. ✉ *32985 Rd. 164, north of Hwy. 216, Ivanhoe* ☎ *559/731–7925* ⊕ *www.mckellarfamilyfarms.com* 🎟 *Tour $100 for up to 2 persons, $10 for each additional person.*

Restaurants

Fugazzi's Bistro

$$ | **ITALIAN** | An upscale restaurant in Visalia's downtown hub, Fugazzi's serves up Italian-American and international-fusion dishes in a slick, contemporary space with leather booths and shiny metal tables. The extensive lunch and dinner menus feature everything from quinoa-and-kale salad and Thai chicken wraps to traditional Italian dishes and filet mignon. **Known for:** full bar with classic and creative cocktails; house-made sauces; upscale yet casual vibe. Ⓢ *Average main: $19* ✉ *127 W. Main St.* ☎ *559/625–0496* ⊕ *www.fugazzisbistro.com.*

Pita Kabob Gastropub

$ | **MEDITERRANEAN** | A large and ever-changing selection of craft beers, a lively dining garden, and authentic Mediterranean and fusion dishes—from kebabs, shawarma, hummus, and gyros to rice bowls and burgers—lure locals and visitors to this popular downtown eatery. Pack in multiple flavors by ordering a combination or sampler plate. **Known for:** daily specials; 31 beers on tap; veggie and vegan options. Ⓢ *Average main: $12* ✉ *227 N. Court St.* ☎ *559/627–2337* ⊕ *pitakabob.com* ◷ *Closed Mon.*

★ The Vintage Press

$$$ | EUROPEAN | Established in 1966, this is one of the best restaurants in the Central Valley. The California–continental cuisine includes dishes such as crispy veal sweetbreads with a port-wine sauce and filet mignon with a cognac-mustard sauce. **Known for:** wine list with more than 900 selections; chocolate Grand Marnier cake and other house-made desserts; sophisticated vibe. $ Average main: $32 ⊠ 216 N. Willis St. ☎ 559/733–3033 ⊕ www.thevintagepress.com.

 Hotels

★ The Darling Hotel

$$ | HOTEL | Developers meticulously restored a dilapidated, three-story, 1930s building to create this hotel, where rooms have a modern take on art-deco style, with plush furnishings, 12-foot ceilings, and spacious bathrooms with period accents. **Pros:** in the heart of downtown; outdoor pool; rooftop lounge and restaurant with panoramic mountain and city views. **Cons:** some rooms on the small side; fronts a busy street; vintage single-pane glass windows don't block urban noise. $ Rooms from: $179 ⊠ 210 N. Court St. ☎ 559/713–2113 ⊕ thedarlingvisalia.com ⇨ 32 rooms ⊚ No meals.

Lamp Liter Inn

$ | HOTEL | FAMILY | A classic, 1960s, roadside motel, Lamp Liter Inn has basic but comfy rooms in several two-story buildings that surround tree-studded gardens and a spacious outdoor pool and terrace. **Pros:** family-owned and operated, personal service; on-site restaurant with full bar; convenient lodging for Sequoia National Park visitors. **Cons:** rooms could use updating; not near downtown; outdoor noise travels through thin walls in some rooms. $ Rooms from: $96 ⊠ 3300 W. Mineral King Ave. ☎ 559/732–4511, 800/662–6692 ⊕ www.lampliter.net ⇨ 100 rooms ⊚ No meals.

Fresno

44 miles north of Visalia.

Fresno, with half a million people, is the center of the richest agricultural county in the United States. Cotton, grapes, and tomatoes are among the major crops; poultry and milk are also important. About 75 ethnic groups, including Armenians, Laotians, and Indians, live here. The city has a relatively vibrant arts scene, several public parks, and many low-price restaurants. The **Tower District**—with its restaurants, coffeehouses, and performance venues—is the town's arts and nightlife nexus. It's the closest large city to Sequoia National Park, though at some 78 miles away it's not that close, so it's an option if there's nothing available in the park itself, Three Rivers, or Visalia.

GETTING HERE AND AROUND

Highway 99 is the biggest road through Fresno. Highways 41 and 180 also bisect the city. Amtrak trains stop here daily (and often).

VISITOR INFORMATION Fresno / Clovis Convention & Visitors Bureau. ⊠ 1180 E. Shaw Ave. ☎ 559/981–5500, 800/788–0836 ⊕ playfresno.org.

 Sights

★ Forestiere Underground Gardens

GARDEN | FAMILY | Sicilian immigrant Baldassare Forestiere spent four decades (1906–46) carving out an odd, subterranean realm of rooms, tunnels, grottoes, alcoves, and arched passageways that once extended for more than 10 acres between Highway 99 and busy, mall-pocked Shaw Avenue. Though not an engineer, Forestiere called on his memories of the ancient Roman structures he saw as a youth and on techniques he learned digging subways in New York and Boston. Only a fraction of his prodigious output is on view, but you can tour his underground living quarters, including bedrooms (one with a fireplace), the kitchen, living room, and bath, as well as a fishpond and auto tunnel. Skylights allow exotic full-grown fruit trees to flourish more than 20 feet belowground. ⊠ *5021 W. Shaw Ave., 2 blocks east of Hwy. 99* ☎ *559/271–0734* ⊕ *www.undergroundgardens.com* ✆ *$19* ⊙ *Closed Dec.–Mar.*

Fresno Art Museum

MUSEUM | The museum's key permanent collections include pre-Columbian Mesoamerican art, Andean pre-Columbian textiles and artifacts, Japanese prints, Berkeley School abstract expressionist paintings, and contemporary sculpture. Temporary exhibits include important traveling shows. ⊠ *Radio Park, 2233 N. 1st St., at E. Yale Ave.* ☎ *559/441–4221* ⊕ *www.fresnoartmuseum.org* ✆ *$10* ⊙ *Closed Mon.–Wed.*

 Restaurants

School House Restaurant & Tavern

$$$ | MODERN AMERICAN | A Wine Country–style establishment that sources ingredients from the on-site gardens and surrounding farms and orchards, this popular restaurant occupies a redbrick 1921 schoolhouse in the town of Sanger. Chef Ryan Jackson, who grew up on local fruit farms, creates seasonal menus from the bounty of familiar backyards, mostly filled with classic American dishes with a contemporary twist. **Known for:** fresh ingredients from neighboring farms and orchards; historic country setting; convenient stop between Kings Canyon and Fresno. $ *Average main: $29* ⊠ *1018 S. Frankwood Ave., at Hwy. 180 (King's Canyon Rd.), 20 miles east of Fresno, Sanger* ☎ *559/787–3271* ⊕ *schoolhousesanger.com* ⊙ *Closed Mon. and Tues.*

 Hotels

Best Western Plus Fresno Inn

$ | HOTEL | With a location near Highway 41 (the main route to Yosemite), Fresno State, and a big mall, this well-run hotel is popular with families, businesspeople, and parents with offspring at the university. **Pros:** convenient location; attentive staff; 24-hour business center. **Cons:** mildly sterile feel; on a busy street; small pool. $ *Rooms from: $130* ⊠ *480 E. Shaw Ave.* ☎ *559/229–5811* ⊕ *bestwestern.com* ✆ *55 rooms* ¶⊙¶ *Free breakfast.*

Hotel Piccadilly

$ | HOTEL | This two-story property has 7½ attractively landscaped acres and a big swimming pool. **Pros:** big rooms; nice pool; on-site restaurant/pub. **Cons:** some rooms show mild wear; neighborhood is somewhat sketchy; no elevator. $ *Rooms from: $119* ⊠ *2305 W. Shaw Ave.* ☎ *559/348–5520* ⊕ *hotel-piccadilly.com* ✆ *187 rooms* ¶⊙¶ *Free breakfast.*

 Activities

WHITE-WATER RAFTING
Kings River Expeditions

TOUR—SPORTS | This outfit arranges one- and two-day white-water rafting trips on the Kings River. The office is in Clovis, but all trips depart from Twin Pines Camp, 60 miles east of Fresno. ⊠ *Twin Pines Camp, Clovis* ☎ *559/233–4881, 800/846–3674* ⊕ *www.kingsriver.com* ✆ *From $145.*

Chapter 6

YOSEMITE NATIONAL PARK

Updated by
Cheryl Crabtree

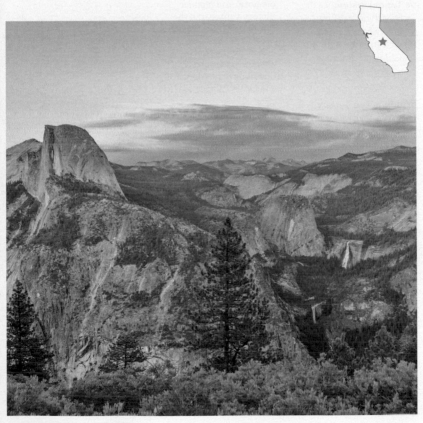

🏕 Camping	🛏 Hotels	🏃 Activities	👁 Scenery	👥 Crowds
★★★★★	★★★★☆	★★★★★	★★★★★	★★★★☆

WELCOME TO YOSEMITE NATIONAL PARK

TOP REASONS TO GO

★ **Scenic falls:** An easy stroll brings you to the base of Lower Yosemite Fall, where roaring springtime waters make for misty lens caps and lasting memories.

★ **Tunnel vision:** Approaching Yosemite Valley, Wawona Road passes through a mountainside and emerges before one of the park's most heart-stopping vistas.

★ **Inhale the beauty:** Pause to take in the light, pristine air as you travel about the High Sierra's Tioga Pass and Tuolumne Meadows, where 10,000-foot granite peaks just might take your breath away.

★ **Walk away:** Leave the crowds behind—but do bring along a buddy—and take a hike somewhere along Yosemite's 800 miles of trails.

★ **Winter wonder:** Observe the snowflakes and stillness of winter in the park.

1 Yosemite Valley. At an elevation of 4,000 feet, in roughly the center of the park, beats Yosemite's heart. This is where you'll find the park's most famous sights and biggest crowds.

2 Wawona. The park's southern tip holds Wawona, with its grand old hotel and pioneer history center, and the Mariposa Grove of Giant Sequoias. These are closest to the south entrance, 35 miles (a one-hour drive) south of Yosemite Village.

3 Tuolumne Meadows. The highlight of east-central Yosemite is this wildflower-strewn valley that's laced with hiking trails and nestled among sharp, rocky peaks. It's a 1½-hour drive northeast of Yosemite Valley along Tioga Road (closed mid-October–late May).

4 Hetch Hetchy. The most remote, least visited part of Yosemite accessible by automobile, this glacial valley is dominated by a reservoir and veined with wilderness trails. It's near the park's western boundary, about a half-hour drive north of the Big Oak Flat entrance.

By merely standing in Yosemite Valley and turning in a circle, you can see more natural wonders in a minute than you could in a full day pretty much anywhere else. Half Dome, Yosemite Falls, El Capitan, Bridalveil Fall, Sentinel Dome, the Merced River, white-flowering dogwood trees, maybe even bears ripping into the bark of fallen trees or sticking their snouts into beehives—it's all here.

Native American nations—including the Miwok, Paiute, Mono, and Ahwahneechee tribes—roamed this wonderland long before other cultures. Indeed, some of the footpaths used by Native Americans to cross mountains and valleys are still used as park hiking trails today.

In the mid-1800s, the valley's special geologic qualities and the giant sequoias of Mariposa Grove 30 miles to the south began attracting visitors. The two areas so impressed a group of influential Californians that they lobbied President Abraham Lincoln to grant them to the state for protection, which he did on June 30, 1864. Further lobbying efforts by naturalist John Muir and Robert Underwood Johnson, editor of *The Century Magazine*, led Congress to set aside an additional 1,500 square miles for Yosemite National Park on October 1, 1890. The valley and Mariposa Grove, which had remained under state control, also became part of the park in 1906.

Yosemite is so large and diverse, it almost seems to be multiple parks. Many visitors spend their time along the southwestern border, between Wawona, which is open all year and is where the giant sequoias stand, and the Big Oak Flat entrance. Also very popular are Yosemite Valley, famous for its waterfalls and cliffs and also open year-round, and the Badger Pass Ski Area, a winter-only destination. The seasonal, east–west Tioga Road spans the park north of the valley and bisects Tuolumne Meadows, the subalpine high country that's open for summer hiking and camping; in winter, it's accessible only via cross-country skis or snowshoes. The northwestern Hetch Hetchy district, home of less-used backcountry trails, is most accessible from late spring through early fall.

Photographers, hikers, and nature enthusiasts visit again and again, lured by the seasonally changing landscapes. In spring, waterfalls are robust thanks to abundant snowmelt. In early summer, wildflowers blanket alpine meadows. In fall, the trees showcase glorious explosions of color. In winter, snows provide a magical setting for activities like ice skating in the valley or cross-country skiing to Glacier Point.

AVERAGE HIGH/LOW TEMPERATURES

JAN.	FEB.	MAR.	APR.	MAY	JUNE
48/29	53/30	55/32	61/36	69/43	78/49
JULY	**AUG.**	**SEPT.**	**OCT.**	**NOV.**	**DEC.**
85/55	84/55	79/49	70/42	56/34	47/29

Planning

When to Go

During extremely busy periods—such as weekends and holidays throughout the year—you will experience delays at the entrance gates. For smaller crowds, visit midweek. Or come January through March, when the park is a bit less busy, and the days usually are sunny and clear.

Summer rainfall is rare. In winter, heavy snows occasionally cause road closures, and tire chains or four-wheel drive may be required on the routes that remain open. The road to Glacier Point beyond the turnoff for the Badger Pass Ski Area is closed after the first major snowfall. Tioga Road is closed from late October through May or mid-June. Mariposa Grove Road is typically closed for a shorter period in winter.

Getting Here and Around

AIR

The closest airport to the south and west entrances is Fresno Yosemite International Airport (FAT). Mammoth Yosemite Airport (MMH) is closest to the east entrance. Sacramento International Airport (SMF) is also close to the north and west entrances.

BUS AND TRAIN

Amtrak's daily *San Joaquins* train stops in Merced and connects with YARTS buses that travel to Yosemite Valley along Highway 140 from there. Seasonal YARTS buses (typically mid-May to late September) also travel along Highway 41 from Fresno, Highway 120 from Sonora, and Highway 395 and Tioga Road from Mammoth Lakes with scheduled stops at towns along the way. Once you're in Yosemite Valley, you can take advantage of the free shuttle buses, which operate on low emissions, have 21 stops, and run from 7 am to 10 pm year-round. Buses run about every 10 minutes in summer, a bit less frequently in winter. A separate (but also free) summer-only shuttle runs out to El Capitan. Also in summer, you can pay to take the "hikers' bus" from Yosemite Valley to Tuolumne or to ride a tour bus up to Glacier Point. During the snow season, buses run regularly between Yosemite Valley and Badger Pass Ski Area.

CAR

Roughly 200 miles from San Francisco, 300 miles from Los Angeles, and 500 miles from Las Vegas, Yosemite takes a while to reach—and its many sites and attractions merit much more time than what rangers say is the average visit: four hours.

Of the park's four entrances, Arch Rock is the closest to Yosemite Valley. The road that goes through it, Route 140 from Merced and Mariposa, is a scenic western approach that snakes alongside the boulder-packed Merced River. Route 41, through Wawona, is the way to come from Los Angeles (or Fresno, if you've flown in and rented a car). Route 120, through Crane Flat, is the most direct route from San Francisco. The only way in from the east is Tioga Road, which may be the best route in terms of scenery— though due to snow accumulation it's open for a frustratingly short amount of time each year (typically early June through mid-October). Once you enter Yosemite Valley, park your car in one of the two main day-parking areas, at Yosemite Village and Yosemite Falls, then visit the sights via the free shuttle bus system. Or walk or bike along the valley's 12 miles of paved paths.

There are few gas stations within Yosemite (Crane Flat and Wawona, none in the valley), so fuel up before you reach the park. From late fall until early spring, the weather is especially unpredictable, and driving can be treacherous. You should carry chains during this period as they are required when roads are icy and when it snows.

Park Essentials

ACCESSIBILITY

Yosemite's facilities are continually being upgraded to make them more accessible. Many of the valley floor trails—particularly at Lower Yosemite Fall, Bridalveil Fall, and Mirror Lake—are wheelchair accessible, though some assistance may be required. The Valley Visitor Center is fully accessible, as are the park shuttle buses. A sign-language interpreter is available for ranger programs. Visitors with respiratory difficulties should take note of the park's high elevations—the valley floor is approximately 4,000 feet above sea level, but Tuolumne Meadows and parts of the high country hover around 10,000 feet.

PARK FEES AND PERMITS

The admission fee, valid for seven days, is $35 per vehicle, $30 per motorcycle, or $20 per individual.

If you plan to camp in the backcountry or climb Half Dome, you must have a wilderness permit. Availability of permits depends upon trailhead quotas. It's best to make a reservation, especially if you will be visiting May through September. You can reserve two days to 24 weeks in advance by phone, mail, or fax (preferred method) (✉ Box 545, Yosemite, CA ☎ 209/372–0826); you'll pay $5 per person plus $5 per reservation if and when your reservations are confirmed. You can apply online via the park website (⊕ www.nps.gov/yose/planyourvisit/backpacking.htm). Without a reservation, you may still get a free permit on a first-come, first-served basis at wilderness permit offices at Big Oak Flat, Hetch Hetchy, Tuolumne Meadows, Wawona, the Wilderness Center in Yosemite Village, and Yosemite Valley in summer. From fall to spring, visit the Valley Visitor Center.

PARK HOURS

The park is open 24/7 year-round. All entrances are open at all hours, except for the Hetch Hetchy entrance, which is open roughly dawn to dusk. Yosemite is in the Pacific Time Zone.

CELL PHONE RECEPTION

Cell phone reception can be hit or miss everywhere in the park. There are public telephones at entrance stations, visitor centers, all park restaurants and lodging facilities, gas stations, and in Yosemite Village.

Hotels

Indoor lodging options inside the park appear more expensive than initially seems warranted, but that premium pays off big-time in terms of the time you'll save—unless you are bunking within a few miles of a Yosemite entrance, you will face long commutes to the park when you stay outside its borders (though the Yosemite View Lodge, on Route 140, is within a reasonable half-hour's drive of Yosemite Valley).

Because of the park's immense popularity—not just with tourists from around the world but with Northern Californians who make weekend trips here—reservations are all but mandatory. Book up to one year ahead. ■TIP→ If you're not set on a specific hotel or camp but just want to stay somewhere inside the park, call the main reservation number to check for availability and reserve (888/413–8869 or 602/278–8888 international). Park lodgings have a seven-day cancellation policy, so you may be able to snag last-minute reservations.

Restaurants

Yosemite National Park has a couple of moderately priced restaurants in lovely (which almost goes without saying) settings: the Mountain Room at Yosemite Valley Lodge and the dining room at the Wawona Hotel. The Ahwahnee hotel provides one of the finest dining experiences in the country.

Otherwise, food service is geared toward satisfying the masses as efficiently as possible. Yosemite Valley Lodge's Base Camp Eatery is the valley's best lower-cost, hot-food option, with Italian, classic American, and world-cuisine counter options. In Curry Village, the offerings at Seven Tents are overpriced and usually fairly bland, but you can get decent pizzas on the adjacent outdoor deck. In Yosemite Valley Village, the Village Grill whips up burgers and fries, Degnan's Kitchen has made-to-order sandwiches, and The Loft at Degnan's has an open, chaletlike dining area in which to enjoy barbecue meals and appetizers.

The White Wolf Lodge and Tuolumne Meadows Lodge—both off Tioga Road and therefore guaranteed open only from early June through September—have small restaurants where meals are competently prepared. Tuolumne Meadows also has a grill, and the gift shop at Glacier Point sells premade sandwiches, snacks, and hot dogs. During ski season, you'll also find one at the Badger Pass Ski Area, off Glacier Point Road.

Hotel and restaurant reviews have been shortened. For full information, visit

Fodors.com. Hotel prices are the lowest cost of a standard double room in high season. Restaurant prices are the average cost of a main course at dinner, or if dinner is not served, at lunch.

What It Costs			
$	$$	$$$	$$$$
RESTAURANTS			
under $17	$17–$26	$27–$36	over $36
HOTELS			
under $150	$150–$250	$251–$350	over $350

Tours

★ Ansel Adams Camera Walks

SPECIAL-INTEREST | Photography enthusiasts shouldn't miss these guided, 90-minute walks offered four mornings (Monday, Tuesday, Thursday, and Saturday) each week by professional photographers. All are free, but participation is limited to 15 people so reservations are essential. Meeting points vary. ☒ Yosemite National Park ☎ 209/372–4413 ⊕ www.anseladams.com ☒ Free.

Discover Yosemite

GUIDED TOURS | This outfit operates daily tours to Yosemite Valley, Mariposa Grove, and Glacier Point in 14- and 29-passenger vehicles. The tour travels along Highway 41 with stops in Bass Lake, Oakhurst, and Fish Camp; rates include lunch. Sunset tours to Sentinel Dome are additional summer options. ☎ 559/642–4400 ⊕ discoveryosemite.com ☒ From $158.

Glacier Point Tour

GUIDED TOURS | This four-hour trip takes you from Yosemite Valley to the Glacier Point vista, 3,214 feet above the valley floor. Some people buy a $29 one-way ticket and hike down. Shuttles depart from the Yosemite Valley Lodge three times a day. ☒ Yosemite National Park ☎ 888/413–8869 ⊕ www.travelyosemite.

com ✉ *From $57* ⊘ *Closed Nov.–late May* ⚠ *Reservations essential.*

Grand Tour

GUIDED TOURS | For a full-day tour of Yosemite Valley, the Mariposa Grove of Giant Sequoias, and Glacier Point, try the Grand Tour, which departs from the Yosemite Valley Lodge in the valley. The tour stops for a picnic lunch (included) at the historic Wawona Hotel. ✉ *Yosemite National Park* ☎ *209/372–1240* ⊕ *www. travelyosemite.com* ✉ *$110* ⚠ *Reservations essential.*

Moonlight Tour

GUIDED TOURS | This after-dark version of the Valley Floor Tour takes place on moonlit nights from June through September, depending on weather conditions. ✉ *Yosemite National Park* ☎ *209/372–4386* ⊕ *www.travelyosemite. com* ✉ *$38.*

Tuolumne Meadows Hikers Bus

BUS TOURS | For a full day's outing to the high country, opt for this ride up Tioga Road to Tuolumne Meadows. You'll stop at several overlooks, and you can connect with another shuttle at Tuolumne Lodge. This service is mostly for hikers and backpackers who want to reach high-country trailheads, but everyone is welcome. ✉ *Yosemite National Park* ☎ *209/372–1240* ⊕ *www.travelyosemite. com* ✉ *$15 one-way, $23 round-trip* ⊘ *Closed Labor Day–mid-June* ⚠ *Reservations essential.*

Valley Floor Tour

GUIDED TOURS | Take a two-hour tour of Yosemite Valley's highlights, complete with narration on the area's history, geology, and flora and fauna. Tours (offered year round) are either in trams or enclosed motor coaches, depending on weather conditions. ✉ *Yosemite National Park* ☎ *209/372–1240, 888/413–8869 reservations* ⊕ *www.travelyosemite.com* ✉ *From $38.*

Visitor Information

PARK CONTACT INFORMATION Yosemite National Park. ☎ *209/372–0200* ⊕ *www. nps.gov/yose.*

Yosemite Valley

Yosemite Valley Visitor Center is 11.5 miles from the Arch Rock entrance and 15 miles east of El Portal.

The glacier-carved Yosemite Valley stretches nearly 8 miles along the Merced River. It holds many of the park's major sights, including El Capitan, Half Dome, Glacier Point, and famous waterfalls. The valley is accessible year-round. Park your car at Yosemite Village (home of the visitor center, museum, market, and other services), Curry Village, or near Yosemite Falls. Free shuttle buses loop through the eastern and western sections of the valley.

◉ Sights

HISTORIC SITES
The Ahwahnee

HOTEL—SIGHT | Gilbert Stanley Underwood, architect of the Grand Canyon Lodge, also designed The Ahwahnee hotel. Opened in 1927, it is generally considered his best work. You can stay here (for about $500 a night), or simply explore the first-floor shops and perhaps have breakfast or lunch in the bustling and beautiful Dining Room or more casual bar. The Great Lounge, 77 feet long with magnificent 24-foot-high ceilings and all manner of artwork on display, beckons with big, comfortable chairs and relative calm. ✉ *Yosemite Valley, Ahwahnee Rd., Yosemite Village* ⊹ *About ¾ mile east of Yosemite Valley Visitor Center* ☎ *209/372–1489* ⊕ *www.travelyosemite. com/lodging/the-ahwahnee.*

Yosemite's Valley Floor

KEY

- Ranger Station
- Campground
- Picnic Area
- Restaurant
- Lodge
- Trailhead
- Restrooms
- Scenic Viewpoint
- Walking/Hiking Trails
- John Muir Trail
- Bicycle Path
- Valley Floor

Half Dome

Liberty Cap

Mist Trail

Nevada Fall

Emerald Pools

Footbridge

John Muir Trail

Vernal Fall

Mist Trail

Clark Point

Panorama Cliff

Mirror Lake

Washington Column

Grizzly Peak

Sierra Point

John Muir Trail

Illilouette Gorge

Road open only to bicycles and shuttlebuses

Happy Isles Bridge

1/2 mi

1/2 km

Royal Arch Cascade

Royal Arches

bicycle path

Upper Pines

North Pines

Clarks Bridge

Happy Isles Art & Nature Center

Lower Pines

Curry Village

Road open only to bicycles and shuttlebuses

Panorama Trail

The Ahwahnee

Curry Village Store

Glacier Point

Wilderness Office

Housekeeping Camp

Staircase Falls

Yosemite Conservation Heritage Center

Glacier Point Road

Pohono Trail

YOSEMITE VILLAGE
Indian Village of Ahwahnee

P.O.

bicycle path

Road open only to bicycles and shuttlebuses

Moran Point

Four Mile Trail

Sentinel Dome

Yosemite Falls

Valley Visitor Center

Yosemite Museum

Chapel

Union Point

Yosemite Valley Lodge

Merced River

bicycle path

Yosemite Valley

Four Mile Trail

Sentinel Rock

Sentinel Fall

Curry Village

HOTEL—SIGHT | A couple of schoolteachers from Indiana founded Camp Curry in 1899 as a low-cost option for staying in the valley, which it remains today. Curry Village's 400-plus lodging options, many of them tent cabins, are spread over a large chunk of the valley's southeastern side. This is one family-friendly place, but it's more functional than attractive. ⊠ *Southside Dr.* ✣ *About ½ mile east of Yosemite Village.*

Indian Village of Ahwahnee

MUSEUM VILLAGE | This solemn smattering of structures, accessed by a short loop trail behind the Yosemite Valley Visitor Center, offers a look at what Native American life might have been like in the 1870s. One interpretive sign points out that the Miwok people referred to the 19th-century newcomers as "Yohemite" or "Yohometuk," which have been translated as meaning "some of them are killers." ⊠ *Northside Dr., Yosemite Village* ⌑ *Free.*

Yosemite Museum

MUSEUM | This small museum consists of a permanent exhibit that focuses on the history of the area and the people who once lived here. An adjacent gallery promotes contemporary and historic Yosemite art in revolving gallery exhibits. A docent demonstrates traditional Native American basket-weaving techniques a few days a week. ⊠ *Yosemite Village* ☎ *209/372–0299* ⌑ *Free.*

SCENIC STOPS

Bridalveil Fall

BODY OF WATER | This 620-foot waterfall is often diverted dozens of feet one way or the other by the breeze. It is the first marvelous site you will see up close when you drive into Yosemite Valley. ⊠ *Yosemite Valley, access from parking area off Wawona Rd.*

El Capitan

NATURE SITE | Rising 3,593 feet—more than 350 stories—above the valley, El Capitan is the largest exposed-granite monolith in the world. Since 1958, people have been climbing its entire face, including the famous "nose." You can spot adventurers with your binoculars by scanning the smooth and nearly vertical cliff for specks of color. ⊠ *Yosemite National Park* ✣ *Off Northside Dr., about 4 miles west of Valley Visitor Center.*

★ Glacier Point

VIEWPOINT | If you lack the time, desire, or stamina to hike more than 3,200 feet up to Glacier Point from the Yosemite Valley floor, you can drive here—or take a bus from the valley—for a bird's-eye view. You are likely to encounter a lot of day-trippers on the short, paved trail that leads from the parking lot to the main overlook. Take a moment to veer off a few yards to the Geology Hut, which succinctly explains and illustrates what the valley looked like 10 million, 3 million, and 20,000 years ago. ⊠ *Yosemite National Park* ✣ *Glacier Point Rd., 16 miles northeast of Rte. 41* ☎ *209/372–0200* ⊘ *Closed late Oct.–mid-May.*

★ Half Dome

NATURE SITE | Visitors' eyes are continually drawn to this remarkable granite formation that tops out at more than 4,700 feet above the valley floor. Despite its name, the dome is actually about three-quarters intact. You can hike to the top of it on an 8½-mile (one-way) trail whose last 400 feet must be ascended while holding onto a steel cable. Permits, available only by lottery, are required and are checked on the trail. Call ☎ *877/444–6777* or visit ⊕ *www.recreation.gov* well in advance of your trip for details. Back down in the valley, see Half Dome reflected in the Merced River by heading to Sentinel Bridge just before sundown. The brilliant orange light on Half Dome is a stunning sight.

✉ *Yosemite National Park* ⊕ *www.nps. gov/yose/planyourvisit/halfdome.htm.*

Nevada Fall

BODY OF WATER | Climb Mist Trail from Happy Isles for an up-close view of this 594-foot cascading beauty. If you don't want to hike (the trail's final approach is quite taxing), you can see it—albeit distantly—from Glacier Point. Stay safely on the trail, as there have been fatalities in recent years after visitors have fallen and been swept away by the water. ✉ *Yosemite Valley, access via Mist Trail from Nature Center at Happy Isles.*

Ribbon Fall

BODY OF WATER | At 1,612 feet, this is the highest single fall in North America. It's also the first waterfall to dry up in summer; the rainwater and melted snow that create the slender fall evaporate quickly at this height. Look just west of El Capitan for the best view of the fall from the base of Bridalveil Fall. ✉ *Yosemite Valley, west of El Capitan Meadow.*

Sentinel Dome

VIEWPOINT | The view from here is similar to that from Glacier Point, except you can't see the valley floor. A moderately steep, 1.1-mile path climbs to the viewpoint from the parking lot. Topping out at an elevation of 8,122 feet, Sentinel is more than 900 feet higher than Glacier Point. ✉ *Glacier Point Rd., off Rte. 41.*

Vernal Fall

BODY OF WATER | Fern-covered black rocks frame this 317-foot fall, and rainbows play in the spray at its base. You can get a distant view from Glacier Point, or hike to see it close up. You'll get wet, but the view is worth it. ✉ *Yosemite Valley, access via Mist Trail from Nature Center at Happy Isles.*

★ Yosemite Falls

BODY OF WATER | Actually three falls, they together constitute the highest combined waterfall in North America and the fifth highest in the world. The water from the top descends a total of 2,425 feet, and

when the falls run hard, you can hear them thunder across the valley. If they dry up—that sometimes happens in late summer—the valley seems naked without the wavering tower of spray. If you hike the mile-long loop trail (partially paved) to the base of the Lower Fall in spring, prepare to get wet. You can get a good full-length view of the falls from the lawn of Yosemite Chapel, off Southside Drive. ✉ *Yosemite Valley, access from Yosemite Valley Lodge or trail parking area.*

TRAILS

Cook's Meadow Loop

TRAIL | **FAMILY** | Take this 1-mile, wheelchair-accessible, looped path around Cook's Meadow to see and learn the basics about Yosemite Valley's past, present, and future. A trail guide (available at a kiosk just outside the entrance) explains how to tell oaks, cedars, and pines apart; how fires help keep the forest floor healthy; and how pollution poses significant challenges to the park's inhabitants. *Easy.* ✉ *Yosemite National Park* ✛ *Trailhead: Across from Valley Visitor Center.*

Four-Mile Trail

TRAIL | If you decide to hike up Four-Mile Trail and back down again, allow about six hours for the challenging, 9½-mile round-trip. (The original 4-mile-long trail, Yosemite's first, has been lengthened to make it less steep.) The trailhead is on Southside Drive near Sentinel Beach, and the elevation change is 3,220 feet. For a considerably less strenuous experience, you can take a morning tour bus up to Glacier Point and enjoy a one-way downhill hike. *Difficult.* ✉ *Yosemite National Park* ✛ *Trailheads: At Glacier Point and on Southside Dr.*

★ John Muir Trail to Half Dome

TRAIL | Ardent and courageous trekkers continue on from Nevada Fall to the top of Half Dome. Some hikers attempt this entire 10- to 12-hour, 16¾-mile round-trip trek in one day; if you're planning to do this, remember that the 4,800-foot elevation gain and the 8,842-foot altitude will cause shortness of breath. Another option is to hike to a campground in Little Yosemite Valley near the top of Nevada Fall the first day, then climb to the top of Half Dome and hike out the next day. Get your wilderness permit (required for a one-day hike to Half Dome, too) at least a month in advance. Be sure to wear hiking boots and bring gloves. The last pitch up the back of Half Dome is very steep—the only way to climb this sheer rock face is to pull yourself up using the steel cable handrails, which are in place only from late spring to early fall. Those who brave the ascent will be rewarded with an unbeatable view of Yosemite Valley below and the high country beyond. Only 300 hikers per day are allowed atop Half Dome, and they all must have permits, which are distributed by lottery, one in the spring before the season starts and another two days before the climb. Contact ⊕ www.recreation.gov for details. *Difficult.* ⊠ *Yosemite National Park* ⊹ *Trailhead: At Happy Isles* ⊕ *www.nps. gov/yose/planyourvisit/halfdome.htm.*

Mirror Lake Trail

TRAIL | FAMILY | Along this trail, you'll look up at Half Dome directly from its base and also take in Tenaya Canyon, Mt. Watkins, and Washington Column. The way is paved for a mile to Mirror Lake itself (total of 2 miles out and back). The trail that loops around the lake continues from there (for a total of 5 miles). Interpretive exhibits provide insight on the area's natural and cultural history. *Easy–Moderate.* ⊠ *Yosemite Village* ⊹ *Trailhead: Shuttle bus stop #17 on the Happy Isles Loop.*

Mist Trail

TRAIL | Except for Lower Yosemite Fall, more visitors take this trail (or portions of it) than any other in the park. The trek up to and back from Vernal Fall is 3 miles. Add another 4 miles total by continuing up to 594-foot Nevada Fall; the trail becomes quite steep and slippery in its

final stages. The elevation gain to Vernal Fall is 1,000 feet, and to Nevada Fall an additional 1,000 feet. The Merced River tumbles down both falls on its way to a tranquil flow through the valley. *Moderate.* ⊠ *Yosemite National Park* ⊹ *Trailhead: At Happy Isles.*

★ Panorama Trail

TRAIL | Few hikes come with the visual punch that this 8½-mile trail provides. It starts from Glacier Point and descends to Yosemite Valley. The star attraction is Half Dome, visible from many intriguing angles, but you also see three waterfalls up close and walk through a manzanita grove. *Moderate.* ⊠ *Yosemite National Park* ⊹ *Trailhead: At Glacier Point.*

★ Yosemite Falls Trail

TRAIL | Yosemite Falls is the highest waterfall in North America. The upper fall (1,430 feet), the middle cascades (675 feet), and the lower fall (320 feet) combine for a total of 2,425 feet, and when viewed from the valley appear as a single waterfall. The ¼-mile trail leads from the parking lot to the base of the falls. Upper Yosemite Fall Trail, a strenuous 7.2-mile round-trip climb rising 2,700 feet, takes you above the top of the falls. Lower trail: *Easy.* Upper trail: *Difficult.* ⊠ *Yosemite National Park* ⊹ *Trailhead: Off Camp 4, north of Northside Dr.*

VISITOR CENTERS

Valley Visitor Center

INFO CENTER | Learn about Yosemite Valley's geology, vegetation, and human inhabitants at this visitor center, which is also staffed with helpful rangers and contains a bookstore with a wide selection of books and maps. Two films, including one by Ken Burns, alternate on the half hour in the theater behind the visitor center. ⊠ *Yosemite Village* ☎ *209/372–0200* ⊕ *www.nps.gov/yose.*

Yosemite Conservation Heritage Center

INFO CENTER | This small but striking National Historic Landmark (formerly Le Conte Memorial Lodge), with its granite walls and steeply pitched shingle roof, is Yosemite's first permanent public information center. Step inside to see the cathedral-like interior, which contains a library and environmental exhibits. To find out about evening programs, check the kiosk out front. ⊠ *Southside Dr., about ½ mile west of Half Dome Village* ⊕ *sierraclub.org/yosemite-heritage-center* ⊗ *Closed Mon., Tues., and Oct.–Apr.*

 ## Restaurants

★ The Ahwahnee Dining Room
$$$$ | EUROPEAN | Rave reviews about The Ahwahnee hotel's dining room's appearance are fully justified—it features towering windows, a 34-foot-high ceiling with interlaced sugar-pine beams, and massive chandeliers. Reservations are always advised, and the attire is "resort casual." **Known for:** lavish $56 Sunday brunch; finest dining in the park; bar menu with lighter lunch and dinner fare at more affordable prices. ⑤ *Average main: $39* ⊠ *The Ahwahnee, Ahwahnee Rd., about ¾ mile east of Yosemite Valley Visitor Center, Yosemite Village* ☎ *209/372–1489* ⊕ *www.travelyosemite.com.*

Base Camp Eatery
$ | AMERICAN | The design of this modern food court, open for breakfast, lunch, and dinner, honors the history of rock climbing in Yosemite. Choose from a wide range of menu options, from hamburgers, salads, and pizzas, to rice and noodle bowls. **Known for:** grab-and-go selections; best casual dining venue in the park; automated ordering kiosks to speed up service. ⑤ *Average main: $12* ⊠ *Yosemite Valley Lodge, about ¾ mile west of visitor center, Yosemite Village* ☎ *209/372–1265* ⊕ *www.travelyosemite.com.*

Curry Village Seven Tents
$$ | AMERICAN | Formerly Curry Village Pavilion, this cafeteria-style eatery serves everything from roasted meats and salads to pastas, burritos, and beyond. Alternatively, order a pizza from the stand on the deck, and take in the views of the valley's granite walls. **Known for:** convenient eats; cocktails at Bar 1899; additional venues (Meadow Grill, Pizza Patio, Coffee Corner). ⑤ *Average main: $18* ⊠ *Curry Village* ☎ *209/372–8303* ⊗ *Closed mid-Oct.–mid-Apr. No lunch.*

★ Mountain Room
$$$ | AMERICAN | Gaze at Yosemite Falls through this dining room's wall of windows—almost every table has a view—as you nosh on steaks, seafood, and classic California salads and desserts. The Mountain Room Lounge, a few steps away in the Yosemite Valley Lodge complex, has about 10 beers on tap. **Known for:** locally sourced, organic ingredients; usually there is a wait for a table (no reservations); vegetarian and vegan options. ⑤ *Average main: $29* ⊠ *Yosemite Valley Lodge, Northside Dr., about ¾ mile west of visitor center, Yosemite Village* ☎ *209/372–1403* ⊕ *www.travelyosemite. com* ⊗ *No lunch except Sun. brunch.*

Village Grill Deck
$ | FAST FOOD | If a burger joint is what you've been missing, head to this bustling eatery in Yosemite Village that serves veggie, salmon, and a few other burger varieties in addition to the usual beef patties. Order at the counter, then take your tray out to the deck, and enjoy your meal under the trees. **Known for:** burgers, sandwiches, and hot dogs; crowds; outdoor seating on expansive deck. ⑤ *Average main: $12* ⊠ *Yosemite Village* ✛ *100 yards east of Yosemite Valley Visitor Center* ☎ *209/372–1207* ⊕ *www.travelyosemite. com* ⊗ *Closed Oct.–Apr. No dinner.*

 ## Hotels

★ The Ahwahnee
$$$$ | HOTEL | This National Historic Landmark is constructed of sugar-pine logs and features Native American design motifs; public spaces are enlivened with art-deco flourishes, Persian rugs, and elaborate iron- and woodwork. **Pros:** best

lodge in Yosemite; helpful concierge; in the historic heart of the valley. **Cons:** expensive rates; some reports that service has slipped in recent years; slow or nonexistent Wi-Fi in some hotel areas. ⑤ *Rooms from: $581* ✉ *Ahwahnee Rd., about ¾ mile east of Yosemite Valley Visitor Center, Yosemite Village* ☎ *801/559–4884* ⊕ *www.travelyosemite.com* ↪ *125 rooms* ⦿ *No meals.*

Curry Village
$ | **HOTEL** | Opened in 1899 as a place for budget-conscious travelers, Curry Village has plain accommodations: standard motel rooms, simple cabins with either private or shared baths, and tent cabins with shared baths. **Pros:** close to many activities; family-friendly atmosphere; surrounded by iconic valley views. **Cons:** community bathrooms need updating; can be crowded; sometimes a bit noisy. ⑤ *Rooms from: $143* ✉ *South side of Southside Dr.* ☎ *888/413–8869, 602/278–8888 international* ⊕ *www.travelyosemite.com* ↪ *583 units* ⦿ *No meals.*

Yosemite Valley Lodge
$$$ | **HOTEL** | This 1915 lodge near Yosemite Falls is a collection of numerous two-story, glass-and-wood structures tucked beneath the trees. **Pros:** centrally located; dependably clean rooms; lots of tours leave from out front. **Cons:** can feel impersonal; high prices; no in-room a/c. ⑤ *Rooms from: $260* ✉ *9006 Yosemite Valley Lodge Dr., Yosemite Village* ☎ *888/413–8869* ⊕ *www.travelyosemite.com* ↪ *245 rooms* ⦿ *No meals.*

 Shopping

Ansel Adams Gallery
ART GALLERIES | Framed prints of the famed nature photographer's best works are on sale here, as are affordable posters. New works by contemporary artists are also available, along with Native American jewelry and handicrafts. The elegant camera shop conducts photography workshops, from free camera walks a few mornings a week to five-day courses. ✉ *Northside Dr., Yosemite Village* ☎ *209/372–4413* ⊕ *anseladams.com.*

Curry Village Gift & Grocery
CONVENIENCE/GENERAL STORES | You can pick up groceries and supplies at this bustling shop at the east end of the valley. ✉ *Curry Village* ☎ *209/372–8391.*

Housekeeping Camp General Store
CONVENIENCE/GENERAL STORES | You'll find the basics here for picnics, campfires, and other outdoor activities. ✉ *Southside Dr., ½ mile west of Half Dome Village* ☎ *209/372–8353.*

Village Store
CONVENIENCE/GENERAL STORES | The Yosemite Valley's largest store has an extensive selection of groceries (including many organic items), household products, and personal-care items. It also has an extensive gift and souvenir shop. ✉ *Yosemite Village* ☎ *209/372–1253.*

Yosemite Bookstore
BOOKS/STATIONERY | An extensive selection of maps and books is available at this store in the Valley Visitor Center. ✉ *Valley Visitor Center, Yosemite Village* ☎ *209/372–0299* ⊕ *shop.yosemite.org.*

Yosemite Museum Shop
CRAFTS | In addition to books on California's Native Americans, this tiny shop sells traditional arts and crafts. ✉ *Yosemite Village* ☎ *209/372–0295.*

Wawona

27 miles from Yosemite Valley Visitor Center, 7½ miles north of Fish Camp.

Wawona is a small village (elevation 4,000 feet) about an hours' drive south of Yosemite Valley. It's rich in pioneer history (visit the Pioneer Yosemite History Center to learn more) and is home to the Victorian-era Wawona Hotel. The park's famous Mariposa Grove of Giant Sequoias is a few miles down the road.

◉ Sights

HISTORIC SIGHTS

Pioneer Yosemite History Center

MUSEUM | FAMILY | These historic buildings reflect different eras of Yosemite's history, from the 1850s through the early 1900s. They were moved to Wawona (the largest stage stop in Yosemite in the late 1800s) from various areas of Yosemite in the '50s and '60s. There is a self-guided-tour pamphlet available for 50 cents. Weekends and some weekdays in the summer, costumed docents conduct free blacksmithing and "wet-plate" photography demonstrations, and for a small fee you can take a stagecoach ride. ☒ *Rte. 41, Wawona* ☎ *209/375–9531* ⊕ *www. nps.gov/yose/planyourvisit/waw.htm* ☎ *Free* ☉ *Closed Mon., Tues., and mid-Sept.–early June.*

Wawona Hotel

HOTEL—SIGHT | Imagine a white-bearded Mark Twain relaxing in a rocking chair on one of the broad verandas of one of the park's first lodges, a whitewashed series of two-story buildings from the Victorian era. Plop down in one of the dozens of white Adirondack chairs on the sprawling lawn, and look across the road at the area's only golf course, one of the few links in the world that does not employ fertilizers or other chemicals. ☒ *Rte. 41, Wawona* ☎ *209/375–1425* ⊕ *www. travelyosemite.com/lodging/wawona-hotel* ☉ *Closed Dec.–Mar. except 2 wks around Christmas and New Year's.*

SCENIC DRIVES

Route 41

SCENIC DRIVE | Entering Yosemite National Park via this road, which follows an ultimately curvy course 55 miles from Fresno through the Yosemite gateway towns of Oakhurst and Fish Camp, presents you with an immediate, important choice: turn right to visit the Mariposa Grove of Giant Sequoias 4 miles to the east, or turn left to travel via Wawona to Yosemite Valley, 31 miles away. Try to do both. (You can get by with an hour in Mariposa Grove if you're really pressed for time.) As you approach the valley, you will want to pull into the Tunnel View parking lot (it's on the east side of the mile-long tunnel) and marvel at what lies ahead: from left to right, El Capitan, Half Dome, and Bridalveil Fall. From here, the valley is another 5 miles. The drive time on Wawona Road alone is about an hour. Make a full day of it by adding Glacier Point to the itinerary; get there via a 16-mile seasonal road that shoots east from Route 41 and passes the Badger Pass Ski Area. ☒ *Yosemite National Park.*

SCENIC STOPS

Mariposa Grove of Giant Sequoias

FOREST | Of Yosemite's three sequoia groves—the others being Merced and Tuolumne, both near Crane Flat and Hetch Hetchy well to the north—Mariposa is by far the largest and easiest to walk around. Grizzly Giant, whose base measures 96 feet around, has been estimated to be one of the world's largest. Perhaps more astoundingly, it's about 1,800 years old. Park at the grove's welcome plaza, and ride the free shuttle (required most of the year). Summer weekends are crowded. ☒ *Yosemite National Park* ⊹ *Rte. 41, 2 miles north of south entrance station* ⊕ *www.nps.gov/ yose/planyourvisit/mg.htm.*

TRAILS

Chilnualna Falls Trail

TRAIL | This Wawona-area trail runs 4 miles one-way to the top of the falls, then leads into the backcountry, connecting with other trails. This is one of the park's most inspiring and secluded—albeit strenuous—trails. Past the tumbling cascade, and up through forests, you'll emerge before a panorama at the top. *Difficult.* ☒ *Wawona* ⊹ *Trailhead: At Chilnualna Falls Rd., off Rte. 41.*

Did You Know?

In mid- to late February, when the conditions are right in the evenings (clear sky, flowing falls), Horsetail Fall, on the eastern edge of El Capitan, experiences Firefall—it looks like the falls are on fire.

Restaurants

Wawona Hotel Dining Room

$$$ | AMERICAN | Watch deer graze in the meadow while you dine in the romantic, candlelit dining room of the whitewashed Wawona Hotel, which dates from the late 1800s. The American-style cuisine favors fresh ingredients and flavors; trout and flatiron steaks are menu staples.
Known for: Saturday-night barbecues on the lawn; historic ambience; Mother's Day and other Sunday holiday brunches. ⑤ *Average main: $28* ✉ *8308 Wawona Rd., Wawona* ☎ *209/375–1425* ⊘ *Closed most of Dec., Jan., Feb., and Mar.*

Hotels

Redwoods in Yosemite

$$$ | RENTAL | This collection of more than 125 homes in the Wawona area is a great alternative to the overcrowded valley.
Pros: sense of privacy; peaceful setting; full kitchens. **Cons:** 45-minute drive from the valley; some units have no a/c; cell phone service can be spotty. ⑤ *Rooms from: $260* ✉ *8038 Chilnualna Falls Rd., off Rte. 41, Wawona* ☎ *209/375–6666 international, 844/355–0039* ⊕ *www.redwoodsinyosemite.com* 🛏 *125 units* ⑩ *No meals.*

Wawona Hotel

$$ | HOTEL | This 1879 National Historic Landmark at Yosemite's southern end is a Victorian-era mountain resort, with whitewashed buildings, wraparound verandas, and pleasant, no-frills rooms decorated with period pieces. **Pros:** lovely building; peaceful atmosphere; historic photos in public areas. **Cons:** few modern amenities, such as phones and TVs; an hour's drive from Yosemite Valley; shared bathrooms in half the rooms. ⑤ *Rooms from: $157* ✉ *8308 Wawona Rd., Wawona* ☎ *888/413–8869* ⊕ *www.travelyosemite.com* ⊘ *Closed Dec.–Mar., except mid-Dec.–Jan. 2* 🛏 *104 rooms, 50 with bath* ⑩ *Free breakfast.*

Shopping

Wawona Store

CONVENIENCE/GENERAL STORES | The Wawona area's only market carries essentials (for some, that means ice cream) in its grocery section. There's also a gift shop. ✉ *Rte. 41 at Forest Dr., Wawona* ☎ *209/375–6574.*

Tuolumne Meadows

56 miles from Yosemite Valley, 21 miles west of Lee Vining via Tioga Rd.

The largest subalpine meadow in the Sierra (at 8,600 feet) is a popular way station for backpack trips along the Pacific Crest and John Muir trails. The setting is not as dramatic as Yosemite Valley, 56 miles away, but the almost perfectly flat basin, about 2½ miles long, is intriguing, and in July it's resplendent with wildflowers. The most popular day hike is to Lembert Dome, atop which you'll have breathtaking views of the basin below. Note that Tioga Road rarely opens before June and usually closes by November.

Sights

SCENIC DRIVES
Tioga Road

SCENIC DRIVE | Few mountain drives can compare with this 59-mile road, especially its eastern half between Lee Vining and Olmstead Point. As you climb 3,200 feet to the 9,945-foot summit of Tioga Pass (Yosemite's sole eastern entrance for cars), you'll encounter broad vistas of the granite-splotched High Sierra and its craggy but hearty trees and shrubs. Past the bustling scene at Tuolumne Meadows, you'll see picturesque Tenaya Lake and then Olmsted Point, where you'll get your first peek at Half Dome. Driving Tioga Road one way takes approximately 1½ hours. Wildflowers bloom here in July and August. By November, the high-altitude road closes for the winter; it sometimes doesn't reopen until early June. ✉ *Yosemite National Park.*

SCENIC STOPS
High Country

NATURE PRESERVE | The high-alpine region east of the valley—a land of alpenglow and top-of-the-world vistas—is often missed by crowds who come to gawk at the more publicized splendors. Summer wildflowers, which pop up mid-July through August, carpet the meadows and mountainsides with pink, purple, blue, red, yellow, and orange. On foot or on horseback are the only ways to get here. For information on trails and backcountry permits, check with the visitor center. ⌂ Yosemite National Park.

 Restaurants

Tuolumne Meadows Grill

$ | FAST FOOD | Serving throughout the day until 5 or 6 pm, this fast-food eatery cooks up basic breakfast, lunch, and snacks. It's possible that ice cream tastes better at this altitude. Known for: soft-serve ice cream; crowds; fresh local ingredients. $ Average main: $8 ⌂ Tioga Rd. (Rte. 120), 1½ miles east of Tuolumne Meadows Visitor Center ☎ 209/372–8426 ⊕ www.travelyosemite. com ☉ Closed Oct.–Memorial Day. No dinner.

Tuolumne Meadows Lodge Restaurant

$$ | AMERICAN | In a central dining tent beside the Tuolumne River, this restaurant serves a menu of hearty American fare at breakfast and dinner. The red-and-white-checkered tablecloths and a handful of communal tables give it the feeling of an old-fashioned summer camp. Known for: box lunches; communal tables; small menu. $ Average main: $24 ⌂ Tioga Rd. (Rte. 120) ☎ 209/372–8413 ⊕ www.travelyosemite.com ☉ Closed late Sept.–mid-June. No lunch.

White Wolf Lodge Restaurant

$$ | AMERICAN | Those fueling up for a day on the trail or famished after a high-country hike will appreciate the all-you-can-eat, family-style breakfasts and dinners in this tiny dining room. Mashed potatoes, big pots of curried vegetables, and heaps of pasta often grace the tables in this cozy out-of-the-way place. Known for: all you can eat; box lunches available; rustic vibe. $ Average main: $24 ⌂ Yosemite National Park ⌖ Tioga Rd. (Rte. 120), 25 miles west of Tuolumne Meadows and 15 miles east of Crane Flat ☎ 209/372–8416 ⊕ www. travelyosemite.com ☉ Closed mid-Sept.–mid-June. No lunch.

 Hotels

White Wolf Lodge

$ | HOTEL | Set in a subalpine meadow, the White Wolf Lodge has rustic accommodations and makes an excellent base camp for hiking the backcountry. Pros: quiet location; near some of Yosemite's most beautiful, less crowded hikes; good restaurant. Cons: far from the valley; tent cabins share bathhouse; remote setting. $ Rooms from: $138 ⌂ Yosemite National Park ⌖ Off Tioga Rd. (Rte. 120), 25 miles west of Tuolumne Meadows and 15 miles east of Crane Flat ☎ 801/559–4884 ☉ Closed mid-Sept.–mid-June ⌖ 28 cabins ⏚ No meals.

 Shopping

Tuolumne Meadows Store

CONVENIENCE/GENERAL STORES | The only retailer in the high country carries backpacking and camping supplies, climbing gear, trail maps and guides, food and beverages, and fishing licenses. ⌂ Yosemite National Park ⌖ Tioga Rd. Rte. 120, 1½ miles east of Tuolumne Meadows Visitor Center ☎ 209/372–8096 ☉ Closed Oct.–early June.

Hetch Hetchy

18 miles from the Big Oak Flat entrance station, 43 miles north of El Portal via Hwy. 120 and Evergreen Rd.

This glacier-carved valley (now filled with water) and surrounding peaks anchor the northwestern section of the park. Drive about 2 miles west of the Big Oak Flat entrance station and turn right on Evergreen Road, which leads down to the Hetch Hetchy entrance and trails along the dam and into the mountains. Two groves of giant sequoia trees—Merced and Tuolumne—grow near Crane Flat, a tiny collection of services south of Big Oak Flat at the intersection of Highway 120 and Tioga Road.

Sights

SCENIC STOPS
Hetch Hetchy Reservoir

BODY OF WATER | When Congress approved the O'Shaughnessy Dam in 1913, pragmatism triumphed over aestheticism. Some 2.5 million residents of the San Francisco Bay Area continue to get their water from this 117-billion-gallon reservoir. Although spirited efforts are being made to restore the Hetch Hetchy Valley to its former, pristine glory, three-quarters of San Francisco voters in 2012 ultimately opposed a measure to even consider draining the reservoir. Eight miles long, the reservoir is Yosemite's largest body of water, and one that can be seen up close from several trails. ⊠ *Hetch Hetchy Rd., about 15 miles north of Big Oak Flat entrance station.*

Tuolumne Grove of Giant Sequoias

FOREST | About two dozen mature giant sequoias stand in Tuolumne Grove in the park's northwestern region, just east of Crane Flat and south of the Big Oak Flat entrance. Park at the trailhead and walk about a mile to see them. The trail descends about 500 feet down to the grove, so it's a relatively steep hike back

up. Be sure to bring plenty of drinking water. ⊠ *On Tioga Rd., just east of Crane Flat, about a 45-minute drive from Yosemite Valley.*

TRAILS
Merced Grove of Giant Sequoias

FOREST | Hike 1½ miles (3 miles round-trip, 500-foot elevation drop and gain) to the small and scenic Merced Grove and its approximately two dozen mature giant sequoias. The setting here is typically uncrowded and serene. Note that you can also park here and hike about 2 miles round-trip to the Tuolumne Grove. Bring plenty of water for either outing. *Moderate.* ⊠ *Big Oak Flat Rd.* ⊹ *East of the Big Oak Flat entrance, about 6 miles west of Crane Flat and a 45-minute drive from Yosemite Valley.*

Hotels

Evergreen Lodge at Yosemite

$$$ | **RESORT** | **FAMILY** | Amid the trees near Yosemite National Park's Hetch Hetchy entrance, this sprawling property is perfect for families. **Pros:** cabin complex includes amphitheater, pool, and more; guided tours available; great roadhouse-style restaurant. **Cons:** no in-room TVs; long, winding access road; spotty cell service. ⑤ *Rooms from: $280* ⊠ *33160 Evergreen Rd., 30 miles east of town of Groveland, Groveland* ☎ *209/379–2606* ⊕ *www.evergreenlodge.com* ⇥ *88 cabins* ⑩ *No meals.*

★ Rush Creek Lodge

$$$$ | **RESORT** | **FAMILY** | Occupying 20 acres on a wooded hillside, this sleek, nature-inspired complex has a saltwater pool and hot tubs, a restaurant and tavern with indoor and outdoor seating, a guided recreation program, a spa and wellness program, a general store, nature trails, and outdoor play areas that include a zip line and a giant slide. **Pros:** close to Yosemite's Big Oak Flat entrance; YARTS bus stops here and connects with Yosemite Valley and Sonora

Half Dome at sunset

spring–fall; year-round evening s'mores. **Cons:** no in-room TVs; pricey in high season; spotty cell service. $ *Rooms from: $410* ✉ *34001 Hwy. 120, Groveland* ✛ *25 miles east of Groveland, 23 miles north of Yosemite Valley* ☎ *209/379–2373* ⊕ *www.rushcreeklodge.com* ⇰ *143 rooms* ⦿ *No meals.*

🛍 Shopping

Crane Flat Store

CONVENIENCE/GENERAL STORES | This small store is a convenient place to get gas and pick up snacks and camping supplies if you're arriving via Route 120. The store is closed November–March. ✉ *Yosemite National Park* ✛ *Intersection of Big Oak Flat Rd. and Tioga Rd., 7 miles east of Big Oak Flat entrance* ☎ *209/379–2742* ⊗ *Closed Dec.–Mar.*

Activities

BIKING

One enjoyable way to see Yosemite Valley is to ride a bike beneath its lofty granite monoliths. The eastern valley has 12 miles of paved, flat bicycle paths across meadows and through woods, with bike racks at convenient stopping points. For a greater challenge, you can ride on 196 miles of paved park roads elsewhere. Note, though, that bicycles are not allowed on hiking trails or in the backcountry, and kids under 18 must wear a helmet.

Yosemite bike rentals

BICYCLING | You can arrange rentals ($12 per hour or $36 per day) at Yosemite Valley Lodge and Curry Village bike stands. Bikes with child trailers, baby-jogger strollers, and wheelchairs are also available. ✉ *Yosemite Valley Lodge or Curry Village* ☎ *209/372–4386* ⊕ *www.travelyosemite.com.*

BIRD-WATCHING

More than 250 bird species have been spotted in the park, including the sage sparrow, pygmy owl, blue grouse, and mountain bluebird. Park rangers lead free bird-watching walks in Yosemite Valley a few days each week in summer; check at a visitor center or information station for times and locations. Binoculars sometimes are available for loan.

Birding seminars

BIRD WATCHING | The Yosemite Conservancy organizes day- and weekend-long seminars for beginner and intermediate birders, as well as bird walks a few times a week. They can also arrange private naturalist-led walks any time of year. ✉ *Yosemite National Park* ⊕ *www.yosemite.org* ✆ *From $99.*

CAMPING

If you are going to concentrate solely on valley sites and activities, you should endeavor to stay in one of the "Pines" campgrounds, which are clustered near Curry Village and within an easy stroll from that busy complex's many facilities. For a more primitive and quiet experience, and to be near many backcountry hikes, try one of the Tioga Road campgrounds.

RESERVATIONS

National Park Service Reservations Office

CAMPING | Reservations are required at many of Yosemite's campgrounds. You can book a site up to five months in advance, starting on the 15th of the month. Unless otherwise noted, book your site through the central National Park Service Reservations Office. If you don't have reservations when you arrive, many sites, especially those outside Yosemite Valley, are available on a first-come, first-served basis. ☎ *877/444–6777 reservations, 518/885–3639 international, 888/448–1474 customer service* ⊕ *www.recreation.gov.*

RECOMMENDED CAMPGROUNDS
YOSEMITE VALLEY

Camp 4. Formerly known as Sunnyside Walk-In, this is the only valley campground available on a walk-in basis—and the only one west of Yosemite Lodge. Open year-round, it's favored by rock climbers and solo campers. From mid-September to mid-May, the camp operates on a first-come, first-served basis; it typically fills early in the morning except in winter. From mid-May to mid-September, campsites are available only by daily lottery (one day in advance via Recreation.gov from midnight to 4 pm Pacific Time) for up to 12 people per application, 6 people per campsite. This is a tents-only campground with 36 sites. ✉ *Base of Yosemite Falls Trail, just west of Yosemite Valley Lodge on Northside Dr., Yosemite Village.*

Housekeeping Camp. Each of the 266 units here consists of three walls (usually concrete) that are covered with two layers of canvas; the open-air side can be closed off with a heavy, white-canvas curtain. Inside, typically, are bunk beds and a full-size bed (dirty mattresses included); outside is a covered patio, fire ring, picnic table, and bear box. You rent "bedpacks," consisting of blankets, sheets, and other comforts in the main building, which also has a small grocery. Lots of guests take advantage of the adjacent Merced River. ✉ *Southside Dr., ½ mile west of Curry Village.*

Lower Pines. This moderate-size campground with 60 small tent/RV sites sits directly along the Merced River; it's a short walk to the trailheads for the Mirror Lake and Mist trails. Expect lots of people. ✉ *At east end of valley.*

Upper Pines. One of the valley's largest campgrounds, with 238 tent and RV sites, is also the closest one to the trailheads. Expect large crowds in the summer—and little privacy. ✉ *At east end of valley, near Curry Village.*

CRANE FLAT

Crane Flat. This 166-site camp for tents and RVs is on Yosemite's western boundary, south of Hodgdon Meadow and just 17 miles from the valley but far from its bustle. A small grove of sequoias is nearby. ⊠ *From Big Oak Flat entrance on Rte. 120, drive 10 miles east to campground entrance on right.*

WAWONA

Bridalveil Creek. This campground sits among lodgepole pines at 7,200 feet, above the valley on Glacier Point Road. From here, you can easily drive to Glacier Point's magnificent valley views. Fall evenings can be cold. The 74 sites can accommodate tents and RVs. ⊠ *From Rte. 41 in Wawona, go north to Glacier Point Rd. and turn right; entrance to campground is 25 miles ahead on right side.*

Wawona. Near the Mariposa Grove, just downstream from a popular fishing spot, this year-round campground's 93 sites for tents and RVs are larger and less densely packed than those at campgrounds in Yosemite Valley. The downside? It's an hour's drive to the valley's attractions. ⊠ *Rte. 41, 1 mile north of Wawona.*

TUOLUMNE MEADOWS

Porcupine Flat. Sixteen miles west of Tuolumne Meadows, this campground sits at 8,100 feet. Sites are close together, but if you want to be in the high country and Tuolumne Meadows is full, this is a good bet. There is no water available. The campground's 52 sites for tents and RVs can't accommodate rigs of 35 feet or longer. ⊠ *Rte. 120, 16 miles west of Tuolumne Meadows.*

Tuolumne Meadows. In a wooded area at 8,600 feet, just south of its namesake meadow, this is one of the most spectacular and sought-after campgrounds in Yosemite. Hot showers can be used at the Tuolumne Meadows Lodge—though only at certain times. Half the 314 tent and RV sites are first-come, first-served,

so arrive early, or make reservations. The campground is open July–September. ⊠ *Rte. 120, 46 miles east of Big Oak Flat entrance station.*

White Wolf. Set in the beautiful high country at 8,000 feet, this is a prime spot for hikers from early July to mid-September. There are 87 tent and RV sites; rigs of up to 27 feet long are permitted. ⊠ *Tioga Rd., 15 miles east of Big Oak Flat entrance.*

EDUCATIONAL OFFERINGS
CLASSES AND SEMINARS
Art Classes

LOCAL SPORTS | Professional artists conduct workshops in watercolor, etching, drawing, and other media. Bring your own materials, or purchase the basics at the Happy Isles Art and Nature Center. Children under 12 must be accompanied by an adult. The center also offers beginner art workshops and children's art and family craft programs ($20–$40 per person). ⊠ *Happy Isles Art and Nature Center* ⊕ *www.yosemite.org* ⊠ *$20* ⊙ *No classes Sun. Closed Dec.–Feb.*

Happy Isles Art and Nature Center

LOCAL SPORTS | **FAMILY** | This family-focused center has a rotating selection of kid-friendly activities and hands-on exhibits that teach tykes and their parents about the park's ecosystem. Books, toys, and T-shirts are stocked in the small gift shop. ⊠ *Yosemite National Park* ⊹ *Off Southside Dr., about ¾ mile east of Curry Village* ⊠ *Free* ⊙ *Closed Oct.–Apr.*

Yosemite Outdoor Adventures

LOCAL SPORTS | Naturalists, scientists, and park rangers lead multihour to multiday outings on topics from woodpeckers to fire management to day hikes and bird-watching. Most sessions take place spring through fall with just a few in winter. ⊠ *Yosemite National Park* ⊕ *www.yosemite.org* ⊠ *From $99.*

RANGER PROGRAMS
Junior Ranger Program
LOCAL SPORTS | FAMILY | Children ages
3 to 13 can participate in the informal,
self-guided Junior Ranger program.
Park activity handbooks ($3.50 for ages
7 to 13 and $3 for Junior Cubs ages 3
to 6) are available at the Valley Visitor
Center, the Happy Isles Art and Nature
Center, the Tuolumne Visitor Center, and
the Wawona Visitor Center. Once kids
complete the book, rangers present
them with a badge and, in some cases,
a certificate. ⊠ *Valley Visitor Center or
the Happy Isles Art & Nature Center*
☎ *209/372–0299.*

Ranger-Led Programs
LOCAL SPORTS | Rangers lead entertaining
walks and give informative talks several
times a day from spring to fall. The
schedule is more limited in winter, but
most days you can find a program somewhere in the park. In the evenings at
Yosemite Valley Lodge and Curry Village,
lectures, slide shows, and documentary
films present unique perspectives on
Yosemite. On summer weekends, campgrounds at Curry Village and Tuolumne
Meadows host sing-along campfire
programs. Schedules and locations are
posted on bulletin boards throughout
the park as well as in the indispensable
Yosemite Guide, which is distributed to
visitors as they arrive at the park. ⊠ *Yosemite National Park* ⊕ *nps.gov/yose.*

Wee Wild Ones
LOCAL SPORTS | FAMILY | Designed for
kids under 10, this 45-minute program
includes naturalist-led games, songs,
stories, and crafts about Yosemite
wildlife, plants, and geology. The event
is held outdoors before the regular
Yosemite Valley Lodge evening programs
in summer and fall. All children must be
accompanied by an adult. ⊠ *Yosemite
National Park* ☎ *209/372–1153* ⊕ *www.
travelyosemite.com* ✉ *Free.*

FISHING
The waters in Yosemite are not stocked;
trout, mostly brown and rainbow, live
here but are not plentiful. Yosemite's fishing season begins on the last Saturday in
April and ends on November 15. Some
waterways are off-limits at certain times;
be sure to inquire at the visitor center
about regulations.

A California fishing license is required;
licenses cost around $17 for one day,
$26.50 for two days, and $53 for 10 days.
Full-season licenses cost $53 for state
residents and $142 for nonresidents
(costs fluctuate year to year). Buy your
license in season at **Yosemite Mountain
Shop in Curry Village** (☎ *209/372–1286*) or
at the **Wawona Store** (☎ *209/375–6574*).

GOLF
The Wawona Golf Course is one of the
country's few organic golf courses; it's
also an Audubon Cooperative sanctuary
for birds. You can play a round or take a
lesson from the pro here.

Wawona Golf Course
GOLF | This organic (one of only a handful
in the United States), 9-hole course has
two sets of tee positions per hole to
provide an 18-hole course. ⊠ *Rte. 41,
Wawona* ☎ *209/375–4386* ⊕ *www.trav-
elyosemite.com* ✉ *$24 for 9 holes; $39
for 18 holes* ⌟ *9 holes, 3011 yards, par 35*
⌖ *Closed Nov.–early May.*

HIKING
Wilderness Center
HIKING/WALKING | This facility provides free
wilderness permits, which are required
for overnight camping (advance reservations are available for $5 per person
plus $5 per reservation and are highly
recommended for popular trailheads in
summer and on weekends). The staff
here also provides maps and advice to
hikers heading into the backcountry. If
you don't have your own bear-resistant
canisters, which are required, you can
buy or rent them here. ⊠ *Between Ansel*

Adams Gallery and post office, Yosemite Village ☎ *209/372–0308.*

Yosemite Mountaineering School and Guide Service

HIKING/WALKING | From April to November, you can rent gear, hire a guide, or join a two-hour to full-day trek with Yosemite Mountaineering School. They also lead backpacking and overnight excursions. Reservations are recommended. In winter, cross-country ski programs are available at Badger Pass Ski Area. ☒ *Yosemite Mountain Shop, Curry Village* ☎ *209/372–8344* ⊕ *yosemitemountaineering.com.*

HORSEBACK RIDING

Reservations for guided trail rides must be made in advance at hotel tour desks or by phone. Scenic trail rides range from two hours to a half day. Four- and six-day High Sierra saddle trips are also available.

Wawona Stable

HORSEBACK RIDING | Two-hour rides at this stable start at $70, and a challenging full-day ride to the Mariposa Grove of Giant Sequoias (for experienced riders in good physical condition only) costs $144. Reservations are recommended. ☒ *Rte. 41, Wawona* ☎ *209/375–6502* ⊕ *www.travelyosemite.com/things-to-do/horseback-mule-riding.*

ICE-SKATING
Curry Village Ice Skating Rink

ICE SKATING | Winter visitors have skated at this outdoor rink for decades, and there's no mystery why: it's a kick to glide across the ice while soaking up views of Half Dome and Glacier Point. ☒ *South side of Southside Dr., Curry Village* ☎ *209/372–8319* ⊕ *www.travelyosemite.com* 🎫 *$11 per session, $5 skate rental.*

RAFTING

Rafting is permitted only on designated areas of the Middle and South forks of the Merced River. Check with the Valley Visitor Center for closures and other restrictions.

Curry Village Recreation Center

WHITE-WATER RAFTING | The per-person rental fee at Curry Village Recreation Center covers the four- to six-person raft, two paddles, and life jackets, plus a return shuttle after your trip. ☒ *South side of Southside Dr., Curry Village* ☎ *209/372–4386* ⊕ *www.travelyosemite.com/things-to-do/rafting* 🎫 *From $33.*

ROCK CLIMBING

The granite canyon walls of Yosemite Valley are world renowned for rock climbing. El Capitan, with its 3,593-foot vertical face, is the most famous, but there are many other options here for all skill levels.

Yosemite Mountain Shop

SPECIALTY STORES | A comprehensive selection of camping, hiking, backpacking, and climbing equipment, along with experts who can answer all your questions, make this store a valuable resource for outdoors enthusiasts. This is the best place to ask about climbing conditions and restrictions around the park, as well as purchase almost any kind of climbing gear. ☒ *Curry Village* ☎ *209/372–8436.*

Yosemite Mountaineering School and Guide Service

CLIMBING/MOUNTAINEERING | The one-day basic lesson offered by this outfit includes some bouldering and rappelling and three or four 60-foot climbs. Climbers must be at least 10 years old and in reasonably good physical condition. Intermediate and advanced classes include instruction in first aid; anchor building; and multipitch, summer-snow, and big-wall climbing. There's a Nordic program in the winter. ☒ *Yosemite Mountain Shop, Curry Village* ☎ *209/372–8444* ⊕ *www.travelyosemite.com* 🎫 *From $172.*

SKIING AND SNOWSHOEING

The beauty of Yosemite under a blanket of snow has long inspired poets and artists, as well as ordinary folks. Skiing and snowshoeing activities in the park center on Badger Pass Ski Area, California's

Ansel Adams's Black-and-White Yosemite

What John Muir did for Yosemite with words, Ansel Adams did with photographs. His photographs have inspired millions of people to visit the park, and his persistent activism helped to ensure its conservation.

Born in 1902, Adams first came to the valley when he was 14, photographing it with a Box Brownie camera. He later said his first visit "was a culmination of experience so intense as to be almost painful. From that day in 1916 my life has been colored and modulated by the great earth gesture of the Sierra." By 1919, he was working in the valley, as custodian of LeConte Memorial Lodge (now called Yosemite Conservation Heritage Center), the Sierra Club headquarters in Yosemite National Park.

Adams had harbored dreams of a career as a concert pianist, but the park sealed his fate as a photographer in 1928, the day he shot *Monolith: The Face of Half Dome,* which remains one of his most famous works. That same year, Adams also married Virginia Best in her father's valley studio (now the Ansel Adams Gallery).

As the photographer's career took off, Yosemite began to sear itself into the American consciousness. David Brower, first executive director of the Sierra Club, later said of Adams's impact, "That Ansel Adams came to be recognized as one of the great photographers of this century is a tribute to the places that informed him."

In 1934, Adams was elected to the Sierra Club's board of directors; he would serve until 1971. As a representative of the conservation group, he combined his work with the club's mission, showing his photographs of the Sierra to influential officials such as Secretary of the Interior Harold L. Ickes, who showed them to President Franklin Delano Roosevelt. The images were a key factor in the establishment of Kings Canyon National Park.

In 1968, the Department of the Interior granted Adams its highest honor, the Conservation Service Award, and, in 1980, he received the Presidential Medal of Freedom in recognition of his conservation work. Until his death in 1984, Adams continued not only to record Yosemite's majesty on film but to urge the federal government and park managers to do right by the park.

In one of his many public pleas on behalf of Yosemite, Adams said, "Yosemite Valley itself is one of the great shrines of the world and—belonging to all our people—must be both protected and appropriately accessible." As an artist and an activist, Adams never gave up on his dream of keeping Yosemite wild yet within reach of every visitor who wants to experience it.

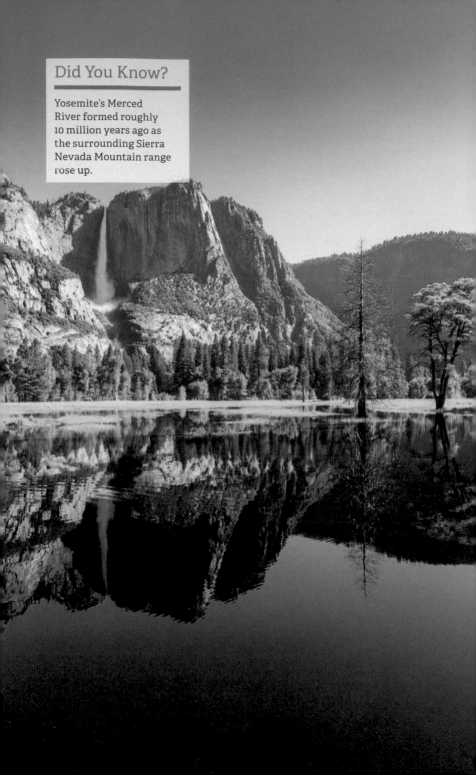

Did You Know?

Yosemite's Merced River formed roughly 10 million years ago as the surrounding Sierra Nevada Mountain range rose up.

oldest snow-sports resort, which is about 40 minutes away from the valley on Glacier Point Road. Here you can rent equipment, take a lesson, have lunch, and join a guided excursion.

Badger Pass Ski Area

SKIING/SNOWBOARDING | California's first ski resort has 10 downhill runs and 90 miles of groomed cross-country trails. Lessons, backcountry guiding, and cross-country and snowshoeing tours are also available. You can rent downhill, tele-mark, and cross-country skis, as well as snowshoes and snowboards. Note that shuttle buses run twice daily between the valley and the ski area. **Facilities:** 10 trails; 90 acres; 800-foot vertical drop; 5 lifts. ⊠ *Yosemite National Park* ⊹ *Badger Pass Rd., off Glacier Point Rd., 18 miles from Yosemite Valley* ☎ *209/372–8430* ⊕ *www.travelyosemite.com/winter/badger-pass-ski-area* ⊠ *Lift ticket: from $62.*

Badger Pass Ski Area School

SKIING/SNOWBOARDING | The gentle slopes of Badger Pass Ski Area make the ski school an ideal spot for children and beginners to learn downhill skiing or snowboarding for as little as $75 for a group lesson. ☎ *209/372–8430* ⊕ *www.travelyosemite.com.*

Badger Pass Ski Area Sport Shop

SKIING/SNOWBOARDING | Stop here to gear (and bundle!) up for downhill and cross-country skiing, snowboarding, and snowshoeing adventures. ⊠ *Yosemite National Park* ⊹ *Yosemite Ski & Snowboard Area, Badger Pass Rd., off Glacier Point Rd., 18 miles from Yosemite Valley* ☎ *209/372–8444* ⊕ *www.travelyosemite.com/winter/badger-pass-ski-area.*

Yosemite Cross-Country Ski School

SKIING/SNOWBOARDING | The highlight of Yosemite's cross-country skiing center is a 21-mile loop from Badger Pass Ski Area to Glacier Point. You can rent cross-country skis for $28 per day at the Cross-Country Ski School, which also rents snowshoes ($26.50 per day) and telemarking

equipment ($36). ☎ *209/372–8444* ⊕ *www.travelyosemite.com.*

Yosemite Mountaineering School

SKIING/SNOWBOARDING | This branch of the Yosemite Mountaineering School, open at the Badger Pass Ski Area during ski season only, conducts snowshoeing, cross-country skiing, telemarking, and skate-skiing classes starting at $44. ⊠ *Badger Pass Ski Area* ☎ *209/372–8444* ⊕ *www.travelyosemite.com.*

What's Nearby

Mariposa

43 miles west of Yosemite's Arch Rock Entrance.

Mariposa marks the southern end of the Mother Lode. Much of the land in this area was part of a 44,000-acre land grant Colonel John C. Fremont acquired from Mexico before gold was discovered and California became a state. Many people stop here on the way to Yosemite National Park, about an hour's drive east on Highway 140.

GETTING HERE AND AROUND

If driving, take Highway 49 or Highway 140. YARTS (⊕ *www.yarts.com*), the regional transit system, can get you to Mariposa from the Central Valley town of Merced (where you can also transfer from Amtrak) or from Yosemite Valley. Otherwise, you'll need a car.

Sights

California State Mining and Mineral Museum

MUSEUM | **FAMILY** | A California state park, the museum has displays on gold-rush history including a replica hard-rock mine shaft to walk through, a miniature stamp mill, and a 13-pound chunk of crystallized gold. ⊠ *5005 Fairground Rd., off Hwy. 49* ☎ *209/742–7625* ⊕ *www.parks.*

Did You Know?

In the Sierra's mixed-conifer forests, telling the many types of pines apart can be difficult if you don't know the trick: sizing up the cones and examining the branches to count how many needles are in discrete clusters. If the needles are paired, you're likely looking at a lodgepole pine. If the needles are long and come in threes, chances are you've come upon a ponderosa pine.

ca.gov/miningandmineralmuseum $4
⏱ *Closed Mon.–Wed.*

Mariposa Museum and History Center
MUSEUM VILLAGE | You'll leave this small museum feeling like you just found your own gold nugget. Detailed exhibits, both indoors and out, tell the history of Mariposa County. Visit a replica of a typical miner's cabin; see a working stamp mill; tour the blacksmith shop. Artifacts, photographs, and maps, along with the knowledgeable staff, will capture your imagination and transport you back to 1849. ✉ *5119 Jessie St.* ☎ *209/966–2924* ⊕ *www.mariposamuseum.com* $5.

 Restaurants

Charles Street Dinner House
$$$ | **AMERICAN** | Centrally located Charles Street, its rustic decor heavy on the wood and Old West adornments, at once evokes gold-rush days and the 1980s, when it opened. The extensive straightforward menu includes hand-cut steaks, honey-barbecue baby back ribs, several pasta dishes, chicken, pork loin, lamb, a few well-adorned burgers, and some vegetarian options. **Known for:** excellent steaks; cheesecake, sundae, crème brûlée for dessert; local feel. ⑤ *Average main: $27* ✉ *Hwy. 140 and 7th St.* ☎ *209/966–2366* ⊕ *www.charlesstreetdinnerhouse.net* ⏱ *Closed Sun. and Mon. No lunch.*

1850 Restaurant & Brewery
$$$ | **AMERICAN** | The name, decor, and menu at this lively brewpub pay homage to California's Gold Rush era and the year the state and county were officially established. Many of the craft beers on tap come from the owners' 1850 Brewing Company, and dishes include everything from traditional Bavarian pretzels and hearty steak-and-ale pie to ahi nachos and salmon cakes. **Known for:** brine-marinated fried chicken; nearly a dozen types of burgers; rotating local seasonal beers on tap. ⑤ *Average main:*

$22 ✉ *5114 Hwy. 140* ☎ *209/966–2229* ⊕ *www.1850restaurant.com* ⏱ *Closed Mon.*

Savoury's
$$ | **AMERICAN** | Seafood, pasta, and portobello mushrooms are some of the savory treats that draw high praise from locals at the kind of refined space you'd expect in an urban environment, not in mellow Mariposa. Contemporary paintings and photography set aglow by track lighting create a gallerylike atmosphere. **Known for:** well-prepared steak and seafood; full bar; vegetarian and vegan options. ⑤ *Average main: $20* ✉ *5034 Hwy. 140* ☎ *209/966–7677* ⏱ *Closed Tues. and Wed. No lunch.*

El Portal

29 miles northwest of Mariposa, 15 miles west of Yosemite's Arch Rock Entrance on Hwy. 140.

The market in town is a good place to pick up provisions before you get to Yosemite. You'll find a post office and a gas station, but not much else.

GETTING HERE AND AROUND
The drive here on Highway 140 from Mariposa and, farther west, Merced, is the prettiest and gentlest route to Yosemite National Park. Much of the road follows the Merced River in a rugged canyon. The Yosemite Area Regional Transportation System (YARTS ⊕ *www.yarts.com*) is a cheap and dependable way to go between Merced and Yosemite Valley; all buses stop in El Portal, where many park employees reside.

 Hotels

Yosemite View Lodge
$$ | **HOTEL** | Two miles outside Yosemite's Arch Rock entrance, this modern property is the most convenient place to spend the night if you are unable to secure lodgings in the valley. **Pros:** great location;

good views; lots of on-site amenities. **Cons:** somewhat pricey; it can be a challenge to get the dates you want; rooms could use an update. $ *Rooms from: $239* ✉ *11136 Hwy. 140* ☎ *209/379–2681, 888/742–4371* ⊕ *www.yosemiteresorts. com/yosemite-view-lodge* ⇴ *335 rooms* ⦿ *No meals.*

Oakhurst

23 miles south of Yosemite's South Entrance.

Motels, restaurants, gas stations, and small businesses line Highway 41 in Oakhurst, the last sizable community before Yosemite National Park and a good spot to find provisions.

GETTING HERE AND AROUND
At the junction of highways 41 and 49, Oakhurst is about an hour's drive north of Fresno. It's the southern gateway to Yosemite, so many people fly into Fresno and rent a car to get here and beyond.

🍴 Restaurants

★ South Gate Brewing Company
$$ | **AMERICAN** | Locals pack this family-friendly, industrial-chic restaurant to socialize and savor small-lot beers, crafted on-site, along with tasty meals. The creative pub fare runs a wide gamut, from thin-crust brick-oven pizzas to fish tacos, fish-and-chips, and vegan black-bean burgers. **Known for:** craft beer; house-made desserts; live-music calendar. $ *Average main: $18* ✉ *40233 Enterprise Dr., off Hwy. 49, north of Von's shopping center* ☎ *559/692–2739* ⊕ *southgatebrewco.com.*

Hotels

Best Western Plus Yosemite Gateway Inn
$$ | **HOTEL** | **FAMILY** | Perched on 11 hillside acres, Oakhurst's best motel has carefully tended landscaping and rooms with stylish contemporary furnishings and hand-painted murals of Yosemite. **Pros:** on-site restaurant; indoor and outdoor swimming pools; frequent deer and wildlife sightings. **Cons:** some rooms on the small side; Internet connection can be slow; some rooms need updating. $ *Rooms from: $249* ✉ *40530 Hwy. 41* ☎ *559/683–2378* ⊕ *www.yosemitegatewayinn.com* ⇴ *149 rooms* ⦿ *No meals.*

Homestead Cottages
$$ | **B&B/INN** | Set on 160 acres of rolling hills that once held a Miwok village, these cottages (the largest sleeps six) have gas fireplaces, fully equipped kitchens, and queen-size beds. **Pros:** remote location; quiet setting; friendly owners. **Cons:** might be too quiet for some; breakfasts on the simple side; 7 miles from center of Oakhurst. $ *Rooms from: $189* ✉ *41110 Rd. 600, 2½ miles off Hwy. 49, Ahwahnee* ☎ *559/683–0495* ⊕ *www. homesteadcottages.com* ⇴ *7 cottages* ⦿ *Free breakfast.*

Sierra Sky Ranch
$$ | **HOTEL** | Off Highway 41 just 10 miles south of the Yosemite National Park, this 19th-century cattle ranch near a hidden grove of giant sequoia trees provides a restful, rustic retreat. **Pros:** peaceful setting; historic property; short drive to giant sequoias. **Cons:** some rooms on the small side; not in town; basic breakfast. $ *Rooms from: $249* ✉ *50552 Rd. 632* ☎ *559/683–8040* ⊕ *www.sierraskyranch. com* ⇴ *26 rooms* ⦿ *Free breakfast.*

Bass Lake

7 miles northwest of Oakhurst via Hwy. 41 to Bass Lake Road 222.

Almost surrounded by the Sierra National Forest, Bass Lake is a reservoir whose waters can reach 80°F in summer. Created by a dam on a tributary of the San Joaquin River, the lake is owned by Pacific Gas and Electric Company and is used to generate electricity as well as for recreation.

🍴 Restaurants

Ducey's on the Lake/Ducey's Bar & Grill

$$$ | **AMERICAN** | With elaborate chandeliers sculpted from deer antlers, the lodge-style restaurant at Ducey's attracts boaters, locals, and tourists with its lake views and standard lamb, beef, seafood, and pasta dishes. It's also open for breakfast: try the Bass Lake seafood omelet, huevos rancheros, or the Rice Krispies–crusted French toast. **Known for:** steaks and fresh fish; lake views; upstairs bar and grill with more affordable eats. $ *Average main: $32* ✉ *Pines Resort, 54432 Rd. 432* ☎ *559/642–3131* ⊕ *www. basslake.com.*

🤸 Activities

BOATING

Bass Lake Boat Rental & Water Sports

BOATING | This outfit on Bass Lake Reservoir, 3 miles north and 6 miles east of Oakhurst, rents ski boats, patio boats, fishing boats, canoes, tubes, and other things that float. The folks here also conduct guided fishing and scenic tours. In summer the noisy reservoir is packed shortly after it opens at 8 am (off-season hours are from 9 to 5). There's also a shop with snacks and gifts. ✉ *54406 Marina Dr.* ☎ *559/642–3200* ⊕ *basslakeboatrentals.com.*

Fish Camp

14 miles north of Oakhurst.

As you climb in elevation along Highway 41 northbound, you see nothing but trees until you get to Fish Camp, where there's a post office and general store. (For gas, head 7 miles north to Wawona, in Yosemite, or 14 miles south to Oakhurst.)

GETTING HERE AND AROUND

Highway 41 is the main drag. YARTS transit stops in Fish Camp on its route between Fresno and Yosemite Valley.

👁 Sights

Yosemite Mountain Sugar Pine Railroad

TRANSPORTATION SITE (AIRPORT/BUS/FERRY/TRAIN) | **FAMILY** | Travel back to a time when powerful steam locomotives hauled massive log trains through the Sierra. This 4-mile, narrow-gauge railroad excursion takes you near Yosemite's south gate. There's a moonlight special ($63), with dinner and entertainment, and you can visit the free museum. ✉ *56001 Hwy. 41, 8 miles south of Yosemite* ☎ *559/683–7273* ⊕ *www.ymsprr.com* 💲 *$28* ⊙ *Closed Nov.–Mar. Closed some weekdays Apr. and Oct.*

🛏 Hotels

Narrow Gauge Inn

$$ | **HOTEL** | Rooms at this family-owned property have balconies with views of the surrounding woods and mountains. **Pros:** close to Yosemite's south entrance; nicely appointed rooms; wonderful balconies. **Cons:** rooms can be a bit dark; dining options are limited, especially for vegetarians; housekeeping service can be spotty. $ *Rooms from: $229* ✉ *48571 Hwy. 41* ☎ *559/683–7720* ⊕ *www. narrowgaugeinn.com* 🛏 *27 rooms* ⭐ *No meals.*

★ Tenaya Lodge

$$$$ | **RESORT** | **FAMILY** | One of the region's largest hotels is ideal for people who enjoy wilderness treks by day but prefer creature comforts at night. **Pros:** close to Yosemite and Mariposa Grove of Giant Sequoias; exceptional spa and exercise facility, 36 miles of mountain bike trails; activities for all ages. **Cons:** so big it can seem impersonal; pricey during summer; daily resort fee. $ *Rooms from: $379* ✉ *1122 Hwy. 41* ☎ *559/683–6555, 888/514–2167* ⊕ *www.tenayalodge.com* 🛏 *352 rooms* ⭐ *No meals.*

Lee Vining

*13 miles northeast of Yosemite's
Tioga Pass Entrance (near Tuolumne
Meadows).*

Tiny Lee Vining is known primarily as the
eastern gateway to Yosemite National
Park (summer only) and the location of
vast and desolate Mono Lake. Pick up
supplies at the general store year-round,
or stop here for lunch or dinner before
or after a drive through the high country.
In winter, the town is all but deserted,
except for the ice climbers who come to
scale frozen waterfalls.

Most people enter Yosemite National
Park from the west, having driven out
from the Bay Area or Los Angeles. The
eastern entrance on Tioga Pass Road
(Highway 120 off Highway 395), however,
provides stunning, sweeping views of
the High Sierra. Gray rocks shine in the
bright sun, with scattered, small vegetation sprinkled about the mountainside.

To drive from Lee Vining to Tuolumne
Meadows is an unforgettable experience,
but keep in mind that the road is closed
for at least seven months of the year.

GETTING HERE AND AROUND
Lee Vining is on U.S. 395, north of the
road's intersection with Highway 120 and
on the south side of Mono Lake. In summer YARTS public transit (⊕ *yarts.com*)
can get you here from Yosemite Valley,
but you'll need a car to explore the area.

**VISITOR INFORMATION Lee Vining
Chamber of Commerce.** ☎ *760/647–6629*
⊕ *www.leevining.com.* **Mono Basin
National Forest Scenic Area Visitor Center.**
✉ *Visitor Center Dr., off U.S. 395, 1 mile
north of Hwy. 120* ☎ *760/647–6595*
⊕ *www.fs.usda.gov/recarea/inyo/
recarea/?recid=20620.*

◉ Sights

June Lake Loop
SCENIC DRIVE | Heading south, U.S. 395
intersects the June Lake Loop. This
gorgeous 17-mile drive follows an old
glacial canyon past Grant, June, Gull, and
Silver lakes before reconnecting with
U.S. 395 on its way to Mammoth Lakes.
■**TIP→ The loop is especially colorful in
fall.** ✉ *Hwy. 158 W.*

★ Mono Lake
BODY OF WATER | Since the 1940s, Los
Angeles has diverted water from this
lake, exposing striking towers of tufa,
or calcium carbonate. Court victories
by environmentalists have meant fewer
diversions, and the lake is rising again.
Although to see the lake from U.S. 395
is stunning, make time to visit South
Tufa, whose parking lot is 5 miles east
of U.S. 395 off Highway 120. There, in
summer, you can join the naturalist-guid-
ed **South Tufa Walk,** which lasts about 90
minutes. The **Scenic Area Visitor Center,**
off U.S. 395, is a sensational stop for its
interactive exhibits and sweeping Mono
Lake views (closed in winter). In town, at
U.S. 395 and 3rd Street, the **Mono Lake
Committee Information Center & Bookstore,**
open from 9 to 5 daily (extended hours
in summer), has more information
about this beautiful area. ✉ *Hwy. 120,
east of Lee Vining* ☎ *760/647–3044
visitor center, 760/647–6595 info center*
⊕ *www.monolake.org* 🆓 *Free.*

🍴 Restaurants

Epic Cafe
$ | AMERICAN | FAMILY | Hungry travelers
and locals feast on fresh, healthy, cooked-
to-order comfort food at this casual café
at Lakeview Lodge, near the Tioga Road
and Highway 395 junction. The menu
changes daily, but you can count on items
like waffles and fritattas for breakfast;
paninis, sandwiches, salads, rice bowls,
and soups for lunch; and three special
dinner entrées, perhaps locally caught

fish, chicken potpie, or braised short ribs. **Known for:** local and organic food sources; cozy indoor dining room and garden patio; fresh-baked scones, muffins, desserts, and other goodies. $ *Average main: $15* ✉ *349 Lee Vining Ave.* ☎ *760/965–6282* ⊕ *epiccafesierra.com* ⊗ *Closed Nov.–early May. Closed Sun.*

Mono Cone

$ | **AMERICAN** | Get soft-serve ice cream, burgers, and fries at this hopping shack in the middle of Lee Vining, but be prepared to wait in line. There's some indoor seating, but unless the clouds are leaking, take your food to nearby (and quiet) Hess Park, whose views of Mono Lake make it one of the best picnic spots in eastern California. $ *Average main: $9* ✉ *51508 U.S. 395* ☎ *760/647–6606* ▭ *No credit cards* ⊗ *Closed in winter.*

Tioga Gas Mart & Whoa Nelli Deli

$$ | **AMERICAN** | This might be the only gas station in the United States serving craft beers and lobster taquitos, but its appeal goes beyond novelty. Order at the counter and grab a seat inside, or sit at one of the picnic tables on the lawn outside and take in the distant view of Mono Lake. **Known for:** fish tacos and barbecued ribs; regular live music; convenient location. $ *Average main: $16* ✉ *Hwy. 120 and U.S. 395* ☎ *760/647–1088* ⊕ *www.whoanelliedeli. com* ⊗ *Closed early Nov.–late Apr.*

 Hotels

Lake View Lodge

$ | **B&B/INN** | Cottages, enormous rooms, and landscaping that includes several shaded sitting areas set this motel apart from its competitors in town. **Pros:** convenient access to Yosemite, Mono Lake, Bodie State Historic Park; peaceful setting; on-site restaurant. **Cons:** could use updating; slow Wi-Fi in some areas; no views from some rooms. $ *Rooms from: $143* ✉ *51285 U.S. 395* ☎ *760/647–6543, 800/990–6614* ⊕ *www.lakeviewlodgeyosemite.com* ⇆ *88 units* ❍ *No meals.*

Bodie State Historic Park

31 miles northeast of Lee Vining.

Bodie State Historic Park's scenery is spectacular, with craggy, snowcapped peaks looming over vast prairies. The town of Bridgeport is the gateway to the park, and the only supply center for miles around. Bridgeport's claims to fame include a courthouse that's been in continuous use since 1880 and excellent fishing—the California state record brown trout, at 26 pounds 12 ounces, was caught in Bridgeport's Twin Lakes. In winter, much of Bridgeport shuts down.

GETTING HERE AND AROUND

A car is the best way to reach this area. Bodie is on Highway 270 about 13 miles east of U.S. 395.

 Sights

★ Bodie Ghost Town

GHOST TOWN | The mining village of Rattlesnake Gulch, abandoned mine shafts, and the remains of a small Chinatown are among the sights at this fascinating ghost town. The town boomed from about 1878 to 1881; by the late 1940s, though, all its residents had departed. A state park was established here in 1962, with a mandate to preserve everything in a state of "arrested decay." Evidence of Bodie's wild past survives at an excellent museum, and you can tour an old stamp mill where ore was crushed into fine powder to extract gold and silver. Bodie lies 13 miles east of U.S. 395 off Highway 270. The last 3 miles are unpaved, and snow may close the highway from late fall through early spring. No food, drink, or lodging is available in Bodie. ✉ *Bodie Rd., off Hwy. 270, Bodie* ☎ *760/616–5040* ⊕ *www.parks.ca.gov/bodie* 🎫 *$8.*

Chapter 7

EASTERN SIERRA

Updated by
Cheryl Crabtree

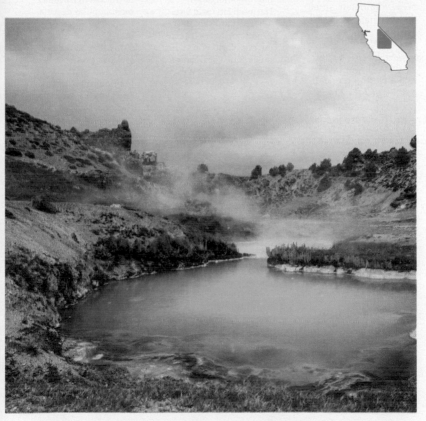

◉ Sights	🞙 Restaurants	🛏 Hotels	💼 Shopping	🍸 Nightlife
★★★★★	★★★★☆	★★★★★	★☆☆☆☆	★☆☆☆☆

WELCOME TO EASTERN SIERRA

TOP REASONS TO GO

★ **Hiking:** Whether you walk the paved loops in the national parks or head off the beaten path into the backcountry, a hike through groves and meadows or alongside streams and waterfalls will allow you to see, smell, and feel nature up close.

★ **Winter fun:** Famous for its incredible snowpack—some of the deepest in the North American continent—the Sierra Nevada has something for every winter-sports fan.

★ **Live it up:** Mammoth Lakes is eastern California's most exciting resort area.

★ **Road trip heaven:** Legendary Highway 395 is one of California's most scenic byways, traveling to Independence, Lone Pine, Bishop, and beyond, for a glimpse of Old West history.

★ **Go with the flow:** Fish, float, raft, and row in the abundant lakes, hot springs, creeks, and rivers.

1 Lone Pine. Mount Whitney and the Alabama Hills in Lone Pine have provided authentic backdrops for hundreds of films and TV shows for nearly a century, as evidenced in the town's Museum of Western Film History.

2 Independence. The moving Manzanar National Historic Site, where 11,000 Japanese-Americans were interned during World War II, lies 6 miles south of Independence, a tiny Old West town.

3 Bishop. One of the largest towns along Highway 395, Bishop is an excellent road stop and base camp for exploration in the surrounding mountains.

4 Mammoth Lakes. Easy access to year-round outdoor adventures has made Mammoth Lakes one of the Sierra Nevada's most popular destinations. The bustling town's many attractions include sprawling Mammoth Mountain Ski and Bike Area and nearby Mammoth Lakes Basin and Devil's Postpile National Monument.

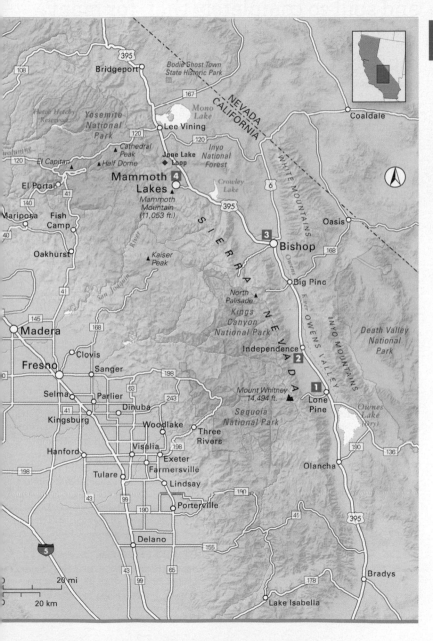

The granite peaks and ancient pines of the Eastern Sierra bedazzle heart and soul so completely that, for many visitors, the experience surpasses that at more famous urban attractions.

This rugged region offers some of the most dramatic sightseeing in California. Highway 395, one of the state's most beautiful routes and generally open year-round, is the main north–south road. It travels the length of the region, from the Mojave Desert in the south to Bridgeport in the north, and along the eastern side of the Sierra Nevada, at the western edge of the Great Basin. Main towns along the route include Lone Pine, Independence, Bishop, and Mammoth Lakes, as well as Lee Vining, a small town at the eastern endpoint of Tioga Road (open only seasonally) into Yosemite National Park.

Pristine lakes and rolling hills outside the parks offer year-round opportunities for rest and relaxation. Or not. In winter, the thrill of Mammoth Lakes slopes—and their relative isolation compared to busy Lake Tahoe—draws a hearty breed of outdoor enthusiasts. From late spring through early fall, a hike through groves and meadows or alongside streams and waterfalls allows you to see, smell, and feel nature up close.

MAJOR REGIONS

Owens Valley. In this undervisited region, the snowcapped Sierra Nevada range rises abruptly and majestically to the west, and the high desert whistles to the east. In between are a series of roadside towns full of character, history, and outfits that cater to adventurers. Along U.S. 395 in this region are Lone Pine, Independence, and Bishop, with Lone Pine

and Bishop having the best selection of dining and lodging options.

Mammoth Lakes. North of Owens Valley, en route to the gateway towns east of Yosemite National Park, is the megaresort of Mammoth Lakes, which lures skiers and snowboarders in winter and hikers and mountain bikers in warmer months.

Planning

Getting Here and Around

AIR

Fresno Yosemite International Airport (FAT) is the main gateway on the western side of the Eastern Sierra. Airports to the region's east and along U.S. 395 include Mammoth–Yosemite (MMH), 6 miles east of Mammoth Lakes; Eastern Sierra Regional (BIH) in Bishop, 45 miles southeast of Mammoth Lakes; and Reno–Tahoe (RNO), 130 miles north of Mammoth Lakes. Alaska, Allegiant, American, Delta, Frontier, JSX, Southwest, United, and a few other carriers serve Fresno and Reno. Advanced Airlines serves Mammoth Lakes, and United and JSX fly into Eastern Sierra Regional.

AIRPORTS Eastern Sierra Regional Airport. (BIH) ⊠ 703 Airport Rd., Bishop ☎ 760/872–2971, 760/937–4017 after business hours. **Fresno Yosemite International Airport.** (FAT) ⊠ 5175 E. Clinton

Ave., Fresno ☎ 800/244–2359 automated information, 559/454–2052 terminal info desk ⊕ www.flyfresno.com. **Mammoth–Yosemite Airport.** (*MMH*) ✉ 1200 Airport Rd., Mammoth Lakes ☎ 760/934–2712, 888/466–2666 ⊕ www.visitmammoth.com/getting-mammoth-lakes. **Reno–Tahoe International Airport.** (*RNO*) ✉ 2001 E. Plumb La., Reno ☎ 775/328–6400 ⊕ www.renoairport.com.

BUS

Eastern Sierra Transit Authority buses serve Mammoth Lakes, Bishop, and other Eastern Sierra towns along Highway 395, from Reno in the north to Lancaster in the south. In summer, YARTS (Yosemite Area Regional Transportation System) connects Yosemite National Park with Mammoth Lakes, June Lake, and Lee Vining, as well as Central Valley cities and towns in the west, including Fresno and Merced. This is a good option during summer, when parking in Yosemite Valley and elsewhere in the park can be difficult.

BUS CONTACTS Eastern Sierra Transit Authority. ☎ 760/872–1901 general, 800/922–1930 toll-free, 760/924–3184 Mammoth Lakes ⊕ www.estransit.com. **YARTS.** ☎ 877/989–2787 ⊕ www.yarts.com.

CAR

Interstate 5 and Highway 99 travel north–south along the western side of the Sierra Nevada. U.S. 395 follows a roughly parallel route on the eastern side. In summer, Tioga Pass Road in Yosemite National Park opens to car and bus travel, intersecting with U.S. 395 at Lee Vining.

From San Francisco: Head east on I–80 to Sacramento, then continue on I–80 to U.S. 395, east of Lake Tahoe's north shore, or take U.S. 50 to Lake Tahoe's south shore and continue on 207E to U.S. 395, then head south.

From Los Angeles: Head north on I–5, exiting and continuing north onto Highway 14 and later onto U.S. 395.

■ TIP→ **Gas stations are few and far between in the Sierra, so fill your tank when you can.** Between October and May, heavy snow may cover mountain roads. Always check conditions before driving. Carry tire chains, and know how to install them. On I–80 and U.S. 50, and at the Mammoth Lakes exit off U.S. 395, chain installers assist travelers (for $40), but elsewhere you're on your own.

TRAIN

Amtrak's daily *San Joaquin* train stops in Fresno and Merced, where you can connect to YARTS for travel to Yosemite National Park and, in summer, to Mammoth Lakes, June Lake, and the Yosemite gateway town of Lee Vining.

Restaurants

Most small towns in the Sierra Nevada have at least one restaurant. Standard American fare is the norm, but you'll also find sophisticated cuisine. With few exceptions, dress is casual. Local grocery stores and delis stock picnic fixings, good to have on hand should the opportunity for an impromptu meal under giant trees emerge.

Hotels

The lodgings in Mammoth Lakes and nearest Yosemite National Park generally fill up the quickest; book hotels everywhere in the Eastern Sierra well in advance in summer.

Restaurant and hotel reviews have been shortened. For full information, visit Fodors.com. Restaurant prices are the average cost of a main course at dinner, or if dinner is not served, at lunch. Hotel prices are the lowest cost of a standard double room in high season.

What It Costs			
$	$$	$$$	$$$$
RESTAURANTS			
under $17	$17–$26	$27–$36	over $36
HOTELS			
under $150	$150–$250	$251–$350	over $350

Tours

MAWS Transportation
BUS TOURS | This outfit (aka Mammoth All Weather Shuttle) operates summer tours from Mammoth Lakes to Yosemite; north to June Lake, Mono Lake, and Bodie Ghost Town; and around the lakes region. The company also transfers passengers from the Bishop and Mammoth–Yosemite airports into Mammoth Lakes, drops off and picks up hikers at trailheads, and runs charters to Los Angeles, Reno, and Las Vegas airports—useful when inclement weather causes flight cancellations at Mammoth's airport. ✉ *Mammoth Lakes* ☎ *760/709–2927* ⊕ *www.mawshuttle. com* ☎ *From $60.*

Visitor Information

CONTACTS Eastern Sierra Visitor Center.
⊕ *2 miles south of Lone Pine, at junctions of U.S. Hwy. 395 and CA Hwy. 136* ☎ *760/876–6200* ⊕ *www.fs.usda. gov/recarea/inyo/recarea/?recid=20698.* **Mammoth Lakes Tourism.** ☎ *760/934–2712, 888/466–2666* ⊕ *www.visitmammoth. com.* **Mono County Tourism.** ☎ *800/845–7922* ⊕ *monocounty.org.*

Lone Pine

100 miles southeast of Mammoth Lakes.

Mt. Whitney towers majestically over this tiny community, which supplied nearby gold- and silver-mining outposts in the 1860s, and for the past century the town has been touched by Hollywood glamour: several hundred movies, TV episodes, and commercials have been filmed here.

GETTING HERE AND AROUND
Arrive via U.S. 395 from the north or south. (If you're heading from Death Valley National Park, you can also take Highway 190 or Highway 138.) Eastern Sierra Transit buses connect Lone Pine to Reno in the north and Lancaster in the south.

ESSENTIALS
VISITOR INFORMATION Lone Pine Chamber of Commerce & Visitor Center.
✉ *120 S. Main St., at Whitney Portal Rd.* ☎ *760/876–4444* ⊕ *www.lonepinechamber.org.*

Sights

Alabama Hills
MOUNTAIN—SIGHT | Drop by the Lone Pine Visitor Center for a map of the Alabama Hills, and drive up Whitney Portal Road (turn west at the light) to this wonderland of granite boulders. Erosion has worn the rocks smooth; some have been chiseled into arches and other formations. The hills have become a popular location for rock climbing. Tuttle Creek Campground sits among the rocks, with a nearby stream for fishing. The area has served as a scenic backdrop for hundreds of films; ask about the self-guided tour of the various movie locations at the Museum of Western Film History. ✉ *Whitney Portal Rd., 4½ miles west of Lone Pine.*

Highway 395
SCENIC DRIVE | For a gorgeous view of the eastern Sierra, travel north of Death Valley along Highway 395 where you'll discover wandering elk herds, trout hatcheries, and breathtaking views of Mt. Whitney, the highest mountain (14,496 feet) in the continental United States. Drive south on Highway 395, between Olancha and Big Pine, and you'll notice the massive salt-crusted Owens Lake, which was drained between 1900 and

1920 as water from the Sierra was diverted to Los Angeles. Today, up to one-fourth of the water flow is being reintroduced to the lake. If you drive to the northwest end of the lake, near the abandoned Pittsburg Plate Glass Soda Ash Plant, you can see brilliant red salt flats, caused by billions of microscopic halobacteria that survive there. Revered by the National Audubon Society, the lake is home to more than 240 migrating birds, including the snowy plover, American white pelican, golden eagle, and countless grebes, bitterns, blue herons, and cranes. ⊠ *Death Valley.*

Mt. Whitney

MOUNTAIN—SIGHT | Straddling the border of Sequoia National Park and Inyo National Forest–John Muir Wilderness, Mt. Whitney (14,496 feet) is the highest mountain in the contiguous United States. A favorite game for travelers passing through Lone Pine is trying to guess which peak is Mt. Whitney. Almost no one gets it right, because Mt. Whitney is hidden behind other mountains. There is no road that ascends the peak, but you can catch a glimpse of the mountain by driving curvy Whitney Portal Road west from Lone Pine into the mountains. The pavement ends at the trailhead to the top of the mountain, which is also the start of the 211-mile John Muir Trail from Mt. Whitney to Yosemite National Park. Day and overnight permits are required to ascend Mt. Whitney. The highly competitive lottery for these permits opens on February 1st. At the portal, a restaurant (known for its pancakes) and a small store cater to hikers and campers staying at Whitney Portal Campground. You can see a waterfall from the parking lot and go fishing in a small trout pond. The portal area is closed from mid-October to early May; the road closes when snow conditions require. ⊠ *Whitney Portal Rd., west of Lone Pine* ⊕ *www.fs.usda.gov/attmain/inyo.*

Museum of Western Film History

MUSEUM | Hopalong Cassidy, Barbara Stanwyck, Roy Rogers, John Wayne—even Robert Downey Jr.—are among the celebrities who have starred in Westerns and other films shot in the Alabama Hills and surrounding dusty terrain. The marquee-embellished museum relates this Hollywood-in-the-desert tale via exhibits and a rollicking 20-minute documentary. ⊠ *701 S. Main St., U.S. 395* ☎ *760/876–9909* ⊕ *www.museumofwesternfilmhistory.org* ⌨ *$5* ⊘ *Closed Tues. and Wed.*

 Restaurants

Alabama Hills Café & Bakery

$ | **AMERICAN** | The extensive breakfast and lunch menus at this eatery just off the main drag include many vegetarian items. Sandwiches are served on homemade bread; choose from up to six varieties baked fresh daily, and get a homemade pie, cake, or loaf to go. **Known for:** house-roasted turkey and beef; huge portions; on-site bakery. ⓢ *Average main: $14* ⊠ *111 W. Post St., at S. Main St.* ☎ *760/876–4675* ⊕ *alabamahillscafe.com.*

The Grill

$$ | **AMERICAN** | **FAMILY** | Open for three meals a day, this small restaurant next to the Dow Villa Motel is a convenient place to stop for a break while driving along Highway 395. The extensive menu includes an array of options, from omelets and French toast for breakfast and sandwiches and burgers for lunch to grilled steaks and fish for dinner. **Known for:** hearty meals with large portions; friendly service; house-made desserts. ⓢ *Average main: $21* ⊠ *446 S. Main St.* ☎ *760/876–4240.*

Mt. Whitney Restaurant

$ | **AMERICAN** | A boisterous family-friendly restaurant with four flat-screen televisions, this place serves the best burgers in town. In addition to the usual beef variety, you can choose from ostrich, elk, venison, and buffalo burgers. **Known for:** burgers; John Wayne memorabilia; convenient fuel-up stop on Highway 395. ⑤ *Average main: $13* ✉ *227 S. Main St.* ☎ *760/876–5751.*

Seasons Restaurant

$$$ | **AMERICAN** | This inviting, country-style diner serves all kinds of traditional American fare. For a special treat, try the medallions of Cervena elk, smothered in port wine, dried cranberries, and toasted walnuts; finish with the Baileys Irish Cream cheesecake or the Grand Marnier crème brûlée for dessert. **Known for:** high-end dining in remote area; steaks and wild game; children's menu. ⑤ *Average main: $27* ✉ *206 S. Main St.* ☎ *760/876–8927* ⊕ *seasonslonepine.club* ⊘ *Closed Mon. Nov.–Mar. No lunch.*

 Hotels

Dow Villa Motel and Dow Hotel

$ | **HOTEL** | Built in 1923 to cater to the film industry, the Dow Villa Motel and the historic Dow Hotel sit in the center of Lone Pine. **Pros:** clean rooms; great mountain views; in-room whirlpool tubs in some motel rooms. **Cons:** some rooms in hotel share bathrooms; sinks in some rooms are in the bedroom, not the bath; on busy highway. ⑤ *Rooms from: $119* ✉ *310 S. Main St.* ☎ *760/876–5521, 800/824–9317* ⊕ *www.dowvillamotel. com* ⇋ *92 rooms* ⦿ *No meals.*

Independence

17 miles north of Lone Pine.

Named for a military outpost that was established near here in 1862, sleepy Independence has some wonderful historic buildings and is worth a stop for another reason: 6 miles south of the small downtown lies the Manzanar National Historic Site, one of 10 camps in the west where people of Japanese descent were confined during World War II.

GETTING HERE AND AROUND

Eastern Sierra Transit buses pass through town, but most travelers arrive by car on U.S. 395.

 Sights

Ancient Bristlecone Pine Forest

FOREST | **FAMILY** | About an hour's drive from Independence or Bishop you can view some of the oldest living trees on Earth, a few of which date back more than 40 centuries. The world's largest bristlecone pine can be found in Patriarch Grove, while the world's oldest known living tree is along Methusula Trail in Schulman Grove. Getting to Patriarch Grove is slow going along the narrow dirt road, especially for sedans with low clearance, but once there you'll find picnic tables, restrooms, and interpretive trails. ✉ *Schulman Grove Visitor Center, White Mountain Rd., Bishop* ✛ *From U.S. 395, turn east onto Hwy. 168 and follow signs for 23 miles* ⊕ *www.fs.usda.gov/ main/inyo/home* ▦ *$3.*

★ Manzanar National Historic Site

HISTORIC SITE | A reminder of an ugly episode in U.S. history, the former Manzanar War Relocation Center is where more than 11,000 Japanese-Americans were confined behind barbed-wire fences between 1942 and 1945. A visit here is both deeply moving and inspiring—the former because it's hard to comprehend that the United States was capable of confining its citizens in such a way, the latter because those imprisoned here showed great pluck and perseverance in making the best of a bad situation. Most of the buildings from the 1940s are gone, but two sentry posts, the auditorium, and numerous Japanese rock gardens remain. One of eight guard towers, two barracks, and a women's latrine have been reconstructed, and a mess hall has been restored. Interactive exhibits inside the barracks include audio and video clips from people who were incarcerated in Manzanar during WWII. You can drive the one-way road on a self-guided tour past various ruins to a small cemetery, where a monument stands. Signs mark where the barracks, a hospital, a school, and the fire station once stood. An outstanding 8,000-square-foot interpretive center has exhibits and documentary photographs and screens a short film. ⌧ *Independence ✛ West side of U.S. 395 between Independence and Lone Pine* ☎ *760/878–2194* ⊕ *www.nps.gov/manz* 💲 *Free.*

Mt. Whitney Fish Hatchery

FISH HATCHERY | FAMILY | A delightful place for a family picnic, the hatchery was one of California's first trout farms. The Tudor Revival–style structure, completed in 1917, is an architectural stunner, its walls nearly 3 feet thick with locally quarried granite. Fish production ceased in 2007 after a fire and subsequent mudslide, but dedicated volunteers staff the facility and raise trout for display purposes in a large pond out front. Bring change for the fish-food machines. ⌧ *1 Golden Trout Circle, 2 miles north of town* ☎ *760/279–1592* ⊕ *www.mtwhitneyfishhatchery.org* 💲 *Free (donations welcome)* ⊙ *Closed mid-Dec.–mid-Apr. Closed Tues. and Wed.*

Bishop

43 miles north of Independence.

One of the biggest towns along U.S. 395, bustling Bishop has views of the Sierra Nevada and the White and Inyo mountains. First settled by the Northern Paiute people, the area was named in 1861 for cattle rancher Samuel Bishop, who established a camp here. Paiute and Shoshone people reside on four reservations in the area. Bishop kicks off the summer season with its Mule Days Celebration. Held over Memorial Day weekend, the five-day event includes mule races, a rodeo, an arts-and-crafts show, and country-music concerts.

GETTING HERE AND AROUND

To fully enjoy the many surrounding attractions, you should get here by car. Arrive and depart via U.S. 395 or, from Nevada, U.S. 6. Local transit provides limited service to nearby tourist sites.

ESSENTIALS

VISITOR INFORMATION Bishop Chamber of Commerce. ⌧ *690 N. Main St., at Park St.* ☎ *760/873–8405* ⊕ *www.bishopvisitor.com.*

 Sights

Laws Railroad Museum

MUSEUM | FAMILY | The laid-back and wholly nostalgic railroad museum celebrates the Carson and Colorado Railroad Company, which set up a narrow-gauge railroad yard here in 1883. Among the exhibits are a self-propelled car from the Death Valley Railroad, a stamp mill from an area mine, and a full village of rescued buildings, including a post office, the original 1883 train depot, and a restored 1900 ranch house. Many of the buildings are full of "modern amenities" of days gone by. ⌧ *200 Silver Canyon Rd., off U.S. 6, 4.5 miles north of town* ☎ *760/873–5950* ⊕ *www.lawsmuseum.org* 💲 *$5 suggested donation.*

 Restaurants

Erick Schat's Bakkerÿ

$ | BAKERY | A bustling stop for motorists traveling to and from Mammoth Lakes, this shop is crammed with delicious pastries, cookies, rolls, and other baked goods. The biggest draw, though, is the sheepherder bread, a hand-shaped and stone hearth–baked sourdough that was introduced during the gold rush by immigrant Basque sheepherders in 1907. **Known for:** sheepherder bread and pastries; convenient place to stock up; hefty sandwiches. 💲 *Average main: $12* ⌧ *763 N. Main St., near Park St.* ☎ *760/873–7156* ⊕ *www.erickschatsbakery.com.*

Great Basin Bakery

$ | **AMERICAN** | Stop at this small, old-world-style community bakery for fresh and healthy salads, sandwiches (made all day), bagels, artisan breads, cookies, pies, and pastries. Savor your goodies indoors and listen to local banter (it's a favorite gathering spot), or take them along to eat at a picnic spot while adventuring nearby. **Known for:** sandwiches on fresh-baked, house-made bread; all items made and packaged by hand; stellar pies and other desserts. ⑤ *Average main: $14* ✉ *275 S. Main St.* ☎ *760/873–9828* ⊕ *greatbasinbakerybishop.com.*

 ## Hotels

Bishop Creekside Inn

$$ | **B&B/INN** | The nicest spot to stay in Bishop, this clean and comfortable mountain-style hotel is a good base from which to explore the town or go skiing and trout fishing nearby. **Pros:** nice pool; spacious and modern rooms; on-site restaurant. **Cons:** pets not allowed; hotel fronts busy road; basic breakfast. ⑤ *Rooms from: $180* ✉ *725 N. Main St.* ☎ *760/872–3044, 800/273–3550* ⊕ *www. bishopcreeksideinn.com* ⇌ *89 rooms* ¶⨂*l Free breakfast.*

 ## Activities

The Owens Valley is trout country; its glistening alpine lakes and streams are brimming with feisty rainbow, brown, brook, and golden trout. Good spots include Owens River, the Owens River gorge, and Pleasant Valley Reservoir. Although you can fish year-round here, some fishing is catch-and-release. Bishop is the site of fishing derbies throughout the year, including the Blake Jones Blind Bogey Trout Derby in March. Rock-climbing, mountain biking, and hiking are also popular Owens Valley outdoor activities.

FISHING

Reagan's Sporting Goods

FISHING | Stop at Reagan's to pick up bait, tackle, and fishing licenses and to find out where the fish are biting. They can also recommend guides. ✉ *963 N. Main St.* ☎ *760/872–3000* ⊕ *www.facebook. com/ReaganSportingGoods.*

HORSE PACKING

Rock Creek Pack Station

HORSEBACK RIDING | The Rock Creek Pack Station outfit runs 3- to 10-day horse-packing trips in the High Sierra, including Mt. Whitney, Yosemite National Park, and other parts of the John Muir Wilderness. One expedition tracks wild mustangs through Inyo National Forest; another is an old-fashioned horse drive between the Owens Valley and the High Sierra. Shorter day rides are also available. Season is mid-June through September. ✉ *Bishop* ☎ *760/872–8331* ⊕ *www.rockcreekpackstation.com.*

TOURS

Sierra Mountain Center

TOUR—SPORTS | The guided experiences Sierra Mountain offers include hiking, skiing, snowshoeing, rock-climbing, and mountain-biking trips for all levels of expertise. ✉ *200 S. Main St.* ☎ *760/873–8526* ⊕ *www.sierramountaincenter.com* ▩ *From $150.*

Sierra Mountain Guides

TOUR—SPORTS | Join expert guides on custom and scheduled alpine adventures, from backcountry skiing and mountaineering to backpacking and mountain running. Programs range from half-day forays to treks that last several weeks. ✉ *312 N. Main St.* ☎ *760/648–1122* ⊕ *www.sierramtnguides.com* ▩ *From $170.*

Twin Lakes, in the Mammoth Lakes region, is a great place to unwind.

Mammoth Lakes

43 miles northwest of Bishop; 30 miles south of the eastern edge of Yosemite National Park.

International real-estate developers joined forces with Mammoth Mountain Ski Area to transform the once sleepy town of Mammoth Lakes (elevation 7,800 feet) into an upscale ski destination. Relatively sophisticated dining and lodging options can be found at the Village at Mammoth complex, and multimillion-dollar renovations to tired motels and restaurants have revived the "downtown" area of Old Mammoth Road. Also here is the hoppin' Mammoth Rock 'n' Bowl, a two-story activity, dining, and entertainment complex. Winter is high season at Mammoth; in summer, the room rates drop.

GETTING HERE AND AROUND

The best way to get to Mammoth Lakes is by car. The town is about 2 miles west of U.S. 395 on Highway 203, signed as Main Street in Mammoth Lakes and Minaret Road west of town. In summer and early fall (until the first big snow), you can drive to Mammoth Lakes east through Yosemite National Park on scenic Tioga Pass Road. Signed as Highway 120 outside the park, this road connects to U.S. 395 north of Mammoth. In summer, YARTS provides once-a-day public transit service between Mammoth Lakes and Yosemite Valley. The shuttle buses of Eastern Sierra Transit Authority serve Mammoth Lakes and nearby tourist sites.

ESSENTIALS

HOTEL CONTACTS Mammoth Reservations. ☎ 800/223–3032 ⊕ *www.mammothreservations.com.*

VISITOR INFORMATION Mammoth Lakes Visitor Center. ✉ *Welcome Center, 2510 Main St., near Sawmill Cutoff Rd.* ☎ *760/934–2712, 888/466–2666* ⊕ *www.visitmammoth.com.*

👁 Sights

★ Devils Postpile National Monument

NATURE SITE | Volcanic and glacial forces sculpted this formation of smooth, vertical basalt columns. For a bird's-eye view, take the short, steep trail to the top of a 60-foot cliff. To see the monument's second scenic wonder, **Rainbow Falls,** hike 2 miles past Devils Postpile. A branch of the San Joaquin River plunges more than 100 feet over a lava ledge here. When the water hits the pool below, sunlight turns the resulting mist into a spray of color. From mid-June to early September, day-use visitors must ride the shuttle bus from the Mammoth Mountain Ski Area to the monument. ⊠ *Mammoth Lakes ✛ 13 miles southwest of Mammoth Lakes off Minaret Rd. (Hwy. 203)* ☎ *760/934–2289, 760/872–1901 shuttle* ⊕ *www.nps.gov/ depo* ⊠ *$10 per vehicle (allowed when the shuttle isn't running, usually early Sept.–mid-Oct.), $15 per person shuttle.*

Hot Creek Geological Site

NATURE SITE | Forged by an ancient volcanic eruption, the geological site is a landscape of boiling hot springs, fumaroles, and occasional geysers. Swimming is prohibited—the water can go from warm to boiling in a short time—but you can look down from the parking area into the canyon to view the steaming volcanic features, a very cool sight indeed. You can also hike the foot path along the creek shores. Fly-fishing for trout is popular upstream from the springs. ⊠ *Hot Creek Hatchery Rd., off U.S. 395 (airport exit), about 10 miles southeast of Mammoth Lakes* ☎ *760/873–2400* ⊕ *www. fs.usda.gov/inyo* ⊠ *Free.*

Hot Creek Trout Hatchery

FISH HATCHERY | FAMILY | This outdoor fish hatchery has the breeding ponds for many of the fish—typically from 3 to 5 million annually—with which the state stocks Eastern Sierra lakes and rivers. In recent years budget cuts have reduced these numbers, but locals have formed foundations to keep the hatchery going. For more details, take the worthwhile self-guided tour. ■TIP➔ **Kids enjoy feeding the fish here.** ⊠ *121 Hot Creek Hatchery Rd., off U.S. 395 (airport exit), about 10 miles southeast of Mammoth Lakes* ☎ *760/934–2664* ⊕ *wildlife.ca.gov/ Fishing/Hatcheries/Hot-Creek* ⊠ *Free.*

June Lake Loop

SCENIC DRIVE | Heading south, U.S. 395 intersects the June Lake Loop. This gorgeous 17-mile drive follows an old glacial canyon past Grant, June, Gull, and Silver lakes before reconnecting with U.S. 395 on its way to Mammoth Lakes. ■TIP➔ **The loop is especially colorful in fall.** ⊠ *Hwy. 158 W, Lee Vining.*

★ Mammoth Lakes Basin

BODY OF WATER | Mammoth's seven main lakes are popular for fishing and boating in summer, and a network of multiuse paths connects them to the North Village. First comes Twin Lakes, at the far end of which is Twin Falls, where water cascades 300 feet over a shelf of volcanic rock. Also popular are Lake Mary, the largest lake in the basin; Lake Mamie; and Lake George. ■TIP➔ **Horseshoe Lake is the only lake in which you can swim.** ⊠ *Lake Mary Rd., off Hwy. 203, southwest of town.*

Mammoth Rock 'n' Bowl

RESTAURANT—SIGHT | FAMILY | A sprawling complex with sweeping views of the Sherwin Mountains, Mammoth Rock 'n' Bowl supplies one-stop recreation, entertainment, and dining. Downstairs are 12 bowling lanes, lounge areas, Ping-Pong and foosball tables, dartboards, and a casual bar-restaurant ($$) serving burgers, pizzas, and small plates. The upstairs floor has three golf simulators, a pro shop, and Mammoth Rock Brasserie ($$$), an upscale dining room and lounge. ■TIP➔ **If the weather's nice, sit on the outdoor patio or the upstairs deck and enjoy the unobstructed vistas.** ⊠ *3029 Chateau Rd., off Old Mammoth Rd.*

☎ 760/934–4200 ⊕ mammothrocknbowl.
com 🍴 Bowling: from $20.

Minaret Vista
NATURE SITE | The glacier-carved sawtooth
spires of the Minarets, the remains of an
ancient lava flow, are best viewed from
the Minaret Vista. Pull off the road, park
your car in the visitors' viewing area, and
walk along the path, which has interpretive signs explaining the spectacular
peaks, ridges, and valleys beyond. ✉ Off
Hwy. 203, 1¼ mile west of Mammoth
Mountain Ski Area.

★ Panorama Gondola
MOUNTAIN—SIGHT | FAMILY | Even if
you don't ski, ride the gondola to see
Mammoth Mountain, the aptly named
dormant volcano that gives Mammoth
Lakes its name. Gondolas serve skiers
in winter and mountain bikers and
sightseers in summer. The high-speed,
eight-passenger gondolas whisk you
from the chalet to the summit, where
you can learn about the area's volcanic
history in the interpretive center, have
lunch in the café, and take in top-of-the-
world views. Standing high above the
tree line, you can look west 150 miles
across the state to the Coastal Range; to
the east are the highest peaks of Nevada
and the Great Basin beyond. You won't
find a better view of the Sierra High
Country without climbing. ⚠ The air is
thin at the 11,053-foot summit; carry water,
and don't overexert yourself. ✉ Boarding area at Main Lodge, off Minaret
Rd. (Hwy. 203), west of village center
☎ 760/934–0745, 800/626–6684 ⊕ www.
mammothmountain.com 🍴 From $40.

Village at Mammoth
TOWN | This huge complex of shops,
restaurants, and luxury accommodations
is the town's tourist center, and the
venue for many special events—check
the website for the weekly schedule.
The complex is also the transfer hub for
the free public transit system, with fixed
routes throughout the Mammoth Lakes
area. The free village gondola starts here
and travels up the mountain to Canyon
Lodge and back. ■TIP→ Unless you're
staying in the village and have access to
the on-site lots, parking can be very difficult
here. ✉ 100 Canyon Blvd. ⊕ villageat-
mammoth.com.

🍴 Restaurants

Black Velvet
$ | CAFÉ | Start your day the way scores of
locals do—with a stop at the slick Black
Velvet espresso bar for Belgian waffles,
baked treats, and coffee drinks made
from small batches of beans roasted
on-site. Then return in the afternoon or
evening to hang out with friends in the
upstairs wine bar (open 4 to 9). Known
for: small-batch coffee roasting; small-
lot wines by the glass; Belgian waffles.
⑤ Average main: $16 ✉ 3343 Main St.,
Suite F ⊕ www.blackvelvetcoffee.com.

Bleu Handcrafted Foods
$$ | MODERN AMERICAN | Handcrafted
artisanal cheeses and meats, wine
and beer tastings, bread baked on-site,
and specialty meats and seafood draw
patrons to Bleu, a combination market,
restaurant (lunch and dinner), and wine
bar. Bleu also cooks up savory pub fare
at The Eatery at Mammoth Brewing
Company. Known for: organic, locally
sourced ingredients; bar and lounge with
cocktails and wine or craft beer tast-
ings; on-site deli, butchery, bakery, and
market. ⑤ Average main: $20 ✉ 106 Old
Mammoth Rd. ☎ 760/914-2530 ⊕ www.
bleufoods.com.

Burgers
$$ | AMERICAN | Don't even think about
coming to this bustling restaurant
unless you're hungry. Burgers is known,
appropriately enough, for its burgers
and sandwiches, and everything comes
in mountainous portions. Known for:
great service; hefty portions; burgers
and seasoned fries. ⑤ Average main:
$17 ✉ 6118 Minaret Rd., across from
the Village ☎ 760/934–6622 ⊕ www.

burgersrestaurant.com ⊙ *Closed 2 wks in May and 4–6 wks in Oct. and Nov.*

Mammoth Brewing Company

$$ | AMERICAN | Steps from the Village gondola and main bus transfer hub, this brewery lures hungry patrons with about a dozen craft beers on tap, tasty grub from the on-site restaurant, tasting flights, a contemporary vibe at two spacious bar areas, and a beer garden. The dining menu changes constantly, but reflects a locals' twist on pub food, for example, wild game sausages, peach-and-goat-cheese flatbread, or house-made sweet-potato tots. **Known for:** craft beer made on-site; upscale pub food; popular après-ski hangout. $ *Average main: $17* ⊠ *18 Lake Mary Rd.* ⊹ *At intersection of Main St. and Minaret Rd.* ☎ *760/934–7141* ⊕ *mammothbrewingco.com.*

The Mogul

$$$ | STEAKHOUSE | FAMILY | Come here for straightforward steaks—top sirloin, New York, filet mignon, and T-bone. The only catch is that the waiters cook them, and the results vary depending on their skill level; but generally things go well, and kids love the experience. **Known for:** traditional alpine atmosphere; servers custom-grill your order; all-you-can-eat salad bar. $ *Average main: $30* ⊠ *1528 Tavern Rd., off Old Mammoth Rd.* ☎ *760/934–3039* ⊕ *www.themogul.com* ⊙ *No lunch.*

Petra's Bistro & Wine Bar

$$$ | AMERICAN | The ambience at Petra's—quiet, dark, and warm (there's a great fireplace)—complements its seductive meat and seafood entrées and smart selection of wines from California and around the world. With its pub grub, whiskies, and craft beers and ales, the downstairs Clocktower Cellar bar provides a lively, if sometimes rowdy, alternative. **Known for:** romantic atmosphere; top-notch service; lively downstairs bar. $ *Average main: $30* ⊠ *Alpenhof Lodge, 6080 Minaret Rd.* ☎ *760/934–3500* ⊕ *www.petrasbistro.com* ⊙ *Closed Mon. No lunch.*

★ Restaurant at Convict Lake

$$$ | AMERICAN | The lake is one of the most spectacular spots in the Eastern Sierra, and the food here lives up to the view. The woodsy room has a vaulted knotty-pine ceiling and a copper-chimney fireplace; natural light abounds in the daytime, but if it's summer, opt for a table outdoors under the white-barked aspens. **Known for:** beef Wellington, rack of lamb, and pan-seared local trout; exceptional service; extensive wine list with reasonably priced European and California bottlings. $ *Average main: $36* ⊠ *Convict Lake Rd. off U.S. 395, 4 miles south of Mammoth Lakes* ☎ *760/934–3800* ⊕ *www.convictlake.com* ⊙ *No lunch early Sept.–mid-June.*

Toomey's

$$ | MODERN AMERICAN | FAMILY | A passionate baseball fan, chef Matt Toomey designed this casual space near the Village Gondola to resemble a dugout, and decorated it with baseball memorabilia. Fill up on buffalo meat loaf, seafood jambalaya, or a New Zealand elk rack chop after an outdoor adventure. **Known for:** lobster taquitos and fish tacos; curbside take-out delivery to your car; homemade organic and gluten-free desserts. $ *Average main: $20* ⊠ *6085 Minaret Rd., at the Village* ☎ *760/924–4408* ⊕ *toomeysmammoth.com.*

★ The Warming Hut

$$ | AMERICAN | FAMILY | Warm up by a crackling fire in the stone fireplace while fueling up on healthy, made-from-scratch breakfast, lunch, and dinner dishes at this ski-lodge-style eatery. The flexible menu allows for lots of choice, including a DIY breakfast with more than 20 mix-and-match items, five types of hash, keto selections, grab-and-go sandwiches, salads, burgers, and soups. **Known for:** nearly everything made in-house, including ketchup; build-your-own pancake stack (batters, mix-ins, toppings); family-owned and operated. $ *Average main: $20* ⊠ *343*

Old Mammoth Rd. ☎ *760/965–0549*
⊕ *www.thewarminghutmammoth.com.*

 Hotels

Alpenhof Lodge

$$ | HOTEL | Across from the Village at
Mammoth, this mom-and-pop motel
(with rooms and a couple of cabins)
offers basic comforts and a few niceties
such as attractive pine furniture. **Pros:**
convenient for skiers; reasonable rates;
excellent dinner at on-site restaurant,
Petra's. **Cons:** some bathrooms are
small; rooms above pub can be noisy; no
elevator. ⑤ *Rooms from: $159* ⊠ *6080
Minaret Rd., Box 1157* ☎ *760/934–6330,
800/828–0371* ⊕ *www.alpenhof-lodge.
com* ⟿ *57 units* ⦿ *Free breakfast.*

★ Convict Lake Resort

$$ | RESORT | The cabins at this resort a
10-minute drive south from Mammoth
Lakes range from rustic to modern and
come with fully equipped kitchens,
including coffeemakers and premium
coffee. **Pros:** great views; tranquil atmosphere; wildlife galore. **Cons:** the smallest
quarters feel cramped; spotty Wi-Fi
and cell service; too remote for some.
⑤ *Rooms from: $219* ⊠ *Convict Rd.,
2 miles off U.S. 395* ☎ *760/934–3800*
⊕ *www.convictlake.com* ⟿ *31 units*
⦿ *No meals.*

★ Double Eagle Resort and Spa

$$ | RESORT | Lofty pines tower over this
June Lake Loop spa retreat with rooms
in four buildings overlooking a pond, as
well as a three-bedroom house and knotty-pine two-bedroom cabins—all with fully equipped kitchens. **Pros:** pretty setting;
spectacular indoor pool; 1½ miles from
June Mountain Ski Area. **Cons:** expensive;
remote; no in-room a/c. ⑤ *Rooms from:
$249* ⊠ *5587 Hwy. 158, Box 736, June
Lake* ☎ *760/648–7004* ⊕ *www.doubleea-
gle.com* ⟿ *34 units* ⦿ *No meals.*

Holiday Haus

$$ | HOTEL | A short walk from the Village,
Holiday Haus is a collection of reasonably
priced, contemporary, mountain-activi-
ty-theme rooms and suites, many with
full kitchens, as well as a separate hos-
tel-style building with private and bunk
rooms (rates start at $42 and include
bedding and linens). **Pros:** free parking
and Wi-Fi; good option for groups and
families; walk to the Village. **Cons:** showers, no tubs in most rooms; no 24-hour
desk; basic breakfast. ⑤ *Rooms from:
$159* ⊠ *3905 Main St.* ☎ *760/934–2414*
⊕ *holidayhausmotelandhostel.com* ⟿ *51
units* ⦿ *No meals.*

Juniper Springs Resort

$$ | RESORT | Tops for slope-side comfort,
these condominium-style units have full
kitchens and ski-in ski-out access to the
mountain. **Pros:** bargain during summer;
direct access to the slopes in winter;
free shuttle to town in winter. **Cons:** no
nightlife within walking distance; no
air-conditioning; property needs updating.
⑤ *Rooms from: $199* ⊠ *4000 Meridian
Blvd.* ☎ *760/924–1102, 800/626–6684*
⊕ *www.mammothmountain.com* ⟿ *184
units* ⦿ *No meals.*

Mammoth Mountain Inn

$$ | RESORT | If you want to be within
walking distance of the Mammoth Mountain Main Lodge, this is the place. **Pros:**
great location; big rooms; a traditional
place to stay. **Cons:** can be crowded in ski
season; needs updating; not in the heart
of town. ⑤ *Rooms from: $199* ⊠ *1 Mina-
ret Rd.* ☎ *760/934–2581, 800/626–6684*
⊕ *www.mammothmountain.com* ⟿ *266
units* ⦿ *No meals.*

Sierra Nevada Resort & Spa

$$ | RESORT | This full-service resort has
it all: Old Mammoth rustic elegance,
three restaurants, four bars, a spa facility,
on-site ski and snowboard rentals, a
seasonal pool and Jacuzzi, seasonal
miniature golf, and room and suite
options in three buildings. **Pros:** kids'

club on weekends from 4 to 9; walk to restaurants on property or downtown; complimentary shuttle service. **Cons:** must drive or ride a bus or shuttle to the slopes; thin walls in older rooms; resort fee. ⑤ *Rooms from: $199* ⊠ *164 Old Mammoth Rd.* ☎ *760/934–2515, 800/824–5132* ⊕ *thesierranevadaresort. com* ⌁ *149 units* ⑩ *No meals.*

★ Tamarack Lodge Resort & Lakefront Restaurant

$$ | **RESORT** | On the edge of the John Muir Wilderness Area, where cross-country ski trails lace the woods, this 1924 lodge looks like something out of a snow globe. **Pros:** rustic; eco-sensitive; many nearby outdoor activities. **Cons:** high price tag; shared bathrooms for some main lodge rooms; spartan furnishings in lodge rooms. ⑤ *Rooms from: $239* ⊠ *Lake Mary Rd., off Hwy. 203* ☎ *760/934–2442, 800/626–6684* ⊕ *www.tamaracklodge. com* ⌁ *46 units* ⑩ *No meals.*

The Village Lodge

$$ | **RESORT** | With their exposed timbers and peaked roofs, these four-story condo buildings at the epicenter of Mammoth's dining and nightlife scene pay homage to Alpine style. **Pros:** central location; big rooms; good restaurants nearby. **Cons:** pricey; can be noisy outside; somewhat sterile decor. ⑤ *Rooms from: $239* ⊠ *1111 Forest Trail* ☎ *760/934–1982, 800/626–6684* ⊕ *www.mammothmountain.com* ⌁ *277 units* ⑩ *No meals.*

★ Westin Monache Resort

$$$$ | **RESORT** | On a hill just steps from the Village at Mammoth, the Westin provides full-service comfort and amenities close to restaurants, entertainment, and free public transportation. **Pros:** full bar, pool, 24-fitness center; prime location; free gondola to the slopes is across the street. **Cons:** long, steep stairway down to village; added resort fee; large property with confusing layout. ⑤ *Rooms from: $359* ⊠ *50 Hillside Dr.* ☎ *760/934–0400, 760/934–4686* ⊕ *www.marriott.com/ mmhwi* ⌁ *230 rooms* ⑩ *No meals.*

NIGHTLIFE

The Village at Mammoth hosts events and has several rockin' bars and clubs.

Clocktower Cellar

BARS/PUBS | Nearly 30 beers on tap and more than 50 by the bottle—plus 160 whiskeys and an extensive, Bavarian-themed pub menu ensure plenty of variety at this lively gathering spot across from the Village Gondola. ⊠ *6080 Minaret Rd.* ☎ *760/934–2725* ⊕ *www.clocktowercellar.com.*

Lakanuki

BARS/PUBS | Sip mai tais at the tiki bar at Lakanuki, which is in the Village near the gondola. ⊠ *6201 Minaret Rd.* ☎ *760/934–7447* ⊕ *lakanuki.net.*

Rafters

BARS/PUBS | Most nights, the upscale lounge in Rafter's Restaurant at the Sierra Nevada Resort has live entertainment. ⊠ *202 Old Mammoth Rd.* ☎ *760/934–2515* ⊕ *raftersmammoth.com.*

Activities

BIKING

★ Mammoth Bike Park

BICYCLING | The park opens when the snow melts, usually by July, and has 80 miles of single-track trails—from mellow to super-challenging. Chairlifts and shuttles provide trail access, and rentals are available. ⊠ *Mammoth Mountain Ski Area* ☎ *760/934–0677, 800/626-6684* ⊕ *www. mammothmountain.com* ⌁ *$55 day pass.*

CLIMBING

Via Ferrata

CLIMBING/MOUNTAINEERING | In Europe, a Via Ferrata is a protected climbing network that allows people to experience the thrills of rock climbing and mountaineering without as much risk. Mammoth's version has six different routes of varying ability, with steel cables, iron rungs, and a suspended bridge, all permanently affixed to the rock. The fully guided tour begins with a gondola ride up the mountain. Clip yourself into a cable and climb

Camping in the Eastern Sierra

Camping in the Sierra Nevada means gazing up at awe-inspiring constellations and awakening to the sights of nearby meadows and streams and the unforgettable landscape of giant granite. More than a hundred campgrounds, from remote, tents-only areas to full-service facilities with RV hookups close to the main attractions, operate in the Eastern Sierra. Be aware that Yosemite National Park's most accessible campgrounds can be jam-packed and claustrophobic in the summer. Luckily, there are many options to the east, including calm and beautiful sites such as Lake Mary Campground in the Mammoth Lakes area. The following campsites are recommended. Reserve sites at ⊕ *www.recreation.gov.*

Convict Lake Campground. A 10-minute drive south of Mammoth, this campground near the Convict Lake Resort is run by the U.S. Forest Service. ⊠ *Convict Lake Rd., 2 miles off U.S. 395* ☎ 760/924 5500 ⌁ *88 campsites.*

Lake Mary Campground. There are few sites as beautiful as this lakeside campground at 8,900 feet, open from June to September. ⊠ *Lake Mary Loop Dr., off Hwy. 203* ☎ 760/924–5500 ▭ *No credit cards* ⌁ *48 sites (tent or RV)* ⏦ *No meals.*

securely to sweeping views of the Sierra Nevada range. If time and group ability allow, you can follow multiple routes during a session. No climbing experience is required. ⊠ *Mammoth Mountain, 10001 Minaret Rd.* ☎ 800/626–6684 ⊕ *www. mammothmountain.com* ⌁ *From $199.*

FISHING

The main fishing season runs from the last Saturday in April until November 15; there are opportunities for catch-and-release fishing in winter. Crowley Lake is the top trout-fishing spot in the area; Convict Lake, June Lake, and the lakes of the Mammoth Basin are other prime spots. One of the best trout rivers is the super-scenic Upper Owens River, near the east side of Crowley Lake. Hot Creek, a designated Wild Trout Stream, is renowned for fly-fishing (catch-and-release only).

Kittredge Sports

FISHING | This outfit rents rods and reels and conducts guided trips. ⊠ *3218 Main St., at Forest Trail* ☎ 760/934–7566 ⊕ *kittredgesports.com.*

Sierra Drifters Guide Service

FISHING | To maximize your time on the water, get tips from local anglers, or better yet, book a guided fishing trip, contact Sierra Drifters. ⊠ *Mammoth Lakes* ☎ 760/935–4250 ⊕ *www.sierradrifters. com.*

HIKING

Hiking in Mammoth is stellar, especially along the trails that wind through alpine scenery around the Lakes Basin. Carry lots of water; and remember, the air is thin at 8,000-plus feet.

You can pick up trail map and permits for backpacking in wilderness areas at the Mammoth Lakes Visitor Center just east of town. For descriptions of more than 300 miles of trails—as well as maps and a wealth of information on recreation in Mammoth Lakes and the Inyo National Forest in all seasons—visit the Mammoth Lakes Trail System website (⊕ *www.mammothtrails.org*).

Convict Lake Loop

HIKING/WALKING | This 2.8-mile trail loops gently around deep blue Convict Lake, a popular site for anglers. Feast your eyes on stunning views of tall peaks, glistening water, and aspen and cottonwood groves while you hike. *Easy.* ⊠ *Trailhead: At Convict Lake, 9 miles south of Mammoth Lakes.*

Duck Lake

HIKING/WALKING | This popular and busy trail (11 miles round-trip) heads up Coldwater Canyon along Mammoth Creek, past a series of spectacular lakes and wildflower meadows over 10,797-foot Duck Pass to dramatic Duck Lake, which eventually links up with the John Muir Trail. *Difficult.* ⊠ *Trailhead: Coldwater Campground.*

Emerald Lake and Sky Meadows

HIKING/WALKING | The first part of this trail travels through shady pine forest along Coldwater Creek to bright-green Emerald Lake (1.8 miles round-trip). Extend the hike by climbing up a trail along an inlet stream up to Gentian Meadow and Sky Meadows (4 miles round-trip), especially beautiful in July and August when various alpine wildflowers, fed by snowmelt, are at their peak splendor. *Moderate.* ⊠ *Trailhead: Coldwater Campground.*

Minaret Falls

HIKING/WALKING | **FAMILY** | Hike along portions of both the Pacific Crest and John Muir trails on this scenic trail (3 miles round-trip), which leads to Devil's Postpile, Minaret Falls, and natural volcanic springs. This is a good family hike, especially in late summer when the water has receded a bit and kids can climb boulders and splash around. *Easy.* ⊠ *Trailhead: At Devil's Postpile National Monument.*

HORSEBACK RIDING

Stables around Mammoth are typically open from June through September.

Mammoth Lakes Pack Outfit

HORSEBACK RIDING | This company runs day and overnight horseback and mule trips and will shuttle you to the high country. ⊠ *Lake Mary Rd., between Twin Lakes and Lake Mary* ☎ *760/934–2434* ⊕ *www.mammothpack.com.*

McGee Creek Pack Station

HORSEBACK RIDING | These folks customize pack trips or will shuttle you to camp alone. ⊠ *2990 McGee Creek Rd., Crowley Lake* ☎ *760/935–4324 summer, 760/874–8314 winter* ⊕ *www.mcgeecreekpackstation.com.*

SKIING

In winter, call the Snow Report (☎ *760/934–7669 or 888/766–9778*) for information about Mammoth weather conditions.

June Mountain Ski Area

SKIING/SNOWBOARDING | **FAMILY** | Snowboarders especially dig June Mountain, a compact, low-key resort north of Mammoth Mountain. Several beginner-to-intermediate terrain areas—including the Surprise Fun Zone and Buckey's Playground—are for both skiers and boarders. There's rarely a line for the lifts here: if you must ski on a weekend and want to avoid the crowds, this is the place to come, and in a storm it's better protected from wind and blowing snow than Mammoth is. (If it starts to storm, you can use your Mammoth ticket at June.) The services include a rental-and-repair shop, a ski school, and a sports shop. There's food, but the options are better at Mammoth. ■**TIP**➔ **Kids 12 and under ski and ride free.** ⊠ *3819 Hwy. 158/June Lake Loop, off U.S. 395, 22 miles northwest of Mammoth, June Lake* ☎ *760/648–7733, 888/586–3686* ⊕ *www.junemountain.com* ☜ *From $120* ⚲ *35 trails on 1,400 acres, rated 35% beginner, 45% intermediate, 20% advanced. Longest run 2 miles, base 7,545 feet, summit 10,190 feet. Lifts: 7.*

★ Mammoth Mountain Ski Area

SKIING/SNOWBOARDING | One of the West's largest and best ski areas, Mammoth has more than 3,500 acres of skiable terrain and a 3,100-foot vertical drop. The

Why Is There So Much Snow?

The Sierra Nevada receives some of the deepest snow anywhere in North America. In winter, houses literally get buried, and homeowners have to build tunnels to their front doors (though many install enclosed wooden walkways). In the high country, it's not uncommon for a single big storm to bring 10 feet of snow and for 30 feet of snow to accumulate at the height of the season. In the enormous bowls of Mammoth Mountain, you might ski past a tiny pine that looks like a miniature Christmas tree—until you remember that more than 30 feet of tree is under the snow.

To understand the weather, you have to understand the terrain. The Sierra Nevada are marked by a gentle western rise from sea level to the Sierra crest, which tops out at a whopping 14,494 feet at Sequoia National Park's Mt. Whitney, the highest point in the continental United States. On the eastern side of the crest, at the escarpment, the mountains drop sharply—as much as 5,000 feet—giving way to the Great Basin and the high-mountain deserts of Nevada and Utah.

When winter storms blow in off the Pacific, carrying vast stores of water with them, they race across the relatively flat, 100-mile-wide Central Valley. As they ascend the wall of mountains, though, the decrease in temperature and the increase in pressure on the clouds force them to release their water. Between October and April, that means snow—lots of it. Storms can get hung up on the peaks for days, dumping foot after foot of the stuff. By the time they finally cross over the range and into the Great Basin, there isn't much moisture left for the lower elevations on the eastern side. This is why, if you cross the Sierra eastward on your way to U.S. 395, you'll notice that brightly colored wildflowers and forest-green trees give way to pale-green sagebrush and brown sand as you drop out of the mountains.

The coastal cities and farmlands of the rest of the state depend heavily on the water from the Sierra snowpack. Most of the spring and summer runoff from the melting snows is caught in reservoirs in the foothills and routed to farmlands and cities throughout the state via a complex system of levees and aqueducts, which you'll no doubt see in the foothills and Central Valley, to the west of the range. But much of the water remains in the mountains, forming lakes, most notably giant Lake Tahoe to the north, Mono Lake to the east, and the thousands of little lakes along the Sierra Crest. The lakes are an essential part of the ecosystem, providing water for birds, fish, and plant life.

views from the 11,053-foot summit are some of the most stunning in the Sierra. Below, you'll find a 6½-mile-wide swath of groomed boulevards and canyons, as well as pockets of tree-skiing and a dozen vast bowls. Snowboarders are everywhere on the slopes; there are seven outstanding freestyle terrain parks of varying difficulty, with jumps, rails, tabletops, and giant super pipes—this is the location of several international snowboarding competitions, and, in summer, mountain-bike meets. Mammoth's season begins in November and often lingers into July. Lessons and equipment are available, and there's a children's ski and snowboard school. Mammoth runs free shuttle-bus routes around town and to the ski area, and the Village Gondola runs from the Village complex to Canyon Lodge. However, only overnight guests are allowed to park at the Village for more than a few hours. **Facilities:** 155 trails; 3,500 acres; 3,100-foot vertical drop; 25 lifts. ⊠ *Minaret Rd., west of Mammoth Lakes, Rte. 203, off U.S. 395* ☏ *760/934–2571, 800/626–6684, 760/934–0687 shuttle* ⊕ *www.mammothmountain.com* ☞ *From $109.*

Tamarack Cross Country Ski Center

SKIING/SNOWBOARDING | Trails at the center, adjacent to Tamarack Lodge, meander around several lakes. Rentals are available. ⊠ *Lake Mary Rd., off Hwy. 203* ☏ *760/934–5293, 760/934–2442* ⊕ *tamaracklodge.com* ☞ *$68 all-inclusive day rate.*

SKI RENTALS
★ Black Tie Ski Rentals

SKIING/SNOWBOARDING | Skiers and snowboarders love this rental outfit whose staffers will deliver and custom-fit equipment for free. They also offer slope-side assistance. ⊠ *501 Old Mammoth Rd.* ☏ *760/934–7009* ⊕ *mammoth.blacktieskis.com.*

Footloose

SKIING/SNOWBOARDING | When the U.S. Ski Team visits Mammoth and needs boot adjustments, everyone heads to Footloose, the best place in town—and possibly all California—for ski-boot rentals and sales, as well as custom insoles. ⊠ *3043 Main St., at Mammoth Rd.* ☏ *760/934–2400* ⊕ *www.footloosesports.com.*

Kittredge Sports

SKIING/SNOWBOARDING | Advanced skiers should consider this outfit, which has been around since the 1960s. ⊠ *3218 Main St.* ☏ *760/934–7566* ⊕ *kittredgesports.com.*

Woolly's Tube Park & Snow Play

SNOW SPORTS | FAMILY | Ride a lift to the top of the hill and whoosh down in a high-speed snow tube as often as you like during a 1¼-hour session. The park has six lanes, a heated deck, and snack shop. Discounts available for a second session if you're not ready to stop riding. Little ones can hang out in the snow play area with sleds and saucers. ⊠ *9000 Minaret Rd.* ☏ *800/626–6684 reservations, 760/934–7533 direct line* ⊕ *www.mammothmountain.com* ☞ *From $45, play area $25.*

SNOWMOBILING
Mammoth Snowmobile Adventures

SNOW SPORTS | Mammoth Snowmobile Adventures conducts guided tours along wooded trails. ⊠ *Mammoth Mountain Main Lodge* ☏ *760/934–9645, 800/626–6684* ⊕ *www.mammothmountain.com* ☞ *From $160.*

ZIP LINING
Mammoth Mega Zip

ZIP LINING | Mammoth Mountain's zipline tour has the tallest vertical drop (2,100 feet) in North America. Ride the Panoramic Gondola up to the summit of Mammoth Mountain, then descend side by side on parallel cables that run more than a mile back down to the base, at speeds of up to 60 mph (minimum weight 75 lbs). ⊠ *Mammoth Adventure Center, 10001 Minaret Rd.* ☏ *800/626–6684* ⊕ *www.mammothmountain.com.*

Chapter 8

SACRAMENTO AND THE GOLD COUNTRY

8

Updated by
Daniel Mangin

● Sights	⑪ Restaurants	🏨 Hotels	● Shopping	♈ Nightlife
★★★★☆	★★★★☆	★★★★☆	★★★☆☆	★★★☆☆

WELCOME TO SACRAMENTO AND THE GOLD COUNTRY

TOP REASONS TO GO

★ **Gold rush:** Marshall Gold Discovery State Park is where it all started—it's a must-see—but there are historic and modern gems all along California Highway 49 from Nevada City to Jamestown.

★ **State capital:** Easygoing Sacramento offers sights like the Capitol and historic Old Sacramento.

★ **Bon appétit:** Sacramento has emerged as a foodie destination, but its celebrations of food, drink, and culture date back to the gold-rush parade of immigrants.

★ **Wine tasting:** With bucolic scenery and friendly tasting rooms, El Dorado County and the Shenandoah Valley are winning acclaim for their diverse offerings.

★ **Rivers, sequoias, and caverns:** Natural beauty here is rich (stream beds are still lined with gold), high (sequoias in Calaveras Big Trees State Park), and deep (the main chamber at Moaning Caverns could hold the Statue of Liberty).

The Gold Country is a sizable rural destination popular with those seeking a reasonably priced escape from Southern California and the Bay Area. Sacramento, Davis, Winters, and Lodi are in enormous valleys just west of the Sierra Nevada range. Foothills communities along Highway 49 tell the gold-rush story, support the nascent wine-growing scene, or serve as gateways to Yosemite or Lake Tahoe. A few function as all three.

1 Sacramento. The capital also serves as a regional hub.

2 Davis. Agriculture meets academics in this university town.

3 Winters. A foodie haven perfect for a day trip.

4 Lodi. "Zinfandel Capital of the World" excels at many other wines.

5 Nevada City. "Queen of the Northern Mines" is a real beauty.

6 Grass Valley. Here, the Empire Mine thrived for years.

7 Auburn. Old Town charms with steep hills, cobblestone streets.

8 Coloma. The gold rush started here.

9 Placerville. Over a million people visit Apple Hill each year.

10 Plymouth. Vines date from 1869 in nearby Shenandoah Valley.

11 Amador City. Shops hold this former mining town's treasures these days.

12 Sutter Creek. Much gold-rush history unfolded here.

13 Volcano. Explorable caverns lie just outside town.

14 Jackson. Two mines produced $70 million in gold in these parts.

15 Mokelumne Hill. Rowdy miners once called "Moke Hill" home.

16 Angels Camp. Mark Twain wrote about this town's famous frog-jumping contest.

17 Murphys. Main Street's vibe is upscale but unpretentious; redwoods and caverns await nearby.

18 Columbia. Experience gold-rush living history in this throwback village.

19 Jamestown. Hollywood often films in or around Railtown 1897.

8

The Gold Country is one of California's less expensive yet still sublime destinations, a region of the Sierra Nevada foothills filled with natural and cultural pleasures. Visitors come for the boomtowns and ghost towns, art galleries and antiques shops, "farm-to-fork" cuisine and delicious wines, and atmospheric inns and historic hotels.

Spring brings wildflowers, and in fall the hills are colored by bright red berries and changing leaves. Because it offers plenty of outdoor diversions, the Gold Country is a great place to take kids. Sacramento is an ethnically diverse city, with significant Mexican, Hmong, and Ukrainian populations, among many others. Many present-day immigrants are relatively recent arrivals, but the capital city has absorbed several waves of newcomers since 1848, when James Marshall turned up a gold nugget in the American River. At the time, Mexico and the United States were still wrestling for ownership of what would become the Golden State. Marshall's discovery provided the incentive for the United States to tighten its grip on the region, and prospectors from all over the world soon came to seek their fortunes in the Mother Lode, a vein of gold-bearing quartz that stretched 150 miles across the foothills.

As gold fever seized the nation, California's population of 15,000 swelled to 265,000 within three years. The mostly young, male adventurers who arrived in search of gold—the '49ers—became part of a culture that discarded many of the button-down conventions of the eastern states. It was also a violent time. Yankee prospectors chased Mexican miners off their claims, and California's leaders initiated a plan to exterminate the local Native American population. Bounties were paid, and private militias were hired to wipe out the Native Americans or sell them into slavery. California was to be dominated by the Anglo.

The gold-rush boom lasted scarcely 20 years, but it changed California forever, producing 546 mining towns, of which fewer than 250 remain. The hills of the Gold Country were alive, not only with prospecting and mining but also with business, the arts, gambling, and a fair share of crime. Opera houses went up alongside brothels, and the California State Capitol, in Sacramento, was built partly with the gold dug out of the hills.

MAJOR REGIONS

Sacramento and Ag Country. The gateway to the Gold Country, the seat of state government, and a key "ag" (agricultural) hub, Sacramento plays many contemporary roles. Nearly 2½ million people live in the metropolitan area, whose sunshine, mild climate, and fertile soil are responsible for the region's current riches: fresh and bountiful food and high-quality wines. There's a growing local craft-beer scene, too. Visits to Sacramento and nearby towns like Davis and Winters provide the broad agricultural perspective, Lodi the wine-making one. Wineries here earn national recognition, yet they're without the high prices of Napa and Sonoma.

Highway 49. Sacramento's museums provide an excellent introduction to the Gold Country's illustrious history, but the region's heart lies along Highway 49, which winds the approximately 300-mile north–south length of the famed Mother Lode mining area past or near the following towns: Nevada City, Grass Valley, Auburn, Coloma, Placerville, Plymouth, Amador City, Sutter Creek, Jackson, Mokelumne Hill, Angels Camp, Murphys, Columbia, and Jamestown. Some can be explored as easy day trips from Sacramento, but to immerse yourself in this storied setting, consider staying overnight at least a day or two, especially if you'll be stopping at the many wineries of the Sierra Foothills appellation. On days when it's not too hot or cold, the highway—a hilly, often twisting two-lane road—begs for a convertible with the top down.

Planning

When to Go

The Gold Country is most pleasant in spring, when the wildflowers are in bloom, and in fall. Summers can be hot in the valley (temperatures of 100°F are fairly common), so head for the hills. Sacramento winters tend to be cool, with occasionally foggy or rainy days. Throughout the year, Gold Country towns stage community and cultural celebrations. In December, many towns are decked out for the holidays.

Getting Here and Around

AIR

Sacramento International Airport (SMF) is served by airlines that include Aeromexico, Air Canada, Alaska/Horizon, American, Delta, Frontier, Hawaiian, JetBlue, Southwest, and United. A taxi from the airport to Downtown Sacramento costs about $40; services like Lyft and Uber often cost less. Public buses are also an option.

CONTACTS Sacramento International Airport. ✉ 6900 Airport Blvd., Sacramento ⊕ 12 miles northwest of Downtown off I–5 ☎ 916/929–5411 ⊕ www.sacramento. aero/smf.

BUS AND LIGHT-RAIL

Greyhound serves Sacramento from San Francisco and Los Angeles. Sacramento Regional Transit serves the capital area with buses and light-rail vehicles. Yolobus public transit connects SMF airport and Downtown Sacramento, West Sacramento, and Davis.

CONTACTS Sacramento Regional Transit. ☎ 916/321–2877 ⊕ www.sacrt.com. **Yolobus.** ☎ 530/666–2877, 916/371–2877 ⊕ www.yolobus.com.

CAR

Interstate 5 (north–south) and I–80 (east–west) are the two main routes into and out of Sacramento. From there, three highways fan out toward the east, all intersecting with historic Highway 49: I–80 heads northeast 34 miles to Auburn; U.S. 50 goes east 40 miles to Placerville; and Highway 16 angles southeast 45 miles to Plymouth. Two-lane Highway 49 winds and climbs through foothills and valleys, linking the principal Gold Country towns. Traveling by car is the only practical way to explore the region.

TRAIN

Amtrak serves Sacramento and Davis from the Bay Area and beyond.

Restaurants

Sacramento's dining scene has experienced a recent changing of the guard. Longtime favorites have closed their doors, and a new generation of chefs has begun capitalizing on inland California's agricultural bounty. American, Italian, Chinese, and Mexican restaurants remain common, but Gold Country chefs also prepare ambitious international and contemporary regional cuisine. Grass Valley's meat- and vegetable-stuffed *pasties,* introduced by 19th-century gold miners from Cornwall, England, are one of the area's more unusual treats.

Hotels

Downtown Sacramento contains boutique and full-service hotels as well as a few small inns. Chain motels predominate in the larger towns—among them Auburn, Grass Valley, and Jackson—along Highway 49, but you'll also find restored historic hotels and luxurious bed-and-breakfasts throughout the Gold Country. Although some 19th-century properties could use sprucing up, they're still appealing for their legacies and lower rates.

Restaurant and hotel reviews have been shortened. For full information, visit Fodors.com. Restaurant prices are the average cost of a main course at dinner, or if dinner is not served, at lunch. Hotel prices are the lowest cost of a standard double room in high season.

What It Costs			
$	$$	$$$	$$$$
RESTAURANTS			
under $17	$17–$26	$27–$36	over $36
HOTELS			
under $150	$150–$250	$251–$350	over $350

Visitor Information

EVENTS AND ENTERTAINMENT Sacramento 365. ⊕ *www.sacramento365.com.*

TOURISM AGENCIES Greater Grass Valley Chamber of Commerce. ✉ *128 E. Main St., Grass Valley* ☎ *530/273–4667* ⊕ *www. grassvalleychamber.com.* **Tuolumne County Visitors Bureau.** ✉ *193 S. Washington St., Sonora* ☎ *209/533–4420, 800/446–1333* ⊕ *www.yosemitegoldcountry.com.* **Visit Amador.** ☎ *209/267–9249* ⊕ *www.visitamador.com.* **Visit El Dorado.** ✉ *542 Main St., Placerville* ☎ *530/621–5885* ⊕ *visit-eldorado.com.*

Sacramento

87 miles northeast of San Francisco, 384 miles north of Los Angeles.

All around the Golden State's seat of government you'll experience echoes of the gold-rush days, most notably in Old Sacramento, whose wooden sidewalks and horse-drawn carriages on cobblestone streets lend the waterfront district a 19th-century feel. The California State Railroad Museum and other venues hold artifacts of state and national significance, and historic buildings house shops and restaurants. River cruises and train rides are fun family diversions.

Due east of Old Sacramento is Downtown, where landmarks include the Capitol building and the surrounding Capitol Park. Golden 1 Center, a sports and concert venue, is part of DOCO, short for Downtown Commons, which also includes shops, restaurants, hotels, and grassy and concrete gathering spaces.

Farther east, starting at about 15th Street, lies Midtown, a mix of Victorian edifices, ultramodern lofts, and innovative restaurants and cozy wine bars. A few intersections are jumping most evenings when the weather's good; they include the corner of 20th and L streets in what's known as Lavender Heights, the center of the city's gay and lesbian community.

GETTING HERE AND AROUND
Most people drive to Sacramento and get around by car. Lyft and Uber tend to work out better than the cab options.

Sacramento Regional Transit buses and light-rail vehicles serve the area. Bus 30 links Old Sacramento, Midtown, and Sutter's Fort.

Assuming that traffic is not a factor (though it often is), Sacramento is a 90-minute drive from San Francisco and a seven-hour drive from Los Angeles. Parking garages serve Old Sacramento and other tourist spots; on-street parking in Downtown can be difficult to find.

TRANSPORTATION CONTACTS Sacramento Regional Transit. ☎ *916/321–2877* ⊕ *www.sacrt.com.*

ESSENTIALS
VISITOR INFORMATION Sacramento Visitor Center. ⊠ *1002 2nd St.* ☎ *916/442 7644* ⊕ *www.oldsacramento.com.* **Visit Sacramento.** ⊠ *1608 I St.* ☎ *916/808–7777* ⊕ *www.visitsacramento.com.*

 Sights

California Automobile Museum
MUSEUM | More than 120 automobiles—from Model Ts, Hudsons, and Studebakers to modern-day electric-powered ones—are on display at this museum that pays tribute to automotive history and

car culture. Check out a replica of Henry Ford's 1896 Quadricycle and a 1920s roadside café and garage exhibit. The docents are ready to explain everything you see. The museum is south of Downtown and Old Sacramento, with ample free parking. ⊠ *2200 Front St., Downtown* ☎ *916/442–6802* ⊕ *www.calautomuseum.org* ⊒ *$10* ☉ *Closed Tues.*

★ California State Railroad Museum
MUSEUM | FAMILY | Sprawling over three floors and taking up the equivalent of 2½ acres of space, this museum celebrates the history of trains from their 19th-century English origins to the pre–jet age glory days of rail travel and the high-speed trains of today's Europe and Asia. A permanent exhibit that debuted in 2019 for the 150th anniversary of the transcontinental railroad's completion (Sacramento was the western terminus) details the contributions of Chinese laborers. Another section contains a cast gold "Last Spike," one of several spikes issued to commemorate the joining in Utah of the west-to-east Central Pacific and east-to-west Union Pacific lines. Twenty-two of the museum's railroad cars and engines—among them Pullman-style cars and steam locomotives—are on display at any one time, and there are interactive displays and a play area for kids. The exhibits of toy trains delight youngsters and adults. ⊠ *125 I St., at 2nd St., Old Sacramento* ☎ *916/323–9280* ⊕ *www.csrmf.org* ⊒ *$12.*

★ Capitol
GOVERNMENT BUILDING | Built in 1869 and topped by a 128-foot gilded dome, the Capitol functions as both a working museum and the active seat of California's government. When the building is open, you can wander freely by reproductions of century-old state offices and into legislative chambers (in session from January to September) decorated in the style of the 1890s. Look for the abstract portrait of Edmund G. "Jerry" Brown, alongside those of fellow former

Sacramento

KEY

1 *Exploring Sights*
1 *Restaurants*
1 *Hotels*

governors Ronald Reagan (who succeeded Brown's father, Edmund G. "Pat" Brown) and Arnold Schwarzenegger. On most days, guides conduct tours of the building and the 40-acre Capitol Park, which contains a rose garden, a fragrant display of camellias (Sacramento's city flower), and California Veterans Memorials. ■TIP→ **The Capitol's diverse trees include more than 1,000 types from around the world.** ✉ *10th St. and L St., Downtown* ☎ *916/324–0333* ⊕ *capitolmuseum. ca.gov* 🖰 *Free.*

Central Pacific Railroad Passenger Station

TRANSPORTATION SITE (AIRPORT/BUS/FERRY/ TRAIN) | FAMILY | At this reconstructed 1876 depot there's rolling stock to admire and a typical waiting room. On summer weekends and a few other times, a train departs from the freight depot, south of the passenger station, making a 45-minute out-and-back trip that starts along the banks of the Sacramento River. ■TIP→ **Cookies and hot chocolate are served aboard sellout Polar Express rides between Thanksgiving and Christmas that include appearances by characters from the famous story.** ✉ *930 Front St., at J St., Old Sacramento* ☎ *916/445–5995* ⊕ *www. csrmf.org/events/train-rides* 🖰 *Train rides from $15* ⊗ *Hrs vary.*

★ Crocker Art Museum

MUSEUM | Established in 1885, Sacramento's premier fine-arts museum specializes in California art, European master drawings, and international ceramics. A highlight is the magnificent *Great Canyon of the Sierra, Yosemite* (1871) by Thomas Hill. Some works are displayed in two architecturally significant 19th-century structures: the original Italianate Crocker residence and a villa-like gallery. A contemporary, 125,000-square-foot space hosts outstanding traveling exhibitions. ✉ *216 O St., at 3rd St., Downtown* ☎ *916/808–7000* ⊕ *www.crockerartmuseum.org* 🖰 *$12* ⊗ *Closed Mon.–Wed. (but check).*

Huntington, Hopkins & Co. Hardware Store

MUSEUM | Picks, shovels, and other paraphernalia used by gold-rush miners are on display at this re-creation of a 19th-century hardware store that also displays tools and accessories for households, farms, and machine shops. Though it's named for two of the Big Four railroad barons, their store was far more elaborate. ✉ *113 I St., at Front St., Old Sacramento* ☎ *916/323–7234* ⊕ *www. csrmf.org/visit/outside-the-museum* 🖰 *Free* ⊗ *Closed Mon.–Wed.*

★ Leland Stanford Mansion State Historic Park

HOUSE | In 1856, this structure's original owner built a modest two-story row house purchased a few years later by Leland Stanford, a railroad baron, California governor, and U.S. senator who expanded it into a 19,000-square-foot mansion. The opulent space is open for touring except on days when California's governor hosts official events. Before Stanford's wife and heir, Jane, died, she donated the mansion to Sacramento's Roman Catholic diocese, whose nuns ran it first as an orphanage and later a home for teenage girls. Luckily for the restoration efforts, which began in 1986 after the state acquired the property, the nuns had stashed many original furnishings and fixtures in the attic, and the renowned photographer Eadweard Muybridge had shot images in the 1870s that made clear what rooms looked like and where things belonged. ■TIP→ **Guided tours of small groups depart hourly from 10 to 4.** ✉ *800 N St., at 8th St., Downtown* ☎ *916/324–0575 recorded info, 916/324– 9266 visitor center* ⊕ *www.parks.ca.gov/ stanfordmansion* 🖰 *Free.*

Old Sacramento Schoolhouse Museum

MUSEUM | FAMILY | A kid-friendly attraction that shows what one-room schoolhouses were like in central California and the Sierra foothills in the late 1800s, this replica built in 1976 is a fun, quick stop a block from the waterfront. ✉ *1200 Front St., at*

L St., Old Sacramento ⊕ www.oldsac-
schoolhouse.org ⊠ Free ☉ Closed Sun.

State Indian Museum

MUSEUM | Adjacent to Sutter's Fort, this
small but engaging museum explores
the lives and history of California's native
peoples. Arts-and-crafts displays, a
demonstration village, and other exhibits
offer a fascinating portrait of the state's
earliest inhabitants. ⊠ 2618 K St., at 26th
St., Midtown ☎ 916/324–0971 ⊕ www.
parks.ca.gov/indianmuseum ⊠ $5.

Sutter's Fort

MUSEUM VILLAGE | **FAMILY** | German-born
Swiss immigrant John Augustus
Sutter founded Sacramento's earliest
Euro-American settlement in 1839. A
self-guided tour includes a blacksmith's
shop, bakery, prison, living quarters,
and livestock areas. Costumed docents
sometimes reenact fort life, demonstrat-
ing crafts, food preparation, and firearms
maintenance. ⊠ 2701 L St., at 27th St.,
Midtown ☎ 916/445–4422 ⊕ www.
suttersfort.org ⊠ From $5.

 Restaurants

Cafeteria 15L

$$ | **AMERICAN** | The exposed brick,
reclaimed wood, mismatched chairs,
and natural light streaming through
large-paned windows of this easygoing
comfort-food hangout make a great first
impression and a lasting one on the
many repeat customers. Favorites like
tater tots (in truffle oil) and chicken and
waffles (with pecan butter, maple syrup,
Tabasco-and-black-pepper pork, and
gravy) prove simultaneously familiar and
intriguing. **Known for:** two outdoor patios;
nostalgic food with a modern twist;
weekend brunch with bottomless mimo-
sas. ⑤ Average main: $20 ⊠ 1116 15th
St., at L St., Downtown ☎ 916/492–1960
⊕ www.cafeteria15l.com.

Camden Spit & Larder

$$$ | **MODERN AMERICAN** | Upscale London
haberdasheries reportedly inspired the
aesthetic of this impeccably designed,
pressed-metal-ceilinged paean to
spit-roasted, Brit-influenced meat dishes.
Near Golden 1 Center and Downtown
Commons, it's a place to share small
offerings like sausage rolls, steak tartare,
and local caviar and crumpets (Sacramento is a center of caviar production)
before proceeding to Loch Duart salmon,
spit-roasted chicken, or the house specialty, roast rib of beef with roasted bone
marrow, horseradish, and Bordelaise.
Known for: beef-fat hash browns with
sour-cream horseradish; wine, beer, and
cider selection; craft cocktails incorporating seasonal fruits, herbs, and vegetables. ⑤ Average main: $34 ⊠ 555 Capitol
Mall, at 6th St., Downtown ☎ 916/619–
8897 ⊕ www.camdenspitandlarder.com
☉ Closed Sun. and Mon. No lunch Sat.

★ Canon

$$$ | **MODERN AMERICAN** | Farmhouse
meets semi-industrial open-kitchen chic
at this light-filled restaurant whose executive chef found success in the Midwest
and the Napa Valley before returning to
Sacramento, where his culinary career
began. Carefully chosen produce and
proteins go into small and large plates,
meant to be shared, that might range
from crispy shrimp heads, caviar, and
smoked-cheddar biscuits to a broccoli
Caesar salad, fondant potatoes, and
roasted duck. **Known for:** alfresco patio
dining in good weather; seasonal cocktails with fresh herbs and fruit; vegan,
vegetarian, and gluten-free options.
⑤ Average main: $29 ⊠ 1719 34th St.
☎ 916/469–2433 ⊕ canoneastsac.com
☉ Closed Mon. and Tues. No lunch.

★ Ella Dining Room and Bar

$$$$ | **MODERN AMERICAN** | This swank res-
taurant and bar near the Capitol is artfully
designed and thoroughly modern. The
California–French, farm-to-table cuisine
changes seasonally, but typical dishes

include oysters on the half shell and a popular steak tartare with garlic popovers as appetizers, the house Caesar, and entrées like wood-fired steaks and pork chops and poached or pan-roasted fish of the day. **Known for:** fresh, seasonal local ingredients; waitstaff's attention to detail; cocktail and wine selection. $ *Average main: $43 ⊠ 1131 K St., at 12th St., Downtown* ☎ *916/443–3772* ⊕ *www. elladiningroomandbar.com* ⊙ *Closed Sun. and Mon. No lunch Sat.*

The Firehouse

$$$$ | AMERICAN | Sacramento's rich and famous, including California governors going back to Ronald Reagan, settle into the elegant spaces within the city's restored first brick firehouse to dine on award-winning contemporary cuisine. The creative fare ranges from carpaccio, seasonal oysters, and braised pork belly to delicately spiced, seared sea bass and herb-crusted rack of lamb, rib eye (with black garlic butter), and other specialty meat cuts. **Known for:** steaks and seafood; happy-hour menu weekdays 4–6; courtyard patio. $ *Average main: $41 ⊠ 1112 2nd St., at L St., Old Sacramento* ☎ *916/442–4772* ⊕ *www. firehouseoldsac.com* ⊙ *No lunch (check on weekdays).*

Fixins Soul Kitchen

$ | AMERICAN | A cheery, sometimes boisterous vibe prevails at this ode to Black cuisine and culture that former NBA star and past Sacramento mayor Kevin Johnson and his wife, Michelle, founded in a high-ceilinged, quasi-industrial space 3½ miles southeast of the Capitol. Expect heapin' helpings of soul food's greatest hits—gumbo, shrimp and grits, oxtails, and fried chicken, catfish, and pork chops among them—that you can pair with sides that include hush puppies, black-eyed peas, candied yams, collard greens (with turkey necks). **Known for:** art on the walls, sports on bar TVs; Kool-Aid for kids and (with alcohol) for adults;

banana pudding for dessert. $ *Average main: $16 ⊠ 3428 3rd Ave., at Broadway ⊹ From Downtown or Midtown take X St. southeast to 34th St. and turn south (right)* ☎ *916/999–7685* ⊕ *fixinssoulkitchen.com.*

★ The Kitchen

$$$$ | MODERN AMERICAN | The chefs and front-of-house staff at this perennial favorite with a prix-fixe menu pull out all the stops to deliver a multisensory gustatory experience. The flamboyant presentation of courses as a series of "Acts"—not to mention the dramatically lit, flower-bestrewn dining room's intentionally buoyant atmosphere—might distract from the modern American cuisine were it not so well conceived and prepared with such panache and precision. **Known for:** one seating each evening (plan on 3½–4 hours); optional wine pairing; impeccably sourced ingredients. $ *Average main: $155 ⊠ 2225 Hurley Way ⊹ 6 miles east of Downtown off Hwy. 160 to Exposition Blvd.* ☎ *916/568–7171* ⊕ *thekitchenrestaurant. com* ⊙ *Closed Mon. and Tues.*

Kru

$$$ | JAPANESE | It's worth the drive a little past Sutter's Fort to this mod Japanese restaurant whose owner-chef fashions fresh, wildly creative sushi for patrons seated at blond-wood tables, a counter, or an open-air patio. Order a sunshine roll—spicy tuna, escolar, and shrimp tempura enlivened by the tart contribution of green apples and lemon—perhaps pairing it with cooked fare like smoked duck *kushiyaki* with plum-wine katsu sauce or hot or cold ramen, including pork belly, poached shrimp, and mushroom broth. **Known for:** smart decor; nearly two dozen rolls; impressive sake, wine, and whiskeys. $ *Average main: $30 ⊠ 3135 Folsom Blvd., at Seville Way* ☎ *916/551–1559* ⊕ *www.krurestaurant. com* ⊙ *No lunch.*

★ Localis

$$$$ | **MODERN AMERICAN** | Exquisite plating and compelling, at times piquant, flavor combinations are the trademarks of this restaurant whose chef-sommelier owner, Chris Barnum-Dann, won the debut (2021) season of the culinary-competition TV show *The Globe*. The open-kitchen choreography of Barnum-Dann and his team deftly preparing one intricate dish after another (7–12 courses, prix-fixe $155–$197) lends the proceedings a balletic air. **Known for:** fresh ingredients from top purveyors creatively combined and presented; thoughtful menu notes; global, well-chosen wines. ⑤ *Average main: $155* ✉ *2031 S St., at 21st St., Midtown* ☎ *916/737–7699* ⊕ *www.localissacramento.com* ☾ *Closed Sun.–Tues. (but check). No lunch.*

★ Magpie Cafe

$$ | **AMERICAN** | This Midtown eatery with a vaguely industrial look and a casual vibe takes its food seriously: nearly all the produce is sourced locally, and the chefs prepare only sustainable seafood. Banh mi sandwiches and grass-fed beef burgers (including a plant-based option) are among the staples, as are steak and fries and pan-roasted fish with seasonal vegetables. **Known for:** outdoor park-view patio; beer, cider, wine, and cocktail lineup; homemade ice-cream sandwiches. ⑤ *Average main: $23* ✉ *1601 16th St., Midtown* ☎ *916/452–7594* ⊕ *www.magpiecafe.com* ☾ *Closed Mon.–Wed. (but check).*

★ The Waterboy

$$$ | **EUROPEAN** | Rural French cooking with locally sourced, seasonal, high-quality, often organic ingredients is the hallmark of this upscale, white-tablecloth, corner storefront restaurant that's as appealing for a casual meal with friends as it is for a drawn-out romantic dinner for two. Among the mains, try the steak, duck breast, or seasonal seafood, and save room for one of the palate-cleansing desserts. **Known for:** exceptional French cooking; quality local ingredients; global wine list. ⑤ *Average main: $32* ✉ *2000 Capitol Ave., at 20th St., Midtown* ☎ *916/498–9891* ⊕ *www.waterboyrestaurant.com* ☾ *Closed Sun.–Tues. (but check). No lunch Sat.*

Zócalo Midtown

$$ | **MEXICAN** | Inside a glamorously renovated Hudson Motor Car showroom from the 1920s that looks out of a movie set, Zócalo puts an upscale spin on Mexican classics. Pair the house margarita or its blackberry variation with a guac or ceviche starter before moving on to a burrito; enchiladas; or a bowl with chicken, salmon, carne asada, or vegetarian ingredients. **Known for:** festive setting; outdoor patio; happy hour daily 3–6 pm. ⑤ *Average main: $18* ✉ *1801 Capitol Ave., at 18th St., Midtown* ☎ *916/441–0303* ⊕ *experiencezocalo.com.*

Hotels

Amber House Inn of Midtown

$$ | **B&B/INN** | Veer from the beaten path of traditional lodging at Amber House Inn's two historic homes—one a 1905 Craftsman, the other an 1895 Dutch colonial–revival—just 1 mile from the Capitol. **Pros:** Midtown location; attentive service; full breakfast served in-room if desired. **Cons:** older buildings and style; B&B regimen not for everyone; lacks spa, fitness center, and other big-hotel amenities. ⑤ *Rooms from: $179* ✉ *1315 22nd St., Midtown* ☎ *916/444–8085* ⊕ *www.amberhouse.com* ⤴ *10 rooms* ⊚| *Free breakfast.*

Citizen Hotel

$$ | **HOTEL** | This boutique hotel within the historic 1926 Cal Western Life building is dapper and refined, with marble stairs, striped wallpaper, and plush velvet chairs, lending the place a Roaring '20s charm. **Pros:** sophisticated decor; smooth service; restaurant and bar. **Cons:** rooms near elevator can be noisy; rates vary widely depending on conventions, legislature, season; expensive parking. $ *Rooms from: $170* ✉ *926 J St., Downtown* ☎ *916/447–2700* ⊕ *www.thecitizenhotel. com* ⇥ *198 rooms* ⦿ *No meals.*

Delta King

$$ | HOTEL | Wake up to the sound of geese taking flight along the river when you book a stay in one of Sacramento's most unusual and historic relics, a carefully restored riverboat hotel permanently moored on Old Sacramento's waterfront. **Pros:** unique lodgings; steps from Old Sacramento shopping and dining; period feel. **Cons:** slanted floors can feel a bit jarring; rooms are cramped; some noise issues. $ *Rooms from: $159* ✉ *1000 Front St., Old Sacramento* ⊕ *At end of K St.* ☎ *916/444–5464, 800/825–5464* ⊕ *www.deltaking.com* ⇥ *44 rooms* ⦿ *Free breakfast.*

★ Fort Sutter Hotel

$$ | HOTEL | Two local restaurateurs are behind this six-story, boutique, Hilton Tapestry Collection whose guest rooms win points for their expansive windows, contemporary style, smartly designed bathrooms, and works by local artists. **Pros:** above-average food for a hotel restaurant; near Midtown dining, entertainment, and shopping; Capitol views from upper floors facing west. **Cons:** diagonally across from a hospital; rooms lack refrigerators and microwaves; more than a mile walk to Downtown. $ *Rooms from: $179* ✉ *1308 28th St, Midtown* ☎ *916/603–2301* ⊕ *www.fortsutterhotel. com* ⇥ *105 rooms* ⦿ *No meals.*

Hyatt Regency Sacramento

$$ | HOTEL | With a marble-and-glass lobby and luxurious rooms, this multitiered, glass-dominated hotel across from the Capitol and adjacent to the convention center has a striking Mediterranean design. **Pros:** best rooms have Capitol Park views; some rooms have small balconies; excellent service. **Cons:** nearby streets can feel dodgy at night; somewhat impersonal; many corporate events. $ *Rooms from: $189* ✉ *1209 L St.,*

Downtown ☎ *916/443–1234* ⊕ *sacramento.regency.hyatt.com* ⇥ *505 rooms* ⦿ *No meals.*

Inn Off Capitol Park

$$ | HOTEL | Business and leisure travelers seeking a touch of style along with comfort and value appreciate the amenities at this Ascend Collection property near the Capitol. **Pros:** convenient location; good value; well run. **Cons:** many rooms are small (220 or 260 square feet); no tub in some rooms; insufficient on-site parking spaces when hotel is full. $ *Rooms from: $154* ✉ *1530 N St., Downtown* ☎ *916/447–8100* ⊕ *www.choicehotels. com* ⇥ *37 rooms* ⦿ *Free breakfast.*

★ Kimpton Sawyer Hotel

$$ | HOTEL | Soft shades of brown and gray and furniture milled from California oak lend an haute-rustic feel to the spacious rooms and suites of this full-service hotel amid Sacramento's Downtown Commons (DOCO) shopping and entertainment complex. **Pros:** pool deck and Revival bar; "living room" lobby; convenient to Downtown and Old Sacramento. **Cons:** pricey in-season; no tubs in many rooms; may be too high-style for some guests. $ *Rooms from: $219* ✉ *500 J St., Downtown* ☎ *916/545–7100 front desk, 877/678–6255 reservations* ⊕ *www.sawyerhotel.com* ⇥ *285 rooms* ⦿ *No meals.*

 Nightlife

Drakes: The Barn

BREWPUBS/BEER GARDENS | Drake's Brewing serves up beer, food, and musical and other events at and around a dramatically curving, cedar-shingled pavilion on 2 acres along the Sacramento River. Chefs prepare pizzas, and there are food trucks. The Barn is closed on Monday. ✉ *985 Riverfront St., at Garden St., West Sacramento* ⊕ *Across Sacramento River from Downtown near Sutter Health Park* ☎ *510/568–2739* ⊕ *drinkdrakes.com/barn.*

Harlow's

MUSIC CLUBS | Blues, rock, and other musicians take to the stage of this restaurant's art-deco bar–nightclub. Repair to the patio when you need to cool off. ⊠ *2708 J St., at 27th St., Midtown* ☎ *916/441–4693* ⊕ *www.harlows.com.*

★ Midtown BierGarten

BREWPUBS/BEER GARDENS | The neighborhood feel and selection of beers, ales, porters, stouts, sours, and ciders make a trip to this boisterous beer garden a fun occasion, with the garlic fries, fresh pretzels with mustard, old-fashioned hot dogs, and other small bites a definite bonus. A 40-foot cargo container holds the bar, and a 20-footer contains the bathrooms, with the rest of the setting alfresco. ⊠ *2332 K St., at 24th St.* ☎ *916/346–4572* ⊕ *beergardensacramento.com.*

★ Midtown's Cantina Alley

BARS/PUBS | Flavorful, colorful, fruity cocktails, some served in hollowed-out pineapples or watermelons, are the specialty of this bar and restaurant whose equally rich-hued decor and corrugated-metal ceiling intentionally evoke spots throughout Mexico. While sipping sangria, a cerveza, or the house margarita in several flavors, you can nibble on street tacos, posole, *elote* (corn on a stick, rolled in mayonnaise and topped with cheese and spices), and other small plates. Closed on Monday, the cantina opens for lunch on Friday and weekends. ⊠ *2320 Jazz Alley, Midtown* ⊹ *Off 24th St. between J and K Sts.* ☎ *833/232–0639* ⊕ *www. cantinaalley.com.*

Punch Bowl Social

BARS/PUBS | This restaurant and entertainment complex offers bowling, billiards, karaoke, Giant Jenga, virtual reality, pinball, and Skee-Ball. After you've worked up an appetite, dine on updated pub grub and sip well-chosen craft beers, wine, specialty cocktails, or boozeless beverages. ⊠ *500 J St., Downtown* ⊹ *At 5th St.* ☎ *916/925–5610* ⊕ *www.punchbowlsocial.com/sacramento*

Tiger

BARS/PUBS | Concrete walls and black-metal beams and railings reinforce the post-industrial mood at this two-level bar, which draws a youngish crowd for craft cocktails based on Sacramento produce, zesty small bites and larger plates, and often live music. ⊠ *722 K St., at 8th St., Downtown* ☎ *916/302–9610* ⊕ *www. tiger700block.com.*

Performing Arts

Broadway Sacramento

THEATER | This group presents Broadway shows at two Downtown venues. Past shows include *Hamilton* and *The Wiz.* ⊠ *SAFE Credit Union Performing Arts Center, 1301 L St., at 13th St., Downtown* ☎ *916/557–1999* ⊕ *www.broadwaysacramento.com.*

Crest Theatre

ARTS CENTERS | It's worth peeking inside the Crest even if you don't catch a show, just to see the swirling art-deco design in the foyer, or to dine at the Empress Tavern restaurant within. It's a beloved venue for classic and art-house films, along with concerts and other cultural events. ⊠ *1013 K St., at 10th St., Downtown* ☎ *916/476–3356* ⊕ *www.crestsacramento.com.*

★ The Sofia

ARTS CENTERS | The long-running B Street Theatre—known for well-staged comedies, dramas, the occasional farce, and productions for children—is the resident company at this industrial-suave performing arts center. The two theaters, plus three rehearsal spaces sometimes used for workshop productions, also present musicians, solo acts, and speakers. ⊠ *2700 Capitol Ave., at 27th St.* ☎ *916/443–5300* ⊕ *bstreettheatre.org.*

Shopping

Downtown Commons (*DOCO*)
SHOPPING CENTERS/MALLS | As its name implies, this multiblock complex adjoining the Golden 1 Center aspires to be a gathering spot for locals and tourists as much as a place to shop, dine, catch a movie, or sip a cocktail. ⊠ *660 J St., Downtown* ⊕ *Between 5th and 7th Sts., J and L Sts.* ☎ *916/273–8124.*

★ Kulture
GIFTS/SOUVENIRS | This vibrant shop sells Mexican art, jewelry, and gifts, along with the pithy Keepin It Paisa line of T-shirts, hoodies, and ball caps. The owners and other vendors sell furniture, clothing, and other items in an adjacent space. ⊠ *2331 K St., Midtown* ⊕ *At 24th St.* ☎ *916/442– 2728* ⊕ *kulturedc.wixsite.com/kulture* ��� *Closed Mon.*

Activities

American River Bicycle Trail
BICYCLING | The Jedediah Smith Memorial Trail, as it's formally called, runs for 32 miles from Old Sacramento to Beals Point in Folsom. Walk or ride a bit of it and you'll see why local cyclists and pedestrians adore its scenic lanes. Enjoy great views of the American River and the bluffs overlooking it. ■**TIP**➔ **Bring lunch or a snack. Parks and picnic areas dot the trail.** ⊠ *Old Sacramento* ⊕ *www.americanriverbiketrail.com.*

Davis

10 miles west of Sacramento.

Davis began as a rich agricultural area and remains one, but it doesn't feel like a cow town. It's home to the University of California at Davis, whose 40,000 or so students hang at downtown cafés, galleries, and bookstores (most of the action takes place between Second and Fourth and B and E streets), lending the city a decidedly college-town feel.

GETTING HERE AND AROUND
Most people arrive by car via I–80, though Yolobus serves the area from Sacramento, and downtown is walkable. Touring by bicycle is also a popular option—Davis is very flat.

◉ Sights

California Agriculture Museum
MUSEUM | **FAMILY** | This gigantic space in the nearby community of Woodland provides a thorough historical overview of motorized agricultural vehicles through dozens and dozens of threshers, harvesters, combines, tractors, and other contraptions. A separate wing surveys the evolution of the truck, with an emphasis on those used for farm work. ⊠ *1958 Hays La., south off Douglas La. from East Main St., Woodland* ⊕ *From Davis, take 5th St. east to Polehill Rd./ County Rd. 102 north 10 miles; from Sacramento, take I–5 for 18 miles northwest to Exit 536* ☎ *530/666–9700* ⊕ *www. californiaagmuseum.org* ☙ *$10* ☙ *Closed Mon. and Tues.*

University of California, Davis
COLLEGE | A top research university, UC Davis educates many of the Wine Country's vintners and grape growers, in addition to farmers, veterinarians, and brewmasters. When offered, campus tours depart from Buehler Alumni and Visitors Center. On a tour or not, worthy stops include the **Arboretum,** the **Manetti Shrem Museum of Art,** and the **Mondavi Center,** a striking modern glass structure that presents top-tier performing artists. ⊠ *Visitor Center, 550 Alumni La.* ☎ *530/752–8111 for tour information* ⊕ *visit.ucdavis.edu.*

🍴 Restaurants

Mustard Seed

$$$ | AMERICAN | Many patrons at this restaurant serving eclectic seasonal California cuisine are attending performing-arts events at the Mondavi Center a short walk away or visiting their kids at UC Davis. With hardwood floors and tables topped with white linen, the dining room is cozy and romantic, but when the weather's fine, the tree-shaded patio out back is the best place to enjoy dishes like tomato bisque topped with a puff pastry and herb-crusted rack of lamb. **Known for:** lunchtime salads and sandwiches; desserts aren't an afterthought; reasonably priced California wines. $ *Average main: $35* ⊠ *222 D St., Suite 11* ☎ *530/758–5750* ⊕ *www.mustardseedofdavis.com* ◔ *No lunch Sat.–Mon.*

🛏 Hotels

Best Western Plus Palm Court Hotel

$$ | HOTEL | Rich accents of gold and cobalt blue add boutique flair to the spacious rooms of this dependable choice for business and leisure travelers. **Pros:** off-campus but nearby; on-site Cafe Bernardo for comfort food; some rooms sleep up to 6 people. **Cons:** pricey during major UC Davis events; no pool; chain's usual free breakfast not offered. $ *Rooms from: $155* ⊠ *234 D St.* ☎ *530/753–7100* ⊕ *bestwestern.com* ⇱ *27 rooms* ⊙ *No meals.*

Hyatt Place UC Davis

$$ | HOTEL | A full-service hotel right on campus, the Hyatt distinguishes itself with an enthusiastic staff and clean, well-designed rooms and suites. **Pros:** generous breakfasts; pool, fitness room, café, and bar; convenient to university and downtown restaurants and shopping. **Cons:** only rooms with queen beds have tubs; noise from campus and nearby train tracks (when booking, ask for a quieter room); only suites have microwaves. $ *Rooms from: $159* ⊠ *173 Old Davis Rd. Extension* ☎ *530/756–9500, 855/516–1090* ⊕ *hyatt.com* ⇱ *127 rooms* ⊙ *Free breakfast.*

Winters

14 miles west of Davis.

Almonds, walnuts, and fruit are the main crops grown in this rural Yolo County town (population 7,300), whose several-block historic district's wine-tasting opportunities and nationally recognized restaurant scene lure tourists and Bay Area and Sacramento Valley day-trippers. The district's Main Street bustles on weekends, especially when music and other events close part of it.

GETTING HERE AND AROUND

It's easiest to drive to Winters, whose main drag, Grant Avenue, doubles as Highway 128 in town. From Davis, follow Russell Boulevard west until it becomes Grant Avenue, from which Railroad Avenue leads south to the historic district. Yolobus serves Winters from Davis.

👁 Sights

Berryessa Gap Vineyards Tasting Room

WINERY/DISTILLERY | Nicole Salengo, the longtime winemaker of this operation whose origins date to the late 1960s, displays a light but knowing touch with even the heaviest reds. A case in point is Berryessa Gap's singular Petite Sirah, whose aromatics and acidity are more pronounced than in most of the wine's California peers. The several rosés poured here make the tasting room a magnet for "drink pink" aficionados. ⊠ *15 E. Main St., near Railroad Ave.* ☎ *539/795–3201* ⊕ *berryessagap.com* 🍷 *Tastings from $15.*

Turkovich Family Wines Tasting Room

WINERY/DISTILLERY | Third-generation farmer Chris Turkovich and his wife, Luciana, whose parents back in her native Argentina are both involved in the wine business, founded this winery known for bold, balanced reds. The two craft many of their wines from Spanish varietals, though Petite Sirah dominates the flagship blend The Boss. Albariño and rosé of Grenache are among the noteworthy lighter wines. The storefront tasting room's sidewalk seating is good for people-watching, the patio in back is good for quieter sipping. ✉ *304 Railroad Ave., near Main St.* ☎ *530/795–3842* ⊕ *turkovichwines.com* ⤷ *Tastings from $8.*

🍴 Restaurants

Ficelle

$$ | ECLECTIC | If you're in Winters on a day this self-proclaimed "delightfully random place to eat" is open, try to score a seat (no reservations) to enjoy internationally inspired small plates that might include chicken tostadas, marinated lamb, empanadas, or baked eggplant. With a few tables indoors, plus counter seating on stools and more tables outside on a wooden deck, Ficelle, run on the whim of its European owners, lives up to its motto. **Known for:** festive ambience; alfresco dining; fanciful flavors. ⑤ *Average main: $25* ✉ *5C E. Main St., east of Railroad Ave.* ⊹ *Behind Steady Eddy's* ☎ *530/795–9593* ⊕ *www.ficelle-restaurant.com* ⊘ *Closed Sun.–Wed. No lunch.*

Preserve

$$ | MODERN AMERICAN | The seasonal produce of nearby purveyors figures in nearly every dish at Preserve, which pairs elevated gastropub fare with artisanal beers, wines, and cocktails. Chicken-fried oysters, grilled sturgeon, slow-roasted pork belly, pizzas, elaborate burgers, fried chicken, and shrimp and grits with aged cheddar are typical menu items, served in the brick-walled, rustic-industrial, semi-chic bar or the plant-laden outdoor patio. **Known for:** fine-dining menu (pricey) some nights; craft cocktails; upscale-casual

feel. ⑤ *Average main: $24* ✉ *200 Railroad Ave., near Russell St.* ☎ *530/795–9963* ⊕ *www.preservewinters.com* ⊘ *Closed Mon. and Tues. No lunch Wed. and Thurs. No dinner Sun.*

Putah Creek Cafe

$$ | AMERICAN | The wood-fired pizza oven blazing away on the sidewalk turns out this café's handmade pies, but the lunch and dinner fare extends well beyond them to tacos, cauliflower buffalo wings, pastrami sandwiches, fish in béarnaise sauce, and fresh salads with ingredients from a local farm. The brick-walled dining room has been a farmers' hangout for breakfast (you name it) for decades. **Known for:** signature corn pie (cornmeal, cheddar, and jack) with roasted tomato sauce; alfresco patio dining; sister restaurant Buckhorn Steakhouse, a Winters culinary anchor, across the street. ⑤ *Average main: $22* ✉ *1 Main St., at Railroad Ave.* ☎ *530/795–2682* ⊕ *www.putahcreekcafe.com.*

🛏 Hotels

Hotel Winters

$$ | HOTEL | Art by regional artists adorns the hallways of this dapper, three-story, downtown historic district boutique property that opened in 2019 and became an instant favorite of business folk, leisure travelers, and local brides. **Pros:** fresh look; spacious rooms with 10-foot ceilings; town and mountain views from rooftop bar. **Cons:** some street-side noise (ask for a room toward the back); shallow "water lounge" has a mesmerizing water feature, but there's no legit pool; irregular hours at rooftop bar. ⑤ *Rooms from: $170* ✉ *12 Abbey St.* ☎ *530/505–9123, 877/514–3870* ⊕ *www.hotelwinters.com* ⤷ *78 rooms* ⦿ *No meals.*

Lodi

34 miles south of Sacramento.

With with more than 100,000 acres of mostly alluvial soils planted to more than 125 grape varietals—more types than in any other California viticultural area—Lodi is a major grape-growing hub. Eighty-five or so wineries do business in Lodi, the self-proclaimed Zinfandel Capital of the World, and neighboring towns. (Although plenty of Zin grows here, these days farmers devote nearly the same amount of land to Cabernet Sauvignon.) Founded on agriculture, Lodi was once the country's watermelon capital. Today it's surrounded by fields of asparagus, pumpkins, beans, safflowers, sunflowers, melons, squashes, peaches, and cherries. Lodi retains an old rural charm. You can stroll downtown or visit a wildlife refuge, all the while benefiting from a Sacramento River delta breeze that keeps this microclimate cooler in summer than anyplace else in the area.

GETTING HERE AND AROUND

Most of Lodi lies west of Highway 99 and east of Interstate 5. Amtrak trains stop here frequently. GrapeLine (☎ 209/333–6806) buses pass by many wineries, but touring by car is more efficient.

ESSENTIALS

VISITOR INFORMATION Visit Lodi. ✉ 25 N. School St. ☎ 209/365–1195, 800/798–1810 ⊕ www.visitlodi.com.

Sights

Acquiesce Winery

WINERY/DISTILLERY | Expect no heavy reds at this boutique operation specializing in Rhône-style whites. The enthusiastic owners, who sourced their grapes' vines from Château de Beaucastel in France's Châteauneuf du Pape appellation, produce Viognier, Roussanne, and Grenache Blanc but also spotlight lower-profile varietals like Bourboulenc and Clairette Blanche. (There's also a Grenache rosé.) Tastings, by appointment only, take place in a 100-year-old barn or just outside it, in either case with vineyard views. ✉ *22353 N. Tretheway Rd., Acampo* ⊹ *From downtown Lodi take Hwy. 12 east, Bruella Rd. north, and E. Peltier Rd. east* ☎ *209/333–6102* ⊕ *www.acquiescevineyards.com* ☞ *Tastings $20.*

Berghold Estate Winery

WINERY/DISTILLERY | The appointment-only tasting room at Berghold recalls an earlier wine era with its vintage Victorian interior, including restored, salvaged mantlepieces, leaded glass, and a 26-foot-long bar. The wines—among them Viognier, Cabernet Sauvignon, Syrah, and Zinfandel—pay homage to French wine-making styles. ✉ *17343 Cherry Rd., off E. Victor Rd./Hwy. 12* ☎ *209/333–9291* ⊕ *bergholdvineyards.com* ☞ *Tastings $10* ⊗ *Closed Mon.–Wed.*

★ Bokisch Vineyards

WINERY/DISTILLERY | This operation 11 miles outside of downtown comes highly recommended for its excellent Spanish varietals and warm hospitality. The Albariño white and Tempranillo and Graciano reds often receive favorable critical notice, but everything is well made, including the non-Spanish Petit Verdot and old-vine Carignane. ■**TIP**➔ **Bokisch welcomes picnickers; pick up fixings in town and enjoy vineyard views while you dine.** ✉ *18921 Atkins Rd.* ⊹ *From Hwy. 99 head east on Hwy. 12, north on Hwy. 88, and east on Brandt Rd.* ☎ *209/642–8880* ⊕ *www. bokischvineyards.com* ☞ *Tastings from $15* ⊗ *Closed Tues. and Wed.*

Harney Lane Winery

WINERY/DISTILLERY | The Harney family has grown grapes in Lodi since the 1900s dawned but only started a winery in 2006. Three Zinfandels star in a lineup that includes Albariño, Chardonnay, two rosés, Cabernet Sauvignon, Petite Sirah, Primitivo, Tempranillo, and an old-vine Zinfandel port-style dessert wine. Extend your tasting with a glass in the "forest" garden, where three-century-old cedars supply the shade. ■ TIP→ **When offered, the Grape to Glass tour is a great way to learn about both the family and Lodi.** ✉ *9010 E. Harney La.* ✛ *About 6½ miles south of downtown, Hwy. 99 to E. Harney La. exit* ☎ *209/365–1900* ⊕ *www.harneylane.com* ✒ *Tastings $10, tour $25.*

Jeremy Wine Co.

WINERY/DISTILLERY | Originally a bank, the downtown tasting room of owner-win-emaker Jeremy Trettevik has the feel of a spiffed-up old-time saloon, though in good weather everyone sips under the bright-red umbrellas shading the patio out back. Creative red blends, most from well-sourced Lodi appellation grapes, are the specialty here, with sweet yet clean-on-the-palate wines like the Orange Muscat and the Bluebonnet Albariño–Orange Muscat blend among the lighter options. There's also a chocolate port-style dessert wine. ✉ *6 W. Pine St. , at S. Sacramento St.* ☎ *209/367–3773* ⊕ *jeremywineco.com* ✒ *Tastings from $10.*

★ Klinker Brick Winery

WINERY/DISTILLERY | The old-vine Zinfan-dels of this winery named for the bricks used to construct Lodi buildings of days past score well in wine competitions for their smooth tannins and complex flavors. Like the Cabernet Sauvignon (among Lodi's best), they're reasonably priced considering the quality. Light-er offerings include sparkling wines, Albariño, Grenache Blanc, and the Vorgänger blend of three white grapes. If the weather's good, taste outside and enjoy garden and vineyard views. ■ TIP→ **Request a reserve tasting ($15) to sample the top-of-the-line reds.** ✉ *15887 N. Alpine Rd.* ☎ *209/333–1845* ⊕ *klinkerbrickwinery.com* ✒ *Tastings from $5.*

Lodi Wine & Visitor Center

WINERY/DISTILLERY | A fine place to sample Lodi wines, the center has a tasting bar and viticultural exhibits. You can also buy wine and pick up a free winery map. ✉ *2545 W. Turner Rd., at Woodhaven La.*

☎ *209/365–0621* ⊕ *www.lodiwine.com* ✒ *Tastings $12* ⊘ *Closed Mon.–Wed. (but check).*

Lucas Winery

WINERY/DISTILLERY | David Lucas was one of the first local producers to start making serious wine, and today the Zinfandels he and his wife, Heather Pyle-Lucas, make are among Lodi's most sought-after vintages. The Lucases, who previously worked at the Robert Mondavi Winery (she also made wine at Opus One), also craft a Chardonnay with subtle oaky flavors and a 100% Zinfandel rosé. Tastings, by appointment only, often take place on a patio with a vineyard view. ✉ *18196 N. Davis Rd., at W. Turner Rd.* ☎ *209/368–2006* ⊕ *www.lucaswinery. com* ✒ *Tastings from $20* ⊘ *Closed Mon. and Tues.*

★ M2 Wines

WINERY/DISTILLERY | With its translu-cent polycarbonate panels, concrete floor, and metal framing, this winery's high ceilinged tasting room strikes an iconoclastic, industrial-sleek pose along an otherwise rural lane north of Lodi. The Soucie Vineyard old-vine Zinfandel and the Trio and Duality red blends are three to seek out, but all the wines here are good. ✉ *2900 E. Peltier Rd., Acampo* ✛ *Take Hwy. 99 north from down-town to Peltier Rd. exit and head west* ☎ *209/339–1071* ⊕ *www.m2wines.com* ✒ *Tastings from $10* ⊘ *Closed Tues.–Thurs. (but check).*

★ McCay Cellars

WINERY/DISTILLERY | Wine critics applaud owner-winemaker Michael McCay's pursuit of balance and restraint with his flagship TruLux Zinfandel and Faith Lot 13 Zin from century-old vines. A longtime grower who started his namesake label in 2007, McCay also makes several rosés and whites, plus Cabernet Franc, Cinsaut, Petite Sirah, Tempranillo, and other reds. He's often on-site at his winery's tasting room. ✉ *18817 E. Hwy. 88* ✛ *From downtown Lodi, take E. Victor*

Rd./Hwy. 12 east to Hwy. 88 north (turn left) ☎ *209/368–9463* ⊕ *www.mccaycellars.com* ⊠ *Tastings $15* ⊘ *Closed Tues. and Wed.*

Michael David Winery

WINERY/DISTILLERY | *Wine Enthusiast* magazine anointed Adam Mettler of Michael David its winemaker of the year in 2018 in recognition of his skill in developing smooth but characterful red blends like Petite Petit (Petite Sirah and Petit Verdot) and Freakshow Zinfandel. Taste these and other wines at the sprawling roadside **Phillips Farms Fruit Stand,** where fifth-generation farmers turned winery owners Michael and David Philips also sell their family's gorgeous produce. ■**TIP**➜ **Breakfast or lunch at the stand's café is a treat.** ⊠ *4580 W. Hwy. 12, at N. Ray Rd.* ☎ *209/368–7384* ⊕ *www.michaeldavidwinery.com* ⊠ *Tastings from $10.*

Micke Grove Regional Park

AMUSEMENT PARK/WATER PARK | **FAMILY** | This 258-acre, oak-shaded park has a Japanese tea garden, picnic tables, children's play areas, an agricultural museum, a zoo, a golf course, and a water-play feature. **Fun Town at Micke Grove,** a family-oriented amusement park, is geared toward younger children. ⊠ *11793 N. Micke Grove Rd.* ✛ *Off Hwy. 99 Armstrong Rd. exit* ☎ *209/953–8800 park info* ⊠ *From $5.*

 Restaurants

The Dancing Fox Winery and Bakery

$ | **AMERICAN** | A good downtown stop especially for lunch, the Dancing Fox also has a tasting room for its eponymous wines. The restaurant, whose decor shimmers with fairy-tale whimsy, serves sandwiches, salads, pizzas, burgers, and wraps and has more than a dozen beers on tap. **Known for:** Sunday brunch; wine tasting; historic downtown setting. ⑤ *Average main: $15* ⊠ *203 S. School St.* ☎ *203/366–2634* ⊕ *www.dancingfoxlodi.com* ⊘ *Closed Mon. No dinner Sun.*

Pietro's Trattoria

$$ | **ITALIAN** | Lodi's go-to spot for Italian American classics wins fans for its quality ingredients, Tuscan-courtyard ambience, and plant-filled outdoor patio (reservations essential on weekends). Expect straightforward, well-executed renditions of chicken piccata and pork Milanese, filling lasagna and seasonal risotto, pizzas, and the like, all delivered with informal good cheer by the cadre of servers. **Known for:** Italian-American classics; meatball and chicken pesto with cheese sandwiches for lunch; Lodi and Italian wines. ⑤ *Average main: $22* ⊠ *317 E. Kettleman La.* ☎ *209/368–0613* ⊕ *www.pietroslodi.com* ⊘ *Closed Sun.*

★ Towne House Restaurant

$$$$ | **MODERN AMERICAN** | Special-occasion dinners often take place in the distinguished rooms of this former residence behind, and part of, the Wine & Roses hotel. Painted in rich, textured hues offset by wide white molding, the rooms exude a subtle sophistication matched by seasonal dishes that might include porcini-dusted lamb chops or fish atop risotto. **Known for:** fresh seasonal local ingredients; weekend brunch with varied offerings; Town Corner Café & Market for breakfast and lunch daily. ⑤ *Average main: $39* ⊠ *2505 W. Turner Rd., at Woodhaven La.* ☎ *209/371–6160* ⊕ *winerose.com/the-restaurant* ⊘ *No lunch.*

 Hotels

Wine & Roses Hotel

$$$ | **HOTEL** | Set on 7 acres amid a tapestry of informal gardens, this hotel has cultivated a sense of refinement that's typically associated with Napa or Carmel. **Pros:** luxurious setting; popular restaurant; spa treatments. **Cons:** expensive for the area; some guests mention that walls are thin; many events. ⑤ *Rooms from: $299* ⊠ *2505 W. Turner Rd.* ☎ *209/334–6988* ⊕ *www.winerose.com* ⇄ *66 rooms* ⦿❙ *No meals.*

Nevada City

61 miles northeast of Sacramento.

Nevada City, once known as the Queen City of the Northern Mines, is the most appealing of the northern Mother Lode towns. The iron-shutter brick buildings that line downtown streets contain antiques shops, galleries, boutiques, B&Bs, restaurants, a winery, and some tasting rooms. Gas street lamps and historic structures like the distinctive 1861 Firehouse No. 1, at 241 Main Street, and the still active 1865 Nevada Theatre, at 401 Broad Street, add to the romance. At one point in the 1850s, Nevada City had a population of nearly 10,000—enough to support much cultural activity. Today, about 3,000 people live here, but the visual and performing-arts scenes remain vibrant.

GETTING HERE AND AROUND
You'll need a car to get here. From Sacramento take I–80 east to Highway 49 north; from Reno take I–80 and Highway 20 west. Nevada County Connects (☎ 530/177–0103) provides public transit.

ESSENTIALS
VISITOR INFORMATION Nevada City Chamber of Commerce. ⊠ *132 Main St.* ☎ *530/265–2692* ⊕ *www.nevadacitychamber.com.*

Sights

Nevada City Winery
WINERY/DISTILLERY | The area's oldest operating winery, established in 1980, pours its wines, many from Sierra Foothills grapes, in a tasting room whose back patio perches over the wine-making facility. Chardonnay is a best seller, with Cabernet Sauvignon and Rhône and Italian reds among the other specialties. ⊠ *321 Spring St., at Bridge St.* ☎ *530/265–9463* ⊕ *www.ncwinery.com* 🍷 *Tastings from $16.*

Szabo Vineyards
WINERY/DISTILLERY | Taste for yourself what makes Sierra Foothills wines unique at the brick-walled sipping salon of owner-winemaker Sándor "Alex" Szabo. In addition to growing the grapes 7 miles west of his downtown tasting room and making the wines, Alex is often the one pouring them. His Zinfandel, Petite Sirah, Grenache, Syrah, and other wines impress with their soft tannins, ample acidity, and long finish. ⊠ *316 Broad St., at York St.* ☎ *530/265–8792* ⊕ *www.szabovineyards.com* 🍷 *Tastings $10* ⊗ *Closed Mon.–Thurs.*

Restaurants

★ Lola
$$$ | **MODERN AMERICAN** | Riffing off the calculated flamboyance of its namesake, the gold-rush-era celebrity Lola Montez, the National Exchange Hotel's restaurant flirts with excess yet retains its composure decorated as it is with Persian rugs, long turquoise banquette benches, and brushed-bronze shepherd's-hook lighting fixtures. The chefs show a similar knack for incorporating unexpected elements, as with a recent entrée of honey-garlic buttermilk fried chicken whose sides— heirloom grits and dinosaur kale with candied kumquats—enlivened the dish but didn't undermine it. **Known for:** Tarantula Dance tequila-mescal specialty-cocktail homage to Lola's stage act; atypical small plates and salads; most ingredients "organic, ethically raised, and locally sourced". ⑤ *Average main: $30* ⊠ *211 Broad St., at Spring St.* ☎ *530/362–7605* ⊕ *thenationalexchangehotel.com/dining* ⊗ *No lunch.*

Sushi in the Raw
$$$ | **JAPANESE** | Landlocked Nevada City might seem like an odd place for a sushi haven, but this brick-walled restaurant with an open kitchen consistently ranks at the top of local "best-of" lists for Japanese cuisine. Owners Susan and Kaoru "Ru" Suzuki (he's the executive

chef and creative whiz), emphasize old-school techniques and ultrafresh ingredients, enlivening the proceedings with offbeat items like truffle sashimi and the signature trout, salmon, and other "shooters" in shot glasses or quail eggs. **Known for:** cooked fish heads in soy marinade; baked and vegetarian items for the non-sushi crowd; gluten-free menu. Ⓢ *Average main: $30* ✉ *315 Spring St., near Pine St.* ☎ *530/478–9503* ⊕ *sushiintheraw.net* ☾ *Closed Sun. and Mon. No lunch.*

Three Forks Bakery & Brewing Co.
$ | **AMERICAN** | Baked goods, wood-fired pizzas, excellent coffee (teas and kombucha, too), and microbrews made on-site draw locals and tourists to this redbrick spot with a high, heavy-beamed open ceiling. The food's ingredients come from nearby organic sources; the beers on tap range from blonde and pale ales to triple IPAs and several porters. **Known for:** lunch and dinner menu changes with the seasons; breads, muffins, scones, cookies, and cakes; soups and salads. Ⓢ *Average main: $14* ✉ *211 Commercial St.* ☎ *530/470–8333* ⊕ *www.threefork-snc.com* ☾ *Closed Tues.*

 Hotels

Madison House Bed & Breakfast
$$ | **B&B/INN** | A convenient downtown location, filling breakfasts showcasing local organic products, and welcoming hosts who exceed expectations make for a winning combination at this northern Gold Country B&B inside a romantic Victorian house. **Pros:** landscaped garden and sun porch; homemade baked goods, historic, romantic atmosphere. **Cons:** no elevator to upper-floor rooms; some noise and sun in front rooms; weekend minimum-stay requirement. Ⓢ *Rooms from: $205* ✉ *427 Broad St.* ☎ *530/470–6127* ⊕ *www.themadisonhouse.net* 🛏 *5 rooms* ⦿ *Free breakfast.*

★ The National Exchange Hotel
$$ | **HOTEL** | Once more proudly anchoring the southern portion of Nevada City's historic district, this three-story boutique property, whose structure dates from 1856, reopened in 2021 following a period-sensitive multiyear makeover. **Pros:** contemporary, boutique-hotel style yet evokes the past; near shops, tasting rooms, and restaurants; as in the 1800s, a swank bar. **Cons:** smaller rooms have full or queen beds and sleep only two; no elevator to third-floor rooms; expensive on summer weekends. Ⓢ *Rooms from: $184* ✉ *211 Broad St.* ☎ *530/362–7605* ⊕ *www.thenationalexchangehotel.com* 🛏 *38 rooms* ⦿ *No meals.*

Outside Inn
$ | **HOTEL** | **FAMILY** | It looks like a typical one-story motel, but the Outside Inn offers a variety of unique accommodations inspired by nature or activities in nature (there's a climbing wall in the rock-climbing suite), in an ideal location to enjoy Northern California's four seasons. **Pros:** fun reinvention of a motel; convenient to trails and hikes; affiliated Inn Town Campground for camping and glamping. **Cons:** rooms are on the small side; might be too funky for some guests; ½-mile walk to downtown. Ⓢ *Rooms from: $99* ✉ *575 E. Broad St.* ☎ *530/265–2233* ⊕ *www.outsideinn.com* 🛏 *15 rooms* ⦿ *No meals.*

🎭 Performing Arts

Miners Foundry
ARTS CENTERS | The foundry, erected in 1856, produced machines for gold mining and logging. The Pelton Water Wheel, a power source for the mines credited with jump-starting the hydroelectric power industry, was invented here. The building is now used to stage art, dance, music, and film events, and there's a combination bar and café. ✉ *325 Spring St.* ☎ *530/265–5040* ⊕ *www.minersfoundry.org.*

Grass Valley

4 miles south of Nevada City.

More than half of California's total gold production was extracted from mines around Grass Valley, including the Empire Mine, among the Gold Country's most fascinating attractions. The mine and the North Star Mining Museum, also worth a stop, are a few miles from the downtown historic district, which though walkable isn't as quaint as nearby Nevada City's.

GETTING HERE AND AROUND

You'll need a car to get here. Highway 49 is the north–south route into town, Highway 20 the east–west one. Nevada County Connects (☎ *530/477–0103*) provides public transit.

Sights

★ Empire Mine State Historic Park

NATIONAL/STATE PARK | FAMILY | Starting with the "secret map" that mine management hid from miners, you can relive the days of gold, grit, and glory, when this mine was one of the biggest and most prosperous hard-rock gold mines in North America. Empire Mine yielded an estimated 5.8 million ounces of gold from 367 miles of underground passages. You can walk into a mine shaft and peer into dark, deep recesses and almost imagine what it felt like to work this vast operation. On some days, you might see tradesfolk in action at the blacksmith shop. The grounds have the Bourn Cottage (exquisite redwood interior; call for tour times), picnic tables, and gentle trails—perfect for a family outing. ✉ *10791 E. Empire St.* ☎ *530/273–8522* ⊕ *www.parks.ca.gov* 💲 *$7.*

North Star Mining Museum

MUSEUM | FAMILY | Inside a former powerhouse, the museum displays a 32-foot-high Pelton Water Wheel said to be the largest ever built. The wheel, used to power mining operations, was a forerunner of modern turbines that generate hydroelectricity. Other exhibits, some geared to children, document life in the mines and the environmental effects mining had on the area. You can picnic nearby. ✉ *10933 Allison Ranch Rd.* ⊹ *Head south from Main St. on Mill St.* ☎ *530/264–7569* ⊕ *www.nevadacounty-history.org* 💲 *Donation requested.*

Restaurants

Cirino's at Main Street

$$ | ITALIAN | FAMILY | A family-owned spot with exposed brick walls, a tall ceiling, and a well-worn bar and floor, Cirino's serves up a vast menu of hefty Italian American favorites like Corsican rosemary chicken, steak à la Gorgonzola, and pork chop Milanese. The bar crew, which slings the signature Bloody Mary and other specialty cocktails, is as friendly as the rest of the team. **Known for:** old-school recipes presented with flair; homemade soups and sauces; family-friendly attitude. 💲 *Average main: $24* ✉ *213 W. Main St.* ☎ *530/477–6000* ⊕ *www.cirino-satmainstreet.com* 🕐 *Closed Mon.–Wed. (but check).*

Grass Valley Pasty Co.

$ | BRITISH | Eat like a 19th-century Cornish miner at this modest restaurant serving home-baked pasties, flaky on the outside with moist and flavorful meat, vegetable, and other fillings. Jammed with skirt steak, potatoes, and turnips, the Cousin Jack, named for a long-time shop on this site, hews closer to tradition, with the vegetarian, barbecued pulled pork, and a recent offering of turkey, pesto, sun-dried tomatoes, and cheese typical of the equally satisfying updates. **Known for:** at least one vegetarian option; family-run business; closes early evening. 💲 *Average main: $10* ✉ *100 S. Auburn St., at W. Main St.* ☎ *530/802–5202* 🕐 *Closed Mon.*

Dancing Her Way to Fame

One of the most colorful personalities of the gold-rush era was Lola Montez (1821–61), a dancer, singer, courtesan, and gender rebel who earned international notoriety for her suggestive "spider dance." By contemporary accounts, her contortions, though not universally admired, were known to inspire approving miners to toss gold nuggets onto the stage.

Countess, Mistress, Possible Witch

Born Eliza Rosanna Gilbert in Ireland, Montez recast herself in young adulthood as a Spanish countess, performing in Europe, where her lovers included the composer Franz Liszt and the ill-fated King Ludwig of Bavaria. Famous, in part, for being famous, the entertainer cooled her heels in the Gold Country not long after her calls for Bavarian democracy contributed to Ludwig's overthrow and her banishment as a witch. Or so one version goes.

Lola Lives On

For a spell, Montez resided in Grass Valley, where a reproduction of her house downtown still stands at 248 Mill Street. Now a family-counseling center, the house isn't accessible, but Lola's memory lives on throughout the Gold Country, where rooms and suites in a few lodgings are named in her honor. Lola, the stylish restaurant in Nevada City's National Exchange Hotel, replicates the opulence of its namesake's glory years.

South Pine Cafe

$ | AMERICAN | Locals flock to this always-busy diner on a Victorian's ground floor for lobster Benedict, a spiced-up Mexican chicken scramble, and other dishes that are anything but your ordinary eggs and pancakes (though you can order those, too, and vegetarian versions of several items). Imaginative burritos, wraps, burgers, and more lobster in the form of a melt sandwich appear for lunch. **Known for:** homemade muffins; vegan and gluten-free options; many ingredients sourced from local family farms. $ *Average main: $14* ✉ *102 Richardson St., at N. Auburn St.* ☎ *707/274–0261* ⊕ *www. southpinecafe.com* ⊘ *No dinner.*

 Hotels

Gold Miners Inn

$$ | HOTEL | Just off Highway 49 and superbly run, this Ascend Collection property provides a comfortable experience, with art and artifacts reflecting the area's mining heritage gracing public areas and guest rooms. **Pros:** clean downtown hotel; art and artifacts reflecting the area's mining heritage; complimentary hot breakfast. **Cons:** no pool; despite stylish touches has a chain-like feel; some light sleepers find highway-side rooms noisy (ask for courtyard accommodations). $ *Rooms from: $155* ✉ *121 Bank St.* ☎ *530/477–1700* ⊕ *www.gold-minersinngrassvalley.com* ⤴ *81 rooms* ⦿*Free breakfast.*

Holbrooke Hotel

$$$ | HOTEL | A Main Street icon from the mid-1800s—when the A-list guest list included entertainer Lola Montez, writer Mark Twain, and Ulysses S. Grant—this two-story, historic-district hotel received a down-to-the-studs (in some cases bricks) makeover and reopened in 2020 as a boutique property. **Pros:** convenient to shops and restaurants; mix of antique, reproduction, and contemporary furnishings; ground-floor saloon is reportedly the West's oldest continuously

operating bar. **Cons:** expensive pet fee; street-side rooms pick up traffic noise; books up well ahead on many weekends. ⑤ *Rooms from: $255* ✉ *212 W. Main St.* ☎ *530/460–3078* ⊕ *www.holbrooke.com* 🛏 *28 rooms* ⦿❘ *No meals.*

Nightlife

The Pour House

BARS/PUBS | The owners of this downtown bar aim to please lovers of beer and wine with a dozen-plus pours of each, many from local and regional craft breweries and boutique wineries. Across from the Holbrooke Hotel, the storefront space (closed on Sunday and Monday) serves soups, dips, soft pretzels, and other comfort bites. There's live music some nights. ✉ *217 W. Main St., at Church St.* ☎ *530/802–5414* ⊕ *www.thepourhousegv.com.*

Auburn

24 miles south of Grass Valley, 34 miles northeast of Sacramento.

Halfway between San Francisco and Reno, Auburn is convenient to gold-rush sites, outdoor recreation opportunities, and wineries. The self-proclaimed "endurance capital of the world" is abuzz almost every summer weekend with running, cycling, rafting, kayaking, and equestrian events. Old Town Auburn has its own gold-rush charm, with narrow climbing streets, cobblestone lanes, wooden sidewalks, and many original buildings.

GETTING HERE AND AROUND

Amtrak serves Auburn, though most visitors arrive by car on Highway 49 or I–80. Once downtown, you can tour on foot.

Sights

Placer County Museum

MUSEUM | Visible from the highway, Auburn's standout structure is the Placer County Courthouse. The classic bronze-domed building houses the Placer County Museum, which documents the area's history—Native American, railroad, agricultural, and mining—from the early 1700s to 1900. Look for the gold nuggets valued at more than $338,000 today, and don't miss the women's cell under the Maple Street staircase. ■TIP➜ **Ask about other nearby county-run history museums.** ✉ *101 Maple St.* ☎ *530/889–6500* ⊕ *www.placer.ca.gov/2489/museums* 🎟 *Free.*

Restaurants

Auburn Alehouse

$ | AMERICAN | FAMILY | Inside the historic American Block building, which dates to 1856, you can see this craft operation's beers being made through glass walls behind the dining room, which serves burgers, nachos, salads, wraps, and other decent gastropub fare. Gold Country Pilsner, Old Town Brown, and Gold Digger IPA are all Great American Beer Festival award winners. **Known for:** chicken, pork, and fish tacos; herb-brined buttermilk fried chicken; kids menu. ⑤ *Average main: $16* ✉ *289 Washington St.* ☎ *530/885–2537* ⊕ *www.auburnalehouse.com.*

Awful Annie's

$ | AMERICAN | FAMILY | One of Auburn's favorite old-time breakfast and lunch spots entices patrons with waffles, pancakes, Monte Cristo French toast, and a slew of egg dishes you can wash down with an award-winning Bloody Mary or two. Feast on burgers, sandwiches, and more Bloody Marys for lunch. **Known for:** heartiest breakfast in the foothills; Grandma's bread pudding with brandy sauce; town-hangout feel. ⑤ *Average main: $13*

Almost 6 million ounces of gold were extracted from the Empire Mine.

⊠ *13460 Lincoln Way* ☎ *530/888–9857* ⊕ *www.awfulannies.com* ⊗ *No dinner.*

Carpe Vino Marketplace & Lounge

$$$ | **MODERN AMERICAN** | What started as a boutique wine retailer inside a restored 19th-century saloon evolved into a must-visit bistro serving imaginative cuisine. By 2022, reboots of both the space and the menu, with the focus reportedly shifting to cocktails and small plates, should be complete. **Known for:** varied wine list; historic setting; imaginative fare. ⑤ *Average main: $27* ⊠ *1568 Lincoln Way* ☎ *530/823–0320* ⊕ *www. carpevinoauburn.com* ⊗ *No lunch (but check).*

The Pour Choice

$ | **AMERICAN** | Black subway tiles, contemporary bistro furniture, and a gray-marble counter lit by orb-shape Edison bulbs lend urban flair to this fine spot for a craft coffee or one of more than two dozen local, national, and international brews on tap. In a space once occupied by a drugstore, the Pour Choice, which bills itself as Auburn's living room, serves light fare that might include a grilled gourmet-cheese sandwich on ciabatta with bacon. **Known for:** upbeat vibe; talented baristas; outdoor terrace in good weather. ⑤ *Average main: $11* ⊠ *177 Sacramento St.* ☎ *530/820–3451* ⊕ *thepourchoice.com.*

Hotels

Holiday Inn Auburn Hotel

$$ | **HOTEL** | **FAMILY** | Above the freeway across from Old Town, this hotel has a welcoming lobby and chain-standard but well-organized rooms with refrigerators, microwaves, and work areas. **Pros:** some rooms sleep four people; suitable base for Gold Country exploring; on site restaurant. **Cons:** lacks style; some traffic noise; can't walk to Old Town restaurants and shops. ⑤ *Rooms from: $153* ⊠ *120 Grass Valley Hwy.* ☎ *530/887–8787, 800/814–8787* ⊕ *www.auburnhi.com* ⇆ *96 rooms* ⑪ *No meals.*

Coloma

18 miles southeast of Auburn.

The California gold rush started in Coloma when James W. Marshall discovered flecks of metal in the bottom of a ditch. "Boys, I believe I've found a gold mine!" he exclaimed in January 1848 to colleagues at John Sutter's mill here. In short order, California's coastal communities began to empty as prospectors flocked to the hills, getting a jump on East Coasters, who didn't hear about the boom until mid-August.

GETTING HERE AND AROUND
A car is the only practical way to get to Coloma, via Highway 49. Once parked, you can walk to all the worthwhile sights.

Sights

★ Marshall Gold Discovery State Historic Park
NATIONAL/STATE PARK | FAMILY | The American River's south fork slices through this park commemorating California's mining history. Trails lead from the parking lot to a statue of James Marshall with sublime views; beyond it to the north stands a working reproduction of an 1840s mill erected near where he first spotted gold. Most of Coloma lies within the park. Though crowded with tourists in summer, the town hardly resembles the mob scene it was in 1849, when 2,000 prospectors staked out claims along the streambed. Coloma's population grew to 4,000, supporting seven hotels, three banks, and many stores and other businesses. But when reserves of the precious metal dwindled, the prospectors left as quickly as they had come. ■TIP→ **For $8 per person, rangers give gold-panning lessons on the hour, year-round.** ⊠ *310 Back St., off Hwy. 49* ☎ *530/622–3470* ⊕ *www.parks.ca.gov/marshallgold* 🖾 *$8 per vehicle.*

Placerville

9 miles south of Coloma, 44 miles east of Sacramento.

It's hard to imagine now, but in 1849 about 4,000 miners staked out every gully and hillside in Placerville, turning the town into a rip-roaring camp of log cabins, tents, and clapboard houses. The area was then known as Hangtown, a graphic allusion to the nature of frontier justice. It took on the name Placerville in 1854 and became an important supply center for the miners.

Many of the always hoppin' downtown historic district's restaurants, indie shops, coffeehouses, and wine bars occupy rehabbed 19th-century buildings. A defining characteristic of nearby El Dorado AVA wineries (⊕ *eldoradowines.org*) is their vineyards' high elevation, from 1,200 to 3,500 feet.

GETTING HERE AND AROUND
You'll need a car to get to and around Placerville. It's a 45-minute drive from Sacramento via U.S. 50.

Sights

Apple Hill
FARM/RANCH | FAMILY | From July to late December, Apple Hill Growers Association members open their orchards and vineyards for apple and berry picking; picnicking; and wine, cider, pressed-juice, and other tastings. Treasure hunts, pond fishing, pie making, and other activities attract families. The Apple Hill website has a map and an events calendar, or download the Official Apple Hill Growers app. ■TIP→ **On autumn weekends, take U.S. 50's Camino exit to avoid some of the traffic congestion.** ⊠ *Placerville* ✛ *Starting 2 miles east of Hwy. 49, Exits 48–57 off U.S. 50* ☎ *530/644–7692* ⊕ *www.applehill.com.*

Boeger Winery

WINERY/DISTILLERY | In 1972, Greg Boeger revived a gold rush–era farm that once supported fruit and nut orchards, a winery, and a distillery. These days Boeger produces estate wines from 30 varietals grown on two parcels totaling 100 acres, with Sauvignon Blanc and Barbera the best sellers and Zinfandel and Primitivo also worth seeking out. Visits are by appointment (same-day often possible). ■TIP→ **The creek-side picnic area fronting the tasting room hosts bands and food vendors on Friday evenings in summer (reserve space well ahead).** ☒ *1709 Carson Rd. ⊹ Head north from U.S. 50, Exit 48, then northeast (right) on Carson Rd.* ☎ *530/622–8094* ⊕ *www.boegerwinery. com* ☕ *Tastings from $10.*

★ Delfino Farms—Edio Vineyards

WINERY/DISTILLERY | Apple growers since 1964, the Delfino family occupies one of El Dorado County's most idyllic sites. The clan gained early notice for Joan Delfino's apple pies and the fun farm events here. In the 2010s, her grandchildren started a winery named for her husband, local agricultural icon Edio Delfino. They pour their superb whites and reds in a gleaming-silver contemporary space whose patio perches over apple trees surrounded by grapevines ringed by a forest. ■TIP→ **Wine tasting takes place year-round; bakery visits and apple events occur seasonally.** ☒ *3205 N. Canyon Rd., off Carson Rd.* ☎ *530/622–0184* ⊕ *delfinofarms.com* ☕ *Tastings from $10* ۞ *Tasting room closed Tues. and Wed.*

Element 79 Vineyards

WINERY/DISTILLERY | This winery's owner envisioned his sleek hospitality space as "a country club" for experiencing wines by the glass or flight, with or without the charcuterie and cheese sold on-site. The glass back wall and adjoining patio edge the 32-acre estate vineyard, which guests can hike on their own (there's a map) or on occasional tours. Winemaker Scott Johnson's red blends and Cabernets stand out, as does the unconventional, canned, dry-hopped Viognier sparkler (Johnson also brews beer). ☒ *7350 Fairplay Rd., southeast 1½ miles off Mt. Aukum Rd., Fair Play* ☎ *530/497–0750* ⊕ *element79vineyards. com* ☕ *Tastings from $5.*

Hangtown's Gold Bug Park & Mine

MINE | **FAMILY** | Take a self-guided tour of this fully lighted mine shaft within a park owned by the City of Placerville. The worthwhile audio tour (included) makes clear what you're seeing. ■TIP→ **A shaded stream runs through the park, and there are picnic facilities.** ☒ *2635 Goldbug La., Exit U.S. 50 at Bedford Ave. and follow signs* ☎ *530/642–5207* ⊕ *www.goldbugpark.org* ☕ *Park free; mine tour $10* ۞ *Closed weekdays late fall–early spring except for a few holidays.*

★ Holly's Hill Vineyards

WINERY/DISTILLERY | The founders of this woodsy hilltop winery 7 miles south of Apple Hill tasted Châteauneuf-du-Pape on their honeymoon, sparking a lifetime passion for Rhône wines made in classic French style. Mourvèdre is a specialty, by itself and in blends with Grenache, Syrah, or both. Carignane, Counoise, and other lower-profile Rhône reds are also made, along with whites that include the Roussanne-dominant Patriarche Blanc blend. By appointment only (same-day usually okay), taste these estate wines in a space with views that extend 75 miles on a clear day. ☒ *3680 Leisure La., off Pleasant Valley Rd. ⊹ From U.S. 50, Exit 49, follow Broadway east to Newtown Rd. and Pleasant Valley Rd. southeast* ☎ *530/344–0227* ⊕ *www.hollyshill.com* ☕ *Tastings $10.*

★ Lava Cap Winery

WINERY/DISTILLERY | Nineteenth-century miners knew if they found the type of volcanic rocks visible everywhere on this winery's property that gold was nearby. These days, the rocky soils and vineyard elevations as high as 2,800 feet play pivotal roles in creating Lava Cap's fruit-forward yet elegant wines. Zinfandel, Grenache, Cabernet Franc, and Petite Sirah star among the reds, Chardonnay and Viognier among the whites. ■TIP→ **After a tasting you can picnic on the patio and enjoy Sierra foothills vistas.** ✉ *2221 Fruitridge Rd.* ☎ *530/621–0175* ⊕ *www. lavacap.com* 🍷 *Tastings from $15.*

★ Starfield Vineyards

WINERY/DISTILLERY | Its many microclimates inspired owner-winemaker Tom Sinton to purchase a 67-acre hillside property he transformed into a magnificent showcase for wines from mostly Rhône and Italian varietals. With a nature trail, a 300-foot-long rose arbor, an amphitheater for events, a lakeside pavilion, and an upper patio with views of trees near and far, the wines could have taken a back seat, but Sinton crafts them with such grace and precision that they more than match the setting and hospitality. ✉ *2750 Jacquier Rd.* ✛ *3 miles northeast of downtown Placerville.* ☎ *530/748–3085* ⊕ *www.starfieldvineyards.com* 🍷 *Tastings from $10.*

Restaurants

★ Allez

$$ | FRENCH | The tale of how the couple running this spot for to-go or dine-in French food came to be husband and wife says all one needs to know about their passion for beautifully crafted cuisine: he won her heart with his escargot sauce. In a casual space with ocher walls, six utilitarian stools at the wine bar, and a few tables inside and out, the two serve baguette sandwiches, salads, crepes, stews, and entrées like coq au vin, cassoulet, and pork tenderloin. **Known for:** all-day prix-fixe menu (a deal), plus à la carte; sandwich, salad, and dessert lunch boxes; many vegetarian and gluten-free items. ⑤ *Average main: $22* ✉ *4242 Fowler La., Diamond Springs* ✛ *Off Hwy. 49, 3 miles south of downtown Placerville* ☎ *530/621–1160* ⊕ *www.allezeldorado. com* ⊗ *Closed Sun. and Mon.*

★ Creekside Cork & Brew

$$ | AMERICAN | At shift's end, workers from Fair Play wineries gather with neighbors at this nouveau rustic roadside watering hole whose chefs prepare elevated farm-to-table comfort cuisine—from soups, salads, and sandwiches to fish, meat, and pasta entrées. Among the crowd-pleasing burgers—served at high-top and regular tables, at the bar, or on the patio outside—is the one with bacon, Brie, and fig, though the prize for decadence goes to the weekend-brunch mash-up with candied maple bacon, a fried egg, and hollandaise. **Known for:** local wines and beers; patio dining; live music on many Fridays and Sundays. ⑤ *Average main: $19* ✉ *7915 Fairplay Rd., at Perry Creek Rd.* ☎ *530/503–0044* ⊕ *creeksidecorkandbrew.com* ⊗ *Closed Tues. and Wed.*

Heyday Cafe

$$ | AMERICAN | Inside an exposed-brick 1857 former assay office where miners exchanged gold nuggets for the coin of the realm, the Heyday is a happy haven for salads, panini, and thin-crust pizzas at lunch and dinner entrées like seared salmon, baby back ribs, and risotto. The mood is casual, but the food is prepared with style. **Known for:** local to international wine list; molasses gingerbread cake; sister restaurant, The Independent, at 629 Main. ⑤ *Average main: $24* ✉ *325 Main St.* ☎ *530/626–9700* ⊕ *www.heydaycafe.com* ⊗ *Closed Mon. (but check).*

★ Smith Flat House

$$$ | MODERN AMERICAN | Carefully sourced ingredients from local purveyors, meticulous execution, and a historic setting at a former mine site 3 miles east of downtown have made this restaurant a hit among locals, Gold Country tourists, and travelers heading to or from Tahoe. The seasonally changing menu might include a wild-mushroom Bordelaise appetizer, jambalaya risotto, and the Black and White entrée of filet mignon and perfectly grilled prawns. **Known for:** waffle Benedict at

Sunday brunch; salads, pizzas, burgers for lunch; outdoor dining area. $ *Average main: $29 ⊠ 2021 Smith Flat Rd. ✛ From U.S. 50, Exit 49, head north on Point View Dr. and Jacquier Rd. and east on Smith Flat Rd. ☎ 530/621–1003 ⊕ www.smith-flathouse.com ☉ Closed Mon. and Tues. No lunch Wed. and Thurs.*

Solid Ground Brewing

$ | **ECLECTIC** | The chef at this brewpub with a no-nonsense industrial decor (high ceilings, concrete floor, huge garage doors) tailors the cuisine to the namesake beers produced by two Sierra foothills natives, one with an enology degree, the other with extensive experience in European beer making. Carnitas tacos, a buttermilk fried-chicken sandwich, and a burger with the cheese of your choice are among the gastropub options. **Known for:** seasonal ciders and spritzers; wine blended into some beers, others aged in wine barrels; good stop for lunch on a hot day. $ *Average main: $13 ⊠ 553 Pleasant Valley Rd., Diamond Springs ✛ Off Hwy. 49, 3 miles south of downtown Placerville ☎ 530/344–7442 ⊕ solidgroundbrewing.com.*

That Little Italian Place

$$ | **ITALIAN** | The chef-owner of this order-at-the-counter restaurant also known as The Place describes the menu's influences as his East Coast grandmother's multicourse Sunday family suppers, his later culinary explorations, and his zeal about creating "fresh and original" Italian cuisine. The country-road setting, butcher-block tables, and open kitchen dominated by a copper-clad, wood-fired oven accentuate the "just like home" feeling, as do the calzones, pizzas, and pasta dishes. **Known for:** antipasti, salads, panini, and "grind-ahs" (submarine sandwiches); vegetarian and gluten-free items; live music on the patio some nights. $ *Average main: $19 ⊠ 2530 Pleasant Valley Rd., at Bucks Bar Rd. ✛ From Main St., take Cedar Ravine Rd. southeast 5¾ miles and turn left (east)*

☎ *530/621–1680 ⊕ thatlittleitalianplace. com/placerville ☉ Closed Mon. and Tues.*

Totem Coffee

$ | **CAFÉ** | The best spot in the historic district to relax over coffee and espresso drinks—or sip tea, kombucha, and sometimes hot chocolate—sources its beans from ethical producers worldwide. Enjoy your beverage inside the informal contemporary-rustic space or on a tree-shaded outdoor patio to the sounds of a large fountain. **Known for:** superb cappuccinos and lattes; pastries, muffins, doughnuts for breakfast; light lunch fare. $ *Average main: $8 ⊠ 312 Main St., Suite 104 ☎ 530/903–3280 ⊕ www. totemcoffeeroasters.com ☉ Closed Tues.*

 Hotels

★ Eden Vale Inn

$$$ | **B&B/INN** | **FAMILY** | This lavish but rustic B&B occupies a converted turn-of-the-20th-century hay barn, the centerpiece of which is a 27-foot slate fireplace that rises to a sloping ceiling of timber beams. **Pros:** exceptionally plush rooms; stunning patio and grounds; romantic setting. **Cons:** expensive for the area; summer weekends book up far ahead; weekend minimum-stay requirement. $ *Rooms from: $309 ⊠ 1780 Springvale Rd. ☎ 530/621–0901 ⊕ www.edenva-leinn.com ⇆ 7 rooms ⦿⃒ Free breakfast.*

★ Lucinda's Country Inn

$$ | **B&B/INN** | Effusive but not intrusive hospitality is the trademark of this contemporary inn between Placerville and Plymouth whose spacious light-filled suites have views of the oaks, firs, and other trees surrounding the property. **Pros:** romantic setting; convenient for wine touring; filling breakfast and catered dinner option. **Cons:** some rooms sleep only two; long drive to Placerville or Plymouth restaurants; lacks amenities of larger properties. $ *Rooms from: $180 ⊠ 6701 Perry Creek Rd., Fair Play ☎ 530/409–4169*

⊕ *www.lucindascountryinn.com* ⌁ *5 rooms* ❍|* Free breakfast.*

Plymouth

20 miles south of Placerville.

The most concentrated Gold Country wine-touring area lies in the hills of the Shenandoah Valley, east of Plymouth—you could easily spend two or three days just hitting the highlights. Zinfandel is the primary grape grown here, but area vineyards produce many other varietals, from Rhônes like Syrah and Mourvèdre to Spanish Tempranillo and Italian Barbera and Sangiovese. Most wineries are open for tastings at least on Friday and weekends, and some of the top ones are open daily; many welcome picnickers.

GETTING HERE AND AROUND
A car is necessary to explore the Shenandoah Valley. Highway 49 runs north–south through Plymouth. To reach the valley from the highway, head east and then north on Shenandoah Road (also signed as E16).

 Sights

Amador Cellars
WINERY/DISTILLERY | Larry and Linda Long made wine out of their home in Truckee for 15 years before opening their downhome Amador County winery. Their son Michael is head winemaker, daughter Ashley his assistant. Estate-grown Zinfandel is the biggest seller, but this small operation also does well with Syrah, Barbera, Tempranillo, and the Portuguese varietal Touriga (one of the Port grapes), and there's a GSM (Grenache, Syrah, and Mourvèdre) Rhône-style blend. Tastings, by appointment, take place in a barn surrounded by grapevines or just outside. ✉ *11093 Shenandoah Rd., Plymouth* ☏ *209/245–6150* ⊕ *amadorcellars.com* ⊙ *Closed Tues. and Wed.*

Helwig Winery
WINERY/DISTILLERY | Splashier than many of its neighbors and a draw as much for its restaurant and seasonal live music as its wines, family-operated Helwig occupies a hilltop steel, wood, and glass tasting space with knockout views. The winery specializes in fruit-forward reds, most notably Barbera, Graciano, and Tempranillo; the sparkling rosé of Sangiovese shines among the lighter wines. ■**TIP→ If the weather's good, it's worth the small extra fee to sip alfresco on the deck.** ✉ *11555 Shenandoah Rd., Plymouth* ☏ *209/245–5200* ⊕ *www.helwigwinery. com* ⊠ *Tastings from $10.*

★ Jeff Runquist Wines
WINERY/DISTILLERY | Judges at the 2018 San Francisco International Wine Competition bestowed Winery of the Year honors on this operation whose tasting room ranks among the Shenandoah Valley's jolliest. Known for elegant, fruit-forward wines with velvety tannins, Jeff Runquist specializes in Barbera, Zinfandel, and Petite Sirah but makes several other reds and Muscat Canelli, Verdelho, and Viognier whites. ✉ *10776 Shenandoah Rd., Plymouth* ☏ *209/245–6282* ⊕ *www. jeffrunquistwines.com* ⊠ *Free.*

Rombauer Sierra Foothills
WINERY/DISTILLERY | For years Rombauer, famous for its Napa Valley Chardonnays, farmed foothills Zinfandel vineyards, so it wasn't a total surprise when the winery acquired an existing facility here. Inside the brightly lit tasting room or at umbrella-shaded tables you can sample the Classic flight—Sauvignon Blanc, Chardonnay, Cabernet Sauvignon, Merlot, and Sierra Foothills Zinfandel—or sip these or other wines by the glass or bottle. ■**TIP→ The winery sells charcuterie and cheeses but also allows outside food.** ✉ *12225 Steiner Rd., Plymouth* ☏ *866/280–2582* ⊕ *www.rombauer.com* ⊠ *Tastings from $13 glass, $20 flight.*

Scott Harvey Wines

WINERY/DISTILLERY | Founder Scott Harvey helped elevate the profile of Amador County wines in the 1970s, later developing two wine programs in the Napa Valley. Harvey describes the foothills as similar to Italy's Piemonte region, where Barbera originated, but with one additional benefit: it's sunnier here, which this grape loves. Barbera, Zinfandel (one from vines planted in 1869), and Syrah are the focus, but you'll also find Cabernet Sauvignon and other reds along with Sauvignon Blanc, Riesling, and sparkling and ice-style wines. ✉ *10861 Shenandoah Rd., Plymouth* ☎ *209/245–3670* ⊕ *www.scottharvey-wines.com* ✉ *Tastings from $15.*

Sobon Estate

WINERY/DISTILLERY | You can sip fruity, robust Zinfandels—old vine and new—and learn about wine making and Shenandoah Valley pioneer life at the museum here. This winery was established in 1856 and has been run since 1989 by the owners of nearby Shenandoah Vineyards, which is open daily. ■**TIP**➜ **To sample the best Zins, pay the modest fee for the reserve tasting.** ✉ *14430 Shenandoah Rd., Plymouth* ☎ *209/245–4455* ⊕ *www.sobon-wine.com* ✉ *Tastings from $5* ☉ *Closed Mon.–Thurs. (but check).*

★ Terre Rouge and Easton Wines

WINERY/DISTILLERY | The winery of Bill Easton and Jane O'Riordan achieves success with two separate labels. Terre Rouge, which focuses on Rhône-style wines, makes some of California's best Syrahs. The Easton label specializes in high-scoring Zinfandels from old and new vines and does well with Sauvignon Blanc and Cabernet Sauvignon. ■**TIP**➜ **You can picnic on the lawn here.** ✉ *10801 Dickson Rd., Plymouth* ☎ *209/245–4277* ⊕ *www.terrerougewines.com* ✉ *Tastings from $10* ☉ *Closed Tues. and Wed.*

★ Turley Wine Cellars

WINERY/DISTILLERY | Zinfandel fans won't want to miss Turley, which makes a dozen and a half single-vineyard wines (collectors love them) from old-vine grapes grown all over California. Some of the wines, including a few from Amador County, are available only in the tasting room. Petite Sirah and Cabernet Sauvignon are two other emphases. All visits are by appointment only. ✉ *10851 Shenandoah Rd., Plymouth* ☎ *209/245–3938* ⊕ *www.turleywinecellars.com/amador* ✉ *Tastings $25* ☉ *Closed Mon.–Wed. (but check).*

Vino Noceto

WINERY/DISTILLERY | Owners Suzy and Jim Gullett draw raves for their Sangioveses, which range from light and fruity to rich and heavy. They also produce Rosato di Sangiovese (aka rosé), old-vine Zinfandel, and a few other varietals. Most tastings take place in the red barn where the couple began operations in the 1980s or on a nearby patio. ✉ *11011 Shenandoah Rd., at Dickson Rd., Plymouth* ☎ *209/245–6556* ⊕ *www.noceto.com* ✉ *Tastings from $10, tour $18.*

Restaurants

Amador Vintage Market

$ | **AMERICAN** | Area caterer Beth Sogaard spiffed up Plymouth's original general store, transforming its handsome red- and sand-color brick building into a dandy stop for gourmet sandwiches and deli specialties like Dijon potato salad and house-smoked salmon. A recent Reuben with pepper Jack cheese, pickled onions, and grain mustard on house-made rosemary focaccia is typical of Sogaard's reimagining of comfort-food staples you can enjoy on-site, at nearby wineries, or in the park next door. **Known for:** homemade truffle potato chips; French dip sandwiches; selection of local wines. ⑤ *Average main: $11* ✉ *9393 Main St., Plymouth* ☎ *209/245–3663* ⊕ *beth-sogaard.com* ☉ *Closed Mon.–Thurs. (but check). No dinner.*

★ Taste

$$$$ | MODERN AMERICAN | A serendipitous find in downtown Plymouth, Taste serves eclectic modern dishes made from fresh local fare. The signature mushroom "cigars"—sautéed shiitake, crimini, and oyster mushrooms rolled with goat cheese in phyllo dough and served with porcini sauce and white truffle oil—are a small-plate staple, and sturgeon, rack of lamb, and duck confit are examples of the sustainably sourced, creative entrées. **Known for:** superb beer and wine list; knowledgeable sommeliers; seasonal cocktails. $ *Average main: $39 ⊠ 9402 Main St., Plymouth ☎ 209/245–3463 ⊕ www.restauranttaste. com ⊘ Closed Tues.–Thurs. No lunch (check for updates).*

Hotels

★ Grand Reserve Inn

$$$$ | B&B/INN | Guests typically leave this B&B gushing over just about everything—the Tuscan-villa atmosphere, the expansive vineyard vistas, the sublime hospitality, the elaborate breakfasts, the luxurious accommodations, even the ultrasoft sheets. **Pros:** idyllic setting; gracious well-trained staff; marvelous special-occasion splurge. **Cons:** pricey for the area; maximum room occupancy two people except for two-bedroom Vineyard House; per website "no children or pets permitted". $ *Rooms from: $449 ⊠ 19890 Shenandoah School Rd., Plymouth ☎ 209/245–5466 ⊕ www. grandreserveinn.com ⇨ 6 suites ⦿ Free breakfast.*

★ Rest Hotel Plymouth

$$ | B&B/INN | The team behind Plymouth's Taste restaurant converted two adjacent run-down buildings into this boutique hotel whose individually decorated rooms rank among the area's finest. **Pros:** attention to detail; continental breakfast's baked goods; evening wine hour. **Cons:** minimum stay requirement some weekends; lacks big-city hotel amenities; some noise in street-side rooms. $ *Rooms from: $165 ⊠ 9372 Main St., Plymouth ☎ 209/245–6315 ⊕ www.hotel-rest.net ⇨ 16 rooms ⦿ Free breakfast.*

Amador City

6 miles south of Plymouth.

The history of tiny Amador City (population less than 200) mirrors the boom-bust-boom cycle of many Gold Country towns. With an output of $42 million in gold, its Keystone Mine was one of the most productive in the Mother Lode. After all the gold was extracted, the miners cleared out, and the area suffered. Amador City now derives its wealth from tourists browsing through its antiques and specialty shops.

GETTING HERE AND AROUND

Park where you can along Old Highway 49 (off Highway 49), and walk around.

Hotels

Imperial Hotel, Saloon & Restaurant

$ | B&B/INN | An 1879 hotel on the bend in this one-block town, the redbrick Imperial charms its guests with six second-floor rooms (two at the front have balconies) whose antique furnishings include iron-and-brass beds, gingerbread flourishes, and, in one instance, art-deco appointments. **Pros:** history-evoking stay; good restaurant and bar; two rooms with balconies. **Cons:** no phones or TVs in rooms; rooms and hotel could use a refresh; noise issues in street-side rooms. $ *Rooms from: $130 ⊠ 14202 Old Hwy. 49 ☎ 209/267–9172 ⊕ www. imperialamador.com ⇨ 9 rooms ⦿ Free breakfast.*

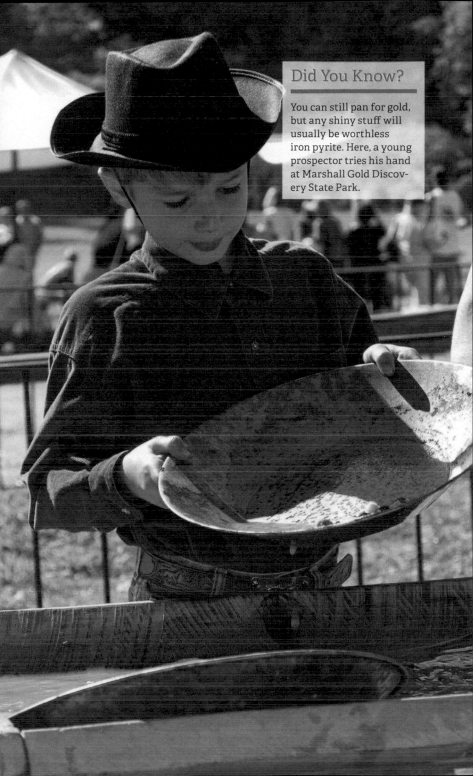

Did You Know?

You can still pan for gold, but any shiny stuff will usually be worthless iron pyrite. Here, a young prospector tries his hand at Marshall Gold Discovery State Park.

Sutter Creek

2 miles south of Amador City.

Sutter Creek is a charming conglomeration of balconied buildings, Victorian homes, and neo–New England structures. At any time of year Main Street (formerly part of Highway 49) is worth a stroll for its shops selling antiques and works by local artists and craftspeople. Tasting rooms of note include Bella Grace, Feist, and Scott Harvey.

GETTING HERE AND AROUND

Arrive here by car on Highway 49. There's no public transit, but downtown is walkable. The visitor center organizes walking tours.

ESSENTIALS

VISITOR INFORMATION Sutter Creek Visitor Center. ⊠ *71A Main St.* ☎ *209/267–5647* ⊕ *www.suttercreek.org.*

Sights

Knight Foundry

FACTORY | Pivotal accomplishments in engineering history occurred at the nation's last functioning water-powered foundry and machine shop, established in 1873 and these days run by volunteers. Namesake Samuel Knight's innovations included a revolutionary system for casting iron and the one-piece Knight Water Wheel for generating power. On the second Saturday of the month or on work days (usually Wednesdays), you can take a tour. ■**TIP→ Plaques and outdoor exhibits are accessible at all hours convey some of this facility's fascinating story.** ⊠ *81 Eureka St., 2 blocks east of Main St.* ☎ *209/560–6160* ⊕ *www.knightfoundry.com* ☜ *Tour $15, outdoor exhibits free.*

Miners' Bend Historic Gold Mining Park

CITY PARK | Volunteers converted a parking lot into a compact open-air tribute to the area's mining legacy. Signs along the path describe 19th-century mining operations and the 16 pieces of equipment on display used to extract or process ore. ⊠ *29 Old Hwy. 49* ☎ *209/560–6880* ⊕ *suttercreekfoundation.org* ☜ *Free.*

Restaurants

Gold Dust Pizza

$$ | PIZZA | Zesty pies like the Miner Moe's BBQ Chicken, with red onions, pineapple, bacon, and cheese, make this casual spot a few steps off Main Street an excellent choice, particularly for lunch or a mid-afternoon snack. You can also build your own pizza or order a sandwich; there's some indoor seating, but when the weather's good most folks eat outside on the front patio or the creekside one out back. **Known for:** ultracrispy crust; chicken wings and calzone; combo meals. ⑤ *Average main: $17* ⊠ *20 Eureka St., off Main St., Davis* ☎ *209/267–1900* ⊕ *www.golddustpizza.org.*

Sina's Backroads Cafe

$ | AMERICAN | Homemade lunches and breakfasts served with warmth and good cheer are the trademarks of this restaurant and coffee shop in Sutter Creek's historic district. Egg scrambles, pancakes, bagel sandwiches, French toast, and biscuits and gravy headline at breakfast, with soups, salads, sandwiches, and wraps on the menu for lunch. **Known for:** quiches and specials; good stop for coffee; cookies, muffins, and pastries. ⑤ *Average main: $9* ⊠ *74 Main St.* ☎ *209/267–0440* ⊕ *sinasbackroadscafe.com* ☼ *Closed Wed. and Thurs. No dinner.*

Hotels

The Foxie

$$ | B&B/INN | A yellow-clapboard house that dates from the mid-1800s contains four of the rooms at this boutique-style historic-district property formerly called the Foxes Inn; a carriage house built more than a century later holds the other three. **Pros:** convenient to shops and tasting rooms; English-style gardens;

private-dinner option. **Cons:** two-night minimum stay requirement; five rooms have queen beds (kings in other two); per website "most suitable" for children over age 12. ⑤ *Rooms from: $209* ✉ *77 Main St.* ☎ *209/267–5882* ⊕ *www.thefoxie. com* ⊋ *7 rooms* ❍ *Free breakfast.*

Inn at 161

$$ | **B&B/INN** | For many years known as the Grey Gables Inn, this property at the northern end of Sutter Creek's historic downtown received a boutique-style makeover following an early-2021 change of ownership. **Pros:** gas-log fireplaces in all rooms; some rooms have a soaking or Jacuzzi tub; landscaped grounds. **Cons:** along town's busy main drag; minimum weekend-stay requirement; some bathrooms could use updating. ⑤ *Rooms from: $159* ✉ *161 Hanford St.* ☎ *209/267–1039* ⊕ *www.innat161.com* ⊋ *11 rooms* ❍ *Free breakfast.*

Volcano

13 miles east of Sutter Creek.

Many roads, all of them winding, all of them scenic, lead to Volcano, an off-the-beaten-path former mining town of about 120 people, the entirety of which is a California Historical Landmark. Black Chasm Cavern is the main attraction.

GETTING HERE AND AROUND

A car is the practical way to get to Volcano. From Sutter Creek or Jackson, pick up Highway 88 heading east. GPS can be sketchy here, so plot and save your route when you have good coverage.

Sights

Black Chasm Cavern National Natural Landmark

CAVE | **FAMILY** | Guided 50-minute tours take you past stalactites, stalagmites, and rare formations of delicate helictites in three underground chambers, one of which also contains a lake. Black Chasm

isn't the largest cave in the Gold Country, but its crystals dazzle both eye and camera—the Landmark Chamber, the tour's third stop, inspired a scene in the 2003 film *The Matrix Reloaded.* Outside is an area where kids can "pan" for crystals. ■**TIP**→ **The same outfit also conducts tours of California Cavern State Historic Landmark, 32 miles south of Volcano, though the days open are less regular.** ✉ *15701 Pioneer Volcano Rd., Volcano* ⊹ *¾ mile south of Volcano off Pine Grove–Volcano Rd.* ☎ *209/296–5007* ⊕ *blackchasmcavern.com* ✉ *$19* ⊙ *Closed Mon.–Thurs. in Jan.*

Hotels

Volcano Pub + Inn

$ | **B&B/INN** | The folks behind Plymouth's Taste restaurant and Rest hotel operate this four-room second-floor inn whose first incarnation, from the 1880s into the 1920s, was as a saloon and boardinghouse for miners and other mostly long-term guests. **Pros:** daily specials at pub; simple but pleasing decor; homemade full breakfast with egg dish, fresh fruit, and baked goods. **Cons:** per website "not suited for small children"; two rooms have a shower but no tub; lacks big-city hotel amenities. ⑤ *Rooms from: $127* ✉ *21375 Consolation St., Volcano* ☎ *209/296–7711* ⊕ *www.volcanounion. com* ⊋ *4 rooms* ❍ *Free breakfast.*

Jackson

8 miles south of Sutter Creek.

Jackson wasn't the Gold Country's rowdiest town, but the party lasted longer here than most anywhere else: "girls' dormitories" (aka brothels) and nickel slot machines flourished until the mid-1950s. Jackson also had the world's deepest and richest gold mines, the Kennedy and the Argonaut, which together produced $70 million in gold. Most of the miners who worked the lode were of Serbian or Italian origin, and they gave the town a European character that persists to this day. A walking-tour map of historic sites, downloadable from the city's website (⊕ *ci.jackson.ca.us*; *click on "Visit Jackson" and then "Things to Do"*), includes the town's steeply terraced Serbian cemetery.

GETTING HERE AND AROUND

Arrive by car on Highway 49. You can walk downtown but otherwise will need a car.

 Sights

Kennedy Gold Mine

HISTORIC SITE | On weekends and some major holidays half the year, docents offer guided 90-minute surface tours of one of the most prolific mines of the gold-rush era and one of the deepest gold mines in the world. Exhibits inside the remaining buildings illustrate how gold flakes were melted for shipment to San Francisco and how "skips" were used to lower miners and materials into the mile-long shaft and carry ore to the surface. ⊠ *Kennedy Mine Rd., at Argonaut La.* ⊕ *½ mile east of Hwy. 49* ☎ *209/223–9542* ⊕ *www.kennedygoldmine.com* ≋ *Free; guided tour $12* ⊗ *Closed most weekdays year-round, all weekends Nov.–Mar.*

Preston Castle

HISTORIC SITE | History buffs and ghost hunters regularly make the trip to this fantastically creepy, 156-room, Romanesque Revival structure erected in 1894 to house troubled youth. Having fallen into disrepair, the building is slowly undergoing a full restoration. On tours, which take place on many Saturdays between April and August, you'll hear all sorts of spine-tingling tales. ⊠ *909 Palm Dr., Ione* ⊕ *12 miles west of Jackson via Hwys. 88 and 104* ☎ *209/256–3623* ⊕ *www.prestoncastle.org* ≋ *From $35 for 1–2 guests* ⊗ *Closed Sept.–Mar.*

🍴 Restaurants

Mel and Faye's Diner

$ | **AMERICAN** | **FAMILY** | Since 1956, the Gillman family has been serving up its famous "Moo Burger" with two patties and special sauce—so big it still makes cow sounds, presumably. The vibe is convivial at this homey diner. **Known for:** hearty breakfasts served until 11 am; milkshakes and floats; freshly baked pies. ⓢ *Average main: $15* ⊠ *31 Hwy. 88* ☎ *209/223–0853* ⊕ *melandfayes. homestead.com.*

Teresa's Place

$$ | **ITALIAN** | Ease back in time at this rustic roadside favorite of Gold Country residents and regulars that dates back to 1921, when its namesake, an Italian immigrant, opened a boardinghouse for local miners. Run by her descendants, the restaurant serves unfussy renditions of Italian-American classics—pastas, wood-fired pizzas, veal and chicken dishes, and steak and seafood. **Known for:** full bar; local wines and microbrews; minestrone from family recipe. ⓢ *Average main: $26* ⊠ *1235 Jackson Gate Rd.* ⊕ *From downtown head north 1¼ miles on N. Main St.; from Hwy. 49 north of town take Jackson Gate Rd. east 1½ miles* ☎ *209/223–1786* ⊗ *Closed Wed. and Thurs. No lunch Sat.–Tues.*

Mokelumne Hill

7 miles south of Jackson.

At first glance you'd never guess that in its 1850s heyday Mokelumne Hill—pronounced *muh-KOHL-ah-mee,* though residents say Moke Hill)—was a whirlwind of mining activity. So rich were the veins of gold in the surrounding countryside that the town's population soared to 15,000. These days, fewer than 700 reside here, but the few-block historic district's galleries and shops and the Hotel Léger's saloon make Moke Hill worth a peek. On

Fridays and weekends, sip a free flight at nearby Renegade Winery's tasting room, which hosts live music some days.

GETTING HERE AND AROUND
Arrive by car on Highway 49. The historic area is walkable.

Hotels

Hotel Léger

$ | HOTEL | A rowdy gold-rush miners' haunt, this hotel anchoring Moke Hill's historic downtown contains rooms and suites decorated with a mishmash of Victorian antiques and utilitarian pieces. **Pros:** rich in history, including a 2013 "Hotel Impossible" makeover; individually decorated rooms; restaurant and 19th-century saloon. **Cons:** some rooms share a bathroom or bathroom is in hallway; rooms above the saloon can be noisy; some rooms feel cramped. ⑤ *Rooms from: $110* ✉ *8304 Main St., Mokelumme Hill* ☎ *209/286–1401* ⊕ *www.hotelleger.com* ⌁ *14 rooms* ❑ *No meals.*

Angels Camp

20 miles south of Jackson.

Angels Camp is famous chiefly for its May jumping-frog contest, based on Mark Twain's short story "The Celebrated Jumping Frog of Calaveras County." The writer reputedly heard the story of the jumping frog from Ross Coon, proprietor of Angels Hotel, which opened in 1856. Sidewalk plaques downtown à la the Hollywood Walk of Fame celebrate the winning frogs in the continuing competition. Either training's gotten way better, or something else is in play—the 1929 victor jumped only 4 feet, but for the last three decades most of the leaps have been from 18- to 20-plus feet. In addition to the contests, Angels Camp's draws include its explorable subterranean caverns and river and lake fishing spots for salmon, trout, and bass.

GETTING HERE AND AROUND
Angels Camp is at the intersection of Highway 49 and Highway 4. You'll need a car to get here and around.

◉ Sights

★ Angels Camp Museum

HISTORIC SITE | FAMILY | Learn a little bit about Mark Twain's "The Celebrated Jumping Frog of Calaveras County"—and Angels Camp's celebrated frog-jumping contests—at this museum's street-side facility, then head to the 3-acre spread behind it for a fascinating survey of gold rush–era mining history. The grounds include a carriage house with pre-automotive farming and passenger coaches and wagons and a large building with mining equipment. Outside, in its original mountings, stands the 27-foot-diameter water wheel that powered machinery at the area's Angels Quartz Mine. ✉ *753 S. Main St.* ☎ *209/736–2963* ⊕ *angelscamp. gov/museum* ⌁ *$15.*

★ Moaning Caverns Adventure Park

CAVE | FAMILY | For a different sort of underground jewel, wander into an ancient limestone cave, where stalactites and stalagmites, not gold and silver, await. Take the 235-step Spiral Tour down a staircase built in 1922 into the vast main cavern, or descend farther on the Expedition Tour caving adventure. Outside are ziplines and a climbing tower. ✉ *5350 Moaning Cave Rd., off Parrotts Ferry Rd./E18, Vallecito* ✛ *Take Hwy. 4 northeast from Angels Camp (7 miles) or south from Murphys (6 miles) and follow signs* ☎ *209/736–2708* ⊕ *www. moaningcaverns.com* ⌁ *Tours from $22, zipline $50* ⊙ *Closed Tues. and Wed. (sometimes varies).*

8

Sacramento and the Gold Country ANGELS CAMP

Murphys

10 miles northeast of Angels Camp.

A well-preserved hamlet of white-picket fences and Victorian houses, compact Murphys has an upscale yet unpretentious vibe. Shops and restaurants line several blocks of Main Street, punctuated by wine-tasting rooms, some open only on Fridays and weekends much of the year. The Calaveras Wine Alliance's staff and volunteers excel at pairing wine lovers with the right winery, in some cases providing discount passes. Horatio Alger, Ulysses S. Grant, and other celebs passed through Murphys when they and other 19th-century tourists came to investigate the giant sequoia groves in nearby Calaveras Big Trees State Park.

GETTING HERE AND AROUND

Murphys is 10 miles northeast of Highway 49 on Highway 4. You'll need to drive here. Parking can be difficult on summer weekends.

CONTACTS Calaveras Wine Alliance.
✉ *202 Main St., at Big Trees Rd.*
☎ *209/728–9467* ⊕ *calaveraswines.org.*

Sights

★ Calaveras Big Trees State Park

NATIONAL/STATE PARK | FAMILY | The park protects hundreds of the largest and rarest living things on the planet—magnificent giant sequoia redwood trees. Some are 3,000 years old, 90 feet around at the base, and 250 feet tall. There are campgrounds, cabin rentals, and picnic areas; swimming, wading, fishing, and sunbathing on the Stanislaus River are popular in summer. Enjoy the "three senses" trail, designated for the blind, with interpretive signs in braille that guide visitors to touch the bark and encourage children to slow down and enjoy the forest in a more sensory way. ✉ *1170 E. Hwy. 4, Arnold* ✛ *15 miles northeast of Murphys, 4 miles northeast of Arnold* ☎ *209/795–2334*

⊕ *www.parks.ca.gov/calaverasbigtrees* ☞ *$10 per vehicle.*

Ironstone Vineyards

WINERY/DISTILLERY | The spectacular, impeccably maintained gardens at 1,150-acre Ironstone—not to mention the 44-pound specimen of crystalline gold on display—make a visit here enjoyable even if you don't drink wine. The winery, known for Lodi and Sierra Foothills Merlot, Cabernet Sauvignon, Cabernet Franc, and old-vine Zinfandel, hosts concerts and other events. Its deli has picnic items. **■ TIP➜ The history-oriented estate tour, conducted on Friday and Saturday, takes in the gardens and wine caverns.** ✉ *1894 6 Mile Rd.* ✛ *From Main St. in town, head south on Scott St.* ☎ *209/728–1251* ⊕ *www.ironstonevineyards.com* ☞ *Tastings $6, estate tour (no tasting) $10* ☉ *Closed Mon.–Wed. (but check).*

Mercer Caverns

CAVE | Light-hearted, well-informed guides lead 45-minute tours (208 steps down, 232 steps up) into caverns a prospector named Walter J. Mercer discovered in 1885. Millions of years in the making, the sheer, draperylike formations and aragonite crystals that resemble snowflakes enthrall visitors. **■ TIP➜ Dress in layers (even in summer) and wear nonskid closed-toe shoes for this mildly strenuous adventure.** ✉ *1665 Sheep Ranch Rd.* ✛ *Head north 1¼ miles from 400 block of Main St.* ☎ *209/728–2101* ⊕ *mercercaverns.net* ☞ *$19.*

Newsome Harlow Wines

WINERY/DISTILLERY | Single-vineyard Sierra Foothills Zinfandels are the passion of Newsome Harlow's owner-winemaker Scott Klann. The ebullient Klann also makes Petite Sirah, Syrah, Carignane, and the Meritage blend of Cabernet Sauvignon and other Bordeaux varietals—whites include a Sauvignon Blanc on several local restaurants' wine lists. The lively in-town tasting room benefits from its upbeat staff, playful atmosphere, and indoor and outdoor tasting spaces. ✉ *403 Main St.* ☎ *209/728–9817* ⊕ *nhvino.com* 🍷 *Tastings $15.*

Villa Vallecito Vineyards Tasting Room

WINERY/DISTILLERY | Winery CEO Ghee Sanchez-Hagedorn's first vineyard memories involve playing amid the Sonoma County grapevines that her migrant-farmer parents tended. After successful Silicon Valley careers, she and her husband began growing Calaveras grapes, later establishing Villa Vallecito, whose Syrah-Grenache Payaso blend often scores high in statewide competitions. The Barbera Reserve and Grenache are two other stars, with Chardonnay and Viognier among the whites. The downtown tasting room's Mexican style honors Sanchez-Hagedorn's heritage. ■TIP➔ **Call or check the website about visiting the winery.** ✉ *263 Main St., Suite C* ☎ *209/890–3157* ⊕ *www.villavallecitovineyards.com* 🍷 *Tastings from $15* ⊙ *Closed Mon.–Thurs.*

★ Vina Moda

WINERY/DISTILLERY | The downtown tasting room of owner-winemaker Nathan Vader's boutique winery occupies a restored 1891 structure made of volcanic rock. Top Sierra Foothills vineyards supply grapes for his primarily reds lineup, led by best sellers Barbera and the Primitivo-based Phoenix blend. Grenache, Syrah, and Mourvèdre, alone or with each other, rank among the other stars, served inside or on the shaded rear patio. ✉ *147 Main St.* ☎ *209/743–6226* ⊕ *vinamoda.com* ⊙ *Closed Tues. and Wed. year-round, closed Mon. and Thurs. early fall–late spring.*

🍴 Restaurants

Alchemy Cafe

$$ | AMERICAN | A casual spot on the eastern edge of town, Alchemy serves sturdy comfort food like braised lamb shank over couscous, seared mahimahi, and meat loaf. Pork belly, fried calamari with roasted jalapeños, and mussels with crusty bread are among the starters that pair well with a bourbon rosemary sour specialty cocktail or an Alchemy Bloody Mary, hopped up with a splash of Firestone Pivo Pilsner. **Known for:** Calaveras County wines well represented; omelets, waffles, French toast for breakfast; mildly pricey but reliable. ⑤ *Average main: $26* ✉ *191 Main St.* ☎ *209/728–0700* ⊕ *alchemymurphys.com* ⊙ *Closed Tues. and Wed. No lunch Thurs. and Mon. (but check).*

Aria Bakery & Espresso Cafe

$ | BAKERY | For a place as small as it is, this bakery-café produces a staggering array of sweet and savory pastries, sandwiches, salads, and desserts you can enjoy with a well-brewed (if not always swiftly made) coffee, espresso drink, or tea. The croissants are golden and flaky, the quiches moist and filling, and the scones large and flavorful; the breads for lunchtime sandwiches include sourdough, focaccia, and polenta wheat. **Known for:** limited seating inside and out; blueberry muffins, savory croissants, and other baked goods; vegetarian, vegan, gluten-free options. ⑤ *Average main: $12* ✉ *458 Main St., Suite B* ☎ *209/728–9250* ⊙ *Closed Mon.–Wed. (but check). No dinner.*

★ Grounds

$$ | AMERICAN | From potato pancakes for breakfast to grilled rib eye for dinner, this bustling bistro with a series of wainscoted rooms and an outdoor back patio has something for all palates. Lighter grilled vegetables, chicken, sandwiches, salads, and homemade soups always shine here, as does heartier fare that might include elk medallions and prawns, forager-mushroom risotto, and cioppino with a relatively delicate yet full-flavored broth. **Known for:** full bar; wines by local producers; attentive service. ⑤ *Average main: $26* ✉ *402 Main St.* ☎ *209/728–8663* ⊕ *www.groundsrestaurant.com* ⊙ *Closed Mon. and Tues. No dinner Sun.*

★ JoMa's Artisan Ice Cream

$ | **AMERICAN** | The smell of waffle cones will direct you to this town treasure whose Portuguese-Swiss namesake has been making ice cream since she was a young lass. Handcrafted flavors include Chill'n Cherry Chip (cherries and dark chocolate) and Wake Up Murphys (coffee, cocoa, and fudge). **Known for:** fruity sorbets; cookies and ice-cream cakes; vegan and gluten-free flavors. ⑤ *Average main: $7* ✉ *386 Main St.* ☎ *209/728–8655* ⊕ *www.jomasicecream.com.*

Rob's Place

$$ | **AMERICAN** | Comfort food crafted with care and served by solicitous staffers makes a trip to this low-slung restaurant on downtown's edge a pleasure whether you dine inside on linen-topped tables or the dog-friendly street-facing patio. Several burgers, one vegetarian, another named for a local winemaker, entice the regulars, but don't overlook dinner entrées that might include shrimp curry, lamb and grits, or grilled Indian-spice tofu with pistachios and Sriracha. **Known for:** clever appetizers; only local wines; plentiful vegetarian, vegan, and gluten-free options. ⑤ *Average main: $23* ✉ *140 Main St.* ☎ *209/813–7003* ⊕ *robsplacerestaurant.com* ⊙ *Closed Tues. and Wed.*

Hotels

★ Dunbar House Inn

$$ | **B&B/INN** | The oversize rooms in this elaborate Italianate-style home have brass beds, down comforters, gas-burning stoves, and claw-foot tubs. **Pros:** great breakfasts; colorful gardens; accommodating staff. **Cons:** expensive in-season; not kid-friendly; minimum-stay requirement on weekends and some holidays. ⑤ *Rooms from: $196* ✉ *271 Jones St.* ☎ *209/728–2897* ⊕ *www.dunbarhouse.com* ⇆ *6 rooms* ⦿*| Free breakfast.*

Murphys Inn Motel

$ | **HOTEL** | Reasonably well run if steadfastly nondescript, this two-story motel built in the late 1990s has three things going for it: a convenient location on the edge of downtown, a pool for hot Gold Country days, and bargain rates most of the year. **Pros:** clean rooms; bargain rates; convenient location. **Cons:** thin walls; some road noise; lacks style and big-hotel amenities. ⑤ *Rooms from: $89* ✉ *76 Main St.* ☎ *209/728–1818, 888/796–1800 reservations* ⊕ *www.murphysinnmotel.com* ⇆ *37 rooms* ⦿*| No meals.*

The Victoria Inn

$$ | **B&B/INN** | Decorated with contemporary furnishings with 19th-century accents, this inn, whose owners also manage 10 area vacation rentals, benefits from a prime Main Street location within walking distance of restaurants, shops, and wine-tasting rooms. **Pros:** convenient location; romantic feel; four spacious rooms with king beds. **Cons:** no TVs in rooms; minimum weekend-stay requirement; noise issues in some rooms. ⑤ *Rooms from: $161* ✉ *420 Main St.* ☎ *209/728–8933* ⊕ *www.victoriainn-murphys.com* ⇆ *13 rooms* ⦿*| No meals.*

Columbia

14 miles south of Angels Camp.

Columbia is the gateway for Columbia State Historic Park, one of the Gold Country's most visited sites. It's a great place for families to participate in living-history activities, like candle dipping and soap making on weekends. There are several inviting spots for a picnic in the area.

GETTING HERE AND AROUND

The only way to get here is by car, via either Highway 4 (the northern route) or Highway 49 (the southern) from Angels Camp.

Sights

★ Columbia State Historic Park

NATIONAL/STATE PARK | **FAMILY** | Columbia, whose mines yielded $87 million in gold, is both a functioning community and a historically preserved town. Usually you can ride a stagecoach, pan for gold, and watch a blacksmith working at an anvil. Street musicians perform in summer. Restored or reconstructed buildings include a Wells Fargo Express office, a Masonic temple, an old-fashioned candy store, saloons, a firehouse, churches, a school, and a newspaper office. At times, all are staffed to simulate a working 1850s town. Also in the park is the **Fallon House Theater,** a gorgeous Victorian structure that sometimes hosts plays and live music. The town's two reasonably priced, historic lodgings, the Fallon Hotel and City Hotel, perch you in the past; reserve a room or cottage at ⊕ *www.reserve-california.com.* ⊠ *11255 Jackson St.* ☎ *209/588–9128* ⊕ *www.parks.ca.gov/columbia* 🖭 *Free.*

🍴 Restaurants

Diamondback Grill and Wine Bar

$ | **AMERICAN** | The bright decor and refined atmosphere suggest more ambitious fare, but massive half-pound burgers and sandwiches like the Ultimate Grilled Cheese with smoked bacon and tomato between three thick slices of sourdough bread are what this place inside a late-19th-century stone-walled building is about. Locals crowd the tables, especially after 6 pm, for the ground-meat patties, beer-battered onion rings, veggie burgers, and fine wines. **Known for:** garlic fries; wine bar and wine club; homemade desserts. 🖭 *Average main: $14* ⊠ *93 S. Washington St., Sonora* ☎ *209/532–6661* ⊕ *diamondback-grillsonora.com.*

🏃 Activities

Zephyr Whitewater Expeditions

WHITE-WATER RAFTING | Challenging rapids and awe-inspiring scenery make white-water rafting trips along the Tuolumne River near Yosemite National Park among California's most popular runs. This well-regarded outfit conducts trips here and on a few other Gold Country rivers. Prices start at $109 for a half day. ⊠ *Headquarters (trips leave from elsewhere), 22517 Parrotts Ferry Rd.* ☎ *209/532–6249, 800/431–3636* ⊕ *zrafting.com.*

Jamestown

7 miles south of Columbia.

Jamestown supplies a touristy view of life during the two gold rushes in these parts. The first took place in the 1850s, the second in the 1880s. Shops in brightly colored buildings along Main Street sell antiques and gift items. You can try your hand at panning for gold in Jamestown or explore a bit of railroad history.

GETTING HERE AND AROUND

Jamestown lies at the intersection of north–south Highway 49 and east–west Highway 108. You'll need a car to tour.

👁 Sights

Gold Prospecting Adventures

TOUR—SIGHT | **FAMILY** | You'll get a real feel (sort of) for the life of a prospector on the three-hour gold-panning excursions (reservations recommended) led by this outfit's congenial tour guides. You might even strike gold at the Jimtown Mine. Even if you're not panning, it's fun to look at the gold-rush artifacts on display here. ⊠ *18170 Main St.* ☎ *209/984–4653* ⊕ *www.goldprospecting.com* 🖭 *Call for prices.*

★ **Railtown 1897 State Historic Park**

NATIONAL/STATE PARK | FAMILY | A must for rail enthusiasts and families with kids, this is one of the most intact early roundhouses (maintenance facilities) in North America. You can hop aboard a steam train for a 40-minute journey— bring along the family dog if you'd like. The docents entertain guests with tales about the history of locomotion. Listen to the original rotor and pulleys in the engine house and take in the smell of axle grease. Walk through a genteel passenger car with dusty-green velvet seats and ornate metalwork, where Grace Kelly and Gary Cooper filmed a scene in *High Noon*. ■**TIP**➜ **When offered, Polar Express excursions at Christmastime sell out quickly.** ✉ *18115 5th Ave.* ☎ *209/984–3953* ⊕ *www.railtown1897.org* 🏞 *Park $5, rides from $15 (includes park fee).*

 Restaurants

Service Station

$$ | AMERICAN | Exposed brick walls and a pressed-metal ceiling lend an air of nostalgia that's heightened by this restaurant's theme, the golden age of road trips and automobile service stations. Half-pounder burgers and pulled-pork, tri-tip, and other sandwiches and wraps count among the menu's highlights, along with small plates like nacho fries and fried calamari and entrées that might include chicken, grilled salmon, or steak. **Known for:** outdoor beer garden; local wines, craft beers on tap; salads and vegetarian wraps and burgers for noncarnivores. $ *Average main: $21* ✉ *18242 Main St.* ☎ *209/782–5122* ⊕ *jamestownservicestation.com.*

 Hotels

1859 Historic National Hotel

$$ | B&B/INN | In business since 1859, the National has survived the gold rush, gambling, prostitution, at least two fires, a ghost named Flo, and Prohibition, and stands today a well-maintained property with all the authentic character and charm its storied past suggests. **Pros:** authentic character—feels straight out of a Western movie; views from odd-numbered rooms (plus Room 2); popular restaurant (good brunches). **Cons:** some rooms are small; most even-numbered rooms have no view; some noise issues. $ *Rooms from: $180* ✉ *18183 Main St.* ☎ *209/984–3446* ⊕ *www.national-hotel.com* ⤳ *9 rooms* ❑ *Free breakfast.*

Jamestown Hotel

$ | HOTEL | The spacious, light-filled rooms above this century-old hotel's saloon and restaurant are decorated simply but with flair, and all have updated bathrooms with a period feel. **Pros:** convenient to shops, restaurants, and tasting rooms; balcony overlooking Main Street; on-site dining. **Cons:** rooms lack refrigerators, microwaves, TVs, and other amenities; noise from restaurant and saloon bleeds through in some rooms; no elevator. $ *Rooms from: $140* ✉ *18153 Main St.* ☎ *209/984–3902* ⊕ *www.thejamestownhotel.com* ⤳ *8 rooms* ❑ *No meals.*

LAKE TAHOE

WITH RENO, NEVADA

Updated by
Cheryl Crabtree

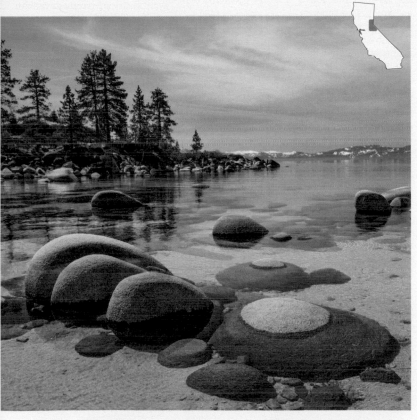

● Sights	⑪ Restaurants	🛏 Hotels	● Shopping	♈ Nightlife
★★★★★	★★★★☆	★★★★★	★☆☆☆☆	★☆☆☆☆

WELCOME TO LAKE TAHOE

TOP REASONS TO GO

★ **The lake:** Blue, deep, and alpine pure, Lake Tahoe is far and away the main reason to visit this High Sierra paradise.

★ **Skiing:** Daring black-diamond runs or baby-bunny bumps—whether you're an expert, a beginner, or somewhere in between, the numerous Tahoe-area ski parks abound with slopes to suit your skills.

★ **The great outdoors:** A ring of national forests and recreation areas linked by miles of trails makes Tahoe excellent for nature lovers.

★ **Dinner with a view:** You can picnic lakeside at state parks or dine in restaurants perched along the shore.

★ **A date with lady luck:** Whether you want to roll dice, play the slots, or hope the blackjack dealer goes bust before you do, you'll find round-the-clock gambling at the casinos on the Nevada side of the lake and in Reno.

1 South Lake Tahoe. This small city is a gateway to nature: swoosh down slopes at Heavenly Mountain, hike or bike scenic trails, or embark on a lake cruise.

2 Pope-Baldwin Recreation Area. Protected forests and several of the west shore's best beaches line the shores here.

3 Emerald Bay State Park. Named for the glistening green waters in its shallow, emerald-shaped cove, this state park is a favorite spot to recreate.

4 D.L. Bliss State Park. Hike the Rubicon Trail along 6 miles of shoreline to access white-sand beaches and spectacular views.

5 Ed Z'berg Sugar Pine Point State Park. Lake Tahoe's largest state park encompasses dense forests and nearly 2 miles of shoreline.

6 Tahoma. This serene lakeshore village reflects early Lake Tahoe, where rustic cottages housed vacationers who sought refuge from urban commotion.

7 Tahoe City. The Truckee River begins its journey to Nevada in this small town, a convenient place to shop and dine.

8 Olympic Valley. The area that hosted the 1960 Winter Olympics is now the north shore's year-round recreation center.

9 Truckee. This Old West city is a trendy town with a historic depot.

10 Carnelian Bay to Kings Beach. Many north shore amenities and services line this scenic stretch.

11 Incline Village. The draws of this ritzy Nevada-side community include Mount Rose and Diamond Peak in winter and beaches and lush hillsides in summer.

12 Zephyr Cove. This tiny Nevada resort occupies a secluded spot edging the eastern shore.

13 Stateline. Towering casinos and 24/7 action give this small city a border-town feel.

14 Reno. This busy city has the Tahoe region's main airport and a revitalized downtown.

Whether you swim, fish, sail, or simply rest on its shores, you'll be wowed by the overwhelming beauty of Lake Tahoe, which is famous for its cobalt-blue water and surrounding snowcapped peaks.

One of the world's largest, clearest, and deepest alpine lakes straddles the border of California and Nevada, giving this popular Sierra Nevada resort region a split personality. About half of its visitors are intent on low-key sightseeing, hiking, camping, and boating; the rest head directly to the Nevada side, lured by bargain dining, big-name entertainment, and glittering casinos.

To explore the lake area and get a feel for its differing communities, drive the 72-mile road that follows the shore through wooded flatlands and past beaches, climbing to vistas on the rugged southwest side of the lake, and passing through busy commercial developments and casinos on its northeastern and southeastern edges. Another option is to travel *on* the 22-mile-long, 12-mile-wide lake via a sightseeing cruise or kayaking trip.

Note, however, that in fall of 2021, the Caldor Fire burned its way along Highway 50 on the western Sierra slopes, over the peaks, and eastward to the Nevada border, coming dangerously close to the lake's southwestern shore. South Lake Tahoe was spared, but evidence of the fire is visible for miles as you drive along Highways 50 and 89.

Although the lake and the region's protected tracts of wilderness are the main draws, other nearby destinations are gaining popularity. Truckee, with an Old West feel and innovative restaurants, entices visitors looking for a relaxed pace and easy access to Tahoe's north shore and Olympic Valley ski parks. And Reno, once known only for its casinos, attracts tourists with its buzzing arts scene, downtown riverfront, and campus events at the University of Nevada.

MAJOR REGIONS

The California Side. The most hotels, restaurants, and ski resorts are on the California side, but you'll also encounter the most congestion and developed areas. From south to north, lakeshore destinations include South Lake Tahoe, Tahoma, Tahoe City, Carnelian Bay, and Kings Beach. Also near the shore are protected lands such as the Pope-Baldwin Recreation Area and Emerald Bay, D.L. Bliss, and Ed Z'berg Sugar Pine Point state parks. West and north of the lake, Olympic Valley beckons with its year-round recreation opportunities, and Truckee charms with its Old West feel.

The Nevada Side. Top stops along the Nevada-side's southern shore include Stateline and its casinos, Zephyr Cove, and Nevada Beach. To the north are Lake Tahoe–Nevada State Park and Sand Harbor Beach as well as the resort area of Incline Village. From there, it's just a short drive northeast to Reno, a long-time gambling town whose revitalized downtown includes interesting museums and the Riverwalk District of shops, galleries, and restaurants.

Planning

When to Go

Christmas week and July 4th are the busiest times, and prices go through the roof, so plan accordingly. If you don't ski, the best times to visit are early fall and late spring. The crowds thin, prices dip, and you can count on Lake Tahoe being beautiful.

In summer, it's crisper and cooler here than in the scorched Sierra Nevada foothills, and the lake's surface temperature is an invigorating 65°F to 70°F (compared with 40°F to 50°F in winter). That said, summer is when visitors—100,000 on peak weekends—clog the lake, its lodgings, and area roads, especially Highway 89 just south of Tahoe City, Highway 28 east of Tahoe City, and U.S. 50 in South Lake Tahoe.

Most Lake Tahoe accommodations, restaurants, and even a handful of parks are open year-round, but many visitor centers, mansions, state parks, and beaches are closed from October through May. During these months, winter-sports enthusiasts pack Tahoe's many downhill resorts and cross-country centers. Note, though, that storms often close roads and force chain requirements on the interstate.

Getting Here and Around

AIR

The nearest airport is Reno–Tahoe International Airport (RNO), in Reno, 50 miles northeast of the closest point on the lake. Airlines serving RNO include Alaska, Allegiant, American, Delta, Frontier, JetBlue, JSX, Southwest, United, and Volaris. Except for Allegiant, these airlines plus Aeromexico, Air Canada, Boutique Air, Contour Airlines, Horizon, Hawaiian, Spirit, and Sun Country serve Sacramento International Airport (SMF), 112 miles from South Lake Tahoe. North Lake Tahoe Express runs buses ($49 each way) between RNO and towns on the western and northern shores, plus Incline Village, Truckee, Palisades Tahoe, and Northstar. South Tahoe Airporter runs buses ($32.75 one-way, $59 round-trip) between Reno–Tahoe Airport and resort hotels in the South Lake Tahoe area.

AIRPORT CONTACTS Reno Tahoe International Airport. *(RNO)* ✉ *2001 E. Plumb La., off U.S. 395/I–580, Reno* ☎ *775/328–6400* ⊕ *www.renoairport. com.* **Sacramento International Airport.** *(SMF)* ✉ *6900 Airport Blvd., Sacramento* ⊹ *Off I–5, 12 miles northwest of downtown* ☎ *916/929–5411* ⊕ *www.sacramento.aero/smf.*

TRANSFER CONTACTS North Lake Tahoe Express. ☎ *833/709–8080* ⊕ *www. northlaketahoeexpress.com.* **South Tahoe Airporter.** ☎ *775/325–8944* ⊕ *southtahoeairporter.com.*

BUS

Greyhound stops in San Francisco, Sacramento, Truckee, and Reno. Tahoe Transportation District ($2 per ride) provides year-round local service in South Lake Tahoe, Stateline, and along the eastern shore to Sand Harbor. On the north shore, Tahoe Area Regional Transit (TART; $1.75) operates buses between Tahoma and Incline Village and runs shuttles to Truckee. RTC RIDE buses ($2) serve the Reno area. All local rides require exact change.

In winter, Tahoe Transportation District provides free ski-shuttle service from South Lake Tahoe hotels and resorts to various Heavenly Mountain ski lodge locations. Most of the major ski resorts offer shuttle service to nearby lodging.

BUS CONTACTS RTC RIDE. ☎ *775/348–7433* ⊕ *www.rtcwashoe.com.* **Tahoe Transportation District.** ☎ *775/ 589–5500, 530/541–7149* ⊕ *www.tahoetransportation.org.* **Tahoe Truckee Area**

Regional Transit (TART). ☎ 530/550–1212, 800/736–6365 ⊕ tahoetruckeetransit. com/contact-us.

CAR

Lake Tahoe is 198 miles northeast of San Francisco, a drive of less than four hours in good weather and light traffic—if possible avoid heavy weekend traffic, particularly leaving the San Francisco area for Tahoe on Friday afternoon and returning on Sunday afternoon. The major route is I–80, a four-lane freeway that cuts through the Sierra Nevada about 14 miles north of the lake. From there Highway 89 and Highway 267 reach the west and north shores, respectively.

U.S. 50, much of which is only two lanes with no center divider, is the more direct route to the south shore, a two-hour drive from Sacramento. From Reno you can get to the north shore by heading south on U.S. 395/I–580 for 10 miles, then west on Highway 431 for 25 miles. For the south shore, head south on U.S. 395/I–580 through Carson City, and then turn west on U.S. 50 (56 miles total).

The scenic 72-mile route around the lake is marked Highway 89 (southwest and west shores), Highway 28 (north and northeast shores), and U.S. 50 (east and southeast shores). During snowy periods, occasional closures along Highway 89 (usually at Emerald Bay because of avalanche danger) make it impossible to complete the lake loop. Interstate 80, U.S. 50, and U.S. 395/I–580 are all-weather highways, but expect snow-removal delays during major storms. Carry tire chains from October through May, though, if you're renting a car, check that the rental agency allows their use. If not, rent a four-wheel-drive vehicle.

TRAIN

Amtrak's cross-country rail service makes stops in Truckee and Reno. Amtrak also operates several buses daily between Reno and Sacramento to connect with coastal train routes.

Restaurants

On weekends and in high season, expect long waits at popular restaurants—and higher prices almost everywhere. In the April–May and September–November "shoulder seasons," some places close or limit their hours, but local papers and websites often feature deals, such as two-for-one coupons.

To attract gamblers, casino marquees often tout "$9.99 prime rib dinners" or "$5.99 breakfast specials." Some of these meals are downright lousy, and they're usually available only in coffee shops or at buffets. The higher prices at finer casino restaurants are offset by reasonable service and a bit of atmosphere. Unless otherwise noted, even the most expensive area restaurants welcome customers in casual clothes.

Hotels

Waterfront inns, slope-side slodges, suburban-style motels, casino hotels, and house and condo rentals constitute Tahoe's lodging choices. In summer and during ski season, reserve as far ahead as possible, especially for holiday periods when prices skyrocket. Spring and fall offer more leeway and lower rates, especially at casinos.

Head to South Lake Tahoe for the most activities and the widest range of lodging options. Heavenly Village, in the heart of town, has an ice rink, cinema, shops, cafés, fine-dining restaurants, and a gondola that will whisk you up to the ski park. Walk two blocks south from downtown, and you can hit the casinos.

Tahoe City, on the west shore, has a small-town atmosphere and is accessible to several ski resorts. A few miles northwest of the lake, Palisades Tahoe has its own self-contained village, an aerial tram to the slopes, and year-round outdoor activities.

Looking for a taste of Old Tahoe? The north shore is your best bet, with Carnelian Bay and Tahoe Vista on the California side. Across the border in Nevada you'll find casino resorts where Hollywood stars once romped.

Restaurant and hotel reviews have been shortened. For full information, visit Fodors.com. Restaurant prices are the average cost of a main course at dinner, or if dinner is not served, at lunch. Hotel prices are the lowest cost of a standard double room in high season.

What It Costs

	$	$$	$$$	$$$$
RESTAURANTS				
	under $17	$17–$26	$27–$36	over $36
HOTELS				
	under $150	$150–$250	$251–$350	over $350

Tours

★ Cruise Tahoe

BOAT TOURS | The captain of the *Tahoe*, a classic wooden boat, takes passengers on an east shore cruise whose highlights are a walking tour and picnic lunch at the Thunderbird Lodge, a historic mansion. A tour of Emerald Bay and Vikingsholm Castle (Sun.–Wed., late May–Sept.) is also available. ⊠ *Departures from Zephyr Cove Pier, 760 U.S. 50, Zephyr Cove* ☎ *775/230–8907* ⊕ *www.cruisetahoe. com/public-cruises* ⊠ *$169 Thunderbird Lodge Cruise, $135 Emerald Bay Cruise.*

Lake Tahoe Balloons

AIR EXCURSIONS | Take a hot-air balloon flight over the lake from mid-May through mid-October with this company that launches and lands its balloons on a boat. The four-hour excursion (the flight is 45–60 minutes) begins shortly after sunrise and ends with a traditional champagne toast. ⊠ *Tahoe Keys Marina,*

2435 Venice Dr. E, South Lake Tahoe ⊕ *Tahoe Keys Blvd. off Lake Tahoe Blvd.* ☎ *530/544–1221, 800/872–9294* ⊕ *www. laketahoeballoons.com* ⊠ *From $325.*

MS *Dixie II*

BOAT TOURS | The 520-passenger MS *Dixie II*, a stern-wheeler, sails year-round from Zephyr Cove to Emerald Bay on sightseeing and dinner cruises. ⊠ *Zephyr Cove Marina, 760 U.S. Hwy. 50, near Church St., Zephyr Cove* ☎ *800/238–2463* ⊕ *www.zephyrcove.com/cruises* ⊠ *From $68.*

North Lake Tahoe Ale Trail

SELF-GUIDED | Bike or walk one of North Lake Tahoe's dozens of trails, then reward yourself with a craft brew at an alehouse near the end of your chosen route. The largest concentration of beer stops is around Incline Village, but you'll find places to stop for a pint from Tahoma to Zephyr Cove. A dedicated website has an interactive map, descriptions, and short videos pairing trails and drinking spots. There are also suggestions for paddleboarders and kayakers. ⊕ *www. gotahoenorth.com/lake-tahoe-activities/ north-lake-tahoe-ale-trail.*

Sierra Cloud

BOAT TOURS | The *Sierra Cloud*, a 41-passenger catamaran, departs from the Hyatt Regency beach at Incline Village and cruises the north and east shore areas for two hours. ⊠ *Hyatt Regency Lake Tahoe, 111 Country Club Dr., Incline Village* ☎ *775/831–4386* ⊕ *www.awsincline. com* ⊠ *From $100* ⊗ *Closed Oct.–Apr.*

South Tahoe Beer Trail

SELF-GUIDED | Download a handy map to find your way to nearly a dozen craft breweries along Lake Tahoe's south shore, from Tahoe Keys to Stateline. ⊕ *tahoesouth.com/beer-trail.*

Tahoe Gal

BOAT TOURS | Docked in Tahoe City this old-style 120-passenger paddle wheeler departs—daily from June through September and some days in May—on brunch, lunch, happy-hour, and sunset tours of Emerald Bay and Lake Tahoe's north and west shores. Specialty excursions feature live music or other entertainment. ⊠ *Departures from Lighthouse Center, 952 N. Lake Blvd., Tahoe City* ☎ *800/218–2464* ⊕ *www.tahoegal.com* ⊠ *From $42.*

Tahoe Cruises *Safari Rose*

BOAT TOURS | This outfit operates year-round cruises on the *Safari Rose*, an 80-foot, wooden motor yacht. Options between mid-May and mid-October include barbecue-lunch, happy-hour, sunset, and champagne cruises. Shuttle-bus pickup service is available. ⊠ *Ski Run Marina, 900 Ski Run Blvd., South Lake Tahoe* ☎ *775/588–1881* ⊕ *www.tahoecruises.com* ⊠ *From $90.*

★ Tahoe Tastings

BOAT TOURS | Taste eight Northern California wines aboard the *Golden Rose*, a 1953 Chris-Craft Venetian Water Taxi, on two-hour cruises from Tahoe Keys to Emerald Bay and back. Charcuterie boards are available for purchase with advance reservation, or you can bring your own snacks along. Tours depart midday, later in the afternoon, and at sunset. ⊠ *2435 Venice Dr., South Lake Tahoe* ⊹ *Rubicon Dock, Tahoe Keys Marina* ☎ *530/494–9222* ⊕ *www.tahoetastings. com* ⊠ *From $65.*

Visitor Information

CONTACTS Go Tahoe North. ☎ *530/581–6900* ⊕ *www.gotahoenorth.com.* **Tahoe South.** ☎ *775/542–4637 California, 800/588–4591 Nevada* ⊕ *tahoesouth. com.*

South Lake Tahoe

60 miles south of Reno, 198 miles north-east of San Francisco.

The city of South Lake Tahoe's raison d'être is tourism: the casinos of adjacent Stateline, Nevada; the ski slopes at Heavenly Mountain; the beaches, docks, bike trails, and campgrounds all around the south shore; and the backcountry of Eldorado National Forest and Desolation Wilderness. The small city's main attributes are its convenient location, bevy of services, and gorgeous lake views.

GETTING HERE AND AROUND

The main route into and through South Lake Tahoe is U.S. 50; signs say "Lake Tahoe Boulevard" in town. Arrive by car or, if coming from Reno airport, take the South Tahoe Express bus. Tahoe Transportation District operates daily bus service in the south shore area year-round.

ESSENTIALS

VISITOR INFORMATION Visit Lake Tahoe South. ⊠ *Visitor Center, 169 U.S. Hwy. 50, at Kingsbury Grade, Stateline* ☎ *775/588–4591* ⊕ *tahoesouth.com* ⊠ *Visitor Center, 4114 Lake Tahoe Blvd.* ☎ *530/542–4637* ⊕ *tahoesouth.com.*

◉ Sights

★ Heavenly Gondola

VIEWPOINT | **FAMILY** | Whether you ski or not, you'll appreciate the impressive view of Lake Tahoe from the Heavenly Gondola. Its eight-passenger cars travel from Heavenly Village 2.4 miles up the mountain in 15 minutes. When the weather's fine, you can take one of three hikes around the mountaintop and then have lunch at Tamarack Lodge. ⊠ *4080 Lake Tahoe Blvd.* ☎ *775/586–7000, 800/432–8365* ⊕ *www. skiheavenly.com* ⊠ *$61.*

Skiing and Snowboarding

The mountains around Lake Tahoe are bombarded by blizzards throughout the winter, and, sometimes, in the fall and spring, as well. Indeed, the Sierras often have the continent's deepest snowpack (10- to 12-foot bases are common), though it can be very heavy and wet owing to relatively mild temperatures over the Pacific. The upside is that you can sometimes ski (either downhill or cross-country) and snowboard (allowed at all Tahoe ski areas) as late as May. Check conditions at OntheSnow.com, or get the inside scoop by talking to waiters and bartenders, many of whom are ski bums.

On weekends, avoid moving with the masses by arriving early and quitting early, with a lunch break at 11 am or 1:30 pm rather than noon. Also consider skiing at areas with few high-speed lifts or limited lodging and real estate at their bases, namely Sugar Bowl, Homewood, Mt. Rose, Sierra-at-Tahoe, Diamond Peak, and Kirkwood.

Cross-country skiing at resorts can be costly, but you get the benefits of machine grooming and trail preparation. If it's bargain Nordic you're after, take advantage of thousands of acres of public forest and parkland trails.

Heavenly Village

STORE/MALL | This lively complex at the base of the Heavenly Gondola has good shopping, an arcade for kids, a cinema, a brewpub, a skating rink in winter, miniature golf in summer, and the Loft for magic shows and other live entertainment. Base Camp Pizza Co., Azul Latin Kitchen, and Kalani's for seafood stand out among the several restaurants. ✉ *1001 Heavenly Village Way, at U.S. 50* ⊕ *www.theshopsatheavenly.com.*

 Restaurants

Artemis Lakefront Cafe

$$ | **MEDITERRANEAN** | A festive marina restaurant with a heated outdoor patio, Artemis reveals its Greek influences in breakfast dishes like baklava French toast and gyros and egg pita wraps. All day, though, the menus encompass more familiar options (eggs Benedict in the morning, burgers and grilled mahimahi later on). **Known for:** heated outdoor patio; outgoing staff; marina location. $ *Average main: $21* ✉ *900 Ski Run Blvd.* ☎ *530/542–3332* ⊕ *www.artemislakefrontcafe.com.*

★ Evan's American Gourmet Cafe

$$$$ | **ECLECTIC** | Its excellent service, world-class cuisine, and superb wine list make this intimate restaurant the top choice for high-end dining in South Lake. Inside a converted cabin, Evan's serves creative American cuisine that might include pan-seared day boat scallops and meat dishes such as rack of lamb marinated with rosemary and garlic and served with raspberry demi-glace. **Known for:** intimate atmosphere; world-class cuisine; superb wine list. $ *Average main: $38* ✉ *536 Emerald Bay Rd., Hwy. 89, at 15th St.* ☎ *530/542–1990* ⊕ *evanstahoe.com* ⊘ *No lunch. Closed Sun. and Mon.*

Kalani's at Lake Tahoe

$$$$ | **ASIAN** | The white-tablecloth dining room at Heavenly's sleekest (and priciest) restaurant is decked out with carved bamboo, a burnt-orange color palette, and a modern-glass sculpture, all of which complement Pacific Rim–influenced dishes like fillet of beef with miso-garlic butter and the signature Chilean sea bass with Thai-basil mash, wilted balsamic greens, and ponzu butter sauce. Sushi selections with inventive rolls and sashimi combos, plus less expensive vegetarian dishes, add depth to the menu. **Known for:** fresh-off-the-plane Hawaiian seafood; thoughtful wine selections; upscale setting. $ *Average main: $38* ⊠ *1001 Heavenly Village Way, #26, at U.S. 50* ☎ *530/544–6100* ⊕ *www. kalanis.com.*

My Thai Cuisine

$ | **THAI** | Fantastic flavors and gracious owners have earned this humble roadside restaurant with river-stone columns, pine-paneled walls and ceilings, Thai statues and ornamentation the loyalty of Tahoe residents and regular visitors. The aromatic dishes include crab pad Thai, basil lamb, sizzling shrimp, and numerous curries. **Known for:** many vegetarian options; lunch specials a steal; lively atmosphere. $ *Average main: $15* ⊠ *2108 Lake Tahoe Blvd., ¼ mile northeast of "Y" intersection of U.S. 50 and Hwy. 89* ☎ *530/544–3232* ⊕ *www. mythaitahoe.com.*

Red Hut Café

$ | **AMERICAN** | A vintage-1959 Tahoe diner, all chrome and red plastic, the Red Hut is a tiny place with a wildly popular breakfast menu: huge omelets; banana, pecan, and coconut waffles; and other tasty vittles. A second South Lake branch has a soda fountain and is the only one that serves dinner, and there's a third location in Stateline. **Known for:** huge omelets; variety of waffles; old-school feel. $ *Average main: $12* ⊠ *2723 Lake Tahoe Blvd., near Blue Lake Ave.* ☎ *530/541–9024* ⊕ *www.facebook.com/TheRedHut* ⊘ *No dinner.*

Scusa! Italian Ristorante

$$ | **ITALIAN** | This longtime favorite turns out big plates of veal scaloppine, chicken piccata, and garlicky linguine with clams—straightforward Italian American food (and lots of it), served in an intimate dining room warmed by a crackling fire on many nights. There's an outdoor patio that's open in warm weather. **Known for:** classic Italian American recipes; fritto

misto, grilled radicchio, and fresh-baked mozzarella appetizers; sticky-bun bread pudding for dessert. $ *Average main: $25* ⊠ *2543 Lake Tahoe Blvd., at Sierra Blvd.* ☎ *530/542–0100* ⊕ *www.scusalaketahoe.com* ⊘ *No lunch.*

★ Sprouts Natural Foods Cafe

$ | **AMERICAN** | If it's in between normal mealtimes and you're hungry for something healthful, head to this order-at-the-counter café for salads, overstuffed wraps, hot sandwiches, homemade vegan soups, all-day breakfasts, and the best smoothies in town. Dine at wooden tables in the cheery contemporary indoor space or out front on the patio, or just order food to go. **Known for:** fresh, healthy cuisine; vegan and vegetarian friendly; congenial staff. $ *Average main: $12* ⊠ *3123 Harrison Ave., U.S. 50 at Alameda Ave.* ☎ *530/541–6969* ⊕ *www.sprouts-cafetahoe.com.*

Hotels

Base Camp South Lake Tahoe

$ | **HOTEL** | This three-floor boutique hotel near the Heavenly Gondola, Stateline casinos, and several good restaurants provides solid value in a hip yet family-friendly setting. **Pros:** convenient location; great for groups; cool public spaces include rooftop hot tub with mountain views. **Cons:** communal dinners won't appeal to all travelers; near a busy area; not on the lake. $ *Rooms from: $143* ⊠ *4143 Cedar Ave., off U.S. 50* ☎ *530/208–0180* ⊕ *www.basecamp-tahoesouth.com* ⊅ *74 rooms* ⏍ *Free breakfast.*

★ Black Bear Lodge

$$ | **B&B/INN** | Built in the 1990s with meticulous attention to detail, this entire complex feels like a grand old Adirondack lodge, with rooms and kitchenette-equipped cabins that feature 19th-century American antiques, fine art, and fireplaces. **Pros:** near Heavenly skiing; within walking distance of good

restaurants; wine and beer bar. **Cons:** no room service; lacks big-hotel amenities; social types may find setting too sedate. ⑤ *Rooms from: $199* ✉ *1202 Ski Run Blvd.* ☎ *530/544–4451* ⊕ *www.tahoe-blackbear.com* ⇌ *9 units* ⑩ *No meals.*

Camp Richardson

$ | **RESORT** | **FAMILY** | An old-fashioned family resort on 120 acres fronting Lake Tahoe, Camp Richardson earns retro cred for its 1920s, log cabin–style lodge, its few dozen cabins, and its small inn—all tucked beneath giant pine trees—but wins no style points for its straightforward accommodations with a dearth of amenities. **Pros:** lakeside location with wide choice of lodgings; great for families; inexpensive daily and weekly rates. **Cons:** dated style; lacks upscale amenities (and even phones and TVs in some rooms); some cabins available in summer only. ⑤ *Rooms from: $115* ✉ *1900 Jameson Beach Rd.* ☎ *530/541–1801, 800/544–1801* ⊕ *www.camprichardson. com* ⇌ *71 units* ⑩ *No meals.*

Hotel Azure

$$$ | **HOTEL** | High-end motel meets boutique hotel at this totally revamped (to the tune of $3.5 million) property across the road from a beach. **Pros:** clean, spacious rooms; good work spaces and tech amenities; short drive to Heavenly Mountain. **Cons:** on busy Lake Tahoe Boulevard; no bell or room service; some sound bleed-through from room to room. ⑤ *Rooms from: $262* ✉ *3300 Lake Tahoe Blvd.* ☎ *530/542–0330, 800/877–1466* ⊕ *www.hotelazuretahoe.com* ⇌ *99 rooms* ⑩ *No meals.*

The Landing Resort & Spa

$$$$ | **RESORT** | Perched at the edge of a semi-private beach that's less than a ½ mile from Heavenly Village, The Landing provides luxe rooms and resort amenities in a prime location—removed from, but close to the Stateline action. **Pros:** across the street from the beach and lake; full-service spa with six treatment rooms, pool, hot tub, fitness center; spacious

rooms, most over 450 square feet. **Cons:** lack of resort grounds; small lobby; busy beach in peak season. ⑤ *Rooms from: $449* ✉ *4104 Lakeshore Blvd.* ☎ *855/700–5263, 530/541–5263* ⊕ *www. thelandingtahoe.com* ⇌ *82 rooms* ⑩ *No meals.*

Marriott's Grand Residence and Timber Lodge

$$$ | **RESORT** | You can't beat the location of these two gigantic, modern condominium complexes right at the base of Heavenly Gondola, smack in the center of town. **Pros:** central location; great for families; near excellent restaurants. **Cons:** can be jam-packed on weekends; no room service; lacks serenity. ⑤ *Rooms from: $245* ✉ *1001 Heavenly Village Way* ☎ *530/542–8400 Marriott's Grand Residence, 800/845–5279, 530/542–6600 Marriott's Timber Lodge* ⊕ *www.marriott. com* ⇌ *431 rooms* ⑩ *No meals.*

★ Wylder Hope Valley

$$$$ | **RESORT** | You can lie on a hammock beneath the aspens, or sit in a rocker on your own front porch at this woodsy, 165-acre resort within the Eldorado National Forest and 20 minutes south of town. **Pros:** gorgeous rustic setting; good on-site café serves three meals a day (nonguests welcome); outdoor activities. **Cons:** nearest nightlife is 20 miles away; lacks amenities of larger properties; basic furnishings. ⑤ *Rooms from: $325* ✉ *14255 Hwy. 88, Hope Valley* ☎ *530/694–2203, 800/423–9949* ⊕ *wylderhotels.com* ⇌ *36 units* ⑩ *No meals.*

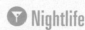 **Nightlife**

Most of the area's nightlife is concentrated in the casinos over the border in Stateline. To avoid slot machines and blinking lights, try the California-side nightspots in and near Heavenly Village.

BARS
The Loft
THEMED ENTERTAINMENT | Crowd-pleasing magic shows and other entertainment and a casual-industrial setting keep patrons happy at this Heavenly Village bar and lounge where kids aren't out of place. The mood is upbeat, the specialty cocktails are potent, and if you're in the mood for dinner the kitchen turns out Italian fare more tasty than one might expect at such a venue. ⌧ *1001 Heavenly Village Way* ☎ *530/523–8024* ⊕ *www. thelofttahoe.com.*

Mc P's Taphouse & Grill
BARS/PUBS | You can hear live bands—rock, jazz, blues, alternative—on most nights at Mc P's while you sample a few of the 40 beers on draft. Lunch and dinner (pub grub) are served daily. ⌧ *4125 Lake Tahoe Blvd., Suite A, near Friday Ave.* ☎ *530/542–4435* ⊕ *www. mcpstahoe.net.*

 Activities

FISHING
Tahoe Sport Fishing
FISHING | One of the area's largest and oldest fishing-charter services offers morning and afternoon trips. Outings include all necessary gear and bait, and the crew cleans and packages your catch. ⌧ *900 Ski Run Blvd., off Lake Tahoe Blvd.* ☎ *530/541–5448* ⊕ *www. tahoesportfishing.com* 🖃 *From $160.*

HIKING
Desolation Wilderness
HIKING/WALKING | Trails within the 63,960-acre wilderness lead to gorgeous backcountry lakes and mountain peaks. It's called Desolation Wilderness for a reason, so bring a topographic map and compass, and carry water and food. You need a permit for overnight camping (☎ *877/444–6777*). In summer you can access this area by boarding a boat taxi ($18 one-way) at **Echo Chalet** (*9900 Echo Lakes Rd., off U.S. 50,* ☎ *530/659–7207,*

⊕ *www.echochalet.com*) and crossing Echo Lake. The Pacific Crest Trail also traverses Desolation Wilderness. ⌧ *El Dorado National Forest Information Center* ☎ *530/644–2349* ⊕ *www.fs.usda. gov/eldorado.*

Pacific Crest Trail
HIKING/WALKING | Hike a couple of miles on this famous mountain trail that stretches from Mexico to Canada. ⌧ *Echo Summit, about 12 miles southwest of South Lake Tahoe off U.S. 50* ☎ *916/285–1846* ⊕ *www.pcta.org.*

ICE-SKATING
Heavenly Village Outdoor Ice Rink
ICE SKATING | **FAMILY** | If you're here in winter, practice your jumps and turns at this rink between the gondola and the cinema. ⌧ *1001 Heavenly Village Way* ☎ *530/542–4230* ⊕ *www.theshopsat-heavenly.com* 🖃 *$22, includes skate rental.*

South Lake Tahoe Ice Arena
ICE SKATING | For year-round fun, head to this NHL regulation–size indoor rink where you can rent equipment and sign up for lessons. ■**TIP➜ Hours vary; call or check website for public skate times**. ⌧ *1176 Rufus Allen Blvd.* ☎ *530/544–7465* ⊕ *www.tahoearena.co* 🖃 *$15; includes skate rental.*

KAYAKING
Kayak Tahoe
KAYAKING | Sign up for lessons and excursions (to the south shore, Emerald Bay, and Sand Harbor), offered from May through September. You can also rent a kayak and paddle solo on the lake. ⌧ *Timber Cove Marina, 3411 Lake Tahoe Blvd., at Balbijou Rd.* ☎ *530/544–2011* ⊕ *www. kayaktahoe.com* 🖃 *Rentals from $35, tours from $80.*

MOUNTAIN BIKING
Tahoe Sports Ltd.
BICYCLING | You can rent road and mountain bikes and get tips on where to ride from the friendly staff at this full-service sports store. ⌧ *Tahoe Crescent*

V Shopping Center, 4000 Lake Tahoe Blvd., Suite 7 ☎ 530/542–4000 ⊕ www.tahoesportsltd.com.

SKIING

★ Heavenly Mountain Resort

SKIING/SNOWBOARDING | Straddling two states, vast Heavenly Mountain Resort—composed of nine peaks, two valleys, and four base-lodge areas, along with the largest snowmaking system in the western United States—pairs terrain for every skier with exhilarating Tahoe Basin views. Beginners can choose wide, well-groomed trails, accessed from the California Lodge or the gondola from downtown South Lake Tahoe; kids have short and gentle runs in the Enchanted Forest area all to themselves. The Sky Express high-speed quad chair whisks intermediate and advanced skiers to the summit for wide cruisers or steep tree-skiing. Mott and Killebrew canyons draw experts to the Nevada side for steep chutes and thick-timber slopes.

The ski school is big and offers everything from learn-to-ski packages to canyon-adventure tours. Call about ski and boarding camps. Skiing lessons are available for children ages four and up; there's day care for infants older than six weeks. Summertime thrill seekers participate in Epic Discovery—fun for the whole family that includes a mountain coaster, zip lines, a climbing wall, ropes courses, hiking opportunities, and a learning center. **Facilities:** 97 trails; 4,800 acres; 3,500-foot vertical drop; 28 lifts. ⊠ *Ski Run Blvd., off U.S. 50 ☎ 775/586–7000, 800/432–8365 ⊕ www.skiheavenly.com* 🎟 *Day pass from $67.*

Kirkwood Ski Resort

SKIING/SNOWBOARDING | Thirty-six miles south of Lake Tahoe, Kirkwood is the hard-core skiers' and boarders' favorite south-shore mountain, known for its craggy gulp-and-go chutes, sweeping cornices, steep-aspect glade skiing, and high base elevation. But there's also fantastic terrain for newbies and intermediates down wide-open bowls, through wooded gullies, and along rolling tree-lined trails. Families often head to the Timber Creek area, a good spot to learn to ski or snowboard. Tricksters can show off in two terrain parks on jumps, wall rides, rails, and a half-pipe. The mountain gets hammered with an average of 354 inches of snow annually. If you're into out-of-bounds skiing, check out Expedition Kirkwood, a backcountry-skills program that teaches basic safety awareness. If you're into cross-country, the resort has 80 km (50 miles) of superb groomed-track skiing, with skating lanes, instruction, and rentals. Nonskiers can snowshoe, snow-skate, and go dogsledding or snow-tubing. The children's ski school has programs for ages 3 to 12. **Facilities:** 86 trails; 2,300 acres; 2,000-foot vertical drop; 15 lifts. ⊠ *1501 Kirkwood Meadows Dr., Kirkwood ⊕ Off Hwy. 88, 14 miles west of Hwy. 89 ☎ 209/258–6000 ⊕ www.kirkwood.com* 🎟 *Day pass from $67.*

Sierra-at-Tahoe

SKIING/SNOWBOARDING | Wind-protected and meticulously groomed slopes, excellent tree-skiing, and gated backcountry skiing are among the draws at this low-key but worthy resort. Extremely popular with snowboarders, Sierra has several terrain parks, including Halfpipe, with 18-foot walls and a dedicated chairlift. For beginners, Sierra-at-Tahoe has more than 100 acres of learning terrain, and there are two snow-tubing lanes. **Facilities:** 46 trails; 2,000-plus acres; 2,250-foot vertical drop; 14 lifts. ⊠ *1111 Sierra-at-Tahoe Rd., Twin Bridges ⊕ 12 miles from South Lake Tahoe off U.S. 50, past Echo Summit ☎ 530/659–7453 information, 530/659–7475 snow phone ⊕ www.sierraattahoe.com* 🎟 *Lift ticket $125.*

Pope-Baldwin Recreation Area

5 miles west of South Lake Tahoe.

To the west of downtown South Lake Tahoe, U.S. 50 and Highway 89 come together, forming an intersection nicknamed "the Y." If you head northwest on Highway 89, also called Emerald Bay Road, and follow the lakefront, commercial development gives way to national forests and state parks. One of these is Pope-Baldwin Recreation Area.

GETTING HERE AND AROUND

The entrance to the Pope-Baldwin Recreation Area is on the east side of Emerald Bay Road. The area is closed to vehicles in winter, but you can cross-country ski here.

Sights

★ Tallac Historic Site

HISTORIC SITE | At this site you can stroll or picnic lakeside year-round, and then in late spring and summer you can also explore three historic estates. The **Pope House** is the magnificently restored 1894 mansion of George S. Pope, who made his money in shipping and lumber and played host to the business and cultural elite of 1920s America. The **Baldwin Museum** is in the estate that once belonged to entrepreneur "Lucky" Baldwin; today it houses a collection of family memorabilia and Washoe Indian artifacts. The **Valhalla** (⊕ *valhallatahoe. com*), with a spectacular floor-to-ceiling stone fireplace, was occupied for years by Walter and Claire Heller (tidbit: after their divorce, each visited the property on alternate weekends, though she held the title). Its Grand Hall, Grand Lawn, and a lakeside boathouse refurbished as a theater, host the summertime Valhalla Art, Music and Theatre Festival of concerts, plays, and cultural activities. Docents conduct tours of the Pope House in summer; call for tour times. ⊠ *Pope Baldwin Recreation Area Hwy. 89* ☎ *530/541–5227 late May–mid-Sept., 530/544–7383 year-round* ⊕ *tahoeheritage.org* ☞ *Free, summer guided site walk $5, Pope House tour $10* ⊘ *House and museum closed late Sept.–late May.*

Taylor Creek Visitor Center

INFO CENTER | FAMILY | At this center operated by the U.S. Forest Service you can visit the site of a Washoe Indian settlement; walk self-guided trails through meadow, marsh, and forest; and inspect the Stream Profile Chamber, an underground display with windows right into Taylor Creek. In fall you may see spawning kokanee salmon digging their nests. In summer Forest Service naturalists organize discovery walks and evening programs. ⊠ *Hwy. 89, 3 miles north of junction with U.S. 50* ☎ *530/543–2674 late May–Oct., 530/543–2600 year-round* ⊕ *www.fs.usda.gov* ☞ *Free.*

Emerald Bay State Park

4 miles west of Pope-Baldwin Recreation Area.

You can hike, bike, swim, camp, scuba dive, kayak, or tour a look-alike Viking castle at this state park. Or you can simply enjoy the most popular tourist stop on Lake Tahoe's circular drive: the high cliff overlooking Emerald Bay, famed for its jewel-like shape and color.

GETTING HERE AND AROUND

The entrance to Emerald Bay State Park is on the east side of a narrow, twisting section of Highway 89. Caution is the key word for both drivers and pedestrians. The park is closed to vehicles in winter.

Fjord-like Emerald Bay is possibly the most scenic part of Lake Tahoe.

Sights

★ Emerald Bay State Park

NATIONAL/STATE PARK | A massive glacier millions of years ago carved this 3-mile-long and 1-mile-wide fjord-like inlet. Famed for its jewel-like shape and colors, the bay surrounds Fannette, Tahoe's only island. Highway 89 curves high above the lake through Emerald Bay State Park; from the Emerald Bay lookout, the centerpiece of the park, you can survey the whole scene. This is one of the don't-miss views of Lake Tahoe. The light is best in mid- to late morning, when the bay's colors really pop. ⊠ *Hwy. 89* ☎ *530/525–7232* ⊕ *www.parks.ca.gov* 🅿 *$10 parking fee.*

Vikingsholm

HOUSE | This 38-room estate was completed in 1929 and built as a precise copy of a 1,200-year-old Viking castle, using materials native to the area. Its original owner, Lora Knight, furnished it with Scandinavian antiques and hired artisans to build period reproductions. The sod roof sprouts wildflowers each spring. There are picnic tables nearby and a gray-sand beach for strolling. A steep 1-mile-long trail from the Emerald Bay lookout leads down to Vikingsholm, and the hike back up is hard (especially if you're not yet acclimated to the elevation), although there are benches and stone culverts to rest on. At the 150-foot peak of Fannette Island are the ruins of a stone structure known as the Tea House, built so that Knight's guests could have a place to enjoy afternoon refreshments after a motorboat ride. The island is off-limits from February through mid-June to protect nesting Canada geese. The rest of the year it's open for day use—kayak and paddleboard rentals are available at Emerald Bay State Park's beach. ⊠ *Hwy. 89* ☎ *530/525–7232* ⊕ *www.vikingsholm. com* 🅿 *Day-use parking fee $10; mansion tour $15* ⊗ *Closed late Sept.–late May.*

Activities

HIKING
Eagle Falls
HIKING/WALKING | To reach these falls, leave your car in the parking lot of the Eagle Falls picnic area (near Vikingsholm; arrive early for a good spot), and walk up the short but fairly steep canyon nearby. You'll have a brilliant panorama of Emerald Bay from this spot near the boundary of Desolation Wilderness. For a strenuous full-day hike, continue 5 miles, past Eagle Lake (a good spot for an alpine swim), to Upper and Middle Velma lakes. Pick up trail maps at Taylor Creek Visitor Center in summer, or year-round at the main U.S. Forest Service Office in South Lake Tahoe, at 35 College Drive. ⊠ *Hwy. 89 at Emerald Bay State Park.*

D.L. Bliss State Park

3 miles north of Emerald Bay State Park, 17 miles south of Tahoe City.

This park shares 6 miles of shoreline with adjacent Emerald Bay State Park and has two white-sand beaches. Hike the Rubicon Trail for stunning views of the lake.

GETTING HERE AND AROUND
The entrance to D.L. Bliss State Park is on the east side of Highway 89 just north of Emerald Bay. No vehicles are allowed in when the park is closed for the season.

Sights

D.L. Bliss State Park
NATIONAL/STATE PARK | This park takes its name from Duane LeRoy Bliss, a 19th-century lumber magnate. At one time Bliss owned nearly 75% of Tahoe's lakefront, along with local steamboats, railroads, and banks. The park shares 6 miles of shoreline with Emerald Bay State Park; combined the two parks cover 1,830 acres, 744 of which the Bliss family donated to the state. At the north end of Bliss is Rubicon Point, which overlooks one of the lake's deepest spots. Short trails lead to an old lighthouse and Balancing Rock, which weighs 250,000 pounds and balances on a fist of granite. The 4.5-mile Rubicon Trail—one of Tahoe's premier hikes—leads to Vikingsholm and provides stunning lake views. Two white-sand beaches front some of Tahoe's warmest water. ⊠ *Hwy. 89* ✛ *Entrance east side of Hwy. 89, 3 miles north of Emerald Bay State Park* ☎ *530/525–3384 visitor information (summer), 530/525–9528 Lake Tahoe sector ranger station/winter conditions, 530/525–7277 D.L. Bliss kiosk (summer)* ⊕ *www.parks.ca.gov* ⊠ *$10 per vehicle, day-use.*

Ed Z'berg Sugar Pine Point State Park

8 miles north of D. L. Bliss State Park, 10 miles south of Tahoe City.

Visitors love to hike, swim, and fish here in the summer, but this park is also popular in winter, when a small campground remains open. Eleven miles of cross-country ski and snowshoe trails allow beginners and experienced enthusiasts alike to whoosh through pine forests and glide past the lake.

GETTING HERE AND AROUND
The entrance to Sugar Pine Point is on the east side of Highway 89, about a mile south of Tahoma. A bike trail links Tahoe City to the park.

Sights

Ed Z'berg Sugar Pine Point State Park
NATIONAL/STATE PARK | Visitors love to hike, swim, and fish in the summer at this park named for a state lawmaker who sponsored key conservation legislation, but it's also popular in winter, when a

A classic lake view at Ed Z'berg Sugar Pine Point State Park.

small campground remains open. Eleven miles of cross-country ski and snowshoe trails allow beginners and experienced enthusiasts alike to whoosh through pine forests and glide past the lake. Rangers lead full-moon snowshoe tours from January to March. With 2,000 densely forested acres and nearly 2 miles of shore frontage, this is Lake Tahoe's largest state park. ⊠ Hwy. 89, 1 mile south of Tahoma ☎ 530/525–7982 summer, 530/525–9528 year-round ⊕ www.parks. ca.gov ✉ $10 per vehicle, day-use.

Hellman-Ehrman Mansion

HOUSE | The main attraction at Sugar Pine Point State Park is the Hellman-Ehrman Mansion, a 1903 stone-and-shingle summer home furnished in period style. In its day the height of modernity, the mansion had electric lights and full indoor plumbing. Also in the park are a trapper's log cabin from the mid-19th century, a nature preserve with wildlife exhibits, a lighthouse, the start of the 10-mile biking trail to Tahoe City, and an extensive system of hiking and cross-country skiing trails. If you're feeling less ambitious, you can relax on the sun-dappled lawn behind the mansion and gaze out at the lake. ■TIP➔ Purchase tour tickets at the Sugar Pine nature center. ⊠ Hwy. 89 ☎ 530/525–7982 summer, 530/525–9528 year-round, 530/583–9911 house tours ⊕ www.parks.ca.gov ✉ $10 per vehicle, day-use; mansion tour $10.

Tahoma

1 mile north of Ed Z'berg Sugar Pine Point State Park, 23 miles south of Truckee.

With its rustic waterfront vacation cottages, Tahoma exemplifies life on the lake in its quiet early days before bright-lights casinos and huge crowds proliferated. In 1960, Tahoma was host of the Olympic Nordic-skiing competitions. Today, there's little to do here except stroll by the lake and listen to the wind in the trees, making it a favorite home base for mellow families and nature buffs.

GETTING HERE AND AROUND

Approach Tahoma by car on Highway 89, called West Lake Boulevard in this section. From the northern and western communities, take a TART bus to Tahoma. A bike trail links Tahoe City to Tahoma.

Hotels

Tahoma Meadows B&B Cottages

$ | B&B/INN | FAMILY | With 16 individually decorated little red cottages sitting beneath towering pine trees, it's hard to beat this serene property for atmosphere and woodsy charm. **Pros:** lovely setting; good choice for families; close to Homewood ski resort. **Cons:** far from the casinos; may be too serene for some guests; old-style decor. ⑤ *Rooms from: $149* ✉ *6821 W. Lake Blvd.* ☎ *530/525–1553* ⊕ *www.tahomameadows.com* ⟳ *16 rooms* ⦿ *No meals.*

Activities

SKIING

Homewood Mountain Resort

SKIING/SNOWBOARDING | Schuss down these slopes for fantastic views—the mountain rises across the road from the Tahoe shoreline. This small, usually uncrowded resort is the favorite area of locals on a snowy day, because you can find lots of untracked powder. It's also the most protected and least windy Tahoe ski area during a storm; when every other resort's lifts are on wind hold, you can almost always count on Homewood's to be open. There's only one high-speed chairlift, but there are rarely any lines. The resort may look small as you drive by, but most of it isn't visible from the road. **Facilities:** 67 trails; 1,260 acres; 1,650-foot vertical drop; 8 lifts. ✉ *5145 W. Lake Blvd., Homewood* ✛ *Hwy. 89, 5 miles south of Tahoe City* ☎ *530/525–2992 information, 530/525–2900 snow phone* ⊕ *www.skihomewood.com* ✉ *Lift ticket $129.*

Tahoe City

9 miles north of Tahoma, 14 miles south of Truckee.

Tahoe City is the only lakeside town with a charming downtown area good for strolling and window-shopping. Stores and restaurants are all within walking distance of the Outlet Gates, where water is spilled into the Truckee River to control the surface level of the lake.

GETTING HERE AND AROUND

Tahoe City is at the junction of Highway 28, also called North Lake Boulevard, and Highway 89 where it turns northwest toward Palisades Tahoe and Truckee. TART buses serve the area.

ESSENTIALS

VISITOR INFORMATION Go Tahoe North. ☎ *530/581–6900* ⊕ *www.gotahoenorth.com.*

Sights

Gatekeeper's Museum

MUSEUM | This museum preserves a little-known part of the region's history. Between 1912 and 1968 the gatekeeper who lived on this site was responsible for monitoring the level of the lake, using a winch system (still used today and visible just outside the museum) to keep the water at the correct level. Also here, the fantastic Marion Steinbach Indian Basket Museum displays intricate baskets from 85 tribes. ✉ *130 W. Lake Blvd.* ☎ *530/583–1762* ⊕ *www.northtahoemuseums.org* ✉ *$5* ⊙ *Closed Mon.–Wed. early-Sept.–late May.*

Watson Cabin Living Museum

MUSEUM | In the middle of Tahoe City sits a 1909 hand-hewn log cabin, the town's oldest structure still on its original site. Now a museum open during the summer, it's filled with century-old furnishings and many reproductions. ✉ *560 N. Lake Blvd.* ☎ *530/583–1762* ⊕ *www.northtahoemuseums.org*

🍴 *Free* ⊘ *Closed Tues. and Wed. and early Sept.–May.*

 Restaurants

Cafe Zenon

$ | **ECLECTIC** | Straightforward Vietnamese pho noodle soup is served all day at this restaurant at Tahoe City's public golf course, but the chef also prepares everything from poutine and kimchi hot dogs to green beans with pork or prawns. The Vietnamese French Dip, a local favorite, substitutes pho broth for the traditional beef. **Known for:** roasted-chicken, Polish sausage, and other sides; Hawaiian buns and gravy with fried egg at weekend brunch; golf course setting (skating rink in winter). ⑤ *Average main: $13* ⊠ *251 N. Lake Blvd.* ⊹ *Behind Bank of America building* ☎ *530/583–1517* ⊕ *www.cafezenon.com.*

★ Christy Hill

$$$$ | **MODERN AMERICAN** | Huge windows reveal stellar lake views at this Euro–Cal restaurant serving seafood, beef, and vegetarian entrées, along with small-plate offerings. The extensive wine list and exceptional desserts earn accolades; the atmosphere is casual. **Known for:** tasting menu a good deal; romantic choice; dinner on the deck in fine weather. ⑤ *Average main: $40* ⊠ *115 Grove St., at N. Lake Blvd.* ☎ *530/583–8551* ⊕ *www.christyhill.com* ⊘ *No lunch. Closed Mon. and Tues.*

Fire Sign Cafe

$ | **AMERICAN** | There's often a wait for breakfast and lunch at this great little diner with pine paneling, hardwood floors, and an exposed-beam ceiling, but it's worth it. The pastries are made from scratch, the salmon is smoked in-house, the salsa is hand cut, and there's real maple syrup for the many types of pancakes and waffles. **Known for:** pastries from scratch; many pancakes and waffles; fruit cobbler for dessert. ⑤ *Average main: $14* ⊠ *1785 W. Lake Blvd.* ⊹ *Hwy. 89, 2 miles south of downtown Tahoe City at Fountain Ave.* ☎ *530/583–0871* ⊕ *www.firesigncafe.com* ⊘ *No dinner.*

Wolfdale's

$$$$ | **ECLECTIC** | Consistent, inspired cuisine served in an elegantly simple dining room makes Wolfdale's one of the top restaurants on the lake, albeit among the most expensive. The imaginative entrées, many involving seafood, merge Asian and European cooking, and everything from teriyaki glaze to smoked fish is made in-house. **Known for:** multiple martinis and other cocktails; lake-view setting; happy hour wines and small plates (5–6:30 except Saturday and holidays). ⑤ *Average main: $44* ⊠ *640 N. Lake Blvd., near Grove St.* ☎ *530/583–5700* ⊕ *www.wolfdales.com* ⊘ *Closed Tues. No lunch.*

 Hotels

Basecamp Tahoe City

$$ | **B&B/INN** | **FAMILY** | A downtown motel for the 21st century, Basecamp charms with a combination of industrial, retro, and rustic styles. **Pros:** lively public spaces; stylish rooms; convenient to commercial strip with restaurants and grocery stores. **Cons:** some road noise; lacks amenities of large properties; eight-minute walk to local beach. ⑤ *Rooms from: $161* ⊠ *955 N. Lake Blvd.* ☎ *530/580–8430* ⊕ *www.basecamptahoecity.com* ⇌ *24 rooms* ⦿ *Free breakfast.*

Cottage Inn

$$ | **B&B/INN** | Avoid the crowds by staying in one of these charming circa-1938 log cottages under the towering pines on the lake's west shore. **Pros:** romantic, woodsy setting; all rooms have gas fireplaces, some two-person tubs; private beach access. **Cons:** guests must be older than 12; most cottages accommodate two people maximum; minimum weekend- and multiple-day stays required in peak. ⑤ *Rooms from: $194* ⊠ *1690 W. Lake Blvd.* ☎ *530/581–4073, 800/581–4073* ⊕ *www.thecottageinn.com* ⇌ *22 rooms* ⦿ *Free breakfast.*

Granlibakken Tahoe

$$ | RESORT | A condo community with its own snow-play area in winter, this secluded 74-acre resort's name means "a hillside sheltered by fir trees" in Norwegian. **Pros:** range of lodging options, from studio condos to town houses; secluded location; pool and spa treatments. **Cons:** some guests find the location too secluded; more for families than romantic interludes; conference activities and weddings. ⑤ *Rooms from: $171* ✉ *725 Granlibakken Rd.* ☎ *530/583–4242 front desk, 800/543–3221 reservations* ⊕ *granlibakken.com* ↩ *165 rooms* ⦿ *Free breakfast.*

★ Sunnyside Restaurant and Lodge

$$ | HOTEL | The views are superb and the hospitality gracious at this lakeside lodge 3 miles south of Tahoe City. **Pros:** complimentary continental breakfast and afternoon tea; most rooms have balconies overlooking the lake; lively bar and restaurant. **Cons:** can be pricey for families; noisy in summer; pricey entrées at restaurant. ⑤ *Rooms from: $199* ✉ *1850 W. Lake Blvd.* ☎ *530/583–7200, 800/822–2754* ⊕ *www.sunnysideresort. com* ↩ *23 rooms* ⦿ *Free breakfast.*

Activities

RAFTING

Truckee River Rafting

WHITE-WATER RAFTING | FAMILY | In summer you can take a self-guided raft trip down a gentle 5-mile stretch of the Truckee River. This outfitter will shuttle you back to Tahoe City at the end of your two- to three-hour trip. ■**TIP**➡ **On a warm day this makes a great family outing.** ✉ *175 River Rd., near W. Lake Blvd.* ☎ *530/583–1111* ⊕ *www.truckeeriverrafting.com* 🎫 *From $60.*

SKIING

AREAS

Alpine Meadows Ski Area

SKIING/SNOWBOARDING | With an average 450 inches of snow annually, Alpine (part of Palisades Tahoe) has some of Tahoe's most reliable conditions. It's usually one of the first areas to open in November and one of the last to close in May or June. Alpine isn't the place for show-offs; instead, you'll find down-to-earth alpine fetishists. The two peaks here are well suited to intermediate skiers, with a number of runs for experts only. Snowboarders and hot-dog skiers will find a terrain park with a super-pipe, rails, and tabletops, as well as a boarder-cross course. Alpine is a great place to learn to ski and has a ski school for kids and adults. On Saturday, because of the limited parking, there's more acreage per person than at other resorts. Lift tickets are good at neighboring Palisades Tahoe; a free shuttle runs all day between the two ski parks. **Facilities:** 100-plus trails; 2,400 acres; 1,802-foot vertical drop; 13 lifts. ✉ *2600 Alpine Meadows Rd.* ⊹ *Off Hwy. 89, 6 miles northwest of Tahoe City, 13 miles south of Truckee* ☎ *530/583–4232, 800/403–0206* ⊕ *www.palisadestahoe. com* 🎫 *Lift ticket $169.*

EQUIPMENT RENTALS

Tahoe Dave's Skis and Boards

SKIING/SNOWBOARDING | You can rent skis, boards, and snowshoes at this shop, which has the area's best selection of downhill rental equipment. ✉ *590 N. Lake Blvd.* ☎ *530/583–6415* ⊕ *www.tahoe-daves.com.*

Palisades Tahoe has runs for skiers of all abilitiy levels, from beginner to expert.

Olympic Valley

7 miles north of Tahoe City to Palisades Tahoe Rd., 8½ miles south of Truckee.

Olympic Valley got its moniker in 1960, when its ski resort, Palisades Tahoe, hosted the Winter Olympics. Snow sports remain the primary activity, but once summer comes, you can hike into the adjacent Granite Chief Wilderness, explore wildflower-studded alpine meadows, or lie by a swimming pool in one of the Sierra's prettiest valleys.

GETTING HERE AND AROUND

Palisades Tahoe Road, the only way into Olympic Valley, branches west off Highway 89 about 8 miles south of Truckee. TART connects the Palisades Tahoe ski area with the communities along the north and west shores, and Truckee, with year-round public transportation. Palisades Tahoe provides a free shuttle to many stops in those same areas.

Sights

High Camp

VIEWPOINT | Ride the Palisades Tahoe Aerial Tram to this activity hub, which at 8,200 feet commands superb views of Lake Tahoe and the surrounding mountains. In summer, go for a hike, sit by the pool, or have a cocktail and watch the sunset. In winter you can ski or snow-tube. There's also a restaurant, a lounge, and a small Olympic museum. Pick up trail maps at the tram building. ⊠ *Aerial Tram Bldg., Palisades Tahoe* ☎ *800/403–0206* ⊕ *www.palisadestahoe. com* ⊠ *Aerial Tram, $46.*

Village at Palisades Tahoe

COMMERCIAL CENTER | FAMILY | The centerpiece of Olympic Valley is a pedestrian mall at the base of several four-story ersatz Bavarian stone-and-timber buildings, where you'll find restaurants, high-end condo rentals, boutiques, and cafés. ⊠ *1750 Village East Rd.* ☎ *530/584–1000, 800/403–0206 information* ⊕ *www. palisadestahoe.com.*

Restaurants

Fireside Pizza Company

$$ | PIZZA | FAMILY | Adults might opt for the signature pear-and-Gorgonzola pizza at this modern Italian restaurant, but most kids clamor for the house favorite: an Italian-sausage-and-pepperoni combo with a bubbly blend of four cheeses. Salads and pasta dishes round out the menu at this family-friendly spot. **Known for:** inventive pizzas; good, inexpensive dining option in a pricey area; family-friendly. ⑤ *Average main: $17* ✉ *The Village at Palisades Tahoe, 1985 Palisades Tahoe Rd., #25* ☎ *530/584–6150* ⊕ *www. firesidepizza.com.*

★ PlumpJack Cafe

$$$$ | AMERICAN | The menu at this silver-tone white-tablecloth restaurant whose wide windows reveal Palisades Tahoe in all its glory changes seasonally, but look for rib-eye steak, seared diver scallops with risotto, and a filling, inventive vegetarian dish. Rather than complicated, heavy sauces, the chef uses simple reductions to complement a dish, resulting in clean, dynamic flavors. **Known for:** specialty cocktails; less expensive but equally adventurous bar menu; varied, reasonably priced wines. ⑤ *Average main: $42* ✉ *1920 Palisades Tahoe Rd.* ☎ *530/583–1586* ⊕ *www.plumpjackcafe. com* ☾ *No lunch (except at bar).*

🛏 Hotels

★ PlumpJack Inn

$$ | HOTEL | Stylish and luxurious, this two-story, cedar-sided inn has a snappy, sophisticated look and laid-back sensibility, perfect for the Bay Area cognoscenti who flock here on weekends. **Pros:** small and intimate; loaded with amenities; personable and attentive service. **Cons:** not the best choice for families with small children; not all rooms have tubs; laid-back sensibility may not work for some guests. ⑤ *Rooms from: $225* ✉ *1920 Palisades Tahoe Rd.* ☎ *530/583–1576,* *800/323–7666* ⊕ *plumpjackinn.com* ⌨ *56 rooms* ⑩ *Free breakfast.*

Resort at Squaw Creek

$$$ | RESORT | This Palisades Tahoe multifacility offers restaurants, a golf course, a spa, heated swimming pool, ice skating rink, chairlift to the mountain, and groomed cross-country ski tracks on the property, plus all the amenities and services you could possibly want in the Tahoe area. **Pros:** every conceivable amenity; chairlift to Palisades Tahoe for ski-in, ski-out; attractive furnishings. **Cons:** so large it can feel impersonal; high in-season rates; a lot of hubbub during ski season. ⑤ *Rooms from: $299* ✉ *400 Squaw Creek Rd.* ☎ *530/412–7034,* *800/404–8006 reservations* ⊕ *www.des-tinationhotels.com/squawcreek* ⌨ *405 rooms* ⑩ *No meals.*

The Village at Palisades Tahoe

$$ | HOTEL | FAMILY | Right at the base of the slopes, at the center point of Olympic Valley, the Village's condominiums (from studio to three bedrooms) come complete with gas fireplaces, daily maid service, and heated slate-tile bathroom and kitchen floors. **Pros:** each condo sleeps at least four people; near Village restaurants and shops; at base of slopes. **Cons:** village often gets crowded on weekends; nicely appointed but not high style; lacks room service and other hotel amenities. ⑤ *Rooms from: $209* ✉ *1750 Village East Rd.* ☎ *530/584–1000,* *888/259–1428* ⊕ *www.palisadestahoe. com* ⌨ *198 rooms* ⑩ *No meals.*

🏃 Activities

GOLF

Resort at Squaw Creek Golf Course

GOLF | For beautiful views of Palisades Tahoe's surrounding peaks, play this narrow, challenging championship course designed by Robert Trent Jones Jr. The design emphasizes accuracy over distance, especially on the front nine. All fees include a golf cart plus valet parking;

rates drop after noon and again after 3 pm. ⊠ *400 Squaw Creek Rd.* ☎ *530/583–6300, 530/581–6637 pro shop* ⊕ *www.destinationhotels.com/squawcreek/recreation* ⌖ *From $127* ⚡ *18 holes, 6931 yards, par 71.*

SKIING
AREAS
★ Palisades Tahoe
SKIING/SNOWBOARDING | Known for some of the toughest skiing in the Tahoe area, this park was the centerpiece of the 1960 Winter Olympics. Today it's the definitive North Tahoe ski resort and among the top-three megaresorts in California (the other two are Heavenly and Mammoth). Although Palisades Tahoe has changed significantly since the Olympics, the skiing is still world-class and extends across vast bowls stretched between six peaks. Experts often head directly to the untamed terrain of the infamous KT-22 face, which has bumps, cliffs, and gulp-and-go chutes, or to the nearly vertical Palisades, where many famous extreme-skiing films have been shot. Fret not, beginners and intermediates: you have plenty of wide-open, groomed trails at High Camp (which sits at the *top* of the mountain) and around the more challenging Snow King Peak. Snowboarders and show-off skiers can tear up the five fantastic terrain parks, which include a giant super-pipe. Ski passes are good at neighboring Alpine Meadows, which is part of Palisades Tahoe; free shuttles run all day between the Alpine and Olympic Valley base camps. (By early 2022, a gondola will connect them.) **Facilities:** 178 trails; 3,600 acres; 2,840-foot vertical drop; 30 lifts. ⊠ *1960 Palisades Tahoe Rd.* ✛ *Off Hwy. 89, 7 miles northwest of Tahoe City* ☎ *800/403–0206* ⊕ *www.palisadestahoe.com* ⌖ *Lift ticket $179.*

EQUIPMENT RENTALS
Tahoe Dave's Skis and Boards
SKIING/SNOWBOARDING | If you don't want to pay resort prices, you can rent and tune downhill skis and snowboards at

this shop. ⊠ *3039 Hwy. 89, at Palisades Tahoe Rd.* ☎ *530/583–5665* ⊕ *www.tahoedaves.com.*

Truckee

13 miles northwest of Kings Beach, 14 miles north of Tahoe City.

Formerly a decrepit railroad town in the mountains, Truckee is now the trendy first stop for many Tahoe visitors. The town was officially established around 1863, and by 1868 it had gone from a stagecoach station to a major stopover for trains bound for the Pacific via the new transcontinental railroad. Every day, freight trains and Amtrak's *California Zephyr* still idle briefly at the depot in the middle of town. The visitor center inside the depot has a walking-tour map of historic Truckee.

Across from the station, where Old West facades line the main drag, you'll find galleries, gift shops, boutiques, a wine-tasting room, old-fashioned diners, and several good restaurants.

GETTING HERE AND AROUND
Truckee is off Interstate 80 between Highways 89 and 267. Greyhound and Amtrak stop here, and TART buses serve the area.

ESSENTIALS
VISITOR INFORMATION Truckee Donner Chamber of Commerce and the California Welcome Center. ⊠ *Amtrak depot, 10065 Donner Pass Rd., near Spring St.* ☎ *530/587–8808* ⊕ *www.truckee.com.*

 Sights

Donner Memorial State Park and Emigrant Trail Museum
NATIONAL/STATE PARK | The park and museum commemorate the 89 members of the Donner Party, westward-bound pioneers who became trapped in the Sierra in the winter of 1846–47 in snow 22 feet

deep. Barely more than half survived, some by resorting to cannibalism. The absorbing Emigrant Trail Museum in the visitor center contains exhibits about the Donner Party, regional Native Americans, and railroad and transportation development in the area. In the park, you can picnic, hike, camp, and go boating, fishing, and waterskiing in summer; winter brings cross-country skiing and snowshoeing on groomed trails. ⊠ *12593 Donner Pass Rd.* ✛ *Off I–80, Exit 184, 2 miles west of Truckee* ☎ *530/582–7892* ⊕ *www.parks. ca.gov/donnermemorial* ⤳ *$10 parking, day-use ($5 in winter).*

🍴 Restaurants

★ Cottonwood Restaurant & Bar

$$$ | ECLECTIC | Perched above town on the site of North America's first chairlift, this local institution has a bar decked out with old wooden skis, sleds, skates, and photos of Truckee's early days. The ambitious menu includes grilled steak, baby-back short ribs with chipotle barbecue jus, and house-special pasta dishes like chicken linguine. **Known for:** early-bird three-course dinner except in high season; wine selection; hilltop views from atmospheric bar. $ *Average main: $31* ⊠ *10142 Rue Hilltop Rd., off Brockway Rd., ¼ mile south of downtown* ☎ *530/587–5711* ⊕ *www.cottonwoodrestaurant.com* ⌚ *No lunch Sept.–May or weekdays in summer.*

FiftyFifty Brewing Company

$$ | AMERICAN | In this brewpub, the warm red tones and comfy booths, plus a pint of the Donner Party porter (or a shot of bourbon), will take the nip out of a cold day on the slopes. The menu includes salads, burgers, inventive pizzas, barbecued ribs, pan-seared salmon, and the house specialty: a pulled-pork sandwich. **Known for:** high-quality burger beef; 2018 Brewery Group of the Year honors at top beer fest; après-ski action. $ *Average main: $24* ⊠ *11197 Brockway Rd., near Martis Valley Rd.* ☎ *530/587–2337* ⊕ *www.fiftyfiftybrewing.com.*

Moody's Bistro, Bar & Beats

$$$ | ECLECTIC | Head here for contemporary-Cal cuisine in a sexy dining room with pumpkin-color walls, burgundy velvet banquettes, and art-deco fixtures. The earthy, sure-handed cooking features organically grown ingredients: look for ahi poke, snazzy pizzas bubbling-hot from a brick oven, braised lamb shanks, pan-roasted wild game, fresh seafood, and organic beef. **Known for:** lighter fare for lunch; summer alfresco dining; live music in bar some nights. $ *Average main: $32* ⊠ *10007 Bridge St., at Donner Pass Rd.* ☎ *530/587–8688* ⊕ *www.moodysbistro.com.*

Pianeta Ristorante

$$$ | ITALIAN | A longtime town favorite, Pianeta serves high-style Italian cuisine in a warmly lit bi-level redbrick space on Truckee's historic main drag. Start with a beef carpaccio antipasto plate or perhaps house-made spicy-fennel and mild sausages, following up with a pasta course of ravioli Bolognese (both pasta and sauce made in-house), an entrée of ragout with spicy sausage and Mexican prawns—or both. **Known for:** welcoming atmosphere; tiramisu and panna cotta for dessert; West Coast and Italian wine selections. $ *Average main: $30* ⊠ *10096 Donner Pass Rd.* ☎ *530/587–4694* ⊕ *www.pianetarestauranttruckee.com* ⌚ *No lunch.*

Squeeze In

$ | AMERICAN | Meet the locals at Truckee's top choice for breakfast, thanks to the dozens of omelets and several variations on eggs Benedict along with banana-walnut pancakes and French toast oozing with cream cheese. At lunch savor homemade soups and sandwiches. **Known for:** cheeseburger omelet; homemade soups; gluten-free variations. $ *Average main: $15* ⊠ *10060 Donner Pass Rd., near Bridge St.* ☎ *530/587–9814* ⊕ *www. squeezein.com* ⌚ *No dinner.*

Truckee Tavern and Grill

$$$ | **AMERICAN** | The wood-fired grill in this second-floor downtown restaurant turns out steaks, chicken, and chops along with fish dishes that might include Mt. Lassen trout with white beans and mushrooms. As with the food, the decor is New West contemporary—bricks line the wall behind the bar, where mixologists craft wiggy drinks like the Salvador (as in Dalí, with rye, mescal, blood orange, and egg white), and, in tribute to Truckee's bootlegging past, pour artisanal small-batch gin and whiskey. **Known for:** buffalo tri-tip; pasta and fish entrées; deck overlooking downtown action. ⑤ *Average main: $29 ⌧ 10118 Donner Pass Rd., near Spring St. ☎ 530/587–3766 ⊕ www.truckeetavern.com ☉ No lunch Wed.*

 ## Hotels

Cedar House Sport Hotel

$$ | **HOTEL** | The clean, spare lines of the Cedar House's wooden exterior evoke a modern European feel, while energy-saving heating, cooling, and lighting systems emphasize the owners' commitment to sustainability. **Pros:** environmentally friendly; hip yet comfortable; heated-tile bathroom floors. **Cons:** some bathrooms on the small side; not all bathrooms have tubs; about a mile from historic downtown Truckee. ⑤ *Rooms from: $215 ⌧ 10918 Brockway Rd. ☎ 530/582–5655, 866/582–5655 ⊕ www.cedarhousesporthotel.com ⇌ 40 rooms ⑩ Free breakfast.*

Northstar California Resort

$$ | **RESORT** | The area's most complete destination resort entices families with its sports activities and concentration of restaurants, shops, and accommodations. **Pros:** array of lodging types; on-site shuttle; several dining options in Northstar Village. **Cons:** family accommodations can be pricey; lacks intimacy; some units not as attractive as others. ⑤ *Rooms from: $220 ⌧ 5001 Northstar*

Dr. ✛ Off Hwy. 267, 6 miles southeast of Truckee ☎ 530/562–1010, 800/466–6784 ⊕ www.northstarcalifornia.com ⇌ 250 units ⑩ No meals.

★ Ritz-Carlton Highlands Court, Lake Tahoe

$$$$ | **RESORT** | Nestled mid-mountain on the Northstar ski resort, the four-story Ritz-Carlton has plush accommodations with floor-to-ceiling windows, fireplaces, cozy robes, and down comforters. **Pros:** superb service; gorgeous setting; ski-in, ski out convenience. **Cons:** in-season prices as breathtaking as the views; resort fee and mandatory valet parking add to cost of stay; must go off-site for golf and tennis. ⑤ *Rooms from: $382 ⌧ 13031 Ritz-Carlton Highlands Court ☎ 530/562–3000, 800/241–3333 ⊕ www.ritzcarlton.com ⇌ 170 rooms ⑩ No meals.*

River Street Inn

$$ | **B&B/INN** | On the banks of the Truckee River, this 1882 wood-and-stone inn has uncluttered, comfortable rooms that are simply decorated, with attractive, country-style wooden furniture and extras like flat-screen TVs. **Pros:** tidy rooms; good value; in historic downtown Truckee. **Cons:** parking is a half block from inn; decor is simple; noise from on-site restaurant and bar and nearby trains. ⑤ *Rooms from: $165 ⌧ 10009 E. River St. ☎ 530/550–9290 inn, 530/550–9222 restaurant ⊕ www.riverstreetinntruckee.com ⇌ 7 rooms ⑩ Free breakfast.*

Truckee Hotel

$$ | **HOTEL** | A four-story hotel in business in various forms since 1873, the Truckee Hotel attracts history buffs and skiers, the latter for the reasonable rates when in-season prices skyrocket at Northstar, Sugar Bowl, and other nearby resorts. **Pros:** historic atmosphere; convenient to shops and restaurants; same owners operate a modern Hampton Inn nearby. **Cons:** no pool, fitness center, elevator; train and other noise issues (when booking ask for a quiet room); most rooms share bathrooms (though all have a sink). ⑤ *Rooms from: $189 ⌧ 10007 Bridge St.*

☎ 530/587–4444 ⊕ www.truckeehotel. com ⇆ 32 rooms ⫟ Free breakfast.

 Activities

GOLF

Coyote Moon Golf Course

GOLF | With pine trees lining the fairways and no houses to spoil the view, this course is as beautiful as it is challenging. Fees include a shared cart; the greens fee drops at 1 pm and dips again at 3. ✉ 10685 Northwoods Blvd., off Donner Pass Rd. ☎ 530/587–0886 ⊕ www.coyotemoongolf.com 🎟 $185 ⛳ 18 holes, 7177 yards, par 72 ⊗ Closed late fall–late spring.

Northstar Golf

GOLF | Robert Muir Graves designed this course that combines hilly terrain and open meadows. The front nine holes here are open-links style, while the challenging back nine move through tight, tree-lined fairways. Rates, which include a cart, drop successively after 11, 1, and 4. ✉ 168 Basque Dr. ✛ Off Northstar Dr., west off Hwy. 267 ☎ 530/562–3290 pro shop ⊕ www.northstarcalifornia.com 🎟 $110 for 18 holes ⛳ 18 holes, 6781 yards, par 72.

MOUNTAIN BIKING

Cyclepaths Mountain Bike Adventures

BICYCLING | This combination full-service bike shop and bike-adventure outfitter offers instruction in mountain biking, guided tours, tips for self-guided bike touring, bike repairs, and books and maps on the area. ✉ Pioneer Center, 10825 Pioneer Trail, Suite 105 ☎ 530/582–1890 ⊕ cyclepaths.com.

Northstar California Bike Park

BICYCLING | From late May through September Northstar's ski slopes transform into a magnificent lift-served bike park with 100 miles of challenging terrain, including the aptly named Livewire trail. Guided tours, multiday retreats, and downhill, cross-country, and endurance races are available for riders of all abilities. ✉ Northstar Dr., off Hwy. 267 ☎ 530/562–1010 ⊕ www.northstarcalifornia.com 🎟 Lift $70.

SKIING

AREAS

★ Northstar California

SKIING/SNOWBOARDING | Meticulous grooming and long cruisers make this resort a paradise for intermediate skiers and a fine choice for families. Although the majority of the trails are intermediate in difficulty, advanced skiers and riders have access to Lookout Mountain's more than two dozen expert trails and 347 acres of gated terrain and steeps. The diversity of terrain in proximity makes it easier for families and groups with varying skills to hang out with each other. As for terrain parks, the ones here are considered among North America's best, with features that include a 420-foot-long super-pipe, a half-pipe, rails and boxes, and lots of kickers. The Cross Country, Telemark and Snowshoe Center, located mid-mountain, is the starting point for a network of 35 km (22 miles) of groomed trails, including double-set tracks and skating lanes. The trails are also fat-bike friendly, so nonskiers can enjoy the park, too. The school has programs for skiers ages three and up, and on-site care is available for tots two and older. **Facilities:** 100 trails; 3,170 acres; 2,280-foot vertical drop; 20 lifts. ✉ 5001 Northstar Dr. ☎ 530/562–2267 ⊕ www.northstarcalifornia.com 🎟 day pass from $67.

★ Royal Gorge

SKIING/SNOWBOARDING | If you love to cross-country, don't miss Royal Gorge, which serves up 140 km (124 miles) of track for all abilities, six trail systems on a whopping 6,000 acres, a ski school, and nine warming huts. Because the complex, affiliated with Sugar Bowl, sits right on the Sierra Crest, the views are drop-dead gorgeous. ✉ 9411 Pahatsi Dr., Soda Springs ✛ Off I–80, Soda Springs/Norden exit ☎ 530/426–3871, 530/426–3871 ⊕ www.royalgorge.com ⇆ All-day pass $40.

Sugar Bowl Ski Resort

SKIING/SNOWBOARDING | Opened in 1939 by Walt Disney, this is the oldest—and one of the best—resorts at Tahoe. Atop Donner Summit, it receives an incredible 500 inches of snowfall annually. Four peaks are connected by 1,650 acres of skiable terrain, with everything from gentle groomed corduroy to wide-open bowls to vertical rocky chutes and outstanding tree skiing. Snowboarders can hit two terrain parks with numerous boxes, rails, and jumps. Because it's more compact than some of the area's megaresorts, there's a gentility here that distinguishes Sugar Bowl from its competitors, making this a great place for families and a low-pressure, low-key place to learn to ski. It's not huge, but there's some very challenging terrain (experts: head to the Palisades). There is limited lodging at the base area. Facilities: 100 trails; 1,650 acres; 1,500-foot vertical drop; 12 lifts. ⊠ 629 Sugar Bowl Rd., Norden ⊹ Off Donner Pass Rd., 3 miles east of I–80 Soda Springs/Norden exit, 10 miles west of Truckee ☎ 530/426–9000, 530/426–1111 snow phone ⊕ www.sugarbowl.com 🎫 Lift ticket from $118.

Tahoe Donner Cross Country Ski Center

SKIING/SNOWBOARDING | Just north of Truckee, the center, which ranks among the nation's best cross-country venues for the skiing and the magnificent Sierra Crest views, includes 65 trails on 100 km (62 miles) of groomed tracks on more than 2,800 acres. In addition to cross-country skiing, there are fat-biking, dog, and snowshoeing trails. ⊠ 15275 Alder Creek Rd. ☎ 530/587–9484 ⊕ www.tahoedonner.com/xc.

EQUIPMENT RENTALS
BackCountry

SKIING/SNOWBOARDING | If you plan to ski or board the backcountry, you'll find everything from crampons to transceivers at this shop. ⊠ 11400 Donner Pass Rd. ☎ 530/582–0909 ⊕ www.thebackcountry.net.

Tahoe Dave's

SKIING/SNOWBOARDING | You can save money by renting skis and boards at this shop, which has the area's best selection and also repairs and tunes equipment. ⊠ 10200 Donner Pass Rd., near Spring St. ☎ 530/582–0900 ⊕ www.tahoedaves.com.

Carnelian Bay to Kings Beach

5–10 miles northeast of Tahoe City.

The small lakeside commercial districts of Carnelian Bay and Tahoe Vista service the thousand or so locals who live in the area year-round and the thousands more who have summer residences or launch their boats here. Kings Beach, the last town heading east on Highway 28 before the Nevada border, is full of basic motels and rental condos, restaurants, and shops.

GETTING HERE AND AROUND

To reach Kings Beach and Carnelian Bay from the California side, take Highway 89 north to Highway 28 north and then east. From the Nevada side, follow Highway 28 north and then west. TART provides public transportation in this area.

 Beaches

Kings Beach State Recreation Area

BEACH—SIGHT | FAMILY | The north shore's 28-acre Kings Beach State Recreation Area, one of the largest such areas on the lake, is open year-round. The 700-foot-long sandy beach gets crowded in summer with people swimming, sunbathing, Jet Skiing, riding in paddleboats, spiking volleyballs, and tossing Frisbees. If you're going to spend the day, come early to snag a table in the picnic area; there's also a good playground. **Amenities:** food and drink; parking (fee); toilets; water sports. **Best for:** sunrise; sunset; swimming; windsurfing. ⊠ 8318 N. Lake Blvd., Kings Beach ☎ 530/523–3203 ⊕ www.parks.ca.gov 🎫 $10 parking fee.

🍴 Restaurants

Gar Woods Grill and Pier

$$$ | ECLECTIC | The view's the thing at this lakeside stalwart, where you can watch the sun shimmer on the water through the dining room's plateglass windows or from the heated outdoor deck. Price wise, this is a better bet for lunch or weekend breakfast than for dinner, at which grilled steak and fish are menu mainstays, but specialties like crab chiles rellenos and pomegranate braised pork ribs also merit consideration. **Known for:** lake views; grilled steak and fish; specialty cocktails. ⑤ *Average main: $36* ✉ *5000 N. Lake Blvd., Carnelian Bay* ✛ *Hwy. 28, 2 miles west of Tahoe Vista* ☎ *530/546–3366* ⊕ *www.garwoods.com.*

Jason's Beachside Grille

$$ | AMERICAN | If the kids want burgers but you want bourbon, area mainstay Jason's has a full bar as well as steaks, 10 kinds of burgers, teriyaki chicken, and a big salad bar. The whole place is wood, from floor to ceiling, lending it an ultrarustic feel. **Known for:** salad bar; summer dining on deck overlooking the lake; tables by fireplace in winter. ⑤ *Average main: $21* ✉ *8338 N. Lake Blvd., Kings Beach* ☎ *530/546–3315* ⊕ *jasonsbeachsidegrille.com.*

Soule Domain

$$$ | ECLECTIC | Rough-hewn wood beams, a vaulted wood ceiling, and in winter, a roaring fireplace, lend high romance to this cozy, 1927, pine-log cabin. Chef-owner Charlie Soule's specialties include curried almond chicken; sea scallops poached in Champagne with a kiwi-and-mango cream sauce; and a vegan sauté judiciously flavored with ginger, jalapeños, sesame seeds, and teriyaki sauce. **Known for:** romance by candlelight; skillfully prepared cuisine; suave service. ⑤ *Average main: $30* ✉ *9983 Cove St., ½ block up Stateline Rd. off Hwy. 28, Kings Beach* ✛ *Restaurant is just west of Tahoe Biltmore casino at California–Nevada border.* ☎ *530/546–7529* ⊕ *www.soule-domain.com* ⊗ *No lunch.*

Spindleshanks American Bistro and Wine Bar

$$$ | AMERICAN | A local favorite on the Old Brockway Golf Course, Spindleshanks serves mostly classic American cooking—ribs, steaks, and seafood updated with adventurous sauces—as well as house-made ravioli. Savor a drink from the full bar or choose a wine from the extensive list while you enjoy views of Lake Tahoe or the historic greens where Bing Crosby hosted his first golf tournament in 1934. **Known for:** classic American cooking; Lake Tahoe views; patio dining. *Average main: $28* ✉ *400 Brassie Ave., Kings Beach* ✛ *At Hwy. 267 and N. Lake Tahoe Blvd.* ☎ *530/546–2191* ⊕ *www.spindleshankstahoe.com.*

🛏 Hotels

Ferrari's Crown Resort

$ | HOTEL | FAMILY | Great for families with kids and all travelers on a budget willing to trade style and amenities for below-average rates and (from some rooms) impressive water views, the family-owned Ferrari's has straightforward rooms in two formerly separate vintage-1950s motels, sitting side-by-side on the lake. **Pros:** family-friendly; lakeside location; a few rooms value-priced. **Cons:** older facility with unappealing exterior; thin walls; uninspired breakfast. ⑤ *Rooms from: $115* ✉ *8200 N. Lake Blvd., Kings Beach* ☎ *530/546–3388, 800/645–2260* ⊕ *www.tahoecrown.com* ⤴ *72 rooms* ⊙ *Free breakfast.*

Mourelatos Lakeshore Resort

$$ | B&B/INN | At first glance this family-run waterfront property looks like a slightly above-average two-story motel, but with a private beach, two hot tubs, ceaselessly alluring lake and mountain vistas, and summertime barbecuing, kayaking, and other extras it legitimately lays claim to the title of resort. **Pros:**

private beach; some rooms have full kitchens; summertime barbecuing and kayaking. **Cons:** decor a tad dated; books up quickly for summer; some rooms lack sufficient heat in winter. $ *Rooms from: $220* ⊠ *6834 N. Lake Blvd., Tahoe Vista* ☎ *530/546–9500* ⊕ *www.mlrtahoe.com* ⇌ *32 rooms* ⊚l *Free breakfast.*

Rustic Cottages

$ | **HOTEL** | **FAMILY** | These charming clapboard cottages sit clustered beneath tall pine trees across the road from Lake Tahoe and a little beach. **Pros:** woodsy Old Tahoe feel; expanded continental breakfast; good value. **Cons:** older facility; some rooms are very small; lacks big-hotel amenities. $ *Rooms from: $134* ⊠ *7449 N. Lake Blvd., Tahoe Vista* ☎ *530/546–3523, 888/778–7842* ⊕ *www.rusticcottages.com* ⇌ *20 rooms* ⊚l *No meals.*

 Activities

KAYAKING
Wild Society

KAYAKING | **FAMILY** | Gaze at the underwater world while paddling a clear-bottom kayak around Kings Beach. Rentals incude (on request) wireless waterproof speakers with a USB plug, waterproof phone cases, binoculars, goggles, snorkels, cooler, cup holders, selfie sticks, and safety equipment. Guided kayak tours from Sand Harbor and SUP rentals (Kings Beach only) are also available. ⊠ *8612 N. Lake Blvd., Kings Beach* ⊹ *At Raccoon St.* ☎ *530/553–1771* ⊕ *www.wildsocietylt.com* ☞ *one-hour single $60, tandem $80.*

Incline Village

5½ miles northeast of Kings Beach.

Incline Village dates from the early 1960s, when an Oklahoma developer bought 10,000 acres north of Lake Tahoe. His idea was to sketch out a plan for a town without a central commercial district, hoping to prevent congestion and to preserve the area's natural beauty. One-acre lakeshore lots originally cost $12,000 to $15,000; today you couldn't buy the same land for less than several million.

GETTING HERE AND AROUND
From the California side, reach Incline Village via Highway 89 or 267 to Highway 28. From South Lake Tahoe, take U.S. 50 north to Highway 28 north. TART serves the communities along Lake Tahoe's north and west shores from Incline Village to Tahoma.

ESSENTIALS
VISITOR INFORMATION Lake Tahoe Incline Village/Crystal Bay Visitors Bureau. ⊠ *969 Tahoe Blvd.* ☎ *775/832–1606, 800/468–2463* ⊕ *www.gotahoenorth.com.*

 Sights

Lakeshore Drive

SCENIC DRIVE | Take this beautiful drive to see some of the most expensive real estate in Nevada. The route is discreetly marked: to find it, start at the Hyatt hotel and drive westward along the lake. ⊠ *Incline Village.*

★ Tahoe Science Center

MUSEUM | **FAMILY** | Learn how Lake Tahoe was formed, why it's so blue, and how its ecosystem is changing at Tahoe's only science center, which is affiliated with UC Davis researchers. Hands-on exhibits include aquariums, a virtual ecology lab and research boat, a watershed map with the 63 streams that flow into the lake (and the only one that flows out, the Truckee River), tables that teach how to identify trees, and a 3D theater. Visitors ages 8 and older will gain the most from the experience. ⊠ *291 Country Club Dr.* ⊹ *At Tahoe Center for Environmental Sciences, Sierra Nevada University campus* ☎ *775/881–7560* ⊕ *tahoesciencecenter.com* ☞ *$5* ⊙ *Closed Sat.–Mon.*

★ Thunderbird Lodge

HOUSE | George Whittell, a San Francisco socialite who once owned 40,000 acres of property along the lake, began building this lodge in 1936, completing it in 1941. You can tour the mansion and the grounds by reservation only, and though it's pricey to do so, you'll be rewarded with a rare glimpse of a time when only the very wealthy had homes at Tahoe. The lodge is accessible via a bus from the Incline Village–Crystal Bay Visitors Bureau, several boats from the Hyatt in Incline Village, and a 1950 wooden cruiser from Zephyr Cove. ⊠ *5000 Hwy. 28* ☎ *800/468–2463 tours, 775/832–8750 lodge* ⊕ *www.thunderbirdtahoe.org/tours* 🎫 *From $50 for bus tour, $169 for boat tours.*

 Beaches

Lake Tahoe–Nevada State Park and Sand Harbor Beach

BEACH—SIGHT | Protecting much of the lake's eastern shore from development, this park comprises several sections that stretch from Incline Village to Zephyr Cove. Beaches and trails provide access to a wilder side of the lake, whether you're into cross-country skiing, hiking, or just relaxing at a picnic. With a gently sloping beach for lounging, crystal-clear water for swimming and snorkeling, and a picnic area shaded by cedars and pines, **Sand Harbor Beach** sometimes reaches capacity by 11 am on summer weekends. A handicap-accessible nature trail has interpretive signs and beautiful lake views. Pets are not allowed on the beach from mid-April through mid-October. **Amenities**: food and drink; parking ($10, $15 for non-NV license plates); toilets; water sports. **Best for**: boating; snorkeling; sunset; swimming; walking. ⊠ *Sand Harbor Beach, Hwy. 28, 3 miles south of Incline Village* ☎ *775/831–0494* ⊕ *parks.nv.gov/parks/lake-tahoe-nevada-state-park.*

 Restaurants

Azzara's

$$ | **ITALIAN** | This dependable if not fabulous Italian family restaurant serves a dozen pasta dishes and many pizzas, as well as chicken, veal, shrimp, and beef. Prices initially might seem high, but once you factor in soup or salad and garlic bread, it's a pretty good value. **Known for:** family run; daily specials; excellent tiramisu. 💲 *Average main: $22* ⊠ *Raley's Shopping Center, 930 Tahoe Blvd., near Village Blvd.* ☎ *775/831–0346* ⊕ *www.azzaras.com* ☾ *Closed Mon. No lunch.*

Le Bistro

$$$$ | **FRENCH** | Incline Village's hidden gem (this restaurant is hard to find, so ask for directions when you book) serves French-country cuisine in a romantic dining room with single-stem roses adorning linen-dressed tables. The five-course prix-fixe menu may include starters like flame-broiled eggplant with ratatouille or escargots, followed by one of several salads (try the gem lettuce Caesar) and lamb loin with lentils and tomato chutney or *coquille St.-Jacques* (scallops in cream sauce), paired with award-winning wines if you choose. **Known for:** romantic setting; five-course prix-fixe meal with wine pairings; gracious, attentive service. 💲 *Average main: $65* ⊠ *120 Country Club Dr., #29* ✛ *Off Lakeshore Blvd.* ☎ *775/831–0800* ⊕ *www.lebistrotahoe.com* ☾ *Closed Sun. and Mon. No lunch.*

★ Mountain High Sandwich Company

$ | **AMERICAN** | A casual plank-floored all-natural deli serving breakfast and lunch, Mountain High may well be the only place in Tahoe to find coconut chia seed pudding and similar delicacies. More familiar fare—biscuits and sausage gravy for breakfast, house-smoked tri-tip sandwiches for lunch—is also on the menu, with many selections gluten-free and vegan or vegetarian friendly. **Known for:** grab-and-go items; inventive soups; sustainable practices. 💲 *Average main: $11* ⊠ *120 Country*

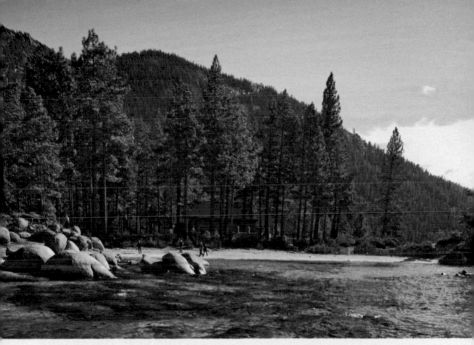

Get to Sand Harbor Beach in Lake Tahoe–Nevada State Park early; the park sometimes fills to capacity before lunchtime in summer.

Club Dr., Suite 28 ☎ *775/298–2636* ⊕ *www.mountainhighsandwichco.com* ⊙ *Closed Mon. No dinner.*

Hotels

Hyatt Regency Lake Tahoe

$$$$ | **RESORT** | A full-service destination resort on 26 acres of prime lakefront property, the Hyatt has a range of luxurious accommodations, from tower-hotel rooms to lakeside cottages. **Pros:** incredible views; low-key casino; luxurious accommodations. **Cons:** pricey (especially for families); feels corporate, smallish beach. [$] *Rooms from: $379* ⊠ *111 Country Club Dr.* ☎ *775/832–1234, 888/899–5019* ⊕ *www.hyatt.com* 🛏 *422 rooms* ⟋⊙⟍ *No meals.*

Activities

GOLF
Incline Championship

GOLF | Robert Trent Jones Sr. designed this challenging course of tightly cut, tree-lined fairways laced with water hazards that demand accuracy as well as distance skills. Greens fee includes a cart. ⊠ *955 Fairway Blvd., at Northwood Blvd., north off Hwy. 28* ☎ *775/832–1146 pro shop* ⊕ *www.yourtahoeplace.com/golf-incline* 🏌 *$199 weekdays, $220 weekends* 🏌 *18 holes, 7106 yards, par 72.*

Incline Mountain

GOLF | Robert Trent Jones Jr. designed this executive (shorter) course that requires accuracy more than distance skills. The greens fee includes a cart. ⊠ *690 Wilson Way, at Golfer's Pass, south off Hwy. 431* ☎ *866/925–4653 reservations, 775/832–1150 pro shop* ⊕ *www.yourtahoeplace.com/golf-incline* 🏌 *From $70* 🏌 *18 holes, 3527 yards, par 58.*

MOUNTAIN BIKING
Flume Trail Bikes

BICYCLING | You can rent bikes and get helpful tips from this company, which also operates a bike shuttle to popular trailheads. ⊠ *1115 Tunnel Creek Rd., at Ponderosa Ranch Rd., off Hwy. 28* ☎ *775/298–2501* ⊕ *www.flumetrailtahoe.com* 🏌 *From $50.*

SKIING
Diamond Peak

SKIING/SNOWBOARDING | Diamond Peak has affordable rates and many special programs. Snowmaking covers 75% of the mountain, and runs are groomed nightly. The ride up the 1-mile Crystal Express rewards you with fantastic views. Diamond Peak is less crowded than Tahoe's larger ski parks and provides free shuttles to nearby lodgings. A great place for beginners and intermediates, it's appropriately priced for families. Though there are some steep-aspect black-diamond runs, advanced skiers may find the acreage too limited. For snowboarders there's a small terrain park. **Facilities:** 30 trails; 655 acres; 1,840-foot vertical drop; 7 lifts. ⊠ *1210 Ski Way, off Country Club Dr.* ☎ *775/832–1177* ⊕ *www.diamondpeak.com* ☒ *Lift ticket from $114.*

Mt. Rose Ski Tahoe

SKIING/SNOWBOARDING | At this park, ski some of Tahoe's highest slopes and take in bird's-eye views of Reno, the lake, and Carson Valley. Though more compact than the bigger Tahoe resorts, Mt. Rose has the area's highest base elevation and consequently the driest snow. The mountain has a wide variety of terrain. The most challenging is the Chutes, 200 acres of gulp-and-go advanced-to-expert vertical. Intermediates can choose steep groomers or mellow, wide-open boulevards. Beginners have their own corner of the mountain, with gentle, wide slopes. Boarders and tricksters have several terrain parks to choose from, on opposite sides of the mountain, allowing them to follow the sun as it tracks across the resort. The mountain gets hit hard in storms; check conditions before heading up during inclement weather or on a windy day. **Facilities:** 61 trails; 1,200 acres; 1,800-foot vertical drop; 8 lifts. ⊠ *22222 Mt. Rose Hwy., Reno* ✛ *Hwy. 431, 11 miles north of Incline Village* ☎ *800/754–7673* ⊕ *www.skirose.com* ☒ *Lift ticket $145.*

Tahoe Meadows Snowplay Area

SKIING/SNOWBOARDING | This is the most popular area near the north shore for noncommercial cross-country skiing, sledding, tubing, snowshoeing, and snowmobiling. ⊠ *Off Hwy. 431* ✛ *From Hwy. 28 at Incline Village, head north about 6½ miles on Hwy. 431 toward Mt. Rose Ski Area.*

Zephyr Cove

22 miles south of Incline Village.

The largest settlement between Incline Village and the Stateline area is Zephyr Cove, a tiny resort. It has a beach, marina, campground, picnic area, coffee shop in a log lodge, rustic cabins, and nearby riding stables.

GETTING HERE AND AROUND

From the north shore communities, reach Zephyr Cove by following Highway 28 along the eastern side of the lake. From South Lake Tahoe, take U.S. 50 north and then west. Public transportation isn't available in Zephyr Cove.

Sights

Cave Rock

NATURE SITE | Near Zephyr Cove, this 75 feet of solid stone at the southern end of Lake Tahoe–Nevada State Park is the throat of an extinct volcano. The impressive outcropping towers over a parking lot, a lakefront picnic ground, and a boat launch. The views are some of the best on the lake; this is a good spot to stop and take a picture. ⚠ **Cave Rock is a sacred burial site for the Washoe Indians. Climbing to it or through it is prohibited.** ⊠ *U.S. 50, 4 miles north of Zephyr Cove* ☎ *775/588–7975* ⊕ *parks.nv.gov/parks* ☒ *$10 ($15 for non-NV vehicles).*

Restaurants

Capisce?

$$$ | **ITALIAN** | The signature mushroom-and-tomato sauce is so thick it's called "gravy" at this roadside restaurant whose menu emphasizes old favorites from the Italian-American side of the family that runs it. The mildly spicy concoction adds zest to cioppino (seafood stew), lasagna, and pasta dishes that include house-made ravioli that some diners prefer slathered instead with a velvety butter-and-Parmesan-cheese sauce. **Known for:** old family recipes; full bar patronized by many locals; desserts including gooey-wonderful cinnamon bun. ⑤ *Average main: $29* ⊠ *178 U.S. 50* ☎ *775/580–7500* ⊕ *www.capiscelaketahoe.com* ⊗ *Closed Mon. No lunch.*

🛏 Hotels

Zephyr Cove Resort

$$ | **RENTAL** | **FAMILY** | Beneath towering pines at the lake's edge stand 28 cozy, modern, vacation cabins with peaked knotty-pine ceilings. **Pros:** family-friendly; cozy cabins; old-school ambience. **Cons:** lodge rooms are basic; can be noisy in summer; not all cabins have fireplaces. ⑤ *Rooms from: $220* ⊠ *760 U.S. 50, 4 miles north of Stateline* ☎ *775/589–4906, 800/238–2463* ⊕ *www.zephyrcove.com* ⇨ *32 units* ⦿ *No meals.*

Stateline

5 miles south of Zephyr Cove.

Stateline is the archetypal Nevada border town. Its four high-rise casinos are as vertical and contained as the commercial district of South Lake Tahoe, on the California side, is horizontal and sprawling. And Stateline is as relentlessly indoors-oriented as the rest of the lake is focused on the outdoors. This small strip is where you'll find the most concentrated action in Lake Tahoe: restaurants (including typical casino buffets), showrooms with semi-famous headliners and razzle-dazzle revues, tower-hotel rooms and suites, and 24-hour casinos.

GETTING HERE AND AROUND

From South Lake Tahoe take U.S. 50 north across the Nevada border to reach Stateline and its casinos. If coming from Reno's airport, take U.S. 395/I–580 south to Carson City, and then head west on U.S. 50 to the lake and head south. Or take the South Tahoe Express bus. Tahoe Transportation District operates daily bus service.

Beaches

Nevada Beach

BEACH—SIGHT | Although less than a mile long, this is the widest beach on the lake and especially good for swimming (many Tahoe beaches are rocky). You can boat and fish here, and there are picnic tables, barbecue grills, and a campground beneath the pines. This is the best place to watch the July 4th or Labor Day fireworks, but most of the summer the subdued atmosphere attracts families and those seeking a less-touristy spot. **Amenities:** parking; water sports; toilets. **Best for:** sunrise; swimming; walking. ⊠ *Elk Point Rd., off U.S. 50, 3 miles north of Stateline* ☎ *530/543–2600* ⊕ *www. fs.usda.gov/recarea/ltbmu/recarea/?recid=11757* ⊘ *$10 day-use fee* ☞ *Dogs permitted on leash in picnic areas but not on beach.*

🍴 Restaurants

★ Edgewood Tahoe

$$$ | **AMERICAN** | The three restaurants at Stateline's classy resort, all in impeccably designed spaces that make the most of the lakeside setting, offer some of the area's best dining, if on the pricey side. Head to the Bistro for casual-fancy breakfast, lunch, and dinner; Brooks Bar & Grill for inventive comfort food during lunch and dinner; and the Edgewood

Restaurant for evening fine dining with views across the lake to Mt. Tallac. **Known for:** a venue for all moods; vegan and gluten-free options; golf-course views from outdoor deck at Brooks. $ *Average main: $30* ⊠ *Edgewood Tahoe, 100 Lake Pkwy.* ☎ *775/588–2787* ⊕ *www.edgewoodtahoe.com/dine-imbibe.*

Hotels

Harrah's Tahoe Hotel/Casino

$ | **HOTEL** | The 18-story hotel's major selling point is that every room has two full bathrooms, a boon if you're traveling with family. **Pros:** lake and mountain views from upper-floor rooms; good midweek values; top-floor steak house with good views from all tables. **Cons:** can get noisy; uneven housekeeping; lacks intimacy. $ *Rooms from: $119* ⊠ *15 U.S. 50, at Stateline Ave.* ☎ *775/588–6611, 800/427–7247* ⊕ *www.caesars.com/harrahs-tahoe* ⇆ *512 rooms* |◎| *No meals.*

Harveys Lake Tahoe Resort Hotel and Casino

$ | **HOTEL** | This resort began as a cabin in 1944, and now it's Tahoe's largest casino-hotel, where premium rooms have custom furnishings, oversize marble baths, minibars, and excellent lake views. **Pros:** live entertainment; great on-site restaurants; lake views from upper-floor rooms. **Cons:** can get loud at night; high summer rates; large property. $ *Rooms from: $119* ⊠ *18 U.S. 50, at Stateline Ave.* ☎ *775/588–2411, 800/648–3361* ⊕ *www.caesars.com/harveys-tahoe* ⇆ *742 rooms* |◎| *No meals.*

★ The Lodge at Edgewood Tahoe

$$$$ | **RESORT** | On a prime lakefront parcel, this hotel makes a bold impression with its stone-and-walnut Great Hall, whose four-story wall of windows frames views across Lake Tahoe to grand Mt. Tallac. **Pros:** prime lakefront location; haute-rustic design; all rooms have balconies and fireplaces. **Cons:** high rates

in-season; some rooms have no lake views; long walk to pool and hot tub from some rooms. $ *Rooms from: $410* ⊠ *100 Lake Pkwy.* ☎ *775/588–2787, 888/769–1924* ⊕ *www.edgewoodtahoe.com/lodge* ⇆ *154 rooms* |◎| *No meals.*

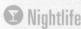 Nightlife

Each of the major casinos has its own showroom, featuring everything from comedy to magic acts to sexy floor shows to Broadway musicals.

LIVE MUSIC

Harveys Outdoor Summer Concert Series

CONCERTS | Headliners such as Trevor Noah, Miranda Lambert, Blake Shelton, and Jackson Browne perform at this weekend concert series. ⊠ *Harveys Lake Tahoe, 18 U.S. 50* ☎ *775/588–2411* ⊕ *www.caesars.com/harveys-tahoe/shows.*

South Shore Room

CABARET | Classic acts like Chris Botti and Todd Rundgren play Harrah's big showroom, along with the psychedelic Pink Floyd Laser Spectacular show and comedians like Sinbad. ⊠ *Harrah's Lake Tahoe, 15 U.S. 50* ☎ *775/586–6244 tickets, 775/588–6611* ⊕ *www.caesars.com/harrahs-tahoe/shows.*

Activities

GOLF
Edgewood Tahoe

GOLF | Golfers of all skill levels enjoy this scenic lakeside course that has four sets of tees, offering a variety of course lengths. The greens fee includes an optional cart. ⊠ *100 Lake Pkwy., at U.S. 50* ☎ *775/588–3566* ⊕ *www.edgewood-tahoe.com/golf* ⇆ *From $150 (varies throughout season)* ⅄ *18 holes, 7529 yards, par 72.*

Reno

38 miles northeast of Incline Village.

Established in 1859 as a trading station at a bridge over the Truckee River, Reno grew along with the silver mines of nearby Virginia City and the transcontinental railroad that chugged through town. Train officials named it in 1868, but gambling—legalized in 1931—put Reno on the map. This is still a gambling town, with most of the casinos crowded into five square blocks downtown, but a thriving university scene and outdoor activities also attract visitors.

Parts of downtown are sketchy, but things are changing. Reno now touts family-friendly activities like kayaking on the Truckee, museums, and a downtown climbing wall. With more than 300 days of sunshine annually, temperatures year-round in this high-mountain-desert climate are warmer than at Tahoe, though rarely as hot as in Sacramento and the Central Valley, making strolling around town a pleasure.

GETTING HERE AND AROUND

Interstate 80 bisects Reno east–west, U.S. 395 north–south (south of town the road is signed U.S. 395/I–580). Greyhound and Amtrak stop here, and several airlines fly into Reno Tahoe International Airport. RTC Ride provides bus service.

ESSENTIALS

BUS CONTACT RTC Ride. ⊠ *Transit Center, E. 4th and Lake Sts.* ☎ *775/348–7433* ⊕ *www.rtcwashoe.com.*

VISITOR INFORMATION Reno Tahoe Visitor Center. ⊠ *135 N. Sierra St.* ☎ *775/682–3800* ⊕ *www.visitrenotahoe.com.*

◉ Sights

★ National Automobile Museum

MUSEUM | FAMILY | One of the best of museums of its kind is filled with antique and classic cars made by obscure and familiar companies like Packard, Studebaker, Maxwell, Oldsmobile, and Lincoln.

Celebrity vehicles include the Lana Turner Chrysler (one of only six made), an Elvis Presley Cadillac, and a Mercury coupe driven by James Dean in the movie *Rebel Without a Cause.* Hard to miss are the experimental and still futuristic-looking 1938 Phantom Corsair and a gold-plated 1980 DeLorean. ⊠ *10 S. Lake St., at Mill St.* ☎ *775/333–9300* ⊕ *www.automuseum.org* ⊑ *$12.*

Nevada Museum of Art

MUSEUM | A dramatic four-level structure designed by Will Bruder houses this splendid museum's collection, which focuses on themes such as the Sierra Nevada/Great Basin and altered-landscape photography. The building's exterior torqued walls are sided with a black zinc-based material that has been fabricated to resemble textures found in the Black Rock Desert. Inside the building, a staircase installed within the central atrium is lit by skylights and suspended by a single beam attached to the atrium ceiling. ⊠ *160 W. Liberty St., and Hill St.* ☎ *775/329–3333* ⊕ *www.nevadaart.org* ⊑ *$10* ۞ *Closed Mon. and Tues.*

Riverwalk District

PROMENADE | A formerly dilapidated section of Reno's waterfront is now the toast of the town. The Riverwalk itself is a half-mile promenade on the north side of the Truckee River, which flows around Wingfield Park, where festivals and other events take place. On the third Saturday of each month, local merchants host a **Wine Walk** between 2 and 5. For $30 you receive a glass and can sample fine wines at participating shops, bars, restaurants, and galleries. In July, look for outdoor art, opera, dance, and kids' performances as part of the monthlong **Artown festival** (⊕ *artown.org*), presented mostly in Wingfield Park. Also at Wingfield is the **Truckee River Whitewater Park.** With activities for all skill levels, it's become a major attraction for water-sports enthusiasts. ⊠ *North side of Truckee River between Lake and Ralston Sts.* ⊕ *www.renoriver.org.*

Restaurants

Beaujolais Bistro

$$$$ | FRENCH | Across from the Truckee River, this Reno favorite serves earthy, country-style French food—escargots, steak frites with red wine sauce, cassoulet, and crisp sweetbreads with Madeira, along with fish and vegetarian selections—with zero pretension. Wood floors, large windows, and brick walls with a fireplace create a welcoming and intimate atmosphere. **Known for:** inventive cocktails; intimate atmosphere; more casual experience at the bar. $ *Average main: $36* ⊠ *753 Riverside Dr., near Winter St.* ☎ *775/323–2227* ⊕ *www.beaujolaisbistro. com* ⊗ *Closed Mon. No lunch.*

Hotels

Eldorado Resort Casino

$ | HOTEL | In the middle of glittering downtown, this resort's huge tower has rooms overlooking either the mountains or the lights of the city. **Pros:** spacious rooms; skywalk connects hotel to casinos; amusingly kitschy decor. **Cons:** noisy atmosphere; some housekeeping lapses; faux-everything decor can overwhelm. $ *Rooms from: $60* ⊠ *345 N. Virginia St.* ☎ *775/786–5700, 800/879–8879* ⊕ *www.eldoradoreno.com* ⇌ *816 rooms* ¶○¶ *No meals.*

Peppermill Reno

$ | HOTEL | A few miles removed from downtown's flashy main drag, this property set a high standard for luxury in Reno, especially in the Tuscany Tower, whose 600 baroque suites have plush king-size beds, marble bathrooms, and European soaking tubs. **Pros:** luxurious rooms; casino decor; good coffee shop. **Cons:** deluge of neon may be off-putting to some; enormous size; mostly expensive dining. $ *Rooms from: $119* ⊠ *2707 S. Virginia St.* ☎ *775/826–2121, 866/821–9996* ⊕ *www.peppermillreno. com* ⇌ *1623 rooms* ¶○¶ *No meals.*

Nightlife

CASINOS

Eldorado Resort Casino

CASINOS | Action-packed, with lots of slots and popular bar-top video poker, this casino also has good coffee-shop and food-court fare. Don't miss the Fountain of Fortune with its massive Florentine-inspired sculptures. ⊠ *345 N. Virginia St., at W. 4th St.* ☎ *775/786–5700, 800/879–8879* ⊕ *www.eldoradoreno.com.*

Peppermill

CASINOS | A few miles from downtown, this casino is known for its excellent restaurants and neon-bright gambling areas. The Fireside cocktail lounge is a blast. ⊠ *2707 S. Virginia St., at Peppermill La.* ☎ *775/826–2121, 866/821–9996* ⊕ *www. peppermillreno.com.*

Silver Legacy

CASINOS | A 120-foot-tall mining rig and video poker games draw gamblers to this razzle-dazzle casino. ⊠ *407 N. Virginia St., at W. 4th St.* ☎ *775/325–7411, 800/215–7721* ⊕ *www.silverlegacyreno. com/gaming.*

Chapter 10

SAN FRANCISCO

Updated by
Trevor Felch, Monique Peterson,
Coral Sisk, and Ava Liang Zhao

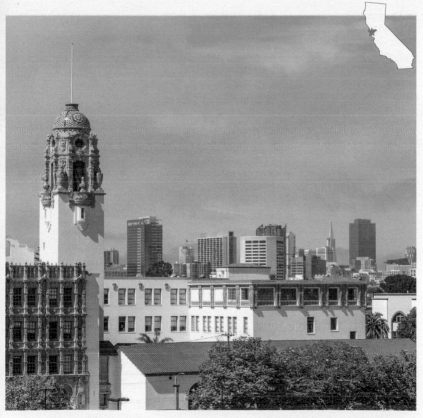

⊙ Sights	🍴 Restaurants	🛏 Hotels	🛍 Shopping	🍸 Nightlife
★★★★★	★★★★☆	★★★★★	★☆☆☆☆	★☆☆☆☆

WELCOME TO SAN FRANCISCO

TOP REASONS TO GO

★ **The bay:** It's hard not to gasp as you catch sight of sunlight dancing on the water when you crest a hill, or watch the Golden Gate Bridge vanish and reemerge in the summer fog.

★ **The food:** San Franciscans are serious about what they eat, and with good reason. Home to some of the nation's best chefs, top restaurants, and finest local produce, it's hard not to eat well here.

★ **The shopping:** Shopaholics visiting the city will not be disappointed—San Francisco is packed with browsing destinations, everything from quirky boutiques to massive malls.

★ **The good life:** A laid-back atmosphere, beautiful surroundings, and oodles of cultural, culinary, and aesthetic pleasures … if you spend too much time here, you might not leave.

★ **The great outdoors:** From Golden Gate Park to sidewalk cafés in North Beach, San Franciscans relish their outdoor spaces.

1 Union Square. Has hotels and upscale stores aplenty.

2 Chinatown. A dense neighborhood full of shops and restaurants.

3 SoMa and Civic Center. A once-industrial, still-in-transition district anchored by SFMOMA and Yerba Buena Gardens.

4 Civic Center. Marked by monumental government buildings.

5 Tenderloin. Situated just north of the Civic Center.

6 Hayes Valley. West is this chic neighborhood.

7 Nob Hill. Old-money San Francisco.

8 Russian Hill. Steep streets lace this classy, au courant district.

9 Polk Gulch. A tiny area next door to Russian Hill.

10 Pacific Heights. Has some of the city's grand Victorians.

11 Japantown. A tight-knit Japanese American community with shopping and dining.

12 Western Addition. South of Japantown is this vibrant residential neighborhood.

13 North Beach. The city's small, historically Italian neighborhood.

14 Fisherman's Wharf. A tourist mecca.

15 Embarcadero. The famous Ferry Building is at the foot of Market Street.

16 Financial District. A district of towering buildings inland from Embarcadero.

17 The Marina. Home to many young professionals.

Golden Gate Bridge

WATERFRONT

Fisherman's
Wharf

14

Pier 39

San Francisco Bay

Marina
Green

MARINA

17

Ghirardelli
Square

Bay St.

13

**NORTH
BEACH**

Lombard St.

**RUSSIAN
HILL**

8

Columbus Ave.

Coit Tower

TELEGRAPH
HILL

The Embarcadero

101

19

**The
Presidio**

**COW
HOLLOW**

18

Broadway

**NOB
HILL**

7

(tunnel)

CHINATOWN

2

**FINANCIAL
DISTRICT**

15

San Francisco-Oakland
Bay Bridge

**PACIFIC
HEIGHTS**

9

Washington St.

Powell St.

16

1

Sacramento St.

California St.

**UNION
SQUARE**

SF MOMA

10

Laguna St.

Franklin St.

Van Ness Ave.

Polk St.

Gough St.

Post St.

Geary St.

SF MOMA

2nd St.

3rd St.

Pine St.

Bush St.

Presidio Ave.

Divisadero St.

Steiner St.

JAPANTOWN

11

Geary Blvd.

Turk St.

Yerba Buena
Gardens

**CIVIC
CENTER**

4

5

Turk St.

Mission St.

4th St.

SOMA

3

80

Golden Gate Ave.

Fulton St.

Hayes St.

6

Market St.

Harrison St.

Folsom St.

5th St.

6th St.

7th St.

8th St.

9th St.

10th St.

Brannan St.

Bryant St.

3rd St.

Townsend St.

Berry St.

Fell St.

12

**WESTERN
ADDITION**

Park Presidio Blvd.

Arguello Blvd.

8th Ave.

**Golden Gate
Park**

22

Stow
Lake

Fulton St.

HAIGHT

23

Haight St.

Clayton St.

Stanyan St.

Duboce

Buena Vista
Park

Market St.

Funston Ave.

7th Ave.

CASTRO

24

17th St.

MISSION

26

Mariposa St.

**PORTRERO
HILL**

27

3rd St.

Indiana St.

Pennsylvania Ave.

**NOE
VALLEY**

25

20th St.

Guerrero St.

Dolores St.

Mission St.

Harrison St.

Van Ness Ave.

Potrero Ave.

Clarendon
Ave.

Twin
Peaks

Castro St.

24th St.

25th St.

Diamond St.

Cesar Chavez St.

101

280

Taraval St.

Dewey Blvd.

**BERNAL
HEIGHTS**

HOW TO EAT LIKE A LOCAL

Several farmers' markets occupy the Ferry Building

San Francisco may well be the most piping-red-hot dining scene in the nation now. After all, with a booming tech industry, there are mouths to feed. Freedom to do what you want. Innovation. Eccentricity. These words define the culture, the food, and the cuisine of the city by the bay. Get in on what locals know by enjoying their favorite foods.

FOOD TRUCKS

This is where experimentation begins, where the overhead is low, and risk-taking is fun. From these mobile kitchens careers are launched. A food meet-up called "Off the Grid" happens in season at Fort Mason where you can have a progressive dinner among the 25 or so trucks. Year-round the convoy roams to different locations, selling things like Korean poutine, Indian burritos, and Vietnamese burgers. Each dish seems to reflect a refusal to follow the norm.

DIM SUM

The tradition of dim sum took hold in San Francisco when Chinese immigrants from Guangdong Province arrived with Cantonese cuisine. These earlier settlers eventually established teahouses and bakeries that sold dim sum, like the steamed dumplings stuffed with shrimp (*har gow*) or pork (*shao mai*). Now carts roll from table to table in Chinatown restaurants—and other parts of the city. Try the grilled and fried bite-size savories but also the sweets like *dan tat*, an egg custard tart.

BARBECUE

Whaaa? San Francisco barbecue? And what would that be? You can bet it's meat from top purveyors nearby. The city is surrounded by grazing lands, where the animals and their minders, the ranchers, are king. Until now, meats came simply plated. Now it's messy, with smokiness, charred crusts, and gorgeous marbling. But you may never hear of a San-Fran-style barbecue because, in the words of one chef, we're "nondenominational." You'll see it all: Memphis, Texas, Carolina, and Kansas City.

ICE CREAM

How ice cream became so popular in a place that spends many of its 365 days below the 75 degree mark is a mystery. But the lines attest to the popularity of the frozen dessert that gets its own San Francisco twist. This is the vanilla-bean vanilla and Tcho chocolate crowd. Bourbon and cornflakes? Reposado tequila? Cheers to that. Diversity and local produce is blended into flavors like ube (purple yam), yuzu, and Thai latte.

BURRITOS

This stuffed tortilla got its Bay Area start in the 1960s in the Mission District. Because the size and fillings distinguish it from other styles, it became

The food truck

known as the Mission burrito. Look for rice (Southern Californians are cringing), beans, salsa, and enough meat in the burrito for two meals. The aluminum foil keeps the interior neat, in theory. Popular choices are *carne asada* (beef) and *carnitas* (pork). But then there's *lengua* (beef tongue) and *birria* (goat). This is a hands-on meal.

COFFEE

Coffee roasters here are like sports teams in other cities. You pick one of the big five or six to be loyal to, and defend it tirelessly. San Francisco favorites source impeccably and blend different beans as if they were wine making. In addition, a few of the big names—Four Barrel, Sightglass, Ritual, Blue Bottle—roast their own to control what they grind and pour at their outlets across the city—and now nationally and internationally

FARMERS' MARKETS

These are our new grocery stores. They're the places to discover the latest in fruits, vegetables, and dried beans—much of it grown within a 60-mile radius. Cheeses, cured salami, breads, and nuts are sampled. Then there are the local ready-to-eat snacks, like pizza and *huevos rancheros*. The most popular market is the one on Saturday at the Ferry Plaza.

Dim sum

On a 46½-square-mile strip of land between San Francisco Bay and the Pacific Ocean, San Francisco has charms great and small. Residents cherish it for the same reasons visitors do: proximity to the bay, rows of hillside Victorian homes, sunsets framed by the Golden Gate Bridge, world-class cuisine.

You can spend hours exploring downtown, Chinatown, North Beach, the northern and western waterfronts, and Golden Gate Park, along with colorful neighborhoods like the Haight, the Mission murals, and the Castro. The city's attraction, though, goes much deeper than its alluring physical space, from the diversity of its neighborhoods to its free-spirited tolerance. All these things together explain why many San Franciscans—despite the dizzying cost of living and the chilly summers—can't imagine calling any place else home.

The City by the Bay's highlights include a cable car ride over Nob Hill, a walk down the Filbert Street Steps, gazing at the thundering Pacific from the cliffs of Lincoln Park, cheering the San Francisco Giants to *beat L.A.* in lively Oracle Park, and eating freshly shucked oysters at the Ferry Building. The diverse wonders of this beautiful metropolis inspire at every turn.

Planning

When to Go

Possibly the best time is September and October, when the city's summer-like weather brings outdoor concerts and festivals. The climate here always feels Mediterranean and moderate, with a foggy, sometimes chilly bite. The temperature rarely drops below 40°F, and anything warmer than 80°F is considered a heat wave. Be prepared for rain in winter, especially December and January. Winds off the ocean can add to the chill factor. That old joke about summer in San Francisco feeling like winter is true at heart, but once you move inland, it gets warmer. (And some locals swear that the thermostat has inched up in recent years.)

Getting Here and Around

AIR

The major gateway to San Francisco is San Francisco International Airport (SFO), 15 miles south of the city. It's off U.S. 101 near Millbrae and San Bruno. Oakland International Airport (OAK) is across the bay, not much farther away from downtown San Francisco (via Interstate 80 east and Interstate 880 south), but rush-hour traffic on the Bay Bridge may lengthen travel times considerably. San Jose International Airport (SJC) is about 40 miles south of San Francisco; travel time depends largely on traffic flow, but plan on an hour and a half with moderate traffic.

AIRPORTS Oakland International Airport. (*OAK*) ⊠ *1 Airport Dr., Oakland* ☎ *510/563–3300* ⊕ *www.oaklandairport. com.* **San Francisco International Airport.** (*SFO*) ⊠ *McDonnell and Links Rds., San Francisco* ☎ *800/435–9736, 650/821–8211* ⊕ *www.flysfo.com.* **San Jose International Airport.** (*SJC*) ⊠ *1701 Airport Blvd., San Jose* ☎ *408/392–3600* ⊕ *www. flysanjose.com.*

BART

BART (Bay Area Rapid Transit) trains, which run until midnight, travel under the bay via tunnel to connect San Francisco with Oakland, Berkeley, and other cities and towns beyond. Within San Francisco, stations are limited to downtown, the Mission, and a couple of outlying neighborhoods.

Trains travel frequently from early morning until evening on weekdays. After 8 pm weekdays and on weekends, there's often a 20-minute wait between trains on the same line. Trains also travel south from San Francisco as far as Millbrae. BART trains connect downtown San Francisco to San Francisco International Airport; the ride costs $9.65.

Intracity San Francisco fares are $2.10; intercity fares are $3.70 to $11.45. BART bases its ticket prices on miles traveled and doesn't offer price breaks by zone. The easy-to-read maps posted in BART stations list fares based on destination, radiating out from your starting point of the current station.

During morning and evening rush hour, trains within the city are crowded—even standing room can be hard to come by. Cars at the far front and back of the train are less likely to be filled to capacity. Smoking, eating, and drinking are prohibited on trains and in stations.

CONTACTS Bay Area Rapid Transit. (*BART*) ☎ *510/465–2278* ⊕ *www.bart.gov.*

BOAT

Several ferry lines run out of San Francisco. Blue & Gold Fleet operates a number of routes, including service to Sausalito ($13 one-way) and Tiburon ($13 one-way). Tickets are sold at Pier 39; boats depart from Pier 41 nearby. Alcatraz Cruises, owned by Hornblower Cruises and Events, operates the ferries to Alcatraz Island ($42, including audio tour and National Park Service ranger-led programs) from Pier 33, about a half-mile east of Fisherman's Wharf. Boats leave 14 times a day (more in summer), and the journey itself takes 30 minutes. Allow at least 2½ hours for a round-trip jaunt. Golden Gate Ferry runs daily to and from Sausalito and Larkspur ($13.50 and $13 one-way), leaving from Pier 1, behind the San Francisco Ferry Building. The Alameda/Oakland Ferry operates daily between Alameda's Main Street Terminal, Oakland's Jack London Square, and San Francisco's Pier 41 and the Ferry Building ($7.20 one-way); some ferries go only to Pier 41 or the Ferry Building, so ask when you board. Purchase tickets on board.

CONTACTS Alameda/Oakland Ferry.
☏ 877/643–3779 ⊕ sanfranciscobayferry.
com. **Alcatraz Cruises.** ☏ 415/981–7625
⊕ www.alcatrazcruises.com. **Blue & Gold
Fleet.** ☏ 415/705–8200 ⊕ www.blueand-
goldfleet.com. **Ferry Building Marketplace.**
✉ 1 Ferry Bldg., at foot of Market St. on
Embarcadero, San Francisco ⊕ www.
ferrybuildingmarketplace.com. **Golden
Gate Ferry.** ☏ 415/923–2000 ⊕ www.
goldengateferry.org.

BUS

Outside the city, AC Transit serves the
East Bay, and Golden Gate Transit serves
Marin County and a few cities in south-
ern Sonoma County.

CABLE-CAR

Don't miss the sensation of moving up
and down some of San Francisco's steepest hills in a clattering cable car. Jump
aboard as it pauses at a designated stop,
and wedge yourself into any available
space. Then just hold on. At this writing,
cable-car service is set to resume later in
fall 2021, but not all lines; check sfmta.
com for updates.

The fare (for one direction) is $8. Buy
tickets in advance at the kiosks at the
cable-car turnarounds at Hyde and
Beach Streets and at Powell and Market
Streets. Or consider MuniMobile or a
Clipper Card; see ⊕ sfmta.com. Cash
purchases require exact change.

The heavily traveled Powell–Mason and
Powell–Hyde lines begin at Powell and
Market Streets near Union Square and
terminate at Fisherman's Wharf; lines for
these routes can be long, especially in
summer. The California Street line runs
east and west from Market and California
Streets to Van Ness Avenue; there's
often no wait to board this route.

CAR

Driving in San Francisco can be a challenge because of the one-way streets,
snarly traffic, and steep hills. The first
two elements can be frustrating enough,
but those hills are tough for unfamiliar

drivers. ■TIP→ **Remember to curb your
wheels when parking on hills—turn wheels
away from the curb when facing uphill,
toward the curb when facing downhill. You
can get a ticket if you don't do this.**

MUNI

The San Francisco Municipal Railway, or
Muni, operates light-rail vehicles, the historic F-line streetcars along Fisherman's
Wharf and Market Street, buses, and the
world-famous cable cars. Light-rail travels
along Market Street to the Mission
District and Noe Valley (J line), Ingleside
(K line), and the Sunset District (L, M,
and N lines) while also passing through
the West Portal, Glen Park, and Castro
neighborhoods. The N line continues
around the Embarcadero to the Caltrain
station at 4th and King Streets; the T-line
light-rail runs from the Castro, down
Market Street, around the Embarcadero,
and south past Mission Bay and Hunters
Point to Sunnydale Avenue and Bayshore
Boulevard. Muni provides 24-hour service
on select lines to all areas of the city.

On buses and streetcars, the fare is
$2.50. Exact change is required, and dollar
bills are accepted in the fare boxes. For
all Muni vehicles other than cable cars,
90-minute transfers are issued free upon
request at the time the fare is paid. These
are valid for unlimited transfers in any
direction until they expire (time is indicated on the ticket). Cable cars cost $8 and
include no transfers (see Cable-Car Travel).

One-day ($13), three-day ($31), and seven-day ($41) Visitor Passports valid on the
entire Muni system can be purchased
at several outlets, including the cable-
car ticket booth at Powell and Market
Streets and the visitor information center
downstairs in Hallidie Plaza. A monthly
ticket is available for $81, which can be
used on all Muni lines (including cable
cars) and on BART within city limits. The
San Francisco CityPass ($76), a discount
ticket booklet to several major city
attractions, also covers all Muni travel for
seven consecutive days.

■TIP→ Save money by purchasing your Passports on MuniMobile, the mobile ticketing app of the San Francisco Metropolitan Transportation Authority (SFMTA).

BUS AND MUNI CONTACTS San Francisco Municipal Transportation Agency . (*Muni*) ☎ 311, 415/701–3000 ⊕ www.sfmta. com.

TAXI

Taxi service is notoriously bad in San Francisco, and finding a cab can be frustratingly difficult. Popular nightlife locales, such as the Mission, SoMa, North Beach, and the Castro, are the easiest places to hail a cab off the street; hotel taxi stands are also an option. If you're going to the airport, make a reservation or book a shuttle instead. Taxis in San Francisco charge $3.50 for the first 0.5 mile (one of the highest base rates in the United States), 55¢ for each additional 0.2 mile, and 55¢ per minute in stalled traffic; a $4 surcharge is added for trips from the airport. There's no charge for additional passengers; there's no surcharge for luggage. For trips farther than 15 miles outside city limits, multiply the metered rate by 1.5; tolls and tip are extra.

That said, San Francisco's poor taxi service was a direct factor in the creation of ridesharing services, such as Uber and Lyft, which are easy to use and prominent throughout the city and its surrounding areas. San Franciscans generally regard taxis as a thing of the past and use ridesharing on a day-to-day basis. If you're willing to share a car with strangers, a trip within the city can run as low as $4; rates go up for private rides and during peak-demand times. These services are especially economical when going to or from the airport, where a shared ride starts at about $25—half the cost of a cab.

CONTACTS Flywheel Taxi. ☎ 415/970–1300 ⊕ flywheeltaxi.com. **Luxor Cab.** ☎ 415/282–4141 ⊕ www.luxorcab.com. **National Veterans Cab.** ☎ 415/648–4444.

Yellow Cab. ☎ 415/333–3333 ⊕ yellowcabsf.com.

COMPLAINTS San Francisco Police Department Taxi Complaints. ☎ 415/701–4400.

TRAIN

Amtrak trains travel to the Bay Area from some cities in California as well as the greater United States. The Coast Starlight travels north from Los Angeles to Seattle, passing the Bay Area along the way, but contrary to its name, the train runs inland through the Central Valley for much of its route through Northern California; the most scenic stretch is in Southern California, between San Luis Obispo and Los Angeles. Amtrak also has several routes between San Jose, Oakland, and Sacramento. The California Zephyr travels from Chicago to the Bay Area, with spectacular alpine vistas as it crosses the Sierra Nevada range. San Francisco doesn't have an Amtrak train station but does have an Amtrak bus stop at the Ferry Building, from which shuttle buses transport passengers to trains in Emeryville, just over the Bay Bridge. Shuttle buses also connect the Emeryville train station with BART and other points in downtown San Francisco. You can buy a California Rail Pass, which gives you 7 days of travel in a 21-day period, for $159.

Caltrain connects San Francisco to Palo Alto, San Jose, Santa Clara, and many smaller cities en route. In San Francisco, trains leave from the main depot, at 4th and Townsend Streets, and a rail-side stop at 22nd and Pennsylvania Streets. One-way fares are $3.75 to $15, depending on the number of zones through which you travel; tickets are valid for four hours after purchase time. A ticket is $8.25 from San Francisco to Palo Alto, at least $10.50 to San Jose. You can also buy a day pass ($7.50–$30) for unlimited travel in a 24-hour period. It's worth waiting for an express train for trips that last from 1 to 1¾ hours. On weekdays, trains depart three or four times per hour during the morning and evening, but only once or twice per hour during daytime non-commute hours and late night. Weekend trains run once per hour, though there are two bullet trains per day, one in late morning and one in early evening The system shuts down after midnight. There are no onboard ticket sales. You must buy tickets before boarding the train or risk paying up to $230 for fare evasion.

CONTACTS Amtrak. ☏ *800/872–7245* ⊕ *www.amtrak.com.* **Caltrain.** ☏ *800/660– 4287* ⊕ *www.caltrain.com.* **San Francisco Caltrain station.** ⊠ *700 4th St., near Townsend St., SoMa* ☏ *800/660–4287* ⊕ *www.caltrain.com/stations.*

Restaurants

Make no mistake, San Francisco is one of America's top food cities. Some of the biggest landmarks are restaurants. In fact, on a Saturday, the Ferry Building—a temple to local eating—may attract more visitors than the Golden Gate Bridge: cheeses, breads, "salty pig parts," homemade delicacies, and sensory-perfect vegetables and fruits attract rabidly dedicated aficionados. You see, San Franciscans are a little loco about their edibles. If you ask them what their favorite season is, don't be surprised if they respond, "tomato season."

Some renowned restaurants are booked weeks or even months in advance. But you can get lucky at the last minute if you're flexible—and friendly. Most restaurants keep a few tables open for walk-ins and VIPs. Show up for dinner early (5:30 pm) or late (after 9 pm) and politely inquire about any last-minute vacancies or cancellations.

The impact of the COVID-19 pandemic on the restaurant scene in the Bay Area, as in many other parts of the globe, has been widespread and severe. Many restaurants and bars have responded with

adjusted hours, changed menus, and limited indoor or only outdoor seating. Call the restaurant or check their website for the latest information. One upside is that temporary parklets and pedestrian-friendly slow streets may become permanent fixtures, lending an air of alfresco European leisure to the streets of San Francisco.

Restaurant reviews have been shortened. For full information, visit Fodors. com. Prices are the average cost of a main course at dinner or, if dinner is not served, at lunch.

What It Costs			
$	$$	$$$	$$$$
RESTAURANTS			
under $16	$16–$22	$23–$30	over $30

Hotels

San Francisco accommodations are diverse, ranging from cozy inns and kitschy motels, to chic little inns and true grande dames, housed in century-old structures and sleek high-rises (though some closed temporarily or permanently due to COVID 19). While the tech boom has skyrocketed the prices of even some of the most dependable low-cost options, luckily, some Fodor's faves still offer fine accommodations without the jaw-dropping prices to match those steep hills. In fact, the number of reasonably priced accommodations is impressive.

Hotel reviews have been shortened. For full information, visit Fodors.com. Prices are the lowest cost of a standard double room in high season.

What It Costs			
$	$$	$$$	$$$$
HOTELS			
under $150	$150–$249	$250–$350	over $350

Nightlife

After hours, the city's business folk and workers give way to costume-clad party-goers, hippies and hipsters, downtown divas, frat boys, and those who prefer something a little more clothing-optional. Downtown and the Financial District remain pretty serious even after dark, and Nob Hill is staid, though you can't beat views from penthouse lounges, the most famous being the Top of the Mark (in the InterContinental Mark Hopkins). Nearby North Beach is an even better starting point for an evening out.

Always lively, North Beach's options include family-friendly dining spots, historic bars from the city's bohemian past (among them Jack Kerouac's old haunts), and even comedy clubs where stars like Robin Williams and Jay Leno cut their teeth. In SoMa there are plenty of places to catch a drink before a Giants game and brewpubs to celebrate in afterward. SoMa also hosts some of the hottest dance clubs, along with some saucy gay bars. While Union Square can be a bit trendy, even the swanky establishments have loosened things up in recent years.

Heading west to Hayes Valley, a more sophisticated crowd dabbles in the burgeoning "culinary cocktail movement." Up-and-coming singles gravitate north of here to Cow Hollow and the Marina. Polk Gulch was the city's gay mecca before the Castro and still hosts some wild bars, but things get downright outlandish in the Castro District. Indie hipsters of all persuasions populate the Mission and Haight Districts by night. Keep in mind, though, that some of the best times San Francisco has to offer are off the beaten path. And a good party can still be found in even the sleepiest of neighborhoods, such as Bernal Heights and Dogpatch.

Sports bars and hotel bars tend to be open on Sunday, but others may be closed. A few establishments—especially wine bars and bars attached to restaurants—also close on Monday.

Performing Arts

The heart of the mainstream theater district lies on or near Geary Street, mostly west of Union Square, though touring Broadway shows land a little farther afield at big houses like the Orpheum and the Golden Gate. But theater can be found all over town. For a bit of culture shock, slip out to eclectic districts, maybe the Mission or the Haight, where smaller theater companies reside and short-run and one-night-only performances happen on a regular basis.

The city's opera house and symphony hall present the musical classics, and venues like the Fillmore and the Warfield host major rock and jazz talents, but the city's extensive festival circuit broadens the possibilities considerably. Stern Grove presents a popular, free summer music festival; Noise Pop is the premier alt-rock showcase; and Hardly Strictly Bluegrass is a beloved celebration of bluegrass, country, and roots music, attracting hundreds of thousands of attendees from all over every year.

Shopping

Each neighborhood has its own distinctive finds, whether it's 1960s housewares, cheeky stationery, or vintage Levi's. If shopping in San Francisco has a downside, it's that real bargains can be few and far between. Sure, neighborhoods like the Lower Haight and the Mission have thrift shops and other inexpensive stores, but you won't find many discount outlets in the city, where rents are sky-high and space is at a premium.

Serious shoppers head straight to Union Square, San Francisco's main shopping area and the site of most of its department stores, including Macy's, Neiman Marcus, and Saks Fifth Avenue. Nearby are such platinum-card international boutiques as Yves Saint Laurent, Cartier, Emporio Armani, Gucci, Hermès, and Louis Vuitton.

Seasonal sales, usually in late January and late July into August, are good opportunities for finding deep discounts on clothing. The *San Francisco Chronicle* and *San Francisco Examiner* advertise sales. For smaller shops, check the free *SF Weekly*, which can be found on street corners every Wednesday. Sample sales are usually held by individual manufacturers, so check your favorite company's website before visiting.

Visitor Information

CONTACTS San Francisco Visitor Information Center. ⊠ *Moscone Center, 749 Howard St. , between 3rd and 4th Sts., SoMa* ☏ *415/391–2000* ⊕ *www.sftravel.com.*

Union Square

The city's finest department stores put on their best faces in Union Square, along with such exclusive emporiums as Tiffany & Co. and Bulgari, and such big-name retailers as Nike, Apple, H&M, and Disney. Visitors lay their heads at several dozen hotels within a three-block walk of the square, and the downtown theater district is nearby. Union Square is shopping-centric; nonshoppers will find fewer enticements here.

 Sights

Maiden Lane

NEIGHBORHOOD | Known as Morton Street in the raffish Barbary Coast era, this former red-light district reported at least one murder a week during the late 19th century, though things cooled down after the 1906 fire: these days Maiden Lane is a chic, designer-boutique-lined pedestrian mall stretching two blocks, between Stockton and Kearny Streets. Wrought-iron gates close the street to traffic most days between 11 and 5, when the lane becomes an alfresco hot spot dotted with umbrella-shaded tables. It's also popular with photographers and Instagrammers for its quaint-chic aesthetic. At **140 Maiden Lane** is the only Frank Lloyd Wright building in San Francisco, fronted by a large brick archway. The curving ramp and skylights of the interior, which houses exclusive Italian menswear boutique Isaia, are said to have been his model for the Guggenheim Museum in New York. ⊠ *Between Stockton and Kearny Sts., Union Sq.*

Union Square

PLAZA | The marquee destination for big-name shopping in the city and within walking distance of many hotels, Union Square is home base for many visitors. The Westin St. Francis hotel and Macy's line two of the square's sides, and Saks, Neiman Marcus, and Tiffany & Co. edge the other two. Four globular contemporary lamp sculptures by the artist R. M. Fischer preside over the landscaped, 2½-acre park anchored by the monument to Admiral George Dewey. The area also has a café with outdoor seating, an open-air stage, and the city's favorite holiday season ice-skating rink—along with a kaleidoscope of characters: office workers sunning and brown-bagging, street musicians, shoppers taking a rest, kids chasing pigeons, and a fair number of homeless people. The constant clang of cable cars traveling up and down Powell Street helps maintain a festive mood. ⊠ *Bordered by Powell, Stockton, Post, and Geary Sts., Union Sq.*

The epicenter of high-end shopping, Union Square is lined with department stores.

The Westin St. Francis San Francisco on Union Square

HOTEL—SIGHT | Built in 1904 and barely established as the most sumptuous hotel in town before it was ravaged by fire following the 1906 earthquake, this grande-dame hotel designed by Walter Danforth Bliss and William Baker Faville reopened in 1907 with the addition of a luxurious Italian Renaissance–style residence designed to attract loyal clients from among the world's rich and powerful. The hotel's checkered past includes the ill-fated 1921 bash in the suite of the silent-film superstar Fatty Arbuckle, at which a woman became ill, leading to her death. Arbuckle endured three sensational trials for rape and murder before being acquitted, by which time his career was kaput. In 1975, Sara Jane Moore, standing among a crowd outside the hotel, attempted to shoot then-President Gerald Ford. Of course, the grand lobby contains no plaques commemorating these events. ■**TIP**→ **Some visitors make the St. Francis a stop whenever they're in town, soaking up the lobby ambience or enjoying** a cocktail at the Clock Bar or lunch at the Oak Room Restaurant. ✉ *335 Powell St., at Geary St., Union Sq.* ☎ *415/397–7000* ⊕ *westinstfrancis.com.*

Restaurants

★ Liholiho Yacht Club

$$$$ | **MODERN AMERICAN** | Inspired but not defined by the chef's native Hawaii, Ravi Kapur's lively restaurant is known for big-hearted, high-spirited cooking, including contemporary riffs on poke and Spam but also squid served with crispy tripe and manila clams in coconut curry. The dining room and front bar area are perpetually packed, and are dominated by an enormous photo of a beaming woman who happens to be none other than the chef's mother. **Known for:** beef tongue on poppy-seed steamed buns "bao"; giant mains that serve two to four people; beautifully composed cocktails. ⑤ *Average main: $42* ✉ *871 Sutter St., Union Sq.* ☎ *415/440–5446* ⊕ *lycsf.com* ⊙ *Closed Sun. No lunch.*

Union Square and Chinatown

| A | B | C | D | E |

RUSSIAN HILL

Bernard St.
John Street
Jackson Street
Washington Street

Tunnel

Broadway

Cable Car

Cable Car

Cable Car Barn

Leavenworth Street
Jones Street
Taylor Street
Mason Street
Powell Street

Pleasant St.

Huntington Park

NOB HILL

California Street

Pine Street

Bush Street

Sutter Street

Post Street

Geary St.

O'Farrell Street

Ellis Street

Eddy Street

Turk Street

Golden Gate Ave.

McAllister St.

Leavenworth Street
Hyde Street
Market Street
7th Street
6th Street
5th Street
Stevenson St.
Mission St.

Stockton St.

Columbus Avenue

CHINATOWN

Vallejo Street

Sonoma St.

Montgomery St.
Sansome St.

Green St.
Battery St.
Front St.
Davis St.

Pacific Ave.
Walton Park

Jackson Square Historic District

Jackson St.

Washington St.
Maritime Plaza

M. Twain Pl.
Clay St.

Commercial St.

FINANCIAL DISTRICT

Embarcadero Center

Cable Car

St. Mary's Sq.

Tunnel

Kearny Street
Grant Avenue
Montgomery Street
Sansome Street

Market Street

1st St.

MONTGOMERY ST.

New Montgomery St.

California Historical Society

2nd St.

Ecker St.
Mission St.
Minna St.
Natoma St.

Transbay Terminal

UNION SQUARE

Market Street

3rd Street
4th Street

POWELL ST.

SOMA

Metréon

Moscone Convention Center

Mission St.
Howard Street
Jessie St.
Minna St.
Natoma St.
Tehama St.
Clementina St.
Folsom Street
Harrison Street
Perry St.

CIVIC CENTER

KEY

- ① *Exploring Sights*
- ① *Restaurants*
- ① *Hotels*
- 🚇 *BART station*

---

0 — 300 m
0 — 1,000 ft

🛣 80 80

Sights ▼

1 Chinatown Gate..........**C4**
2 Golden Gate Fortune Cookie Factory **C2**
3 Maiden Lane **D5**
4 Portsmouth Square......**C2**
5 Tin How Temple..........**C3**
6 Union Square.............**C5**

7 The Westin St. Francis San Francisco on Union Square.............**B5**

Restaurants ▼

1 Liholiho Yacht Club **A5**
2 Mister Jiu's **C3**
3 Sam Wo Restaurant.....**C3**

Hotels ▼

1 Cornell Hotel De France.................**B4**

2 Hotel Adagio, Autograph Collection... **A5**
3 Hotel Emblem San Francisco...........**B4**
4 Hotel Triton **C4**
5 The Westin St. Francis San Francisco on Union Square...........**B5**

🛏 Hotels

★ Cornell Hotel de France

$ | **HOTEL** | In their six-story, 1910 structure, hosts Claude and Micheline Lambert have created a bit of Paris a few blocks from Union Square, with rooms individually decorated with pastel colors, a stenciled ceiling, and prints of works by Picasso, Chagall, Klimt, and other European artists. **Pros:** excellent room quality and design for the price; updated bathrooms; special packages and discounts. **Cons:** several blocks from the center of things; surrounding area mildly dodgy after dark; small lobby. ⑤ *Rooms from: $144* ⊠ *715 Bush St., Union Sq.* ☎ *415/421–3154* ⊕ *www.cornellhotel. com* ⮑ *50 rooms* ⦿ *Free breakfast.*

Hotel Adagio, Autograph Collection

$ | **HOTEL** | The Spanish-colonial facade of this 16-story theater-row hotel complements its chic interior, with good-size rooms that have beautiful sea-blue carpets and plenty of tech amenities for working or relaxing after sightseeing. **Pros:** Marriott-run property with boutique-hotel charm; central location for lots of sightseeing; good drinks and scene at lobby bar, the Mortimer. **Cons:** street noise; area can be dicey at night; adjacent to a popular outdoor bar. ⑤ *Rooms from: $159* ⊠ *550 Geary St., Union Sq.* ☎ *415/775–5000* ⊕ *www.hoteladagiosf. com* ⮑ *171 rooms* ⦿ *No meals.*

Hotel Emblem San Francisco

$ | **HOTEL** | Inspiration is everywhere at this intimate hotel, with a prominent literary theme that celebrates San Francisco's Beat poets, from its lobby wall of books and poetry-laced carpet to in room libraries and typewriters. **Pros:** fun, creative vibe; excellent eating and drinking options; amenities available by request include diffusers, a humidifier, and bath bombs. **Cons:** some guests might feel the hotel is trying too hard to be hip; no on-site fitness option; some rooms on the small side. ⑤ *Rooms from: $159* ⊠ *562 Sutter*

Cable Car Terminus

Two of the three cable-car lines begin and end their runs at Powell and Market streets, a couple blocks south of Union Square. These two lines are the most scenic, and both pass near Fisherman's Wharf, so they're usually clogged with first-time sightseers. The wait to board a cable car at this intersection is longer than at any other stop in the system. If you'd rather avoid the mob, board the less-touristy California line at the bottom of Market Street, at Drumm Street.

St., Union Sq. ☎ *415/433–4434* ⊕ *www. viceroyhotelsandresorts.com/en/emblem* ⮑ *96 rooms* ⦿ *No meals.*

Hotel Triton

$ | **HOTEL** | With a strong location at the convergence of Chinatown, the Financial District, and Union Square, this boutique anchor attracts a design-conscious crowd and is highlighted by its intricately decorated lobby featuring marble floors, a wood-beam ceiling, and art from around the world. **Pros:** arty environs; Carrara marble bathrooms and showers; beautiful Café de la Presse next door offers discount for guests. **Cons:** rooms and baths are on the small side; hallways feel cramped; room decor feels a bit dated to some guests. ⑤ *Rooms from: $160* ⊠ *342 Grant Ave., Union Sq.* ☎ *415/394–0500* ⊕ *www.hoteltriton.com* ⮑ *140 rooms* ⦿ *No meals.*

The Westin St. Francis San Francisco on Union Square

$$ | **HOTEL** | The survivor of two major earthquakes, some headline-grabbing scandals, and even an attempted presidential assassination, this richly appointed and superbly located grande

dame dating to 1904 is comprised of the landmark building, renovated in 2018, and a modern 32-story tower whose glass elevators reveal Union Square views from the upper floors. **Pros:** prime Union Square location; correctly named Heavenly Bed; Chateau Montelena wine-tasting room and the excellent Clock Bar. **Cons:** rooms in original building can be small; public spaces lack the panache of days gone by; no dinner at on-site Oak Room Restaurant. ⑤ *Rooms from: $209* ⊠ *335 Powell St., Union Sq.* ☎ *415/397–7000, 888/627–8546* ⊕ *www.marriott.com* ⌦ *1,195 rooms* ⦿ *No meals.*

Nightlife

Mikkeller Bar San Francisco
BARS/PUBS | Beer nerds rejoice every time they step through the door from the dicey sidewalk of Mason Street and are greeted by 40 shiny taps serving the celebration creations of the namesake Danish brewer plus some of the world's most in-demand small production beers. This is hardly a proper pub or beer dive—the exposed-brick interior and zigzag-shape bar are as chic as any fashionable drinking spot in town. Don't miss the house-made sausages. ⊠ *34 Mason St., Union Sq.* ☎ *415/984–0279* ⊕ *mikkeller.com.*

Redwood Room
BARS/PUBS | Opened in 1933 and updated many times, including in 2019, this lounge at the Clift Hotel is a San Francisco icon. The art-deco bar itself and the wood-paneled room are constructed from a single old redwood tree, giving a distinct only-in-California sense of place. Cocktails are a mix of high-quality classics and slightly creative newcomers. ⊠ *The Clift Royal Sonesta Hotel, 495 Geary St., at Taylor St., Union Sq.* ☎ *415/929–2372 for table reservations* ⊕ *redwoodroomsf.com.*

Performing Arts

TIX Bay Area
TICKETS | Half-price, same-day tickets for many local and touring shows go on sale (cash only) at the TIX booth in Union Square, which is open daily from 10 to 6. Discount purchases can also be made online. ⊠ *350 Powell St., at Geary St., Union Sq.* ☎ *415/433–7827* ⊕ *www.tixbayarea.org.*

THEATER
American Conservatory Theater
THEATER | One of the nation's leading regional theater companies presents about eight plays a year, from classics to contemporary works, often in repertory. The season runs from early fall to late spring. In December ACT stages a beloved version of Charles Dickens's *A Christmas Carol*. ⊠ *415 Geary St., Union Sq.* ☎ *415/749–2228* ⊕ *www.act-sf.org.*

Shopping

Union Square is still San Francisco's main shopping area and the site of most of its department stores, including Macy's, Neiman Marcus, and Saks Fifth Avenue. Nearby are such platinum-card international boutiques as Yves Saint Laurent, Cartier, Emporio Armani, Gucci, Hermès, and Louis Vuitton.

The **Westfield San Francisco Centre,** anchored by Bloomingdale's and Nordstrom, is notable for its gorgeous atriums and top-notch dining options.

■ TIP→ **Most retailers in the square don't open until 10 am or later, so there isn't much advantage to getting an early start unless you're grabbing breakfast nearby. If you're on the prowl for art, be aware that many galleries are closed on Sunday and Monday.**

ART GALLERIES
Hang Art
ART GALLERIES | A spirit of fun imbues this inviting space that showcases local, emerging artists. Prices range from a

few hundred dollars to several thousand, making it an ideal place for novice collectors to get their feet wet. ⊠ *567 Sutter St., 2nd fl., near Mason St., Union Sq.* ☎ *415/434–4264* ⊕ *hangart.com.*

Chinatown

A few blocks uphill from Union Square is the abrupt beginning of dense and insular Chinatown—the oldest such community in the country. When the street signs have Chinese characters, produce stalls crowd pedestrians off the sidewalk, and whole roast ducks hang in deli windows, you'll know you've arrived. (The neighborhood huddles together in the 17 blocks and 41 alleys bordered roughly by Bush, Kearny, and Powell streets and Broadway.) A number of neighborhood businesses closed or struggled during the COVID-19 pandemic, and, as in other parts of San Francisco and in cities around America, the community is seeing an unfortunate rise in anti–Asian American incidents. The city is trying hard to support this landmark neighborhood and keep its largely elderly population safe.

◉ Sights

Chinatown Gate
BUILDING | At the official entrance to Chinatown, stone lions flank the base of the pagoda-topped gate; the lions, dragons, and fish up top symbolize wealth, prosperity, and other good things. The four Chinese characters immediately beneath the pagoda represent the philosophy of Sun Yat-sen, the leader who unified China in the early 20th century. Sun Yat-sen, who lived in exile in San Francisco for a few years, promoted the notion of friendship and peace among all nations based on equality, justice, and goodwill. The vertical characters under the left pagoda read "peace" and "trust," the ones under the right pagoda "respect" and "love."

Look Up!

When wandering around Chinatown, don't forget to look up! Above the chintziest souvenir shop might loom an ornate balcony or a curly pagoda roof. The best examples are on the 900 block of Grant Avenue (at Washington Street) and at Waverly Place.

The whole shebang telegraphs the internationally understood message of "photo op." Immediately beyond the gate, dive into souvenir shopping on Grant Avenue, Chinatown's tourist strip. ⊠ *Grant Ave. at Bush St., Chinatown.*

Golden Gate Fortune Cookie Factory
FACTORY | FAMILY | Follow your nose down Ross Alley to this tiny but fragrant cookie factory. Two workers sit at circular motorized griddles and wait for dollops of batter to drop onto a tiny metal plate, which rotates into an oven. A few moments later, out comes a cookie that's pliable and ready for folding. It's easy to peek in for a moment, and hard to leave without getting a few free samples and then buying a bagful of fortune cookies for snacks and wisdom later. ⊠ *56 Ross Alley, between Washington and Jackson Sts., west of Grant Ave., Chinatown* ☎ *415/781–3956* ⊕ *www.goldengatefortunecookies.com* ⊠ *Free.*

Portsmouth Square
PLAZA | Chinatown's living room buzzes with activity: the square, with its pagoda-shape structures, is a favorite spot for morning tai chi, and by noon dozens of men huddle around Chinese chess tables, engaged in competition. Kids scamper about the square's two grungy playgrounds. Back in the late 19th century this land was near the waterfront. The square is named for the USS *Portsmouth* , the ship helmed by Captain John Montgomery, who in 1846 raised

the American flag here and claimed the then-Mexican land for the United States. A couple of years later, Sam Brannan kicked off the gold rush at the square when he waved his loot and proclaimed, "Gold from the American River!" Robert Louis Stevenson, the author of *Treasure Island,* often dropped by, chatting up the sailors who hung out here. Some of the information he gleaned about life at sea found its way into his fiction. A bronze galleon sculpture, a tribute to Stevenson, anchors the square's northwest corner. A plaque marks the site of California's first public school, built in 1847. ⊠ *Bordered by Walter Lum Pl. and Kearny, Washington, and Clay Sts., Chinatown* ⊕ *sfrecpark.org.*

★ Tin How Temple

RELIGIOUS SITE | In 1852, Day Ju, one of the first three Chinese to arrive in San Francisco, dedicated this temple to the Queen of the Heavens and the Goddess of the Seven Seas, and the temple looks largely the same today as it did more than a century ago. Duck into the inconspicuous doorway, climb three flights of stairs, and be surrounded by the aroma of incense in this tiny, altar-filled room. In the entryway, elderly ladies can often be seen preparing "money" to be burned as offerings to various Buddhist gods or as funds for ancestors to use in the afterlife. Hundreds of red-and-gold lanterns cover the ceiling; the larger the lamp, the larger its donor's contribution to the temple. Gifts of oranges, dim sum, and money left by the faithful, who kneel while reciting prayers, rest on altars to different gods. Tin How presides over the middle back of the temple, flanked by one red and one green lesser god. Taking photographs is not allowed. ⊠ *125 Waverly Pl., between Clay and Washington Sts., Chinatown* ☛ *Free, donations accepted.*

🍴 Restaurants

Mister Jiu's

$$$ | CHINESE | Brandon Jew's ambitious, graceful restaurant offers the chef's delicious contemporary, farm-to-table interpretation of Chinese cuisine that sometimes tweaks classic dishes with a California spin (hot-and-sour soup with nasturtiums) or enhances fresh produce with unique Chinese flavors (local asparagus with smoked tofu). The elegant dining room—accented with plants and a chrysanthemum chandelier—provides beautiful views of Chinatown, while the menu breathes new life into it. **Known for:** sea urchin cheong fun (rice noodle rolls); standout cocktails; large-format roast duck with pancakes. ⑤ *Average main: $29* ⊠ *28 Waverly Pl., Chinatown* ☎ *415/857–9688* ⊕ *misterjius.com* ⊘ *Closed Sun. and Mon. No lunch.*

Sam Wo Restaurant

$ | CHINESE | Few restaurants in San Francisco—or the country—can match the history of this city treasure that has been around since 1908 (with a brief closure in 2012) and now resides in a narrow, two-story space across the street from Portsmouth Square. You'll want to try as much as possible from the menu, which is a unique mix of Cantonese dishes, a few items from other regions of China, a couple Southeast Asia–inspired noodles, and more familiar Chinese American fare. **Known for:** iconic sign; jook (rice porridge); BBQ pork noodle roll, a great appetizer to share. ⑤ *Average main: $11* ⊠ *713 Clay St., Chinatown* ☎ *415/989–8898* ⊕ *samworestaurant.com* ⊘ *Closed Tues.*

SoMa

SoMa is less a neighborhood than a sprawling area of wide, traffic-heavy boulevards lined with office skyscrapers and ultrachic condo high-rises. Aside from the fact that many of them work in the area, locals are drawn to the cultural offerings, destination restaurants, and concentration of bars and restaurants. In terms of sightseeing, gigantic and impressive SFMOMA tops the list, followed by the specialty museums of the Yerba Buena arts district.

◉ Sights

Contemporary Jewish Museum (CJM)

MUSEUM | Noted architect Daniel Libeskind designed the postmodern CJM, whose impossible-to-ignore diagonal blue cube juts out of a painstakingly restored power substation. A physical manifestation of the Hebrew toast *l'chaim* (to life), the cube may have obscure philosophical origins, but Libeskind created a unique, light-filled space that merits a stroll through the lobby even if the current exhibits (the museum is non-collecting and does not have permanent holdings, so they change regularly) don't entice you into the galleries. Exhibits, usually two or three at a time, vary, from a look at the history of Levi Strauss to an immersive series about the 19th-century Jewish immigrant and photographer Shimmel Zohar. ■TIP→ San Francisco's best Jewish deli, Wise Sons, operates a counter in the museum. Try the company's popular smoked salmon bagel sandwich or a slice of chocolate babka. ⊠ *736 Mission St., between 3rd and 4th Sts., SoMa* ☎ *415/655–7800* ⊕ *www.thecjm.org* 🖾 *$16* ⊗ *Closed Mon.–Wed.*

Museum of the African Diaspora (MoAD)

MUSEUM | Dedicated to the influence that people of African descent have had in places all over the world, MoAD focuses on temporary exhibits in its four galleries over three floors. With floor-to-ceiling windows onto Mission Street, the museum fits perfectly into the cultural scene of Yerba Buena and is well worth a 30-minute foray. Most striking is its front-window centerpiece: a three-story mosaic, made from thousands of photographs, that forms the image of a young girl's face. ■TIP→ Walk up the stairs inside the museum to view the mosaic photographs up close—Malcolm X is there, Muhammad Ali, too, along with everyday folks—but the best view is from across the street. ⊠ *685 Mission St., SoMa* ☎ *415/358–7200* ⊕ *www.moadsf.org* 🖾 *$10* ⊗ *Closed Mon. and Tues.*

★ San Francisco Museum of Modern Art (SFMOMA)

MUSEUM | Opened in 1935, the San Francisco Museum of Modern Art was the first museum on the West Coast dedicated to modern and contemporary art, and after a three-year expansion designed by Snøhetta, it emerged in 2016 as one of the largest modern art museums in the country and the revitalized anchor of the Yerba Buena arts district. With gallery space over seven floors, the museum displays only a portion of its more than 33,000-work collection and has numerous temporary exhibits. You could spend a day here, but allow at least two hours; three is better. The museum's holdings include art from the Doris and Donald Fisher Collection, one of the world's greatest private collections of modern and contemporary art. Highlights here include deep collections of works by German abstract expressionist Gerhard Richter and American painter Ellsworth Kelly and an Agnes Martin gallery. The third floor is dedicated to photography. Also look for seminal works by Diego Rivera, Alexander Calder, Matisse, and Picasso. Don't miss the third-floor sculpture terrace. The first floor is free to the public and contains four large works as well as the museum's shop and expensive restaurant. Ticketing, information, and one gallery are on the second floor; save time and reserve timed tickets online. ⊠ *151 3rd St., SoMa* ☎ *415/357–4000* ⊕ *www.sfmoma.org* 🖾 *$25.*

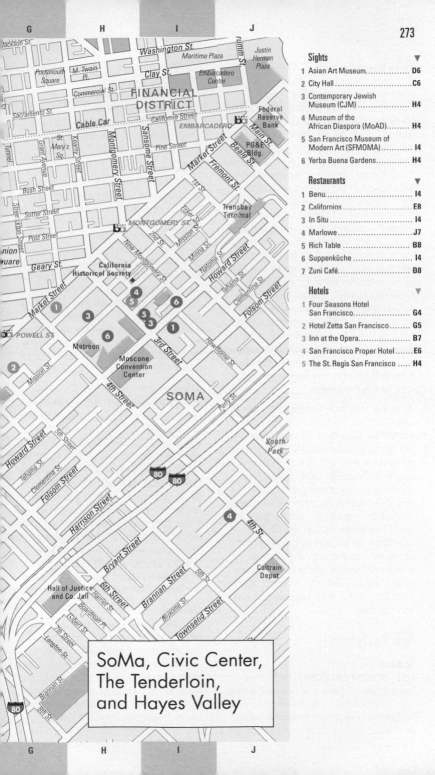

Yerba Buena Gardens

CITY PARK | FAMILY | Not much south of Market Street encourages lingering outdoors, with this notable exception: these two blocks encompass the Yerba Buena Center for the Arts, the Metreon, and Moscone Convention Center, but the gardens themselves are the everyday draw. Office workers and convention-goers escape to the green swath of the East Garden, the focal point of which is the memorial to Martin Luther King Jr. Powerful streams of water surge over large, jagged stone columns, mirroring the enduring force of King's words, which are carved on the stone walls and on glass blocks behind the waterfall. Moscone North is behind the memorial, and an overhead walkway leads to Moscone South and its rooftop attractions. ■TIP→ **The gardens are liveliest during the week and especially during the Yerba Buena Gardens Festival, from May through October (www.ybgfestival.org), with free performances.**

Atop the Moscone Center perch a few lures for kids. The historic Looff carousel (*$5 for two rides; $3 with museum admission*) twirls daily 10–5. The carousel is attached to the Children's Creativity Museum (☎ *415/820–3320* ⊕ *creativity.org*), a high-tech, interactive arts-and-technology center (*$13*) geared to children ages 3–12. Just outside, kids adore the slides, including a 25-foot tube slide, at the play circle. Also part of the rooftop complex are gardens, an ice-skating rink, and a bowling alley. ✉ *Bordered by 3rd, 4th, Mission, and Folsom Sts., SoMa* ⊕ *yerbabuenagardens. com* 🖃 *Free.*

🍴 Restaurants

★ Benu

$$$$ | MODERN AMERICAN | Chef Corey Lee's three-Michelin-star fine dining mecca is a must-stop for those who hop from city to city collecting memorable meals. At this tasting menu–only restaurant, each course is impossibly meticulous, a marvel of textures and flavors. **Known for:** high-end dining; phenomenal wine pairings and list of bottles; stellar service. $ *Average main: $325* ✉ *22 Hawthorne St., SoMa* ☎ *415/685–4860* ⊕ *www.benusf.com* ⊗ *Closed Sun. and Mon. No lunch.*

★ Californios

$$$$ | MODERN MEXICAN | Most restaurant discussion in San Francisco during the COVID-19 pandemic sadly revolved around the closings, except for a few exciting openings like this Californian-Mexican tasting-menu concept by chef Val M. Cantu that relocated in 2021 from its Mission District digs to a larger, ultrachic home in SoMa's former Bar Agricole space. **Known for:** house-made tortillas used in brilliant ways; wonderful patio; hard to get reservations. $ *Average main: $223* ✉ *355 11th St., SoMa* ☎ *415/757–0994* ⊕ *www.californiossf. com* ⊗ *Closed Sun. and Mon. No lunch.*

★ In Situ

$$$ | CONTEMPORARY | Benu chef Corey Lee's restaurant at SFMOMA is an exhibition of its own, with a rotating menu comprised of dishes from 80 famous chefs around the world. You might taste David Chang's sausage and rice cakes, René Redzepi's wood sorrel granita, or Wylie Dufresne's shrimp grits. **Known for:** global culinary influences; sleek space that fits the modern art vibe; most refined daytime option in an area without many sit-down lunch choices. $ *Average main: $30* ✉ *151 3rd St., SoMa* ☎ *415/941–6050* ⊕ *insitu.sfmoma.org* ⊗ *Closed Tues. and Wed. No dinner Mon.*

Marlowe

$$$ | AMERICAN | Hearty American bistro fare and hip design draw crowds to this Anna Weinberg–Jennifer Puccio enterprise. The menu boasts one of the city's best burgers, and the dining room gleams with white penny-tile floors and marble countertops. **Known for:** refined takes on comfort food like roast chicken and deviled eggs; strong drinks; festive atmosphere. $ *Average main: $29* ⊠ *500 Brannan St., SoMa* ☎ *415/777–1413* ⊕ *marlowesf.com.*

Hotels

Four Seasons Hotel San Francisco

$$$$ | **HOTEL** | Occupying floors 5 through 17 of a skyscraper, the Four Seasons delivers subdued elegance in rooms with contemporary artwork, fine linens, floor-to-ceiling windows that overlook Yerba Buena Gardens or downtown, and bathrooms with soaking tubs and glass-enclosed showers. **Pros:** near museums, galleries, restaurants, shopping, and clubs; terrific fitness facilities; luxurious rooms and amenities. **Cons:** in-house restaurant/bar has delicious eats and drinks but lacks personality; rooms can feel sterile; Market Street entrance can have aggressive street life outside. $ *Rooms from: $490* ⊠ *757 Market St., SoMa* ☎ *415/633–3000* ⊕ *www.fourseasons.com/sanfrancisco* ⇆ *277 rooms* ❙○❙ *No meals.*

★ Hotel Zetta San Francisco

$ | **HOTEL** | With a playful lobby lounge, London-style brasserie The Cavalier, and slick-yet-homey tech-friendly rooms, this trendy redo behind a stately 1913 neoclassical facade is a leader on the SoMa hotel scene. **Pros:** tech amenities and arty design; in-room spa services; noteworthy fitness center. **Cons:** lots of hubbub and traffic; no bathtubs; aesthetic too frenetic for some guests. $ *Rooms from: $198* ⊠ *55 5th St., SoMa* ☎ *415/543–8555* ⊕ *hotelzetta.com* ⇆ *116 rooms* ❙○❙ *No meals.*

★ The St. Regis San Francisco

$$$$ | **HOTEL** | Across from Yerba Buena Gardens and SFMOMA, the luxurious and modern St. Regis is favored by celebrities, such as Lady Gaga and Al Gore, and others drawn to guest rooms and suites decorated with subdued cream colors, leather-textured walls, and window seats offering city views. **Pros:**

excellent views; stunning lap pool and luxe spa; art by local artists on display. **Cons:** expensive rates; restaurant isn't on par with the rest of the hotel; cramped space for passenger unloading. $ *Rooms from: $489* ⊠ *125 3rd St., SoMa* ☎ *415/284–4000* ⊕ *st-regis.marriott.com* ⇆ *260 rooms* ❙○❙ *No meals.*

Nightlife

★ City Beer Store

BARS/PUBS | Called CBS by locals, this friendly tasting room meets liquor mart has a wine bar's sensibility. Perfect for both connoisseurs and the merely beer curious, CBS stocks hundreds of different bottled beers, and more than a dozen are on tap to enjoy on the patio or the bar seats in front of a whimsical mural depicting aquatic animals flying around the Bay Bridge. ⊠ *1148 Mission St., between 7th and 8th Sts., SoMa* ☎ *702/941–0349* ⊕ *www.citybeerstore.com.*

Terroir

WINE BARS—NIGHTLIFE | The focus at this quaint wine bar is on natural (and mostly old-world) vintages, though it's not impossible to find local offerings, too. The space may be small, but the selection is not: hundreds of different wines, stacked along the walls, compete for your attention. Not sure about Jura wines or the difference between Poulsard and Trousseau? The staff is always eager to help. The bar also serves a small selection of artisanal cheeses and charcuterie to pair with the wines. ■**TIP**→ **Go on a weekday and head to the candlelit loft above the bar. It's the best seat in the house.** ⊠ *1116 Folsom St., at 7th St., SoMa* ☎ *415/558–9946* ⊕ *terroirsf.com.*

21st Amendment Brewery

BREWPUBS/BEER GARDENS | Known for its range of beer types, this popular brewery has multiple taps going at all times. In the summer, the Hell or High Watermelon—a wheat beer—gets rave reviews.

■ **TIP→ Serious beer drinkers should try the Back in Black, a black IPA-style beer this brewpub helped pioneer.** The space has an upmarket warehouse feel, though exposed wooden ceiling beams, framed photos, whitewashed brick walls, and hardwood floors help keep it cozy. It's a good spot to warm up before a Giants game and an even better place to party after they win. ⊠ *563 2nd St., between Bryant and Brannan Sts., SoMa* ☎ *415/369–0900* ⊕ *www.21st-amendment.com.*

Performing Arts

Yerba Buena Center for the Arts
ARTS CENTERS | Across the street from SFMOMA and abutting a lovely urban garden, this performing arts complex schedules interdisciplinary art exhibitions, touring and local dance troupes, music, film programs, and contemporary theater events. You can depend on the quality of the productions at Yerba Buena. Film buffs often come here for screenings by the San Francisco Cinematheque (⊕ *www.sfcinematheque.org*), which showcases experimental film and digital media. And dance enthusiasts can attend concerts by a roster of city companies that perform here, including Smuin Ballet (⊕ *www.smuinballet.org*), ODC/Dance (⊕ *www.odcdance.org*), and Alonzo King's LINES Ballet (⊕ *www.linesballet.org*). Lamplighters (⊕ *www.lamplighters.org*), an alternative opera that specializes in Gilbert & Sullivan, also performs here. ⊠ *701 Mission St., SoMa* ☎ *415/978–2787* ⊕ *ybca.org.*

Shopping

BOOKS
★ Chronicle Books
BOOKS/STATIONERY | A local beacon of publishing produces inventively designed fiction, cookbooks, art books, and other titles, as well as diaries, planners, and address books—all of which you can purchase at its home near Oracle Park in an old maritime machine shop and warehouse. ⊠ *680 2nd St., SoMa* ☎ *415/537–4200* ⊕ *www.chroniclebooks.com.*

FOOD AND DRINK
K&L Wine Merchants
WINE/SPIRITS | More than any other wine store in the city, this one has an ardent cult following around town. The friendly staffers promise not to sell what they don't taste themselves, and weekly events—on Friday from 5 pm to 6:30 pm and Saturday from noon to 3 pm—open the tastings to customers. The best-seller list for varietals and regions for both the under- and over-$30 categories appeals to the wine lover in everyone. ⊠ *855 Harrison St., near 4th St., SoMa* ☎ *415/896–1734* ⊕ *www.klwines.com.*

Civic Center

The eye-catching, gold-domed City Hall presides over this patchy neighborhood bordered roughly by Franklin, McAllister, Hyde, and Grove streets. The optimistic "City Beautiful" movement of the early 20th century produced the Beaux Arts–style complex for which the area is named, including City Hall, the War Memorial Opera House, the Veterans Building, and the old public library, now the home of the Asian Art Museum. The wonderful Main Library on Larkin Street between Fulton and Grove streets is a modern variation on the Civic Center's architectural theme.

Sights

★ Asian Art Museum
MUSEUM | You don't have to be a connoisseur of Asian art to appreciate a visit to this museum whose monumental exterior conceals a light, open, and welcoming space. The fraction of the museum's collection on display (about 2,500 pieces out of 18,000-plus total) is laid out

thematically and by region, making it easy to follow historical developments.

Begin on the third floor, where highlights of Buddhist art in Southeast Asia and early China include a large, jewel-encrusted, exquisitely painted 19th-century Burmese Buddha and clothed rod puppets from Java. On the second floor you can find later Chinese works, as well as exquisite pieces from Korea and Japan. The ground floor is devoted to temporary exhibits and the museum's wonderful gift shop. During spring and summer, visit on Thursday evenings for extended programs and sip drinks while a DJ spins tunes. ⊠ *200 Larkin St., between McAllister and Fulton Sts., Civic Center* ☎ *415/581–3500* ⊕ *asianart.org* ⊡ *$15, free 1st Sun. of month; $8 Thurs. 5–8* ☉ *Closed Tues. and Wed.*

★ **City Hall**

GOVERNMENT BUILDING | This imposing 1915 structure with its massive gold-leaf dome—higher than the U.S. Capitol's—is about as close to a palace as you're going to get in San Francisco: the classic granite-and-marble behemoth was modeled after St. Peter's Basilica in Rome. Architect Arthur Brown Jr., who was also behind Coit Tower and the War Memorial Opera House, designed an interior with grand columns and a sweeping central staircase. The 1899 structure it replaced had taken 27 years to erect, but it collapsed in about 27 seconds during the 1906 earthquake.

City Hall was seismically retrofitted in the late 1990s, but the sense of history remains palpable, and you can learn about it on a tour. Some noteworthy events that have taken place here include the hosing of civil-rights and freedom-of-speech protesters (1960); the assassinations of Mayor George Moscone and openly gay supervisor Harvey Milk (1978); the torching of the lobby by angry members of the gay community in response to the light sentence given to the former supervisor who killed both men (1979); and the first domestic partnership registrations of gay couples (1991). In 2004, Mayor Gavin Newsom took a stand against then-current state and federal law by issuing marriage licenses to same-sex partners.

Across Polk Street from City Hall is **Civic Center Plaza,** with lawns, walkways, seasonal flower beds, a playground, and an underground parking garage. This sprawling space is generally clean but somewhat grim, as many homeless people hang out here. ⊠ *1 Dr. Carlton B. Goodlett Pl. , bordered by Van Ness Ave. and Polk, Grove, and McAllister Sts., Civic Center* ☎ *415/554–4000, 415/554–6139 tour reservations* ⊕ *sfgov.org/cityhall/city-hall-tours* ⊡ *Free* ☉ *Closed weekends.*

🎭 Performing Arts

DANCE
★ **San Francisco Ballet**

DANCE | For ballet lovers, the nation's oldest professional company is reason alone to visit the Bay Area, as SFB's performances under the direction of Helgi Tomasson have won critical raves. The primary season runs from February through May. The repertoire includes full-length ballets such as *Don Quixote* and *Sleeping Beauty*; the December presentation of *The Nutcracker* is truly spectacular. The company also performs bold new dances from star choreographers such as William Forsythe and Mark Morris, alongside modern classics by George Balanchine and Jerome Robbins. Tickets are available at the **War Memorial Opera House.** ⊠ *War Memorial Opera House, 301 Van Ness Ave., at Grove St., Civic Center* ☎ *415/865–2000* ⊕ *www.sfballet.org.*

MUSIC
★ **San Francisco Symphony**

MUSIC | One of America's top orchestras performs from September through May, with additional summer performances of light classical music and show tunes.

The symphony is known for its daring programming of 20th-century American works, often performed with soloists of the caliber of André Watts, Gil Shaham, and Renée Fleming. Legendary maestro Michael Tilson Thomas retired in 2020, and music lovers are eager to listen to the opening postpandemic concerts of the new music director, Esa-Pekka Salonen. ⊠ *Louise M. Davies Symphony Hall, 201 Van Ness Ave., at Grove St., Civic Center* ☎ *415/864–6000* ⊕ *www. sfsymphony.org.*

OPERA
★ San Francisco Opera
OPERA | Founded in 1923, this internationally recognized organization has occupied the War Memorial Opera House since the building's completion in 1932. From September through December and June through July, the company presents a wide range of operas, from *Carmen* to an operatic version of *It's a Wonderful Life* . The opera often takes on ambitious world premieres and sometimes presents unconventional, edgy projects designed to attract younger audiences. Translations are projected above the stage during most non-English productions. ⊠ *War Memorial Opera House, 301 Van Ness Ave., at Grove St., Civic Center* ☎ *415/864–3330 tickets* ⊕ *sfopera.com.*

The Tenderloin

Stretching west of Union Square and north of Civic Center, the Tenderloin is not an attractive neighborhood. So why would anyone go out of their way to come here? Trendy watering holes and coffee shops are springing up, with a handful of intrepid hipsters moving into the hood after them. The Tenderloin may be on its way to becoming the next Mission, but for now it remains a gritty slice of San Francisco.

 Hotels

★ San Francisco Proper Hotel
$$ | HOTEL | Inside the magnificent, flatiron-shape Beaux-Arts building—given a modern refresh in the mid-2010s—is one of the city's most spectacular places to stay, a sharp, upscale, ultra-hip boutique hotel; in contrast, outside is one of the roughest intersections for streetlife in San Francisco. **Pros:** gorgeous lobby; excellent restaurant and cocktails; tech elements like wireless speakers and smart TV. **Cons:** price may seem high for difficult location; too cool for many tastes; $30 daily fee for amenities. Ⓢ *Rooms from: $220* ⊠ *1100 Market St., Tenderloin* ✛ *Entrance at 45 McAllister St.* ☎ *415/737–7777, 888/730–4299 reservations* ⊕ *properhotel.com/san-francisco* ⬏ *131 rooms* �🍽 *No meals.*

Ⓨ Nightlife

★ Bourbon & Branch
BARS/PUBS | Although this spot reeks of Prohibition-era speakeasy cool, it's not exclusive: everyone is granted a password, though it's *highly* recommended to book a reservation. The place has sex appeal, with tin ceilings, bordello-red silk wallpaper, intimate booths, and low lighting; loud conversations and cell phones are not allowed. The menu of expertly mixed cocktails and quality bourbon and whiskey is substantial, with cocktails leaning more in the spirit-forward direction. A speakeasy within the speakeasy called Wilson & Wilson is more exclusive, but just as funky. ⊠ *501 Jones St., at O'Farrell St., Tenderloin* ☎ *415/346–1735* ⊕ *www.bourbonandbranch.com.*

Great American Music Hall
MUSIC CLUBS | You can find top-drawer entertainment at this eclectic concert venue. Acts range from the best in blues, folk, and jazz to up-and-coming college-radio and American-roots artists to indie rockers. The colorful marble-pillared club, built in 1907 as a

bordello, also accommodates dancing at some shows. Pub grub is available most nights. ✉ *859 O'Farrell St., between Polk and Larkin Sts., Tenderloin* ☎ *415/885–0750* ⊕ *slimspresents.com/great-american-music-hall.*

Hayes Valley

A chic neighborhood due west of Civic Center, Hayes Valley has terrific eateries, cool watering holes, and great browsing in its funky clothing, home-decor, and design boutiques. Locals love this quarter, but without any big-name draws it remains off the radar for many visitors.

🍴 Restaurants

★ Rich Table
$$$ | MODERN AMERICAN | Sardine chips and porcini doughnuts are popular bites at co-chefs (and husband and wife) Evan and Sarah Rich's lively, creative restaurant; mains are also clever stunners, including pastas like the sea urchin *cacio e pepe.* The room's weathered-wood wallboards repurposed from a Northern California sawmill give it a homey vibe. **Known for:** tough-to-get reservations; freshly baked bread; seasonal ingredients. ⑤ *Average main: $34* ✉ *199 Gough St., Hayes Valley* ☎ *415/355–9085* ⊕ *www.richtablesf.com* ⊗ *No lunch.*

Suppenküche
$$ | GERMAN | Nobody goes hungry—and no beer drinker goes thirsty—at this lively, hip outpost of simple German cooking in Hayes Valley. The hearty food—bratwurst and sauerkraut, potato pancakes with house-made applesauce, meat loaf, braised beef, pork loin, schnitzel, spaetzle—is tasty and kind to your wallet, and the imported brews are first-rate. **Known for:** seating at common tables; any of the sausages; quick service. ⑤ *Average main: $26* ✉ *525 Laguna St., Hayes Valley* ☎ *415/252–9289* ⊕ *www.suppenkuche.com* ⊗ *Closed Mon. No lunch weekdays.*

★ Zuni Café
$$$ | MODERN AMERICAN | After one bite of Zuni's succulent brick-oven-roasted whole chicken with warm bread salad, you'll understand why the two-floor café is a perennial star. Its long copper bar is a hub for a disparate mix of patrons who commune over oysters on the half shell and cocktails and wine. **Known for:** seasonal Californian cooking at its best; under-the-radar lunch and late-night burger; beloved margarita. ⑤ *Average main: $35* ✉ *1658 Market St., Hayes Valley* ☎ *415/552–2522* ⊕ *zunicafe.com* ⊗ *Closed Mon. and Tues.*

🛏 Hotels

Inn at the Opera
$$ | B&B/INN | Within walking distance of Davies Symphony Hall and the War Memorial Opera House, this inn with small rooms with dark wood furnishings caters to season-ticket holders for the opera, ballet, and symphony; it's also been the choice for stars of the music, dance, and opera worlds, from Luciano Pavarotti to Mikhail Baryshnikov. **Pros:** staff goes the extra mile; good on-site dining; prime location but a quiet block. **Cons:** no air-conditioning; sold out far in advance during opera season; difficult parking. ⑤ *Rooms from: $215* ✉ *333 Fulton St., Hayes Valley* ☎ *415/863–8400* ⊕ *www.shellhospitality.com/inn-at-the-opera* ⇄ *48 rooms* ⦿ *Free breakfast.*

📶 Nightlife

The Mint Karaoke Lounge
BARS/PUBS | A mixed gay-straight crowd that's drop-dead serious about its karaoke—to the point where you'd think an *American Idol* casting agent was in attendance—comes here seven nights a week. Regulars sing everything from Simon and Garfunkel songs to disco classics in front of an attentive audience. Do *not* walk onstage unprepared! Check out the songbook online to perfect

your debut before you attempt to take the mic. Hit the ATM beforehand, as everything here is cash-only. ✉ *1942 Market St., between Duboce Ave. and Laguna St., Hayes Valley* ☎ *415/626–4726* ⊕ *themint.net.*

★ Smuggler's Cove

BARS/PUBS | With the decor of a pirate ship and a slew of rum-based cocktails, you half expect Captain Jack Sparrow to sidle up next to you at this offbeat, Disney-esque hangout. But the folks at Smuggler's Cove take rum so seriously they've even had it made for them from distillers around the world, which you can sample along with more than 550 other offerings. A punch card is provided so you can try the entire menu (featuring 80-plus cocktails). The small space fills up quickly, so arrive early. The same owner also has a gin-centric cocktail bar, Whitechapel, a few blocks away on Polk Street, where the cocktails are equally special and the outrageous decor echoes a vintage London Underground station. ✉ *650 Gough St., at McAllister St., Hayes Valley* ☎ *415/869–1900* ⊕ *www.smugglerscovesf.com.*

◉ Performing Arts

★ SFJAZZ Center

MUSIC | Jazz legends Branford Marsalis and Herbie Hancock have performed at the snazzy center, as have Rosanne Cash, Dianne Reeves, and world-music favorite Esperanza Spalding. The sight lines and acoustics here are impressive, as are the second-floor tile murals. Shows often sell out quickly. ✉ *201 Franklin St., Hayes Valley* ☎ *866/920–5299* ⊕ *www.sfjazz.org.*

◎ Shopping

BOOKS

Isotope Comic Book Lounge

BOOKS/STATIONERY | For full-frontal nerdity in a chic modern setting, pay a visit to SF's premier comic book hangout. You'll find a great selection of graphic novels and artwork by popular and local artists, as well as lively after-hours events. ✉ *326 Fell St., at Gough St., Hayes Valley* ☎ *415/621–6543* ⊕ *www.isotopecomics.com.*

FOOD AND DRINK

Miette Patisserie & Confiserie

FOOD/CANDY | There is truly nothing sweeter than a cellophane bag tied with colorful ribbon and filled with malt balls or floral meringues from this Insta-friendly candy and pastry store. Grab a gingerbread cupcake or a tantalizing macaron or some shortbread. The pastel-color cake stands make even window-shopping a treat. It's open Thursday–Sunday. ✉ *449 Octavia Blvd., between Hayes and Linden Sts., Hayes Valley* ☎ *415/626–6221* ⊕ *www.miette.com.*

Nob Hill

Nob Hill was officially dubbed during the 1870s when the "Big Four"—Charles Crocker, Leland Stanford, Mark Hopkins, and Collis P. Huntington, who were involved in the construction of the transcontinental railroad—built their hilltop estates. The lingo is thick from this era: those on the hilltop were referred to as "nabobs" (originally meaning a provincial governor from India) and "swells," and the hill itself was called Snob Hill, a term that survives to this day. By 1882 so many estates had sprung up on Nob Hill that Robert Louis Stevenson called it "the hill of palaces." The 1906 earthquake and fire, though, destroyed all the palatial mansions except for portions of the James Flood brownstone. History buffs may choose to

Nob Hill, Russian Hill, and Polk Gulch

KEY

- **1** Exploring Sights
- **1** Restaurants
- **1** Hotels
- **bart** BART station

Sights ▼	Restaurants ▼	Hotels ▼
1 Cable Car Museum..... **D4**	**1** Acquerello.............. **A5**	**1** Fairmont San Francisco........... **D5**
2 Grace Cathedral **D5**	**2** Sons & Daughters....... **E5**	
3 Lombard Street **B2**	**3** Swan Oyster Depot..... **B5**	**2** The Ritz-Carlton, San Francisco........... **E5**
4 Macondray Lane........ **C3**		
5 San Francisco Art Institute.............. **C1**		

linger here, but for most visitors, a casual glimpse from a cable car will be enough.

 Sights

Cable Car Museum

MUSEUM | FAMILY | One of the city's best free offerings, this museum is an absolute must for kids. You can even ride a cable car here—all three lines stop between Russian Hill and Nob Hill. The facility, which is inside the city's last remaining cable-car barn, takes the top off the system to let you see how it all works. Eternally humming and squealing, the massive powerhouse cable wheels steal the show. You can also climb aboard a vintage car and take the grip, let the kids ring a cable-car bell (briefly), and check out vintage gear dating from 1873. ✉ *1201 Mason St., at Washington St., Nob Hill* ☎ *415/474–1887* ⊕ *www.cablecarmuseum.org* ⊒ *Free.*

★ Grace Cathedral

RELIGIOUS SITE | Not many churches can boast an altarpiece by Keith Haring and two labyrinths, but this one, the country's third-largest Episcopal cathedral, does. The soaring Gothic-style structure took 14 (often interrupted) years to build, beginning in 1927 and eventually wrapping up in 1964. The gilded bronze doors at the east entrance were taken from casts of Lorenzo Ghiberti's incredible *Gates of Paradise*, designed for the Baptistery in Florence, Italy. A sculpture of St. Francis by Beniamino Bufano greets you as you enter.

The 34-foot-wide limestone labyrinth is a replica of the 13th-century stone maze on the floor of Chartres Cathedral. All are encouraged to walk the 1/8-mile-long labyrinth, a ritual based on the tradition of meditative walking. There's also a granite outdoor labyrinth on the church's northeast side. The AIDS Interfaith Chapel, to the right as you enter Grace, contains a bronze triptych by the late artist

Keith Haring and panels from the AIDS Memorial Quilt. ■**TIP→ Especially dramatic times to view the cathedral are during Tuesday-evening yoga (6 pm), Thursday-night evensong (5:15 pm), and special holiday programs.** ✉ *1100 California St., at Taylor St., Nob Hill* ☎ *415/749–6300* ⊕ *www.gracecathedral.org* ⊒ *Free; tours $25.*

🍴 **Restaurants**

★ Sons & Daughters

$$$$ | AMERICAN | The constantly evolving tasting menu that chef-owner Teague Moriarty serves at his standout restaurant serves as a primer for how to do highly seasonal cuisine the right way. Though the preparations are intricate and often luxurious, there is a pretension-free, contemporary type of elegance on the plate and throughout the small, immaculate space that makes this one of the most relaxed (and fun) fine-dining experiences in the city. **Known for:** refined, cozy but chic dining room anchored by an ornate fireplace; excellent house-made bread; attentive service. ⑤ *Average main: $175* ✉ *708 Bush St., Nob Hill* ☎ *415/994–7933* ⊕ *www.sonsanddaughterssf.com* ☯ *Closed Mon. and Tues. No lunch.*

🛏 **Hotels**

Fairmont San Francisco

$$$ | HOTEL | Dominating the top of Nob Hill like a European palace, the Fairmont indulges guests in luxury: rooms in the main building, adorned in sapphire blues with platinum and pewter accents, have high ceilings, decadent beds, and marble bathrooms; rooms in the newer Tower, many with fine views, have a neutral color palette with bright-silver notes. **Pros:** huge bathrooms; stunning lobby; great location. **Cons:** some older rooms are small; hills can be challenging for those on foot; $30 per night Urban Experience amenities fee. ⑤ *Rooms*

Continued on page 287

SAN FRANCISCO'S CABLE CARS

The moment it dawns on you that you severely underestimated the steepness of the San Francisco hills will likely be the same moment you look down and realize those tracks aren't just for show—or just for tourists.

Van Ness Ave., California
59
& Market Streets

Sure, locals rarely use the cable cars for commuting these days. (That's partially due to the $8 fare—hear that, Muni?) So you'll likely be packed in with plenty of fellow sightseers. You may even be approaching cable-car fatigue after seeing its image on so many souvenirs. But if you fear the magic is gone, simply climb on board, and those jaded thoughts will dissolve. Grab the pole and gawk at the view as the car clanks down an insanely steep grade toward the bay. Listen to the humming cable, the clang of the bell, and the occasional quip from the gripman. It's an experience you shouldn't pass up, whether on your first trip or your fiftieth.

HOW CABLE CARS WORK

The mechanics are pretty simple: cable cars grab a moving subterranean cable with a "grip" to go. To stop, they release the grip and apply one or more types of brakes. Four cables, totaling 9 miles, power the city's three lines. If the gripman doesn't adjust the grip just right when going up a steep hill, the cable will start to slip and the car will have to back down the hill and try again. This is an extremely rare occurrence—imagine the ribbing the gripman gets back at the cable car barn!

Gripman: Stands in front and operates the grip, brakes, and bell. Favorite joke, especially at the peak of a steep hill: "This is my first day on the job, folks . . ."

Conductor: Moves around the car, deals with tickets, alerts the grip about what's coming up, and operates the rear wheel brakes.

❶ Cable: Steel wrapped around flexible sisal core; 2 inches thick; runs at a constant 9½ mph.

❷ Bells: Used for crew communication; alerts other drivers and pedestrians.

❸ Grip: Vice-like lever extends through the center slot in the track to grab or release the cable.

❹ Grip Lever: Left-hand lever; operates grip.

❺ Car: Entire car weighs 8 tons.

❻ Wheel Brake: Steel brake pads on each wheel.

❼ Wheel Brake Lever: Foot pedal; operates wheel brakes.

❽ Rear Wheel Brake Lever: Applied for extra traction on hills.

❾ Track Brake: 2-foot-long sections of Monterey pine push down against the track to help stop the car.

❿ Track Brake Lever: Middle lever; operates track brakes.

⓫ Emergency Brake: 18-inch steel wedge, jams into street slot to bring car to an immediate stop.

⓬ Emergency Brake Lever: Right-hand lever, red; operates emergency brake.

ROUTES

Cars run at least every 15 minutes, from around 6 am to about 1 am.

Powell–Hyde line: Most scenic, with classic Bay views. Begins at Powell and Market streets, then crosses Nob Hill and Russian Hill before a white-knuckle descent down Hyde Street, ending near the Hyde Street Pier.

Powell–Mason line: Also begins at Powell and Market streets, but winds through North Beach to Bay and Taylor streets, a few blocks from Fisherman's Wharf.

California line: Runs from the foot of Market Street, at Drumm Street, up Nob Hill and back. Great views (and aromas and sounds) of Chinatown on the way up. Sit in back to catch glimpses of the bay. ■TIP→ **Take the California line if it's just the cable-car experience you're after— the lines are shorter, and the grips and conductors say it's friendlier and has a slower pace.**

RULES OF THE RIDE

Tickets. There are ticket booths at all three turnarounds. You must purchase your ticket in advance.

■TIP→ **If you're planning to use public transit a few times, or if you'd like to ride back and forth on the cable car without worrying about the price, consider a one-day (or multiday) Muni Visitor Passport. You can get passports online, at the Powell Street turnaround, the TIX booth on Union Square, or the Fisherman's Wharf cable-car ticket booth at Beach and Hyde streets. Also consider Muni Mobile or a Clipper Card; see sfmta.com. Cash purchases require exact change.**

All Aboard. You can board on either side of the cable car. It's legal to stand on the running boards and hang on to the pole, but keep your ears open for the gripman's warnings. ■TIP→ **Grab a seat on the outside bench for the best views.**

Most people wait (and wait) in line at one of the cable car turnarounds, but you can also hop on along the route. Board wherever you see a white sign showing a figure climbing aboard a brown cable car; wave to the approaching driver, and wait until the car stops.

Riding on the running boards can be part of the thrill.

CABLE CAR HISTORY

HALLIDIE FREES THE HORSES

In the 1850s and '60s, San Francisco's streetcars were drawn by horses. Legend has it that the horrible sight of a car dragging a team of horses downhill to their deaths roused Andrew Smith Hallidie to action. The English immigrant had invented the "Hallidie Ropeway," essentially a cable car for mined ore, and he was convinced that his invention could also move people. In 1873, Hallidie and his intrepid crew prepared to test the first cable car high on Russian Hill. The anxious engineer peered down into the foggy darkness, failed to see the bottom of the hill, and promptly turned the controls over to Hallidie. Needless to say, the thing worked . . . but rides were free for the first two days because people were afraid to get on.

SEE IT FOR YOURSELF

The Cable Car Museum (✉ 1201 Mason St, ⊕ cablecarmusem.org) is one of the city's best free offerings and an absolute must for kids. (You can even ride a cable car there, since all three lines stop between Russian Hill and Nob Hill.) The museum, which is inside the city's last cable-car barn, takes the top off the system to let you see how it all works. Eternally humming and squealing, the massive powerhouse cable wheels steal the show. You can also climb aboard a vintage car and take the grip, let the kids ring a cable-car bell (briefly, please!), and check out vintage gear dating from 1873.

■ TIP→ The gift shop sells cable car paraphernalia, including an authentic gripman's bell (it'll sound like Powell Street in your house every day). For significantly less, you can pick up a key chain made from a piece of worn-out cable. Books, T-shirts, hats, and models are also on sale.

CHAMPION OF THE CABLE CAR BELL

Each fall (though the month can vary widely : check ⊕ sfmta.com for update) the city's best and brightest come together to crown a bell-ringing champion at Union Square. The crowd cheers gripmen and conductors as they stomp, shake, and riff with the rope. But it's not a popularity contest; the ringers are judged by former bell-ringing champions and others who take each ping and gong very seriously.

from: $301 ✉ *950 Mason St., Nob Hill* ☎ *415/772–5000, 866/550–4491* ⊕ *www.fairmont.com/san-francisco* ➷ *606 rooms* ⦿ *No meals.*

★ The Ritz-Carlton, San Francisco

$$$ | HOTEL | A tribute to beauty and attentive, professional service, the Ritz-Carlton emphasizes luxury and elegance, which are evident in the Ionic columns that grace the neoclassical facade and the crystal chandeliers that illuminate marble floors and walls in the lobby. **Pros:** terrific service; beautiful furnishings throughout; lobby wine-tasting lounge. **Cons:** nothing is a bargain; hilly location; no pool. Ⓢ *Rooms from: $364* ✉ *600 Stockton St., at Pine St., Nob Hill* ☎ *415/296–7465, 800/542–8680* ⊕ *www.ritzcarlton.com/sanfrancisco* ➷ *336 rooms* ⦿ *No meals.*

Russian Hill

Essentially a tony residential neighborhood of spiffy pieds-à-terre, Victorian flats, Edwardian cottages, and boxlike condos, Russian Hill has some of the city's loveliest stairway walks, hidden garden ways, and steepest streets—not to mention those bay views.

◉ Sights

★ Lombard Street

NEIGHBORHOOD | The block-long "Crookedest Street in the World" makes eight switchbacks down the east face of Russian Hill between Hyde and Leavenworth Streets. Residents bemoan the traffic jam outside their front doors, but the throngs continue. Join the line of cars waiting to drive down the steep hill, or avoid the whole mess and walk down the steps on either side of Lombard. You take in super views of North Beach and Coit Tower whether you walk or drive—though if you're the one behind the wheel, you'd better keep your eye on the road lest you become yet another of the many folks who ram the garden barriers.

■ **TIP→ Can't stand the traffic? Thrill seekers of a different stripe may want to head two blocks south of Lombard to Filbert Street. At a gradient of 31.5%, the hair-raising descent between Hyde and Leavenworth Streets is one of the city's steepest. Go slowly!** ✉ *Lombard St. between Hyde and Leavenworth Sts., Russian Hill.*

★ Macondray Lane

NEIGHBORHOOD | San Francisco has no shortage of impressive, grand homes, but Macondray Lane is the quintessential hidden garden. Enter under a lovely wooden trellis and proceed down a quiet, cobbled pedestrian lane lined with Edwardian cottages and flowering plants and trees. A flight of steep wooden stairs at the end of the lane leads to Taylor Street—on the way down you can't miss the bay views. If you've read any of Armistead Maupin's *Tales of the City* books, you may find the lane vaguely familiar. It's the thinly disguised setting for parts of the series' action. ✉ *Between Jones and Taylor Sts., and Union and Green Sts., Russian Hill.*

San Francisco Art Institute

COLLEGE | The number-one reason for a visit to this art college is Mexican master Diego Rivera's *The Making of a Fresco Showing the Building of a City* (1931), in the student gallery to your immediate left inside the entrance. Rivera himself is in the fresco—his broad behind is to the viewer—and he's surrounded by his assistants. They in turn are surrounded by a construction scene, laborers, and city notables, such as sculptor Ralph Stackpole and architect Timothy Pflueger. *Making* is one of three San Francisco murals painted by Rivera. The school itself has seen substantial changes on the academic side because of budget issues and the COVID-19 pandemic, but the mural still remains, as does the panoramic view from the courtyard café.

The Walter & McBean Galleries

(☎ *415/749–4563;* ☾ *closed Sun. and Mon.*) exhibit the often provocative works of established artists. ⊠ *800 Chestnut St., Russian Hill* ☎ *415/771–7020* ⊕ *sfai. edu* ⊠ *Galleries free.*

Polk Gulch

Polk Gulch, the microhood surrounding north–south Polk Street, hugs the western edges of Nob Hill and Russian Hill but is nothing like either. It's actually two microhoods: Upper Polk Gulch, fairly classy in its northern section, runs from about Union Street south to California Street; Lower Polk Gulch, the rougher southern part, continues south from California to Geary or so. Polk Gulch was the Castro before the Castro. It was the city's gay neighborhood into the 1970s, hosting San Francisco's first pride parade in 1972 and several festive Halloween extravaganzas.

Restaurants

★ Acquerello

$$$$ | **ITALIAN** | At this true San Francisco dining gem, chef and co-owner Suzette Gresham has elicited plenty of swoons over the years with high-end but soulful Italian cooking that is worth every penny. Her cuttlefish "tagliatelle" is a star of the menu, which features both classic and cutting-edge dishes. **Known for:** sensational prix-fixe dining with a variety of options; city's premier Italian cheese selection; extensive Italian wine list. ⑤ *Average main: $115* ⊠ *1722 Sacramento St., Polk Gulch* ☎ *415/567–5432* ⊕ *www.acquerellosf.com* ⊗ *Closed Sun., Mon. and Tues. No lunch.*

★ Swan Oyster Depot

$$ | **SEAFOOD** | Half fish market and half diner, this small, slim, family-run seafood operation, open since 1912, has no tables, just a narrow marble counter with about 18 stools. Some locals come in to buy perfectly fresh salmon, halibut, crabs, and other seafood to take home; everyone else hops onto one of the rickety stools to enjoy a dozen oysters, other shellfish, or a bowl of clam chowder—the only hot food served. **Known for:** memorable Dungeness crab Louie salad; long lines; payment is cash only. ⑤ *Average main: $26* ⊠ *1517 Polk St., Polk Gulch* ☎ *415/673–1101* ⊕ *swanoysterdepot.us* ⊟ *No credit cards* ⊗ *Closed Sun. No dinner.*

Pacific Heights

Pacific Heights defines San Francisco's most expensive and dramatic real estate. Grand Victorians line the streets, mansions and town houses are priced in the millions, and there are magnificent views from almost any point in the neighborhood. Old money and new, personalities in the limelight and those who prefer absolute media anonymity live here, and few outsiders see anything other than the pleasing facades of Queen Anne charmers, English Tudor imports, and baroque bastions. Nancy Pelosi and Dianne Feinstein, Larry Ellison, and Gordon Getty all own impressive homes here, but not even pockets as deep as those can buy a large garden—space in the city is simply at too much of a premium. Luckily, two of the city's most spectacular parks are located in the area. The boutiques and restaurants along Fillmore Street, which range from glam to funky, are a draw for the whole city as well.

Sights

Haas-Lilienthal House

HOUSE | A small display of photographs on the bottom floor of this elaborate, gray 1886 Queen Anne house makes clear that despite its lofty stature and striking, round third-story tower, the house was modest compared with some of the giants that fell victim to the 1906 earthquake and fire. San Francisco Heritage, a foundation to preserve San Francisco's architectural history, operates the home, whose carefully kept rooms provide a glimpse into late-19th-century life through period furniture, authentic details (like the antique dishes in the kitchen built-in), and photos of the Haas family, who occupied the house for three generations until 1972. ■TIP➔ **You can admire hundreds of gorgeous San Francisco Victorians from the outside, but this is the only one that's open to the public, and it's worth a visit.** You can download free maps of two nearby walking tours highlighting the neighborhood's historic architecture on the house's website. ✉ *2007 Franklin St., Pacific Heights ✣ Between Washington and Jackson Sts.* ☎ *415/441–3000* ⊕ *www.haas-lilienthalhouse.org* 🎫 *Tours $10.*

🍴 Restaurants

★ Octavia

$$$ | **MODERN AMERICAN** | Regardless of the time of year, Melissa Perello's second and more upscale restaurant (Frances is the first) is a perennial favorite for diners seeking out what California cuisine really tastes like. The warm, immaculate dining room is a perfect setting for edgier dishes like the popular chilled squid ink noodles starter, along with more comforting produce-driven small plates and entrées. **Known for:** exciting preparations with peak-of-season produce; spicy deviled egg starter; truly professional service. ⑤ *Average main: $32* ✉ *1701 Octavia St., at Bush St., Lower Pacific Heights* ☎ *415/408-7607* ⊕ *www.octavia-sf.com* ☾ *No lunch.*

Sociale

$$$ | **NORTHERN ITALIAN** | The COVID-19 pandemic's outdoor dining requirement led San Francisco diners to discover the city's premier patios—like the one that regulars have known about for years at this Presidio Heights stalwart, hidden from the street down a little alley, almost like a posh, aboveground speakeasy. Whether you're dining on that patio or in the elegant dining room,

Italian and seasonal Californian cooking mingle together on the menu. **Known for:** fantastic pastas; chocolate oblivion cake for dessert; Barolo and Barbaresco wine choices. ⑤ *Average main: $28* ✉ *3665 Sacramento St., Presidio Heights* ☎ *415/921–3200* ⊕ *sfsociale.com* ☾ *Closed Sun. and Mon.*

🛏 Hotels

★ Hotel Drisco

$$$$ | **HOTEL** | You can pretend you're a denizen of one of San Francisco's wealthiest residential neighborhoods while you stay at this understated, elegant Edwardian hotel built in 1903. **Pros:** gorgeous rooms and public spaces; great service and many amenities; quiet residential neighborhood retreat. **Cons:** not a close walk to restaurants or major sights; room prices are as steep as nearby hill; no complimentary chauffeur service in the afternoon or evening. ⑤ *Rooms from: $499* ✉ *2901 Pacific Ave., Pacific Heights* ☎ *415/346-2880, 800/634-7277* ⊕ *hoteldrisco.com* ⇌ *48 rooms* ❌ *Free breakfast.*

🍸 Nightlife

The Snug

BARS/PUBS | A welcoming yet refined drinking destination, this Lower Pac Heights bar is exactly what the well-heeled and fun-loving neighborhood needed. It's the rare bar that emphasizes clever cocktails, in-high-demand local craft beer, and smartly selected wine in equal parts. Come hungry, as well, because elevated takes on bar bites like yellowtail poke and sesame naan with shiitake mushroom hummus are created by a chef formerly at some of the country's gastronomic heavyweights (Benu, Alinea). ✉ *2301 Fillmore St., Lower Pacific Heights* ⊕ *www.thesnugsf.com.*

Shopping

Browser Books

BOOKS/STATIONERY | FAMILY | Opened in 1976, one of the city's most beloved independent bookstores resides quietly among the chic fashion boutiques lining Fillmore Street. All ages will find ample choices for their next reading material, from contemporary fiction to children's books to a large selection of Buddhist Dharma literature. The store was recently sold to the small, local Green Apple Books group (with two other bookstores in the city), but barely anything has changed at the store with the transition. ⊠ *2195 Fillmore St., Lower Pacific Heights* ☎ *415/567–8027* ⊕ *www. greenapplebooks.com.*

★ Verve Wine

WINE/SPIRITS | Wine nerds will fall in love with this trendy, upscale destination from one of the country's few master sommeliers, Dustin Wilson. Many wine drinkers will also recognize him from the popular 2012 documentary *Somm* (and its sequels). High-quality, smaller producers from prominent and lesser-known regions share wall space in this exceptionally organized boutique. ⊠ *2358 Fillmore St., between Washington St. and Jackson St., Lower Pacific Heights* ☎ *415/896–4935* ⊕ *vervewine.com.*

Japantown

Though still the spiritual center of San Francisco's Japanese American community, Japantown feels somewhat adrift. The Japan Center mall, for instance, comes across as rather sterile, and whereas Chinatown is densely populated and still largely Chinese, Japantown struggles to retain its unique character.

 Sights

Japan Center

STORE/MALL | FAMILY | Cool and curious trinkets, noodle houses and sushi joints, a destination bookstore, and a peek at Japanese culture high and low await at this 5-acre complex designed in 1968 by noted American architect Minoru Yamasaki. The Japan Center includes the shop- and restaurant-filled Kintetsu Mall and Kinokuniya Building; the excellent Kabuki Springs & Spa; the Hotel Kabuki; and the AMC Kabuki reserved-seating cinema/restaurant complex. ⊠ *Bordered by Geary Blvd. and Fillmore, Post, and Laguna Sts., Japantown* ⊕ *www.japan-centersf.com.*

★ Kabuki Springs & Spa

SPA—SIGHT | The serene spa is one Japantown destination that draws locals from all over town, from hipsters to grandmas, Japanese American or not. Balinese urns decorate the communal bath area of this house of tranquility. The extensive service menu includes facials, salt scrubs, and mud and seaweed wraps, in addition to massage. You can take your massage in a private room with a bath or in a curtained-off area. The communal baths ($30) contain hot and cold tubs, a large Japanese-style bath, a sauna, a steam room, and showers. Bang the gong for quiet if your fellow bathers are speaking too loudly. The clothing-optional baths are open for men only on Monday, Thursday, and Saturday; women bathe on Wednesday, Friday, and Sunday. Bathing suits are required on Tuesday, when the baths are coed. Men and women can reserve a private room daily. ⊠ *1750 Geary Blvd., Japantown* ☎ *415/922–6000* ⊕ *kabukisprings.com.*

🍴 Restaurants

Marufuku Ramen

$$ | **RAMEN** | Hakata-style *tonkotsu* (pork) and extra-intense chicken *paitan* ramen are the specialties of this modern-looking Japan Center restaurant that serves what many San Franciscans consider the city's finest bowl of ramen. As a result, long lines can be daunting, but luckily tables move pretty quickly inside the bustling yet relaxed space decorated with wood design elements and dangling Edison bulbs. **Known for:** no reservations, but there's an online wait list; gyoza (pan-fried dumplings) and pork buns to snack on; lively, contemporary vibe. ⑤ *Average main: $18* ✉ *Kinokuniya Bldg., 1581 Webster St., #235, Japantown* ☎ *415/872–9786* ⊕ *www.marufukuramen.com* ⊘ *Closed Mon.*

Sasa

$$ | **SUSHI** | Japantown has a host of sushi options at all price points, but this long-time staple on the second floor of the Japan Center stands out from the crowd for its excellent rolls, nigiri, and sashimi. The *omakase* (selections chosen by the chef) menu, with eight pieces of sushi and nigiri, is a fraction of the cost of its downtown peers, but close to equal in quality and diner satisfaction. **Known for:** "mystery box" mini chirashi (rice and raw fish) bowl; uni spoon with quail egg and ikura (cured salmon roe); an oasis in a busy mall. ⑤ *Average main: $26* ✉ *Japan Center East Mall, 22 Peace Plaza, Suite 530, Japantown* ☎ *628/600–6945* ⊕ *sasasf.com*.

🛍 Shopping

BOOKS

Kinokuniya Bookstore

BOOKS/STATIONERY | FAMILY | The selection of English-language books about Japanese culture—everything from medieval history to origami instructions—is one of the finest in the country. Kinokuniya is also the city's biggest seller of Japanese-language books. Dozens of glossy Asian fashion magazines attract the young and trendy; the manga and anime books and magazines are wildly popular, too. ✉ *Kinokuniya Bldg., 1581 Webster St., at Geary Blvd., Japantown* ☎ *415/567–7625* ⊕ *usa.kinokuniya.com*.

Western Addition

Part of the Western Addition, the Lower Fillmore in its post–World War II heyday was known as the Harlem of the West for its profusion of jazz night spots, where such legends as Billie Holliday, Duke Ellington, and Charlie Parker would play. These days the neighborhood tries to maintain its African American core and its link to that heritage; one success is the annual Fillmore Jazz Festival in June. More live music rings at the Fillmore Auditorium, made famous in the 1960s by Bill Graham and the iconic bands he booked there, and at the blues-centric Boom Boom Room.

👁 Sights

★ Alamo Square Park

CITY PARK | FAMILY | Whether you've seen them on postcards or on the old TV show *Full House*, the colorful "Painted Ladies" Victorian houses are some of San Francisco's world-renowned icons. The signature view of these beauties with the downtown skyline in the background is from the east side of this hilly park. Tourists love the photo opportunities, but locals also adore the park's tennis courts, dog runs, and ample picnic area—with great views, of course. After taking plenty of photos, swing by the park's northwest corner and admire the William Westerfeld House (*1198 Fulton St.*), a splendid five-story late-19th-century Victorian mansion. ■**TIP→ If it's a sunny day, grab picnic provisions from Bi-Rite Market (*550 Divisadero St., at Hayes St.*). On Fridays and weekends, the Lady Falcon Coffee**

Sights ▼

1	Alamo Square Park	**D7**
2	Cathedral of Saint Mary of the Assumption	**G5**
3	Haas-Lilienthal House	**G1**
4	Japan Center	**E4**
5	Kabuki Springs & Spa	**D4**

Restaurants ▼

1	Che Fico	**C7**
2	4505 Burgers & BBQ	**B7**
3	Marufuku Ramen	**E4**
4	Merchant Roots	**D5**
5	The Mill	**C7**
6	Nopa	**C8**
7	Octavia	**F3**
8	SaSa	**E4**
9	Sociale	**A3**
10	State Bird Provisions	**D5**

Hotels ▼

1	Hotel Drisco	**A2**

Club truck is stationed in the park, offering a great caffeine pick-me-up. ⊠ *Western Addition* ✛ *Bordered by Steiner, Hayes, Scott, and Fulton Sts.* ⊕ *sfrecpark.org.*

Cathedral of Saint Mary of the Assumption

RELIGIOUS SITE | Residing at the prominent intersection of two busy thoroughfares (Geary Boulevard and Gough Street), this striking cathedral stands out with its sweeping contemporary design. Italian architects Pietro Belluschi and Pier Luigi Nervi intended to create a spectacular cathedral that reflects both the Catholic faith and modern technology. It was controversial when it opened in 1971, yet now is applauded for its grand, curving roof that rises to a height of 190 feet, with sections that form a cross highlighted with intricate stained-glass work. The cathedral is open daily for visitors other than during Mass, and it usually has docents on duty in the late morning hours. ⊠ *1111 Gough St., at Geary St., Western Addition* ⊕ *smcsf.org.*

Restaurants

Che Fico

$$$ | MODERN ITALIAN | In a city full of Italian restaurants, this consistently popular Divisadero spot on the second floor of a revamped auto body shop sets itself apart with homemade charcuterie, plus antipasti, pastas, and pizza that often take traditional standbys for a creative spin or a California slant from local produce. The clever, beautifully balanced cocktails and fun twists on homey desserts are both must-orders. **Known for:** pineapple pizza; loud space and hard-to-get reservations; Roman Jewish specialties. ⑤ *Average main: $32* ⊠ *838 Divisadero St., Western Addition* ☎ *415/416–6959* ⊕ *www.chefico.com* ⊙ *Closed Sun. and Mon. No lunch.*

4505 Burgers & BBQ

$$ | BARBECUE | FAMILY | The smoker works overtime from noon to night at this hipster-chic barbecue shack, churning out an array of succulent meats that can be had by the plate, the pound, or as a sandwich. Every plate comes with two sides, and you should certainly make the frankaroni one of them: possibly the work of the devil, this is macaroni-and-cheese with pieces of hot dog … deep fried. **Known for:** partially outdoor seating in shipping containers; decadent sides; self-named and possibly correct "Best Damn Cheeseburger". ⑤ *Average main: $20* ⊠ *705 Divisadero St., between Grove and Fulton Sts., Western Addition* ☎ *415/231–6993* ⊕ *www.4505burger-sandbbq.com.*

Merchant Roots

$$$$ | CONTEMPORARY | After starting as part grocer/part lunch café/part tasting menu, this tiny Fillmore spot is now fully devoted to the elaborate tasting menus of chef-owner Ryan Shelton. Themes and dishes change every few months (it could be "flowers" or "Alice in Wonderland"), but the one constant is Shelton's incredible imagination and ability to transform those themes into elaborate, technique-driven composed dishes. **Known for:** SF's best chocolate chip cookies available as a takeout supplement; warm and welcoming ambience; excellent wine program. ⑤ *Average main: $128* ⊠ *1365 Fillmore St., Western Addition* ☎ *530/574–7365* ⊕ *www.merchantroots. com* ⊙ *Closed Sun. and Mon. No lunch.*

★ The Mill

$ | BAKERY BAKERY | "Four-dollar toast" is a phrase used around San Francisco referring to gentrification—and it was inspired by this sun-drenched, Wi-Fi-less café. At this project between one of the city's leading bakers, Josey Baker (yes, that's really his last name and profession!), and the Mission's Four Barrel Coffee, toasts slathered with jam or spreads are the specialty during the day. **Known for:** stellar loaves of bread; precious, post-yoga vibe; one pizza topping served most nights. ⑤ *Average main: $8* ⊠ *736 Divisadero*

St., Western Addition ☎ *415/345–1953* ⊕ *www.themillsf.com.*

★ Nopa

$$$ | AMERICAN | This is the good-food granddaddy of the hot corridor of the same name (it's hard to tell which came first—Nopa the restaurant or NoPa the North of the Panhandle neighborhood). The Cali-rustic fare here draws dependable crowds regardless of the night, with attractions including a beloved Moroccan vegetable tagine; crisp-skin rotisserie chicken; a juicy hamburger with thick-cut fries; and an outstanding weekend brunch. **Known for:** high-quality comforting food with smart twists; actually good food after 11 pm; a constant and diverse crowd. ⑤ *Average main: $28* ⊠ *560 Divisadero St., Western Addition* ☎ *415/864–8643* ⊕ *nopasf.com* ⊘ *No lunch weekdays.*

★ State Bird Provisions

$$ | MODERN AMERICAN | It's more or less impossible to score a reservation for a normal dinner hour at Lower Fillmore's game-changing restaurant, but once you nab a golden ticket, you'll be rewarded with fascinating bites served from roving carts and an à la carte printed menu. The food has an artsy bent to it, and the colorful dining room with pegboard walls adds to a vibe that's part high-school art room, part bohemian dinner party. **Known for:** "State Bird" namesake buttermilk fried quail; long lines at opening time for the no-reservation tables; "World Peace" peanut milk dessert drink. ⑤ *Average main: $26* ⊠ *1529 Fillmore St., Western Addition* ☎ *415/795–1272* ⊕ *www. statebirdsf.com* ⊘ *No lunch.*

Nightlife

Boom Boom Room

MUSIC CLUBS | One of San Francisco's liveliest music spots is this Fillmore blues favorite, opened in 1997 by the "King of the Boogie," John Lee Hooker. The club has a fun blend of blues, funk,

and hip-hop shows most nights of the week. ⊠ *1601 Fillmore St., at Geary Blvd., Western Addition* ☎ *415/673–8000* ⊕ *boomboomroom.com.*

The Fillmore

MUSIC CLUBS | This is *the* club that all the big names, from Coldplay to Clapton, want to play. San Francisco's most famous rock-music hall presents national and local acts: rock, reggae, grunge, jazz, folk, acid house, and more. Go upstairs to view the amazing collection of rock posters lining the walls. At the end of each show, free apples are set near the door, and staffers hand out collectible posters. ■ **TIP→ Avoid steep service charges by purchasing tickets at the club's box office on Sunday from 10 to 4.** ⊠ *1805 Geary Blvd., at Fillmore St., Western Addition* ☎ *415/346–6000* ⊕ *www. thefillmore.com.*

Horsefeather

BARS/PUBS | Creative, produce-driven cocktails and a chic, low-key vibe make this Divisadero drinking destination a locals' frequent top choice for a fun night out. The always interesting (but never too bizarre) cocktails range from a breezy California Cooler with celery juice to the rum-and-whiskey-based Breakfast Punch featuring clarified Cinnamon Toast Crunch–infused milk. Weekend brunch is excellent, as is the delightfully messy double cheeseburger. As an added bonus, the kitchen stays open late nightly. ⊠ *528 Divisadero St., Western Addition* ☎ *415/817–1939* ⊕ *www.horse-featherbar.com.*

North Beach

San Francisco novelist Herbert Gold called North Beach "the longest-running, most glorious, American bohemian operetta outside Greenwich Village." Indeed, to anyone who has spent some time in its eccentric old bars and cafés, North Beach evokes everything from the Barbary Coast days to the no-less-rowdy Beatnik era.

Sights

Beat Museum

MUSEUM | "Museum" might be a stretch for this tiny storefront that's half bookstore, half memorabilia collection. You can see the 1949 Hudson from the movie version of *On the Road* and the shirt Neal Cassady wore while driving Ken Kesey's Merry Prankster bus, "Further." There are also manuscripts, letters, and early editions by Jack Kerouac, Allen Ginsberg, and Lawrence Ferlinghetti; but the true treasure here is the passionate and well-informed staff, which often includes the museum's founder, Jerry Cimino: your short visit may turn into an hours-long trip through the Beat era. ■**TIP→ The excellent Saturday walking tour goes beyond the museum to take in favorite Beat watering holes and hangouts in North Beach.** ⊠ *540 Broadway, North Beach* ☎ *415/399–9626* ⊕ *www.thebeat-museum.org* ⊠ *$8* ⊘ *Closed Tues. and Wed.*

★ City Lights Bookstore

STORE/MALL | The exterior of this famous literary bookstore is iconic in itself, from the replica of a revolutionary mural destroyed in Chiapas, Mexico, by military forces to the art banners hanging above the windows. Designated a landmark by the city, the hangout of Beat-era writers and independent publishers remains a vital part of San Francisco's literary scene. Browse the three levels of poetry, philosophy, politics, fiction, history, and local zines, to the beat of creaking wood floors.

Back in the day, writers like Allen Ginsberg and Jack Kerouac would do their reading here (and even receive mail in the basement). The late poet Lawrence Ferlinghetti, who cofounded City Lights in 1953, cemented its place in history by publishing Ginsberg's *Howl and Other Poems* in 1956. The small volume was ignored in the mainstream … until Ferlinghetti and the bookstore manager were arrested for obscenity and corruption of youth. In the landmark First Amendment trial that followed, the judge exonerated both men. *Howl* went on to become a classic.

Stroll Kerouac Alley, branching off Columbus Avenue next to City Lights, to read the quotes from Ferlinghetti, Maya Angelou, Confucius, John Steinbeck, and the street's namesake embedded in the pavement. ⊠ *261 Columbus Ave., North Beach* ☎ *415/362–8193* ⊕ *www. citylights.com.*

Coit Tower

VIEWPOINT | Among San Francisco's most distinctive skyline sights, this 210-foot tower is often considered a tribute to firefighters because of the donor's special attachment to the local fire company. As the story goes, a young gold rush–era girl, Lillie Hitchcock Coit (known as Miss Lil), was a fervent admirer of her local fire company—so much so that she once deserted a wedding party and chased down the street after her favorite engine, Knickerbocker No. 5, while clad in her bridesmaid finery. When Lillie died in 1929, she left the city $125,000 to "expend in an appropriate manner … to the beauty of San Francisco." You can ride the elevator to the top of the tower to enjoy the 360° view of the Bay Bridge and the Golden Gate Bridge; due north is Alcatraz Island. Most visitors saunter past the 27 fabulous Depression-era murals inside the tower that depict California's economic and political life, but take the time to appreciate the first New Deal art project, supported by taxpayer money. It's also possible to walk up and down (if you're in shape): a highlight is the descent toward the Embarcadero via the **Filbert Steps,** a series of stairways that are a shaded green oasis in the middle of the city. ⊠ *Telegraph Hill Blvd., at Greenwich St. or Lombard St., North Beach* ☎ *415/362–0808* ⊕ *sfrecpark.org* ⊠ *Free; elevator to top $9.*

Grant Avenue

NEIGHBORHOOD | Originally called Calle de la Fundación, Grant Avenue is the oldest street in the city, but it's got plenty of young blood. Here, dusty bars such as the Saloon mix with independent boutiques and odd curio shops, as well as curated gourmet shops such as Italian Slow Food import store Sotto Casa and fancy wine and cheese shop Little Vine. While the street runs from Union Square through Chinatown, North Beach, and beyond, the fun stuff in this neighborhood is jammed into the four blocks from Columbus Avenue north to Filbert Street. ✉ *North Beach.*

★ Telegraph Hill and the Filbert Steps

NEIGHBORHOOD | Residents here have some of the city's best views, as well as the most difficult ascents to their aeries. The hill rises from the east end of Lombard Street to a height of 284 feet and is capped by Coit Tower. If you brave the slope, though, you can be rewarded with a "secret treasure" San Francisco moment. Filbert Street starts up the hill, then becomes the **Filbert Steps** when the going gets too steep. You can cut between the Filbert Steps and another flight, the **Greenwich Steps,** on up to the hilltop. As you climb, you pass some of the city's oldest houses and are surrounded by beautiful, flowering private gardens. In some places the trees grow over the stairs, so it feels like you're walking through a green tunnel; elsewhere, you'll have wide-open views of the bay. The cypress trees that grow on the hill are a favorite roost of local avian celebrities, the wild parrots of Telegraph Hill; you'll hear the cries of the cherry-headed conures if they're nearby. And the telegraphic name? It comes from the hill's status as the first Morse code signal station back in 1853. ✉ *Bordered by Lombard, Filbert, Kearny, and Sansome Sts., North Beach.*

Washington Square

PLAZA | Once the daytime social heart of San Francisco's Italian district, this grassy patch has changed character numerous times over the years. The Beats hung out here in the 1950s, hippies camped out in the 1960s and early '70s, and nowadays you're more likely to see picnickers and residents doing community dance, yoga, or tai chi. You might also see homeless people hanging out on the benches and young locals sunbathing or running their dogs. Lillie Hitchcock Coit, in yet another show of affection for San Francisco's firefighters, donated the statue of two firemen with a rescued child. Camera-toting visitors focus on the Romanesque splendor of **Saints Peter and Paul Church** (Filbert St. side of square), a 1924 building with Disneyesque stone-white towers that are local landmarks. Mass reflects the neighborhood; it's given in English, Italian, and Chinese. ✉ *Bordered by Columbus Ave. and Stockton, Filbert, and Union Sts., North Beach* ⊕ *sfrecpark. org.*

🍴 Restaurants

The Italian Homemade Company

$ | ITALIAN | FAMILY | In Italy, the bastion of fresh pasta is Emilia-Romagna, and a trio of entrepreneurs hailing from the region give respect to its claim to carb fame in a mini-empire of fast-casual pasta eateries, with the one in North Beach as its flagship. Come for treats like slabs of lasagna that fool you into thinking you're caloric loading in Bologna, as well as stuffed ravioli and gnocchi. **Known for:** varieties of piadina (Italian flatbreads with meats, cheeses, and vegetables); mix-and-match pastas and sauces; great quality for the price. ⑤ *Average main: $13* ✉ *716 Columbus Ave., North Beach* ☎ *415/712–8874* ⊕ *italianhomemade.com.*

Tony's Pizza Napoletana

$$ | PIZZA | FAMILY | Repeatedly crowned the World Champion Pizza Maker at the World Pizza Cup in Naples, Tony

North Beach, Fisherman's Wharf, Embarcadero, and Financial District

Sights ▼

1	Alcatraz	F1
2	Beat Museum	F6
3	City Lights Bookstore	F6
4	Coit Tower	F4
5	Exploratorium	I4
6	Ferry Building	J6
7	F-line	C2
8	Grant Avenue	F6
9	Hyde Street Pier	B2
10	Jackson Square Historic District	G6
11	Musée Mécanique	C2
12	Pier 39	E1
13	San Francisco National Maritime Museum	A2
14	San Francisco Railway Museum	J7
15	Telegraph Hill and the Filbert Steps	F4
16	Washington Square	E5

Restaurants ▼

1	Angler	J7
2	Cotogna	G6
3	Gary Danko	B3
4	Hog Island Oyster Company	J6
5	The Italian Homemade Company	D4
6	Perbacco	H7
7	Tony's Pizza Napoletana	E5
8	Tosca Cafe	F6
9	Waterbar	J7
10	Yang Sing	H8

Hotels ▼

1	Argonaut Hotel	B2
2	Columbus Motor Inn	C4
3	Hotel Vitale	J7
4	Hotel Zoe Fisherman's Wharf	D3
5	Le Méridien San Francisco	H7

Gemignani is a carb-friendly legend in the city for his flavorful dough and myriad versions. The multiple gas, electric, and wood-burning ovens in his casual, modern pizzeria turn out many different styles of pies—the famed Neapolitan-style Margherita, but also Sicilian, Roman, and Detroit styles—with salads, antipasti, homemade pastas, and calzone rounding out the menu. **Known for:** Cal-Italia pie with aged balsamic drizzle; vibes like an NYC pizza parlor; slice stand next door if you can't wait. ⑤ *Average main: $26 ⊠ 1570 Stockton St., North Beach ☎ 415/835–9888 ⊕ tonyspizzanapoletana. com.*

Tosca Cafe

$$$$ | ITALIAN | The leather booths and chairs are in high demand at this dark and clubby boho classic from 1919, where well-heeled locals and visitors delight in food that skews to the Cal-Italian genre, meaning local catches and seasonal produce as well as Italian flair in dishes such as halibut crudo and meatballs swimming in red sauce. The dinner menu is prix fixe, and there's a stylish Sunday brunch with choices like polenta pancakes and salt cod hash. **Known for:** Italian cocktails; raw bar and caviar menu; Tuscan fried chicken. ⑤ *Average main: $75 ⊠ 242 Columbus Ave., North Beach ☎ 415/986–9651 ⊕ toscacafesf.com ⊘ No lunch.*

Hotels

Columbus Motor Inn

$ | HOTEL | FAMILY | Close to Chinatown and Fisherman's Wharf, this affordable lodging with basic rooms decked out with oversize pillows, earth-toned bedding, and large flat-screen TVs is a great pick if you brought your family and have a car to park. **Pros:** free parking; affordable rooms deep-cleaned regularly; lively location. **Cons:** lacks amenities; decor is not stylish; street-facing accommodations can be noisy. ⑤ *Rooms from: $120 ⊠ 1075 Columbus Ave., North Beach*

☎ *415/885–1492 ⊕ www.columbusmotorinn.com ⇌ 45 rooms ⚭ No meals.*

Nightlife

Bimbo's 365 Club

MUSIC CLUBS | The plush main room and adjacent lounge of this club, here since 1951, retain a retro vibe perfect for the "Cocktail Nation" programming that keeps the crowds entertained. For a taste of the original San Francisco nightclub scene, you can't beat it. Indie low-fi and pop bands such as Mustache Harbor and Tainted Love have played here. ⊠ *1025 Columbus Ave., at Chestnut St., North Beach ☎ 415/474–0365 ⊕ www. bimbos365club.com.*

Tony Nik's

BARS/PUBS | For a dive bar with old San Francisco soul (considering there are few legends like this left), go no further for a nightcap involving an old-fashioned, martini, or Negroni after a night of pizza crushing or any carb-fueled meal, really. If you can, hang out at the bar with and quickly become acquainted with the charming owner/bartender. Tony Nik's is an icon to local bar history, around since Prohibition and with a lot of the same details intact. ⊠ *1534 Stockton St., North Beach ☎ 415/693–0990.*

★ Vesuvio

BARS/PUBS | If you're hitting only one bar in North Beach, it should be this one. The low-ceilinged second floor of this raucous boho saloon hangout, little altered since its 1960s heyday (when Jack Kerouac frequented the place), is a fine vantage point for watching the colorful Broadway and Columbus Avenue intersection. Another part of Vesuvio's appeal is its diverse clientele, from older neighborhood regulars and young couples to bacchanalian posses. ⊠ *255 Columbus Ave., at Broadway, North Beach ☎ 415/362–3370 ⊕ www.vesuvio.com.*

Thousands of visitors take ferries to Alcatraz each day to walk in the footsteps of the notorious criminals who were held on "The Rock."

Shopping

Knitz and Leather

CLOTHING | Local artisans Julia Relinghaus and Katharina Ernst have been producing one-of-a-kind and custom products of extraordinary craftsmanship for over 30 years. Ernst's bold knitted sweaters and accessories will help you stand out from the crowd, and Relinghaus's exquisite, high-quality leather jackets for men and women are the kind of investment you make for fine leather. ⊠ *1453 Grant Ave., North Beach* ☎ *415/391–3480.*

Fisherman's Wharf

The crack of fresh Dungeness crab, the aroma of sourdough warm from the oven, the cry of the gulls—in some ways you can experience Fisherman's Wharf today as it has been for more than 100 years.

⊙ Sights

★ Hyde Street Pier

MUSEUM | FAMILY | If you want to get to the heart of the Wharf, there's no better place to do it than at this pier. Don't pass up the centerpiece collection of historic vessels, part of the **San Francisco Maritime National Historical Park,** almost all of which can be boarded. The *Balclutha,* an 1886 full-rigged three-masted sailing vessel that's more than 250 feet long, sailed around Cape Horn 17 times. Kids especially love the *Eureka,* a side-wheel passenger and car ferry, for her onboard collection of vintage cars. The *Hercules* is a steam-powered tugboat, and the *C. A. Thayer* is a beautifully restored three-masted schooner.

Across the street from the pier and a museum in itself is the maritime park's **Visitor Center** (*499 Jefferson St., 415/447–5000*), whose fun, large-scale exhibits make it an engaging stop. See a huge First Order Fresnel lighthouse lens and a shipwrecked boat. Then stroll through time in the exhibit "The Waterfront," where you can touch the timber from a gold rush–era ship recovered from below the Financial District, peek into 19th-century storefronts, and see the sails of an Italian fishing vessel. ⊠ *Hyde and Jefferson Sts., Fisherman's Wharf* ☏ *415/561–7100* ⊕ *www.nps.gov/safr* 🎫 *Ships $15 (ticket good for 7 days).*

Musée Mécanique

MUSEUM | FAMILY | Once a staple at Playland at the Beach, San Francisco's early 20th-century amusement park, the antique mechanical contrivances at this time-warp arcade—including peep shows and nickelodeons—make it one of the most worthwhile attractions at the Wharf. Some favorites are the giant and rather creepy "Laffing Sal"; an arm-wrestling machine; the world's only steam-powered motorcycle; and mechanical fortune-telling figures that speak from their curtained boxes. Note the depictions of race that betray the prejudices of the time: stoned Chinese figures in the "Opium-Den" and clown-faced African Americans eating watermelon in the "Mechanical Farm." ■TIP→ **Admission is free, but you'll need quarters to bring the machines to life.** ⊠ *Pier 45, Shed A, Fisherman's Wharf* ☏ *415/346–2000* ⊕ *museemecaniquesf.com* 🎫 *Free.*

Pier 39

STORE/MALL | FAMILY | The city's most popular waterfront attraction draws millions of visitors each year, who come to browse through its shops and concessions hawking every conceivable form of souvenir. The pier can be quite crowded, and the numerous street performers may leave you feeling more harassed than entertained. Arriving early in the morning ensures you a front-row view of the sea lions that bask here, but if you're at Pier 39 to shop, be aware that most stores don't open until 9:30 or 10 (later in winter).

Follow the sound of barking to the northwest side of the pier to view the **sea lions** flopping about the floating docks. During the summer, orange-clad naturalists answer questions and offer fascinating facts about the playful pinnipeds—for example, that most of the animals here are males.

At the **Aquarium of the Bay** (☏ *415/623–5300 or 888/732–3483* ⊕ *www.aquariumofthebay.org* 🎫 *$29.95*), moving walkways transport you through a space surrounded on three sides by water filled with indigenous San Francisco Bay marine life, from fish and plankton to sharks. ⊠ *Beach St., at Embarcadero, Fisherman's Wharf* ⊕ *www.pier39.com.*

San Francisco National Maritime Museum

MUSEUM | FAMILY | You'll feel as if you're out to sea when you step aboard, er, inside this sturdy, ship-shape (literally), Streamline-Moderne structure, dubbed the Bathhouse Building and built in 1939 as part of the New Deal's Works Progress Administration. The first floor of the museum, part of the **San Francisco Maritime National Historical Park,** has stunningly restored undersea dreamscape murals and some of the museum's intricate ship models. The first-floor balcony overlooks the beach and has lovely WPA-era tile designs. ■TIP→ **If you've got young kids in tow, the museum makes a great quick, free stop. Then pick up ice cream at Ghirardelli Square across the street and enjoy it on the beach or next door in Victorian Park, where you can watch the cable cars turn around.** ⊠ *Aquatic Park, foot of Polk St., Fisherman's Wharf* ☏ *415/447–5000* ⊕ *www.nps.gov/safr* 🎫 *Donation suggested.*

🍴 Restaurants

Gary Danko

$$$$ | AMERICAN | This San Francisco classic for prix-fixe dining has earned a legion of fans—and a Michelin star—for its namesake chef's refined and creative seasonal California cooking, displayed in dishes like glazed oysters with Ossetra caviar and juniper-crusted bison. The

banquette-lined rooms, with stunning floral arrangements, are as memorable as the food and impeccable service. **Known for:** tableside cheese cart; soufflé for dessert; reservations are hard to get. $ *Average main: $97* ✉ *800 N. Point St., Fisherman's Wharf* ☎ *415/749–2060* ⊕ *garydanko.com* ⊗ *No lunch* 🏛 *Jacket required.*

🛏 Hotels

★ Argonaut Hotel

$$ | HOTEL | FAMILY | The nautically themed Argonaut's spacious guest rooms have exposed-brick walls, wood-beam ceilings, and best of all, windows that open to the sea air and the sounds of the waterfront; many rooms enjoy Alcatraz and Golden Gate Bridge views. **Pros:** hotel's seafood restaurant is above average for the neighborhood; near Hyde Street cable car; toys for the kids. **Cons:** nautical theme isn't for everyone; cramped public areas; far from crosstown attractions. $ *Rooms from: $269* ✉ *495 Jefferson St., at Hyde St., Fisherman's Wharf* ☎ *415/563–0800, 800/790–1415 reservations* ⊕ *www.argonauthotel.com* ⇌ *252 rooms* ❍ *No meals.*

Hotel Zoe Fisherman's Wharf

$$ | HOTEL | A little removed from the heart of the wharf area craziness, this smart-looking boutique hotel with guest-room interiors inspired by luxury Mediterranean yachts aims for subtle contemporary elegance in the form of lightly stained woods and soft-brown and cream fabrics and walls. **Pros:** cozy feeling; nice desks and sitting areas in rooms; open-air courtyard with firepits. **Cons:** rather congested touristy area; smaller rooms can feel too tight; resort fee catches some guests off guard. $ *Rooms from: $239* ✉ *425 N. Point St., at Mason St., Fisherman's Wharf* ☎ *415/561–1100, 800/648–4626* ⊕ *www.hotelzoesf.com* ⇌ *221 rooms* ❍ *No meals.*

🍸 Nightlife

★ Buena Vista Cafe

BARS/PUBS | At the end of the Hyde Street cable-car line, the Buena Vista packs 'em in for its famous Irish coffee—which, according to owners, was the first served stateside (in 1952). The place oozes nostalgia with its white-jacketed bartenders and timeless atmosphere, drawing devoted locals as well as out-of-towners relaxing after a day of sightseeing. It's narrow and can get crowded, but this spot is a sip of history and provides a fine alternative to the overpriced tourist joints nearby. ✉ *2765 Hyde St., at Beach St., Fisherman's Wharf* ☎ *415/474–5044* ⊕ *www.thebuenavista.com.*

Embarcadero

Stretching from below the Bay Bridge to Fisherman's Wharf, San Francisco's flat, accessible waterfront invites you to get up close and personal with the bay, the picturesque and constant backdrop to this stunning city. For decades the Embarcadero was obscured by a raised freeway and known best for the giant buildings on its piers that further cut off the city from the water. With the freeway gone and a few piers restored for public access, the Embarcadero has been given a new lease on life. Millions of visitors may come through the northern waterfront every year, lured by Fisherman's Wharf and Pier 39, but locals tend to stop short of these, opting instead for the gastronomic pleasures of the Ferry Building or using the palm-tree-lined sidewalks as a jogging route. Between the wharf and South Beach Park, though, you'll find tourists and San Franciscans alike soaking up the sun, walking out over the water on a long pier to see the sailboats, savoring the excellent restaurants and old-time watering holes, and watching the street performers that crowd Embarcadero Plaza on a sunny day—these are the simple joys that make you happy you're in San Francisco, whether for a few days or a lifetime.

★ Alcatraz

JAIL | FAMILY | Thousands of visitors come every day to walk in the footsteps of Alcatraz's notorious criminals. The stories of life and death on "the Rock" may sometimes be exaggerated, but it's almost impossible to resist the chance to wander the cell block that tamed the country's toughest gangsters and saw daring escape attempts. Some infamous inmates included Al "Scarface" Capone, Robert "The Birdman" Stroud, and George "Machine Gun Kelly." The boat ride to the island is brief (15 minutes) but affords beautiful views, and the audio tour is highly recommended. Allow at least three hours for the visit and boat rides combined. Tour options include a regular daytime one, plus a Night Tour and an evening Behind the Scenes Tour.
■TIP→ Booking your tour ahead is absolutely essential to avoid disappointment. ⊠ Pier 33, Embarcadero ☎ 415/981–7625 ⊕ www.nps.gov/alca ⊠ From $41.

★ Exploratorium

MUSEUM | FAMILY | Walking into this fascinating "museum of science, art, and human perception" is like visiting a mad-scientist's laboratory, but one in which most of the exhibits are supersize and you can play with everything. Signature experiential exhibits include the Tinkering Studio and a glass Bay Observatory building, where the exhibits inside help visitors better understand what they see outside. Get an Alice-in-Wonderland feeling in the Distorted Room, where you seem to shrink and grow as you walk across the slanted, checkered floor. In the Shadow Box, a powerful flash freezes an image of your shadow on the wall; jumping is a favorite pose. More than 650 other exhibits focus on sea and insect life, computers, electricity, patterns and light, language, the weather, and more. One surefire hit is the pitch-black, hands-on Tactile Dome ($15 extra; reservations required): crawl through ladders, slides, and tunnels, relying solely on your sense of touch. Don't miss a walk around the outside of the museum afterward for superb views and a lesson about the bay's sediment and water motion in the Bay Windows presentation. ⊠ Piers 15–17, Embarcadero ☎ 415/528–4444 general information, 415/528–4407 Tactile Dome reservations ⊕ www.exploratorium.edu ⊠ $30.

★ Ferry Building

MARKET | The jewel of the Embarcadero, erected in 1896 and now home to an outstanding food marketplace, is topped by a 230-foot clock tower modeled after the campanile of the cathedral in Seville, Spain. On the morning of April 18, 1906, the tower's four clock faces stopped at 5:17—the moment the great earthquake struck—and stayed still for 12 months.

Today San Franciscans flock to the street-level marketplace, stocking up on supplies from local favorites, such as Acme Bread, Blue Bottle Coffee, El Porteño (empanadas), the gluten-free Mariposa Baking Company, and Humphry Slocombe (ice cream). The Slanted Door, the city's beloved high-end Vietnamese restaurant, is the fine dining favorite here, along with Hog Island Oyster Company and the seasonal Californian duo of Bouli Bar and Boulette's Larder. On the plaza side, the outdoor tables at Gott's Roadside offer great people-watching and famous burgers. On Saturday morning the plazas outside the building buzz with an upscale farmers' market. Extending south from the piers north of the building to the Bay Bridge, the waterfront promenade out front is a favorite among joggers and picnickers, with a view of sailboats plying the bay. True to its name, the Ferry Building still serves actual ferries: from its eastern flank they sail to Sausalito, Larkspur, Tiburon, and the East Bay. ⊠ Embarcadero, 1 Ferry Bldg., at foot of Market St.,

Embarcadero ☎ *415/983–8030* ⊕ *www.
ferrybuildingmarketplace.com.*

F-line

**TRANSPORTATION SITE (AIRPORT/BUS/FERRY/
TRAIN)** | The city's system of vintage electric trolleys, the F-line, gives the cable cars a run for their money as a beloved mode of transportation. The beautifully restored streetcars—some dating from the 19th century—run from the Castro District down Market Street to the Embarcadero, then north to Fisherman's Wharf. Each car is unique, restored to the colors of its city of origin, from New Orleans and Philadelphia to Melbourne and Milan. ■**TIP→ Pay with a Clipper card or purchase tickets on board; exact change is required.** ⊠ *San Francisco* ⊕ *www.
streetcar.org* ⊒ *$3.*

San Francisco Railway Museum

MUSEUM | **FAMILY** | A labor of love brought to you by the same vintage-transit enthusiasts responsible for the F-line's revival, this one-room museum and store celebrates the city's streetcars and cable cars with photographs, models, and artifacts. The permanent exhibit includes the replicated end of a streetcar with a working cab—complete with controls and a bell—for kids to explore; the cool, antique Wiley birdcage traffic signal; and models and display cases to view. Right on the F-line track, just across from the Ferry Building, this is a great quick stop. ⊠ *77 Steuart St., Embarcadero* ☎ *415/974–1948* ⊕ *www.streetcar.org/
museum/* ⊒ *Free* ☉ *Closed Mon.*

🍴 Restaurants

Angler

$$$ | **SEAFOOD** | Immaculately fresh seafood and a wood-burning hearth are the centerpieces of this bustling yet luxurious Embarcadero sibling to Saison. The menu descriptions might be brief, but it's really all about the ingredients—whether it's "fresh from the live tank" geoduck (a large Pacific clam) or peak seasonal baby

artichokes—fulfilling their full potential on the plate with a few smart embellishments. **Known for:** taxidermy-filled back room with Bay Bridge views; bigeye tuna tartare; Instagram-favorite radicchio salad. ⑤ *Average main: $36* ⊠ *132 The Embarcadero, Embarcadero* ☎ *415/872–
9442* ⊕ *anglerrestaurants.com/san-fran-
cisco* ☉ *Closed Sun. and Mon. No lunch.*

Hog Island Oyster Company

$$ | **SEAFOOD** | A thriving oyster farm north of San Francisco in Tomales Bay serves up its harvest at this raw bar and restaurant in the Ferry Building, where devotees come for impeccably fresh oysters and clams on the half shell. Other mollusk-centered options include a first-rate seafood stew, grilled oysters, clam chowder, and "steamer" dishes, but the bar also turns out one of the city's best grilled cheese sandwiches, made with three artisanal cheeses on artisanal bread. **Known for:** crowds slurping dozens of oysters; local produce salads; superior Bloody Mary. ⑤ *Average main:
$21* ⊠ *1 Ferry Bldg., Embarcadero at Market St., Embarcadero* ☎ *415/391–7117* ⊕ *hogislandoysters.com.*

Waterbar

$$$$ | **SEAFOOD** | You come for seafood with a view: sky-high aquariums dominate the dining room, and the bay is just beyond, but the biggest attraction is the food. Every fin and shell of the sea, from the oak-roasted Petrale sole to the roasted Sacramento sturgeon, is sustainably sourced. **Known for:** cured fish starters; ample oyster bar; delightful Pat Kuleto–designed interior. ⑤ *Average main:
$38* ⊠ *399 The Embarcadero, between Folsom and Harrison Sts., Embarcadero* ☎ *415/284–9922* ⊕ *www.waterbarsf.com.*

🛏 Hotels

Hotel Vitale

$$$ | **HOTEL** | The emphasis on luxury and upscale relaxation at this eight-story property across the street from the bay is apparent: limestone-lined baths

stocked with top-of-the-line products; the penthouse-level day spa with soaking tubs set in a rooftop bamboo forest; terraces on the fifth, seventh, and eighth floors with great waterfront views. **Pros:** excellent Americano Restaurant & Bar; spacious rooms; well-designed work-from-room setups with ergonomic chairs. **Cons:** not close to much nightlife; steep $40 per day amenities fee adds expense to an already pricey property; yet another charge for Wi-Fi beyond basic. ⑤ *Rooms from: $319* ⊠ *8 Mission St., Embarcadero* ☎ *415/278–3700* ⊕ *www.hotelvitale.com* ⇨ *200 rooms* ⦿ *No meals.*

Nightlife

Hard Water

BARS/PUBS | The waterfront restaurant and bar with a stunning horseshoe-shape bar centerpiece pays homage to America's most iconic spirit—bourbon—with a wall of whiskeys and a lineup of specialty cocktails. The menu, crafted by Charles Phan of Slanted Door fame, is an ode to New Orleans cuisine and includes spicy pork-belly cracklings, BBQ oysters, must-try Nashville hot fried chicken, and other fun snacks. ⊠ *Pier 3, at The Embarcadero, Embarcadero* ☎ *415/392–3021* ⊕ *www.hardwaterbar.com.*

Shopping

FARMERS' MARKETS
★ **Ferry Plaza Farmers' Market**

OUTDOOR/FLEA/GREEN MARKETS | The partylike Saturday edition of the city's most upscale and expensive farmers' market places baked goods, gourmet cheeses, smoked fish, and fancy pots of jam alongside organic basil, specialty mushrooms, heirloom tomatoes, and juicy-ripe locally grown fruit. Smaller markets also take place on Tuesday and Thursday year-round, rain or shine—and the many passionate San Francisco home cooks who frequent them will come even in a rainstorm. ⊠ *Ferry Plaza, at Market St.,*

Embarcadero ☎ *415/291–3276* ⊕ *www. ferrybuildingmarketplace.com.*

Financial District

During the latter half of the 19th century, when San Francisco was a brawling, extravagant gold-rush town, today's Financial District (FiDi, for short) was underwater. Yerba Buena Cove reached all the way up to Montgomery Street, and what's now Jackson Square was the heart of the Barbary Coast, bordering some of the roughest wharves in the world.

These days, Jackson Square is a genteel and upscale neighborhood wedged between North Beach and the Financial District, but buried below Montgomery Street lie remnants of those wild days: more than 100 ships abandoned by frantic crews and passengers caught up in gold fever rest under the foundations of buildings here. The Financial District of the 21st century is a decidedly less exciting affair: it's all office towers with mazes of cubicles now. When the sun sets, this quarter empties out fast. The few sights here will appeal mainly to gold-rush history enthusiasts; others can spend time elsewhere.

Sights

Jackson Square Historic District

NEIGHBORHOOD | This was the heart of the Barbary Coast of the Gay '90s—the 1890s, that is. Although most of the red-light district was destroyed in the fire that followed the 1906 earthquake, the remaining old redbrick buildings, many of them now occupied by advertising agencies, law offices, and antiques firms, retain hints of the romance and rowdiness of San Francisco's early days.

With its gentrified gold rush–era buildings, the 700 block of **Montgomery Street** just barely evokes the Barbary Coast days, but this was a colorful block in the 19th century and on into the 20th. Writers Mark Twain and Bret Harte were among the contributors to the spunky *The Golden Era* newspaper, which occupied No. 732 (now part of the building at No. 744).

Restored 19th-century brick buildings line Hotaling Place, which connects Washington and Jackson Streets, named for the **A. P. Hotaling Company whiskey distillery** (*451 Jackson St., at Hotaling Pl.*), the largest liquor repository on the West Coast in its day. The exceptional Gold Rush City walking tour offered by City Guides (☎ *415/557–4266* ⊕ *www.sfcityguides.org*) covers this area and brings its history to life. ✉ *Bordered by Columbus Ave., Broadway, and Washington and Sansome Sts., Financial District.*

 ## Restaurants

Cotogna

$$$ | ITALIAN | The draw at this urban trattoria—just as in demand as its fancier big sister, Quince, next door—is chef Michael Tusk's flavorful, rustic, seasonally driven Italian cooking, headlined by pastas, beautifully grilled or spit-roasted meats, and homemade gelato. The look is comfortably chic, with wood tables, quality stemware, and fantastic Italian and under-the-radar Californian wines by the bottle and glass. **Known for:** raviolo with brown butter and egg in center; very tough to get prime reservations; peak seasonal produce in antipasti. ⑤ *Average main: $29* ✉ *490 Pacific Ave., Financial District* ☎ *415/775–8508* ⊕ *www.cotognasf.com* ⊗ *Closed Mon. and Tues.*

Perbacco

$$ | ITALIAN | From the complimentary basket of skinny, brittle breadsticks to the pappardelle with short rib *ragù,* chef Staffan Terje's entire menu is a delectable paean to northern Italy. With a long marble bar and open kitchen, this brick-lined two-story space oozes big-city charm, attracting business types and Italian food aficionados alike to the FiDi well after evening rush hour ends. **Known for:** agnolotti del plin (a type of pasta filled with meat); house-made cured meats; vitello tonnato (cold veal with a tuna-flavored sauce) appetizer. ⑤ *Average main: $26* ✉ *230 California St., Financial District* ☎ *415/955–0663* ⊕ *www.perbaccosf.com* ⊗ *Closed Sun.–Tues. No lunch Sat.*

Yank Sing

$$ | CHINESE | FAMILY | This bustling, lunch-only restaurant serves some of San Francisco's best dim sum to office workers on weekdays and boisterous families on weekends, and the take-out counter makes a meal on the run a satisfying compromise when office duties—or sightseeing—won't wait. The several dozen varieties prepared daily include the classic and the creative; steamed pork buns, shrimp dumplings, scallion-skewered prawns tied with bacon, and basil seafood dumplings are among the many delights. **Known for:** Peking duck; Shanghai soup dumplings; energetic vibe in dining room. ⑤ *Average main: $18* ✉ *49 Stevenson St., Financial District* ☎ *415/541–4949* ⊕ *yanksing.com* ⊗ *No dinner.*

Hotels

Le Méridien San Francisco

$ | HOTEL | The stylishly contemporary Le Méridien scores well on both form and function, with compelling artwork throughout the lobby and guest rooms outfitted with polished granite sinks, wall-size San Francisco maps, and floor-to-ceiling windows. **Pros:** spacious rooms; interesting artwork throughout; accommodating staff. **Cons:** this FiDi neighborhood grows sleepy after dark; restaurant and bar merely adequate; not a lot of amenities. ⑤ *Rooms from: $169* ✉ *333 Battery St., Financial District* ☎ *415/296–2900* ⊕ *lemeridiensanfrancisco.com* ⮑ *360 rooms* ⦿ *No meals.*

The Marina

Well-funded postcollegiates and the nou-veau riche flooded the Marina after the 1989 Loma Prieta earthquake had sent many residents running for more-solid ground, changing the tenor of this for-merly low-key neighborhood. The number of yuppie coffee emporiums skyrocketed, a bank became a Williams-Sonoma store, and the local grocer gave way to a Pot-tery Barn. On weekends a young, fairly homogeneous, well-to-do crowd floods the cafés and bars.

Sights

★ Palace of Fine Arts

BUILDING | At first glance this stunning, rosy rococo palace on a lagoon seems to be from another world, and indeed, it's the sole survivor of the many tinted-plaster structures (a temporary neoclassical city of sorts) built for the 1915 Panama-Pacific International Expo-sition, the world's fair that celebrated San Francisco's recovery from the 1906 earthquake and fire. The expo buildings originally extended about a mile along the shore. Bernard Maybeck designed this faux-Roman classic beauty, which was reconstructed in concrete and reopened in 1967. A victim of the elements, the Pal-ace required a piece-by-piece renovation that was completed in 2008.

The pseudo-Latin language adorning the Palace's exterior urns continues to stump scholars. The massive columns (each topped with four "weeping maidens"), great rotunda, and swan-filled lagoon have been used in countless fashion lay-outs, films, and wedding photo shoots. Other than its use for major events and exhibitions inside the building, it's really an outdoor architecture attraction that's perfect for an hour of strolling and relaxing. After admiring the lagoon, look across the street to the house at 3460 Baker Street. If the statues out front look

familiar, they should—they're original casts of the "garland ladies" you can see in the Palace's colonnade. ⊠ *3301 Lyon St., at Beach St., Marina* ☎ *415/886–1296* ⊕ *palaceoffinearts.com* ⊠ *Free.*

Restaurants

A16

$$$ | ITALIAN | Named after a highway that runs through southern Italy, this trattoria specializes in the food from that region, done very, very well. The menu is stocked with pizza and rustic pastas like *maccaronara* with *ragù Napole-tano* (a meat sauce) and house-made salted ricotta, as well as entrées like roasted chicken with caper salsa *verde*. **Known for:** spicy arrabbiata pizza; one of the city's best Italian wine programs; dark chocolate budino tart. Ⓢ *Average main: $36* ⊠ *2355 Chestnut St., Marina* ☎ *415/771–2216* ⊕ *www.a16pizza.com* ⊗ *Closed Mon.*

Causwells

$$ | AMERICAN | There are two personali-ties to Chestnut Street's sleek grown-up diner—the double-stack burger that draws burger hounds from dozens of miles away, and the rest of the honest, spruced-up comfort-food menu. It's a local institution that feels partially like a bistro and partially like a modern tavern, and a place where the buzz from signa-ture mezcal paloma cocktails and deli-cious eats never disappears. **Known for:** house-made ricotta; excellent wine list full of bottles from lesser-known regions; feels like a party even on weeknights. Ⓢ *Average main: $24* ⊠ *2346 Chestnut St., Marina* ☎ *415/447–6081* ⊕ *www. causwells.com* ⊗ *Closed Mon. No lunch Tues.–Thurs.*

Greens

$$$ | VEGETARIAN | Owned and operated by the San Francisco Zen Center, this leg-endary vegetarian restaurant gets some of its fresh produce from the center's organic Green Gulch Farm. Despite the lack of meat, the hearty and often creative dishes—such as root vegetable *biryani* (mixed rice) with tamarind chutney—really satisfy, and floor-to-ceiling windows give diners a sweeping view of the Marina and the Golden Gate Bridge. **Known for:** magnificent wood-heavy decor headlined by a large redwood sculpture; mesquite-grilled tofu entrée; seasonal produce–driven pizzas. $ *Average main: $27 ⊠ Bldg. A, Fort Mason, 2 Marina Blvd., Marina ☎ 415/771–6222 ⊕ greens-restaurant.com ⊗ Closed Mon.*

☲ Nightlife

California Wine Merchant
WINE BARS—NIGHTLIFE | Part cluttered shop, part cozy bar, Chestnut Street's marquee wine destination is a longtime favorite for grabbing a glass or three. Wines featured always come from some of the state's most highly regarded vintners of all sizes and celebrity standings. The neighborhood has many wine bars, but this is where the locals go when the focus is on the wine itself. ⊠ *2113 Chestnut St., Marina ☎ 415/567–0646 ⊕ www. californiawinemerchant.com.*

The Interval
BARS/PUBS | Even many locals don't realize that the Fort Mason Center is home to one of the city's most impressive and scene-free cocktail bars. As part of the Long Now Foundation, a nonprofit devoted to long-term thinking, the bar serves cocktails that reflect the group's approach, finding innovative ways to serve tried-and-true libations. The Navy Gimlet with clarified lime juice is a modern-day San Francisco classic. ⊠ *Fort Mason Center, 2 Marina Blvd., Bldg. A, Marina ☎ 415/496–9187 ⊕ www. theinterval.org.*

Cow Hollow

Between old-money Pacific Heights and the well-heeled, postcollegiate Marina lies comfortably upscale Cow Hollow. The neighborhood's name harks back to the 19th-century dairy farms whose owners eked out a living here despite the fact that there was more sand than grass.

☱ Restaurants

★ Atelier Crenn
$$$$ | MODERN FRENCH | Dinner at the spectacularly inventive flagship of San Francisco's most celebrated chef of the moment, Dominique Crenn, starts with the presentation of a poem. Each course, many of which include produce from Crenn's own Bleu Belle Farm, and some of which have a slight French influence, is described by a line in the poem: the "Hidden beneath the bluffs" might be whole grilled Monterey abalone with a purée of its own liver and a grilled mussel sauce. **Known for:** extraordinary, whimsical tasting menu with fish and seafood but no meat; stellar desserts; hip-elegant atmosphere. $ *Average main: $365 ⊠ 3127 Fillmore St., Cow Hollow ☎ 415/440–0460 ⊕ www.ateliercrenn. com ⊗ Closed Sun. and Mon. No lunch.*

Bar Crenn
$$$ | FRENCH | Dominique Crenn's sumptuous salon decked out with fur-draped bar stools, chandeliers, and lush velvet drapes is really a bar only in name. Yes, there's a bar pouring outstanding wines and it's possible to graze on warm *gougères* (savory cheese puffs) and oysters. **Known for:** Versailles-style furnishings; canelés de Bordeaux (a type of small pastry); fine Champagne. $ *Average main: $36 ⊠ 3131 Fillmore St., Cow Hollow ☎ 415/440–0460 ⊕ www. barcrenn.com ⊗ Closed Sun. and Mon. No lunch.*

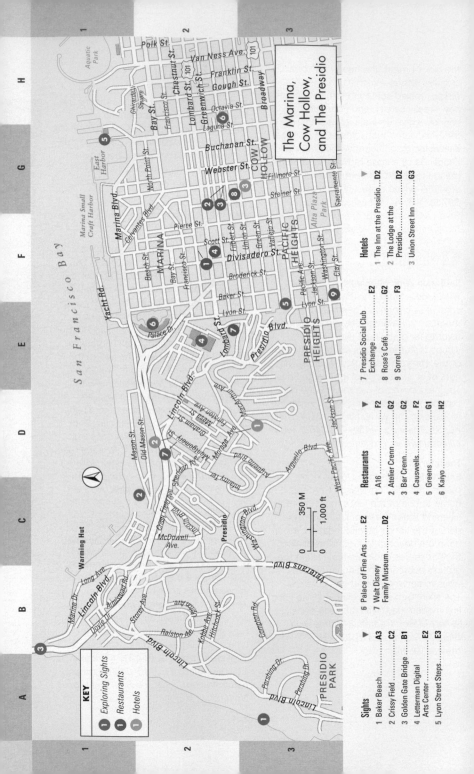

The Marina, Cow Hollow, and The Presidio

KEY
- 1 Exploring Sights
- 1 Restaurants
- 1 Hotels

Sights ▶
1 Baker Beach A3
2 Crissy Field C2
3 Golden Gate Bridge B1
4 Letterman Digital
  Arts Center E2
5 Lyon Street Steps E3
6 Palace of Fine Arts E2
7 Walt Disney
  Family Museum D2

Restaurants ▶
1 A16 .... F2
2 Atelier Crenn G2
3 Bar Crenn G2
4 Causwells F2
5 Greens G1
6 Kaiyo H2
7 Presidio Social Club
  Exchange E2
8 Rose's Café G2
9 Sorrel F3

Hotels ▶
1 The Inn at the Presidio ... D2
2 The Lodge at the
  Presidio D2
3 Union Street Inn G3

0 ─── 350 M
0 ─── 1,000 ft

Kaiyo

$$ | PERUVIAN | San Francisco has a handful of Peruvian restaurants, but this uber-hip Union Street spot is the first "Nikkei" (Japanese-Peruvian) cuisine restaurant for diners to explore. Skip the pedestrian *pollo a la brasa* (rotisserie chicken) and have fun sampling around the *tiraditos* (dishes with raw fish) and sushi rolls. **Known for:** creative pisco cocktails; shrimp tempura and yellowtail Lima roll; no reservations, so lines can be long. $ *Average main: $18* ⊠ *1838 Union St., Cow Hollow* ☎ *415/525–4804* ⊕ *kaiyosf. com* ⊘ *Closed Mon.*

Rose's Café

$$ | AMERICAN | FAMILY | Although it's open morning until night, this cozy café is most synonymous with brunch. Sleepy-headed locals turn up for delights like the smoked ham, fried egg, and Gruyère breakfast sandwich, and evening favorites lean toward roast chicken, pastas, and seasonal-rustic fare. **Known for:** pizzas for the morning and night; house-baked goods; wonderful sidewalk patio. $ *Average main: $25* ⊠ *2298 Union St., Cow Hollow* ☎ *415/775–2200* ⊕ *rosescafesf.com.*

Hotels

★ Union Street Inn

$$ | B&B/INN | Antiques, unique artwork, fine linens, and windows opening to a lovely courtyard or Union Street view make this charming Edwardian inn popular with honeymooners and those looking for a romantic getaway with an English countryside ambience. **Pros:** personal service; afternoon wine and cheese; beautiful secret garden. **Cons:** parking garage is two blocks away; old-fashioned decor not for all tastes; no elevator. $ *Rooms from: $270* ⊠ *2229 Union St., Cow Hollow* ☎ *415/346–0424* ⊕ *unionstreetinn.com* ➦ *6 rooms* ❑ *Free breakfast.*

Nightlife

The Black Horse London Pub

BARS/PUBS | Barely seven stools fit in San Francisco's smallest bar. Plus, there are just as many bottled beers (no taps) as seats, and be sure to bring some cash since credit cards aren't accepted. It's as bare-bones as it gets, but there's sports on TV, a fun dice game, and most important, a neighborhood camaraderie that is increasingly hard to find. ⊠ *1514 Union St., Cow Hollow* ☎ *415/678–5697* ⊕ *www.blackhorselondon.com.*

West Coast Wine & Cheese

WINE BARS—NIGHTLIFE | Whether you're in the mood for a Mendocino County rosé or an Oregon Pinot Noir, as the name suggests, you'll find it at this narrow, sleek locals' favorite. The kitchen isn't much more than a stovetop but does some pretty impressive work beyond cheese and charcuterie. Take advantage of the ability to order half pours and sample more wines. ⊠ *2165 Union St., Cow Hollow* ☎ *415/376–9720* ⊕ *www. westcoastsf.com.*

Shopping

The Caviar Company

FOOD/CANDY | "The Caviar Sisters" Petra and Saskia Bergstein created this sustainability-minded brand that has developed a cult following among caviar connoisseurs and chefs in the Bay Area. Their chic above-street-level boutique on Union Street allows the public to pick out some of the finest caviar products in town—and feel good about it. ⊠ *1954 Union St., Cow Hollow* ☎ *415/580–7986* ⊕ *thecaviarco.com.*

Presidio

At the foot of the Golden Gate Bridge, one of city residents' favorite in-town getaways is the 1,400-plus-acre Presidio, which combines accessible nature-in-the-raw with a window into the past.

Sights

★ Baker Beach

BEACH—SIGHT | FAMILY | West of the Golden Gate Bridge is a mile-long stretch of soft sand beneath steep cliffs, beloved for its spectacular views and laid-back vibe (read: good chance you'll see naked people here on the northernmost end). Its isolated location makes it rarely crowded, but many San Franciscans know that there is no better place to take in the sunset than this beach. Kids love climbing around the old Battery Chamberlin. This is truly one of those places that inspires local pride. **Amenities:** parking (free); toilets. **Best for:** nudists; solitude; sunsets. ⊠ *Baker Beach, Presidio* ✛ *Accessed from Bowley St. off Lincoln Blvd.* ⊕ *www.parksconservancy. org* 🎫 *Free.*

Crissy Field

NATIONAL/STATE PARK | FAMILY | One of the most popular places for San Franciscans to get fresh air is this stretch of restored marshland along the sand of the bay, part of the Golden Gate National Recreation Area. Kids on bikes, folks walking dogs, and joggers share the paved path along the shore, often winding up at the Warming Hut, a combination café and fun gift store at its end, for a hot chocolate in the shadow of the Golden Gate Bridge. Midway along the Golden Gate Promenade that winds along the shore is the Greater Farallones National Marine Sanctuary Visitor Center, where kids can get a close-up view of small sea creatures and learn about the rich ecosystem offshore. Alongside the main green of Crissy Field, several renovated airplane hangars and warehouses are now home to the likes of rock-climbing gyms, an air trampoline park, and a craft brewery (the latter is not open to the public). The Quartermaster Reach Marsh by Crissy Field was reclaimed as wetland ecosystem in 2020 after being asphalt. It nicely connects the Presidio with Crissy Field for pedestrians. ⊠ *1199 E. Beach, Presidio* ✛ *Area north of Mason St. between Baker St. and Marine Dr.* ⊕ *www.presidio.gov/places/ crissy-field.*

★ Golden Gate Bridge

BRIDGE/TUNNEL | Instantly recognizable as an icon of San Francisco, the two reddish-orange towers of the majestic Golden Gate Bridge rise 750 feet over the Golden Gate at the mouth of San Francisco Bay, linking the city and Marin County. Designed in simple but powerful art-deco style and opened in 1937, the 1.7-mile suspension span and the towers were built to handle winds of more than 100 mph. Crossing the bridge under your own power, by foot or bicycle, is exhilarating, a bit scary—and definitely chilly. From the bridge's eastern-side walkway, the panoramic views of the city skyline, Marin Headlands, and Pacific Ocean are magnificent. ⊠ *Lincoln Blvd., near Doyle Dr. and Fort Point, Presidio* ☎ *415/921–5858* ⊕ *www.goldengate.org* 🎫 *Free.*

Letterman Digital Arts Center

LOCAL INTEREST | FAMILY | Bay Area filmmaker George Lucas's 23-acre **Letterman Digital Arts Center,** a digital studio "campus" along the eastern edge of the land, is exquisitely landscaped and largely open to the public. If you have kids in tow or are a *Star Wars* fan yourself, make the pilgrimage to the **Yoda Fountain** (*Letterman Dr. at Dewitt Rd.*), between two of the arts-center buildings, then take your picture with the life-size Darth Vader statue in the lobby, open to the public on weekdays. The center's public restaurant, **Sessions,** is a good stop for a craft beer and some satisfying eats that often include produce or beef from

Lucas's Skywalker Ranch. ✉ *1 Letterman Dr., Presidio* ⊕ *www.presidio.gov/places/letterman-digital-arts-center* ⊗ *Lobby closed weekends.*

Lyon Street Steps

VIEWPOINT | Get ready for a workout—and a spectacularly rewarding view at the top—when tackling the 332 steps at the eastern edge of the Presidio. There will likely be no shortage of exercise seekers bounding up the steps, but feel free to conquer the climb slowly. The trimmed hedge landscaping is worthy of its own visit, but the views of the Presidio forests and the bay are the reason these steps are a top attraction. Equally stunning, though, are the opulent mansions surrounding them. ✉ *2545 Lyon St., Presidio Heights* ✚ *Between Green St. and Broadway* ⊕ *www.nps.gov/places/000/lyon-street-steps.htm.*

Walt Disney Family Museum

MUSEUM | **FAMILY** | This beautifully refurbished brick barracks is a tribute to the man behind Mickey Mouse, the Disney Studios, and Disneyland. The smartly organized displays include hundreds of family photos, and well-chosen videos play throughout. Disney's legendary attention to detail becomes evident in the cels and footage of Fantasia, Sleeping Beauty, and other animation classics. "The Toughest Period in My Whole Life" exhibit sheds light on lesser-known bits of history: the animators' strike at Disney Studios, the films Walt Disney made for the U.S. military during World War II, and his testimony before the U.S. House Un-American Activities Committee during its investigation of Communist influence in Hollywood. The liveliest exhibit, and the largest gallery, documents the creation of Disneyland with a fun, detailed model of what Disney imagined the park would be. Teacups spin, the Matterhorn looms, and that world-famous castle leads the way to Fantasyland. You won't be the first to leave humming "It's a Small World." In the final gallery, titled simply "December 15, 1966," a series of cartoons chronicles the world's reaction to Disney's sudden death. Worth checking for are periodic special exhibitions that take a deep dive into film themes or historical periods surrounding Disney's life. ✉ *Main Post, 104 Montgomery St., off Lincoln Blvd., Presidio* ☎ *415/345–6800* ⊕ *www.waltdisney.org* 🎫 *$25* ⊗ *Closed Mon.–Wed.*

🍴 Restaurants

Presidio Social Club Exchange

$$ | **AMERICAN** | **FAMILY** | American comfort classics meet seasonal California cooking in this restaurant in an old barracks building at the eastern edge of the Presidio. Like the military base/national park itself, the restaurant has a blend of the nostalgic past and the trendy present (spice-fried Cornish game hen; a Thursday prime rib special; shrimp cocktail), as well as a substantial "exchange" shop/takeout café and ample patio seating that allows diners to soak up the Presidio outdoor beauty. **Known for:** East–West chicken soup; French onion burger; barrel-aged cocktails. ⑤ *Average main: $26* ✉ *563 Ruger St., Presidio* ☎ *415/885–1888* ⊕ *www.presidiosocialclub.com* ⊗ *Closed Mon.–Wed. No brunch Thurs.–Fri. No dinner Sun.*

★ Sorrel

$$$ | **MODERN AMERICAN** | After a long run as one of San Francisco's most important dining pop-ups, Alex Hong's refined seasonal Californian cooking can be found in one of San Francisco's most dramatic dining settings, with a skylight and floral arrangements that epitomize California "good life" architecture. That vibe is reflected in dishes like a springtime dry-aged duck with green garlic and kumquat, where Hong beautifully blends contemporary techniques and local ingredients. **Known for:** exemplary pastas; beautifully composed tasting menu; upscale dinner party vibe. ⑤ *Average main: $36* ✉ *3228 Sacramento*

St., Presidio Heights ☎ *415/525–3765* ⊕ *www.sorrelrestaurant.com* ⊘ *Closed Mon. and Tues.*

Hotels

The Inn at the Presidio

$$$ | **B&B/INN** | Built in 1903, this two-story, Georgian revival–style structure once served as officers' quarters but these days is a standout boutique hotel where the rooms and suites have a nice sense of modern refinement and historical touches varying by the room, such as wrought-iron beds, vintage black-and-white photos, and Pendleton blankets. **Pros:** beautifully designed rooms, some with gas fireplaces; peaceful place away from the city's frenetic vibe; evening wine-and-cheese reception by firepits. **Cons:** lack of noise blocking because of old building; 2-night minimum on weekends; challenging to get a taxi/ride-share. ⑤ *Rooms from: $320* ✉ *42 Moraga Ave., Presidio* ☎ *415/800–7356* ⊕ *www. presidiolodging.com* 📧 *26 rooms* ⧓ *Free breakfast.*

★ The Lodge at the Presidio

$$$ | **B&B/INN** | The three-story Lodge occupies former Army barracks, built in the 1890s, and is at the Main Post green's northwestern edge, allowing some rooms to have Golden Gate Bridge views; all rooms are far more upscale and chic than military accommodations, with large flat-screen TVs, well-appointed bathrooms, work stations, and dreamy, custom-made pillow-top mattresses. **Pros:** gorgeous, spacious rooms; charming staff; feels like a vacation from the city but within the city. **Cons:** traffic noise is fairly loud in rooms facing the Golden Gate Bridge; isolated from restaurants and nightlife; similar prices to downtown's more lavish luxury hotels. ⑤ *Rooms from: $320* ✉ *105 Montgomery St., Presidio* ☎ *415/561–1234* ⊕ *www. presidiolodging.com* 📧 *42 rooms* ⧓ *Free breakfast.*

The Richmond

In the mid-19th century, the western section of town just north of Golden Gate Park was known as the Outer Lands, covered in sand dunes and seen fit for cemeteries and little else. Today it's the Richmond, comprised of two distinct neighborhoods: the Inner Richmond, from Arguello Boulevard to about 20th Avenue, and the Outer Richmond, from 20th to the ocean.

Sights

★ Legion of Honor

MUSEUM | Built to commemorate soldiers from California who died in World War I and set atop cliffs overlooking the ocean, the Golden Gate Bridge, and the Marin Headlands, this beautiful Beaux Arts building in Lincoln Park displays an impressive collection of 4,000 years of ancient and European art. A pyramidal glass skylight in the entrance court illuminates the lower-level galleries, which exhibit prints and drawings, European porcelain, and ancient Assyrian, Greek, Roman, and Egyptian art. The 20-plus galleries on the upper level display European art (paintings, sculpture, decorative arts, and tapestries) from the 14th century to the present day. The noteworthy Auguste Rodin collection includes two galleries devoted to the master and a third with works by Rodin and other 19th-century sculptors. An original cast of Rodin's *The Thinker* welcomes you as you walk through the courtyard. Also impressive is the 4,526-pipe Spreckels Organ; live concerts take advantage of the natural sound chamber produced by the building's massive rotunda. As fine as the museum is, the setting and view outshine the collection and also make a trip here worthwhile. ✉ *100 34th Ave., at Clement St., Richmond* ☎ *415/750–3600* ⊕ *legionofhonor.famsf.org* 🎟 *$15, free 1st Tues. of month; free Sat. for Bay Area residents* ⊘ *Closed Mon.*

Armed with only helmets, safety harnesses, and painting equipment, a full-time crew of 38 painters keeps the Golden Gate Bridge clad in International Orange.

★ Lincoln Park

CITY PARK | Although many of the city's green spaces are gentle and welcoming, Lincoln Park is a wild, 275-acre park in the Outer Richmond with windswept cliffs and panoramic views. The **Coastal Trail,** the park's most dramatic one, leads out to **Lands End**; pick it up west of the Legion of Honor (at the end of El Camino del Mar) or from the parking lot at Point Lobos and El Camino del Mar. Time your hike to hit Mile Rock at low tide, and you might catch a glimpse of two wrecked ships peeking up from their watery graves. ⚠ **Be careful if you hike here; landslides are frequent, and people have fallen into the sea by standing too close to the edge of a crumbling bluff top.**

Lincoln Park's 18-hole golf course (⊕ *www.lincolnparkgolfcourse.com)* is on land that in the 19th century was the Golden Gate Cemetery. (When digging has to be done in the park, human bones still occasionally surface.) Next door to the golf course on 33rd Avenue and California Street are the dazzling, mosaic Lincoln Park Steps, which rival the 16th Avenue Steps and the Hidden Garden Steps in the Sunset District. They provide a delightful backdrop for contemplation or an Instagram photo op. ⊠ *Entrance at 34th Ave. at Clement St., Richmond* ⊕ *sfrecpark.org.*

Sutro Baths

LOCAL INTEREST | Along the oceanfront, to the north of the Cliff House, lie the ruins of the once-grand glass-roof Sutro Baths. Today visitors can explore this evocative historical site and listen to the pounding surf. Adolph Sutro, eccentric onetime San Francisco mayor and Cliff House owner, built the bath complex in 1896 so that everyday folks could enjoy the benefits of swimming. Six enormous baths—freshwater and seawater—and more than 500 dressing rooms plus several restaurants covered 3 acres and accommodated 25,000 bathers. Likened to Roman baths in a European glass palace, the baths were for decades a favorite destination of San Franciscans. The complex fell into disuse after World War II, was closed in

Sights ▼

1 California Academy of
  Sciences.................. **G4**

2 Conservatory of
  Flowers **H3**

3 de Young Museum...... **G4**

4 Legion of Honor......... **C1**

5 Lincoln Park **B1**

6 Sutro Baths.............. **A2**

Restaurants ▼

1 Hook Fish Co **B5**

2 Tenglong **H2**

KEY

1 *Exploring Sights*

1 *Restaurants*

The Richmond, The Sunset, and Golden Gate Park

E F G H

1

2

3

4

5

Lake Street

California Street

SEACLIFF

Clement Street

Geary Blvd.

27th Ave. 26th Ave. 25th Ave. 24th Ave. 23rd Ave. 22nd Ave. 21st Ave. 20th Ave. 19th Ave. 18th Ave. 17th Ave. 16th Ave. 15th Ave. 14th Ave. Park Presidio Blvd. Funston Ave. 12th Ave. 11th Ave. 10th Ave. 9th Ave. 8th Ave. 7th Ave. 6th Ave. 5th Ave. 4th Ave. 3rd Ave. 2nd Ave. Arguello Blvd.

Balboa Street

Cabrillo Street

Fulton Street

Crossover Dr.

Marx
Meadow

Lindley
Meadow

Portals of
the Past

Boat
House

J.F. Kennedy Dr.

Stow Lake

Speedway
Meadow

Strawberry
Hill

Golden   Gate   Park

Middle Dr. W.

Crossover Dr.

Japanese
Tea Garden

National AIDS
Memorial
Grove

Shakespeare
Garden

Koret Children's
Quarter

Mallard
Lake

San Francisco
Botanical Garden at
Strybing Arboretum

M.L. King Jr. Dr.

Lincoln Way

Irving St.

29th Ave. 27th Ave. 26th Ave. 25th Ave. 24th Ave. 23rd Ave. 22nd Ave. 20th Ave. 19th Ave. 18th Ave. 17th Ave. 16th Ave. 15th Ave. 14th Ave. Funston Ave. 12th Ave. 11th Ave. 10th Ave. 9th Ave. 8th Ave. 7th Ave. 6th Ave. 5th Ave. 4th Ave. 3rd Ave.

Parnassus Avenue

Judah St.

SUNSET

1952, and burned down (under questionable circumstances) during demolition in 1966. To get here, park in the main Lands End parking lot and walk down toward the ruins by the ocean. ⊠ *1004 Point Lobos Ave., Richmond* ☎ *415/426–5240* ⊕ *www.nps.gov/goga.*

 ## Restaurants

Tenglong

$ | CHINESE | Plenty of locals come to this tidy space known for remarkably friendly service and the dry chicken wings, fried in garlic and roasted red peppers, as well as for thinly sliced Mongolian beef and *dan dan* noodles. Run by two former Hong Kong restaurant owners, it specializes in mostly southern Chinese fare, like Cantonese cuisine, and has a few Sichuan specialties, too. **Known for:** honey-walnut prawns; spicy seafood noodle soup; local hot spot. ⑤ *Average main: $14* ⊠ *208 Clement St., Richmond* ☎ *415/666–3515* ⊕ *www.tenglongchinese.com* ⊙ *Closed Tues.*

The Sunset

Hugging the southern edge of Golden Gate Park and built atop the sand dunes that covered much of western San Francisco into the 19th century, the Sunset is made up of two distinct neighborhoods—the popular Inner Sunset, from Stanyan Street to 19th Avenue, and the foggy Outer Sunset, from 19th to the beach. The Inner Sunset is perhaps the perfect San Francisco "suburb": not too far from the center of things, reachable by public transit, and home to main streets—Irving Street and 9th Avenue just off Golden Gate Park—packed with excellent dining options, with Asian food particularly well represented. Long the domain of surfers and others who love the laid-back beach vibe and the fog, the slow-paced Outer Sunset finds itself newly on the radar of locals, with high-quality cafés and

restaurants and quirky shops springing up along Judah Street between 42nd and 46th avenues. The zoo is the district's main tourist attraction.

 ## Restaurants

★ Hook Fish Co

$ | SEAFOOD | Unpretentious yet undeniably chic, this neighborhood beach shack is famous for its simple, fresh seafood. The menu changes daily depending on the day's catch, so join hungry surfers and locals as they gobble up tacos, burritos, or fish-and-chips; wash your choice down with beer or wine. **Known for:** serves possibly the best fish-and-chips in San Francisco; blackboard oysters and specials; lines can be long, so come early. ⑤ *Average main: $16* ⊠ *4542 Irving St., Sunset* ☎ *415/569–4984* ⊕ *www. hookfishco.com.*

Nightlife

The Riptide

BARS/PUBS | A cozy cabin bar that's the perfect finale for beachgoers, the Riptide is a surfer favorite, but you don't have to own a board to feel at home. You'll find classic beers and good food, all at wallet-friendly prices. There's live music most nights, often country, bluegrass, honky-tonk, and open mic. Many tourists fooled by San Francisco's version of summer end up warming their popsicle toes at the bar's fireplace. Sunday features a bacon Bloody Mary, great for hangovers. ⊠ *3639 Taraval St., Sunset* ☎ *415/681–8433* ⊕ *www.riptidesf.com.*

Golden Gate Park

Jogging, cycling, skating, picnicking, going to a museum, checking out a concert, dozing in the sunshine … Golden Gate Park is the perfect playground for fast-paced types, laid-back dawdlers, and everyone in between.

◉ Sights

★ California Academy of Sciences

MUSEUM | **FAMILY** | With its native plant–covered living roof, retractable ceiling, three-story rain forest, gigantic planetarium, living coral reef, and frolicking penguins, the California Academy of Sciences is one of the city's most spectacular treasures. Dramatically designed by Renzo Piano, it's an eco-friendly, energy-efficient adventure in biodiversity and green architecture. Moving away from a restrictive role as a museum that cataloged natural history, the academy these days is all about sustainability and the future, but the locally beloved dioramas in African Hall remain.

It's best to look at the academy's floor plan to design your visit before you arrive. Here's the quick version: head left from the entrance to the wooden walkway over otherworldly rays in the Philippine Coral Reef, then continue to the Swamp to see Claude, the famous albino alligator. Swing through African Hall and study the penguins, take the elevator up to the living roof, then return to the main floor and get in line to explore the Rainforests of the World. You'll end up below ground in the Amazonian Flooded Rainforest, where you can explore the academy's other aquarium exhibits. The popular adults-only NightLife event, held every Thursday evening, includes after-dark access to all exhibits, as well as special programming and a full bar. ■ **TIP**→ **Considering the hefty price of admission, start early and take advantage of in-and-out privileges to take a break.** ⊠ 55 Music Concourse Dr., Golden Gate Park 🕾 415/379–8000 ⊕ www.calacademy.org 🖭 From $30; free one Sun. per quarter; save $3 if you bike, walk, or take public transit here.

Conservatory of Flowers

GARDEN | **FAMILY** | Whatever you do, be sure to at least drive by the Conservatory of Flowers—it's too darn pretty to miss.

The gorgeous, white-framed 1878 glass structure is topped with a 14-ton glass dome. Stepping inside the giant greenhouse is like taking a quick trip to the rain forest, with its earthy smell and humid warmth. The undeniable highlight is the Aquatic Plants section, where lily pads float and carnivorous plants dine on bugs to the sounds of rushing water.

On the east side of the conservatory (to the right as you face the building), cypress, pine, and redwood trees surround the **Dahlia Garden,** which blooms in summer and fall. Adding to the allure are temporary special exhibits; a recurring holiday-season model-train display punctuated with mini buildings, found objects, and dwarf plants; night blooms; and a butterfly garden that returns periodically. To the west is the **Rhododendron Dell,** which contains 850 varieties, more than any other garden of its kind in the country. It's a favorite local Mother's Day picnic spot. ⊠ 100 John F. Kennedy Dr., at Conservatory Dr., Golden Gate Park 🕾 415/831–2090 ⊕ conservatoryofflowers.org 🖭 $10 Tues.–Thurs., $12 Fri.–Sun., free 1st Tues. of month 🕤 Closed Mon. ⚞ No food, drink, tripods, or strollers are allowed inside.

de Young Museum

MUSEUM | It seems that everyone in town has a strong opinion about the de Young museum: some adore its striking copper facade, while others just hope that the green patina of age will mellow the effect. Most maligned is the 144-foot tower, but the view from its ninth-story observation room, ringed by floor-to-ceiling windows and free to the public, is worth a trip here by itself. The building almost overshadows the de Young's respected collection of American, African, and Oceanic art. The museum also plays host to major international exhibitions; there's often an extra admission charge for these. The annual Bouquets to Art is a fanciful tribute to the museum's collection by notable Bay Area floral designers. On many Friday evenings in the fall, admission is free and the museum hosts fun events, with live music and a wine and beer bar (the café stays open late, too). ⊠ *50 Hagiwara Tea Garden Dr., Golden Gate Park* ☎ *415/750–3600* ⊕ *deyoung.famsf.org* ⊜ *$15, good for same-day admittance to the Legion of Honor; free 1st Tues. of month, free Sat. for Bay Area residents* ⊙ *Closed Mon.*

Nightlife

BARS
Beach Chalet
BARS/PUBS | Renovated in 2021, this restaurant-microbrewery, on the second floor of a historic building filled with 1930s Works Project Administration murals (on the first floor), has a stunning view of the Pacific Ocean. It's open for lunch and dinner, but you may want to time your visit and a drink to coincide with the sunset. ■**TIP**→ **Arrive at least 30 minutes before sunset to beat the dinner crowd.** The house brews are rich and flavorful, and there's a good selection of California wines by the glass. ⊠ *1000 Great Hwy., near John F. Kennedy Dr., Golden Gate Park* ☎ *415/386–8439* ⊕ *www.beachchalet.com.*

The Haight

During the 1960s the siren song of free love, peace, and mind-altering substances lured thousands of young people to the Haight, a neighborhood just east of Golden Gate Park. By 1966 the area had become a hot spot for rock artists, including the Grateful Dead, Jefferson Airplane, and Janis Joplin. Some of the most infamous flower children, including Charles Manson and People's Temple founder Jim Jones, also called the Haight home.

Sights

Haight-Ashbury Intersection
NEIGHBORHOOD | On October 6, 1967, hippies took over the intersection of Haight and Ashbury Streets to proclaim the "Death of Hip." If they thought hip was dead then, they'd find absolute confirmation of it today, what with the only tie-dye in sight on the famed corner being a Ben & Jerry's storefront. ⊠ *Haight.*

Restaurants

Parada 22
$$ | **PUERTO RICAN** | A small, colorful space sandwiched between larger restaurants on either side, Parada 22 serves up heaping plates of home-style Puerto Rican cuisine—think plantains, seafood, and slow-roasted pork. This still being the Haight, there's also plenty of vegetarian fare on offer. **Known for:** delicious yuca fries; marinated meats and vegetables; lunch specials. Ⓢ *Average main: $17* ⊠ *1805 Haight St., near Shrader St., Haight* ☎ *415/750–1111.*

Nightlife

Magnolia Brewing Company
BREWPUBS/BEER GARDENS | Known for its food as much as its beers, Magnolia is a San Francisco institution, thanks in part to its prime location one block away from the famous Haight-Ashbury intersection. Come for the smoked trout croquettes, falafel salad, and famed burgers, or just grab any one of the over a dozen beers on tap, many made right here in the in-house brewery. There is also a second popular location on 3rd Street in the Dogpatch. ⊠ *1398 Haight St., at Masonic St., Haight* ☎ *415/864–7468* ⊕ *magnolia-brewing.com.*

🛍 Shopping

MUSIC
★ Amoeba Music

MUSIC STORES | With well over a million new and used CDs, DVDs, and records at bargain prices, this warehouselike offshoot of the Berkeley original carries titles you likely can't find on Amazon. No niche is ignored—from electronica and hip-hop to jazz and classical—and the stock changes frequently. ■**TIP→ Weekly in-store performances attract large crowds.** ⊠ *1855 Haight St., between Stanyan and Shrader Sts., Haight* ☎ *415/831–1200* ⊕ *www.amoeba.com.*

The Castro

The Castro district—the social, political, and cultural center of San Francisco's thriving gay community— stands at the western end of Market Street. This neighborhood is one of the city's liveliest and most welcoming, especially on weekends. Streets teem with folks out shopping, pushing political causes, heading to art films, and lingering in bars and cafés. It's also one of the city's most expensive neighborhoods to live in, with an influx of tech money exacerbating an identity crisis that's been simmering for a couple of decades.

👁 Sights

★ Castro Theatre

ARTS VENUE | Here's a classic way to join in a beloved Castro tradition: grab some popcorn and catch a flick at this 1,500-seat art-deco theater built in 1922, the grandest of San Francisco's few remaining movie palaces. The neon marquee, which stands at the top of the Castro strip, is the neighborhood's great landmark. The Castro was the fitting host of 2008's red-carpet preview of Gus Van Sant's film *Milk*, starring Sean Penn as openly gay San Francisco supervisor Harvey Milk. The theater's elaborate Spanish baroque interior is fairly well preserved. Before many shows, the theater's pipe organ rises from the orchestra pit and an organist plays pop and movie tunes, usually ending with the Jeanette MacDonald standard "San Francisco" (go ahead, sing along). The crowd can be enthusiastic and vocal, talking back to the screen as loudly as it talks to them. Flicks such as *Who's Afraid of Virginia Woolf?* take on a whole new life, with the assembled beating the actors to the punch and fashioning even snappier comebacks for Elizabeth Taylor. There are often family-friendly sing-alongs to classics like *Mary Poppins*, as well as the occasional niche film festival. ⊠ *429 Castro St., Castro* ☎ *415/621–6120* ⊕ *www.castrotheatre.com* ☎ *$14.*

Harvey Milk Plaza

PLAZA | An 18-foot-long rainbow flag, the symbol of gay pride, flies above this plaza named for the man who electrified the city in 1977 by being elected to its Board of Supervisors as an openly gay candidate. In the early 1970s, Milk's camera store on Castro Street became the center for his campaign to open San Francisco's social and political life to gays and lesbians.

The liberal Milk hadn't served a full year of his term before he and Mayor George Moscone, also a liberal, were shot to death in November 1978 at City Hall. The murderer was a conservative ex-supervisor named Dan White, who had resigned his post and then became enraged when Moscone wouldn't reinstate him. Milk and White had often been at odds on the board. The gay community became infuriated when the "Twinkie defense"—that junk food had led to diminished mental capacity—resulted in only a manslaughter verdict for White. During the so-called White Night Riot of May 21, 1979, gays and their allies stormed City Hall, torching its lobby.

KEY

- ① Exploring Sights
- ① Restaurants
- ① Quick Bites
- ① Hotels
- 🅱️ BART station

The Haight, The Castro, Noe Valley, and The Mission

Milk, who had feared assassination, left behind a tape recording in which he urged the community to continue his work. His legacy is the high visibility of gay people throughout city government; a bust of him was unveiled at City Hall in 2008, and the 2008 film *Milk* gives insight into his life. Keep your visiting expectations in check: sandwiched between SoulCycle and a Muni bus stop, this is more of a historical site than an Instagrammable spot. ⊠ *Southwest corner of Castro and Market Sts., Castro.*

Restaurants

Frances

$$$ | **MODERN AMERICAN** | Still one of the hottest tickets in town, chef Melissa Perello's simple, sublime restaurant is a consummate date-night destination. Perello's seasonal California-French cooking is its own enduring love affair, with menu standouts including the savory *bavette* steak, grilled Sakura pork chop, and *panisse frites*. For dessert, the lumberjack cake is a perennial favorite. **Known for:** lumberjack cake for dessert; neighborhood gem; tough reservation due to intimate size. ⑤ *Average main: $34* ⊠ *3870 17th St., Castro* ☎ *415/621–3870* ⊕ *www.frances-sf.com* ⊙ *Closed Mon. No lunch.*

Performing Arts

FILM

★ Castro Theatre

FILM | A large neon sign marks the exterior of this 1,400-plus-seat art-deco movie palace whose exotic interior transports you back to 1922, when the theater first opened. High-profile festivals present films here, along with classic revivals and foreign flicks. There are a few cult-themed drag shows every month. ■**TIP→** Lines for the Castro's popular sing-along movie musicals often trail down the block. ⊠ *429 Castro St., near Market St., Castro* ☎ *415/621–6120* ⊕ *www. castrotheatre.com.*

Noe Valley

This upscale but relaxed enclave just south of the Castro is among the city's most desirable places to live, with laid-back cafés, kid-friendly restaurants, and comfortable, old-time shops along Church Street and 24th Street, its main thoroughfares. You can also see remnants of Noe Valley's agricultural beginnings: Billy Goat Hill (at Castro and 30th streets), a wild-grass hill often draped in fog and topped by one of the city's best rope-swinging trees, is named for the goats that grazed here right into the 20th century.

Sights

Seward Street Slides

CITY PARK | **FAMILY** | A teenager designed these two long, concrete slides back in 1973, saving this mini park from development. Aimed at older kids and adults rather than little ones, the slides offer a fun, steep ride down, so wear sturdy pants. ⊠ *Seward Mini Park, 30 Seward St., Noe Valley* ⊕ *www.sfrecpark.org* ⊙ *Closed Mon.*

Restaurants

Barney's Gourmet Hamburgers

$ | **AMERICAN** | **FAMILY** | The Noe Valley location of this family-friendly California burger chain offers a cozy indoor-outdoor dining area, the latter really a patio encased in glass windows for watching foot traffic along 24th Street. The ample menu is loaded with fancier versions of diner classics—think the Gastropub burger, with a fried egg and a pretzel bun, or the Maui Waui, with a teriyaki glaze and grilled pineapple. **Known for:** all kinds of fries; vegetarian options; delicious milk shakes. ⑤ *Average main: $14* ⊠ *4138 24th St., near Castro St., Noe Valley* ☎ *415/282–7770* ⊕ *www.barneyshamburgers.com.*

A colorful mosaic mural in the Castro

Mission District

The Mission has a number of distinct personalities: it's the Latino neighborhood, where working-class folks raise their families and where gangs occasionally clash; it's the hipster hood, where tattooed and pierced twenty- and thirtysomethings hold court in the coolest cafés and bars in town; it's a culinary epicenter, with the strongest concentration of destination restaurants and affordable ethnic cuisine; it's the face of gentrification, where high-tech money prices out longtime commercial and residential renters; and it's the artists' quarter, where murals adorn literally blocks of walls long after the artists have moved to cheaper digs. It's also the city's equivalent of the Sunshine State—this neighborhood's always the last to succumb to fog.

Sights

Balmy Alley murals

PUBLIC ART | Mission District artists have transformed the walls of their neighborhood with paintings, and Balmy Alley is one of the best-executed examples. Many murals adorn the one-block alley, with newer ones continually filling in the blank spaces. In 1971, artists began teaming with local children to create a space to promote peace in Central America, community spirit, and (later) AIDS awareness; since then dozens of muralists have added their vibrant works. The alley's longtime popularity has grown exponentially thanks to its Instagram appeal. ⚠ **Be alert here: the 25th Street end of the alley adjoins a somewhat dangerous area.**

Once you're done at Balmy Alley, head a couple blocks west on 24th Street to another prominent alley of murals on Cypress Street (also between 24th and 25th Streets). ✉ *24th St. between and parallel to Harrison and Treat Sts., alley runs south to 25th St., Mission District* ⊕ *balmyalley.org.*

★ Dolores Park

CITY PARK | A two-square-block microcosm of life in the district, Mission Dolores Park is one of San Francisco's liveliest green spaces: dog lovers and their pampered pups congregate, kids play at the extravagant playground, and hipsters hold court, drinking beer and rosé cans on sunny days. (Fair warning: if it's over 70°, the place can get packed like traffic at rush hour for picnic-blanket space.) During the summer, Dolores Park hosts movie nights, performances by the San Francisco Mime Troupe, and any number of pop-up events and impromptu parties. Spend a warm day here—maybe sitting at the top of the park with a view of the city and the Bay Bridge —surrounded by locals and that laid-back, still-abundant San Francisco energy, and you may well find yourself plotting your move to the city. The best views are in the southeast corner, near the historic **golden fire hydrant** that saved the neighborhood after the 1906 earthquake. ⊠ *Between 18th and 20th Sts. and Dolores and Church Sts., Mission District* ⊕ *sfrecpark.org.*

Golden fire hydrant

LOCAL INTEREST | When all the other fire hydrants went dry during the fire that followed the 1906 earthquake, this one kept pumping. Noe Valley and the Mission District were thus spared the devastation wrought elsewhere in the city, which explains the large number of prequake homes here. Every year on April 18th (the anniversary of the quake), folks gather here to share stories about the disaster, and the famous hydrant gets a fresh coat of gold paint. ⊠ *Church and 20th Sts., southeastern corner of intersection, across from Dolores Park, Mission.*

Mission Dolores

RELIGIOUS SITE | Two churches stand side by side here, a newer multidomed basilica and the small adobe **Mission San**

Francisco de Asís, the latter being the city's oldest standing structure along with the Presidio Officers' Club. Completed in 1791, it's the sixth of the 21 California missions founded by Franciscan friars in the 18th and early 19th centuries. Its ceiling depicts original Ohlone Indian basket designs, executed in vegetable dyes. The tiny chapel includes frescoes and a hand-painted wooden altar.

There's a hidden treasure here, too, a mural forgotten and rediscovered: an original 20-by-22-foot mural with images including a dagger-pierced Sacred Heart of Jesus, painted with natural dyes by Native Americans in 1791, was found in 2004 behind the altar. Interesting fact: Mission San Francisco de Asís was founded on June 29, 1776, five days before the Declaration of Independence was signed.

The small museum in the mission complex covers its founding and history, and the pretty cemetery—which appears in Alfred Hitchcock's film *Vertigo*—contains the graves of mid-19th-century European immigrants. The remains of an estimated 5,000 Native Americans who died at the mission lie in unmarked graves. ⊠ *3321 16th St., at Dolores St., Mission District* ☎ *415/621–8203* ⊕ *www.missiondolores. org* ✉ *Suggested donation $7.*

Museum of Craft and Design

MUSEUM | Right at home in this once-industrial neighborhood now bursting with creative energy, this small, four-room space—definitely a quick view—mounts temporary art and design exhibitions. The focus might be sculpture, metalwork, furniture, or jewelry, though it might also be industrial design, architecture, or very on-trend 2020s subjects like data and computer encoding. The beautifully curated shop is a perfect place for unique souvenirs and imagination-spurring items for the home office. ⊠ *2569 3rd St., near 22nd St., Dogpatch* ☎ *415/773–0303* ⊕ *sfmcd.org* ✉ *$10* ☉ *Closed Mon. and Tues.*

Did You Know?

These pastel Victorian homes in Pacific Heights are closer to the original hues sported back in the 1900s. It wasn't until the 1960s that the bold, electric colors now seen around San Francisco gained popularity. Before that, the most typical house paint color was a standard gray.

🍴 Restaurants

★ AL's Place

$$ | **MODERN AMERICAN** | AL is chef Aaron London, and his place is a sunny, whitewashed corner spot that serves Michelin-starred, vegetable-forward cooking. London's menu changes frequently, but some dishes, like yellow eye bean stew and grits with goat's milk curd and seasonal produce, stick around, and the wine list is packed with some of the world's finest, largely under-the-radar small producers. **Known for:** fries with a cult following; inventive, vegetable-heavy menu; wonderful sherry and vermouth cocktails. ⓢ *Average main: $22* ⊠ *1499 Valencia St., Mission* ☎ *415/416–6136* ⊕ *www.alsplacesf.com* ⊗ *Closed Mon. and Tues. No lunch.*

★ Delfina

$$$ | **ITALIAN** | Crowds are a constant fixture at Craig and Annie Stoll's cultishly adored northern Italian spot, where aluminum-topped tables are squeezed into a casual chic interior with hardwood floors, a room-length mirror, and a tile bar that seems to radiate happiness. Deceptively simple, exquisitely flavored dishes include excellent pastas and consistently great roast chicken; the *panna cotta* is best in class. **Known for:** signature spaghetti with plum tomatoes; hard to get reservations; Monterey Bay calamari with white bean salad. ⓢ *Average main: $29* ⊠ *3621 18th St., Mission District* ☎ *415/552–4055* ⊕ *www.delfinasf.com* ⊗ *No lunch.*

★ flour + water

$$ | **MODERN ITALIAN** | This handsome and boisterous hot spot with slate-gray walls, sturdy wooden tables, and a tiny bar is synonymous with pasta and also serves top-notch, blistery thin-crust Neapolitan pizzas, but the grand experience here is the seven-course pasta-tasting menu (extra charge for wine pairings). Pastas on both menus change constantly with the seasons, but the one standby is a meatless Taleggio *scarpinocc* with aged balsamic drizzled over the bow tie–shaped pasta. **Known for:** difficult-to-get reservations; rarely seen pasta shapes; Italian wines from small producers. ⓢ *Average main: $25* ⊠ *2401 Harrison St., Mission District* ☎ *415/826–7000* ⊕ *www.flourandwater.com* ⊗ *No lunch.*

★ Lazy Bear

$$$$ | **MODERN AMERICAN** | There's no end to the buzz around chef David Barzelay's 12-plus-course prix-fixe seasonal and imagination-driven dinners, which might include grilled lamb covered in spring herbs and flowers or delicate San Francisco coast king salmon with English peas and cured roe. An ode to the Western lodge, the high-ceilinged, spacious dining room includes a fireplace, charred wood walls, and wooden rafters. **Known for:** brown bread rolls with butter cultured in-house; sensational friendly yet formal service; dinner-party vibe. ⓢ *Average main: $245* ⊠ *3416 19th St., Mission District* ☎ *415/874–9921* ⊕ *www.lazybearsf. com* ⊗ *Closed Mon. and Tues.*

Mission Chinese Food

$$ | **CHINESE** | While the setting is a bit confusing (the awning still bears the name of its predecessor) and notably informal, the food draws throngs for its bold, cheerfully inauthentic riffs on Chinese cuisine made with quality meats and ingredients, including the fine and super-fiery kung pao pastrami, salt cod fried rice with mackerel confit, and sour chili chicken. Some of the food spikes hot (Chongqing chicken wings), while milder dishes (Westlake rice porridge) are homey and satisfying. **Known for:** thrice-cooked bacon and rice cakes; mapo tofu (tofu in a spicy sauce); party vibe. ⓢ *Average main: $20* ⊠ *2234 Mission St., Mission District* ☎ *415/863–2800* ⊕ *www.missionchinesefood.com.*

SanJalisco

$ | **MEXICAN** | **FAMILY** | This colorful old-time, sun-filled, family-run restaurant has been a neighborhood favorite since 1988, and not only because it serves breakfast all day—though the hearty *chilaquiles* always hits the spot. On weekends, longtime regulars opt for *birria,* a spicy barbecued goat stew, or *menudo,* a tongue-searing soup made from beef tripe, complemented by beer and sangria. **Known for:** huevos "con amor"; soups change based on day of the week; friendly service. $ *Average main: $13* ✉ *901 S. Van Ness Ave., Mission District* ☎ *415/648-8383* ⊕ *www.sanjaliscorestaurant.com.*

Coffee and Quick Bites

★ Tartine Bakery
$ | **BAKERY** | **FAMILY** | Chad Robertson is America's first modern cult baker, and this tiny Mission District outpost is where you'll find his famed loaves of tangy country bread, beloved pastries like croissants and morning buns, and near-constant lines out the door—good luck finding a seat. They're longest in the morning when locals (and plenty of tourists) need a pastry punch to start the day, and later in the afternoon when the famed loaves emerge freshly baked. **Known for:** anything bread-related; chocolate soufflé cake; indecisive guests who want to order everything. $ *Average main: $15* ✉ *600 Guerrero St., at 18th St., Mission District* ☎ *415/487-2600* ⊕ *tartinebakery.com* ⊙ *No dinner.*

Hotels

★ The Parker Guest House
$$ | **B&B/INN** | Two yellow 1909 Edwardian houses enchant travelers wanting an authentic San Francisco experience; dark hallways and steep staircases lead to bright, earth-toned rooms with tiled baths (most with tubs), comfortable sitting areas, and cozy linens. **Pros:** handsomely designed, affordable rooms; close to the Castro and Dolores Park; evening wine social hour. **Cons:** long walk or short car ride from the main Mission nightlife;

economy rooms have private baths in a hallway; standard rooms are a little tight. $ *Rooms from: $229* ✉ *520 Church St., Mission District* ☎ *415/621-3222* ⊕ *www.parkerguesthouse.com* ⇆ *21 rooms* ⊙| *Free breakfast.*

Nightlife

ABV
BARS/PUBS | One of the city's top cocktail bars offers elevated small plates (the burger has a devoted following) late into the night to pair with the excellent cocktail menu, which includes such favorites as a Mumbai Mule featuring saffron vodka. A knowledgeable and friendly staff serves a diverse, energetic crowd that knows their drinks, in a smart modern setting with hard surfaces, bar-stool seating, and a giant mural. The sidewalk tables are popular on sunny days. ■**TIP→ Pay attention to the schedule of the upstairs loft, Over Proof. When open, it's one of the city's best themed cocktail-pairing dinner experiences.** ✉ *3174 16th St., Mission District* ☎ *415/294-1871* ⊕ *www.abvsf.com.*

★ El Rio
BARS/PUBS | A dive bar in the best sense, El Rio has a calendar chock-full of events, from free bands and films to Salsa Sunday (seasonal), all of which keep Mission kids coming back. No matter what day you attend, expect to find a diverse gay and straight crowd enjoying local beers and margaritas. When the weather's warm, the large patio out back is especially popular, and the midday dance parties are *the* place to be. ✉ *3158 Mission St., between César Chavez and Valencia Sts., Mission District* ☎ *415/282-3325* ⊕ *www.elriosf.com.*

Martuni's
BARS/PUBS | A mixed crowd enjoys cocktails in the semi-refined environment of this piano bar where the Castro, the Mission, and Hayes Valley intersect; variations on the martini and different

fruit-flavored lemon drops are a specialty. This is not the place for innovative mixology. In the intimate back room a pianist plays nightly, and patrons take turns boisterously singing show tunes. Martuni's often gets busy after symphony and opera performances—Davies Hall and the Opera House are both within walking distance. ⊠ *4 Valencia St., at Market St., Mission District* ☎ *415/241–0205.*

★ **Zeitgeist**

BARS/PUBS | It's a dive but one of the city's best beer bars—there are almost 50 on tap—and a great place to relax with a cold one or an ever-popular Bloody Mary in the large "garden" (there's not much greenery) on a sunny day. Burgers and brats are available, and if you own a trucker hat, a pair of Vans, and a Pabst Blue Ribbon T-shirt, you'll fit right in. This is one of the city's quintessential experiences, both in terms of bars and of simply having fun. ⊠ *199 Valencia St., at Duboce Ave., Mission District* ☎ *415/255–7505* ⊕ *www.zeitgeistsf.com.*

🛍 Shopping

FURNITURE, HOUSEWARES, AND GIFTS

★ **Paxton Gate**

GIFTS/SOUVENIRS | Elevating gardening to an art, this serene shop offers beautiful earthenware pots, amaryllis and narcissus bulbs, decorative garden items, and coffee-table books, such as a composting book called *Let It Rot!* The collection of taxidermy and preserved bugs provides more unusual gift ideas. A couple storefronts away is too-cute Paxton Gate Curiosities for Kids, jam-packed with retro toys, books, and other stellar finds. ⊠ *824 Valencia St., between 19th and 20th Sts., Mission District* ☎ *415/824–1872* ⊕ *paxtongate.com.*

Potrero Hill

Tucked between two freeways east of the Mission and south of SoMa, warm and sunny Potrero Hill is a laid-back, family-friendly neighborhood that can feel like a place apart from the rest of the city. The longtime music club Bottom of the Hill has always been a draw, but the area is still off the tourist radar.

 Nightlife

Bottom of the Hill

MUSIC CLUBS | This is a great live-music dive—in the best sense of the word—and truly the epicenter of Bay Area indie rock. The club has hosted some great acts over the years, including the Strokes and the Throwing Muses. Rap and hip-hop acts occasionally make it to the stage. ⊠ *1233 17th St., at Missouri St., Potrero Hill* ☎ *415/626–4455* ⊕ *www.bottomofthehill.com.*

Chapter 11

THE BAY AREA

Updated by
Monique Peterson

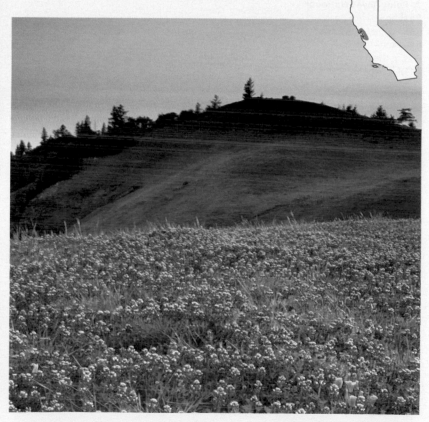

⊙ Sights	🍴 Restaurants	🛏 Hotels	⊖ Shopping	🍸 Nightlife
★★★★☆	★★★★☆	★★☆☆☆	★★☆☆☆	★★★★☆

WELCOME TO THE BAY AREA

TOP REASONS TO GO

★ **Berkeley's culinary mecca:** Eat your way through this area of North Berkeley, starting with a slice of perfect pizza from Cheese Board Pizza (just look for the line).

★ **Point Reyes National Seashore:** Hike beautifully rugged—and often deserted—beaches at one of the most beautiful places on Earth.

★ **Sitting on a dock by the bay:** Admire the beauty of the Bay Area from the rocky, picturesque shores of Sausalito or Tiburon.

★ **"Beer-hopping" in Oakland's hippest hoods:** Spend time discovering the wealth of unique brewers and award-winning craft-beer makers along the Oakland Ale Trail in a city that takes its beer seriously.

★ **Giant redwoods:** Walking into Muir Woods National Monument, a mere 12 miles north of the Golden Gate Bridge, is like entering a cathedral built by God.

1 Berkeley. Independent bookstores, excellent coffee spots, and thousands of cyclists.

2 Oakland. A diverse, multifaceted city with a lively arts, nightlife, and food scene.

3 The Marin Headlands. Stretching from the Golden Gate Bridge to Muir Beach, these headlands offer spectacular vistas.

4 Sausalito. This Marin County city has stunning views and a bohemian feel.

5 Tiburon. Scenic and quaint, this town has good dining and hiking.

6 Mill Valley. A superb natural setting with a bustling downtown area. Nearby are the towering redwoods of Muir Woods National Monument and breathtaking panoramas of the entire Bay Area from Mt. Tamalpais State Park.

7 Muir Beach. The quiet beach here has a distinctly local feel.

8 Stinson Beach. An expansive stretch of beach and a town with a nonchalant surfer vibe.

9 Point Reyes National Seashore. A dramatic and rocky coastline with miles of sandy beaches.

It's rare for a metropolis to compete with its suburbs for visitors, but the view from any of San Francisco's hilltops shows that the Bay Area's temptations extend far beyond the city limits.

MAJOR REGIONS

East of the city are the energetic urban centers of Berkeley and Oakland. Famously radical Berkeley is also comfortably sophisticated, while Oakland has an arts and restaurant scene so hip that it pulls San Franciscans across the bay. To the north is Marin County with its dramatic coastal beauty and chic, affluent villages.

The East Bay. The college town of Berkeley has long been known for its liberal ethos, stimulating university community (and perhaps even more stimulating coffee shops), and activist streak. But these days, the lively restaurant and arts scenes are luring even those who wouldn't be caught dead in Birkenstocks. Meanwhile, life in the diverse, harborfront city of Oakland is strongly defined by a turbulent history. Today, progressive Oakland is an incubator for artisans of all kinds, and the thriving culinary and creative scenes are taking off.

Marin County. Marin is considered the prettiest of the Bay Area counties, primarily because of its wealth of open space. Anchored by water on three sides, the county is mostly parkland, including long stretches of undeveloped coastline along the Marin Headlands, recognizable by the distinguished peak of Mt. Tamalpais. The coastal treasures of Muir Woods National Monument, "Mt. Tam," Stinson and Muir Beaches, and the entire Point Reyes National Seashore are among the country's greatest natural beauties. It's no wonder that the picturesque small towns here—Sausalito, Tiburon, Mill Valley, and Bolinas among them—may sometimes look rustic, but most are home to a dizzyingly high tax bracket.

Planning

When to Go

As with San Francisco, you can visit the rest of the Bay Area any time of year, and it's especially nice in late spring and fall. Unlike San Francisco, though, the surrounding areas are reliably sunny in summer—it gets hotter as you head inland. Even the rainy season has its charms, as otherwise golden hills turn a rich green and wildflowers become plentiful. Precipitation is usually the heaviest between November and March. Berkeley is a university town, so it's easier to navigate the streets and find parking near the university between semesters, but there's also less buzz around town then.

Getting Here and Around

Seamless travel from train to ferry to bus with one fare card is possible—and often preferable to driving on congested freeways and over toll bridges. For trips from one city to the next across the bay, take a tip from locals and save time and money with a Clipper card. They work

with BART, Muni, buses, and ferries.
■**TIP→ Order a Clipper card before you travel:** ⊕ *www.clippercard.com.*

BART

Using public transportation to reach Berkeley or Oakland is ideal. The under- and aboveground BART (Bay Area Rapid Transit) trains make stops in both cities as well as other East Bay destinations. Trips to either take about a half hour one-way from the center of San Francisco. BART does not serve Marin County.
■**TIP→ Check ahead for safety measures and service advisories.**

CONTACTS BART. ☎ *510/465–2278* ⊕ *www.bart.gov.*

BOAT AND FERRY

For sheer romance, nothing beats the ferry; there's service from San Francisco to Sausalito, Tiburon, and Larkspur in Marin County, and to Alameda and Oakland in the East Bay.

The Golden Gate Ferry crosses the bay to Larkspur and Sausalito from San Francisco's Ferry Building (⊠ *Market St. and the Embarcadero*). Blue & Gold Fleet ferries depart daily for Sausalito and Tiburon from Pier 41 at Fisherman's Wharf; weekday commuter ferries leave from the Ferry Building for Tiburon. The trip to either Sausalito or Tiburon takes from 25 minutes to an hour. Purchase tickets from terminal vending machines.

The Angel Island–Tiburon Ferry sails to the island daily from April through October and on weekends the rest of the year. Call ahead to book and to check schedules.

The San Francisco Bay Ferry runs several times daily between San Francisco's Ferry Building or Pier 41 and Oakland's Jack London Square, by way of Alameda. The trip lasts from 25 to 45 minutes and leads to Oakland's waterfront shopping and restaurant district. Purchase tickets on board.

CONTACTS Angel Island–Tiburon Ferry. ☎ *415/435–2131* ⊕ *angelislandferry. com.* **Blue & Gold Fleet.** ☎ *415/705–8200* ⊕ *www.blueandgoldfleet.com.* **Golden Gate Ferry.** ☎ *415/921–5858* ⊕ *www. goldengate.org.* **San Francisco Bay Ferry.** ☎ *707/643–3779, 877/643–3779* ⊕ *sanfranciscobayferry.com.*

BUS

Golden Gate Transit buses travel north to Sausalito, Tiburon, and elsewhere in Marin County from Perry and 3rd Streets and other points in San Francisco. For Mt. Tamalpais State Park and West Marin (Stinson Beach, Bolinas, and Point Reyes Station), take any route to Marin City and then transfer to the West Marin Stagecoach. San Francisco Muni buses primarily serve the city. ■**TIP→ Several other bus options exist for local and regional travel throughout the Bay Area, including Amtrak, Greyhound, California Shuttle, and more (www.bayareatransit.net/regional).**

Though less speedy than BART, more than 30 AC Transit bus lines provide service to and from San Francisco throughout the East Bay, even after BART shuts down. The F and FS lines will get you to Berkeley, while lines C, P, B, and O take you to Oakland and Piedmont. Many lines have been temporarily suspended due to COVID-19, so check ahead. At this writing, face masks are required.

CONTACTS AC Transit. ☎ *510/891–4777* ⊕ *www.actransit.org.* **Golden Gate Transit.** ☎ *511* ⊕ *www.goldengate.org.* **SamTrans.** ☎ *800/660–4287* ⊕ *www.samtrans. com.* **San Francisco Muni.** ☎ *311* ⊕ *www. sfmta.com.* **West Marin Stagecoach.** ☎ *511* ⊕ *marintransit.org/stagecoach.*

CAR

To reach the East Bay from San Francisco, take Interstate 80 East across the San Francisco–Oakland Bay Bridge. For U.C. Berkeley, merge onto Interstate 580 West and take Exit 11 for University Avenue. For Oakland, merge onto Interstate 580 East. To reach downtown Oakland,

11

The Bay Area PLANNING

take Interstate 980 West from Interstate 580 East and exit at 14th Street. Travel time varies depending on traffic but should take about 30 minutes (or more than an hour if it's rush hour).

For all points in Marin, head north on U.S. 101 and cross the Golden Gate Bridge. Sausalito, Tiburon, the Marin Headlands, and Point Reyes National Seashore are all accessed off U.S. 101. The scenic coastal route, Highway 1, also called Shoreline Highway (and briefly, Panoramic Highway) for certain stretches, can be accessed off U.S. 101 as well. Follow this road to Muir Woods, Mt. Tamalpais State Park, Muir Beach, Stinson Beach, and Bolinas. From Bolinas, you can continue north on Highway 1 to Point Reyes.

Restaurants

The Bay Area is home to many popular and innovative restaurants, such as Chez Panisse in Berkeley and Commis in Oakland—for which reservations must be made well in advance. There are also many casual but equally tasty eateries to test out; expect an emphasis on organic seasonal produce, locally raised meats, craft cocktails, and curated wine menus. Marin's dining scene trends toward the sleepy side, so be sure to check hours ahead of time.

Hotels

With a few exceptions, hotels in Berkeley and Oakland tend to be standard-issue, but many Marin hotels package themselves as cozy retreats. Summer in Marin is often booked well in advance, despite weather that can be downright chilly. Check for special packages during this season.

Restaurant and hotel reviews have been shortened. For full information, visit Fodors.com. Restaurant prices are the average cost of a main course at dinner or, if dinner is not served, at lunch. Hotel prices are the lowest cost of a standard double room in high season.

What It Costs			
$	$$	$$$	$$$$
RESTAURANTS			
under $17	$17–$26	$27–$36	over $36
HOTELS			
under $200	$200–$300	$301–$400	over $400

Tours

★ **Best Bay Area Tours**
SPECIAL-INTEREST | FAMILY | Morning and afternoon tours of Muir Woods and Sausalito include at least 90 minutes in the redwoods before heading on to Sausalito. On returning to the city, tours make a scenic stop in the Marin Headlands to enjoy fantastic views. Knowledgeable guides lead small tours in comfortable vans, and hotel pickup is included, though park entrance is not. Another tour option includes a visit to Muir Woods plus Wine Country exploration. ☎ 415/543–8687 ⊕ bestbayareatours. com ✉ From $110.

Berkeley

2 miles northeast of Bay Bridge.

Berkeley is the birthplace of the Free Speech Movement, the radical hub of the 1960s, the home of arguably the nation's top public university, and a frequent site of protests and political movements. The city of 103,000 is also a culturally diverse breeding ground for social trends, a bastion of the counterculture, and an important center for Bay Area writers, artists, and musicians. Berkeley residents, students, and faculty spend hours nursing coffee concoctions while they read, discuss, and debate at the dozens of cafés that surround campus. It's the quintessential university town, with numerous independent bookstores, countless casual eateries, myriad meetups, and thousands of cyclists.

Oakland may have the edge over Berkeley when it comes to ethnic diversity and cutting-edge arts, but unless you're accustomed to sipping hemp-milk lattes while taking in a spontaneous street performance prior to yoga, you'll likely find Berkeley charmingly offbeat.

GETTING HERE AND AROUND

BART is the easiest way to get to Berkeley from San Francisco. Exit at the Downtown Berkeley Station, and walk a block up Center Street to get to the western edge of campus. AC Transit buses F and FS lines stop near the university and Fourth Street shopping. By car, take Interstate 80 East across the Bay Bridge, merge onto Interstate 580 West, and take the University Avenue exit through downtown Berkeley or take the Ashby Avenue exit and turn left on Telegraph Avenue. Once you arrive, explore on foot. Berkeley is very pedestrian-friendly.

TOURS

Edible Excursions

WALKING TOURS | For an unforgettable foodie experience in Berkeley, book a culinary walking tour, maybe one of North Berkeley. Come hungry for knowledge and noshing. Tours take place Thursday, Saturday, and Sunday. The company also offers tours of San Francisco and Oakland. ☎ 415/806–5970 ⊕ www.edibleexcursions.net ☒ From $114.

ESSENTIALS

VISITOR INFORMATION Koret Visitor Center. ☒ 2227 Piedmont Ave., at California Memorial Stadium, Downtown ☎ 510/642–5215 ⊕ visit.berkeley. edu. **Visit Berkeley.** ☒ 2030 Addison St., Suite 102, Downtown ☎ 510/549 7040, 800/847–4823 ⊕ www.visitberkeley.com.

Sights

★ BAMPFA (Berkeley Art Museum and Pacific Film Archive)

MUSEUM | This combined art museum, repertory movie theater, and film archive, known for its extensive collection of some 28,000 works of art and 18,000 films and videos, is now also home to the world's largest collection of African American quilts, thanks to the bequest of art scholar Eli Leon. Artworks span five centuries and include modernist notables Mark Rothko, Jackson Pollock, David Smith, and Hans Hofmann. The Pacific Film Archive includes the largest selection of Japanese films outside Japan and specializes in international films, offering regular screenings, programs, and performances. ☒ 2155 Center St., Downtown ☎ 510/642–0808 ⊕ bampfa.org ☒ $14; free 1st Thurs. of month ♡ Closed Mon. and Tues.

Fourth Street

NEIGHBORHOOD | Once an industrial area, this walkable stretch of Fourth Street north of University Avenue has transformed into the busiest few blocks of refined shopping and eating in Berkeley. A perfect stop for lovers of design, curated taste experiences, artful living, and fashion, the vibrant district boasts more than 70 shops, specialty stores, cafés, and restaurants. See creation and find inspiration at Castle in the Air, Builders Booksource, and Stained Glass Garden, or sip a "live roast" at Artís, where you can watch small-batch coffee roasting in progress—one pound at a time. ☒ 4th St. between University Ave. and Virginia St., 4th Street ⊕ www.fourthstreet.com.

★ Shattuck & Vino Street Neighborhood

NEIGHBORHOOD | The success of Alice Waters's Chez Panisse defined California cuisine and attracted countless food-related enterprises to a stretch of Shattuck Avenue. Foodies will do well here poking around the shops, grabbing a quick bite, or indulging in a feast.

Berkeley

KEY

- b — BART station
- ① Exploring Sights
- ① Restaurants
- ① Quick Bites
- ① Hotels

Sights ▶

1 BAMPFA (Berkeley Art Museum and Pacific Film Archive)...... **F2**
2 Fourth Street...... **C2**
3 Shattuck & Vine Street Neighborhood...... **F1**
4 Tilden Regional Park...... **H1**
5 University of California...... **G2**
6 University of California Botanical Garden...... **H2**

Restaurants ▶

1 Agrodolce Osteria...... **F1**
2 Bette's Oceanview Diner...... **C1**
3 Cheese Board Pizza...... **F1**
4 Chez Panisse Café & Restaurant...... **F1**
5 Comal...... **F2**
6 Gather...... **F2**
7 Gaumenkitzel...... **D1**
8 Ippuku...... **F2**
9 Iyasare...... **C1**
10 La Marcha Tapas Bar...... **D1**
11 La Note...... **F2**
12 Rivoli...... **E1**
13 Saul's...... **F1**

Quick Bites ▶

1 1951 Coffee Company...... **F2**

Hotels ▶

1 Aiden by Best Western @ Berkeley...... **E1**
2 The Bancroft Hotel...... **G2**
3 Berkeley City Club...... **F2**
4 The Graduate Berkeley...... **F2**
5 Hotel Shattuck Plaza...... **F2**
6 Residence Inn by Marriott Berkeley...... **F2**

Tigerlily (✉ *1513 Shattuck*) dishes up authentic modern Indian cuisine along with signature cocktails and light fare on the patio. Neighboring **Epicurious Garden** (✉ *1509–1513 Shattuck*) food stands sell everything from sushi to gelato. A small terraced garden winds up to the **Imperial Tea Court,** a Zen-like teahouse rife with imports and teaware.

Across Vine Street, the **Vintage Berkeley** (✉ *2113 Vine*) wine shop offers regular tastings and reasonably priced bottles within the walls of a historic former pump house. Coffee lovers can head to the original **Peet's Coffee & Tea** at the corner of Walnut and Vine (*2124 Vine*).

South of Cedar Street, **The Local Butcher Shop** (✉ *No. 1600*) sells locally sourced meat and hearty sandwiches of the day. For high-end food at takeout prices, try the salads, sandwiches, and signature potato puffs at **Grégoire,** around the corner on Cedar Street (✉ *No. 2109*). **Masse's Pastries** (✉ *No. 1469 Shattuck*) is a museum of edible artwork. We could go on, but you get the idea. ✉ *Shattuck Ave. between Delaware and Rose Sts., North Berkeley* ⊕ *www.northshattuckas-sociation.org.*

★ **Tilden Regional Park**
NATIONAL/STATE PARK | FAMILY | Stunning bay views, a scaled-down steam train, and a botanic garden with the nation's most complete collection of California plant life are the hallmarks of this 2,077-acre park in the hills just east of the U.C. Berkeley campus. The garden's visitor center offers tours as well as information about Tilden's other attractions, including its picnic spots, Lake Anza swimming site, golf course, and hiking trails (the paved **Nimitz Way,** at Inspiration Point, is a popular hike with wonderful sunset views). ■**TIP**➔ **Children love Tilden's interactive Little Farm and vintage carousel.** ✉ *Tilden Regional Park, 2501 Grizzly Peak Blvd., Tilden Park* ☎ *510/544–2747 park office* ⊕ *www.ebparks.org* ✍ *Free parking and botanic garden.*

University of California
COLLEGE | Known simply as "Cal," the founding campus of California's university system is one of the leading intellectual centers in the United States and a major site for scientific research. Chartered in 1868, the university sits on 178 oak-covered acres split by Strawberry Creek; it's bounded by Bancroft Way to the south, Hearst Avenue to the north, Oxford Street to the west, and Gayley Road to the east. Campus highlights include bustling and historic **Sproul Plaza** (✉ *Bancroft Way and Sather Rd.*), the seven floors and 61-bell carillon of **Sather Tower** (✉ *Campanile Esplanade*), the nearly 3 million artifacts in the **Phoebe A. Hearst Museum of Anthropology** (Kroeber Hall), hands-on **Lawrence Hall of Science** (✉ *1 Centennial Dr.*), the vibrant 34-acre **Botanical Gardens** (✉ *200 Centennial Dr.*), and the historic **Hearst Greek Theatre** (✉ *2001 Gayley Rd.*), the classic outdoor amphitheater designed by John Galen Howard. ✉ *Downtown* ☎ *510/642–6000* ⊕ *www.berkeley.edu.*

University of California Botanical Garden
GARDEN | FAMILY | Thanks to Berkeley's temperate climate, more than 10,000 types of plants from all corners of the world flourish in the 34-acre University of California Botanical Garden. Free garden tours are given regularly with paid admission. Benches and shady picnic tables make this a relaxing place for a snack with a breathtaking view. Call or go online before you travel to reserve your visit. ✉ *200 Centennial Dr., Downtown* ☎ *510/643–2755* ⊕ *www.botanicalgar-den.berkeley.edu* ✍ *$15* ⊘ *Closed 1st Tues. every month*

🍴 Restaurants

Dining in Berkeley may be low-key when it comes to dress, but it's top-of-class in quality, even in less fancy spaces. Late diners beware: Berkeley is an "early to bed" kind of town.

The University of California is the epicenter of Berkeley's energy and activism.

Agrodolce Osteria

$$ | **ITALIAN** | **FAMILY** | Angelo D'Alo's family brings Sicilian flavors and their love for preparing them freshly to the heart of the Shattuck & Vine Street neighborhood, in a setting with black-and-white photos and Italian home decor that add to the old-world atmosphere. The menu features local, sustainable, and organic ingredients in such dishes as housemade orecchiette, seafood risotto, and free-range *pollo allo scarpariello*. **Known for:** oven-roasted heritage pork shoulder; spicy arrabiata; antipasti specialties. ⑤ *Average main: $22* ✉ *1730 Shattuck Ave., North Berkeley* ☎ *510/848–8748* ⊕ *www.agrodolceberkeley.com* ⊗ *Closed Tues. No lunch.*

Bette's Oceanview Diner

$ | **DINER** | **FAMILY** | Checkered floors, vintage burgundy booths, and an old-time jukebox set the scene at this retro-chic diner in the heart of Berkeley's fashionable Fourth Street shopping district. The wait for a seat at breakfast can be quite long; luckily Bette's To Go is always an option. **Known for:** soufflé pancakes; poached egg specialties; meat loaf and gravy. ⑤ *Average main: $13* ✉ *1807 4th St., near Delaware St., 4th Street* ☎ *510/644–3230* ⊕ *bettesdiner.com* ⊗ *No dinner.*

★ Cheese Board Pizza

$ | **PIZZA** | A jazz combo often entertains the line that usually snakes down the block outside Cheese Board Pizza; it's that good. The cooperatively owned vegetarian and vegan takeout spot and restaurant draws devoted customers with the smell of just-baked garlic on the pie of the day. **Known for:** cheese varieties; green sauce; live music. ⑤ *Average main: $12* ✉ *1504–1512 Shattuck Ave., at Vine St., North Berkeley* ☎ *510/549–3183* ⊕ *cheeseboardcollective.coop/pizza* ⊗ *Pizza closed Sun. and Mon., bakery closed Sun.*

★ Chez Panisse Café & Restaurant

$$$$ | **MODERN AMERICAN** | Alice Waters's legendary eatery, the birthplace of California cuisine, first opened its doors on August 28, 1971. It's still known for a

passionate dedication to locally sourced heirloom varieties of fruits and vegetables, heritage breeds, and ethically farmed or foraged ingredients. **Known for:** sustainably sourced meats; attention to detail; simpler fare in upstairs café. ⑤ *Average main: $150* ✉ *1517 Shattuck Ave., at Vine St., North Berkeley* ☎ *510/548–5525 restaurant, 510/548–5049 café* ⊕ *www.chezpanisse.com* ⊘ *Closed Sun. No lunch in restaurant.*

★ Comal

$ | **MODERN MEXICAN** | Relaxed yet trendy, Comal's cavernous indoor dining space and intimate back patio and firepit draw a diverse, decidedly casual crowd for creative Oaxacan-inspired fare and well-crafted cocktails. The modern Mexican menu centers on small dishes that lend themselves to sharing and are offered alongside more than 100 tequilas and mezcals. **Known for:** margaritas and mezcal; house-made chicharróns; wood-fired entrées. ⑤ *Average main: $16* ✉ *2020 Shattuck Ave., near University Ave., Downtown* ☎ *510/926–6300* ⊕ *www.comalberkeley.com* ⊘ *No lunch.*

Gather

$ | **MODERN AMERICAN** | All things local, organic, seasonal, and sustainable reside harmoniously under one roof at Gather. This haven for vegans, vegetarians, and carnivores alike serves up market and grain salads, shareable grilled local vegetables or cheese plates, roast chicken, and more in a vibrant, well-lit space that boasts funky light fixtures, shiny wood furnishings, and banquettes made of recycled leather belts. **Known for:** heirloom varietals; wood-fired pizzas; house-made liqueurs. ⑤ *Average main: $16* ✉ *2200 Oxford St., at Allston Way, Downtown* ☎ *510/809–0400* ⊕ *www.gatherberkeley.com.*

Gaumenkitzel

$$ | **GERMAN** | **FAMILY** | This award-winning, convivial locale for organic, slow-food German fare is also the spot for the Bay Area's best variety of German beers.

With dishes like spätzle and caramelized onions, house-made *brezel* with bratwurst, *jägerschnitzel* with braised red cabbage, and panfried rainbow trout, this kitchen puts a fresh stamp on traditional German favorites. **Known for:** German wine and beer selection; house-made German breads; fresh, sustainable, zero-waste ingredients. ⑤ *Average main: $20* ✉ *2121 San Pablo Ave., Downtown* ☎ *510/647–5016* ⊕ *www.gaumenkitzel. net* ⊘ *Closed Mon.*

★ Ippuku

$$ | **JAPANESE** | More Tokyo street chic than standard sushi house, this *izakaya*—the Japanese equivalent of a bar with appetizers—is decked with bamboo-screen booths. Servers pour an impressive array of sakes and *shōchū* and serve up surprising fare. **Known for:** shōchū selection; charcoal-grilled yakitori skewers; selection of small dishes. ⑤ *Average main: $18* ✉ *2130 Center St., Downtown* ☎ *510/665–1969* ⊕ *ippuku-berkeley.com* ⊘ *Closed Mon. No lunch.*

Iyasare

$$ | **JAPANESE** | Reservations are recommended at this Fourth Street hot spot where the outdoor seating is ideal for people-watching and the Japanese country food is uniquely prepared. Locals come back for seasonally changing, eclectic dishes made with a blend of local ingredients, such as burdock root tempura and tamari-kombu cured salmon or sake-steamed Asari clams with squid-ink pasta. **Known for:** Japanese whiskey and specialty sakes; donburi (rice-bowl dishes) and small plates; cured salads. ⑤ *Average main: $20* ✉ *1830 4th St., 4th Street* ☎ *510/845–0100* ⊕ *iyasare-berkeley.com* ⊘ *Closed Sun. and Mon.*

La Marcha Tapas Bar

$$ | **SPANISH** | Delectable samplings of Spanish cuisine and a lively setting with expanded outdoor seating keep this tapas bar brimming with energy amid savory smells of seafood dishes and small plates of peel-and-eat prawns, wild

Famed Berkeley restaurant Chez Panisse focuses on seasonal local ingredients.

boar meatballs, or goat cheese–stuffed *piquillos rellenos*. The bar's passion for Spanish cuisine and culture is evident in the wines, the Mediterranean flavors, and the cozy setting. **Known for:** paella varieties; happy hour specials; churros con chocolate. $ *Average main: $18* ✉ *2026 San Pablo Ave., Downtown* ☎ *510/647–9525* ⊕ *www.lamarchaberkeley.com.*

★ La Note

$$ | **FRENCH** | A charming taste of Provence in a 19th-century locale with stone floors, country tables, and a seasonal flowering patio, La Note serves rustic French food that is as thoughtfully prepared as the space is lovely. Enjoy breakfast and brunch outdoors with fresh, crusty breads and pastries, eggs Lucas with house-roasted tomatoes, and lemon gingerbread pancakes, or romantic dinners including mussels *mouclade*, ratatouille, and fondue. **Known for:** rustic sandwiches; house-made Merguez sausage; brioche pain perdu. $ *Average main: $20* ✉ *2377 Shattuck Ave., Downtown* ✛ *Between Channing Way and Durant Ave.* ☎ *510/843–1525* ⊕ *www.lanoterestaurant.com* ⊗ *No dinner Sun.–Wed.*

Rivoli

$$$ | **MODERN AMERICAN** | Italian-inspired dishes using fresh California ingredients star on a menu that changes regularly. Inventive offerings are served in a Zen-like modern dining room with captivating views of the lovely back garden. **Known for:** line-caught fish and sustainably sourced meats; curated wine list and specialty cocktails; thoughtfully combined ingredients. $ *Average main: $30* ✉ *1539 Solano Ave., at Neilson St., North Berkeley* ☎ *510/526–2542* ⊕ *www.rivolirestaurant.com* ⊗ *Closed Mon. and Tues. No lunch.*

★ Saul's

$ | **AMERICAN** | **FAMILY** | High ceilings and red-leather booths add to the friendly, retro atmosphere of Saul's deli, a Berkeley institution that is well known for its house-made celery tonic sodas and enormous sandwiches made with Acme bread. Locals swear by the pastrami Reubens, stuffed-cabbage rolls, and challah French toast. **Known for:** hand-rolled organic bagels; chicken schnitzel; corned beef brisket. $ *Average main: $14 ✉ 1475 Shattuck Ave., near Vine St., North Berkeley* ☎ *510/848–3354* ⊕ *www. saulsdeli.com.*

Coffee and Quick Bites

★ 1951 Coffee Company

$ | **CAFÉ** | Taking its name from the 1951 Refugee Convention at which the United Nations first set guidelines for refugee protections, 1951 Coffee Company is a nonprofit coffee shop inspired and pow-ered by refugees. In addition to crafting high-caliber coffee drinks and dishing out local pastries and savory bites, the color-ful café also serves as an inspiring advo-cacy space and barista training center for refugees. Just three blocks south of campus, this community hub is a favorite meetup spot for locals and students alike. **Known for:** hand-roasted blends; Third Culture Bakery mochi doughnuts and muffins; matcha lattes. $ *Average main: $8 ✉ 2410 Channing Way, at Dana St., Downtown* ☎ *510/280–6171* ⊕ *www.1951coffee.com* ☻ *No dinner.*

Hotels

For inexpensive lodging, investigate University Avenue, west of campus. The area can be noisy, congested, and somewhat dilapidated, but it does include a few decent motels and chain properties. All Berkeley lodgings are strictly mid-range.

Aiden by Best Western @ Berkeley

$ | **HOTEL** | One of Berkeley's newest hotels, the Aiden is the first of Best Western's boutique lines to open in California; within a mile of campus and the heart of downtown, it celebrates the culture of Berkeley with posters and wall art that showcase the campus life and spirit the town is known for. **Pros:** private parking; rooftop terrace with firepits and San Francisco Bay views; free bikes. **Cons:** no pets; no capacity for cribs or extra beds; congested area. $ *Rooms from: $189 ✉ 1499 University Ave., Downtown* ☎ *800/528–1234 toll-free* ⊕ *www.bestwestern.com* ☞ *39 rooms* ⦿ *No meals.*

The Bancroft Hotel

$$ | **HOTEL** | This eco-friendly boutique hotel—across from the U.C. campus—is quaint, charming, and completely green. **Pros:** closest hotel in Berkeley to U.C. campus; friendly staff; many rooms have good views. **Cons:** some rooms are quite small; despite renovation, the building shows its age with thin walls; no eleva-tor. $ *Rooms from: $230 ✉ 2680 Ban-croft Way, Downtown* ☎ *510/549–1000, 800/549–1002* ⊕ *bancrofthotel.com* ☞ *22 rooms* ⦿ *Free breakfast.*

★ Berkeley City Club

$$ | **HOTEL** | Moorish design and Gothic architecture join with modern amen-ities at this historic locale steps from the campus, arts venues, and eateries. **Pros:** art gallery and courtyard seating; laundry facilities; on-site salon and skin care. **Cons:** no nonservice pets allowed; limited, fee-only parking; no televisions in rooms. $ *Rooms from: $245 ✉ 2315 Durant Ave., Downtown* ☎ ⊕ *www. berkeleycityclub.com* ☞ *38 rooms* ⦿ *Free breakfast.*

The Graduate Berkeley

$ | **HOTEL** | Fresh, colorful design and Bohemian flair set the tone at this hotel in one of Berkeley's registered historic places, just steps from campus and downtown eating, shopping, and entertainment. **Pros:** convenient location; pet-friendly; complimentary bikes. **Cons:** rooms can be noisy; rooms can be small; fee parking only. $ *Rooms from: $159 ✉ 2600 Durant Ave., Downtown* ☎ *510/845–8981* ⊕ *www.graduatehotels. com/berkeley* ☞ *144 rooms* ⦿ *No meals.*

★ Hotel Shattuck Plaza

$ | **HOTEL** | This historic boutique hotel sits amid Berkeley's downtown arts district, just steps from the U.C. campus and a short walk from North Berkeley's best bites. **Pros:** central location near public transit; special date night and B&B packages; modern facilities. **Cons:** public and street parking only; limited on-site fitness center; street-facing rooms may be noisy. ⑤ *Rooms from: $173* ✉ *2086 Allston Way, at Shattuck Ave., Downtown* ☎ *510/845–7300* ⊕ *www.hotelshattuck-plaza.com* ⇨ *199 rooms* ⑩ *No meals.*

Residence Inn by Marriott Berkeley

$$$ | **HOTEL** | **FAMILY** | One of Berkeley's newest hotels (planned opening is September 2021), in the heart of the city's arts and cultural district, this Residence Inn reflects the community's dedication to green living, as evident in its Gold LEED certification, use of recycled materials, organic design, and vibrant art that celebrates the city and campus life. **Pros:** views from bar and terrace on 12th floor; steps from campus, arts, fine dining, and sights; state-of-the-art technology. **Cons:** no swimming pool; no free parking; traffic gets very congested in the area. ⑤ *Rooms from: $301* ✉ *2121 Center St., Downtown* ☎ *510/982–2100* ⊕ *www.marriott.com* ⇨ *331 suites* ⑩ *Free breakfast.*

🍸 Nightlife

★ The Freight & Salvage Coffeehouse

MUSIC CLUBS | Since 1968, the Freight has been a venue for some of the world's finest practitioners of folk, jazz, gospel, blues, world-beat, bluegrass, and storytelling. The nonprofit organization grew from an 87-seat coffee house to a thriving, 500-seat venue in the heart of Berkeley's Arts District. Many tickets cost less than $30. ✉ *2020 Addison St., between Shattuck Ave. and Milvia St., Downtown* ☎ *510/644–2020* ⊕ *thefreight.org.*

★ Tupper & Reed

BARS/PUBS | Housed in the former music shop of John C. Tupper and Lawrence Reed, this music-inspired cocktail haven presents a symphony of carefully crafted libations, which are mixed with live music performed by local musicians. The historic 1925 building features a balcony bar, cozy nooks, antique fixtures, a pool table, and romantic fireplaces. ✉ *2271 Shattuck Ave., at Kitteredge St., Downtown* ☎ *510/859–4472* ⊕ *www.tupperandreed.com.*

 ## Performing Arts

Aurora Theatre Company

ARTS CENTERS | Known for critically acclaimed productions like David Mamet's *American Buffalo* and Toni Morrison's *The Bluest Eye*, the Aurora is at the heart of Berkeley storytelling and community engagement. The theater's Alafi Auditorium seats 150 on three sides of the stage for premium viewing, and the smaller Harry's UpStage offers a more intimate experience for 49. New play development and storytelling continue beyond the stage with collaborative audio dramas broadcast weekly. ✉ *2081 Addison St., Downtown* ☎ *510/843–4822* ⊕ *www.auroratheatre.org.*

Berkeley Repertory Theatre

THEATER | One of the region's most highly respected and innovative repertory theaters, Berkeley Rep performs the work of classic and contemporary playwrights. Well-known pieces mix with world premieres and edgier fare, like steamy Afro-jazz musicals. The theater's complex, which includes the 400-seat Peet's Theatre and the 600-seat Roda Theatre, is in the heart of downtown Berkeley's arts district, near BART's Downtown Berkeley station. ✉ *2025 Addison St., near Shattuck Ave., Downtown* ☎ *510/647–2949* ⊕ *www.berkeleyrep.org.*

★ California Jazz Conservatory

MUSIC | What started as a music education program in 1977, offering classes with the Bay Area's best jazz players, has become the area's top concert venue for the freshest sounds in jazz from around the world. Two 100-seat performance venues across the street from each other, Hardymon Hall (*2087 Addison St.*) and Rendon Hall (*2040 Addison St.*), offer intimate viewing of some of the world's most influential musicians. Classes and workshops continue to serve as the foundation of the conservatory, with regular, affordably priced weekend concerts and weekly performances for the public. ⊠ *2087 Addison St., Downtown* ☎ *510/845–5373* ⊕ *cjc.edu.*

Cal Performances

ARTS CENTERS | Based out of U.C. Berkeley, this autumn and spring series runs from September/October through May/June. It features a varied bill of internationally acclaimed artists ranging from classical soloists to the latest jazz, world-music, theater, and dance ensembles. ⊠ *101 Zellerbach Hall , Suite 4800, Downtown* ⊹ *Dana St. and Bancroft Way* ☎ *510/642–9988* ⊕ *calperformances.org.*

The UC Theatre Taube Family Music Hall

MUSIC | One of Berkeley's oldest theaters opened its doors in 1917 as a first-run movie house with seating for 1,466 filmgoers. For years it served as a famous venue for foreign and domestic classics, closing in 2001. The theater's programming and ongoing renovation are now run by the nonprofit Berkeley Music Group, dedicated to bringing local, national, and international talent to Berkeley's arts district. Limited outdoor drinks and dining are available at the street bar, Out Front at the UC. ⊠ *2036 University Ave., Downtown* ☎ *510/356–4000* ⊕ *theuctheatre. org.*

🛍 Shopping

★ ACCI Gallery

ART GALLERIES | The Arts & Crafts Cooperative, Inc., a collective of Berkeley artists and artisans, has been a stalwart gallery and retail store showcasing ceramics, textiles, paintings, photography, jewelry, and various media since 1959. Explore the amazing range of local talent in a well-lit historic space, and find truly one-of-a-kind gems to take home. ⊠ *1652 Shattuck Ave., North Berkeley* ⊹ *At Lincoln St.* ☎ *510/843–2527* ⊕ *www. accigallery.com.*

★ Amoeba Music

MUSIC STORES | Heaven for audiophiles and movie collectors, this legendary Berkeley favorite is *the* place to head for new and used CDs, vinyl, cassettes, VHS tapes, Blu-ray discs, and DVDs. The massive and ever-changing stock includes thousands of titles for all music tastes, as well as plenty of Amoeba merch. There are branches in San Francisco and Hollywood, but this is the original. ⊠ *2455 Telegraph Ave., at Haste St., Downtown* ☎ *510/549–1125* ⊕ *www.amoeba.com.*

Hammerling Wines

WINE/SPIRITS | Offering a curated taste of Central Coast sparkling wines, winemaker Josh Hammerling sources his grapes from responsibly farmed vineyards with distinctive fruit. Old-world techniques are part of the practice for these wines made entirely by hand. Drop in on weekends for wines by the glass; it's first come, first served. ⊠ *1350 5th St., 4th Street* ☎ *510/984–0340* ⊕ *www.hammerling-wines.co.*

★ Moe's Books

BOOKS/STATIONERY | The spirit of Moe—the creative, cantankerous, cigar-smoking late proprietor—lives on in this world-famous four-story house full of new and used books. Since its doors first opened in 1959, students and professors have flocked here to browse the large selection, which includes literary and cultural criticism, art titles, and literature in foreign languages. ⊠ *2476 Telegraph Ave., near Haste St., Downtown* ☎ *510/849–2087* ⊕ *www.moesbooks.com.*

Oakland

East of Bay Bridge.

In contrast to San Francisco's buzz and beauty and Berkeley's storied counterculture, Oakland's allure lies in its amazing diversity. Here you can find a Nigerian clothing store, a Gothic revival skyscraper, a Buddhist meditation center, and a lively salsa club, all within the same block.

Oakland's multifaceted nature reflects its colorful and tumultuous history. Once a cluster of Mediterranean-style homes and gardens that served as a bedroom community for San Francisco, the town had a major rail terminal and port by the turn of the 20th century. Already a hub of manufacturing, Oakland became a center for shipbuilding and industry when the United States entered World War II. New jobs in the city's shipyards, railroads, and factories attracted thousands of laborers from across the country, including sharecroppers from the Deep South, Mexican Americans from the Southwest, and some of the nation's first female welders. Neighborhoods were imbued with a proud but gritty spirit, along with heightened racial tension. In the wake of the civil rights movement, racial pride gave rise to militant groups like the Black Panther Party, but they were little match for the economic hardships and racial tensions that plagued Oakland. In many neighborhoods the reality was widespread poverty and gang violence—subjects that dominated the songs of such Oakland-bred rappers as the late Tupac Shakur. The protests of the Occupy Oakland movement in 2011 and 2012 and the Black Lives Matter movement more

recently illustrate just how much Oakland remains a mosaic of its past.

Oakland's affluent reside in the city's hillside homes and wooded enclaves like Claremont, Piedmont, and Montclair, which provide a warmer, more spacious alternative to San Francisco. A constant flow of newcomers ensures continued diversity, vitality, and growing pains. Neighborhoods to the west and south of the city center show signs of gentrification as the renovated downtown and vibrant arts scene continue to inject new life into the city. Even San Franciscans, often loath to cross the Bay Bridge, come to Uptown and Temescal for the nightlife, arts, and restaurants.

Everyday life here revolves around the neighborhood. In some areas, such as Piedmont and Rockridge, you'd swear you were in Berkeley or San Francisco's Noe Valley. Along Telegraph Avenue just south of 51st Street, Temescal is littered with hipsters and pulsing with creative culinary and design energy. These are perfect places for browsing, eating, or relaxing between sightseeing trips to Oakland's architectural gems, rejuvenated waterfront, and numerous green spaces.

GETTING HERE AND AROUND

Driving from San Francisco, take Interstate 80 East across the Bay Bridge, then take Interstate 580 East to the Grand Avenue exit for Lake Merritt. To reach downtown and the waterfront, take Interstate 980 West from Interstate 580 East and exit at 12th Street; exit at 18th Street for Uptown. For Temescal, take Interstate 580 East to Highway 24 and exit at 51st Street.

By BART, use the Lake Merritt Station for the Oakland Museum and southern Lake Merritt; the Oakland City Center–12th Street Station for downtown, Chinatown, and Old Oakland; and the 19th Street Station for Uptown, the Paramount Theatre, and the north side of Lake Merritt.

By bus, take the AC Transit's C and P lines to get to Piedmont in Oakland. The

O bus stops at the edge of Chinatown near downtown Oakland.

Oakland's Jack London Square is an easy hop on the ferry from San Francisco. Those without cars can take advantage of the free Broadway Shuttle, which runs from Jack London Square to Grand Avenue weekdays, with continued service to 27th Street weeknights from 7 to 10 pm. There's no weekend service.

Be aware of how quickly neighborhoods can change. Walking is generally safe downtown and in the Piedmont and Rockridge areas, but be mindful when walking west and southeast of downtown, especially at night.

CONTACTS Broadway Shuttle. ⊕ *www. oaklandca.gov.*

ESSENTIALS
VISITOR INFORMATION Visit Oakland. ✉ *481 Water St., near Broadway, Jack London Square* ☎ *510/839–9000* ⊕ *www. visitoakland.com.*

 ## Sights

★ Lake Merritt
NATURE PRESERVE | In the center of Oakland just east of downtown, this tidal lagoon with its unique habitat for more than 100 bird species became the country's first wildlife refuge in 1870. Today the 3.1-mile path around the lake is also a free refuge for walkers, bikers, joggers, and nature lovers. **Lakeside Park** has **Children's Fairyland** (✉ *699 Bellevue*) and the **Rotary Nature Center** (✉ *600 Bellevue*), where monthly bird walks commence every fourth Wednesday. For views from the water, the **Lake Merritt Boating Center** (✉ *568 Bellevue*) rents kayaks and rowboats (⊕ *www.lakemerritt.org*). Venetian gondolas cruise from the Oakland Boathouse (☎ *Basic tours start at $75 for 45 mins* ⊕ *gondolaservizio. com*), where visitors can also indulge in local artisanal chocolates.

On the lake's south side, the **Cam-ron-Stanford House** (✉ *1418 Lakeside Dr.*) is the last of the grand Victorians that once dominated the area; it's open Sundays for tours. Nearby, bold **Oakland mural art** offers a more modern feast for the eyes (✉ *Between Madison and Webster Sts. and 7th and 11th Sts.*).

The lake's necklace of lights adds allure for diners heading to the art-deco **Terrace Room** (✉ *1800 Madison St.*) or **Lake Chalet** (✉ *1520 Lakeside Dr.*), as well as to a host of tasty options along Grand Avenue, from Ethiopian cuisine at **Enssaro** (✉ *357a*) and Korean BBQ at **Jong Ga House** (✉ *372*) to comfort gourmet at **Grand Lake Kitchen** (✉ *576*). ✉ *Lake Merritt* ☎ *Free.*

★ Oakland Museum of California (*OMCA*)
MUSEUM | FAMILY | Designed by Kevin Roche, this museum is one of the country's quintessential examples of mid-century modern architecture and home to a capacious collection of nearly 2 million objects in three distinct galleries celebrating California's history, natural sciences, and art. Listen to native species and environmental soundscapes in the Library of Natural Sounds and engage in stories of the state's past and future, from Ohlone basket making to emerging technologies and current events. Not to be missed are the photographs from Dorothea Lange's personal archive and a worthy collection of Bay Area figurative painters, including David Park and Joan Brown. The museum is also home to Oakland's freshest culinary destination—star chef Tanya Holland's Town Fare café. Experience vegetable-centric California soul food raised to an art form. ■**TIP→ On Friday evening, the museum bustles with live music, food trucks, and after-hours gallery access.** ✉ *1000 Oak St., at 10th St., Downtown* ☎ *510/318–8400, 888/625–6873 toll-free* ⊕ *museumca.org* ☎ *$16, free 1st Sun. of month* ⊗ *Closed Mon.–Thurs.*

KEY

bↄ *BART station*

❶ *Exploring Sights*

❶ *Restaurants*

❶ *Hotels*

Rockridge

NEIGHBORHOOD | **FAMILY** | One of Oakland's most desirable places to live is this fashionable, upscale neighborhood. Explore the tree-lined streets that radiate out from **College Avenue,** just north and south of the Rockridge BART station for a look at California Craftsman bungalows at their finest. By day, College Avenue between Broadway and Alcatraz Avenue is crowded with shoppers buying fresh flowers, used books, and clothing; by night, the same folks are back for hand-crafted meals, artisanal wines, and locally brewed ales. With its specialty food shops and quick bites to go, **Market Hall,** an airy European-style marketplace at Shafter Avenue, is a hub of culinary activity. ⊠ *Market Hall, 5655 College Ave., between Alcatraz Ave. and Broadway, Rockridge* ⊕ *www.rockridgedistrict.com.*

★ Temescal

NEIGHBORHOOD | Centering on Telegraph Avenue between 40th and 51st Streets, Temescal (the Aztec term for "sweat house") is a low-pretension, moneyed-hipster hood with young families and middle-aged folks thrown into the mix. Newly redesigned protected bike lanes, bus islands, and a pedestrian plaza add to the vibrancy of this neighborhood. A critical mass of excellent eateries draws diners from around the Bay Area; there are newer favorites like **Co Nam Noodle Bar** (⊠ *3936 Telegraph Ave.*) and **Smokin Woods BBQ** (⊠ *4307 Telegraph Ave.*), as well as standbys like **Pizzaiolo** (⊠ *5008 Telegraph Ave.*) and **Rose's Taproom** (⊠ *4930 Telegraph Ave.*). Old-time dive bars and smog-check stations share space with public art installations of murals, sculptures, and mosaic trash cans.

Temescal Alley (✉ *Off 49th St.*), a tucked-away lane of tiny storefronts, crackles with the creative energy of local makers. Find botanical wonders at **Crimson Horticultural Rarities** (✉ *No. 470*) or get an old-fashioned straight-edge shave at **Temescal Alley Barbershop** (✉ *No. 470B*). Don't miss grabbing a sweet scoop at **Curbside Creamery** (✉ *No. 482*). ✉ *Temescal ✛ Telegraph Ave. between 40th and 51st Sts.* ⊕ *www.temescaldistrict.org.*

Uptown/KONO

NEIGHBORHOOD | Uptown and KONO (Koreatown/Northgate) is where nightlife and cutting-edge art merge. Dozens of galleries cluster around Telegraph Avenue and north of Grand Avenue into KONO, exhibiting everything from photography and installations to glasswork and fiber arts. The first Friday of each month, thousands of people descend for **Art Murmur** (⊕ *www.oaklandartmurmer.org*), a late-night gallery event that has expanded into **First Fridays** (⊕ *www.oaklandfirstfridays.org*), a festival of food trucks, street vendors, and live music along Telegraph Avenue.

Restaurants with a distinctly urban vibe make Uptown/KONO a dining destination every night of the week. Favorites include eclectic Japanese-inspired fare at **Hopscotch** (✉ *1915 San Pablo Ave.*), ramen and *izakaya* offerings at **Shinmai** (✉ *1825–3 San Pablo Ave.*), Oaxacan cuisine at **Agave Uptown** (✉ *2135 Franklin St.*), and soul food with a French-inspired twist at **Brown Sugar Kitchen** (✉ *2295 Broadway*), to name just a few.

Toss in the bevy of bars and there's plenty within walking distance to keep you busy all evening, such as **Drake's Dealership** (✉ *2325 Broadway*), with its spacious, hipster-friendly beer garden, and **Somar** (✉ *1727 Telegraph Ave.*), a bar, music lounge, and art gallery in one. ✉ *Uptown ✛ Telegraph Ave. and Broadway from 14th to 27th Sts.*

🍴 Restaurants

À Côté

$$ | MEDITERRANEAN | This Mediterranean hot spot is all about seasonal small plates, cozy tables, family-style eating, and excellent wine. Heavy wooden tables, intimate dining nooks, natural light, and a heated patio make this an ideal destination for couples, families, and the after-work crowd. **Known for:** Pernod mussels; Wed. and Thurs. happy hour specials; global and regional wine list. $ *Average main: $23* ✉ *5478 College Ave., at Taft Ave., Rockridge* ☎ *510/655–6469* ⊕ *www.acoterestaurant.com* ⊗ *No lunch.*

★ Brown Sugar Kitchen

$$ | SOUTHERN | FAMILY | Distinguished chef Tanya Holland dishes up soul food flavored by her African American heritage and French culinary training. This bright, airy, modern Uptown venue is a beloved and bustling community-favorite dining spot, serving local, organic ingredients and sweet and savory dishes—from sweet potato pie to Creole meat loaf—paired with house cocktails and sumptuous wines. **Known for:** fried chicken and cornmeal waffles; bacon-cheddar-scallion biscuits; catfish and oyster po'boys. $ *Average main: $1/* ✉ *2295 Broadway, Uptown* ☎ *510/839–7685* ⊕ *www.brownsugarkitchen.com* ⊗ *Closed Mon. No dinner Tues. and Wed.*

Calavera

$$ | MODERN MEXICAN | FAMILY | This Oaxacan-inspired hot spot offers inventive and elevated plates in an industrial-chic space with lofty ceilings, warm wooden tables, exposed brick walls, and heated outdoor dining. Innovative cocktails like the salt-air margarita come from a beautiful bar with a library of more than 100 agaves. **Known for:** fresh ceviches with shrimp or mushrooms; family-style, wood-fired chicken and whole fish; carnitas tacos in nixtamal heirloom-corn tortillas. $ *Average main: $22* ✉ *2337 Broadway, at 24th*

St., Uptown ☏ 510/338–3273 ⊕ calaver-aoakland.com ⊙ Closed Mon.

Comal Next Door

$ | MEXICAN | A sister restaurant to Berkeley's creative, Oaxacan-inspired Comal, this modern Mexican taqueria centers on mouthwatering, quick-service dishes with freshly grilled ingredients and house-made tortillas, sauces, and salsas. It's easy to see why the lines can be long, thanks to unique bottled mezcal libations and takeaway favorites like cenas televisiónes—frozen TV dinners of chicken enchiladas with mole or rajas (sliced poblano peppers) and zucchini tamales. **Known for:** burrito bowls and tortas; bottled cocktails and house-made frescas; buttermilk fried chicken and chipotle aioli. ⑤ Average main: $11 ✉ 550 Grand Ave., Grand Lake ☏ 510/422–6625 ⊕ comalnextdoor.com.

★ Commis

$$$$ | AMERICAN | A slender, unassuming storefront houses the first East Bay restaurant with a Michelin star (two of them, in fact). The room is minimalist and polished: nothing distracts from the artistry of chef James Syhabout, who creates a multicourse prix-fixe dining experience based on the season and his distinctive vision of modern and classic creations. **Known for:** inventive tasting menu; dizzying variety of wines from around the world; reservations needed well in advance. ⑤ Average main: $73 ✉ 3859 Piedmont Ave., at Rio Vista Ave., Piedmont ☏ 510/653–3902 ⊕ commisrestaurant.com ⊙ Closed Sun. and Mon. No lunch.

Miss Ollie's

$ | CARIBBEAN | FAMILY | Centrally located in the city's historic district, Miss Ollie's is a colorful, community-minded Afro-Caribbean gem in Swan's Market that packs in mouthwatering flavors. Lunch specialties include the likes of Bajan fried chicken or eggplant sandwiches and Creole salads with persimmon and jicama, while heartier dishes are jerk

hen with coconut rice, spicy goat curry, and split-pea and okra fritters. **Known for:** skillet-fried chicken and collard greens; Caribbean meat and vegetable patties; pea and pumpkin soups. ⑤ Average main: $16 ✉ 901 Washington St., Old Oakland ☏ 510/285–6188 ⊕ www.realmissolliesoakland.com ⊙ Closed Tues.

Pizzaiolo

$$ | ITALIAN | FAMILY | Chez Panisse alum Charlie Hallowell helms the kitchen of this rustic-chic Oakland institution. Diners of all ages perch on wooden chairs with red-leather backs and nosh on farm-to-table Italian fare from a daily-changing menu. **Known for:** seasonal wood-fired pizza; daily house-made breads; California-Italian entrées. ⑤ Average main: $21 ✉ 5008 Telegraph Ave., at 51st St., Temescal ☏ 510/652–4888 ⊕ www.pizzaiolooakland.com ⊙ No lunch. Closed Mon. and Tues.

Plank

$$ | AMERICAN | FAMILY | Food and entertainment come together in an expansive indoor-outdoor space with a waterfront view. Sip from more than 50 handcrafted local beers while playing boccie in the beer garden, lunch on Cuban sandwiches and Cajun mahi tacos during a bowling or billiards match, or try your hand at the arcade before biting into baby back ribs. **Known for:** fun outdoor space with firepits; generous portions; burgers and pizzas with local ingredients. ⑤ Average main: $17 ✉ 98 Broadway, Jack London Square ☏ 510/817–0980 ⊕ www.plankoakland.com.

★ Shakewell

$$ | MEDITERRANEAN | Two Top Chef vets opened this stylish Lakeshore restaurant, which serves creative and memorable Mediterranean small plates in a lively setting that features an open kitchen, wood-fired oven, communal tables, and snug seating. As the name implies, well-crafted cocktails are shaken (or stirred) and poured with panache. **Known for:** wood-oven paella; Spanish and

Mediterranean small plates; vegetarian options. $ *Average main: $20* ✉ *3407 Lakeshore Ave., near Mandana Blvd., Grand Lake* ☎ *510/251–0329* ⊕ *www. shakewelloakland.com* ⊘ *Closed Mon.*

Hotels

Best Western Plus Bayside Hotel
$ | **HOTEL** | Sandwiched between the serene Oakland Estuary and an eight-lane freeway, this all-suites property has handsome accommodations with balconies or patios, many overlooking the water. **Pros:** attractive, budget-conscious choice; estuary walkways and views; easy access to and from airport, Jack London Square, and downtown. **Cons:** few shops or restaurants in walking distance; freeway-side rooms can be noisy; some rooms have no views or patios/balconies. $ *Rooms from: $189* ✉ *1717 Embarcadero, off I–880, at 16th St. exit, San Antonio* ☎ *510/356–2450* ⊕ *www. baysidehoteloakland.com* ⇦ *81 rooms* ⎮◎⎮ *Free breakfast*

★ Claremont Club & Spa, a Fairmont Hotel
$$$ | **HOTEL** | **FAMILY** | Straddling the Oak-land–Berkeley border, this amenities-rich property dating from 1915 beckons like a gleaming white castle in the hills. **Pros:** amazing spa and outdoor fitness pavilion; daily events and special programs for children; solid business amenities. **Cons:** parking is pricey; mandatory facilities charge; remote from shops and restaurants. $ *Rooms from: $339* ✉ *41 Tunnel Rd., at Ashby and Domingo Aves., Clare-mont* ☎ *510/843–3000, 800/257–7544 reservations* ⊕ *www.fairmont.com/ claremont-berkeley* ⇦ *276 rooms* ⎮◎⎮ *No meals.*

★ Waterfront Hotel
$$ | **HOTEL** | **FAMILY** | Thoroughly modern and pleasantly appointed, this JdV by Hyatt hotel sits among the many high-caliber restaurants of Jack London Square and is both a favorite place for locals' family members and a sweet spot for business travelers with its proximity to the square and downtown. **Pros:** outdoor dining in Jack London Square; lovely views, including some water views; free shuttle service to downtown and easy access to SF ferry. **Cons:** passing trains can be noisy on the city side; parking is pricey; limited amenities. $ *Rooms from: $200* ✉ *10 Washington St., Jack London Square* ☎ *510/836–3800 front desk, 888/842–5333 reservations* ⊕ *www. jdvhotels.com* ⇦ *145 rooms* ⎮◎⎮ *No meals.*

Nightlife

BARS

★ Heinold's First and Last Chance Saloon
BARS/PUBS | Arguably California's longest continuously active saloon since it opened in 1884, this watering hole, built from the hull of a flat-bottomed stern-wheeler, is the famous place where young Jack London got his start as a writer. Historic photos, artifacts, and turn-of-the-20th-century curios hang from the crooked walls and ceilings, which have been atilt since the 1906 earthquake. Get a peek at the slanted bar, where beers on tap and bottomless stories of Oakland history abound. If the proprietor is in, you'll be in for a treat: a trip through time into the Oakland of old is well worth a visit. ✉ *48 Webster St., Jack London Square* ☎ *510/839–6761* ⊕ *www.hein-oldsfirstandlastchance.com.*

Make Westing
BARS/PUBS | Named for a short story by Oakland native Jack London, this sprawling industrial-chic space is always abuzz with hipsters playing bocce, the postwork crowd sipping old-fashioneds, or pretheater couples passing Mason jars of unexpected delectables like Cajun shrimp boil. The patio's your best bet for a conversation on a busy evening. ✉ *1741 Telegraph Ave., at 18th St., Uptown* ☎ *510/251–1400* ⊕ *makewesting.com.*

BREWPUBS AND BEER GARDENS

★ Brotzeit Lokal

BREWPUBS/BEER GARDENS | Wonderfully situated, this tucked-away German *biergarten* is in Oakland's Brooklyn Basin along the waterfront Bay Trail, with lovely views of the marina, estuary, and Coast Guard Island. Known for its select German beers and a delectable offering of Bavarian dishes, including house-made sausage, schnitzel, sauerkraut, and sandwiches, this family-friendly spot is especially popular on nice days. ✉ *1000 Embarcadero, at 10th Ave., Lake Merritt* ☎ *510/ 645–1905* ⊕ *brotzeitbiergarten. com.*

Buck Wild Brewing

BREWPUBS/BEER GARDENS | Oakland's Jack London District is home to a luxurious taproom that is California's first 100%-gluten-free brewery, specializing in craft beers made without rye, wheat, or barley. The brewery has also partnered with San Francisco's Kitava, which provides a menu with fare (such as fish and chips, loaded fries, Cuban bowls, and small bites) completely free of inflammatory ingredients. ✉ *401 Jackson St., at 4th St., Jack London Square* ☎ *510/350–7938* ⊕ *www.buckwildbrew.com.*

Federation Brewing Company

BREWPUBS/BEER GARDENS | Part of Oakland's Ale Trail, the brewery has a convivial tasting room in the Jack London District with plenty of games for extended sipping of their pilsners, saisons, sours, and hoppy IPAs. Wednesday happy hours and regular rotating comedy and music entertainment usually pack the place, so it's good to check ahead and reserve advance tickets. ✉ *420 3rd St., Jack London Square* ☎ *510/496–4228* ⊕ *www.federationbrewing.com.*

Line 51 Brewing—The Terminal Taproom

BREWPUBS/BEER GARDENS | The bright, airy, 7,500-square-foot brewery and taproom is in many ways a tribute to its early history, when the brewers hauled their kegs on public transit line 51 to their warehouse. Now, Oakland Ale Trail explorers can enjoy freshly tapped beer from a vintage 1971 AC transit bus that serves as a refrigeration unit for their brews. Fermentation tanks are on full display: the owners are passionate about their Red Death ale, IPAs, Short Dog ale, and porters. ✉ *303 Castro St., at 3rd St., Jack London Square* ☎ *510/985–4181* ⊕ *www.line51beer.com.*

Original Pattern Brewing

BREWPUBS/BEER GARDENS | The love for beer of all varieties is evident in the selection of award-winners at this employee-owned brewery in a brick warehouse space in the Jack London District. The list of IPAs, lagers, sours, fruit-infused beers, Belgian-style ales, and porters is ever changing as the latest brews are tapped. Food pop-ups from Good to Eat Dumplings make outdoor dining possible with dumplings, wontons, and noodles. ✉ *292 4th St., Jack London Square* ☎ *510/844–4833* ⊕ *www.originalpatternbeer.com.*

★ The Trappist

BREWPUBS/BEER GARDENS | Brick walls, dark wood, soft lighting, and a hum of conversation set a warm and mellow tone inside this Old Oakland Victorian space that has been renovated to resemble a traditional Belgian pub. The setting (which includes two bars and a back patio) is a draw, but the real stars are the artisanal beers—more than 100 Belgian, Dutch, and North American brews. Experience guided tastings and curated offerings by passionate staff well versed in the styles of Trappist and European craft brewing. ✉ *460 8th St., near Broadway, Old Oakland* ☎ *510/238–8900* ⊕ *www.thetrappist.com.*

CAFÉS

Mua

CAFES—NIGHTLIFE | Cuisine, cocktails, and culture—husband-and-wife-owned Mua puts it all together in an airy converted garage decked out with works by owner/artist Hi-Suk Dong as well as pieces from his personal collection. The chefs serve up beautifully crafted dishes like blackened catfish and garlic prawns; the bartenders shake up elegant cocktails; and a lively crowd enjoys cultural offerings that include community sketch nights, art shows, and weekend DJ music. This is the perfect stop for any foodie who supports the arts. ⊠ *2442a Webster St., between 24th and 26th Sts., Uptown* ☎ *510/238–1100* ⊕ *muaoakland.com.*

ROCK, POP, HIP-HOP, FOLK, AND BLUES CLUBS

Fox Theater

MUSIC CLUBS | This renovated 1928 theater, Oakland's favorite performance venue, is a remarkable feat of Mediterranean Moorish architecture and has seen the likes of Willie Nelson, the Magnetic Fields, Rebelution, and B.B. King, to name a few. The venue boasts good sight lines, a state-of-the-art sound system, brilliant acoustics, and a restaurant and bar, among other amenities. ⊠ *1807 Telegraph Ave., between 18th and 19th Sts., Uptown* ☎ *510/302–2250* ⊕ *thefoxoakland.com.*

★ Yoshi's

MUSIC CLUBS | Opened in 1972 as a sushi bar, Yoshi's has evolved into one of the area's best jazz and live music venues. The full Yoshi's experience includes traditional Japanese and Asian fusion cuisine in the adjacent restaurant. ⊠ *510 Embarcadero W, between Washington and Clay Sts., Jack London Square* ☎ *510/238–9200* ⊕ *yoshis.com.*

Performing Arts

Paramount Theatre

ARTS CENTERS | A glorious art-deco specimen, the Paramount operates as a venue for concerts and performances of all kinds, from the Oakland Ballet and Oakland Symphony to Jerry Seinfeld and Elvis Costello. The popular classic movie nights start off with a 30-minute Wurlitzer concert. ∎**TIP→ Docent-led**

tours ($5), offered the first and third Saturday of the month, are fun and informative. ⊠ *2025 Broadway, at 20th St., Uptown* ☎ *510/465–6400* ⊕ *paramounttheatre. com.*

🛍 Shopping

Bay-Made

GIFTS/SOUVENIRS | Owned and operated by women artists, this gift shop showcases the delightful works of more than 120 Oakland artisans and makers. Browse offerings such as handcrafted paper and print art, collage art, chocolate, waxworks, jewelry, ceramics, herbs and oils, and quality art and printing supplies. A rotating gallery wall features the latest works from local artists. ⊠ *3295 Lakeshore Ave., Grand Lake* ☎ *510/520–4600* ⊕ *www.bay-made.com.*

Maison d'Etre

GIFTS/SOUVENIRS | Close to the Rockridge BART station, this store epitomizes the Rockridge neighborhood's funky-chic shopping scene. Look for high-end housewares along with impulse buys like whimsical watches, imported fruit-tea blends, one-of-a-kind gifts, and funky slippers. ⊠ *5640 College Ave., at Keith Ave., Rockridge* ☎ *510/658–2801* ⊕ *www. maisondetre.com.*

★ Oaklandish

CLOTHING | The ultimate place for Oakland swag started in 2000 as a public art project of local pride and has become a celebrated brand around the bay, with clothing and accessories for men, women, and kids. A portion of the proceeds from hip Oaklandish-brand T-shirts and accessories supports grassroots non profits committed to bettering the local community. It's good-looking stuff for a good cause. ⊠ *1444 Broadway, near 15th St., Uptown* ☎ *510/251–9500* ⊕ *oaklandish.com.*

⚡ Activities

Oakland Athletics

BASEBALL/SOFTBALL | FAMILY | Baseball's Oakland Athletics, also called the Oakland A's, has a loyal following among locals in Oakland and enjoys a fierce rivalry with the San Francisco Giants just across the bay. The team hopes to move from its RingCentral Coliseum stadium to a proposed new waterfront ballpark at Jack London Square, perhaps in 2023, but Major League Baseball is also allowing the team to consider relocating to another city; stay tuned. ⊠ *RingCentral Coliseum, 7000 Coliseum Way* ☎ *877/493–2255 box office* ⊕ *mlb. com/athletics.*

The Marin Headlands

Due west of the Golden Gate Bridge's northern end.

The term "Golden Gate" has become synonymous with the world-famous bridge, but it was first given to the narrow waterway that connects the Pacific and San Francisco Bay. To the north of the Golden Gate Strait lie the Marin Headlands, part of the Golden Gate National Recreation Area (GGNRA), with some of the area's most dramatic scenery.

GETTING HERE AND AROUND

Driving from San Francisco, head north on U.S. 101. Just after you cross the Golden Gate Bridge, take Exit 442 for Alexander Avenue. Keep left at the fork and follow signs for San Francisco/U.S. 101 South. Go through the tunnel under the freeway, and turn right up the hill. On weekends and major holidays, Muni bus 76X runs hourly from Sutter and Sansome Streets in the city to the Marin Headlands Visitor Center.

⊙ Sights

Marin Headlands

NATIONAL/STATE PARK | FAMILY | The stunning headlands stretch from the Golden Gate Bridge to Muir Beach, drawing photographers who perch on the southern heights for spectacular shots of the city and bridge. Equally remarkable are the views north along the coast and out to the ocean, where the Farallon Islands are visible on clear days. Hawk Hill (accessed from Conzelman Rd.) has a trail with panoramic views and is a great place to watch the fall raptor migration; it's also home to the mission blue butterfly.

The headlands' strategic position at the mouth of San Francisco Bay made them a logical site for military installations from 1890 through the Cold War. Today you can explore the crumbling concrete batteries where naval guns once protected the area. Main attractions are centered on Forts Barry and Cronkhite, which are separated by Rodeo Lagoon and Rodeo Beach, a dark stretch of sand that attracts sandcastle builders and dog owners.

The visitor center is a worthwhile stop for its exhibits on the area's history and ecology, and kids enjoy the educational installations and small play area inside. You can pick up guides to historic sites and wildlife and get information about programming and guided walks. ⊠ *Golden Gate National Recreation Area, Visitor Center, Fort Barry Chapel, Fort Barry, Bldg. 948, Field and Bunker Rds., Sausalito* ☎ *415/331–1540* ⊕ *www.nps. gov/goga* ⊠ *Free* ☉ *Closed Tues.*

Sausalito

2 miles north of Golden Gate Bridge.

Bougainvillea-covered hillsides and an expansive yacht harbor give Sausalito the feel of an Adriatic resort. The town sits on the northwestern edge of San Francisco Bay, where it's sheltered from the ocean by the Marin Headlands; the mostly mild weather here is perfect for strolling and outdoor dining. Nevertheless, morning fog and afternoon winds can roll over the hills without warning, funneling through the central part of Sausalito once known as Hurricane Gulch.

South of Bridgeway, which snakes between the bay and the hills, a waterside esplanade is lined with restaurants on piers that lure diners with good seafood and even better views. Stairs along the west side of Bridgeway and throughout town climb into wooded hillside neighborhoods filled with both rustic and opulent homes. Back on the northern portion of the shoreline, harbors shelter a community of more than 400 houseboats. As you amble along Bridgeway past shops and galleries, you'll notice the absence of basic services. Find them and more on Caledonia Street, which runs parallel to Bridgeway and inland a couple of blocks. While ferry-side shops flaunt kitschy souvenirs, smaller side streets and narrow alleyways offer eccentric jewelry and handmade crafts.

■TIP→ **The ferry is the best way to get to Sausalito from San Francisco; you get more romance (and less traffic) and disembark in the heart of downtown.**

First occupied by the Coast Miwok tribe and later visited by Spanish explorers who called the area Saucito (Little Willow) for the trees growing along its streams, Sausalito was developed as a ranch in 1838 under the ownership of English mariner William Richardson. It served as a port for whaling ships during the 19th century and became a major terminus for transport by rail, ferry, and, eventually, car. By the mid-1800s, wealthy San Franciscans had made Sausalito their getaway across the bay and built lavish Victorian summer homes in the hills. Meanwhile, an influx of hardworking, fun-loving merchants and working-class folk populated the waterfront area, which grew thick with saloons, gambling dens, and bordellos. Bootleggers flourished

during Prohibition, and shipyard workers swelled the town's population in the 1940s, at the height of World War II.

Sausalito developed its bohemian flair in the 1950s and '60s, when creative types, including artist Jean Varda, poet Shel Silverstein, and madam Sally Stanford, established an artists' colony and a houseboat community here (this is Otis Redding's "Dock of the Bay"). Both the spirit of the artists and the neighborhood of floating homes persist. For a close-up view of the quirky community, head north on Bridgeway, turn right on Gate Six Road, park where it dead-ends, and enter through the unlocked gates.

GETTING HERE AND AROUND
From San Francisco by car or bike, follow U.S. 101 North across the Golden Gate Bridge and take Exit 442 for Alexander Avenue, just past Vista Point; continue down the winding hill toward the water to where the road becomes Bridgeway. Golden Gate Transit buses will drop you off in downtown Sausalito, and the ferries dock downtown as well. The center of town is flat, with plenty of sidewalks and bay views. It's a pleasure and a must to explore on foot.

ESSENTIALS
VISITOR INFORMATION Sausalito Chamber of Commerce. ✉ *1913 Bridgeway* ☎ *415/331–7262* ⊕ *www.sausalito.org.*

 ## Sights

The Marine Mammal Center
COLLEGE | FAMILY | This hospital for distressed, sick, and injured marine animals is a leading center for ocean conservancy in the Bay Area and the largest rehabilitation center of its kind in the world. Dedicated to pioneering education, rehabilitation, and research, the center is free and open daily to the public. Tour the facilities and see how elephant seals, sea lions, and pups are cared for and meet the scientists who care for them. Bonus: you'll catch some of the best views of the

Marin County

Marin Headlands and San Francisco Bay along the way. ■ TIP➜ Call ahead or check their website for tour availability. ✉ 2000 Bunker Rd. ☎ 415/289–7325 ⊕ www. marinemammalcenter.org ⊠ Free.

Sally Stanford Drinking Fountain

FOUNTAIN | There's an unusual historic landmark on the Sausalito Ferry Pier—a drinking fountain inscribed "Have a drink on Sally" in remembrance of Sally Stanford, the former San Francisco brothel madam who became Sausalito's mayor in the 1970s. Sassy Sally would have appreciated the fountain's eccentric attachment: a knee-level basin with the inscription "Have a drink on Leland," in memory of her beloved dog. ✉ Sausalito Ferry Pier, Anchor St. at Humboldt St., off southwest corner of Gabrielson Park ⊕ www.oursausalito.com.

Sausalito Ice House Museum and Visitor Center

INFO CENTER | The local historical society operates this dual educational exhibit and visitor center, where you can get your bearings, learn some history, and find out what's happening around town. The artifacts of indigenous Miwok peoples and photography of turn-of-the-20th-century Sausalito are worth a peek. ✉ 780 Bridgeway, at Bay St. ☎ 415/332–0505 ⊕ www.sausalitohistoricalsociety.com ⊗ Closed Mon.

Viña del Mar Plaza and Park

PLAZA | The landmark Plaza Viña del Mar, named for Sausalito's sister city in Chile, marks the center of town. Adjacent to the parking lot and ferry pier, the plaza is flanked by two 14-foot-tall statues of elephants, which were created for the Panama–Pacific International Exposition world's fair held in San Francisco in 1915. A picture-perfect fountain here is great for people-watching. ⊠ *Bridgeway and El Portal St.* ⊕ *www.oursausalito.com.*

🍴 Restaurants

Arawan Thai
$ | **THAI** | Tucked along the restaurant row of Caledonia Street for decades, Arawan Thai has been a stalwart destination for some of the tastiest Thai dishes in Marin County. The elegant and cozy interior lends an intimate quality to this hidden gem known for its generous variety of authentic soups, salads, and grilled specialties, along with shareable dishes, such as spicy angel wings (stuffed chicken wings) and prawn and cream cheese puffs. **Known for:** panang, red, and green coconut curries; papaya and mango salads; sizzling wok dishes. ⑤ *Average main: $14* ⊠ *47 Caledonia St.* ☎ *415/729–9395* ⊕ *www.arawansausalito.com.*

Fast Food Français
$ | **BISTRO** | **FAMILY** | F3, as it's known, puts a French twist on classic American fast food and dishes up some French nibbles, too, in this casual bistro. The same folks who started Le Garage branch out here with quick bites like French onion burgers with cheddar fondue and double-cream mac-and-cheese, along with Brussels sprouts chips, deviled eggs, and ratatouille. **Known for:** fries and frites; spacious locale; excellent brunch spot. ⑤ *Average main: $16* ⊠ *39 Caledonia St.* ☎ *415/887–9047* ⊕ *www.eatf3.com.*

★ Fish
$$ | **SEAFOOD** | **FAMILY** | Unsurprisingly, fish—specifically, fresh, sustainably caught fish—is the focus at this gleaming dockside fish house a mile north of downtown. Order at the counter—cash only—and then grab a seat by the floor-to-ceiling windows or at a picnic table on the pier, overlooking the yachts and fishing boats. **Known for:** taco plate; barbecued oysters; fire-grilled entrées. ⑤ *Average main: $23* ⊠ *350 Harbor Dr., at Gate 5 Rd., off Bridgeway* ☎ *415/331–3474* ⊕ *www.331fish.com* ▬ *No credit cards.*

The Joinery
$$ | **AMERICAN** | Sausalito's popular beer hall and rotisserie offers ample, open, airy indoor seating at long tables and expanded outdoor deck dining with exceptional views of the bay. It's a relaxing spot to enjoy burgers, sandwiches, soups, and salads along with a selection of Belgian beers, IPAs, lagers, and ciders on tap. **Known for:** fried chicken sandwich and grilled cheese; Joinery burger with special sauce; dirty fries and fried Brussels sprouts. ⑤ *Average main: $18* ⊠ *300 Tourney St.* ☎ *415/766–8999* ⊕ *www.joineryca.com.*

Le Garage
$$$ | **FRENCH** | Brittany-born Olivier Souvestre serves traditional French bistro fare in a relaxed, bayside setting that feels more sidewalk café than the converted garage that it is. The restaurant seats only 35 inside and 15 outside, so make reservations or arrive early. **Known for:** PEI mussels and house-cut fries; no-reservation weekend brunch; outstanding bouillabaisse. ⑤ *Average main: $27* ⊠ *85 Liberty Ship Way, Suite 109* ☎ *415/332–5625* ⊕ *www.legarage-sausalito.com.*

Poggio
$$ | **ITALIAN** | A hillside dining destination, Poggio serves modern Tuscan-style comfort food in a handsome, old world–inspired space whose charm spills onto the sidewalks. An extensive and ever-changing menu, with ingredients sourced from the restaurant's garden and local farms, features house-made capellini, grilled fish, and wood-fired pizzas. **Known for:** traditional northern Italian dishes; rotisserie chicken with property-grown organic herbs and vegetables; lobster-roe pasta. ⑤ *Average main: $25* ⊠ *777 Bridgeway, at Bay St.* ☎ *415/332–7771* ⊕ *www.poggiotrattoria.com.*

Sausalito Seahorse

$$ | ITALIAN | Live music and dancing complement Tuscan seafood and pasta specialties here and make the Seahorse one of Sausalito's most spirited supper clubs. Sample an abundant antipasti menu and homemade focaccia on outdoor patios or enjoy the band inside with traditional seafood stew or lasagna *classica*. **Known for:** happy hour; schiacciata (a type of Tuscan bread) panini; fun atmosphere. ⑤ *Average main: $23* ⊠ *305 Harbor Dr.* ☎ *415/331–2899* ⊕ *www.sausalitoseahorse.com.*

★ Sushi Ran

$$ | JAPANESE | Sushi aficionados swear that this tiny, stylish restaurant—in business since 1986—is the Bay Area's finest option for raw fish, but don't overlook the excellent Pacific Rim fusions, a melding of Japanese ingredients and French cooking techniques. Book in advance or expect a wait, which you can soften by sipping one of the bar's 30 by-the-glass sakes. **Known for:** fish imported from Tokyo's famous Tsukiji market; local miso-glazed black cod; outstanding sake and wine list. ⑤ *Average main: $25* ⊠ *107 Caledonia St., at Pine St.* ☎ *415/332–3620* ⊕ *sushiran.com* ⊘ *No lunch Mon.–Thurs.*

Taste of Rome

$$ | ITALIAN | FAMILY | From early-morning espresso and frittatas to late-night wine and marsalas, there's something just right at Taste of Rome any time of day. With spacious indoor and outdoor seating and a bountiful menu of fresh and homemade Italian specialties, it's easy to see why this family-owned café is beloved among locals. **Known for:** coffee drinks and desserts; locally sourced organic produce and sustainable seafood; house-made pasta. ⑤ *Average main: $17* ⊠ *1000 Bridgeway* ☎ *415/332–7660* ⊕ *tasteofrome.co.*

☕ Coffee and Quick Bites

★ Hamburgers Sausalito

$ | BURGER | Patrons queue up daily outside this tiny street-side shop for organic Angus beef patties that are made to order on a wheel-shaped grill. Brave the line (it moves fast) and take your food to the esplanade to enjoy fresh air and bayside views. **Known for:** legendary burgers; bay views; local following. ⑤ *Average main: $9* ⊠ *737 Bridgeway, at Anchor St.* ☎ *415/332–9471* ⊘ *No dinner.*

Venice Gourmet Deli & Pizza

$ | ITALIAN | The traditional Italian deli sandwiches, pizzas made daily, and a shop filled with gourmet delectables, wines, kitchenware, and local flavor have enticed taste buds along picturesque Bridgeway since 1969. Enjoy a meal alfresco at the sidewalk tables, or take a picnic a few steps away to Yee Toch Chee Park for a waterside bite. **Known for:** picnic-perfect sandwiches; service and quality from family owners; plentiful selections. ⑤ *Average main: $12* ⊠ *625 Bridgeway* ☎ *415/332–3544* ⊕ *www.venicegourmet.com.*

Hotels

The Inn Above Tide

$$$$ | B&B/INN | The balconies at the inn literally hang over the water, and each of its rooms has a "perfect 10" view that takes in wild Angel Island as well as the city lights across the bay. **Pros:** generous continental breakfast; free bikes to tour the area; in-room spa services available. **Cons:** costly daily parking; some rooms are on the small side; ferry-side rooms can be noisy. ⑤ *Rooms from: $425* ⊠ *30 El Portal* ☎ *415/332–9535, 800/893–8433* ⊕ *www.innabovetide.com* ⇆ *33 rooms* ⑨ *Free breakfast.*

Tiburon

7 miles north of Sausalito, 11 miles north of Golden Gate Bridge.

On a peninsula that was named Punta de Tiburón (Shark Point) by 18th-century Spanish explorers, this beautiful Marin County community retains the feel of a village—it's more low-key than Sausalito—despite the encroachment of commercial establishments from the downtown area. The harbor faces Angel Island across Raccoon Strait, and San Francisco is directly south across the bay, making the views from the decks of harbor restaurants major attractions. Since 1884, when the San Francisco and North Pacific Railroad relocated their ferry terminal facilities to the harbor town, Tiburon has centered on the waterfront. The ferry is the most relaxing (and fastest) way to get here and allows you to skip traffic and parking problems.

One of the bay's best secrets in plain sight, Angel Island State Park (📞 *415/435–1915* ⊕ *www.parks.ca.gov*) offers 13 miles of roads and trails from the perimeter up to Mt. Livermore (788 feet), with magnificent panoramic views. The 12-minute ferry ride to Angel Island from Tiburon ($15 round-trip) includes the cost of park admission. ■ **TIP→ To see the sites by bike, rent on the island (www. angelisland.com/bike-rentals) or in Tiburon at Pedego Electric Bikes (10 Main St.).**

GETTING HERE AND AROUND

Blue & Gold Fleet ferries travel between San Francisco and Tiburon daily. By car, head north from San Francisco on U.S. 101 and get off at CA 131/Tiburon Boulevard/East Blithedale Avenue (Exit 447). Turn right onto Tiburon Boulevard and drive just over 4 miles to downtown. Golden Gate Transit serves downtown Tiburon from San Francisco; watch for changes during evening rush hour. Tiburon's Main Street is perfect for wandering, as are the footpaths that frame the water's edge.

ESSENTIALS

VISITOR INFORMATION destination: Tiburon. ✉ *Town Hall, 1505 Tiburon Blvd.* 📞 *415/435–2298* ⊕ *www.destinationtiburon.org.*

 Sights

Ark Row

NEIGHBORHOOD | The historic second block of Main Street is known as Ark Row and has a tree-shaded walk lined with antiques shops, restaurants, and specialty stores. The quaint stretch gets its name from the 19th-century ark houseboats that floated in Belvedere Cove before being beached and transformed into stores. ■ **TIP→ If you're curious about architectural history, the Tiburon Heritage & Arts Commission has a self-guided walking-tour map, available online and at local businesses.** ✉ *Ark Row, Main St., south of Juanita La.* ⊕ *www.townoftiburon.org.*

Old St. Hilary's Landmark and John Thomas Howell Wildflower Preserve

HISTORIC SITE | The architectural centerpiece of this attraction is a stark-white 1888 Carpenter Gothic church that overlooks the town and the bay from its hillside perch. Surrounding the church, which was dedicated as a historical monument in 1959, is a wildflower preserve that's spectacular in May and June, when the rare Tiburon paintbrush and Tiburon black jewel flower bloom. Expect a steep walk uphill to reach the preserve. The Landmarks Society will arrange guided tours by appointment. ■ **TIP→ The hiking trails behind the landmark wind up to a peak that has views of the entire Bay Area.** ✉ *201 Esperanza St., off Mar West St. or Beach Rd.* 📞 *415/435–1853* ⊕ *landmarkssociety.com* 🕑 *Church closed Mon.–Sat. and Nov.–Mar.*

Railroad & Ferry Depot Museum

MUSEUM | A short waterfront walk from the ferry landing, this free museum in Shoreline Park is a well-preserved time capsule of the city's industrial history, complete with working trains. The landmark building has a detailed scale model of Tiburon and its 43-acre rail yard at the turn of the 20th century, when the city served as a major railroad and ferry hub for San Francisco Bay. The Depot House Museum on the second floor showcases a restoration of the stationmaster's living quarters. ✉ *1920 Paradise Dr.* ☎ *415/435– 1853* ⊕ *landmarkssociety.com* ⏱ *Closed Mon.–Sat. and Oct.–Apr.*

🍴 Restaurants

Caffè Acri

$ | CAFÉ | This Italian espresso bar and café at the end of the Tiburon Ferry dock is a sweet spot to enjoy a leisurely breakfast or lunch with a cup of locally roasted coffee while waiting for the ferry. In addition to daily-baked pastries and desserts, the menu ranges from omelets and toasted sandwiches to smoothies. **Known for:** farm-fresh salads; espresso drinks; soups and paninis. ⑤ *Average main: $10* ✉ *1 Main St.* ☎ *415/435–8515* ⊕ *www.caffeacri.com* ⏱ *No dinner.*

★ Luna Blu

$$ | SICILIAN | Friendly, informative staff serve Sicilian-inspired seafood in this lively Italian restaurant just a stone's throw from the ferry. Recent renovations have opened up 1,000 square feet of new patio and tripled the capacity of the original dining space. **Known for:** sustainably caught seafood and local, organic ingredients; homemade pastas; rock crab bisque. ⑤ *Average main: $20* ✉ *35 Main St.* ☎ *415/789–5844* ⊕ *lunablurestaurant. com* ⏱ *Closed Tues. No lunch weekdays.*

Salt & Pepper

$$ | AMERICAN | FAMILY | Bright and welcoming, this American bistro on Ark Row is known for its seafood starters (oyster poppers, crab stacks, scallops, and steamers) and salads as well as shareable dishes and burgers, chops, and ribs. The airy, rustic space has a pleasant café-like atmosphere that makes it easy to stay and even consider returning for a breakfast of Dungeness crab omelet or ricotta pancakes. **Known for:** clam chowder; kabocha squash and vegetable curry; Mongolian pork chops and rib-eye steaks. ⑤ *Average main: $24* ✉ *38 Main St.* ☎ *415/435–3594* ⊕ *www.saltandpeppertiburon.com.*

★ Sam's Anchor Cafe

$$ | AMERICAN | Open since 1920, this beloved dockside restaurant is the town's most famous eatery, and after 99 years, a bright remodel includes floor-to-ceiling sliding-glass doors and an 80-foot heated bench for deck views on cool days. Remnants of Sam's history are evident in some vintage decor, the hamburger and champagne specials, and the free popcorn. **Known for:** excellent raw bar; pink lemonade and margarita "bowls"; hurricane fries. ⑤ *Average main: $22* ✉ *27 Main St.* ☎ *415/435–4527* ⊕ *samscafe.com.*

Servino Ristorante

$$ | SOUTHERN ITALIAN | FAMILY | This family-owned eatery specializes in southern Italian recipes, including lobster agnolotti, seafood stew, pork sausage fondue, house-made pastas, and pizza made with local, sustainable ingredients. With spacious indoor and outdoor seating and waterfront views, the scene is cozy and welcoming even in cooler weather, when there's heated patio dining. **Known for:** alfresco waterfront dining; wines from Italy and California; black truffle raviolacci. ⑤ *Average main: $23* ✉ *9 Main St.* ☎ *415/435–2676* ⊕ *www.servino.com.*

☕ Coffee and Quick Bites

Waypoint Pizza

$ | PIZZA | FAMILY | A nautical theme and a tasty "between the sheets" pizza-style sandwich are signatures of this creative pizzeria, which is housed in the 19th-century landmark building that was once home to the Pioneer Boathouse and is now owned by two sailing aficionados. Booths are brightened with blue-checkered tablecloths, and a playful air is added by indoor deck chairs and a picnic table complete with umbrella. **Known for:** pizza-style sandwiches; wild shrimp pesto pizza; soft-serve organic ice cream. $ *Average main: $15* ⊠ *15 Main St.* ☎ *415/435–3440* ⊕ *www. waypointpizza.com.*

Hotels

Waters Edge Hotel
$$$ | B&B/INN | Checking into this stylish downtown hotel feels like tucking away into an inviting retreat by the water—the views are stunning, and the lighting is perfect. **Pros:** complimentary wine and cheese for guests every evening; restaurants and sights are steps away; free bike rentals for guests. **Cons:** downstairs rooms lack privacy and balconies; paid self-parking; 2-night minimum weekends, 3-night minimum holidays. $ *Rooms from: $309* ⊠ *25 Main St., off Tiburon Blvd.* ☎ *415/789–5999, 877/789–5999* ⊕ *www.marinhotels.com* ⊋ *23 rooms* ⦿⏐ *Free breakfast.*

🛍 Shopping

Local Spicery
FOOD/CANDY | This is the place for spices of all varieties from around the world, from adobo to za'atar. Where historic Ark Row curves uphill, the apothecary-like storefront features an aromatic library of assorted loose teas and spices milled in small quantities and prepared in smallbatch hand blends to obtain maximum freshness and quality. Not sure where to begin? Ask about pairing flavors with your favorite ingredients and ways of cooking. ⊠ *80 Main St.* ☎ *415/435–1100* ⊕ *www. localspicery.com.*

Schoenberg Guitars
MUSIC STORES | Small, narrow, and chockablock with handmade guitars alongside fine vintage classics, this shop is a treat even for those who don't play music. Dozens, if not hundreds, of guitars

varying in size, shape, and color hang from the walls and stand against the polished wood floor. There is an organized beauty to the layout of this place and a comforting sense of musical harmony. You may even enjoy an impromptu concert or workshop. ⊠ *Ark Row Shopping Center, 106 Main St.* ☎ *415/789–0846* ⊕ *www.om28.com.*

Tiburon Wine
WINE/SPIRITS | Some 200 regional and international wines as well as local Marin Rieslings and pinot noirs line the walls of this cozy shop, which has an indoor tasting room where you can sample more than two dozen. There's also an outdoor seating space for sipping by the glass or bottle. ⊠ *84 Main St.* ☎ *415/435–3499* ⊕ *tiburonwine.net.*

Mill Valley

2 miles north of Sausalito, 4 miles north of Golden Gate Bridge.

Chic and woodsy Mill Valley has a dual personality. Here, as elsewhere in the county, the foundation is a superb natural setting. Virtually surrounded by parkland, the town lies at the base of Mt. Tamalpais and contains dense redwood groves traversed by countless creeks. But this is no lumber camp. Smart restaurants and chichi boutiques line streets that have been roamed by more rock stars than one might suspect.

The rustic village flavor isn't a modern conceit, but a holdover from the town's early days as a center for the lumber industry. In 1896, the Mt. Tamalpais Scenic Railroad—dubbed the "Crookedest Railroad in the World" because of its curvy tracks— began transporting visitors from Mill Valley to the top of Mt. Tam and down to Muir Woods, and the town soon became a vacation retreat for city slickers. The trains stopped running in the 1930s as cars became more popular, but the old railway depot still serves as the center of town:

the 1929 building has been transformed into the popular Depot Café & Bookstore, at 87 Throckmorton Avenue.

The small downtown area has the constant bustle of a leisure community; even at noon on a Tuesday, people are out shopping for fancy cookware, eco-friendly home furnishings, and boutique clothing.

GETTING HERE AND AROUND
By car from San Francisco, head north on U.S. 101 and get off at CA 131/Tiburon Boulevard/East Blithedale Avenue (Exit 447). Turn left onto East Blithedale Avenue and continue west to Throckmorton Avenue; turn left to reach Depot Plaza, then park. Golden Gate Transit buses serve Mill Valley from San Francisco. Once here, explore the town on foot.

ESSENTIALS
VISITOR INFORMATION Mill Valley Chamber of Commerce & Visitor Center. ⊠ *85 Throckmorton Ave.* ☎ *415/388–9700* ⊕ *www.millvalley.org.*

 # Sights

Lytton Square
PLAZA | FAMILY | Mill Valley locals congregate on weekends to socialize in the coffeehouses and cafés near the town's central square, but it's buzzing most of the day. The Mill Valley Depot Café & Bookstore at the hub of it all is the place to grab a coffee and sweet treat while reading or playing a game of chess. Shops, restaurants, and cultural venues line the nearby streets. ⊠ *Miller and Throckmorton Aves.*

★ Marin County Civic Center
BUILDING | A wonder of arches, circles, and skylights just 10 miles north of Mill Valley, the Civic Center was Frank Lloyd Wright's largest public project and has been designated a national and state historic landmark, as well as a UNESCO World Heritage Site. It's a performance venue and the locale for the fun and funky Marin County Fair. One-hour docent-led tours leave from the café on the second floor Wednesday and Friday morning at 10:30. ⊠ *3501 Civic Center Dr., off N. San Pedro Rd., San Rafael* ☎ *415/473–6400 Cultural Services department* ⊕ *www.marincounty.org* 🖼 *Free; tour $10* 🕑 *Closed weekends; no tours Mon., Tues., Thurs.*

★ Mill Valley Lumber Yard
HISTORIC SITE | FAMILY | The lumber yard, once a vital center of the region's logging industry, is now a vibrant micro-village of craftsfolk, bread bakers, textile makers, and lifestyle designers, and their boutiques and restaurants. You'll even find a chocolate art studio where custom-designed chocolates and truffles may look almost too good to eat. The preserved brick-red historic structures are hard to miss along Miller Avenue, and with plenty of parking in the area, plus picnic tables and outdoor space, it's well worth a visit. ⊠ *129 Miller Ave.* ⊕ *www. millvalleylumberyard.com.*

★ Mt. Tamalpais State Park
NATIONAL/STATE PARK | FAMILY | The view of Mt. Tamalpais from all around the bay can be a beauty, but that's nothing compared to the views *from* the mountain, which take in San Francisco, the East Bay, the coast, and beyond. Although the summit of Mt. Tamalpais is only 2,571 feet high, the mountain rises practically from sea level, dominating the topography of Marin County. For years the 6,300-acre park has been a favorite destination for hikers, with more than 200 miles of trails. The park's major thoroughfare, Panoramic Highway, snakes its way up from U.S. 101 to the **Pantoll Ranger Station** and down to Stinson Beach. Parking is free along the roadside, but there's an $8 fee (cash or check only) at the ranger station and additional charges for walk-in campsites and group use.

The **Mountain Theater,** also known as the Cushing Memorial Amphitheatre, is a natural 3,750-seat amphitheater that has showcased summer "Mountain Plays" since 1913.

The **Rock Spring Trail** starts at the Mountain Theater and gently climbs for 1½ miles to the **West Point Inn,** where you can relax at picnic tables before forging ahead via Old Railroad Grade Fire Road and the Miller Trail to Mt. Tam's Middle Peak.

From the Pantoll Ranger Station, the precipitous **Steep Ravine Trail** brings you past stands of coastal redwoods. Hike the connecting **Dipsea Trail** to reach Stinson Beach. ■TIP➔ If you're too weary to make the 3½-mile trek back up, Marin Transit Bus 61 takes you from Stinson Beach back to the ranger station. ⊠ *Pantoll Ranger Station, 3801 Panoramic Hwy., at Pantoll Rd. ✛ on Mt. Tamalpais* ☎ *415/388–2070* ⊕ *www.parks.ca.gov.*

★ **Muir Woods National Monument**
NATIONAL/STATE PARK | FAMILY | One of the last old-growth stands of redwood (*Sequoia sempervirens*) giants, Muir Woods is nature's cathedral: awe-inspiring and not to be missed. The nearly 560 acres of Muir Woods National Monument contain some of the most majestic redwoods in the world—some more than 250 feet tall.

Part of the Golden Gate National Recreation Area, Muir Woods is a pedestrian's park. The popular 2-mile main trail begins at the park headquarters and provides easy access to streams, ferns, azaleas, and redwood groves. Summer weekends can prove busy, so consider taking a more challenging route, such as the **Dipsea Trail,** which climbs west from the forest floor to soothing views of the ocean and the Golden Gate Bridge. For a complete list of trails, check with rangers.

Picnicking and camping aren't allowed, and neither are pets. Crowds can be large, especially from May through October, so come early in the morning or late in the afternoon. The **Muir Woods Visitor Center** has books and exhibits about redwood trees and the woods' history as well as the latest info on trail conditions; the **Muir Woods Trading Company** serves hot food, organic pastries, and other tasty snacks, and the gift shop offers plenty of souvenirs. ■TIP➔ Muir Woods has no cell service or Wi-Fi, so plan directions and communication ahead of time.

For parking reservations (required) and shuttle information, visit ⊕ *gomuirwoods. com.* To drive directly from San Francisco, take U.S. 101 North across the Golden Gate Bridge to Exit 445B for Mill Valley/Stinson Beach, then follow signs for Highway 1 North and Muir Woods. ⊠ *1 Muir Woods Rd., off Panoramic Hwy.* ☎ *415/561–2850 park reservations,* ⊕ *www.nps.gov/muwo* ⊠ *$15.*

Old Mill Park
CITY PARK | FAMILY | To see one of the numerous outdoor oases that make Mill Valley so appealing, follow Throckmorton Avenue a quarter mile west from Lytton Square to Old Mill Park, a shady patch of redwoods that shelters a playground and reconstructed sawmill. The park also hosts September's annual Mill Valley Fall Arts Festival. From the park, Cascade Way winds its way past creek-side homes to the trailheads of several forest paths. ⊠ *Throckmorton Ave. and Cascade Dr.* ☎ *415/383–1370 for rental information.* ⊕ *www.millvalleyrecreation.org.*

🍽 Restaurants

Boo Koo
$ | ASIAN | Southeast Asian street food with local flair is fired up in this hip and modern street café, where there's outdoor seating and a 10-tap bar. Summer rolls, satays, and skewers complement pho and wok specialties, and the locally sourced, vegan-based menu still has plenty for carnivores, who can customize dishes with grass-fed beef, wild salmon, and free-range chicken. **Known for:** green curry noodles; mint salad; Asian Brussels

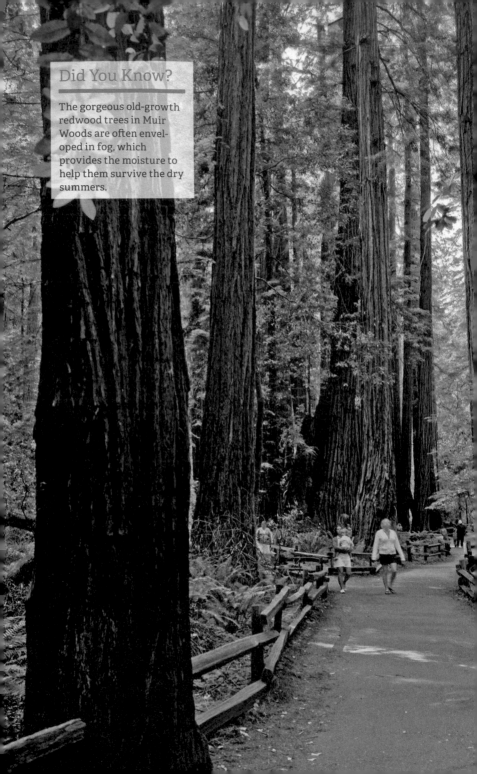

Did You Know?

The gorgeous old-growth redwood trees in Muir Woods are often enveloped in fog, which provides the moisture to help them survive the dry summers.

sprouts. ⑤ *Average main: $11* ✉ *25 Miller Ave.* ☎ *415/888–8303* ⊕ *eatbookoo.com.*

Buckeye Roadhouse

$$$ | **AMERICAN** | House-smoked meats and fish, grilled steaks, classic salads, and decadent desserts bring locals and visitors back again and again to this 1937 lodge-style roadhouse. Enjoy a Marin martini at the cozy mahogany bar or sip local wine beside the river-rock fireplace. **Known for:** oysters bingo; chili-lime "brick" chicken; ribs and chops. ⑤ *Average main: $29* ✉ *15 Shoreline Hwy., off U.S. 101* ☎ *415/331–2600* ⊕ *www. buckeyeroadhouse.com.*

Bungalow 44

$$ | **AMERICAN** | An open, well-lit space with booths and countertop seating from which diners can watch the cooks in action sets the scene at this lively eatery, which serves contemporary California cuisine and inventive cocktails. The menu focuses on locally sourced veggies and seafood. **Known for:** $1 oyster daily happy hour; fresh Marin Farmers' Market ingredients; kickin' fried chicken. ⑤ *Average main: $24* ✉ *44 E. Blithedale Ave., at Sunnyside Ave.* ☎ *415/381–2500* ⊕ *www. bungalow44.com* ⊙ *No lunch.*

La Ginestra

$$ | **ITALIAN** | **FAMILY** | In business since 1964, La Ginestra—named for the flowers that grow on Mt. Vesuvius, in the owners' homeland—is a Mill Valley institution renowned for its no-pretense, family-style Italian meals and impressive wine list. The Sorrento Bar, off the dining room, serves up a delectable array of bar bites, pizzas, and sweets to enjoy while sipping wines and cocktails inspired by the Aversa family's home country. **Known for:** handmade pasta and gnocchi; excellent ravioli; daily fish and small plates. ⑤ *Average main: $20* ✉ *127 Throckmorton Ave., off Miller Ave.* ☎ *415/388–0224* ⊕ *www.laginestramv.com* ⊙ *Closed Mon. and Tues. No lunch.*

Piazza D'Angelo

$$ | **ITALIAN** | **FAMILY** | In the heart of downtown, busy D'Angelo's is known for its authentic and fresh pastas; there are even gluten-free options. Another draw is the scene, especially in the lounge area, which hosts a lively cocktail hour in a traditional trattoria setting. **Known for:** fresh seafood; homemade pasta; top-notch tiramisu. ⑤ *Average main: $22* ✉ *22 Miller Ave., off Throckmorton* ☎ *415/388–2000* ⊕ *www.piazzadangelo.com.*

Playa

$$ | **MODERN MEXICAN** | Modern Mexican farm-to-table creations and inspired cocktails are the focus of this festive indoor-outdoor space that's popular for its firepit, made-to-order masa station, and happy hour. An open kitchen serves up locally sourced, organic, and sustainable dishes like ceviche and flautas, grilled octopus tacos, and braised pork tortas. **Known for:** taco Tuesdays; rare tequilas and mezcals; moles and salsas. ⑤ *Average main: $18* ✉ *41 Throckmorton Ave.* ☎ *415/384–8871* ⊕ *www.playamv.com.*

Vasco

$ | **ITALIAN** | With its wood-fired pizza oven, wine bar, and live music in the evening, this lovely corner restaurant has serious neighborhood charm. Authentic Italian specialties include chicken marsala, seafood stew, and calamari steak. **Known for:** great atmosphere; gluten-free pizza and pasta; memorable tiramisu. ⑤ *Average main: $16* ✉ *106 Throckmorton Ave.* ☎ *415/381–3343* ⊕ *vascorestaurantmillvalley.com* ⊙ *No lunch.*

☕ Coffee and Quick Bites

Avatar's Restaurant

$ | **INDIAN** | The lines can get long at this hole-in-the-wall, no-frills kitchen, where Indian curries are served burrito style while you wait (note: it's cash only). Punjabi burritos or rice plates come with savory lamb, chicken, fish, vegetarian, and vegan ingredients flavored with seasonal fruit chutneys, tamarind sauce, and aromatic blends. **Known for:** curried pumpkin; smoked eggplant; mostly take-out dining. $ *Average main: $8* ✉ *15 Madrona St.* ☎ *415/381–8293* 🕑 *Closed Sun.* 🚫 *No credit cards.*

Equator Coffees

$ | **CAFÉ** | This is the prime spot for a pick-me-up (and people-watching) over a picturesque view of downtown Mill Valley and Mt. Tam. The owners are as serious about coffee as they are about social responsibility, from their fair-chain single-origin beans and organic loose teas down to the locally recycled wood and metal decor. **Known for:** espresso and cappuccino drinks; breakfast sandwiches; strawberry and chocolate waffles. $ *Average main: $9* ✉ *2 Miller Ave.* ☎ *415/383–1651* 🌐 *www.equatorcoffees. com* 🕑 *No dinner.*

 ## Hotels

Acqua Hotel

$$ | **HOTEL** | Alongside Richardson Bay, this stylish boutique hotel has modern, elegant rooms decorated in soft Zen-like color schemes. **Pros:** evening wine service; free parking and Wi-Fi; hearty breakfast buffet. **Cons:** next to freeway; traffic audible in rooms facing east; limited amenities within walking distance. $ *Rooms from: $259* ✉ *555 Redwood Hwy., off U.S. 101* ☎ *415/388–9353* 🌐 *www.marinhotels.com* 🛏 *49 rooms* 🍴 *Free breakfast.*

Mill Valley Inn

$$$ | **B&B/INN** | The only hotel in downtown Mill Valley is comprised of one of the area's first homes, the Creek House, which has smart-looking Victorian rooms, and two small cottages nestled in a grove beyond a creek. **Pros:** unique rooms in private yet central location; some rooms have balconies, soaking tubs, and fireplaces; free mountain bikes. **Cons:** limited room service; dark in winter because of surrounding trees; some rooms are not accessible via elevator. $ *Rooms from: $329* ✉ *165 Throckmorton Ave., near Miller Ave.* ☎ *415/389–6608, 855/334–7946* 🌐 *millvalleyinn.com* 🛏 *25 rooms* 🍴 *Free breakfast.*

Mountain Home Inn

$$ | **B&B/INN** | Abutting 40,000 acres of state and national parks, this airy wooden inn sits on the skirt of Mt. Tamalpais, where you can follow hiking trails all the way to Stinson Beach. **Pros:** amazing terrace and views; peaceful, remote setting; cooked-to-order breakfast. **Cons:** nearest town is a 12-minute drive away; restaurant can get crowded on sunny weekend days; some rooms are tiny and have no TVs. $ *Rooms from: $243* ✉ *810 Panoramic Hwy., at Edgewood Ave.* ☎ *415/381–9000* 🌐 *www.mtnhomeinn. com* 🛏 *10 rooms* 🍴 *Free breakfast.*

 ## Nightlife

BREWPUBS AND BEER GARDENS

The Junction Beer Garden & Bottle Shop

BREWPUBS/BEER GARDENS | With more than a hundred styles of canned and bottled beers and 30 beers on tap, plus wine and hard kombucha, this enormous indoor and outdoor beer garden is perfectly situated along the Dipsea Trail for a visit before or after a Mt. Tam hike or Tennessee Valley beach visit. The brewers partnered with PizzaHacker, a cult-favorite pizzeria in San Francisco's Bernal Heights, to provide classic pies like their "top-shelf" Margherita, as well as salads and meatballs. The landscaped outdoor space is lined with picnic tables, Adirondack chairs, and firepits. ✉ *226 Shoreline Hwy.* ☎ *415/888–3544* 🌐 *thejunc.com.*

Performing Arts

★ Throckmorton Theatre

ARTS CENTERS | A vibrant cultural hub in the region, the restored cinema and vaudeville house in Mill Valley is known for fostering exceptional arts and education. The darling playhouse seats upward of 260 and features live theater, comedy, and concerts. Two smaller street-side halls, the Tivoli and Crescendo, feature free classical concerts on Wednesday, along with Sunday evening sessions, jazz performances, and new art exhibits every month. ⊠ *142 Throckmorton Ave.* ☎ *415/383–9600* ⊕ *www.throckmortont-heatre.org.*

Shopping

Mill Valley Market

FOOD/CANDY | This family-owned market has been the go-to stop for specialty foods, groceries, deli items, and hot food since 1929. Known for the notable beer and wine selection alongside local and organic produce and healthy grab-and-go foods, this is an ideal place to prepare for a picnic or seek out gourmet gifts, like imported chocolates and 100-year-old balsamic vinegars. ⊠ *12 Corte Madera Ave.* ☎ *415/388–3222* ⊕ *millvalleymarket. com.*

Muir Beach

12 miles northwest of Golden Gate Bridge, 6 miles southwest of Mill Valley.

Except on the sunniest of weekends, Muir Beach is relatively quiet, but the drive to this community and beach is a scenic adventure.

GETTING HERE AND AROUND

A car is the best way to reach Muir Beach. From Highway 1, follow Pacific Way southwest ¼ mile.

Beaches

Muir Beach

BEACH—SIGHT | **FAMILY** | Small but scenic, this beach—a rocky patch of shoreline off Highway 1 in the northern Marin Headlands—is a good place to stretch your legs and gaze out at the Pacific Ocean. Locals often walk their dogs

here; families and cuddling couples come for picnicking and sunbathing. At the northern end of the beach are waterfront homes (and occasional nude sunbathers), and at the other are the bluffs of the Golden Gate National Recreation Area. A land bridge connects directly from the parking lot to the beach, as well as to a short trail that leads to a scenic overlook and connects to other coastal paths. There are no lifeguards on duty and the currents can be challenging, so swimming is not advised. **Amenities:** parking (free); toilets. **Best for:** solitude; sunset; walking. ⊠ *100 Pacific Way, off Shoreline Hwy.* ⊕ *www.nps.gov/gogo.*

Hotels

The Pelican Inn

$$ | **B&B/INN** | From its slate roof to its whitewashed plaster walls, this Tudor-style inn built in the 1970s is English to the core, with its cozy upstairs guest rooms (no elevator) and draped half-tester beds, a sun-filled solarium, and bangers and grilled tomatoes for breakfast. **Pros:** five-minute walk to the beach; great bar and restaurant; peaceful setting. **Cons:** 20-minute drive to nearby attractions; rooms are quite small and rustic; workout and steam room access not on-site. Ⓢ *Rooms from: $224* ⊠ *10 Pacific Way, off Hwy. 1* ☎ *415/383–6000* ⊕ *www.pelicaninn.com* ⤴ *7 rooms* ⦿ *Free breakfast.*

Stinson Beach

20 miles northwest of Golden Gate Bridge.

This laid-back hamlet is all about the beach, and folks come from all over the Bay Area to walk its sandy, often windswept shore. An ideal day trip would include a morning hike at Mt. Tamalpais followed by lunch at one of Stinson's unassuming eateries and a leisurely beach stroll.

GETTING HERE AND AROUND

If you're driving, take U.S. 101 to the Mill Valley/Stinson Beach/Highway 1 exit and follow the road west and then north. By bus, take Golden Gate Transit to Marin City and then transfer to the West Marin Stagecoach (61) for Bolinas.

 Beaches

Stinson Beach

BEACH—SIGHT | FAMILY | When the fog hasn't rolled in, this expansive stretch of sand is about as close as you can get in Marin to the stereotypical feel of a Southern California beach. There are several clothing-optional areas, among them a section south of Stinson Beach called Red Rock Beach. ⚠ **Swimming at Stinson Beach can be dangerous; the undertow is strong, and shark sightings, though infrequent, have occurred; lifeguards are on duty May–September.** Pets are not allowed on the national park section of the beach.

On any hot summer weekend, roads to Stinson are packed and the parking lot fills, so factor this into your plans. The town itself—population 600, give or take—has a nonchalant surfer vibe, with a few good eating options and pleasant hippie-craftsy browsing. **Amenities:** food and drink; lifeguards (summer); parking (free); showers; toilets. **Best for:** nudists; sunset; surfing; swimming; walking; windsurfing. ⊠ *Hwy. 1, 1 Calle Del Sierra* ☎ *415/868–0942 lifeguard tower* ⊕ *www. nps.gov/goga.*

 Restaurants

Parkside Cafe

$$ | AMERICAN | FAMILY | Though this place is popular for its 1950s beachfront snack bar, the adjoining café, coffee bar, marketplace, and bakery shouldn't be missed either. The full menu serves up fresh ingredients, local seafood, and wood-fired pizzas. **Known for:** espresso and pastry bar; tasty fish-and-chips; rustic house-made breads. ⑤ *Average main: $26* ⊠ *43 Arenal Ave., off Shoreline Hwy.* ☎ *415/868–1272* ⊕ *www.parksidecafe.com.*

Stinson Beach Breakers Cafe

$$ | AMERICAN | Hard to miss along the tiny stretch of Main Street, this café is an easy prebeach destination for coffee and griddle specialties or postsurf bar bites and cocktails on the heated patio in the afternoon. Beach-cottage hardwood floors and a woodstove add to the warmth of the rustic seaside interior, while a mountain view and firepit enhance the deck. **Known for:** hearty egg breakfast dishes with a Latin twist; fresh oysters; fish tacos. ⑤ *Average main: $19* ⊠ *3465 Hwy. 1* ☎ *415/868–2002* ⊘ *Closed Tues. and Wed. Nov.–Mar.*

 Hotels

Sandpiper Lodging

$$ | B&B/INN | FAMILY | Recharge, rest, and enjoy the local scenery at this ultrapopular lodging that books up months, even years, in advance. **Pros:** beach chairs, towels, and toys provided; lush garden with grill; minutes from the beach and town. **Cons:** walls are thin; limited amenities; charge for rollaway beds and extra persons. ⑤ *Rooms from: $262* ⊠ *1 Marine Way, off Arenal Ave.* ☎ *415/868–1632* ⊕ *www.sandpiperstinsonbeach. com* ➭ *11 rooms* ⦿ *No meals.*

Point Reyes National Seashore

Bear Valley Visitor Center is 14 miles north of Stinson Beach.

With sandy beaches stretching for miles, a dramatic rocky coastline, a gem of a lighthouse (Point Reyes Lighthouse: closed at this writing, but check online), and idyllic, century-old dairy farms, Point Reyes National Seashore is one of the most varied and strikingly beautiful corners of the Bay Area.

GETTING HERE AND AROUND

From San Francisco, take U.S. 101 North, head west at Sir Francis Drake Boulevard (Exit 450B) toward San Anselmo, and follow the road just under 20 miles to Bear Valley Road. From Stinson Beach or Bolinas, drive north on Highway 1 and turn left on Bear Valley Road. If you're going by bus, take one of several Golden Gate Transit buses to Marin City; in Marin City, transfer to the West Marin Stagecoach (you'll switch buses in Olema). Once at the visitor center, the best way to get around is on foot.

Sights

Bear Valley Visitor Center

INFO CENTER | FAMILY | Tucked in the Olema Valley, this welcoming center is a perfect point of orientation for trails and roads throughout the region's unique and diverse ecosystem. It offers a rich glimpse of local cultural and natural heritage with engaging exhibits about the wildlife, history, and ecology of the Point Reyes National Seashore. The rangers at the barnlike facility share their in-depth knowledge about beaches, whale-watching, hiking trails, and camping. Restrooms are available, as well as trailhead parking and a picnic area with barbecue grills. Winter hours may be shorter and summer weekend hours may be longer; call or check the website for details. ⊠ *Bear Valley Visitor Center, 1 Bear Valley Visitor Center Access Rd., west of Hwy. 1, off Bear Valley Rd., Point Reyes Station* ☎ *415/464–5100* ⊕ *www. nps.gov/pore.*

★ Duxbury Reef

NATURE PRESERVE | FAMILY | Excellent tide pooling can be had along the 3-mile shoreline of Duxbury Reef; it's the most extensive tide pool area near Point Reyes National Seashore, as well as one of the largest shale intertidal reefs in North America. Look for sea stars, barnacles, sea anemones, purple urchins, limpets, sea mussels, and the occasional abalone.

But check a tide table (⊕ *tidesandcurrents.noaa.gov*) or the local papers if you plan to explore the reef—it's accessible only at low tide. The reef is a 30-minute drive from the Bear Valley Visitor Center. Take Highway 1 South from the center, turn right at Olema Bolinas Road (keep an eye peeled; the road is easy to miss), left on Horseshoe Hill Road, right on Mesa Road, left on Overlook Drive, and then right on Elm Road, which dead-ends at the Agate Beach County Park parking lot.

Excellent tide pooling can be had along the 3-mile shoreline of Duxbury Reef; it's the most extensive tide pool area near Point Reyes National Seashore, as well as one of the largest shale intertidal reefs in North America. Look for sea stars, barnacles, sea anemones, purple urchins, limpets, sea mussels, and the occasional abalone. But check a tide table (⊕ *tidesandcurrents.noaa.gov*) or the local papers if you plan to explore the reef—it's accessible only at low tide. The reef is a 30-minute drive from the Bear Valley Visitor Center. Take Highway 1 South from the center, turn right at Olema Bolinas Road (keep an eye peeled; the road is easy to miss), left on Horseshoe Hill Road, right on Mesa Road, left on Overlook Drive, and then right on Elm Road, which dead-ends at the Agate Beach County Park parking lot. ⊕ *At Duxbury Point, 1 mile west of Bolinas* ⊕ *www.ptreyes.org* ⊠ *Free.*

Palomarin Field Station & Point Reyes Bird Observatory

NATURE PRESERVE | FAMILY | Birders adore Point Blue Conservation Science, which maintains the Palomarin Field Station and the Point Reyes Bird Observatory that are located in the southernmost part of Point Reyes National Seashore. The Field Station has excellent interpretive exhibits, including a comparative display of real birds' talons. The surrounding woods harbor some 200 bird species. As you hike the quiet trails through forest and along ocean cliffs, you're likely to see biologists banding birds to aid in the study of their life cycles. ■TIP➔ Visit Point Blue's website for detailed directions and to find out when banding will occur. ⊠ *999 Mesa Rd., Bolinas* ☎ *415/868–0655 field station, 707/781–2555 headquarters* ⊕ *www. pointblue.org.*

★ Point Reyes National Seashore
NATIONAL/STATE PARK | FAMILY | One of the Bay Area's most spectacular treasures and the only national seashore on the West Coast, the 71,000-acre Point Reyes National Seashore encompasses hiking trails, secluded beaches, and rugged grasslands, as well as Point Reyes itself, a triangular peninsula that juts into the Pacific. The Point Reyes Lighthouse occupies the peninsula's tip and is a scenic 21-mile drive from Bear Valley Visitor Center; at this writing it is closed for renovations, but check online. The town of **Point Reyes Station** is a one-main-drag affair, with some good places to eat.

When explorer Sir Francis Drake sailed along the California coast in 1579, he allegedly missed the Golden Gate Strait and San Francisco Bay, but he did land at what he described as a convenient harbor. In 2012 the federal government recognized Drake's Bay, which flanks the point on the east, as that harbor, designating the spot a National Historic Landmark.

The infamous San Andreas Fault runs along the park's eastern edge; take the **Earthquake Trail** from the visitor center to see the impact near the epicenter of the 1906 earthquake that devastated San Francisco. A half-mile path from the visitor center leads to **Kule Loklo,** a reconstructed Miwok village of the region's first known inhabitants.

You can experience the diversity of Point Reyes's ecosystems on the scenic **Coast Trail** through eucalyptus groves and pine forests and along seaside cliffs to beautiful and tiny Bass Lake.

The 4.7-mile-long (one-way) **Tomales Point Trail** follows the spine of the park's northernmost finger of land through the Tule Elk Preserve, providing spectacular ocean views from high bluffs. ⊠ *Bear Valley Visitor Center, 1 Bear Valley Visitor Center Access Rd., Point Reyes Station* ✛ *West of Hwy. 1, off Bear Valley Rd.* ☎ *415/464–5100* ⊕ *www.nps.gov/pore* 🎫 *Free.*

 Restaurants

Cafe Reyes
$ | PIZZA | FAMILY | Sunny patio seating, hand-tossed pizza, and organic local ingredients are the selling points of this laid-back café. The semi-industrial dining room, built around a brick oven, features glazed concrete floors, warm-painted walls, and ceilings high enough to accommodate full-size market umbrellas. **Known for:** wood-fired pizza; Tomales Bay fresh oysters; good salads. ⑤ *Average main: $15* ⊠ *11101 Hwy. 1, Point Reyes Station* ☎ *415/663–9493* ⊕ *cafe-reyes. com* ☾ *Closed Mon. and Tues.*

Due West
$$ | AMERICAN | A convivial atmosphere and local, sustainable culinary provisions keep this classic Point Reyes tavern a favorite stop among locals. Refurbished and modernized since its days as a horse-and-wagon stop in the 1860s, it now has a farm-to-fork seasonal menu including American classics from burgers and brick-roasted chicken to seafood specialties like shrimp scampi and steamed mussels. **Known for:** artisanal cheese plate; steak frites; regional wine list. ⑤ *Average main: $23* ⊠ *10021 Coastal Hwy. 1, Olema* ☎ *415/663–1264* ⊕ *olemahouse.com/due-west-restaurant/.*

Eleven
$$ | WINE BAR | For a true taste of local culture, this sisters-owned venture welcomes you to sit back, relax, sip some wine, and enjoy the flavors and scene Bolinas is known for, from the town's

laid-back lifestyle and quirky decor to the natural beauty and the fresh coastal air. The wine bar and bistro's short but ever-changing creative and thoughtful menus change daily based on what's available and reflect the richness of this region's foodshed—considered one of the nation's most diverse. **Known for:** house-made, locally sourced ingredients; local natural wine selections; pizzas and oysters. $ *Average main: $17* ✉ *11 Wharf Rd., Bolinas* ☎ *415/868–1133* ⊕ *www.11wharfroad.com* ☾ *Closed Sun.–Wed.*

★ **Hog Island Oyster Co. Marshall Oyster Farm and the Boat Oyster Bar**
$$ | **SEAFOOD** | **FAMILY** | Take a short trek north on Highway 1 to the gritty mecca of Bay Area oysters—the Hog Island Marshall Oyster Farm. For a real culinary adventure, arrange to shuck and barbecue your own oysters on one of the outdoor grills (all tools supplied, reservations required); or for the less adventurous, the Boat Oyster Bar is an informal outdoor café that serves raw and grilled oysters, local snacks, and tasty beverages. **Known for:** fresh, raw, and grilled oysters; farm tours; Hog Shack shellfish to go. $ *Average main: $24* ✉ *20215 Shoreline Hwy.* ☎ *415/663–9218* ⊕ *hogislandoysters.com* ☾ *Oyster Bar closed Tues.–Thurs. No dinner.*

Inverness Park Market & Tap Room
$$ | **AMERICAN** | An organic oasis in the region, this deli, restaurant, and taproom offers a true taste of the Point Reyes foodshed. Classic sandwiches, breakfast bites, burritos, grilled Niman Ranch beef, wild-caught salmon, and vegan burgers are all prepared with fresh local ingredients. **Known for:** Tuesday tacos and Wednesday sushi specials; house-cooked tri-tip and smoked pastrami; grilled oysters. $ *Average main: $18* ✉ *12301 Sir Francis Drake Blvd., Inverness Park* ☎ *415/663–1491* ⊕ *invernessparkmarket.com.*

Saltwater Oyster Depot
$$ | **SEAFOOD** | Oysters shucked moments after they're taken out of Tomales Bay and French and California wines sourced from small producers are the keystones of this neighborhood oyster bar. True to the spirit of the region, it is dedicated to sustainable farming, foraging, and fishing. **Known for:** broiled, baked, and chili oysters; clam chowder; natural wines. $ *Average main: $20* ✉ *12781 Sir Francis Drake Blvd., Inverness* ☎ ⊕ *www.saltwateroysterdepot.com* ☾ *Closed Mon.–Wed.*

★ **Side Street Kitchen**
$ | **AMERICAN** | **FAMILY** | Rotisserie meats and veggies sourced from local farms steal the show at this former mid-20th-century truck stop and diner. It's a go-to for tri-tip and pork belly sandwiches or house-seasoned roasted chicken, best eaten with a host of sides, sips, and sweets, like crispy Parmesan Brussels sprouts, ginger lemonade, and butterscotch pudding. **Known for:** cold smoked seafood and rotisserie chicken; dog-friendly outdoor patio; apple fritters. $ *Average main: $16* ✉ *60 4th St., Point Reyes Station* ☎ *415/663–0303* ⊕ *sidestreet-prs.com* ☾ *No dinner after 6 pm.*

★ **Station House Café**
$$ | **AMERICAN** | Relocated to the space where the restaurant originally opened its doors in 1974, the Station House Café has been a stalwart venue for local music and a staunch supporter of local farms and food artisans. The community-centric eatery serves a blend of modern and classic California dishes comprised of organic seasonal ingredients, sustainable hormone-free meats, and wild-caught seafood. **Known for:** signature popovers and bread pudding; hearty breakfast items; fresh local seafood. $ *Average main: $17* ✉ *11285 Hwy. 1, at 3rd St., Point Reyes Station* ☎ *415/663–1515* ⊕ *www.stationhousecafe.com* ☾ *Closed Wed. and Thurs.*

Hotels

★ Olema House

$$$$ | B&B/INN | FAMILY | Once a historic 1860s stagecoach stopover, this renovated, luxurious getaway offers just as many reasons to stay on property—with its views of Mt. Wittenberg and garden setting—as to explore the 71,000 acres of national seashore just steps away. **Pros:** steps from trails; convenient parking and horse hitching; friendly and informative staff. **Cons:** steps to some rooms may be steep; street-facing rooms above restaurant may be noisy; Wi-Fi and cell service may be spotty. ⑤ *Rooms from: $480* ✉ *10021 Coastal Hwy. 1, Olema* ☎ *415/663–9000* ⊕ *olemahouse.com* ⤳ *25 rooms* ⏛ *Free breakfast.*

 Shopping

★ Cowgirl Creamery

FOOD/CANDY | FAMILY | In this former hay barn, a couple of Berkeley foodies (from Chez Panisse and Bette's Oceanview Diner) started their original creamery for artisanal cheeses. In addition to more than 200 specialty cheeses—local, regional, and international—you'll find Tomales Bay Foods offerings featuring West Marin farm wares. Cowgirl Creamery cheeses harness flavors unique to Point Reyes, such as their award-winning Red Hawk and Mt. Tam made with Straus Family organic milk. Sample seasonal cheeses and see how the cheese is made or order a hot mac-and-cheese at the cantina and stay for a bite at the picnic tables. Abundant deli items, gourmet goodies, and wine selections are perfect for picnicking. ✉ *80 4th St., Point Reyes Station* ☎ *415/663–9335* ⊕ *cowgirlcreamery.com.*

Gospel Flat Farm Stand

LOCAL SPECIALTIES | This combination art gallery, farm stand, and flower shop captures the true essence of the Bolinas and Olema area, with its dedication to community arts and a bounty of local organic vegetables, fruits, and eggs. The colorful self-serve site is open 24 hours, but what makes it truly special is that the entire stand operates on the honor system. Weigh and log your produce, and slip your payment (cash or check) in the box. The ever-rotating local art on exhibit adds to the allure of this roadside treasure. ✉ *140 Olema-Bolinas Rd., Bolinas* ☎ *415/868–0921* ⊕ *gospelflatfarm.com.*

★ Toby's Feed Barn

LOCAL SPECIALTIES | The heart of the community since 1942, the barn has a bounty of local gifts and produce, plus an art gallery, yoga studio, and Toby's Coffee Bar for espresso drinks and sell-out pastries. See and hear what's happening locally, catch a live band or literary event, and explore the garden. The internationally renowned all-local, all-organic Point Reyes Farmers' Market is held here on Saturdays during the growing season. ✉ *11250 Hwy. 1, Point Reyes Station* ☎ *415/663–1223* ⊕ *www.tobysfeedbarn.com.*

Chapter 12

NAPA AND SONOMA

Updated by
Daniel Mangin

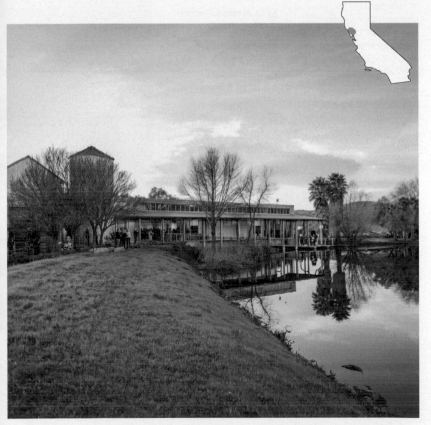

⊙ Sights	🍴 Restaurants	🛏 Hotels	🛍 Shopping	🍸 Nightlife
★★★★★	★★★★★	★★★★☆	★★★☆☆	★★★☆☆

WELCOME TO NAPA AND SONOMA

TOP REASONS TO GO

★ **Touring wineries:** Let's face it: this is the reason you're here, and the range of excellent sips to sample would make any oeno-phile (or novice drinker, for that matter) giddy.

★ **Biking:** Gentle hills and vineyard-laced farmland make Napa and Sonoma perfect for combining lei-surely back-roads cycling with winery stops.

★ **Spa treatments:** Work-hard, play-hard types and inveterate sybarites flock to Wine Country spas for pampering.

★ **Fine dining:** A meal at a top-tier restaurant can be a revelation about the level of artistry intuitive chefs can achieve and how successfully quality wines pair with food.

★ **Viewing the art:** Several wineries, among them the Hess Collection in Napa, The Donum Estate in Sonoma, and Hall St. Helena, dis-play museum-quality artworks indoors and on their grounds.

1 **Napa.** Good base, with tasting rooms, dining, shopping, nightlife.

2 **Yountville.** Walkable downtown, must-visit restaurants.

3 **Oakville.** Cabernet central.

4 **Rutherford.** Find out what "Rutherford dust" is.

5 **St. Helena.** Genteel downtown amid wineries.

6 **Calistoga.** Spas—from rustic to chic.

7 **Sonoma.** Anchored by a historic mission and plaza.

8 **Glen Ellen.** Creekside village with a rural flavor.

9 **Kenwood.** Top of Sonoma Valley.

10 **Petaluma.** Farming town, proud of it.

11 **Healdsburg.** Northern Sonoma's swank hub.

12 **Geyserville.** Alexander Valley wineries, fun downtown.

13 **Forestville.** Woodsy river enclave.

14 **Guerneville.** A Russian River vacation spot.

15 **Sebastopol.** West County's HQ.

16 **Santa Rosa.** Sonoma County's largest city.

In California's premier wine region, the pleasures of eating and drinking are celebrated daily. It's easy to join in at famous wineries and rising newcomers off country roads, or at trendy in-town tasting rooms. Chefs transform local ingredients into feasts, and gourmet groceries sell perfect picnic fare.

Yountville, Healdsburg, and St. Helena have small-town charm as well as luxurious inns, hotels, and spas. Yet the natural setting is equally sublime, whether experienced from a canoe on the Russian River or the deck of a winery overlooking endless rows of vines.

The Wine Country is also rich in history. In Sonoma you can explore California's Spanish and Mexican pasts at the Sonoma Mission, and the origins of modern California wine making at Buena Vista Winery. Some wineries, among them St. Helena's Beringer and Rutherford's Inglenook, have cellars or tasting rooms dating to the late 1800s. Calistoga is a flurry of late-19th-century Steamboat Gothic architecture, though the town's oldest-looking building, the medieval-style Castello di Amorosa, is a 21st-century creation.

Visits to the Napa Valley's Beringer, Robert Mondavi, and Inglenook—and at Buena Vista in the Sonoma Valley—provide an entertaining overview of Wine Country history. Through the glass walls at Hall St. Helena's tasting room you may glimpse 21st-century wine-making technology in action, and over in Glen Ellen's Benziger Family Winery you can learn how its vineyard managers apply biodynamic farming principles to grape

growing. At numerous facilities you can play winemaker at seminars in the fine art of blending wines. If that strikes you as too much effort, you can always pamper yourself at a luxury spa.

To delve further into the fine art of Wine Country living, pick up a copy of *Fodor's Napa and Sonoma*.

MAJOR REGIONS

Napa Valley. Practically speaking, the valley can be divided into its southern and northern parts. The southern Napa Valley encompasses cooler grape-growing areas and the tasting rooms, restaurants, and hotels of **Napa** and **Yountville**, along with slightly warmer **Oakville.** The northern valley begins around **Rutherford,** like Oakville blessed with Cabernet-friendly soils. Beyond it lies hotter **St. Helena,** whose downtown entices with boutiques, galleries, and restaurants. Warmer still is **Calistoga,** known for spas and hot springs.

Sonoma Valley and Petaluma. Modern California wine making began in Sonoma Valley. North of the tasting rooms, restaurants, and lodgings near Sonoma Plaza in downtown **Sonoma** lie the wineries of more pastoral **Glen Ellen** and **Kenwood.** To the valley's west, **Petaluma,** with a burgeoning dining scene, has come into its own as a Wine Country destination.

Northern Sonoma, Russian River, and West County. Its walkable downtown, swank hotels, and restaurant scene make **Healdsburg** the tourist hub of Sonoma County's northern section. North of Healdsburg, mostly rural **Geyserville** has a small, engaging downtown. The Russian River winds through or near **Forestville, Guerneville,** and **Sebastopol,** three West County towns where Chardonnay and Pinot Noir grow well. The county's largest city, **Santa Rosa,** contains nonwine attractions and affordable lodgings.

Planning

When to Go

High season extends from late May through October. In summer, expect the days to be hot and dry. Hotel rates are highest during the height of harvest, in September and October. Then and in summer, book lodgings well ahead. November, except for Thanksgiving week, and December before Christmas are less busy. The weather in Napa and Sonoma is pleasant nearly year-round. Daytime temperatures average from about 55°F during winter to the 80s and 90s (occasionally 100s) in summer. April, May, and October are milder but still warm. The rainiest months are usually from December through March.

Getting Here and Around

AIR
Wine Country regulars often bypass San Francisco and Oakland and fly into Santa Rosa's Charles M. Schulz Sonoma County Airport (STS), which receives direct flights from several western cities. The airport is 15 miles from Healdsburg.
■ TIP→ **Alaska Airlines allows passengers flying out of STS to check up to one case of wine for free.**

BUS
Bus travel is an inconvenient way to explore the Wine Country, though it is possible. Take Golden Gate Transit from San Francisco to connect with Sonoma County Transit buses. VINE connects with BART commuter trains in the East Bay and the San Francisco Bay Ferry in Vallejo. VINE buses serve the Napa Valley.

CAR
A car is the most convenient way to navigate Napa and Sonoma. If you're flying into the area, it's almost always easiest to pick up a car at the airport. You'll also find rental companies in major Wine Country towns. A few rules to note: smartphone use for any purpose is prohibited, including mapping applications unless the device is mounted to a car's windshield or dashboard and can be activated with a single swipe or finger tap. A right turn after stopping at a red light is legal unless posted otherwise.

If you base yourself in the Napa Valley towns of Napa, Yountville, or St. Helena, or in Sonoma County's Healdsburg or Sonoma, you can visit numerous tasting rooms and nearby wineries on foot or by bicycle on mostly flat terrain. The free Yountville trolley loops through town, and ride sharing is viable there and in Napa. Sonoma County sprawls more, but except for far west the public transit and ride-sharing generally work well.

■ TIP→ **When wine tasting, select a designated driver or monitor your intake—the police keep an eye out for tipsy drivers.**

Restaurants

Top Wine Country chefs tend to apply French and Italian techniques to dishes incorporating fresh, local products. Menus are often vegan- and vegetarian-friendly, with gluten-free options. At pricey restaurants you can save money by having lunch instead of dinner. With a few exceptions (noted in individual restaurant listings), dress is informal.

Hotels

The fanciest accommodations are concentrated in the Napa Valley towns of Yountville, Rutherford, St. Helena, and Calistoga; Sonoma County's poshest lodgings are in Healdsburg. The cities of Napa, Petaluma, and Santa Rosa are the best bets for budget hotels and inns. On weekends, two- or even three-night minimum stays are commonly required at smaller lodgings. Book well ahead for stays at such places in summer or early fall. Some accommodations aren't suitable for kids, so ask before you book.

Restaurant and hotel reviews have been shortened. For full information, visit Fodors.com. Restaurant prices are the average cost of a main course at dinner, or if dinner is not served, at lunch. Hotel prices are the lowest cost of a standard double room in high season.

What It Costs			
$	$$	$$$	$$$$
RESTAURANTS			
under $17	$17–$26	$27–$36	over $36
HOTELS			
under $200	$200–$300	$301–$400	over $400

Napa

46 miles northeast of San Francisco.

After many years as a blue-collar burg detached from the Wine Country scene, the Napa Valley's largest town (population about 80,000) has evolved into one of its shining stars. Masaharu Morimoto and other chefs of note operate restaurants here, swank hotels and inns can be found downtown and beyond, and the nightlife options include the West Coast edition of the famed Blue Note jazz club. A walkway that follows the Napa River has made downtown more pedestrian-friendly, and the Oxbow Public Market, a complex of high-end food purveyors, is popular with locals and tourists. The market is named for the nearby oxbow bend in the Napa River, a bit north of where Napa was founded in 1848. The first wood-frame building was a saloon, and the downtown area still projects an old-river-town vibe.

GETTING HERE AND AROUND

Downtown Napa lies a mile east of Highway 29—take the 1st Street exit and follow the signs. Ample parking, much of it free for the first three hours and some for the entire day, is available on or near Main Street. Several VINE buses serve downtown and beyond.

Sights

★ Ashes & Diamonds

WINERY/DISTILLERY | Barbara Bestor's sleek white design for this appointment-only winery's glass-and-metal tasting space evokes mid-century modern architecture and with it the era and wines predating the Napa Valley's rise to prominence. Two much-heralded pros lead the wine-making team assembled by record producer Kashy Khaledi: Steve Matthiasson, known for his classic, restrained style and attention to viticultural detail, and Diana Snowden Seysses, who draws on experiences in Burgundy, Provence, and California. Bordeaux varietals are the focus, most notably Cabernet Sauvignon and Cabernet Franc but also the white blend of Sauvignon Blanc and Sémillon and even the rosé (of Cabernet Franc). With a label designer who was also responsible for a Jay-Z album cover and interiors that recall the *Mad Men* in the Palm Springs story arc, the pitch seems unabashedly intended to millennials, but the wines, low in alcohol and with high acidity (good for aging the wines),

enchant connoisseurs of all stripes.
⊠ *4130 Howard La., Napa* ✛ *Off Hwy. 29*
☎ *707/666–4777* ⊕ *ashesdiamonds.com*
🍷 *Tastings from $75.*

CIA at Copia

COLLEGE | Full-fledged foodies and the merely curious achieve gastronomical bliss at the Culinary Institute of America's Oxbow District campus, its facade brightened by a wraparound mural inspired by the colorful garden that fronts the facility. When everything's going full tilt, you could easily spend a few hours dining at the indoor and outdoor restaurants; checking out the shop, themed exhibitions, and Vintners Hall of Fame wall; or attending (book ahead) classes and demonstrations. If it's open, head upstairs to the Chuck Williams Culinary Arts Museum. Named for the Williams-Sonoma kitchenwares founder, it holds a fascinating collection of cooking, baking, and other food-related tools, tableware, gizmos, and gadgets, some dating back more than a century. ⊠ *500 1st St., Napa* ✛ *Near McKinstry St* ☎ *707/967–2500* ⊕ *www.ciaatcopia. com* 🍷 *Facility/museum free, class/demo fees vary.*

★ Domaine Carneros

WINERY/DISTILLERY | A visit to this majestic château is an opulent way to enjoy the Carneros District—especially in fine weather, when the vineyard views are spectacular. The château was modeled after an 18th-century French mansion owned by the Taittinger family. Carved into the hillside beneath the winery, the cellars produce sparkling wines reminiscent of those made by Taittinger, using only Los Carneros AVA grapes. Enjoy flights of sparkling wine or Pinot Noir with cheese and charcuterie plates, caviar, or smoked salmon. Tastings are by appointment only. ⊠ *1240 Duhig Rd., Napa* ✛ *At Hwy. 121* ☎ *707/257–0101, 800/716–2788* ⊕ *www.domainecarneros. com* 🍷 *Tastings from $40.*

Etude Wines

WINERY/DISTILLERY | You're apt to see or hear hawks, egrets, Canada geese, and other wildlife on the grounds of Etude, known for sophisticated Pinot Noirs. Although the winery and its light-filled tasting room are in Napa County, the grapes for its flagship Carneros Estate Pinot Noir come from the Sonoma portion of Los Carneros, as do those for the rarer Heirloom Carneros Pinot Noir. Longtime winemaker Jon Priest also excels at single-vineyard Napa Valley Cabernets. In good weather, hosts pour Priest's reds, plus Chardonnay, Pinot Gris, and a few others, on the patio outside the contemporary tasting room. ⊠ *1250 Cuttings Wharf Rd., Napa* ✛ *1 mile south of Hwy. 121* ☎ *707/257–5782* ⊕ *www.etudewines.com* 🍷 *Tastings from $30* ⊙ *Closed Tues. and Wed.*

★ Fontanella Family Winery

WINERY/DISTILLERY | Six miles from the downtown Napa whirl, husband-and-wife Jeff and Karen Fontanella's hillside spread seems a world apart. In addition to his formal studies, Jeff learned about wine making at three prestigious wineries before he and Karen, a lawyer, established their own operation on 81 south-facing Mt. Veeder acres. The couple braved an economic recession, an earthquake, and wildfires in the first decade but emerged tougher, if no less gracious to guests lucky enough to find themselves tasting Chardonnay, Zinfandel, and Cabernet Sauvignon on the patio here. Tastings often end with a Zinfandel-based port-style wine. With the barnlike production facility in the foreground and nearby Cabernet vines ringing a large irrigation pond, the setting represents the very picture of Napa Valley life many visitors imagine. ■**TIP**➔ **If offered the chance to stroll the estate, take it—the views south to San Francisco and east to Atlas Peak reward the exertion.** ⊠ *1721 Partrick Rd., Napa* ✛ *1st St. to Browns Valley Rd. west of Hwy. 29* ☎ *707/252–1017* ⊕ *www. fontanellawinery.com* 🍷 *Tasting $45.*

Continued on page 386

12

Napa and Sonoma NAPA

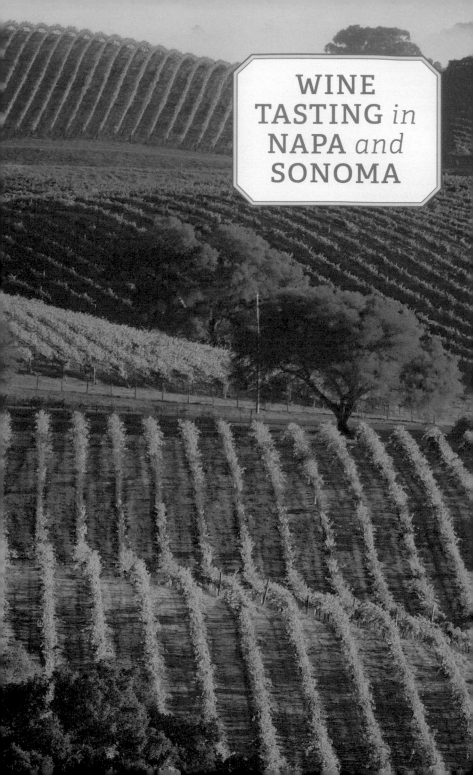

WINE
TASTING *in*
NAPA *and*
SONOMA

VISITING WINERIES

Tasting rooms range from the grand to the humble, offering everything from a few sips of wine to in-depth tours of facilities and vineyards. Some are open for drop-in visits, usually daily from around 10 or 11 am to 5 pm. Many require guests to make reservations. First-time visitors frequently enjoy the history-oriented focus at Charles Krug, Inglenook, and Buena Vista. The environments at some wineries reflect their owners' or founders' other interests: art at The Donum Estate and Hall St. Helena, movie making at Francis Ford Coppola, and medieval history at the Castello di Amorosa.

Many wineries describe their pourers as "wine educators," and indeed some of them have taken online or other classes and have passed an exam to prove basic knowledge of appellations, grape varietals, vineyards, and wine-making techniques. The one constant, however, is a deep, shared pleasure in the experience of wine tasting.

Fees. Most wineries charge for tasting. In the Napa Valley, expect to pay $35–$65 to sample current releases, $75–$100 or more for reserve, estate, or library wines. Sonoma County tastings generally cost $20–$40 for the former, $40–$75 for the latter. To experience wine making at its highest level, consider splurging for at least one special tasting.

Some wineries waive tasting fees if you join the wine club, purchase a few bottles, or spend a particular dollar amount. At others, the fees are "exclusive of purchase."

Tipping. Many guests tip out of instinct, but it isn't required. Instances when you might consider tipping include when your server has given a few extra pours or a discount on your purchases or has otherwise provided outstanding service. For a basic tasting, $5–$10 per couple will suffice; for a hosted seated tasting, $5–$10 per person, perhaps a little more for extra attention.

Whether you're a serious wine collector making your annual pilgrimage to Northern California's Wine Country or a newbie who doesn't know the difference between a Merlot and Mourvèdre but is eager to learn, you can have a great time touring Napa and Sonoma wineries. Your gateway to the wine world is the tasting room, where staff members are happy to chat with curious guests.

(opposite page) Carneros vineyards in autumn, Napa Valley. (top) Pinot Gris grapes. (bottom) Bottles from Far Niente winery.

WINE TASTING 101

TAKE A GOOD LOOK.
Hold your glass by the stem, raise it to the light, and take a close look at the wine. Check for clarity and color. (This is easiest to do if you can hold the glass in front of a white background.) Any tinge of brown usually means that the wine is over the hill or has gone bad.

BREATHE DEEP.
1. Sniff the wine once or twice to see if you can identify any smells.

2. Swirl the wine gently in the glass. Aerating the wine this way releases more of its aromas. (It's called "volatilizing the esters," if you're trying to impress someone.)

3. Take another long sniff. You might notice that experienced wine tasters spend more time sniffing the wine than drinking it. This is because this step is where the magic happens. The number of scents you might detect is almost endless, from berries, apricots, honey, and wildflowers to leather, cedar, or even tar. Does the wine smell good to you? Do you detect any "off" flavors, like wet dog or sulfur?

AT LAST! TAKE A SIP.
1. Swirl the wine around your mouth so that it makes contact with all your taste buds and releases more of its aromas. Think about the way the wine feels in your mouth. Is it watery or rich? Is it crisp or silky? Does it have a bold flavor, or is it subtle? The weight and intensity of a wine are called its body.

2. Hold the wine in your mouth for a few seconds and see if you can identify any developing flavors. More complex wines will reveal many different flavors as you drink them.

SPIT OR SWALLOW.
The pros typically spit, since they want to preserve their palate (and sobriety) for the wines to come, but you'll find that swallowers far outnumber the spitters in the winery tasting rooms. Whether you spit or swallow, notice the flavor that remains after the wine is gone (the finish).

Swirl

Sniff

Sip

MAKE AN APPOINTMENT

Most Napa and Sonoma wineries accept visitors by appointment only to serve patrons better, though some welcome walk-ins if space is available. To avoid disappointment, make reservations at least a day or two ahead. In summer and early fall, try to visit on weekdays or before 11 am or so when it's less crowded. Also look for wineries off the main drags of Highway 29 in Napa and Highway 12 in Sonoma.

HOW WINE IS MADE

1. CRUSHING

Harvested grapes go into a stemmer-crusher, which separates stems from fruit and crushes the grapes to release "free-run" juice.

2. PRESSING

Remaining juice is gently extracted from grapes. Usually done by pressing grapes against the walls of a tank with an inflatable bladder.

3. FERMENTING

Extracted juice (and also grape skins and pulp, when making red wine) goes into stainless-steel tanks or oak barrels to ferment. During fermentation, sugars convert to alcohol.

4. AGING

Wine is stored in stainless-steel or oak casks or barrels, or sometimes in concrete vessels, to develop flavors.

5. RACKING

Wine is transferred to clean barrels; sediment is removed. Wine may be filtered and fined (clarified) to improve its clarity, color, and sometimes flavor.

6. BOTTLING

Wine is bottled either at the winery or at a special facility, then stored again for bottle-aging.

WHAT'S AN APPELLATION?

American Viticultural Area (AVA) or, more commonly, an appellation. What can be confusing is that some appellations encompass smaller subappellations. The Rutherford, Oakville, and Mt. Veeder AVAs, for instance, are among the Napa Valley AVA's 16 subappellations. Wineries often buy grapes from outside their AVA, so their labels might reference different appellations. A winery in the warmer Napa Valley, for instance, might source Pinot Noir grapes from the cooler Russian River Valley, where they grow better. The appellation listed on a label always refers to where a wine's grapes were grown, not to where the wine was made.

By law, if a label bears the name of an appellation, 85% of the grapes must come from it.

Napa Valley

KEY

① *Exploring Sights*

Sights ▼

Hess Collection

WINERY/DISTILLERY | About 9 miles northwest of Napa, up a winding road ascending Mt. Veeder, this winery is a delightful discovery. The limestone structure, rustic from the outside but modern and airy within, contains Swiss founder Donald Hess's world-class art collection, including large-scale works by contemporary artists such as Andy Goldsworthy, Anselm Kiefer, and Robert Rauschenberg. Cabernet Sauvignon and Chardonnay are strengths, along with small-lot reds (Petite Sirah, Pinot Noir, Syrah, and blends). All visits are by appointment. ■TIP→ **Guided or self-guided gallery tours are part of most tastings.** ⊠ 4411 Redwood Rd., Napa ✛ West off Hwy. 29 at Trancas St./Redwood Rd. exit ☎ 707/255–1144 ⊕ www. hesscollection.com ☞ Tastings from $45.

★ Mayacamas Downtown

WINERY/DISTILLERY | Cabernets from Mayacamas Vineyards placed second and fifth respectively on _Wine Spectator_ magazine's 2019 and 2020 "Top 100" lists of the world's best wines, two accolades among many for this winery founded atop Mt. Veeder in 1889. One of Napa's leading viticulturists, Annie Favia farms the organic vineyards, elevation 2,000-plus feet, without irrigation; her husband, Andy Favia, is the consulting winemaker. The grapes for the Chardonnay come from 40-year-old vines. Aged in mostly neutral (previously used) French oak barrels to accentuate mountain minerality, the wine is a Napa Valley marvel. The Cabernet Sauvignon ages for three years, spending part of the time in oak barrels more than a century old. Erin Martin, a Napa Valley resident with a hip international reputation, designed the light-filled storefront tasting space. ■TIP→ **Experiencing these magnificent wines at this downtown tasting room may entice you to visit the estate.** ⊠ First Street Napa, 1256 1st St., Napa ✛ At Randolph St. ☎ 707/294–1433 ⊕ www.mayacamas. com ☞ Tastings from $35 ☽ Closed Mon. and Tues.

Napa Valley Wine Train

TOUR—SIGHT | Guests on this Napa Valley fixture ride the same 150-year-old rail corridor along which trains once transported passengers as far north as Calistoga's spas. The rolling stock includes restored Pullman cars and a two-story Vista Dome coach with a curved glass roof. The train travels a leisurely, scenic route between Napa and St. Helena. Patrons on some tours enjoy a multicourse meal and tastings at one or more wineries. Some rides involve no winery stops, and themed trips are occasionally scheduled. ■TIP→ **It's best to make this trip during the day, when you can enjoy the vineyard views.** ⊠ 1275 McKinstry St., Napa ✛ Off 1st St. ☎ 707/253–2111, 800/427–4124 ⊕ www.winetrain.com ☞ From $160.

★ Oxbow Public Market

MARKET | The 40,000-square-foot market's two dozen stands provide an introduction to Northern California's diverse artisanal food products. Swoon over decadent charcuterie at the Fatted Calf (great sandwiches, too), slurp oysters at Hog Island, enjoy empanadas at El Porteño, or chow down on vegetarian, duck, or salmon tacos at C Casa. Sample wine (and cheese) at the Oxbow Cheese & Wine Merchant, ales at Fieldwork Brewing's taproom, and barrel-aged cocktails at the Napa Valley Distillery. The owner of Kara's Cupcakes operates the adjacent Bar Lucia for (mostly) sparkling wines and rosés. Napa Bookmine is among the few nonfood vendors here. ■TIP→ **Five Dot Ranch and Cookhouse sells quality steaks and other meat to go; if you don't mind eating at the counter, you can order from the small menu and dine on the spot.** ⊠ 610 and 644 1st St., Napa ✛ At McKinstry St. ⊕ www.oxbowpublicmarket.com.

★ Robert Biale Vineyards

WINERY/DISTILLERY | Here's a surprise: a highly respected Napa Valley winery that doesn't sell a lick of Cabernet. Zinfandel from heritage vineyards, some with vines more than 100 years old, holds the spotlight, with luscious Petite Sirahs in supporting roles. Nearly every pour comes with a fascinating backstory, starting with the flagship Black Chicken Zinfandel. In the 1940s, the Biale family sold eggs, walnuts, and other farm staples, with bootleg Zinfandel a lucrative sideline. Because neighbors could eavesdrop on party-line phone conversations, "black chicken" became code for a jug of Zin. These days the wines are produced on the up-and-up by valley native Tres Goetting, whose vineyard and cellar choices bring out the best in two unsung varietals. The 10-acre property's open-air tasting setting—a stone's throw from Zinfandel vines, with far-off views of two mountain ranges—has a back-porch feel. Visits are by appointment; call ahead for same-day. ⊠ 4038 Big Ranch Rd., at Salvador Ave., Napa ☎ 707/257–7555 ⊕ biale.com ⊠ Tastings from $35.

Stag's Leap Wine Cellars

WINERY/DISTILLERY | A 1973 Stag's Leap Wine Cellars S.L.V. Cabernet Sauvignon put this winery and the Napa Valley on the enological map by placing first in the famous Judgment of Paris tasting of 1976. The grapes for that wine came from a vineyard visible from the stone-and-glass Fay Outlook & Visitor Center, which has broad views of a second fabled Cabernet vineyard (Fay) and the promontory that gives both the winery and the Stags Leap District AVA their names. The top-of-the-line Cabernets from these vineyards are poured at appointment-only tastings (call ahead for same-day visits), some of which include perceptive food pairings by the winery's executive chef. ■TIP→ When the weather's right, two patios with the same views as the tasting room fill up quickly. ⊠ 5766 Silverado Trail, Napa ✦ At Wappo Hill Rd. ☎ 707/261–6410 ⊕ www.stagsleapwine-cellars.com ⊠ Tastings from $50.

🍴 Restaurants

Angèle

$$$ | FRENCH | A vaulted wood-beamed ceiling and paper-topped tables set the scene for romance at this softly lit French bistro inside an 1890s boathouse. Look for clever variations on classic dishes such as croque monsieur (grilled Parisian ham and Gruyère) and Niçoise salad for lunch, with veal sweetbreads and, in season, steamed mussels with white wine–and–saffron broth for dinner. **Known for:** classic bistro cuisine; romantic setting; outdoor seating under bright-yellow umbrellas. ⑤ Average main: $33 ⊠ 540 Main St., Napa ✦ At 5th St. ☎ 707/252–8115 ⊕ www.angelerestaurant.com.

★ Compline

$$$ | MODERN AMERICAN | The full name of this enterprise put together by master sommelier Matt Stamp and restaurant wine vet Ryan Stetins is Compline Wine Bar, Restaurant, and Merchant, and indeed you can just sip wine or purchase it here. The place evolved into a hot spot, though, for its youthful vibe and eclectic small and large plates that might include shrimp lumpia (essentially a type of fried spring roll) and citrus-brined chicken but always the Compline burger, best enjoyed with duck-fat fries—and, per Stamp, champagne. **Known for:** upbeat vibe; pastas and vegetarian dishes; by-the-glass wines. ⑤ Average main: $29 ⊠ 1300 1st St., Suite 312, Napa ☎ 707/492–8150 ⊕ complinewine.com ⊗ Closed Tues.

Grace's Table

$$ | ECLECTIC | A dependable, varied menu makes this modest corner restaurant occupying a brick-and-glass storefront many Napans' go-to choice for a simple meal. Fish tacos and iron-skillet corn bread with lavender honey and butter show up at all hours, with buttermilk pancakes and chilaquiles scrambled eggs among the brunch staples and cassoulet and roasted young chicken popular for

dinner. **Known for:** congenial staffers; good beers on tap; eclectic menu focusing on France, Italy, and the Americas. ⑤ *Average main: $26* ⊠ *1400 2nd St., Napa* ✛ *At Franklin St.* ☎ *707/226–6200* ⊕ *www.gracestable.net.*

★ La Toque

$$$$ | **MODERN AMERICAN** | Chef Ken Frank's La Toque is the complete package: his imaginative French-inspired cuisine, served in a formal dining space, is complemented by a wine lineup that consistently earns the restaurant a coveted *Wine Spectator* Grand Award. Ingredients appearing on the prix-fixe multicourse tasting menu often include caviar, sea scallops, squab, and lamb saddle, in dishes prepared and seasoned to pair with wines jointly chosen by the chefs and master sommelier. **Known for:** chef's tasting menu (à la carte also possible); astute wine pairings; vegetarian tasting menu. ⑤ *Average main: $150* ⊠ *Westin Verasa Napa, 1314 McKinstry St., Napa* ✛ *Off Soscol Ave.* ☎ *707/257–5157* ⊕ *www.latoque.com* ⊙ *Closed Mon. and Tues. No lunch.*

Morimoto Napa

$$$$ | **JAPANESE** | *Iron Chef* star Masaharu Morimoto is the big name behind this downtown Napa restaurant where everything is delightfully over the top, including the desserts. Organic materials such as twisting grapevines above the bar and rough-hewn wooden tables seem simultaneously earthy and modern, creating a fitting setting for the gorgeously plated Japanese fare, from straightforward sashimi to more elaborate seafood, chicken, pork, and beef entrées. **Known for:** theatrical ambience; gorgeous plating; cocktail and sake menu. ⑤ *Average main: $42* ⊠ *610 Main St., Napa* ✛ *At 5th St.* ☎ *707/252–1600* ⊕ *www.morimotonapa.com.*

Oenotri

$$ | **ITALIAN** | Often spotted at local farmers' markets and his restaurant's gardens, Oenotri's ebullient chef-owner and Napa native Tyler Rodde is ever on the lookout for fresh produce to incorporate into his rustic southern-Italian cuisine. His restaurant, a brick-walled contemporary space with tall windows and wooden tables, is a lively spot to sample housemade salumi and pastas, thin-crust pizzas, and entrées that might include seared fresh fish or grilled skirt steak. **Known for:** lively atmosphere; Margherita pizza with San Marzano tomatoes; desserts with flair. ⑤ *Average main: $26* ⊠ *1425 1st St., Napa* ✛ *At Franklin St.* ☎ *707/252–1022* ⊕ *www.oenotri.com.*

★ Torc

$$$ | **MODERN AMERICAN** | *Torc* means "wild boar" in an early Celtic dialect, and owner-chef Sean O'Toole, who formerly helmed kitchens at top Manhattan, San Francisco, and Yountville establishments, occasionally incorporates the restaurant's namesake beast into his eclectic offerings. A recent menu featured baked-stuffed Maine lobster, nettle risotto, three hand-cut pasta dishes, and pork-belly with pole beans, all prepared by O'Toole and his team with style and precision. **Known for:** gracious service; specialty cocktails; Bengali sweet-potato pakora and deviled-egg appetizers. ⑤ *Average main: $36* ⊠ *1140 Main St., Napa* ✛ *At Pearl St.* ☎ *707/252–3292* ⊕ *www.torcnapa.com* ⊙ *Closed Sun. and Mon.*

★ ZuZu

$$$ | **SPANISH** | At festive ZuZu the focus is on cold and hot tapas, paella, and other Spanish favorites often downed with cava or sangria. Regulars revere the paella, made with Spanish *bomba* rice, and small plates that might include garlic shrimp, jamón Ibérico, lamb chops with Moroccan barbecue glaze, and white anchovies with sliced egg and rémoulade on grilled bread. **Known for:** singular flavors and spicing; Spanish jazz on the stereo; sister restaurant La Taberna three doors south for beer, wine, and bar bites. ⑤ *Average main: $32* ⊠ *829 Main St., Napa* ✛ *Near 3rd St.* ☎ *707/224–8555* ⊕ *www.zuzunapa.com* ⊙ *Closed Mon. and Tues.*

Hotels

Andaz Napa

$$$ | HOTEL | Part of the Hyatt family, this boutique hotel with an urban-hip vibe has spacious guest rooms with white-marble bathrooms stocked with high-quality products. **Pros:** casual-chic feel; proximity to downtown restaurants, theaters, and tasting rooms; cheery, attentive service. **Cons:** unremarkable views from some rooms; expensive on weekends in high season; some room show wear and tear. ⑤ *Rooms from: $304 ⊠ 1450 1st St., Napa ☎ 707/687–1234 ⊕ andaznapa.com ⬐ 141 rooms ⦿ No meals.*

★ Archer Hotel Napa

$$$ | HOTEL | Ideal for travelers seeking design pizzazz, a see-and-be-seen atmosphere, and first-class amenities, this five-story downtown Napa property fuses New York City chic and Las Vegas glamour. **Pros:** restaurants and room service by chef Charlie Palmer; Sky & Vine rooftop bar; great views from upper-floor rooms (especially south and west). **Cons:** not particularly rustic; expensive in high season; occasional service, hospitality lapses. ⑤ *Rooms from: $324 ⊠ 1230 1st St., Napa ☎ 707/690–9800, 855/200–9052 ⊕ archerhotel.com/napa ⬐ 183 rooms ⦿ No meals.*

★ Carneros Resort and Spa

$$$$ | RESORT | A winning combination of glamour, service, and pastoral seclusion makes this resort with freestanding board-and-batten cottages the perfect getaway for active lovebirds or families and groups seeking to unwind. **Pros:** cottages have lots of privacy; beautiful views from hilltop pool and hot tub; heaters on private patios. **Cons:** long drive to upvalley destinations; least expensive accommodations pick up highway noise; pricey pretty much year-round. ⑤ *Rooms from: $749 ⊠ 4048 Sonoma Hwy./Hwy. 121, Napa ☎ 707/299–4900, 888/400–9000 ⊕ www.carnerosresort.com ⬐ 100 rooms ⦿ No meals.*

★ The Inn on First

$$ | B&B/INN | Guests gush over the hospitality at this inn where the painstakingly restored 1905 mansion facing 1st Street contains five rooms, with five additional accommodations, all suites, in a building behind a secluded patio and garden. **Pros:** full gourmet breakfast by hosts-with-the-most owners; gas fireplaces and whirlpool tubs in all rooms; away from downtown but not too far. **Cons:** no TVs; owners "respectfully request no children"; lacks pool, fitness center, and other amenities of larger properties. ⑤ *Rooms from: $225 ⊠ 1938 1st St., Napa ☎ 707/253 1331 ⊕ www.theinnonfirst.com ⬐ 10 rooms ⦿ Free breakfast.*

★ Inn on Randolph

$$$ | B&B/INN | A few calm blocks from the downtown action on a nearly 1-acre lot with landscaped gardens, the Inn on Randolph—with a Gothic Revival–style main house and its five guest rooms plus five historic cottages out back—is a sophisticated haven celebrated for its gourmet gluten-free breakfasts and snacks. **Pros:** quiet residential neighborhood; spa tubs in cottages and two main-house rooms; romantic setting. **Cons:** a bit of a walk from downtown; expensive in-season; weekend minimum-stay requirement. ⑤ *Rooms from: $339 ⊠ 411 Randolph St., Napa ☎ 707/257–2886 ⊕ www.innonrandolph.com ⬐ 10 rooms ⦿ Free breakfast.*

 # Nightlife

Blue Note Napa

MUSIC CLUBS | The famed New York jazz room's intimate West Coast club hosts national headliners such as Kenny Garrett, KT Tunstall, and Jody Watley. There's a full bar, and you can order a meal or small bites from the kitchen. The larger JaM Cellars Ballroom upstairs books similar artists. ⊠ *Napa Valley Opera House, 1030 Main St., Napa ⊹ At 1st St. ☎ 707/880–2300 ⊕ www.bluenotenapa.com.*

Cadet Wine + Beer Bar

WINE BARS—NIGHTLIFE | Cadet plays things urban-style cool with a long bar, high-top tables, and a low-lit, generally loungelike feel. When they opened their bar, the two owners described their outlook as "unabashedly pro-California," but their wine-and-beer lineup circles the globe. The crowd here is youngish, the vibe festive. ⊠ *930 Franklin St., Napa* ✢ *At end of pedestrian alley between 1st and 2nd Sts.* ☎ *707/224–4400* ⊕ *www. cadetbeerandwinebar.com* ⌨ *Closed Mon. and Tues.*

 ## Shopping

First Street Napa

SHOPPING CENTERS/MALLS | The Archer Hotel Napa anchors this open-air downtown complex of mostly ground-level restaurants, tasting rooms, and national (Anthropologie, Lululemon) and homegrown (Bennington Napa Valley, Habituate Lifestyle + Interiors, Napa Stäk) design, clothing, housewares, and culinary shops. Copperfield's Books and the Visit Napa Valley Welcome Center are also here, along with Milo and Friends for pet necessities and accessories. ⊠ *1300 1st St., Napa* ✢ *Between Franklin and Coombs Sts.* ☎ *707/257–6900* ⊕ *www. firststreetnapa.com.*

 ## Activities

Napa Valley Gondola

TOUR—SPORTS | Rides in authentic gondolas that seat up to six depart from downtown Napa's municipal dock. You'll never mistake the Napa River for the Grand Canal, but on a sunny day this is a diverting excursion that often includes a serenade. ⊠ *Main Street Boat Dock, 680 Main St., Napa* ✢ *Riverfront Promenade, south of 3rd St. Bridge* ☎ *707/373–2100* ⊕ *napavalleygondola.com* ⌨ *From $145 (up to 6 people).*

Yountville

9 miles north of the town of Napa.

Yountville (population 3,000) is something like Disneyland for food lovers. You could stay here several days and not exhaust all the options—a few of them owned by The French Laundry's Thomas Keller—and the tiny town is full of small inns and high-end hotels that cater to those who prefer to walk (not drive) after an extravagant meal. It's also well located for excursions to many big-name Napa wineries, especially those in the Stags Leap District, from which big, bold Cabernet Sauvignons helped make the Napa Valley's wine-making reputation.

GETTING HERE AND AROUND

Downtown Yountville sits just off Highway 29. Approaching from the south take the Yountville exit—from the north take Madison—and proceed to Washington Street, home to the major shops and restaurants. Yountville Cross Road connects downtown to the Silverado Trail, along which many noted wineries do business. The free Yountville Trolley serves the town daily 10 am–7 pm (on-call service until 11 pm except on Sunday).

 ## Sights

★ Cliff Lede Vineyards

WINERY/DISTILLERY | Inspired by his passion for classic rock, owner and construction magnate Cliff Lede named the blocks in his Stags Leap District vineyard after hits by the Grateful Dead and other bands. Rock memorabilia and contemporary art like Jim Dine's outdoor sculpture *Twin 6′ Hearts,* a magnet for the Instagram set, are two other Lede obsessions. The vibe at his efficient, high-tech winery is anything but laid-back, however. Cutting-edge agricultural and enological science informs the vineyard management and wine making here. Lede produces Sauvignon Blanc, Cabernet Sauvignon, and Bordeaux-style red blends; tastings often include a Chardonnay, Pinot Gris, or Pinot Noir from sister winery FEL. All the wines are well crafted, though the Cabs really rock. ✉ *1473 Yountville Cross Rd., Yountville* ✦ *Off Silverado Trail* ☎ *707/944–8642* ⊕ *cliffledevineyards.com* ✉ *Tastings from $60 (sometimes $40 for weekend garden tastings).*

★ Elyse Winery

WINERY/DISTILLERY | One of his colleagues likens Elyse's winemaker, Russell Bevan, to "a water witch without the walking stick" for his ability to assess a vineyard's weather, soil, and vine positioning and intuit how particular viticultural techniques will affect wines' flavors. Bevan farms judiciously during the growing season, striving later in the cellar to preserve what nature and his efforts have yielded rather than rely on heavy manipulation. Under previous owners for three-plus decades (until 2018), Elyse became known for single-vineyard Zinfandels and Cabernet Sauvignons, with Merlot, Petite Sirah, and red blends other strong suits. A country lane edged by vines leads to this unassuming winery, whose tastings, often outdoors, have a backyard-casual feel. ■ **TIP→ Costing much less than the average Napa Valley Cab, Elyse's Holbrook Mitchell Cabernet Sauvignon holds its own against peers priced appreciably higher**. ✉ *2100 Hoffman La., Napa* ✦ *1¾ miles south of central Yountville, off Hwy. 29 or Solano Ave.* ☎ *707/944–2900* ⊕ *elysewinery.com* ✉ *Tastings from $50.*

★ Heron House Yountville

WINERY/DISTILLERY | Nine family-owned wineries specializing in small-batch Cabernet Sauvignon showcase their output at this southern Yountville tasting space that doubles as a boutique for contemporary art, fashion accessories, and household items. Several heavy-duty Napa names are involved, starting with Richard Steltzner, who began growing grapes here in 1965. His daughter, Allison, Heron House's founder, represents his Steltzner Vineyards and her Bench Vineyards, and well-known vintners and winemakers are behind the other operations: Eponymous, Hobel, Lindstrom, Myriad, Perchance, Switchback Ridge, and Zeitgeist. The wineries also make whites, rosés, and other reds. Tasting fees vary depending on the flight, which hosts are happy to adjust to match guests' preferences. Visits are by appointment, but walk-ins are accommodated when possible. ■ **TIP→ The King of Kings Cabernet Experience suits collectors and Napa Valley Cab lovers eager to up their game.** ✉ *6484 Washington St., Suite G, Yountville* ✦ *At Oak Circle* ☎ *707/947–7039* ⊕ *heronhouseyountville.com* ✉ *Tastings from $65* ⊗ *Closed Tues. and Wed.*

★ Oasis by Hoopes

WINERY/DISTILLERY | Vineyards surround the walk-through organic garden and corral for rescue animals that anchor second-generation vintner Lindsay Hoopes's playfully pastoral, cool-bordering-on-chic wine venue. In conceiving this family- and dog-friendly outdoor-oriented spot— with ample patio and garden seating, an Airstream trailer Instagrammers love, and even a tent—Hoopes aimed to expand the notion of what a Napa Valley wine tasting can entail. To that end, each group or solo visitor pays a table charge the hosts apply to bottles purchased for sipping on-site or later. If you prefer a traditional flight, the fee can go toward that, too. Lindsay's father started Hoopes Vineyard in the 1980s, selling his Oakville AVA Cabernet Sauvignon grapes to A-list producers before starting his boutique label in 1999. The lineup now includes Sauvignon Blanc, Chardonnay, rosé, Merlot, and Syrah. Most are gems, particularly two Oakville Cabs and a Howell Mountain Merlot. ✉ *6204 Washington St., Yountville* ✦ *1 mile south of downtown* ☎ *707/944–1869* ⊕ *hoopesvineyard.com/oasis-by-hoopes* ✉ *Tastings from $75.*

RH Wine Vault

WINERY/DISTILLERY | Gargantuan crystal chandeliers, century-old olive trees, and strategically placed water features provide visual and aural continuity at Restoration Hardware's quadruple-threat food, wine, art, and design compound. An all-day café fronts two steel, glass, and concrete home-furnishings galleries, with a bluestone walkway connecting them to a reboot of the former Ma(i) sonry wine salon here. Centered on a two-story 1904 manor house constructed from Napa River stone, it remains an excellent spot to learn about small-lot Napa and Sonoma wines, served by the glass, flight, or bottle. Collector-revered labels like Corison, Fisher, Lail, Matthiasson, Melka, and Spottswoode are all represented, the wines in good weather poured in "outdoor living rooms" behind the stone structure. Oozing RH fabulousness as it does, the Wine Vault can feel like a scene on a busy day, but the wines are the real deal. All tastings are by appointment. ⊠ *6725 Washington St., Yountville* ✛ *At Pedroni St.* ☎ *707/339–4654* ⊕ *www.restorationhardware.com* ▭ *Tastings from $50.*

Robert Sinskey Vineyards

WINERY/DISTILLERY | Although the winery produces a Stags Leap Cabernet Sauvignon (SLD Estate), two Bordeaux-style red blends (Marcien and POV), and white wines, Sinskey is best known for its intense, brambly Carneros District Pinot Noirs. All the grapes are grown in organic, certified biodynamic vineyards. The influence of Robert's wife, Maria Helm Sinskey—a chef and cookbook author and the winery's culinary director—is evident during the tastings, all of which are accompanied by at least a few bites of food. The elevated Terroir Tasting explores the winery's land and farming practices. Chef's Table takes in the winery's culinary gardens and ends with a seated wine-and-food pairing. All visits require an appointment, wisely made a day or two ahead. ⊠ *6320 Silverado Trail, Napa* ✛ *At Yountville Cross Rd.* ☎ *707/944–9090* ⊕ *www.robertsinskey.com* ▭ *Tastings from $40.*

 ## Restaurants

Ad Hoc

$$$$ | MODERN AMERICAN | At this low-key dining room with zinc-top tables and wine served in tumblers, superstar chef Thomas Keller offers a single, fixed-price, nightly menu that might include smoked beef short ribs with creamy herb rice and charred broccolini or sesame chicken with radish kimchi and fried rice. Ad Hoc also serves a small but decadent Sunday brunch, and Keller's Addendum annex, in a separate small building behind the restaurant, sells boxed lunches to go (including moist buttermilk fried chicken) from Thursday to Saturday except in winter. **Known for:** casual cuisine at great prices for a Thomas Keller restaurant; don't-miss buttermilk-fried-chicken night; Burgers & Half Bottles (of wine) pop-up. ⑤ *Average main: $56* ⊠ *6476 Washington St., Yountville* ✛ *At Oak Circle* ☎ *707/944–2487* ⊕ *www.thomaskeller.com/adhoc* ⊗ *Closed Tues. and Wed. No lunch Mon. and Thurs.* ☞ *Check website or call a day ahead for next day's menu.*

★ Bistro Jeanty

$$$ | FRENCH | Escargots, cassoulet, *steak au poivre* (pepper steak), and other French classics are prepared with the utmost precision inside this tan-brick country bistro whose flower-filled window boxes, extra-wide shutters, and red-and-white-striped awning hint at the Old World flair and joie de vivre that infuse the place. Regulars often start with the rich tomato soup in a flaky puff pastry before proceeding to sole meunière or coq au vin, completing the French sojourn with a lemon meringue tart or other authentic dessert. **Known for:** traditional preparations; oh-so-French atmosphere; patio seating. ⑤ *Average main: $30* ⊠ *6510 Washington St., Yountville* ✛ *At Mulberry St.* ☎ *707/944–0103* ⊕ *www.bistrojeanty.com.*

★ Bouchon Bistro

$$$ | FRENCH | The team that created The French Laundry is also behind this place, where everything—the zinc-topped bar, antique sconces, suave waitstaff, and traditional French onion soup—could have come straight from a Parisian bistro. Pan-seared rib eye with béarnaise and mussels steamed with white wine, saffron, and Dijon mustard—both served with crispy, addictive fries—are among the perfectly executed entrées. **Known for:** bistro classics; raw bar; Bouchon Bakery next door. $ *Average main: $35* ✉ *6534 Washington St., Yountville* ✛ *Near Humboldt St.* ☎ *707/944–8037* ⊕ *thomaskeller.com/bouchonyountville.*

Ciccio

$$ | MODERN ITALIAN | The ranch of Ciccio's owners, Frank and Karen Altamura, supplies some of the vegetables and herbs for the modern Italian cuisine prepared in the open kitchen of this remodeled former grocery store. Seasonal growing cycles dictate the menu, with fried-seafood appetizers (calamari, perhaps, or softshell crabs), a few pasta dishes, herb-crusted fish, and several pizzas among the likely offerings. **Known for:** Negroni bar; pizzas' flavorful cheeses; mostly Napa Valley wines, some from owners' winery. $ *Average main: $23* ✉ *6770 Washington St., Yountville* ✛ *At Madison St.* ☎ *707/945–1000* ⊕ *www.ciccionapavalley.com* ⊗ *Closed Mon. and Tues. No lunch.*

Coqueta Napa Valley

$$$ | SPANISH | From *pintxos* (small plates) and paellas to Iberian cheeses and fish *a la plancha* (flat-grilled), the chefs at this Wine Country offspring of Michael Chiarello's successful San Francisco restaurant Coqueta reimagine Spanish classics with a 21st-century farm-to-table sensibility. The frenetic pace in the flame-happy open kitchen, inside Yountville's redbrick former railroad depot, keeps the mood lively in the relatively small dining space, with the vibe on the patio out back even more so. **Known for:** sensual flavors; dynamic spicing; seasonal cocktails inspired by Spain and the Napa Valley. $ *Average main: $32* ✉ *6525 Washington St., Yountville* ✛ *Near Yount St.* ☎ *707/244–4350* ⊕ *www.coquetanv.com/home* ⊗ *Closed Tues. and Wed.*

★ The French Laundry

$$$$ | AMERICAN | An old stone building laced with ivy houses chef Thomas Keller's destination restaurant. Some courses on the two prix-fixe menus, one of which highlights vegetables, rely on luxe ingredients such as *calotte* (cap of the rib eye); others take humble elements like carrots or fava beans and elevate them to art. **Known for:** signature starter "oysters and pearls"; sea urchin, black truffles, and other "supplements"; superior wine list. $ *Average main: $350* ✉ *6640 Washington St., Yountville* ✛ *At Creek St.* ☎ *707/944–2380* ⊕ *www.frenchlaundry.com* ⊗ *No lunch Mon.–Thurs.* 🎩 *Jacket required* ☞ *Reservations essential wks ahead.*

Mustards Grill

$$$ | AMERICAN | Cindy Pawlcyn's Mustards Grill fills day and night with fans of her hearty cuisine, equal parts updated renditions of traditional American dishes—what Pawlcyn dubs "deluxe truck stop classics"—and fanciful contemporary fare. Barbecued baby back pork ribs and a lemon-lime tart piled high with brown-sugar meringue fall squarely in the first category, and sweet corn tamales with tomatillo-avocado salsa and wild mushrooms represent the latter. **Known for:** roadhouse setting; convivial mood; hoppin' bar. $ *Average main: $30* ✉ *7399 St. Helena Hwy./Hwy. 29, Napa* ✛ *1 mile north of Yountville* ☎ *707/944–2424* ⊕ *www.mustardsgrill.com.*

North Block

$$$ | MODERN AMERICAN | In his California debut, chef Nick Tamburo, previously of two Manhattan locations of celeb chef David Chang's Momofuku, prepares farm-to-table cuisine with intriguing flavors and ingredients. A recent starter paired oro blanco (a grapefruitlike citrus) and ever-so-thinly sliced kohlrabi (a type of turnip) spiced to marvelous effect with the mildly minty Japanese herb shiso, the chef's artistry repeating itself on the menu's wood-fired pizzas and fish and meat entrées. **Known for:** courtyard patio seating; cocktails and wine list; atmospheric interior. ⑤ *Average main: $35 ⊠ North Block Hotel, 6757 Washington St., Yountville ✥ Near Madison St. ☎ 707/944–8080 ⊕ www.northblockhotel.com/dining.*

★ Perry Lang's

$$$$ | STEAKHOUSE | An 1870 redbrick former mansion holds this contemporary chophouse whose art-deco accents recall an old-school gentlemen's club—the kind of place to order a stiff cocktail, a wedge salad topped with thick maple-glazed bacon, and a dry-aged rib eye or tomahawk. Chef Adam Perry Lang, a grilling and barbecue artiste, seduces patrons with culinary drama and hand-tooled steak knives so exquisite it's a felony to swipe them, delivering the goods with an experience that satisfies appetite and soul. **Known for:** St. Louis pork ribs with peach barbecue sauce; Cabernet bone-marrow jus and béarnaise and horseradish sauces for steaks; potent craft cocktails. ⑤ *Average main: $40 ⊠ 6539 Washington St., Yountville ✥ Just south of Vintage House ☎ 707/945–4522 ⊕ perrylangs.com ⊙ No lunch.*

 Hotels

★ Bardessono

$$$$ | RESORT | Tranquillity and luxury with a low carbon footprint are among the goals of this ultragreen wood, steel, and glass resortlike property in downtown Yountville, but there's nothing spartan about the accommodations, arranged around four landscaped courtyards. **Pros:** large rooftop lap pool; in-room spa treatments; three luxury villas for extra privacy. **Cons:** expensive year-round; limited view from some

rooms; a bit of street traffic on hotel's west side. ⑤ *Rooms from: $750 ⊠ 6526 Yount St., Yountville ☎ 707/204–6000, 855/232–0450 ⊕ www.bardessono.com ⊅ 65 rooms ⫶⊘⫶ No meals.*

Maison Fleurie

$$ | B&B/INN | A stay at this comfortable, reasonably priced inn, said to be the oldest hotel in the Napa Valley, places you within walking distance of Yountville's fine restaurants. **Pros:** smallest rooms a bargain; outdoor hot tub and pool; free bike rental. **Cons:** lacks amenities of a full-service hotel; some rooms pick up noise from nearby Bouchon Bakery; hard to book in high season. ⑤ *Rooms from: $229 ⊠ 6529 Yount St., Yountville ☎ 707/944–2056 ⊕ www.maisonfleurienapa.com ⊅ 13 rooms ⫶⊘⫶ Free breakfast.*

Napa Valley Lodge

$$ | HOTEL | Clean rooms in a convenient motel-style setting draw travelers willing to pay more than at comparable lodgings in the city of Napa to be within walking distance of Yountville's tasting rooms, restaurants, and shops. **Pros:** well-maintained rooms; vineyard-view rooms on north and west sides; large pool area. **Cons:** no elevator; nice enough but lacks panache; pricey on weekends in high season. ⑤ *Rooms from: $285 ⊠ 2230 Madison St., Yountville ☎ 707/944–2468, 888/944–3545 ⊕ www.napavalleylodge.com ⊅ 55 rooms ⫶⊘⫶ Free breakfast.*

★ North Block Hotel

$$$$ | HOTEL | A two-story boutique property near downtown Yountville's northern edge, the North Block attracts sophisticated travelers who appreciate the clever but unpretentious style and offhand luxury. **Pros:** extremely comfortable beds; personalized service; spacious bathrooms. **Cons:** outdoor areas get some traffic noise; weekend minimum-stay requirement; rates soar on high-season weekends. ⑤ *Rooms from: $540 ⊠ 6757 Washington St., Yountville ☎ 707/944–8080 ⊕ northblockhotel.com ⊅ 20 rooms ⫶⊘⫶ No meals.*

Vintage House

$$$$ | RESORT | Part of the 22-acre Estate Yountville complex—other sections include sister lodging Hotel Villagio, the 13,000-square-foot Spa at the Estate, and shops and restaurants—this downtown hotel consists of two-story brick buildings along verdant landscaped paths shaded by mature trees. **Pros:** aesthetically pleasing accommodations; private patios and balconies; secluded feeling yet near shops, tasting rooms, and restaurants. **Cons:** highway noise audible in some exterior rooms; very expensive on summer and fall weekends; weekend minimum-stay requirement. ⑤ *Rooms from: $429* ⊠ *6541 Washington St., Yountville* ☎ *707/944–1112, 877/351–1153* ⊕ *www.vintagehouse.com* ⟿ *80 rooms* ⦿ *Free breakfast.*

Shopping

The Conservatory

CLOTHING | The New York City–based lifestyle company's heavily curated "considered luxury" comes in the form of clothing, accessories, and decor and well-being items created by small, quality-oriented brands for a discerning clientele. Local products include Vintner's Daughter Active Botanical Serum face oil, whose adherents swear nearly stops time. ⊠ *6540 Washington St., Yountville* ✛ *Near Humboldt St.* ☎ *707/415–5015* ⊕ *theconservatorynyc.com/pages/ napa-store.*

Activities

BALLOONING
Napa Valley Aloft

BALLOONING | Passengers soar over the Napa Valley in balloons that launch from downtown Yountville. Flights are from 40 minutes to an hour-plus, depending on the wind speed, with the entire experience taking from three to four hours. ⊠ *The Estate Yountville, 6525 Washington St., Yountville* ✛ *Near Mulberry St.*

☎ *707/944–4400, 855/944–4408* ⊕ *www. nvaloft.com* ⊠ *$250 per person.*

BICYCLING
Napa Valley Bike Tours

BICYCLING | With dozens of wineries within 5 miles, this shop makes a fine starting point for guided and self-guided vineyard and wine-tasting excursions. Rental bikes are also available. ⊠ *6500 Washington St., Yountville* ✛ *At Mulberry St.* ☎ *707/251–8687* ⊕ *www.napavalleybiketours.com* ⊠ *From $124 (½-day guided tour).*

SPAS
The Spa at The Estate

FITNESS/HEALTH CLUBS | The joint 13,000-square-foot facility of Vintage House and the Hotel Villagio is a five-minute walk from the former's lobby, even less from the latter's. Private spa suites are popular with couples, who enjoy the separate relaxation areas, indoor and outdoor fireplaces, steam showers, saunas, and extra-large tubs. Many treatments involve Omorovicza products based on Hungarian thermal waters and minerals. For a quick uplift, book 20 minutes in the spa's oxygen chair, designed to optimize breathing and promote relaxation. Facials, lip plumping, and massages are among the other à la carte services. The ground-floor retail area, open to the public, is well stocked with beauty products. ⊠ *The Estate Yountville, 6481 Washington St., Yountville* ✛ *At Oak Circle* ☎ *707/948–5050* ⊕ *www.villagio. com/spa* ⊠ *Treatments from $85.*

Oakville

2 miles northwest of Yountville.

A large butte that runs east–west just north of Yountville blocks the cooling fogs from the south, facilitating the myriad microclimates of the Oakville AVA, home to several high-profile wineries.

GETTING HERE AND AROUND

Driving along Highway 29, you'll know you've reached Oakville when you see the Oakville Grocery on the east side of the road. You can reach Oakville from the Sonoma County town of Glen Ellen by heading east on Trinity Road from Highway 12. The twisting route, along the mountain range that divides Napa and Sonoma, eventually becomes the Oakville Grade. The views on this drive are breathtaking, though the continual curves make it unsuitable for those who suffer from motion sickness.

 ## Sights

B Cellars

WINERY/DISTILLERY | The chefs take center stage in the open-hearth kitchen of this boutique winery's hospitality house, and with good reason: creating food-friendly wines is B Cellars's raison d'être. Visits to the Oakville facility—all steel beams, corrugated metal, and plate glass yet remarkably cozy—often begin with a tour of the winery's culinary garden and vineyard, with a pause for sips of wine still aging in barrel. A seated tasting of finished wines paired with small bites follows the tour. Kirk Venge, whose fruit-forward style suits the winery's food-oriented approach, crafts red and white blends and single-vineyard Cabernets from estate fruit and grapes from Beckstoffer and other noteworthy vineyards. All visits are strictly by appointment. ⊠ *703 Oakville Cross Rd., Oakville* ✛ *West of Silverado Trail* ☎ *707/709–8787* ⊕ *www. bcellars.com* ✉ *Tastings from $80* ⊗ *Closed Tues. and Wed.*

Far Niente

WINERY/DISTILLERY | Hamden McIntyre, a prominent winery architect of his era also responsible for Inglenook and what's now the Culinary Institute of America at Greystone, designed the centerpiece 1885 stone winery here. Abandoned in the wake of Prohibition and only revived beginning in 1979, Far Niente now

ranks as one of the Napa Valley's most beautiful properties. Guests participating in the Estate Tasting learn some of this history while sipping the flagship wines, a Chardonnay and a Cabernet Sauvignon blend, along with Russian River Valley Pinot Noir from the affiliated EnRoute label and Dolce, a late-harvest Sémillon and Sauvignon Blanc wine. The Extended Estate Tasting takes in the winery and its aging caves, while the Library Wine Tasting compares older vintages. ⊠ *1350 Acacia Dr., Oakville* ✛ *Off Oakville Grade Rd.* ☎ *707/944–2861* ⊕ *www.farniente. com* ✉ *Tastings from $80.*

Robert Mondavi Winery

WINERY/DISTILLERY | Arguably the most influential participant in the Napa Valley's rise to international prominence, the late Robert Mondavi established his namesake winery in the 1960s after losing a battle with his brother over the direction of their family's Charles Krug Winery. In an era when tasting rooms were mostly downscale affairs, Mondavi commissioned architect Cliff May to create a grand Mission-style space to receive visitors. May's design still resonates, the graceful central arch framing the lawn and the vineyard behind, inviting a stroll under the arcades. The Estate Tour & Tasting and Vintner's Tasting provide an introduction to the winery, its portfolio, and Mondavi's life. Another offering focuses on whites and caviar, with a third involving Cabernet Sauvignon from the Mondavi section of the famed To Kalon Vineyard. All visits require a reservation, with last-minute requests often granted. ⊠ *7801 St. Helena Hwy./Hwy. 29, Oakville* ☎ *888/766–6328* ⊕ *www. robertmondaviwinery.com* ✉ *Tastings and tours from $40.*

★ Silver Oak

WINERY/DISTILLERY | The first review of this winery's Napa Valley Cabernet Sauvignon declared the debut 1972 vintage not all that good and, at $6 a bottle, overpriced. Oops. The celebrated Bordeaux-style

Cabernet blend, still the only Napa Valley wine bearing its winery's label each year, evolved into a cult favorite, and founders Ray Duncan and Justin Meyer received worldwide recognition for their signature use of exclusively American oak to age the wines. At the Oakville tasting room, constructed out of reclaimed stone and other materials from a 19th-century Kansas flour mill, the Silver Oak Tasting includes sips of the current Napa Valley vintage, its counterpart from Silver Oak's Alexander Valley operation in Sonoma County, and a library wine. Hosts of vertical tastings pour six Cabernet vintages. All visits require an appointment. ⊠ *915 Oakville Cross Rd., Oakville* ⊹ *Off Hwy. 29* ☎ *707/942-7022* ⊕ *www.silveroak. com* ⌂ *Tastings from $30.*

Rutherford

2 miles northwest of Oakville.

With its singular microclimate and soil, Rutherford is an important viticultural center, with more big-name wineries than you can shake a corkscrew at. Cabernet Sauvignon is king here. The well-drained, loamy soil is ideal for those vines, and since this part of the valley gets plenty of sun, the grapes develop exceptionally intense flavors.

GETTING HERE AND AROUND
Wineries around Rutherford are dotted along Highway 29 and the parallel Silverado Trail north and south of Rutherford Road/Conn Creek Road, on which wineries can also be found.

◉ Sights

★ Frog's Leap
WINERY/DISTILLERY | If you're a novice, the tour at eco-friendly Frog's Leap is a fun way to begin your education. Conducted by hosts with a sense of humor, the tour stops by a barn built in 1884, 5 acres of organic gardens, and a frog pond topped with lily pads. The winery produced its first vintage, small batches of Sauvignon Blanc and Zinfandel, in 1981, adding Chardonnay and Cabernet Sauvignon the next year. These days Chenin Blanc is another white, with Merlot, Petite Sirah, and the Heritage Blend of classic Napa Valley varietals among the other reds. All visits require a reservation. ■ TIP→ **The tour is recommended, but you can forgo it and taste on a garden-view porch.** ⊠ *8815 Conn Creek Rd., Rutherford* ☎ *707/963-4704* ⊕ *www.frogsleap.com* ⌂ *Tastings from $45, tour and tasting $75.*

★ Inglenook
WINERY/DISTILLERY | *Wine Enthusiast* magazine bestowed a lifetime-achievement award on vintner-filmmaker Francis Ford Coppola, whose wine-world contributions include resurrecting the historic Inglenook estate. Over the decades he reunited the original property acquired by Inglenook founder Gustave Niebaum, remodeled Niebaum's ivy-covered 1880s château, and purchased the rights to the Inglenook name. The winery's place in Napa Valley history is among the topics discussed at tastings, some of which involve cheese, charcuterie, or other wine-food pairings. Most sessions see a pour of the signature Rubicon wine, a Cabernet Sauvignon–based blend. All visits require an appointment; call the winery or check at the visitor center for same-day. ■ TIP→ **In lieu of a tasting, you can book a table at The Bistro, a wine bar with a picturesque courtyard, to sip wine by the glass or bottle.** ⊠ *1991 St. Helena Hwy./Hwy. 29, Rutherford* ⊹ *At Hwy.128* ☎ *707/968-1100* ⊕ *www.inglenook. com* ⌂ *Tastings from $60* ⊗ *Closed Mon.–Wed.*

Mumm Napa
WINERY/DISTILLERY | When Champagne Mumm of France set about establishing a California sparkling-wine outpost, its winemaker chose the Napa Valley, where today the winery sources grapes from more than 50 local producers. Made

Frog's Leap's picturesque country charm extends all the way to the white picket fence.

in the *méthode traditionelle* style from Chardonnay, Pinot Noir, Pinot Meunier, and occasionally Pinot Gris, the wines are all fermented in the bottle. Most guests enjoy them alfresco, by the glass or flight, on a patio above the surrounding vineyards or one at eye level. Book an Oak Terrace Tasting to sample top-of-the-line cuvées under the sprawling branches of a blue oak nearly two centuries old. Tasting is by appointment only. ⊠ *8445 Silverado Trail, Rutherford* ✛ *1 mile south of Rutherford Cross Rd.* ☎ *707/967–7700* ⊕ *www.mummnapa.com* ☒ *Tastings from $40.*

ZD Wines

WINERY/DISTILLERY | Founded in 1969 and still run by the same family, this winery specializing in Chardonnay, Pinot Noir, and Cabernet Sauvignon is respected for its organic practices, local philanthropy, and Abacus blend. Made "solera-style," Abacus contains wine from every ZD Reserve Cabernet Sauvignon vintage since 1992. The Chardonnay and Pinot Noir come from a Carneros property, the

Cabernet from the winery's Rutherford estate, where the wines are made and presented to the public. Appointment-only tastings (same-day often possible) take place in a second-floor space with broad valley views west to the Mayacamas Mountains. For an introduction to ZD and its wine-making philosophy, book a current-release flight. Barrel tastings, small bites, and small-batch reserve wines are all part of the Abacus Experience, which concludes with a current and older Abacus blend. ⊠ *8383 Silverado Trail, Rutherford* ☎ *800/487–7757* ⊕ *www. zdwines.com* ☒ *Tastings from $40.*

🍴 Restaurants

★ Restaurant at Auberge du Soleil

$$$$ | **MODERN AMERICAN** | Possibly the most romantic roost for brunch or dinner in all the Wine Country is a terrace seat at the Auberge du Soleil resort's illustrious restaurant, and the Mediterranean-inflected cuisine more than matches the dramatic vineyard views. The prix-fixe dinner menu (three or four courses), which relies mainly on local produce, might include caviar or diver scallop starters, delicately prepared fish or vegetable middle-course options, and mains like prime beef pavé with béarnaise, spiced lamb loin, or Japanese Wagyu. **Known for:** polished service; comprehensive wine list; special-occasion feel. $ Average main: $135 ✉ Auberge du Soleil, 180 Rutherford Hill Rd., Rutherford ⊹ Off Silverado Trail ☎ 707/963–1211, 800/348–5406 ⊕ www.aubergedusoleil.com.

Rutherford Grill

$$$ | AMERICAN | Dark-wood walls, subdued lighting, and red-leather banquettes make for a perpetually clubby mood at this Rutherford hangout where the patio, popular for its bar, fireplace, and rocking chairs, opens for full meal service or drinks and appetizers when the weather's right. Many entrées—steaks, burgers, fish, rotisserie chicken, and barbecued pork ribs—emerge from an oak-fired grill operated by master technicians. **Known for:** iron-skillet corn bread direct from the oven; signature French dip sandwich and grilled jumbo artichokes; reasonably priced wine list with rarities. $ Average main: $29 ✉ 1180 Rutherford Rd., Rutherford ⊹ At Hwy. 29 ☎ 707/963–1792 ⊕ www.rutherfordgrill.com.

 Hotels

★ Auberge du Soleil

$$$$ | RESORT | Taking a cue from the olive-tree-studded landscape, this hotel with a renowned restaurant and spa cultivates a luxurious look that blends French and California style. **Pros:** stunning valley views; spectacular pool and spa areas; Deluxe-category suites fit for a superstar. **Cons:** stratospheric prices; least expensive rooms get some noise from the bar and restaurant; weekend minimum-stay requirement. $ Rooms from: $925 ✉ 180 Rutherford Hill Rd., Rutherford ☎ 707/963–1211, 800/348–5406 ⊕ www.

aubergedusoleil.com ⇦ 52 rooms ⦿ Free breakfast.

★ Rancho Caymus Inn

$$$ | HOTEL | A romantic hacienda-away-from-home that off-season may well be the Napa Valley's best value in its price range, this upscale-contemporary boutique hotel near Inglenook and the Rutherford Grill contains rooms whose decor and artworks evoke the area's Mexican heritage. **Pros:** courtyard pool area; smallest rooms are 400 square feet, with several 600 or more; well-trained staff. **Cons:** all rooms have only showers (albeit nice ones); king beds in all rooms (no sofa beds, though a few rollaways available); no spa or fitness center. $ Rooms from: $396 ✉ 1140 Rutherford Rd., Rutherford ☎ 707/200–9300 ⊕ www.ranchocaymusinn.com ⇦ 26 rooms ⦿ Free breakfast.

St. Helena

2 miles northwest of Oakville.

Downtown St. Helena is the very picture of good living in the Wine Country. Sycamore trees arch over Main Street (Highway 29), where visitors flit between boutiques, cafés, and storefront tasting rooms housed in sun-faded redbrick buildings. The genteel district pulls in rafts of tourists during the day, though like most Wine Country towns St. Helena more or less rolls up the sidewalks after dark.

The Napa Valley floor narrows between the Mayacamas and Vaca mountains around St. Helena. The slopes reflect heat onto the vineyards below, and since there's less fog and wind, things get pretty toasty. This is one of the valley's hottest AVAs, with midsummer temperatures often reaching the mid-90s. Bordeaux varietals are the most popular grapes grown here—especially Cabernet Sauvignon but also Merlot, Cabernet Franc, and Sauvignon Blanc.

GETTING HERE AND AROUND

Downtown stretches along Highway 29, called Main Street here. Many wineries lie north and south of downtown along Highway 29. More can be found off Silverado Trail, and some of the most scenic spots are on Spring Mountain, which rises southwest of town.

Sights

Beringer Vineyards

WINERY/DISTILLERY | Brothers Frederick and Jacob Beringer opened the winery that still bears their name in 1876. One of California's earliest bonded wineries, it's the oldest one in the Napa Valley never to have missed a vintage—no mean feat, given Prohibition. Reserve tastings of a limited release Chardonnay, a few big Cabernets, and a Sauterne-style dessert wine take place on the veranda (also inside when possible) at Frederick's grand Rhine House Mansion, built in 1884 and surrounded by mature landscaped gardens. Beringer is known for several widely distributed wines, but many poured here are winery exclusives. Visits require a reservation; same-day guests are accommodated if possible. ⊠ 2000 Main St./Hwy. 29, St. Helena ✢ Near Pratt Ave. ☎ 707/963–8989 ⊕ www.beringer.com ☒ Tastings from $35.

Charles Krug Winery

WINERY/DISTILLERY | A historically sensitive renovation of its 1874 Redwood Cellar Building transformed the former production facility of the Napa Valley's oldest winery into an epic hospitality center. Charles Krug, a Prussian immigrant, established the winery in 1861 and ran it until his death in 1892. Italian immigrants Cesare Mondavi and his wife, Rosa, purchased Charles Krug in 1943, operating it with their sons Peter and Robert (who later opened his own winery). Still run by Peter's family, Charles Krug specializes in small-lot Yountville and Howell Mountain Cabernet Sauvignons plus Sauvignon Blanc, Chardonnay, Merlot, and Pinot Noir. All visits are by appointment. ⊠ 2800 Main St./Hwy. 29, St. Helena ✢ Across from Culinary Institute of America ☎ 707/967–2229 ⊕ www.charleskrug. com ☒ Tasting $45, tour $75 (includes tasting).

Hall St. Helena

WINERY/DISTILLERY | The Cabernet Sauvignons produced here are works of art born of the latest in organic-farming science and wine-making technology. A glass-walled tasting room allows guests to see some of the high-tech equipment winemaker Megan Gunderson employs to craft wines that also include Merlot, Cabernet Franc, and Sauvignon Blanc. Looking westward from the second-floor tasting area, rows of neatly spaced Cabernet vines capture the eye, beyond them the tree-studded Mayacamas Mountains. Hard to miss as you arrive along Highway 29, Lawrence Argent's 35-foot-tall *Bunny Foo Foo,* a stainless-steel sculpture of a rabbit leaping out of the vineyard, is one of many museum-quality artworks on display at appointment-only Hall (call for same-day). ■TIP→ **Sister winery Hall Rutherford hosts an exclusive wine-and-food pairing atop a Rutherford hillside.** ⊠ 401 St. Helena Hwy./Hwy. 29, St. Helena ✢ Near White La. ☎ 707/967–2626 ⊕ www.hallwines. com ☒ Tastings from $40.

★ Joseph Phelps Vineyards

WINERY/DISTILLERY | An appointment is required for tastings at the winery started by the late Joseph Phelps, but it's worth the effort—all the more so after an inspired renovation of the main redwood structure, a classic of 1970s Northern California architecture. Phelps produces very fine whites, along with Pinot Noir from its Sonoma Coast vineyards, but the blockbusters are the Bordeaux reds, particularly the Cabernet Sauvignons and Insignia, a luscious-yet-subtle Cab-dominant blend. Insignia, which often receives high-90s scores from respected wine publications, is always among the current releases poured at the one-hour seated Terrace Tasting overlooking grapevines and oaks. Several other experiences involve food pairings; participants in the blending seminar mix the varietals that go into Insignia. ⊠ *200 Taplin Rd., St. Helena* ⊕ *Off Silverado Trail* ☎ *707/963–2745, 800/707–5789* ⊕ *www.joseph-phelps.com* ⊠ *Tastings from $90.*

Prager Winery & Port Works

WINERY/DISTILLERY | "If door is locked, ring bell," reads a sign outside the weathered-redwood tasting shack at this family-run winery known for red, white, and tawny ports. The sign, the bell, and the thousands of dollar bills tacked to the walls and ceilings inside are your first indications that you're drifting back in time with the old-school Pragers, who have been making regular and fortified wines in St. Helena since the late 1970s. Five members of the second generation, along with two spouses, run this homespun operation founded by Jim and Imogene Prager. In addition to ports the winery makes Petite Sirah and Sweet Claire, a late-harvest Riesling dessert wine. Some tastings take place in a garden outside the tasting room or on the crush pad. ⊠ *1281 Lewelling La., St. Helena* ⊕ *Off Hwy. 29* ☎ *707/963–7678* ⊕ *www.pragerport.com* ⊠ *Tastings $40 (includes glass).*

★ Pride Mountain Vineyards

WINERY/DISTILLERY | This winery 2,200 feet up Spring Mountain straddles Napa and Sonoma counties, confusing enough for visitors but even more complicated for the wine-making staff: government regulations require separate wineries and paperwork for each side of the property. It's one of several Pride Mountain quirks, but winemaker Sally Johnson's "big red wines," including a Cabernet Sauvignon that earned 100-point scores from a major wine critic two years in a row, are serious business. On a visit, by appointment only, you can learn about

the farming and cellar strategies behind Pride's acclaimed Cabs (the winery also produces Syrah, a Cab-like Merlot, Viognier, and Chardonnay among others). ■**TIP**➜ **The views here are knock-your-socks-off gorgeous.** ⊠ *4026 Spring Mountain Rd., St. Helena* ⊕ *Off St. Helena Rd. (extension of Spring Mountain Rd. in Sonoma County)* ☎ *707/963–4949* ⊕ *www.pridewines.com* ⊠ *Tastings from $30* ⊗ *Closed Tues.*

The Prisoner Wine Company

WINERY/DISTILLERY | The iconoclastic brand opened an industrial-chic space with interiors by the wildly original Napa-based designer Richard Von Saal to showcase its flagship The Prisoner red blend. "Getting the varietals to play together" is winemaker Chrissy Wittmann's mission with that wine (Zinfandel, Cabernet Sauvignon, Petite Sirah, Syrah, Charbono) and siblings like the Blindfold white (Chardonnay plus Rhône and other varietals). The Line-up Tasting of current releases unfolds either in the Tasting Lounge (more hip hotel bar than traditional tasting room) or outside in the casual open-air The Yard. When offered, The Makery Experience (indoors) involves boldly flavored plates that pair well with Wittman's fruit-forward wines. The Prisoner's tasting space is quite the party, for which a reservation is required. ⊠ *1178 Galleron Rd., St. Helena* ⊕ *At Hwy. 29* ☎ *707/967–3823, 877/283–5934* ⊕ *www.theprisonerwinecompany.com* ⊠ *Tastings from $45.*

★ Tres Sabores Winery

WINERY/DISTILLERY | A long, narrow lane with two sharp bends leads to splendidly workaday Tres Sabores, where the sight of sheep, golden retrievers, guinea hens, pomegranate and other trees and plants, a slew of birds and bees, and a heaping compost pile reinforce a simple point: despite the Napa Valley's penchant for glamour this is, first and foremost, farm country. Owner-winemaker Julie Johnson specializes in single-vineyard wines that include Cabernet Sauvignon and Zinfandel from estate-grown certified-organic Rutherford bench vines. She also excels with Petite Sirah from dry-farmed Calistoga fruit, Sauvignon Blanc, and the zippy ¿Por Qué No? (Why not?) red blend. *Tres sabores* is Spanish for "three flavors," which to Johnson represents the land, her vines, and, as she puts it, "the spirit of the company around the table." Tastings by appointment only are informal and usually held outside. ⊠ *1620 S. Whitehall La., St. Helena ✛ West of Hwy. 29* ☎ *707/967–8027* ⊕ *www.tressabores. com* ⊒ *Tasting $50.*

🍴 Restaurants

Brasswood Bar + Bakery + Kitchen

$$$ | ITALIAN | After Napa Valley fixture Tra Vigne lost its lease, many staffers regrouped a few miles north at the restaurant (the titular Kitchen) of the Brasswood complex, which also includes a bakery, shops, and a wine-tasting room. Along with dishes developed for the new location, chef David Nuno incorporates Tra Vigne favorites such as mozzarella-stuffed *arancini* (rice balls) into his Mediterranean-leaning menu. **Known for:** mostly Napa-Sonoma wine list; no corkage on first bottle; Tra Vigne favorites. ⑤ *Average main: $31* ⊠ *3111 St. Helena Hwy. N, St. Helena ✛ Near Ehlers La.* ☎ *707/968–5434* ⊕ *www.brasswood. com.*

The Charter Oak

$$$ | MODERN AMERICAN | Christopher Kostow's reputation rests on his swoonworthy haute cuisine for The Restaurant at Meadowood, but he and his Charter Oak team adopt a more straightforward approach—fewer ingredients chosen for maximum effect—at this high-ceilinged, brown-brick downtown restaurant. On the ever-evolving menu this strategy might translate into dishes like celery-leaf chicken with preserved lemon, herbs, and pan drippings, and red kuri squash with caramelized koji and goat cheese (or

just go for the droolworthy cheeseburger and thick fries). **Known for:** exceedingly fresh produce from nearby Meadowood farm; patio dining in brick courtyard; top chef's affordable cuisine. ⑤ *Average main: $29* ⊠ *1050 Charter Oak Ave., at Hwy. 29, St. Helena* ☎ *707/302–6996* ⊕ *www.thecharteroak.com* ⊗ *No lunch Mon. and Tues.*

★ Cook St. Helena

$$ | ITALIAN | A curved marble bar spotlit by contemporary art-glass pendants adds a touch of style to this downtown restaurant whose northern Italian cuisine pleases with understated sophistication. Mussels with house-made sausage in a spicy tomato broth, chopped salad with pancetta and pecorino, and the daily changing risotto are among the dishes regulars revere. **Known for:** top-quality ingredients; reasonably priced local and international wines; intimate dining. ⑤ *Average main: $26* ⊠ *1310 Main St., St. Helena ✛ Near Hunt Ave.* ☎ *707/963–7088* ⊕ *www.cooksthelena. com* ⊗ *Closed weekends (check website for updates).*

★ Farmstead at Long Meadow Ranch

$$$ | MODERN AMERICAN | In a highceilinged former barn with plenty of outside seating, Farmstead revolves around an open kitchen whose chefs prepare meals with grass-fed beef and lamb, fruits and vegetables, and eggs, olive oil, wine, honey, and other ingredients from nearby Long Meadow Ranch. Entrées might include wood-grilled trout with fennel, mushroom, onion, and bacon-mustard vinaigrette; caramelized beets with goat cheese; or a wood-grilled heritage pork chop with jalapeño grits. **Known for:** Tuesday fried-chicken night; housemade charcuterie; on-site general store, café, and Long Meadow Wines tasting space. ⑤ *Average main: $27* ⊠ *738 Main St., St. Helena ✛ At Charter Oak Ave.* ☎ *707/963–4555* ⊕ *www.longmeadowranch.com/eat-drink/restaurant.*

Goose & Gander

$$$ | MODERN AMERICAN | A Craftsman bungalow whose 1920s owner reportedly used the cellar for bootlegging during Prohibition houses this restaurant where the pairing of food and drink is as likely to involve a craft cocktail as a sommelier-selected wine. Main courses such as brick-cooked chicken, a heritage-pork burger, and dry-aged New York steak with black-lime and pink-peppercorn butter follow starters that might include blistered Brussels sprouts and roasted octopus. **Known for:** intimate main dining room with fireplace; alfresco patio dining; basement bar among Napa's best watering holes. $ *Average main: $31* ✉ *1245 Spring St., St. Helena* ✛ *At Oak St.* ☎ *707/967–8779* ⊕ *www.goosegander. com* ⊗ *No lunch.*

Gott's Roadside

$ | AMERICAN | A 1950s-style outdoor hamburger stand goes upscale at this spot whose customers brave long lines to order breakfast sandwiches, juicy burgers, root-beer floats, and garlic fries. Choices not available a half century ago include ahi tuna and Impossible burgers and kale and Vietnamese chicken salads. **Known for:** tasty 21st-century diner cuisine; shaded picnic tables (arrive early or late for lunch to get one); second branch at Napa's Oxbow Public Market. $ *Average main: $14* ✉ *933 Main St./ Hwy. 29, St. Helena* ✛ *Near Charter Oak Ave.* ☎ *707/963–3486* ⊕ *www.gotts.com* ↻ *Reservations not accepted.*

★ Press

$$$$ | MODERN AMERICAN | For years this cavernous restaurant with a contempo-barn interior and wraparound patio steps from neighboring vineyards was northern Napans' preferred stop for a top-shelf cocktail, grass-fed dry-aged steak, and high-90s-scoring local Cabernet. It still is, but since arriving in 2019, chef Philip Tessier, formerly of Yountville's The French Laundry and Bouchon Bistro and New York City's Le Bernardin, has

expanded the menu to include more refined preparations, much of whose produce is grown nearby. **Known for:** extensive wine cellar; impressive cocktails; casual-chic ambience. $ *Average main: $45* ✉ *587 St. Helena Hwy./Hwy. 29, St. Helena* ✛ *At White La.* ☎ *707/967–0550* ⊕ *www.pressnapavalley.com* ⊗ *No lunch Mon.–Thurs.*

 # Hotels

Alila Napa Valley

$$$$ | HOTEL | An upscale-casual ultracontemporary adults-only resort formerly known as Las Alcobas Napa Valley but as of 2021 in the Hyatt Alila brand's fold, this hillside beauty sits adjacent to Beringer Vineyards six blocks north of Main Street shopping and dining. **Pros:** vineyard views from most rooms; Acacia House restaurant; pool, spa, and fitness center. **Cons:** expensive much of the year; per website no children under age 18 permitted; no self-parking. $ *Rooms from: $700* ✉ *1915 Main St., St. Helena* ☎ *707/963–7000* ⊕ *www.alilanapavalley. com* ➦ *68 rooms* ⦿ *No meals.*

El Bonita Motel

$ | HOTEL | A classic 1950s-style neon sign marks the driveway to this well-run roadside motel that—when it isn't sold out—offers great value to budget-minded travelers. **Pros:** cheerful rooms; family-friendly; microwaves and mini-refrigerators. **Cons:** noise issues in roadside and ground-floor rooms; expensive on high-season weekends; lacks amenities of fancier properties. $ *Rooms from: $160* ✉ *195 Main St./Hwy. 29, St. Helena* ☎ *707/963–3216* ⊕ *www.elbonita.com* ➦ *52 rooms* ⦿ *Free breakfast.*

Harvest Inn

$$$ | HOTEL | Although this inn sits just off Highway 29, its patrons remain mostly above the fray, strolling 8 acres of gardens, enjoying views of the vineyards adjoining the property, partaking in spa services, and drifting to sleep in beds adorned with fancy linens and down pillows. **Pros:** garden setting; spacious rooms; near choice wineries, restaurants, and shops. **Cons:** some lower-price rooms lack elegance; high weekend rates; occasional service lapses. ⑤ *Rooms from: $359* ⊠ *1 Main St., St. Helena* ☎ *707/963–9463* ⊕ *www.harvestinn.com* ⌁ *81 rooms* ❤️❗ *No meals.*

Inn St. Helena

$$$ | **B&B/INN** | A large room at this spiffed-up downtown St. Helena inn is named for author Ambrose Bierce *(The Devil's Dictionary)*, who lived in the main Victorian structure in the early 1900s, but sensitive hospitality and modern amenities are what make a stay worth writing home about. **Pros:** aim-to-please staff and owner; outdoor porch and swing; convenient to shops, tasting rooms, restaurants. **Cons:** no pool, gym, room service, or other typical amenities; two-night minimum on weekends (three with Monday holiday); per website "children 16 and older are welcome". ⑤ *Rooms from: $309* ⊠ *1515 Main St., St. Helena* ☎ *707/963–3003* ⊕ *www. innsthelena.com* ⌁ *8 rooms* ❤️❗ *Free breakfast.*

Meadowood Napa Valley

$$$$ | **RESORT** | This elite 250-acre resort's celebrated restaurant and more than half its accommodations were destroyed in the 2020 Glass Fire, but the spa, pools, tennis courts, fitness center, and a fair number of cottages in one part survived and reopened in 2021, with reconstruction in other areas not expected to affect the guest experience. **Pros:** scrupulously maintained rooms; all-organic spa; gracious service. **Cons:** still recovering from fire; far from downtown St. Helena; weekend minimum-stay requirement. ⑤ *Rooms from: $825* ⊠ *900 Meadowood La., St. Helena* ☎ *707/963–3646, 866/987–8212* ⊕ *www.meadowood.com* ⌁ *36 rooms* ❤️❗ *No meals.*

Wine Country Inn

$$$ | **B&B/INN** | Vineyards flank the three buildings, containing 24 rooms, and five cottages of this pastoral retreat, where blue oaks, maytens, and olive trees provide shade, and gardens feature lantana (small butterflies love it) and lavender. **Pros:** staff excels at anticipating guests' needs; good-size swimming pool; vineyard views from most rooms. **Cons:** some rooms let in noise from neighbors; expensive in high season; weekend minimum-stay requirement. ⑤ *Rooms from: $329* ⊠ *1152 Lodi La., St. Helena* ✛ *East of Hwy. 29* ☎ *707/963–7077, 888/465–4608* ⊕ *www.winecountryinn.com* ⌁ *29 rooms* ❤️❗ *Free breakfast.*

★ Wydown Hotel

$$$ | **HOTEL** | This smart boutique hotel near downtown shopping and dining delivers comfort with a heavy dose of style: the storefront lobby's high ceiling and earth tones, punctuated by rich-hued splashes of color, hint at the relaxed grandeur owner-hotelier Mark Hoffmeister and his design team achieved in the rooms upstairs. **Pros:** well run; eclectic decor; downtown location. **Cons:** lacks the amenities of larger properties; large corner rooms pick up some street noise; two-night minimum on weekends. ⑤ *Rooms from: $339* ⊠ *1424 Main St., St. Helena* ☎ *707/963–5100* ⊕ *www. wydownhotel.com* ⌁ *12 rooms* ❤️❗ *No meals.*

Nightlife

The Saint

WINE BARS—NIGHTLIFE | This high-ceilinged downtown wine bar benefits from the grandeur and gravitas of its setting inside a stone-walled late-19th-century former bank. Lit by chandeliers and decked out in contemporary style with plush sofas and chairs and Lucite stools at the bar, it's a classy, loungelike space to expand your enological horizons. ⊠ *1351 Main St., St. Helena* ✛ *Near Adams St.* ☎ *707/302–5130* ⊕ *www.*

thesaintnapavalley.com ☞ Closed Mon.–Wed. (but check).

Calistoga

3 miles northwest of St. Helena.

With false-fronted, Old West–style shops and 19th-century inns and hotels lining its main drag, Lincoln Avenue in Calistoga comes across as more down-to-earth than its more polished neighbors. Don't be fooled, though. On its outskirts lie some of the Wine Country's swankest (and priciest) resorts and its most fanciful piece of architecture, the medieval-style Castello di Amorosa winery.

Calistoga was developed as a spa-oriented getaway from the start. Sam Brannan, a gold rush–era entrepreneur, planned to use the area's natural hot springs as the centerpiece of a resort complex. His venture failed, but old-time hotels and bathhouses—along with some glorious new spas—still operate. You can come for an old-school mud bath, or go completely 21st century and experience lavish treatments based on the latest innovations in skin and body care.

GETTING HERE AND AROUND

Highway 29 heads east (turn right) at Calistoga, where in town it is signed as Lincoln Avenue. If arriving via the Silverado Trail, head west at Highway 29/Lincoln Avenue.

Sights

Castello di Amorosa

WINERY/DISTILLERY | An astounding medieval structure complete with drawbridge and moat, chapel, stables, and secret passageways, the Castello commands Diamond Mountain's lower eastern slope. Some of the 107 rooms contain artist Fabio Sanzogni's replicas of 13th-century frescoes (cheekily signed with his website address), and the dungeon has an iron maiden from Nuremberg, Germany.

You must pay for a tour, when offered, to see most of Dario Sattui's extensive eight-level property, though with general admission you'll have access to part of the complex. Bottlings of note include several Italian-style wines, including La Castellana, a robust "super Tuscan" blend of Cabernet Sauvignon, Sangiovese, and Merlot; and Il Barone, a deliberately big Cab primarily of Rutherford grapes. All visits are by appointment. ⊠ *4045 N. St. Helena Hwy./Hwy. 29, Calistoga ✛ Near Maple La.* ☎ *707/967–6272* ⊕ *www.castellodiamorosa.com* ⓢ *Check with winery for tasting and tour prices.*

Chateau Montelena

WINERY/DISTILLERY | Set amid a bucolic northern Calistoga landscape, this winery helped establish the Napa Valley's reputation for high-quality wine making. At the pivotal Paris tasting of 1976, the Chateau Montelena 1973 Chardonnay took first place, beating out four white Burgundies from France and five other California Chardonnays, an event immortalized in the 2008 movie *Bottle Shock*. A 21st century Napa Valley Chardonnay is always part of A Taste of Montelena—the winery also makes Sauvignon Blanc, Riesling, a fine estate Zinfandel, and Cabernet Sauvignon—or you can opt for the Montelena Estate Collection tasting of Cabernets from several vintages. When tours are offered, there's one that takes in the grounds and covers the history of this stately property whose stone winery building was erected in 1888. All visits require a reservation. ⊠ *1429 Tubbs La., Calistoga ✛ Off Hwy. 29* ☎ *707/942–5105* ⊕ *www.montelena.com* ⓢ *Tastings from $40.*

Frank Family Vineyards

WINERY/DISTILLERY | As a former Disney film and television executive, Rich Frank knows a thing or two about entertainment, and it shows in the chipper atmosphere that prevails in the winery's bright-yellow Craftsman-style tasting room. The site's wine-making history dates from the 19th century, and portions of an original 1884 structure, reclad in stone in 1906, remain standing today. From 1952 until 1990, Hanns Kornell made sparkling wines on this site. Frank Family makes sparklers itself, but the high-profile wines are the Carneros Chardonnay and several Cabernet Sauvignons, particularly the Rutherford Reserve and the Winston Hill red blend. Tastings are sit-down affairs, indoors, on the back veranda, or under 100-year-old elms. Reservations are required. ⊠ 1091 Larkmead La., Calistoga ✛ Off Hwy. 29 ☎ 707/942–0859 ⊕ www.frankfamilyvineyards.com ⊠ Tastings from $50.

★ **Schramsberg**
WINERY/DISTILLERY | On a Diamond Mountain site the German-born Jacob Schram planted to grapes in the early 1860s, Schramsberg pours its esteemed *méthode traditionnelle* (aka *méthode champenoise*) sparkling wines. Author Robert Louis Stevenson was among Schram's early visitors. After the vintner's death in 1905 the winery closed and fell into disrepair, but in 1965 Jack and Jamie Davies purchased the 200-acre Schramsberg property and began restoring its buildings and caves. Chinese laborers dug some of the latter in the 1870s. In the 1990s, the family set about replanting the vineyard to Cabernet Sauvignon and other Bordeaux varietals for the Davies Vineyards label's still red wines. Tastings at Schramsberg can include pours of only sparkling wines, only still wines, or a combination of the two. All visits are by appointment. ⊠ 1400 Schramsberg Rd., Calistoga ✛ Off Hwy. 29 ☎ 707/942–4558, 800/877–3623 ⊕ www.schramsberg.com ⊠ Tastings from $50.

Tamber Bey Vineyards
WINERY/DISTILLERY | Endurance riders Barry and Jennifer Waitte share their passion for horses and wine at their glam-rustic winery north of Calistoga. Their 22-acre Sundance Ranch remains a working equestrian facility, but the site has been revamped to include a state-of-the-art winery with separate fermenting tanks for grapes from Tamber Bey's vineyards in Yountville, Oakville, and elsewhere. The winemakers produce Chardonnay, Sauvignon Blanc, and Pinot Noir, but the showstoppers are several subtly powerful reds, including the flagship Oakville Cabernet Sauvignon and a Yountville Merlot. The top-selling wine, Rabicano, is a Cabernet Sauvignon-heavy Bordeaux-style blend. Visits here require an appointment. ⊠ 1251 Tubbs La., Calistoga ✛ At Myrtledale Rd. ☎ 707/942–2100 ⊕ www.tamberbey.com ⊠ Tastings from $45.

🍴 Restaurants

★ **Lovina**
$$$ | **MODERN AMERICAN** | A vintage-style neon sign outside this bungalow restaurant announces "Great Food," and the chefs deliver with imaginative, well-plated dishes served on two floors or a streetside patio that in good weather is especially festive during weekend brunch. Entrée staples on the seasonally changing menu include cioppino and slow-roasted half-chicken, with heirloom-tomato gazpacho a summer starter and chicken-dumpling soup its warming winter counterpart. **Known for:** imaginative cuisine; weekend brunch scene; Wine Wednesdays no corkage, discounts on wine list. $ *Average main: $34* ⊠ 1107 Cedar St., Calistoga ✛ At Lincoln Ave. ☎ 707/942–6500 ⊕ www.lovinacalistoga.com ⊗ No lunch weekdays.

Sam's Social Club
$$$ | **MODERN AMERICAN** | Tourists, locals, and spa guests—some of the latter in bathrobes after treatments—assemble inside this resort restaurant or on its extensive patio for breakfast, lunch, bar snacks, or dinner. Lunch options include thin-crust pizzas, sandwiches, an aged-cheddar burger, and entrées such as chicken paillard, with the burger reappearing for dinner along with pan-seared

The astounding Castello di Amorosa has 107 rooms.

fish, rib-eye steak frites, and similar fare. **Known for:** casual atmosphere; cocktail-friendly starters; hearty salads. ⑤ *Average main: $31* ✉ *Indian Springs Resort and Spa, 1712 Lincoln Ave., Calistoga* ✛ *At Wappo Ave.* ☎ *707/942–4969* ⊕ *www.samssocialclub.com.*

★ Solbar

$$$$ | MODERN AMERICAN | The restaurant at Solage attracts the resort's clientele, upvalley locals, and guests of nearby lodgings for sophisticated farm-to-table cuisine served in the high-ceilinged dining area or alfresco on a sprawling patio warmed by shapely heaters and a mesmerizing fire pit. Dishes on the lighter side might include house-made pasta or well-executed sole, with duck breast, crispy pork, or prime New York steak among the heartier options. **Known for:** artisanal cocktails; festive patio; Sunday brunch. ⑤ *Average main: $40* ✉ *Solage, 755 Silverado Trail, Calistoga* ✛ *At Rosedale Rd.* ☎ *866/942–7442* ⊕ *solage. aubergeresorts.com/dine.*

Hotels

★ Embrace Calistoga

$$$ | B&B/INN | Extravagant hospitality defines the Napa Valley's luxury properties, but Embrace Calistoga takes the prize in the "small lodging" category. **Pros:** attentive owners; marvelous breakfasts; restaurants, tasting rooms, and shopping within walking distance. **Cons:** light hum of street traffic; no pool or spa; two-night minimum some weekends. ⑤ *Rooms from: $309* ✉ *1139 Lincoln Ave., Calistoga* ☎ *707/942–9797* ⊕ *embracecalistoga.com* ⤴ *5 rooms* ⦿*◆ Free breakfast.*

Four Seasons Resort and Residences Napa Valley

$$$$ | RESORT | Opened in 2021, this suave luxury resort entices high rollers with farmhouse-eclectic interiors and amenities that include a spa, a destination restaurant, two pools, 7-plus acres of vines, and a working winery. **Pros:** estate villa and one-bedroom suites offer maximum luxury and privacy; destination restaurant

Truss; on-site vineyard and winery. **Cons:** expensive year-round; casual-chic yet may feel too formal for some guests; minimum two-night weekend requirement. ⑤ *Rooms from: $1400* ⊠ *400 Silverado Trail N, Calistoga* ☎ *707/709–2100, 800/819–5053 for reservations* ⊕ *www.fourseasons.com/napavalley* ⇌ *83 rooms* ⑩ *No meals.*

Indian Springs Calistoga

$$$ | **RESORT** | Palm-studded Indian Springs—operating as a spa since 1862—ably splits the difference between laid-back and chic in accommodations that include lodge rooms, suites, cottages, stand-alone bungalows, and two houses. **Pros:** palm-studded grounds with outdoor seating areas; on-site Sam's Social Club restaurant; enormous mineral pool. **Cons:** lodge rooms are small; many rooms have showers but no tubs; two-night minimum on weekends (three with Monday holiday). ⑤ *Rooms from: $309* ⊠ *1712 Lincoln Ave., Calistoga* ☎ *707/709–8139* ⊕ *www.indianspringscalistoga.com* ⇌ *113 rooms* ⑩ *No meals.*

★ Solage

$$$$ | **RESORT** | The aesthetic at this 22-acre property, where health and wellness are priorities, is Napa Valley barn meets San Francisco loft: guest rooms have high ceilings, sleek contemporary furniture, all-natural fabrics in soothingly muted colors, and an outdoor patio. **Pros:** great service; complimentary bikes; separate pools for kids and adults. **Cons:** vibe might not suit everyone; longish walk from some lodgings to spa and fitness center; expensive in-season. ⑤ *Rooms from: $749* ⊠ *755 Silverado Trail, Calistoga* ☎ *866/942–7442, 707/226–0800* ⊕ *www.solagecalistoga.com* ⇌ *89 rooms* ⑩ *No meals.*

 # Shopping

Mad Mod Shop

CLOTHING | Find the new polka-dotted, patent-leathered you at this quirky stop for vintage-inspired dresses, skirts, tops, and accessories in all sizes. ⊠ *1410 Lincoln Ave., Calistoga* ✛ *At Washington St.* ☎ *707/942–1059* ⊕ *madmodshop.com.*

 # Activities

BICYCLING

Calistoga Bikeshop

BICYCLING | Options here include regular and fancy bikes that rent for $28 and up for two hours, and there's a self-guided Cool Wine Tour ($110) with stops for tastings at three or four small wineries. ⊠ *1318 Lincoln Ave., Calistoga* ✛ *Near Washington St.* ☎ *707/942–9687* ⊕ *www.calistogabikeshop.net.*

SPAS

Indian Springs Spa

FITNESS/HEALTH CLUBS | Even before Sam Brannan constructed a spa on this site in the 1860s, the Wappo Indians built sweat lodges over its thermal geysers. Treatments include a Calistoga-classic, pure volcanic-ash mud bath followed by a mineral bath, after which clients are wrapped in a flannel blanket for a 15-minute cool-down session or until called for a massage if they've booked one. Oxygen-infusion facials are another specialty. Before or following a treatment, guests unwind at the serene Buddha Pool, fed by one of the property's four geysers. ⊠ *1712 Lincoln Ave., Calistoga* ✛ *At Wappo Ave.* ☎ *707/942–4913* ⊕ *indianspringscalistoga.com/spa-overview* ⊠ *Treatments from $95.*

★ Spa Solage

FITNESS/HEALTH CLUBS | This 20,000-square-foot eco-conscious spa reinvented the traditional Calistoga mud-and-mineral-water regimen with the hour-long "Mudslide." The three-part treatment includes a mud body mask applied in a heated lounge, a soak in a thermal bath, and a power nap in a sound-vibration chair. The mud here, less gloppy than at other resorts, is a mix of clay, volcanic ash, and essential oils. Traditional spa services—combination Shiatsu-Swedish and other massages, foot reflexology, facials, and waxes—are available, as are yoga and wellness sessions. ⊠ *755 Silverado Trail, Calistoga* ⊹ *At Rosedale Rd.* ☎ *707/226–0825* ⊕ *solage.aubergeresorts.com/spa* ⊒ *Treatments from $110.*

Sonoma

14 miles west of Napa, 45 miles northeast of San Francisco.

One of the few towns in the valley with multiple attractions unrelated to food and wine, Sonoma has plenty to keep you busy for a couple of hours before you head out to tour the wineries. And you needn't leave town to taste wine. About three dozen tasting rooms are within steps of tree-filled Sonoma Plaza. The valley's cultural center, Sonoma was founded in 1835 when California was still part of Mexico.

GETTING HERE AND AROUND
Highway 12 (signed as Broadway near Sonoma Plaza) heads north into Sonoma from Highway 121 and south from Santa Rosa into downtown Sonoma. Parking is relatively easy to find on or near the plaza, and you can walk to many restaurants, shops, and tasting rooms. Signs point the way to several wineries a mile or more east of the plaza. Sonoma County Transit buses serve the town.

⊙ Sights

★ Bedrock Wine Co.
WINERY/DISTILLERY | Zinfandel and other varietals grown in heritage vineyards throughout California are the focus of Bedrock, a young winery whose backstory involves several historical figures. Tastings take place in a home east of Sonoma Plaza owned in the 1850s by General Joseph Hooker. By coincidence, Hooker planted grapes at what's now the estate Bedrock Vineyard a few miles away. General William Tecumseh Sherman was his partner in the vineyard (a spat over it affected their Civil War interactions), which newspaper magnate William Randolph Hearst's father, George, replanted in the late 1880s. Some Hearst vines still produce grapes, whose current owner-winemaker, Morgan Twain-Peterson, learned about Zinfandel from his dad, Ravenswood founder Joel Peterson. Twain-Peterson's bottlings, many of them field blends containing multiple varietals grown and fermented together, are as richly textured as his winery's prehistory. ⊠ *General Joseph Hooker House, 414 1st St. E, Sonoma* ⊹ *Near E. Spain St.* ☎ *707/343–1478* ⊕ *www.bedrockwineco.com* ⊒ *Tastings from $30* ⊙ *Closed Mon. and Tues.*

Buena Vista Winery
WINERY/DISTILLERY | A local actor in top hat and 19th-century garb often greets guests as Count Agoston Haraszthy at this entertaining homage to the birthplace of modern California wine making. Haraszthy's rehabilitated former press house (used for pressing grapes into wine), completed in 1864, is the architectural focal point, with photos, banners, plaques, and artifacts providing historical context. Chardonnay, Pinot Noir, and several red blends are the strong suits among the two-dozen-plus wines produced. During appointment-only visits (walk-ins sometimes possible), you can taste some of them solo or preorder a box lunch from the affiliated Oakville Grocery. ⊠ *18000 Old Winery Rd., Sonoma* ⊹ *Off E. Napa St.* ☎ *800/926–1266* ⊕ *www.buenavistawinery.com* ⊒ *Tastings from $20.*

Sonoma County

KEY

1 Exploring Sights

Sights ▼

Corner 103

WINERY/DISTILLERY | After leading an effort to revive a troubled local winery, Lloyd Davis, an African American financier and oenophile, turned his attention to a new passion: making the experience of learning about wine and food-wine pairings less daunting. To that end he opened a light-filled space, diagonally across from Sonoma Plaza, for tastings of Sonoma County wines usually paired with cheeses or other pertinent bites. The lineup includes a Brut Rosé sparkler, Chardonnay and Marsanne-Roussanne whites, a rosé of Pinot Noir, and several reds. Corner 103's welcoming atmosphere, which earned it the top slot on *USA Today's* Best Tasting Room list for 2020, makes it an excellent choice for wine novices seeking to expand their knowledge. Visits are by appointment only, though hosts usually accommodate drop-ins seeking wine-only tastings. ⊠ *103 W. Napa St., Sonoma* ✛ *At 1st St. W* ☎ *707/931–6141* ⊕ *www.corner103. com* ⌧ *Tastings from $20.*

★ The Donum Estate

WINERY/DISTILLERY | The wine-making team of this prominent Chardonnay and Pinot Noir producer prizes viticulture—selecting vineyards with superior soils and microclimates, planting compatible clones, then farming with rigor—over wine-making wizardry. The Donum Estate, whose white board-and-batten tasting room affords guests hilltop views of Los Carneros, San Pablo Bay, and beyond, farms two vineyards surrounding the structure, one in the Russian River Valley, and another in Mendocino County's Anderson Valley. All the wines exhibit the "power yet elegance" that sealed the winery's fame in the 2000s. Tastings are by appointment only. Forty large-scale museum-quality contemporary sculptures placed amid the vines, including works by Ai Weiwei, Lynda Benglis, Louise Bourgeois, Keith Haring, and Anselm Kiefer, add a touch of high culture to a visit here. ■TIP➔ The winery

offers an invigorating 1½-hour guided stroll past the artworks without the tasting. ⊠ *24500 Ramal Rd., Sonoma* ✛ *Off Hwy. 121/12* ☎ *707/732–2200* ⊕ *www.thedonumestate.com* ⌧ *Tastings from $95, art tour $50.*

Gloria Ferrer Caves and Vineyards

WINERY/DISTILLERY | On a clear day this Spanish hacienda–style winery's Vista Terrace lives up to its name as guests at seated tastings sip delicate sparkling wines while taking in views of gently rolling Carneros hills and beyond them San Pablo Bay. The Chardonnay and Pinot Noir grapes from the vineyards in the foreground are the product of old-world wine-making knowledge—generations of the founding Ferrer family made cava in Spain—but also contemporary soil management techniques and clonal research. Hosts well-acquainted with the winery's sustainability practices and history as the Carneros District's first sparkling-wine house serve the wines accompanied by food that varies from cheese and charcuterie to caviar or a full lunch. All visits are by appointment. ■TIP➔ For the cheese-and-charcuterie option you can upgrade from the standard flight, which includes still wines, to an all-bubbles one. ⊠ *23555 Carneros Hwy./Hwy. 121, Sonoma* ☎ *707/933–1917* ⊕ *www.gloriaferrer. com* ⌧ *Tastings from $55.*

Hanson of Sonoma Distillery

WINERY/DISTILLERY | The Hanson family makes grape-based organic vodkas, one traditional, the rest infused with cucumbers, ginger, mandarin oranges, Meyer lemons, or habanero and other chili peppers. A surprise to many visitors, the Hansons make a blended white wine before distilling it into vodka. The family pours its vodkas, along with single-malt whiskey, in an industrial-looking tasting room heavy on the steel, with wood reclaimed from Deep South smokehouses adding a rustic note. In good weather some sessions take place on the landscaped shore of a small pond. Per state law, there's a limit to the amount poured, but it's sufficient to get to know the product. ✉ *22985 Burndale Rd., Sonoma ⚓ At Carneros Hwy. (Hwy. 121)* 🕾 *707/343–1805* ⊕ *hansonofsonoma. com* 🍷 *Tastings from $25, tours from $50 (includes tasting).*

★ Sangiacomo Family Wines

WINERY/DISTILLERY | Several dozen wineries produce vineyard-designate Chardonnays and Pinot Noirs from grapes grown by the Sangiacomo family, whose Italian ancestors first started farming in Sonoma in 1927. The family didn't establish its own label until 2016, but its cool-climate wines and a Napa Valley Cabernet are already earning critical plaudits. Chardonnay vines and the Carneros District's western hills form the backdrop for tastings, usually outdoors, at the 110-acre Home Ranch, the first of a dozen-plus vineyards the Sangiacomos acquired or lease. At appointment-only visits you're apt to encounter one or more third-generation members, all of whom enjoy meeting guests and sharing their family's legacy. ■**TIP→ On Fridays, the winery hosts Sunset on the Terrace, with wines served by the glass or bottle from 3:30 pm until sundown.** ✉ *21545 Broadway, Sonoma ⚓ 2½ miles south of Sonoma Plaza* 🕾 *707/934–8445* ⊕ *www.sangiacomowines.com* 🍷 *Tastings from $30.*

Sonoma Mission

RELIGIOUS SITE | The northernmost of the 21 missions established by Franciscan friars in California, Sonoma Mission was founded in 1823 as Mission San Francisco Solano. These days it serves as the centerpiece of **Sonoma State Historic Park,** which includes several other sites in Sonoma and nearby Petaluma. Some early mission structures fell into ruin, but all or part of several remaining buildings date to the era of Mexican rule over California. The **Sonoma Barracks,** a half block west of the mission at 20 East Spain Street, housed troops under the command of General Mariano Guadalupe

Vallejo, who controlled vast tracts of land in the region. **General Vallejo's Home,** a Victorian-era structure, is a few blocks west. ✉ *114 E. Spain St., Sonoma ⚓ At 1st St. E* 🕾 *707/938–9560* ⊕ *www.parks.ca.gov* 🍷 *$3, includes same-day admission to other historic sites.*

Restaurants

★ Cafe La Haye

$$$ | **AMERICAN** | In a postage-stamp-size open kitchen (the dining room, its white walls adorned with contemporary art, is nearly as compact), chef Jeffrey Lloyd turns out understated, sophisticated fare emphasizing seasonally available local ingredients. Meats, pastas, and seafood get deluxe treatment without fuss or fanfare—and the daily risotto special is always worth trying. **Known for:** Napa-Sonoma wine list with French complements; signature butterscotch pudding; owner Saul Gropman on hand to greet diners. ⑤ *Average main: $27* ✉ *140 E. Napa St., Sonoma ⚓ East of Sonoma Plaza* 🕾 *707/935–5994* ⊕ *www. cafelahaye.com* 🕙 *Closed Sun. and Mon. No lunch.*

El Dorado Kitchen

$$$ | **MODERN AMERICAN** | This restaurant owes its visual appeal to its clean lines and handsome decor, but the eye inevitably drifts westward to the open kitchen, where longtime chef Armando Navarro and his team craft dishes full of subtle surprises. The menu might include cod ceviche or fried calamari with spicy marinara sauce as starters and pan-roasted salmon or paella awash with seafood and dry-cured Spanish chorizo sausage among the entrées. **Known for:** subtle tastes and textures; truffle-oil fries with Parmesan; bar menu's pizzas and burger. ⑤ *Average main: $29* ✉ *El Dorado Hotel, 405 1st St. W, Sonoma ⚓ At W. Spain St.* 🕾 *707/996–3030* ⊕ *eldoradokitchen.com.*

★ Girl & the Fig

$$ | FRENCH | At this hot spot for inventive French cooking inside the historic Sonoma Hotel bar, you can always find a dish with the signature figs on the menu, whether it's a fig-and-arugula salad or an aperitif blending sparkling wine with fig liqueur. Also look for duck confit, a burger with matchstick fries, and wild flounder meunière. **Known for:** Rhône-wines emphasis; artisanal cheese platters; Sunday brunch. ⑤ *Average main: $26 ⊠ Sonoma Hotel, 110 W. Spain St., Sonoma ✣ At 1st St. W ☎ 707/938–3634 ⊕ www.thegirlandthefig.com.*

★ LaSalette Restaurant

$$$ | PORTUGUESE | Born in the Azores and raised in Sonoma, chef-owner Manuel Azevedo serves cuisine inspired by his native Portugal in this warmly decorated spot. The wood-oven-roasted fish is always worth trying, and there are usually boldly flavored pork dishes, along with stews, salted cod, and other hearty fare. **Known for:** authentic Portuguese cuisine; sophisticated spicing; local and Portuguese wine flights. ⑤ *Average main: $29 ⊠ 452 1st St. E, Sonoma ✣ Near E. Spain St. ☎ 707/938–1927 ⊕ www.lasaletterestaurant.com ☉ Closed Wed.*

Taub Family Outpost

$$ | AMERICAN | Its varied initiatives and location across from Sonoma Plaza's southwest corner ensure steady traffic to this combination all-day restaurant, gourmet marketplace, wine shop, café, bar, and wine-tasting space whose updated-country-store decor suits its 1912 building's Mexican period/Old West flourishes. Items that might appear on the menu range from the healthful (ancient-grain burgers; smoked-beet salad) to the sinfully delicious (grilled cheese with bacon; fried chicken) and in-between (prosciutto with honeydew melon). **Known for:** coffee and cocktails; wines from many lands; patio dining. ⑤ *Average main: $22 ⊠ 497 1st St. W, Sonoma ✣ At*

W. Napa St. ☎ 707/721–1107 ⊕ taubfamilyoutpost.com ☉ Closed Mon.

★ Wit & Wisdom Tavern

$$$ | MODERN AMERICAN | A San Francisco culinary star with establishments worldwide, Michael Mina debuted his first Wine Country restaurant in 2020, its interior of charcoal grays, browns, and soft whites dandy indeed, if by evening vying with outdoor spaces aglow with fire pits and lighted water features. Seasonal regional ingredients—Pacific Coast fish, pasture-raised meats, freshly plucked produce—go into haute-homey dishes, prepared open-fire, that include pizzas, handmade pastas, and the signature lobster potpie with brandied lobster cream and black truffle. **Known for:** shellfish and duck-wing apps; extensive local wines; large outdoor patio. ⑤ *Average main: $35 ⊠ The Lodge at Sonoma, 1325 Broadway, Sonoma ✣ At Leveroni Rd. ☎ 707/931–3405 ⊕ www.witandwisdomsonoma.com.*

 Hotels

Inn at Sonoma

$$ | B&B/INN | Little luxuries delight at this well-run inn ¼-mile south of Sonoma Plaza whose guest rooms, softly lit and done in pastels, have comfortable beds topped with feather comforters and plenty of pillows. **Pros:** last-minute specials are a great deal; afternoon wine, cheese, and freshly baked cookies; good soundproofing blocks out Broadway street noise. **Cons:** on a busy street rather than right on the plaza; pet-friendly rooms book up quickly; some rooms on the small side. ⑤ *Rooms from: $259 ⊠ 630 Broadway, Sonoma ☎ 707/939–1340 ⊕ www.innatsonoma.com ⬠ 27 rooms ❑ Free breakfast.*

★ Ledson Hotel

$$$ | B&B/INN | With just six rooms the Ledson feels intimate, and the furnishings and amenities—down beds, mood lighting, gas fireplaces, whirlpool tubs, and balconies for enjoying breakfast or a glass of wine—stack up well against Wine Country rooms costing more, especially in high season. **Pros:** convenient Sonoma Plaza location; spacious, individually decorated rooms; whirlpool tub in all rooms. **Cons:** two people maximum occupancy in all rooms; children must be at least 12 years old; front rooms have plaza views but pick up some street noise. $ *Rooms from: $350* ✉ *480 1st St. E, Sonoma* ☎ *707/996–9779* ⊕ *www.ledsonhotel.com* ⬤ *6 rooms* ❘◯❘ *No meals.*

★ MacArthur Place Hotel & Spa
$$$$ | **HOTEL** | Guests at this 7-acre boutique property five blocks south of Sonoma Plaza bask in ritzy seclusion in plush accommodations set amid landscaped gardens. **Pros:** verdant garden setting; restaurant among Sonoma's best; great for a romantic getaway. **Cons:** a bit of a walk from the plaza; some traffic noise audible in street-side rooms; pricey in high season. $ *Rooms from: $459* ✉ *29 E. MacArthur St., Sonoma* ☎ *707/938–2929, 800/722–1866* ⊕ *www.macarthurplace.com* ⬤ *64 rooms* ❘◯❘ *Free breakfast.*

Nightlife

Sigh!
WINE BARS—NIGHTLIFE | From the oval bar and walls the color of a fine Blanc de Blancs to retro chandeliers that mimic champagne bubbles, everything about this sparkling-wine bar's frothy space screams "have a good time." That owner Jayme Powers and her posse are trained in the fine art of *sabrage* (opening a bottle of sparkling with a saber) only adds to the festivity. ■TIP→ **Sigh! opens at noon, so it's a good daytime stop, too.** ✉ *120 W. Napa St., Sonoma* ✚ *At 1st St. W* ☎ *707/996–2444* ⊕ *www.sighsonoma.com.*

Shopping

Chateau Sonoma
HOUSEHOLD ITEMS/FURNITURE | The fancy furniture, lighting fixtures, and objets d'art at this upscale shop make it a dangerous place to enter: within minutes you may find yourself reconsidering your entire home's aesthetic. The owner's keen eye for French style makes a visit here a pleasure. ✉ *453 1st St. W, Sonoma* ✚ *Between W. Napa and W. Spain Sts.* ☎ *707/309–1993* ⊕ *www.chateausonoma.com.*

Activities

SPAS
Willow Stream Spa at Fairmont Sonoma Mission Inn & Spa
FITNESS/HEALTH CLUBS | By far the Wine Country's largest spa, the Fairmont resort's 40,000-square-foot facility provides every amenity you could want, including pools and hot tubs fed by local thermal springs. Each of the three signature treatments achieves a specific objective. Starting with a lavender bubble bath, followed by a botanical body wrap and a massage, the Couples Lavender Kur focuses on pampering, whereas the Neroli Blossom Kur—a body polish, a full-body massage, a moisture mask, and a facial and scalp massage—is all about restoring balance. For clients in need of a detox, the Wine Country Kur begins with exfoliation, a soak, and a wrap, concluding with a grape-seed oil massage. ✉ *100 Boyes Blvd./Hwy. 12, Sonoma* ✚ *2½ miles north of Sonoma Plaza* ☎ *707/938–9000* ⊕ *www.fairmont.com/sonoma/willow-stream* ⬤ *Treatments from $79.*

Glen Ellen

7 miles north of Sonoma.

Craggy Glen Ellen epitomizes the difference between the Napa and Sonoma valleys. Whereas small Napa towns like St. Helena get their charm from upscale boutiques and restaurants lined up along well-groomed sidewalks, Glen Ellen's crooked streets are shaded with stands of old oak trees and occasionally bisected by the Sonoma and Calabazas creeks. Tucked among the trees of a narrow canyon where Sonoma Mountain and the Mayacamas pinch in the valley floor, Glen Ellen looks more like a town of the Sierra foothills gold country than a Wine Country village.

GETTING HERE AND AROUND

Glen Ellen sits just off Highway 12. From the north or south, take Arnold Drive west and follow it south less than a mile. The walkable downtown straddles a half-mile stretch of Arnold Drive. Sonoma County Transit buses serve Glen Ellen.

Sights

Benziger Family Winery

WINERY/DISTILLERY | One of the best-known Sonoma County wineries sits on a sprawling estate in a bowl with 360-degree sun exposure. Hosts conducting popular tram tours explain the benefits of the vineyard's natural setting and how biodynamic farming yields healthier, more flavorful fruit. The eco-friendly agricultural practices include extensive plantings to attract beneficial insects and the deployment of sheep to trim vegetation between the vines while simultaneously tilling the soil with their hooves and fertilizing to boot. Known for Chardonnay, Cabernet Sauvignon, Merlot, Pinot Noir, and Sauvignon Blanc, the winery is a beautiful spot for an alfresco tasting, whether you take the tour or not. All visits are by appointment; in summer and early fall, reserve a tram tour at least a day or two ahead. ⊠ *1883 London Ranch Rd., Glen Ellen ✛ Off Arnold Dr.* ☎ *888/490–2739* ⊕ *www.benziger.com* ⊠ *Tasting $30, tram tour and tasting $60* ⊗ *Closed Tues. and Wed.*

★ Jack London State Historic Park

NATIONAL/STATE PARK | The pleasures are pastoral and intellectual at author Jack London's beloved Beauty Ranch, where you could easily spend the afternoon hiking some of the 30-plus miles of trails that loop through meadows and stands of oaks, redwoods, and other trees. Manuscripts and personal artifacts depicting London's travels are on view at the House of Happy Walls Museum, which provides an overview of the writer's life, literary passions, humanitarian and conservation efforts, and promotion of organic farming. A short hike away lie the ruins of Wolf House, which burned down just before London was to move in. Also open to visitors are a few outbuildings and the restored wood-framed cottage where London penned many of his later works. He's buried on the property. ■**TIP→** **The park's Broadway Under the Stars series, a hot summer ticket, is expected to resume in 2021.** ⊠ *2400 London Ranch Rd., Glen Ellen ✛ Off Arnold Dr.* ☎ *707/938–5216* ⊕ *www.jacklondonpark.com* ⊠ *Parking $10 ($5 walk-in or bike), includes admission to museum; cottage $4.*

★ Lasseter Family Winery

WINERY/DISTILLERY | Immaculately groomed grapevines dazzle the eye at John and Nancy Lasseter's secluded winery, and it's no accident: Phil Coturri, Sonoma Valley's premier organic vineyard manager, tends them. Even the landscaping, which includes an insectary to attract beneficial bugs, is meticulously maintained. Come harvest time, the wine-making team oversees gentle processes that transform the fruit into wines of purity and grace, among them a Sémillon–Sauvignon Blanc blend, two rosés, and Bordeaux and Rhône reds. Evocative labels illustrate the tale behind each wine. In good weather, guests enjoy these well-told stories at tastings on the winery's outdoor patio, whose views include the vineyard and the Mayacamas Mountains. All visits are by appointment. ⊠ *1 Vintage La., Glen Ellen ✛ Off Dunbar*

Benziger tram tours take to the fields to show biodynamic farming techniques in action.

Rd. ☎ *707/933–2814* ⊕ *www.lasseter-familywinery.com* ☐ *Tastings from $25.*

 Restaurants

★ Glen Ellen Star

$$$ | ECLECTIC | Chef Ari Weiswasser honed his craft at The French Laundry, Daniel, and other bastions of culinary finesse, but at his Wine Country outpost he prepares haute-rustic cuisine, much of it emerging from a wood-fired oven that burns a steady 600°F. Crisp-crusted, richly sauced Margherita and other pizzas thrive in the torrid heat, as do tender whole fish entrées and vegetables roasted in small iron skillets. **Known for:** outdoor dining area; prix-fixe Wednesday "neighborhood night" menu with free corkage; Weiswasser's sauces, emulsions, and spices. Ⓢ *Average main: $30* ✉ *13648 Arnold Dr., Glen Ellen* ✛ *At Warm Springs Rd.* ☎ *707/343–1384* ⊕ *glenellenstar.com* ⊙ *No lunch.*

★ Les Pascals

$ | FRENCH | A bright-yellow slice of France in downtown Glen Ellen, this combination pâtisserie, boulangerie, and café takes its name from its husband-and-wife owners, Pascal and Pascale Merle. Pascal whips up croissants, breads, turnovers, and sweet treats like Napoleons, galettes, and eclairs, along with quiches, potpies, and other savory fare; Pascale creates an upbeat environment for customers to enjoy them. **Known for:** memorable French onion soup; shaded back patio; high-test French and Italian coffee drinks. Ⓢ *Average main: $10* ✉ *13758 Arnold Dr., Glen Ellen* ✛ *Near London Ranch Rd.* ☎ *707/934–8378* ⊕ *www.lespascalspatisserie.com* ⊙ *Closed Wed. No dinner.*

 Hotels

★ Gaige House + Ryokan

$$$ | B&B/INN | There's no other place in Sonoma or Napa quite like the Gaige House + Ryokan, which blends the best elements of a traditional country inn, a boutique hotel, and a longtime expat's

classy Asian hideaway. **Pros:** short walk to Glen Ellen restaurants, shops, and tasting rooms; freshly baked cookies; full breakfasts, afternoon wine and appetizers. **Cons:** sound carries in the main house; the least expensive rooms are on the small side; oriented more toward couples than families with children. ⑤ *Rooms from: $302* ✉ *13540 Arnold Dr., Glen Ellen* ☎ *707/935–0237, 800/935–0237* ⊕ *www.thegaigehouse.com* ⌁ *23 rooms* ⦿I *Free breakfast.*

★ Olea Hotel

$$$ | B&B/INN | Husband-and-wife team Ashish and Sia Patel operate this down-home country casual yet sophisticated boutique lodging. **Pros:** beautiful style; complimentary wine; filling two-course breakfasts. **Cons:** minor road noise in some rooms; fills up quickly on weekends; weekend minimum-stay requirement. ⑤ *Rooms from: $309* ✉ *5131 Warm Springs Rd., Glen Ellen* ⊹ *West off Arnold Dr.* ☎ *707/996–5131* ⊕ *www.olea-hotel.com* ⌁ *15 rooms* ⦿I *Free breakfast.*

Kenwood

4 miles north of Glen Ellen.

Tiny Kenwood consists of little more than a few restaurants, shops, tasting rooms, and a historic train depot, now used for private events. But hidden in this pretty landscape of meadows and woods at the north end of Sonoma Valley are several good wineries, most just off the Sonoma Highway. Varietals grown here at the foot of the Sugarloaf Mountains include Sauvignon Blanc, Chardonnay, Zinfandel, and Cabernet Sauvignon.

GETTING HERE AND AROUND

To get to Kenwood from Glen Ellen, head northeast on Arnold Drive and north on Highway 12. Sonoma Transit buses serve Kenwood from Glen Ellen and Sonoma.

◉ Sights

★ En Garde Winery

WINERY/DISTILLERY | Sommeliers, critics, and collectors extol the Pinot Noirs and Cabernet Sauvignons of Csaba Szakál, En Garde's Hungarian-born winemaker and owner. Striving to create what he describes as "aromatic, complex, lush, and juicy" wines, Szakál selects top Sonoma County vineyards for the Pinots and the Napa Valley's Diamond Mountain, Mt. Veeder, and other high-elevation sites for the Cabernets. Not afraid to heavy up the oak on the Cabernets, he nevertheless achieves elegance as well. The winemaker is equally precise about hiring staffers for his modest highway's-edge tasting room along Kenwood's brief commercial strip. Well-acquainted with his goals and methods, they provide a wealth of knowledge about wine making and California viticulture. If you're lucky, Szakál himself will be around to discuss his wines (he loves to), which also include Chardonnay, Viognier, and rosé of Pinot Noir. Visits are by reservation, with same-day appointments sometimes possible. ✉ *9077 Sonoma Hwy., Kenwood* ⊹ *At Shaw Ave.* ☎ *707/282–9216* ⊕ *www.engardewinery.com* ✉ *Tastings from $25.*

St. Francis Winery

WINERY/DISTILLERY | Nestled at the foot of Mt. Hood, St. Francis has earned national acclaim for its pairings of wines and small bites. With its red-tile roof and bell tower and views of the Mayacamas Mountains to the east, the winery's California Mission–style visitor center occupies one of Sonoma County's most scenic locations. The charm of the surroundings is matched by the mostly red wines, among them rich, earthy Zinfandels from the Dry Creek, Russian River, and Sonoma valleys. The five-course pairings might include Chardonnay with lobster bisque or Cabernet Sauvignon with wine-braised beef ribs. ✉ *100 Pythian Rd., Kenwood* ⊹ *Off Hwy. 12*

☎ 707/538–9463, 888/675–9463 ⊕ www.stfranciswinery.com ➦ Tastings from $20 ⊗ Closed Tues. and Wed.

 Restaurants

Salt & Stone

$$$ | **MODERN AMERICAN** | The menu at this upscale roadhouse with a sloping wood-beamed ceiling focuses on seafood and meat —beef, lamb, chicken, duck, and other options—with many dishes in both categories grilled. Start with the classics, perhaps a martini and oysters Rockefeller, before moving on to well-plated contemporary entrées that might include crispy-skin salmon or duck breast, a fish stew, or grilled rib-eye. **Known for:** mountain-view outdoor seating area; weekend brunch; weekday happy hour 2:30–5:30 except holidays. ⑤ Average main: $29 ✉ 9900 Sonoma Hwy., Kenwood ✛ At Kunde Winery Rd. ☎ 707/833–6326 ⊕ www.saltstonekenwood.com ⊗ No lunch Tues. and Wed.

 Hotels

⭐ **Kenwood Inn and Spa**

$$$ | **B&B/INN** | Fluffy feather beds, custom Italian furnishings, and French doors in most cases opening onto terraces or balconies lend this inn's uncommonly spacious guest rooms a romantic air—more than a few guests are celebrating honeymoons or anniversaries. **Pros:** large rooms; lavish furnishings; romantic setting. **Cons:** far from nightlife; expensive in high season; geared more to couples than families with children. ⑤ Rooms from: $381 ✉ 10400 Sonoma Hwy.,/ Hwy. 12, Kenwood ☎ 707/833–1293, 800/353–6966 ⊕ www.kenwoodinn.com ➥ 29 rooms ⦿ Free breakfast.

Petaluma

24 miles southwest of Kenwood, 39 miles north of San Francisco.

The first thing you should know about Petaluma is that this is a farm town—with more than 62,500 residents, a large one—and the residents are proud of it. Recent years have seen an uptick in the quality of Petaluma cuisine, fueled in part by the proliferation of local organic and artisanal farms and boutique wine production. With the 2018 approval of the Petaluma Gap AVA, the city even has its name on a wine appellation.

GETTING HERE AND AROUND

Petaluma lies west of Sonoma and southwest of Glen Ellen and Kenwood. From Highway 12 or Arnold Drive, take Watmaugh Road west to Highway 116 west. Sonoma Transit buses serve Petaluma. From San Francisco take U.S. 101 (or Golden Gate Transit Bus 101) north.

👁 Sights

Lagunitas Brewing Company

WINERY/DISTILLERY | These days owned by Heineken International, Lagunitas began as a craft brewery in Marin County in 1993 before moving to Petaluma in 1994. In addition to its large facility, the company operates a taproom, the Schwag Shop for gifts, and an outdoor beer garden that in good weather bustles even midday. Guides leading the brewery tour, which when offered includes a beer flight, provide an irreverent version of the company's rise to international acclaim. An engaging tale involves the state alcohol board's sting operation commemorated by Undercover Investigation Shut-down Ale, one of several small-batch brews made here. ■**TIP**➜ **The taproom closes on Monday and Tuesday, but the gift shop stays open and tours may take place.** ✉ 1280 N. McDowell Blvd., Petaluma ✛ ½ mile north of Corona Rd. ☎ 707/769–4495 ⊕ lagunitas.com/

taproom/petaluma ⌂ *Tour free* ⊙ *Taproom closed Mon. and Tues.*

★ McEvoy Ranch

WINERY/DISTILLERY | The late Nan McEvoy's retirement project after departing as board chair of the *San Francisco Chronicle,* the ranch produces organic extra virgin olive oil as well as Pinot Noir and other wines, the estate ones from the Petaluma Gap AVA. Relaxing tastings of oils or wines unfold on a pond's-edge flagstone patio with views of alternating rows of Syrah grapes and mature olive trees. Two wine tastings include a simple lunch; the Taste of the Season spread involves wine served with artisanal cheeses, charcuterie, and other items. Walkabout Ranch Tours of four guests or more take in vineyards, gardens, and a Chinese pavilion. All visits require an appointment. ⌂ *5935 Red Hill Rd., Petaluma* ⌖ *6½ miles south of downtown* ☎ *866/617–6779* ⊕ *www.mcevoyranch. com* ⌂ *Tastings from $25 (olive oil), $35 (wine); tours from $55.*

Restaurants

★ Central Market

$$ | **MODERN AMERICAN** | A participant in the Slow Food movement, Central Market serves creative, upscale Cal-Mediterranean dishes—many of whose ingredients come from the restaurant's organic farm—in a century-old building with an exposed brick wall and an open kitchen. The menu, which changes daily depending on chef Tony Najiola's inspiration and what's ripe and ready, might include smoked duck wings as a starter, a slow-roasted-beets salad, pizzas, stews, two or three pasta dishes, and wood-grilled fish and meat. **Known for:** chef's tasting menus; superior wine list; historic setting. ⑤ *Average main: $26* ⌂ *42 Petaluma Blvd. N, Petaluma* ⌖ *Near Western Ave.* ☎ *707/778–9900* ⊕ *www. centralmarketpetaluma.com* ⊙ *Closed Mon. and Tues. No lunch.*

★ Pearl Petaluma

$$ | **MEDITERRANEAN** | Regulars of this southern Petaluma "daytime café" with indoor and outdoor seating rave about its eastern Mediterranean–inflected cuisine—then immediately downplay their enthusiasm lest this unassuming gem become more popular. The menu changes often, but mainstays include *shakshuka* (a tomato-based stew with baked eggs) and a lamb burger dripping with tzatziki. **Known for:** weekend brunch; fun beverage lineup, both alcoholic and non; menu prices include gratuity. ⑤ *Average main: $20* ⌂ *500 1st St., Petaluma* ⌖ *At G St.* ☎ *707/559–5187* ⊕ *pearlpetaluma. com* ⊙ *Closed Tues. No dinner.*

Healdsburg

17 miles north of Santa Rosa, 32 miles northwest of Petaluma.

Sonoma County's ritziest town and the star of many a magazine spread or online feature, Healdsburg is located at the intersection of the Dry Creek Valley, Russian River Valley, and Alexander Valley AVAs. Several dozen wineries bear a Healdsburg address, and around downtown's plaza you'll find fashionable boutiques, spas, hip tasting rooms, and art galleries, and some of the Wine Country's best restaurants.

Especially on weekends, you'll have plenty of company as you tour the downtown area. You could spend a day just exploring the tasting rooms and shops surrounding Healdsburg Plaza, but be sure to allow time to venture into the surrounding countryside. With orderly rows of vines alternating with beautifully overgrown hills, this is the setting you dream about when planning a Wine Country vacation.

GETTING HERE AND AROUND

Healdsburg sits just off U.S. 101. Heading north, take the Central Healdsburg exit to reach Healdsburg Plaza; heading south, take the Westside Road exit and pass

21

east under the freeway. Sonoma County Transit buses serve Healdsburg from Santa Rosa.

Sights

★ Aperture Cellars

WINERY/DISTILLERY | As a youth, Jesse Katz tagged along with his photographer father, Andy Katz, to wineries worldwide, stimulating curiosity about wine that led to stints at august operations like the Napa Valley's Screaming Eagle and Bordeaux's Petrús. In 2009, still in his 20s, Katz started Aperture, a success from the get-go for his single-vineyard Cabernets and Bordeaux blends. Among the whites are Sauvignon Blanc and an old-vine Chenin Blanc that's one of California's best. Katz's wines, which benefit from rigorous farming and cellar techniques, are presented by appointment only in an ultracontemporary hospitality center that opened in 2020 about 2½ miles south of Healdsburg Plaza. One tasting explores Aperture's various wine-growing sites, the other the single vineyard wines. The center's shutterlike windows and other architectural elements evoke Andy Katz's photography career; his images of the Russian River Valley and beyond hang on the walls. ⊠ *12291 Old Redwood Hwy.* ✛ *¼ mile south of Limerick La.* ☎ *707/200–7891* ⊕ *www.aperture-cellars.com* 🍷 *Tastings from $50.*

Breathless Wines

WINERY/DISTILLERY | The mood's downright bubbly (pardon that pun) at the oasis-like garden patio of this sparkling-wine producer tucked away in an industrial park northwest of Healdsburg Plaza. Established by three sisters in memory of their mother, Breathless sources grapes from appellations in Sonoma, Napa, and Mendocino counties that find their way into sparklers and a few still wines. The small indoor tasting area, decorated flapper-era-style, was ingeniously fashioned out of shipping containers, though nearly everyone sips in the umbrella-shaded garden in fine weather. You can sample wine by the glass, flight, or bottle; all visits require an appointment, with same-day reservations sometimes possible. ■**TIP**➜ **Splurge on the Sabrage Experience to learn how to open a bottle with a saber, a tradition supposedly initiated by Napoléon's soldiers.** ⊠ *499 Moore La.* ✛ *Off North St.* ☎ *707/395–7300* ⊕ *www.breathless-wines.com* 🍷 *Tastings from $13 per glass, $20 per flight* ⊗ *Closed Tues. and Wed. (sometimes changes).*

Dry Creek Vineyard

WINERY/DISTILLERY | Loire-style Sauvignon Blanc marketed as Fumé Blanc brought instant success to the Dry Creek Valley's first new winery since Prohibition, but this stalwart established in 1972 also does well with Zinfandel and Cabernet Sauvignon and other Bordeaux-style reds. Founder David Stare's other contributions include leading the drive to develop the Dry Creek Valley appellation and coining the term "old-vine Zinfandel." The winery's history and wine-making evolution are among the topics addressed at tastings—outdoors under the shade of a magnolia and several redwood trees or in the nautical-themed tasting room. ⊠ *3770 Lambert Bridge Rd.* ✛ *Off Dry Creek Rd.* ☎ *707/433–1000, 800/864–9463* ⊕ *www.drycreekvineyard.com* 🍷 *Tastings from $25.*

Gary Farrell Vineyards & Winery

WINERY/DISTILLERY | Pass through an impressive metal gate and wind your way up a steep hill to reach this winery with knockout Russian River Valley views from the elegant two-tiered tasting room and terrace outside. In 2017 *Wine Enthusiast Magazine* named a Gary Farrell Chardonnay wine of the year, one among many accolades for this winery known for sophisticated single-vineyard Chardonnays and Pinot Noirs. Farrell departed in the early 2000s, but current winemaker Theresa Heredia acknowledges that her philosophy has much in common with his. For the Pinots, this means picking on the early side to preserve acidity and focusing on "expressing the site." The Elevation Tasting of single-vineyard wines provides a good introduction. All visits are by appointment; same-day reservations are possible during the week, but call ahead. ✉ *10701 Westside Rd.* ☎ *707/473–2909* ⊕ *www.garyfarrellwinery.com* 🍷 *Tastings from $35.*

★ Jordan Vineyard and Winery

WINERY/DISTILLERY | Founders Tom and Sally Jordan erected the French-style château here in part to emphasize their goal of producing Sonoma County Chardonnays and Cabernet Sauvignons—one of each annually—to rival those from the Napa Valley and France itself. Their son John, now at the helm, has instituted numerous improvements, among them the replanting of many vines and a shift to all-French barrels for aging. Most tastings revolve around executive chef Todd Knoll's small bites, whose ingredients come mainly from Jordan's organic garden. The Library Tasting of current releases concludes with an older Cabernet for comparison. An enchanting themed lunch and wine pairing, Paris on the Terrace, unfolds on the château's terrace from spring to early fall, when the winery often hosts a three-hour Estate Tour & Tasting. The latter's pièce de résistance is the stop at a 360-degree vista point overlooking the 1,200-acre property's vines, olive trees, and countryside. Visits are strictly by appointment. ✉ *1474 Alexander Valley Rd.* ✛ *1½ miles east of Healdsburg Ave.* ☎ *800/654–1213, 707/431–5250* ⊕ *www.jordanwinery.com* 🍷 *Tastings from $45* ⊙ *Closed Tues. and Wed. Dec.–Mar.*

MacRostie Estate House

WINERY/DISTILLERY | A driveway off Westside Road curls through undulating vineyard hills to the steel, wood, and heavy-on-the-glass tasting space of this longtime Chardonnay and Pinot Noir producer. Moments after you've arrived and a host has offered a glass of wine, you'll already feel transported to a genteel, rustic world. Hospitality is clearly a priority, but so, too, is seeking out top-tier grape sources—30 for the Chardonnays, 15 for the Pinots—among them Dutton Ranch, Sangiacomo, and owner Steve MacRostie's Wildcat. With fruit this renowned, current winemaker Heidi Bridenhagen downplays the oak and other tricks of her trade, letting the vineyard settings, grape clones, and vintage do the talking. Tastings, inside or on balcony terraces with views across the Russian River Valley, are all seated and by appointment. ✉ *4605 Westside Rd.* ✛ *Near Frost Rd.* ☎ *707/473–9303* ⊕ *macrostiewinery.com* 🍷 *Tastings from $35.*

★ Ridge Vineyards

WINERY/DISTILLERY | Ridge stands tall among local wineries, and not merely because its 1971 Monte Bello Cabernet Sauvignon rated second-highest among California reds competing with French ones at the famous Judgment of Paris blind tasting of 1976. The winery built its reputation on Cabernets, Zinfandels, and Chardonnays of unusual depth and complexity, but you'll also find blends of Rhône varietals. Ridge makes wines using grapes from several California locales—including the Dry Creek Valley, Sonoma Valley, Napa Valley, and Paso Robles—but the focus is on single-vineyard estate wines such as the Lytton Springs Zinfandel from fruit grown near the tasting room. In good weather you can sit outside, taking in views of rolling vineyard hills while you sip. ✉ *650 Lytton Springs Rd.* ✛ *Off U.S. 101* ☎ *408/867–3233* ⊕ *www.ridgewine.com/visit/lytton-springs* 🍷 *Tastings from $20.*

★ Silver Oak

WINERY/DISTILLERY | The views and architecture are as impressive as the wines at the Sonoma County outpost of the same-named Napa Valley winery. In 2018, six years after purchasing a 113-acre parcel with 73 acres planted to grapes, Silver Oak debuted its ultramodern, environmentally sensitive winery and glass-walled tasting pavilion. As in Napa, the Healdsburg facility produces just one wine each year: a well-balanced Alexander Valley Cabernet Sauvignon aged in American rather than French oak barrels. One tasting includes the current Alexander Valley and Napa Valley Cabernets plus an older vintage. Two or more wines of sister operation Twomey Cellars, which produces Sauvignon Blanc, Pinot Noir, and Merlot, begin a second offering that concludes with the current Cabernets. Hosts at a third pour current and older Cabernets from either Napa or Sonoma. Make a reservation for all visits. ⊠ 7300 Hwy. 128 ✛ Near Chaffee Rd. ☎ 707/942–7082 ⊕ www.silveroak.com ⌖ Tastings from $40.

★ Tongue Dancer Wines

WINERY/DISTILLERY | Down a country lane less than 2 miles south of Healdsburg Plaza, James MacPhail's modest production facility seems well away from the upscale fray. MacPhail makes wines for The Calling, Sangiacomo, and other labels, but Tongue Dancer's Chardonnays and Pinot Noirs are his handcrafted labors of love. Made from small lots of grapes from choice vineyard sites, the wines impress, sometimes stun, with their grace, complexity, and balance. The flagship Sonoma Coast Pinot Noir, a blend from two or more vineyards, is poured at most tastings, in a mezzanine space above oak-aging barrels or on an outdoor patio. Either the winemaker or his co-owner and wife, Kerry Forbes-MacPhail—she's credited on bottles as the "Knowledgeable One" (and she is)—will host you. As James describes it, they aim to "create an approachable experience for guests we hope will leave as friends." Appointment-only visits are best made a day or more ahead. ⊠ 851 Magnolia Dr. ✛ Off Westside Rd. ☎ 707/433–4780 ⊕ tonguedancerwines. com ⌖ Tastings from $25 ☯ Closed Sun.

Restaurants

★ Barndiva

$$$$ | AMERICAN | Music plays quietly in the background while servers carry inventive seasonal cocktails at this restaurant that abandons the homey vibe of many Wine Country spots in favor of a more urban feel. Make a light meal out of yellowtail tuna crudo or homemade linguine, or settle in for the evening with pan-seared day scallops or a grass-fed strip loin. **Known for:** good cocktails; stylish cuisine; open-air patio. ⑤ Average main: $38 ⊠ 231 Center St. ✛ Near Matheson St. ☎ 707/431–0100 ⊕ www.barndiva. com ☯ Closed Mon. and Tues. No lunch weekdays.

Bravas Bar de Tapas

$$$ | SPANISH | Spanish-style tapas and an outdoor patio in perpetual party mode make this restaurant, headquartered in a restored 1920s bungalow, a popular downtown perch. Contemporary Spanish mosaics set a perky tone inside, but unless something's amiss with the weather, nearly everyone heads out back for flavorful croquettes, paella, jamón, pan tomate (tomato toast), grilled octopus, skirt steak, and crispy fried chicken. **Known for:** casual small plates; specialty cocktails, sangrias, and beer; sherries from dry to sweet. ⑤ Average main: $28 ⊠ 420 Center St. ✛ Near North St. ☎ 707/433–7700 ⊕ www.barbravas.com ☯ Closed Mon. and Tues.

Campo Fina

$$ | ITALIAN | Chef Ari Rosen serves up contemporary-rustic Italian cuisine at this converted storefront that once housed a bar notorious for boozin' and brawlin'. Sandblasted red brick, satin-smooth walnut tables, and old-school lighting fixtures (and a large back patio) strike a retro note for a menu built around pizzas and gems such as Rosen's variation on his grandmother's tomato-braised chicken with creamy-soft polenta. **Known for:** outdoor patio's boccie court out of an Italian movie set; lunch sandwiches; wines from California and Italy. $ *Average main: $23* ⊠ *330 Healdsburg Ave.* ⊹ *Near North St.* ☎ *707/395–4640* ⊕ *www.campofina.com.*

Costeaux French Bakery

$ | FRENCH | Breakfast, served all day at this bright-yellow French-style bakery and café, includes the signature omelet (sun-dried tomatoes, bacon, spinach, and Brie) and French toast made from thick slabs of cinnamon-walnut bread. French onion soup and cranberry-turkey, French dip, and (on the cinnamon-walnut bread) Monte Cristo sandwiches are among the lunch favorites. **Known for:** breads, croissants, and fancy pastries; quiche and omelets; front patio. $ *Average main: $15* ⊠ *417 Healdsburg Ave.* ⊹ *At North St.* ☎ *707/433–1913* ⊕ *www.costeaux.com* ⊗ *Closed Mon. and Tues. (check to be sure). No dinner.*

★ SingleThread Farms Restaurant

$$$$ | ECLECTIC | The seasonally oriented, multicourse Japanese dinners known as *kaiseki* inspired the prix-fixe vegetarian, meat, and seafood menu at the spare, elegant restaurant—redwood walls, walnut tables, mesquite-tile floors, muted-gray yarn-thread panels—of internationally renowned culinary artists Katina and Kyle Connaughton (she farms, he cooks). As Katina describes the endeavor, the microseasons of their nearby farm (ask about visiting it) plus SingleThread's rooftop garden of fruit trees and greens dictate Kyle's rarefied fare, prepared in a theatrically lit open kitchen. **Known for:** culinary precision; instinctive service; impeccable wine pairings. $ *Average main: $295* ⊠ *131 North St.* ⊹ *At Center St.* ☎ *707/723–4646* ⊕ *www.singlethreadfarms.com* ⊗ *No lunch weekdays.*

★ Valette

$$$ | MODERN AMERICAN | Northern Sonoma native Dustin Valette opened this homage to the area's artisanal agricultural bounty with his brother, who runs the high-ceilinged dining room, where the playful contemporary lighting tempers the austerity of the exposed concrete walls and butcher-block-thick wooden tables. Charcuterie is an emphasis, but also consider the signature day-boat scallops *en croûte* (in a pastry crust) or dishes that might include Szechuan-crusted duck breast or a variation on Niçoise salad with albacore poached in olive oil. **Known for:** "Trust me" (the chef) tasting menu; mostly Northern California and French wines; chef's nearby The Matheson for wine tasting, pairings, and rooftop dining. $ *Average main: $36* ⊠ *344 Center St.* ⊹ *At North St.* ☎ *707/473–0946* ⊕ *www.valettehealdsburg.com* ⊗ *No lunch.*

Hotels

★ Harmon Guest House

$$$ | HOTEL | A boutique sibling of the h2hotel two doors away, this downtown delight debuted in late 2018 having already earned LEED Gold status for its eco-friendly construction and operating practices. **Pros:** rooftop bar's cocktails, food menu, and views; connecting rooms and suites; similarly designed sister property h2hotel two doors south. **Cons:** minor room-to-room noise bleed-through; room gadgetry may flummox some guests; minimum-stay requirements some weekends. $ *Rooms from: $389* ⊠ *227 Healdsburg Ave.* ☎ *707/922–5262* ⊕ *harmonguesthouse.com* ⊿ *39 rooms* ⊙ *Free breakfast.*

Hotel Trio Healdsburg

$$ | HOTEL | Named for the three major wine appellations—the Russian River, Dry Creek, and Alexander valleys—whose confluence it's near, this Residence Inn by Marriott 1¼ miles north of Healdsburg Plaza caters to families and extended-stay business travelers with spacious rooms equipped with full kitchens. **Pros:** cute robot room service; full kitchens; rooms sleep up to four or six. **Cons:** 30-minute walk to downtown; slightly corporate feel; pricey in high

season. $\boxed{S}$ *Rooms from: $242* ⊠ *110 Dry Creek Rd.* ☎ *707/433–4000* ⊕ *www. hoteltrio.com* ⇆ *122 rooms* ⦿ *Free breakfast.*

★ **Montage Healdsburg**

$$$$ | RESORT | Its bungalowlike guest rooms deftly layered into oak- and Cabernet-studded hills a few miles north of Healdsburg Plaza, this architectural sensation that opened fully in 2021 significantly upped Sonoma County's ultraluxury game. **Pros:** vineyard views from spa, restaurant, and swimming pool; outdoor living spaces with daybeds and fire pits; recreational options on-property or nearby. **Cons:** expensive year-round; hefty resort fee; car trip required for off-property visits. $\boxed{S}$ *Rooms from: $845* ⊠ *100 Montage Way* ☎ *707/979–9000* ⊕ *www. montagehotels.com/healdsburg* ⇆ *130 bungalows* ⦿ *No meals.*

★ **River Belle Inn**

$$ | B&B/INN | An 1875 Victorian with a storied past and a glorious colonnaded wraparound porch anchors this boutique property along the Russian River. **Pros:** riverfront location near a dozen-plus tasting rooms; cooked-to-order full breakfasts; attention to detail. **Cons:** about a mile from Healdsburg Plaza; minimum-stay requirement on weekends; lacks on-site pool, fitness center, and other amenities. $\boxed{S}$ *Rooms from: $280* ⊠ *68 Front St.* ☎ *707/955–5724* ⊕ *www. riverbelleinn.com* ⇆ *12 rooms* ⦿ *Free breakfast.*

🛍 Shopping

ART GALLERIES
★ **Gallery Lulo**

ART GALLERIES | A collaboration between a local artist and jewelry maker and a Danish-born curator, this gallery presents changing exhibits of jewelry, sculpture, and objets d'art. ⊠ *303 Center St.* ⊹ *At Plaza St.* ☎ *707/433–7533* ⊕ *www. gallerylulo.com.*

FOOD AND WINE
Dry Creek General Store

FOOD/CANDY | For breakfasts, sandwiches, bread, cheeses, and picnic supplies, stop by the general store, established in 1881 and still a popular spot for locals to hang out on the porch or in the bar. Beer and wine are also for sale, along with artisanal sodas, ciders, and juices. ⊠ *3495 Dry Creek Rd.* ⊹ *At Lambert Bridge Rd.* ☎ *707/433–4171* ⊕ *www.drycreekgeneralstore1881.com.*

🏃 Activities

SPAS
★ **A Simple Touch Spa**

FITNESS/HEALTH CLUBS | Skilled in Swedish, deep-tissue, sports, and other massage modalities, this soothing but unpretentious day spa's therapists routinely receive post-session raves. The most popular treatment involves heated basalt stones applied to the client's body, followed by a massage of choice. Foot reflexology, reiki, and facials are among the other specialties. ■**TIP→ Couples can enjoy any of the massages performed side-by-side by two therapists.** ⊠ *239 Center St., Suite C* ⊹ *Near Matheson St.* ☎ *707/433–6856* ⊕ *asimpletouchspa.com* ⧉ *Treatments from $55.*

Geyserville

8 miles north of Healdsburg.

Several high-profile Alexander Valley AVA wineries, including the splashy Francis Ford Coppola Winery, can be found in the town of Geyserville, a small part of which stretches west of U.S. 101 into northern Dry Creek. Not long ago this was a dusty farm town, and downtown Geyserville retains its rural character, but the restaurants, shops, and tasting rooms along the short main drag hint at Geyserville's growing sophistication.

GETTING HERE AND AROUND

From Healdsburg, the quickest route to downtown Geyserville is north on U.S. 101 to the Highway 128/Geyserville exit. Turn right at the stop sign onto Geyserville Avenue and follow the road north to the small downtown. For a more scenic drive, head north from Healdsburg Plaza along Healdsburg Avenue. About 3 miles north, jog west (left) for a few hundred feet onto Lytton Springs Road, then turn north (right) onto Geyserville Avenue. In town the avenue merges with Highway 128. Sonoma County Transit buses serve Geyserville from downtown Healdsburg.

 Sights

Francis Ford Coppola Winery

WINERY/DISTILLERY | The fun at what the film director has called his "wine wonderland" is all in the excess. You may find it hard to resist having your photo snapped standing next to Don Corleone's desk from *The Godfather* or beside other memorabilia from Coppola films (including some directed by his daughter, Sofia). A bandstand reminiscent of one in *The Godfather Part II* is the centerpiece of a large pool area where you can rent a changing room, complete with shower, and spend the afternoon lounging poolside, perhaps ordering food from the adjacent café. A more elaborate restaurant, Rustic, overlooks the vineyards. As for the wines, the excess continues in the cellar, where Coppola's team produces several dozen varietal bottlings and blends. ⊠ *300 Via Archimedes* ⊕ *Off U.S. 101* ☎ *707/857–1400* ⊕ *www.franciscopolawinery.com* 🍷 *Tastings from $35.*

★ Locals Tasting Room

WINERY/DISTILLERY | If you're serious about wine, Carolyn Lewis's tasting room is worth the trek 8 miles north of Healdsburg Plaza to downtown Geyserville. Connoisseurs who appreciate Lewis's ability to spot up-and-comers head here regularly to sample the output of a dozen or so small wineries, most without tasting rooms of their own. There's no fee for tasting—extraordinary for wines of this quality—and the extremely knowledgeable staff are happy to pour you a flight of several wines so you can compare, say, different Cabernet Sauvignons. ⊠ *21023A Geyserville Ave.* ⊕ *At Hwy. 128* ☎ *707/857–4900* ⊕ *www.localstastingroom.com* 🍷 *Tasting free.*

★ Robert Young Estate Winery

WINERY/DISTILLERY | Panoramic Alexander Valley views unfold at Scion House, the stylish yet informal knoll-top tasting space of this longtime Geyserville grower. The first Youngs began farming this land in the mid-1800s, raising cattle and growing wheat, prunes, and other crops. In the 1960s the late Robert Young, of the third generation, began cultivating grapes, eventually planting two Chardonnay clones now named for him. Grapes from them go into the Area 27 Chardonnay, among the best whites. The reds—small-lot Cabernet Sauvignons plus individual bottlings of Cabernet Franc, Malbec, Merlot, and Petit Verdot—shine even brighter. Tastings at Scion House, named for the fourth generation, whose members built on Robert Young's legacy and established the winery, are by appointment. Call ahead for same-day reservations. ■TIP→ **Cab fanatics should consider the Ultimate Cabernet Lovers Experience of top-tier estate wines.** ⊠ *5120 Red Winery Rd.* ⊕ *Off Hwy. 128* ☎ *707/431–4811* ⊕ *www.ryew.com* 🍷 *Tastings from $30* ⊙ *Closed Tues.*

★ Zialena

WINERY/DISTILLERY | Sister-and-brother team Lisa and Mark Mazzoni (she runs the business, he makes the wines) debuted their small winery's first vintage in 2014, but their Italian American family's wine-making heritage stretches back more than a century. Named for the siblings' great aunt Lena, known for her hospitality, Zialena specializes in estate-grown Zinfandel and Cabernet Sauvignon, some of whose lush mouthfeel derives from techniques Mark absorbed while working for the international consultant Philippe Melka. The Zin and Cab grapes, along with those for the Chardonnay and seductive rosé of Sangiovese, come from the 120-acre Mazzoni Vineyard, from which larger labels like Jordan also source fruit. Tastings are by appointment only, with same-day visits often possible. ✉ 21112 River Rd. ✛ Off Hwy. 128 ☎ 707/955-5992 ⊕ www.zialena.com ✑ Tastings from $15.

🍴 Restaurants

Diavola Pizzeria & Salumeria
$$ | ITALIAN | A dining area with hardwood floors, a pressed-tin ceiling, and exposed-brick walls provides a fitting setting for the rustic cuisine at this Geyserville mainstay. Chef Dino Bugica studied with artisanal cooks in Italy before opening this restaurant specializing in wood-fired pizzas and house-cured meats, with a few salads and meaty main courses rounding out the menu. **Known for:** talented chef; smoked pork belly, pancetta, and spicy Calabrese sausage; casual setting. ⑤ Average main: $23 ✉ 21021 Geyserville Ave. ✛ At Hwy. 128 ☎ 707/814-0111 ⊕ www.diavolapizzeria.com.

🛏 Hotels

Geyserville Inn
$$ | HOTEL | Clever travelers give the Healdsburg hubbub and prices the heave-ho but still have easy access to outstanding Dry Creek and Alexander Valley wineries from this modest, motel-like inn with a boutique-hotel sensibility. **Pros:** outdoor pool; vineyard-view decks from second-floor rooms in back; picnic area. **Cons:** rooms facing pool or highway can be noisy; weekend two-night minimum requirement; not for party types. ⑤ Rooms from: $209 ✉ 21714 Geyserville Ave. ☎ 707/857-4343, 877/857-4343 ⊕ www.geyservilleinn.com ⇆ 41 rooms ⏐◎⏐ No meals.

Forestville

13 miles southwest of Healdsburg.

To experience the Russian River Valley AVA's climate and rusticity, follow the river's westward course to the town of Forestville, home to a highly regarded restaurant and inn and a few wineries producing Pinot Noir from the Russian River Valley and well beyond.

GETTING HERE AND AROUND
To reach Forestville from U.S. 101, drive west from the River Road exit north of Santa Rosa. From Healdsburg, follow Westside Road west to River Road and then continue west. Sonoma County Transit buses serve Forestville.

👁 Sights

★ Hartford Family Winery
WINERY/DISTILLERY | Pinot Noir lovers appreciate the subtle differences in the wines Hartford's team crafts from grapes grown in several Sonoma County AVAs, along with fruit from nearby Marin and Mendocino counties and Oregon. The winery also produces highly rated Chardonnays and old-vine Zinfandels. If the weather's good, enjoy a flight on the patio outside the opulent main winery building. At private library tastings, guests sip current and older vintages. All visits are by appointment; call ahead on the same day. ✉ 8075 Martinelli Rd. ✛ Off Hwy. 116 or River Rd. ☎ 707/887-8030 ⊕ www.hartfordwines.com ✑ Tastings from $25 ⏰ Closed Tues. and Wed.

Joseph Jewell Wines
WINERY/DISTILLERY | Pinot Noirs from the Russian River Valley and Humboldt County to the north are the strong suit of this winery sourcing from prestigious vineyards like Bucher and Hallberg Ranch. Owner-winemaker Adrian Manspeaker, a Humboldt native, spearheaded the foray into Pinot Noir grown in the coastal redwood country. His playfully rustic

storefront tasting room in downtown Forestville (visits by appointment) provides the opportunity to experience what's unique about the varietal's next Northern California frontier. There are plenty of whites here, too—Sauvignon Blanc, two Chardonnays, Pinot Gris, and Vermentino—plus rosé of Pinot, and Zinfandel from 1970s vines. ■TIP→ **In 2021 the winery expects to begin offering outdoor tastings and vineyard tours at Raymond Burr Vineyards in Healdsburg.** ⊠ 6542 Front St. ✛ Near 1st St. ☎ 707/820–1621 ⊕ www. josephjewell.com ⊠ Tastings from $25 ⊗ Closed Mon.–Wed.

Restaurants

Backyard

$$$ | MODERN AMERICAN | The couple behind this casually rustic modern American restaurant, who met while working at Thomas Keller restaurants in Yountville, regard Sonoma County's farms and gardens as their "backyard." Dinner entrées, which change seasonally, usually include buttermilk fried chicken with buttermilk biscuits, coleslaw, and honey butter. **Known for:** husband-and-wife chef-owners; ingredients from high-quality local purveyors; poplar-shaded outdoor front patio. ⓢ Average main: $28 ⊠ 6566 Front St./Hwy. 116 ✛ At 1st St. ☎ 707/820–8445 ⊕ backyardforestville.com ⊗ Closed Tues.–Thurs.

🛏 Hotels

★ The Farmhouse Inn

$$$$ | B&B/INN | With a farmhouse-meets-modern-loft aesthetic, this low-key but upscale getaway with a pale-yellow exterior contains spacious rooms filled with king-size four-poster beds, whirlpool tubs, and hillside-view terraces. **Pros:** fantastic restaurant; luxury bath products; full-service spa. **Cons:** mild road noise audible in rooms closest to the street; two-night minimum on weekends; pricey, especially during high season. ⓢ Rooms from: $518 ⊠ 7871 River Rd. ☎ 707/887–3300, 800/464–6642 ⊕ www.farmhouseinn. com ⌂ 25 rooms ⎮⊙⎮ Free breakfast.

Activities

Burke's Canoe Trips

CANOEING/ROWING/SKULLING | You'll get a real feel for the Russian River's flora and fauna on a leisurely 10-mile paddle downstream from Burke's to Guerneville. A shuttle bus returns you to your car at the end of the journey, which is best taken from late May through mid-October and, in summer, on a weekday—summer weekends can be crowded and raucous. ⊠ 8600 River Rd. ✛ At Mirabel Rd. ☎ 707/887–1222 ⊕ www.burkescanoetrips.com ⊠ $75 per canoe.

Guerneville

7 miles northwest of Forestville, 15 miles southwest of Healdsburg.

Guerneville's tourist demographic has evolved over the years—Bay Area families in the 1950s, lesbians and gays starting in the 1970s, and these days a mix of both groups, plus techies and outdoorsy types—with coast redwoods and the Russian River always central to the town's appeal. The area's most famous winery is Korbel Champagne Cellars, established nearly a century and a half ago. Even older are the stands of trees that except on the coldest winter days make Armstrong Redwoods State Natural Reserve such a perfect respite from wine tasting.

GETTING HERE AND AROUND

To get to Guerneville from Healdsburg, follow Westside Road south to River Road and turn west. From Forestville, head west on Highway 116; alternatively, you can head north on Mirabel Road to River Road and then head west. Sonoma County Transit buses serve Guerneville.

Sights

★ Armstrong Redwoods State Natural Reserve

NATIONAL/STATE PARK | **FAMILY** | Here's your best opportunity in the western Wine Country to wander amid *Sequoia sempervirens,* also known as coast redwood trees. The oldest example in this 805-acre state park, the Colonel Armstrong Tree, is thought to be more than 1,400 years old. A half mile from the parking lot, the tree is easily accessible, and you can hike a long way into the forest before things get too hilly. ■**TIP→ During hot summer days, Armstrong Redwoods's tall trees help the park keep its cool.** ⊠ *17000 Armstrong Woods Rd.* ⊹ *Off River Rd.* ☎ *707/869–2958 for visitor center, 707/869–2015 for park headquarters* ⊕ *www.parks.ca.gov* ⊠ *$8 per vehicle, free to pedestrians and bicyclists.*

⟊ Restaurants

★ boon eat+drink

$$ | **MODERN AMERICAN** | A casual storefront restaurant on Guerneville's main drag, boon eat+drink has a menu built around salads, smallish shareable plates, and entrées that might include a vegan bowl, chili-braised pork shoulder, and local cod with beluga lentils. Like many of chef-owner Crista Luedtke's dishes, the signature polenta lasagna—creamy ricotta salata cheese and polenta served on greens sautéed in garlic, all of it floating upon a spicy marinara sauce—deviates significantly from the lasagna norm but succeeds on its own merits. **Known for:** adventurous culinary sensibility; Sonoma County wine selection; local organic ingredients. ⑤ *Average main: $23* ⊠ *16248 Main St.* ⊹ *At Church St.* ☎ *707/869–0780* ⊕ *eatatboon.com* ⊘ *Closed Mon. and Tues.*

🛏 Hotels

boon hotel+spa

$$ | **HOTEL** | Redwoods, Douglas firs, and palms supply shade and seclusion at this lushly landscaped resort ¾ mile north of downtown Guerneville. **Pros:** filling breakfasts; pool area and on-site spa; complimentary bikes. **Cons:** lacks amenities of larger properties; pool rooms too close to the action for some guests; can be pricey in high season. ⑤ *Rooms from: $213* ⊠ *14711 Armstrong Woods Rd.* ☎ *707/869–2721* ⊕ *boonhotels.com* ⇌ *15 rooms* ⎡◎⎤ *Free breakfast.*

Sebastopol

14 miles southeast of Guerneville.

A stroll through downtown in Sebastopol—formerly known more for Gravenstein apples than for grapes but these days a burgeoning wine hub—reveals glimpses of the past and, perhaps, the future, too. Many hippies settled here in the '60s and '70s and, as the old Crosby, Stills, Nash & Young song goes, they taught their children well: the town remains steadfastly countercultural.

GETTING HERE AND AROUND

From Guerneville, take Highway 116 south. From Santa Rosa, head west on Highway 12. Sonoma County Transit buses serve Sebastopol.

Sights

The Barlow

MARKET | A multibuilding complex on a former apple-cannery site, The Barlow celebrates Sonoma County's "maker" culture with tenants who produce or sell wine, beer, spirits, crafts, clothing, art, and artisanal food and herbs. The anchor wine tenant, Kosta Browne, receives only club members and allocation-list guests, but other tasting rooms are open to the public, and Region wine bar promotes small Sonoma County producers. Crooked Goat Brewing makes and sells ales, Golden State Cider pours apple-driven beverages, and you can have a nip of vodka, gin, sloe gin, or wheat and rye whiskey at Spirit Works Distillery. Over at Fern Bar, the zero-proof (as in nonalcoholic) cocktails entice as much as the traditional ones. The bar serves food, as do Sushi Koshō, Blue Ridge Kitchen (Southern-influenced comfort fare), and a few other spots. ⊠ 6770 McKinley St. ✛ At Morris St., off Hwy. 12 ☎ 707/824–5600 ⊕ www.thebarlow.net ⊠ Complex free; fees for tasting.

★ Dutton-Goldfield Winery

WINERY/DISTILLERY | An avid cyclist whose previous credits include developing the wine-making program at Hartford Court, Dan Goldfield teamed up with fifth-generation farmer Steve Dutton to establish this small operation devoted to cool-climate wines. Goldfield modestly strives to take Dutton's meticulously farmed fruit and "make the winemaker unnoticeable," but what impresses the most about these wines, which include Chardonnay, Gewürztraminer, Riesling, Pinot Noir, and Zinfandel, is their sheer artistry. Among the ones to seek out are the Angel Camp Pinot Noir, from Anderson Valley (Mendocino County) grapes, and the Morelli Lane Zinfandel, from fruit grown on the remaining 1.8 acres of an 1880s vineyard Goldfield helped revive. One tasting focuses on current releases, another on single-vineyard Pinot Noirs. ⊠ 3100 Gravenstein Hwy. N/Hwy. 116 ✛ At Graton Rd. ☎ 707/827–3600 ⊕ www.duttongoldfield.com ⊠ Tastings from $30.

★ Iron Horse Vineyards

WINERY/DISTILLERY | A meandering one-lane road leads to this winery known for its sparkling wines and estate Chardonnays and Pinot Noirs. The sparklers have made history: Ronald Reagan served them at his summit meetings with Mikhail Gorbachev; George H. W. Bush took some along to Moscow for treaty talks; and Barack Obama included them at official state dinners. Despite Iron Horse's brushes with fame, a casual rusticity prevails at its outdoor tasting area (large heaters keep things comfortable on chilly days), which gazes out on acres of rolling, vine-covered hills. Tastings are by appointment only. ⊠ 9786 Ross Station Rd. ✛ Off Hwy. 116 ☎ 707/887–1507 ⊕ www.ironhorsevineyards.com ⊠ Tasting $30.

 Restaurants

★ Handline Coastal California

$ | MODERN AMERICAN | FAMILY | Sebastopol's former Foster's Freeze location, now a 21st-century fast-food palace, won design awards for its rusted-steel frame and translucent panel-like windows. The menu, a paean to coastal California cuisine, includes oysters raw and grilled, fish tacos, ceviche, tostadas, three burgers (beef, vegetarian, and fish), and, honoring the location's previous incarnation, chocolate and vanilla soft-serve ice cream. **Known for:** upscale comfort food; outdoor patio; sustainable seafood and other ingredients. ⑤ Average main: $14 ⊠ 935 Gravenstein Hwy. S ✛ Near Hutchins Ave. ☎ 707/827–3744 ⊕ www.handline.com.

Ramen Gaijin

$$ | JAPANESE | Inside a tall-ceilinged, brick-walled, vaguely industrial-looking space with reclaimed wood from a coastal building backing the bar, the chefs at Ramen Gaijin turn out richly flavored ramen bowls brimming with crispy pork belly, woodear mushrooms, seaweed, and other well-proportioned ingredients. *Izakaya* (Japanese pub grub) dishes like *donburi* (meat and vegetables over rice) are another specialty, like the ramen made from mostly local proteins and produce. **Known for:** artisanal cocktails, beer, wine, and cider; gluten-free, vegetarian dishes; karage (fried chicken) and other small plates. ⑤ Average main: $18 ⊠ 6948 Sebastopol Ave. ✛ Near Main St.

☎ 707/827–3609 ⊕ www.ramengaijin. com ⊗ Closed Sun. and Mon. No lunch.

Santa Rosa

6 miles east of Sebastopol, 55 miles north of San Francisco.

Urban Santa Rosa isn't as popular with tourists as many Wine Country destinations—not surprising, as there are more office parks than wineries within its limits. Still, this hardworking town has a couple of interesting cultural offerings and a few noteworthy restaurants and vineyards. The city's chain motels and hotels can be handy if everything else is booked, especially since Santa Rosa is roughly equidistant from Sonoma, Healdsburg, and the western Russian River Valley, three of Sonoma County's most popular wine-tasting destinations.

GETTING HERE AND AROUND

From Sebastopol, drive east on Highway 12. From San Francisco, cross the Golden Gate Bridge and continue north on U.S. 101. Santa Rosa's hotels, restaurants, and wineries are spread over a wide area; factor in extra time when driving around the city, especially during rush hours. From San Francisco or Marin County, take Golden Gate Transit Bus 101. Sonoma County Transit buses serve Santa Rosa and the surrounding area.

◉ Sights

Balletto Vineyards

WINERY/DISTILLERY | A few decades ago Balletto was known more for quality produce than grapes, but the now millennium saw vineyards emerge as the core business. About 90% of the fruit from the family's 650-plus acres goes to other wineries, with the remainder destined for Balletto's estate wines. The house style is light on the oak, high in acidity, and low in alcohol content, a combination that yields exceptionally food-friendly wines.

Sipping a Pinot Gris, rosé of Pinot Noir, or brut rosé sparkler on the outdoor patio can feel transcendent on a warm day, though the Chardonnays and Pinot Noirs, starting with the very reasonably priced Teresa's Unoaked Chard and flagship Estate Pinot, steal the show. ⊠ 5700 Occidental Rd. ✚ 2½ miles west of Hwy. 12 ☎ 707/568–2455 ⊕ www.ballettovineyards.com ⊡ Tastings from $15.

★ Belden Barns

WINERY/DISTILLERY | Experiencing the enthusiasm this winery's owners radiate supplies half the pleasure of a visit to Lauren and Nate Belden's Sonoma Mountain vineyard, where at elevation 1,000 feet they grow fruit for their all-estate lineup. Grüner Veltliner, a European white grape, isn't widely planted in California, but the crisp yet softly rounded wine they produce from it makes a case for an increase. Critics also hail the Grenache, Pinot Noir, Syrah, and a nectarlike late-harvest Viognier, but you're apt to like anything poured. Tastings take place in a high-ceilinged former milking barn whose broad doorway frames a view of grape vines undulating toward a hilltop. The Beldens tailor visits to guests' interests but will nearly always whisk you into the vineyard, past a 2-acre organic garden, and over to a wishing tree whose results Lauren swears by. ■TIP→ **The tasting fee here is a two-bottle purchase per adult.** ⊠ 5561 Sonoma Mountain Rd. ✚ 10 miles south of downtown off Bennett Valley Rd.; 5½ miles west of Glen Ellen off Warm Springs Rd. ☎ 415/577–8552 ⊕ www.beldenbarns.com ⊡ Tastings from $50 (for two bottles).

★ Martinelli Winery

WINERY/DISTILLERY | In a century-old hop barn with the telltale triple towers, Martinelli has the feel of a traditional country store, but sophisticated wines are made here. The winery's reputation rests on its complex Pinot Noirs, Syrahs, and Zinfandels, including the Jackass Hill Vineyard Zin, made with grapes from vines planted mostly in the 1880s. Noted winemaker Helen Turley set the Martinelli style—fruit-forward, easy on the oak, reined-in tannins—in the 1990s, and the current team continues this approach. Tastings held (weather permitting) on a vineyard's-edge terrace survey the current releases. All visits are by appointment, best made online. ■TIP➔ **Call the winery directly about library or collector flights.** ⊠ *3360 River Rd., Windsor* ✢ *East of Olivet Rd.* ☎ *707/525–0570, 800/346–1627* ⊕ *www.martinelliwinery. com* ⊠ *Tastings from $25* ⊙ *Closed days may vary; check with winery.*

Safari West

NATURE PRESERVE | FAMILY | An unexpected bit of wilderness in the Wine Country, this preserve with African wildlife covers 400 acres. Begin your visit with a stroll around enclosures housing lemurs, cheetahs, giraffes, and rare birds like the brightly colored scarlet ibis. Next, climb with your guide onto open-air vehicles that spend about two hours combing the expansive property, where more than 80 species—including gazelles, cape buffalo, antelope, wildebeests, and zebras—inhabit the hillsides. ■TIP➔ **If you'd like to extend your stay, lodging in swank Botswana-made tent cabins is available.** ⊠ *3115 Porter Creek Rd.* ✢ *Off Mark West Springs Rd.* ☎ *707/579–2551, 800/616–2695* ⊕ *www.safariwest.com* ⊠ *From $93 Sept.–May, from $108 June–Aug.*

 Restaurants

Grossman's Noshery and Bar

$$ | DELI | The menu at this homage to Jewish delicatessens plays the greatest hits—blintzes, latkes, lox, chopped liver, and knishes, plus pastrami, corned beef, and Reuben sandwiches—but mashes things up with chicken shawarma kebabs, fish-and-chips, and other atypical deli dishes. It's all executed with panache, and the retro-eclectic decor (black-and-white ceramic tile floors, colorful tropical-bird-print wallpaper, chunky stone fireplace) feels nostalgic yet of the moment. **Known for:** baked goods; happy-hour (daily 3–5) frozen vodka shots; picnic-table seating beside the building. ⑤ *Average main: $18* ⊠ *Hotel La Rose, 308½ Wilson St.* ✢ *Near 4th St.* ☎ *707/595–7707* ⊕ *grossmanssr.com.*

★ Walter Hansel Wine & Bistro

$$$ | FRENCH | Tabletop linens and lights softly twinkling from this ruby-red roadhouse restaurant's low wooden ceiling raise expectations the Parisian-style bistro cuisine consistently exceeds. A starter of cheeses or lobster bisque in a puff pastry awakens the palate for entrées like chicken cordon bleu, steak au poivre, or what this place does best: seafood dishes that might include scallops in white-truffle cream sauce or subtly sauced wild Alaskan halibut. **Known for:** romantic setting for classic cuisine; prix-fixe option; vegan and vegetarian dishes. ⑤ *Average main: $35* ⊠ *3535 Guerneville Rd.* ✢ *At Willowside Rd., 6 miles northwest of downtown* ☎ *707/546–6462* ⊕ *walterhanselbistro.com* ⊙ *Closed Mon. and Tues. No lunch.*

 Hotels

★ Vintners Resort

$$$$ | HOTEL | With a countryside location, a reserved sense of style, and spacious rooms with comfortable beds, the Vintners Resort further seduces with a slew of amenities and a scenic vineyard landscape. **Pros:** John Ash & Co. restaurant; vineyard jogging path; personalized service. **Cons:** occasional noise from adjacent events center; trips to downtown Santa Rosa or Healdsburg require a car; pricey on summer and fall weekends. ⑤ *Rooms from: $415* ⊠ *4350 Barnes Rd.* ☎ *707/575–7350, 800/421–2584* ⊕ *www. vintnersresort.com* ⇄ *78 rooms* ❏❍| *No meals.*

Chapter 13

13

THE NORTH COAST

FROM SONOMA TO THE REDWOODS

Updated by
Daniel Mangin

 Sights
★★★★★

 Restaurants
★★★★☆

 Hotels
★★★★★

 Shopping
★☆☆☆☆

 Nightlife
★☆☆☆☆

WELCOME TO THE NORTH COAST

TOP REASONS TO GO

★ **Scenic coastal drives:** There's hardly a road here that *isn't* scenic.

★ **Wild beaches:** This stretch of California is one of nature's masterpieces. Revel in the unbridled, rugged coastline, without a building in sight.

★ **Dinnertime:** When you're done hiking the beach, refuel with delectable food; you'll find everything from fresh-off-the-boat seafood to haute French-inspired cuisine.

★ **Fine wine:** Sip wines at family-owned tasting rooms—cool-climate Pinot Noirs and Chardonnays in the Anderson Valley, then wines from Zinfandel and other heat-loving varietals as you move inland.

★ **Wildlife:** Watch for migrating whales, sunbathing sea lions, and huge Roosevelt elk with majestic antlers.

It's all but impossible to explore the Northern California coast without a car. Indeed, you wouldn't want to—driving here is half the fun. The main road is Highway 1, two lanes that twist and turn (sometimes 180 degrees) up cliffs and down through valleys in Sonoma and Mendocino counties, with U.S. 101 proceeding parallel inland until the two roads join northward in the Redwood Country of Humboldt County.

1 Bodega Bay. Harbor seals bask on Bodega Bay's windswept beaches.

2 Jenner. Cliffs here overlook the estuary where the Russian River empties into the Pacific.

3 Elk. Perched high above the ocean, Elk entices with a downscale roadhouse café and an ultraluxurious resort.

4 Little River. Bask in breathtaking ocean views at inns and restaurants in Little River and nearby Albion.

5 Mendocino. Artsy Mendocino is all about aesthetics, from sweeping coastal vistas to stylishly plated cuisine

6 Ft. Bragg. Travelers love this down-to-earth town for its botanical garden, working harbor, and water's-edge trail.

7 Philo. Chardonnay and Pinot Noir star in scenic Philo.

8 Boonville. Sip beer at a famous brewery or drop by family-owned wineries at this town with a certified language all its own.

9 Hopland. This wisp of a town has acquired a hip cachet for its tasting rooms, restaurants, and lodgings.

10 Ukiah. Wine making in and around Mendocino County's largest city dates back a century-plus.

11 Avenue of the Giants. This glorious stretch of redwoods passes through tiny Weott.

12 Eureka. Ornate Victorians line downtown blocks of this gateway to national and state parks.

13 Trinidad. A former trading post, Trinidad trades these days on its beauty and proximity to ocean and redwoods.

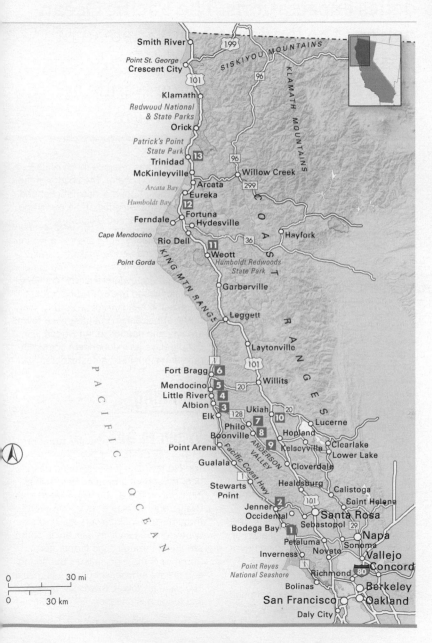

The spectacular coastline of Sonoma, Mendocino, and Humboldt counties defies expectations. The Pacific Ocean defines the landscape, but instead of boardwalks and bikinis there are ragged cliffs and pounding waves—and the sunbathers are mostly sea lions.

Two-lane Highway 1 follows the fickle shoreline. Although coastal towns vary from deluxe spa retreat to hippie hideaway, all are reliably sleepy—and that's precisely why many Californians escape here to enjoy nature unspoiled. On a detour inland, you can explore redwoods and sip wines at tasting rooms rarely too crowded or pricey. When you travel the North Coast, turn off your phone; you won't have much of a signal anyway, and this stretch of Highway 1 has numerous little worlds, each different from the last, waiting to be discovered. ■TIP→ **Don't plan to drive too far in one day. Some drivers stop frequently to appreciate the views, and you can't safely drive faster than 30 or 40 mph on many stretches.**

MAJOR REGIONS

The Sonoma Coast. As you enter Sonoma County from the south on Highway 1, you pass through rolling pastureland. North of Bodega Bay dramatic shoreline takes over. The road snakes up, down, and around sheer cliffs and steep inclines—some without guardrails—where cows seem to cling precariously. Stunning vistas (or cottony fog) and hairpin turns make for an exhilarating drive.

The Mendocino Coast. The timber industry gave birth to most of the small towns along this stretch of coastline. Although tourism now drives the economy,

the region has retained much of its old-fashioned charm. The beauty of the landscape, of course, has not changed. Inland lie the wineries of the Anderson Valley, Hopland, and Ukiah.

Redwood Country. For a pristine encounter with giant redwoods, make the trek to Humboldt County's national and state parks, where even casual visitors have easy access to thick redwood forests. Eureka and nearby Arcata, both former ports, are sizeable, but otherwise towns are tiny and nestled in the woods, and people have an independent spirit that recalls the original homesteaders.

Planning

When to Go

The North Coast is a year-round destination, though when you go determines what you will see. The migration of Pacific gray whales lasts from November through April. Wildflowers follow the winter rain, as early as January in southern areas through June farther north. Summer is the high season, but spring and fall are arguably better times to visit. The pace is slower, towns are quieter, and lodging is cheaper.

The coastal climate is similar to San Francisco's, although winter nights are colder than in the city. In July and August, thick fog can drop temperatures to the high 50s, but fear not: you need only drive inland a few miles to find temperatures that are often 20 degrees higher.

Getting Here and Around

AIR
Arcata/Eureka Airport (ACV), 14 miles north of Eureka in McKinleyville, is served by United Express and a few other small carriers. Most visitors rent a car, with ride-sharing (starting at $25 or so to Eureka) the next best option.

AIRPORT CONTACTS Arcata/Eureka Airport. ✉ *3561 Boeing Ave., McKinleyville* ☎ *707/445–9651* ⊕ *flyhumboldt.org.*

GROUND TRANSPORTATION CONTACTS City Cab. ☎ *707/442–4551* ⊕ *citycab-humboldt.com.* **Door-to-Door Airporter.** ☎ *707/839–4186* ⊕ *www.doortodoorairporter.com.*

BUS
Greyhound buses serve Eureka. Mendocino Transit Authority serves its county plus a few Sonoma County towns. Humboldt Transit Authority connects Eureka and Trinidad.

BUS CONTACTS Humboldt Transit Authority. ☎ *707/443–0826* ⊕ *www.hta.org.* **Mendocino Transit Authority.** ☎ *707/462–1422* ⊕ *mendocinotransit.org.*

CAR
U.S. 101 has excellent services, but long stretches separate towns along Highway 1. ■**TIP→ If you're running low on fuel and see a gas station, stop for a refill.** Twisting Highway 1 is the scenic route to Mendocino from San Francisco, but the fastest one is U.S. 101 north to Highway 128 west (from Cloverdale) to Highway 1 north. The quickest route to the far North Coast is straight up U.S. 101 past Cloverdale to Hopland and Ukiah and on into Humboldt County.

Restaurants

Restaurants here entice diners with dishes fashioned from fresh seafood and locally grown vegetables and herbs. Attire is usually informal, though at pricier places dressy casual is the norm. Most kitchens close at 8 or 8:30 pm, and few places serve past 9:30 pm.

Hotels

Restored Victorians, rustic lodges, country inns, and vintage motels are among the accommodations available here. Few have air-conditioning (the ocean breezes make it unnecessary), and many lack in-room phones or TVs. Except in Fort Bragg and a few other towns, budget accommodations are rare, but in winter you're likely to find reduced rates. In summer and on weekends, make reservations at small inns as far ahead as possible—rooms at the best ones often sell out months in advance.

Restaurant and hotel reviews have been shortened. For full information, visit Fodors.com. Restaurant prices are the average cost of a main course at dinner, or if dinner is not served, at lunch. Hotel prices are the lowest cost of a standard double room in high season.

What It Costs			
$	$$	$$$	$$$$
RESTAURANTS			
under $17	$17–$26	$27–$36	over $36
HOTELS			
under $150	$150–$250	$251–$350	over $350

Visitor Information

CONTACTS Humboldt County Visitors Bureau. ☎ *707/443–5097, 800/346–3482* ⊕ *www.visitredwoods.com.* **Sonoma County Tourism.** ☎ *707/522–5800, 800/576–6662* ⊕ *www.sonomacounty. com.* **Visit Mendocino County.** ☎ *707/964–9010, 866/466–3636* ⊕ *www.visitmendocino.com.*

Bodega Bay

23 miles west of Santa Rosa.

Pockets of modernity notwithstanding, this commercial fishing town retains the workaday vibe of its cinematic turn in Alfred Hitchcock's *The Birds* (1963). Little from the film's era remains save the windswept bay and ocean views. (For the ocean ones, drive west from Highway 1, Eastshore to Bay Flat to Westshore.) To the east in the town of Bodega, the film's schoolhouse still stands, at Bodega Lane off Bodega Highway.

GETTING HERE AND AROUND

To reach Bodega Bay, exit U.S. 101 at Santa Rosa and take Highway 12 west (called Bodega Highway west of Sebastopol) 23 miles to the coast. A scenic alternative is to take U.S. 101's East Washington Street/Central Petaluma exit and follow signs west to Bodega Bay; just after you merge onto Highway 1, you'll pass through down-home Valley Ford. Mendocino Transit Authority buses serve Bodega Bay.

Sights

Sonoma Coast Vineyards

WINERY/DISTILLERY | This winery with an ocean-view tasting room makes small-lot wines from grapes grown close to the Pacific. The Petersen Vineyard Chardonnay and Antonio Mountain Pinot Noir stand out among cool-climate bottlings that also include Sauvignon Blanc, rosé of Pinot Noir, and a Blanc de Noirs sparkler. ✉ *555 Hwy. 1* ☎ *707/921–2860* ⊕ *www. sonomacoastvineyards.com* 🍷 *Tastings from $10 glass.*

Beaches

★ Sonoma Coast State Park

BEACH—SIGHT | The park's gorgeous sandy coves stretch for 17 miles from Bodega Head to 4 miles north of Jenner. **Bodega Head** is a popular whale-watching perch in winter and spring, and **Rock Point, Duncan's Landing,** and **Wright's Beach,** at about the halfway mark, have good picnic areas. Rogue waves have swept people off the rocks at Duncan's Landing Overlook, so don't stray past signs warning you away. Calmer **Shell Beach,** about 2 miles north, is known for beachcombing, tidepooling, and fishing. Walk part of the bluff-top **Kortum Trail** or drive about 2½ miles north of Shell Beach to **Blind Beach.** Near the mouth of the Russian River just north of here at **Goat Rock Beach,** you'll find harbor seals; pupping season is from March through August. Bring binoculars and walk north from the parking lot to view the seals. During summer, lifeguards are on duty at some beaches, but strong rip currents and heavy surf keep most visitors onshore. **Amenities:** parking (fee); toilets. **Best for:** solitude; sunset; walking. ✉ *Park Headquarters/ Salmon Creek Ranger Station, 3095 Hwy. 1* ⊹ *2 miles north of Bodega Bay* ☎ *707/875–3483* ⊕ *www.parks.ca.gov* 🚗 *$8 per vehicle.*

🍴 Restaurants

Spud Point Crab Company

$ | SEAFOOD | Crab sandwiches, New England or Manhattan clam chowder, and homemade crab cakes with roasted red-pepper sauce star on this food stand's brief menu. Place your order and enjoy your meal to go or, when possible, at one of the marina-view picnic tables outside. **Known for:** family operation;

opens at 9 am; seafood cocktails, superb chowder. ⑤ *Average main: $10* ✉ *1910 Westshore Rd.* ✛ *West off Hwy. 1, East-shore Rd. to Bay Flat Rd.* ☎ *707/875–9472* ⊕ *www.spudpointcrabco.com* ⊘ *No dinner.*

★ Terrapin Creek Cafe & Restaurant
$$$ | **MODERN AMERICAN** | Intricate but not fussy cuisine based on locally farmed ingredients and *fruits de mer* has made this casual yet sophisticated restaurant with an open kitchen a West County darling. Start with raw oysters, rich potato-leek soup, or (in season) Dungeness crab before moving on to halibut or other fish pan-roasted to perfection. **Known for:** intricate cuisine of chefs Liya and Andrew Truong; Bay Area food-lovers' choice; great starters and salads. ⑤ *Average main: $34* ✉ *1580 Eastshore Rd.* ✛ *Off Hwy. 1* ☎ *707/875–2700* ⊕ *www.terrapincreekcafe.com* ⊘ *Closed Mon.–Wed. No lunch Thurs.*

 Hotels

Bodega Bay Lodge
$$$ | **HOTEL** | Looking out to the ocean across a wetland, the lodge's shingle-and-river rock buildings contain Bodega Bay's finest accommodations. **Pros:** spacious rooms with ocean views; on-site Drakes Sonoma Coast restaurant for seafood; fireplaces and patios or balconies in most rooms. **Cons:** pricey in-season; parking lot in foreground of some rooms' views; fairly long drive to other fine dining. ⑤ *Rooms from: $349* ✉ *103 Coast Hwy. 1* ☎ *707/875–3525* ⊕ *www.bodegabaylodge.com* ⊴ *83 rooms* ⦿ *No meals.*

Jenner

10 miles north of Bodega Bay.

The Russian River empties into the Pacific Ocean at Jenner, a wide spot in the road where houses dot a mountain-side high above the sea. Facing south, the village looks across the river's mouth to Sonoma Coast State Park's Goat Rock Beach. North of the village, Fort Ross State Historic Park provides a glimpse into Russia's early-19th-century foray into California. South of the fort a winery named for it grows Chardonnay and Pinot Noir above the coastal fog line. North of the fort lie more beaches and redwoods to hike and explore.

GETTING HERE AND AROUND
Jenner is north of Bodega Bay on Highway 1. From Guerneville head west on Highway 116 (River Road). Mendocino Transit Authority buses serve Jenner.

 Sights

Fort Ross State Historic Park
NATIONAL/STATE PARK | **FAMILY** | With its reconstructed Russian Orthodox chapel, stockade, and officials' quarters, Fort Ross looks much the way it did after the Russians made it their major California coastal outpost in 1812. Russian settlers established the fort on land they leased from the native Kashia people. The Russians hoped to gain a foothold in the Pacific coast's warmer regions and to produce crops and other supplies for their Alaskan fur-trading operations. In 1841, with the local marine mammal population depleted and farming having proven unproductive, the Russians sold their holdings to John Sutter, later of gold-rush fame. The land, privately ranched for decades, became a state park in

The Sonoma and Mendocino Coasts

Leggett

Westport
Pacific Star Winery
Fort Bragg
Noyo
Mendocino Coast Botanical Gardens
Point Cabrillo Light Station
Mendocion Headlands State Park
Mendocino
Little River
Albion
Navarro River Redwoods State Park
Greenwood State Beach
Elk

Laytonville

Willits

Caspar

See inset below
Navarro

Calpella
Testa Vineyards
Ukiah

Lucerne

Philo

Rivino Winery
Nelson Family Vineyards
Graziano Family of Wines
Blue Quail Tasting Room

Clear Lake

Manchester

Boonville

Saracina Vineyards
Brutocao Cellars

Hopland
Campovida

Kelseyville

Point Arena
Point Arena Lighthouse
Point Arena

Yorkville

Clearlake
Lower Lake

Anchor Bay
Gualala

Cloverdale
Geyserville

Middletown

Sea Ranch
Stewarts Point

Healdsburg

Calistoga

Salt Point State Park
Fort Ross State Historic Park
Fort Ross Vineyard Winery

Fort Ross

Guerneville
Santa Rosa

Saint Helena

Napa Valley

Jenner
Sonoma Coast State Park
Salmon Creek
Bodega Bay

Occidental
Freestone
Sebastopol

Bodega Bay
Dillon Beach
Tomales Point

Sonoma Coast Vineyards
Valley Ford
Tomales

Sonoma Valley
Sonoma

Petaluma
Novato

Tomales Bay

Marshall

Inverness
Point Reyes Station
Olema

Saint Rafael

Point Reyes
Drakes Bay

Bolinas
Stinson Beach

Mt. Tamalpais

Marin Ci

San Francisco
Daly City

PACIFIC OCEAN

ANDERSON VALLEY

Pacific Coast Highway

ALEXANDER VALLEY

0   15 mi
0   15 km

Anderson Valley

Navarro
Lula Cellars
Handley Cellars
Roederer Estate
Phillips Hill Winery
Husch Vineyards
Navarro Vineyards
Toulouse Vineyards

Montgomery Woods State Natural Reserve

Philo
Goldeneye Winery

Hendy Woods State Park
The Madrones Tasting Rooms

Bee Hunter Wine

Boonville
Foursight Wines

Pennyroyal Farm
Anderson Valley Brewing Company

ANDERSON VALLEY

5 mi
5 km

Yorkville

1909. One original Russian-era structure remains, as does a cemetery. The rest of the compound has been reconstructed to look much as it did during Russian times. An excellent small museum documents the history of the fort, the Kashia people, and the ranch and state-park eras. No dogs are allowed past the parking lot and picnic area. ⊠ *19005 Hwy. 1 ⊕ 11 miles north of Jenner village* ☎ *707/847–3437* ⊕ *www.fortross.org* ⊠ *$8 per vehicle.*

Fort Ross Vineyard & Winery

WINERY/DISTILLERY | The Russian River and Highway 116 snake west from Guerneville through redwood groves to the coast, where Highway 1 twists north past rocky cliffs to this windswept ridgetop winery. Until recently many experts deemed the weather this far west too chilly even for cool-climate varietals, but Fort Ross Vineyard and other Fort Ross–Seaview AVA wineries are proving that Chardonnay and Pinot Noir can thrive above the fog line. The sea air and rocky soils here produce wines generally less fruit forward than their Russian River Valley counterparts but equally sophisticated and no less vibrant. With its rustic-chic, barnlike tasting room and outdoor patio overlooking the Pacific, Fort Ross provides an appealing introduction to its region's wines. Tastings include a cheese and charcuterie plate (vegetarian option possible). Appointments are required; for same-day visits call before 11 am. ⊠ *15725 Meyers Grade Rd. ⊕ Off Hwy. 1, 6 miles north of Jenner* ☎ *707/847–3400* ⊕ *www. fortrossvineyard.com* ⊠ *Tastings from $55* ⊙ *Closed Tues. and Wed.*

🍴 Restaurants

River's End

$$$ | AMERICAN | The hot tip at this low-slung cliff's-edge restaurant is to come early or reserve a window table, where the Russian River and Pacific Ocean views alone, particularly at sunset, might make your day (even more so if you're a birder). Seafood is the specialty—during the summer the chef showcases local king salmon—but filet mignon, duck, elk, a vegetarian napoleon, and pasta with prawns are often on the dinner menu. **Known for:** majestic setting; international wine list; burgers, fish-and-chips for lunch. ⑤ *Average main: $34* ⊠ *11048 Hwy. 1 ⊕ 1½ miles north of Hwy. 116* ☎ *707/865–2484* ⊕ *www.ilovesunsets. com.*

Hotels

★ Timber Cove Resort

$$$ | RESORT | Restored well beyond its original splendor, this resort anchored to a craggy oceanfront cliff is by far the Sonoma Coast's coolest getaway. **Pros:** dramatic sunsets; grand public spaces; patio dining at Coast Kitchen restaurant. **Cons:** some service lapses; pricey ocean-view rooms; far from nightlife. ⑤ *Rooms from: $340* ⊠ *21780 Hwy. 1* ☎ *707/847–3231* ⊕ *www.timbercoveresort.com* ⊠ *46 rooms* ⑩ *No meals.*

Elk

70 miles north of Jenner, 17 miles south of Mendocino.

In this quiet town on the cliff above Greenwood Cove, just about every spot has a view of the rocky coastline and stunning Pacific sunsets. There's a museum, and few restaurants and inns do business here, but the main attraction is highly walkable Greenwood State Beach, accessed via a trail that starts across Highway 1 from the town's general store.

GETTING HERE AND AROUND

Elk is along Highway 1, 6 miles south of Highway 128. Mendocino Transit Authority buses serve Elk.

Surfers check out the waves near Bodega Bay on the Sonoma Coast.

Sights

Greenwood State Beach

BEACH—SIGHT | If you're not staying at one of Elk's cliff-top lodgings, the easiest access to the sandy shore below them is at this state beach whose parking lot sits across Highway 1 from the town's general store. A trail leads from the lot down to the beach, where the waves crashing against the huge offshore rocks are the perfect backdrop. **Amenities:** parking (free). **Good for:** sunset; walking. ⊠ *6150 Hwy. 1* ☎ *707/937–5804* ⊕ *www. parks.ca.gov* ✍ *Free.*

★ Point Arena Lighthouse

LIGHTHOUSE | For an outstanding view of the ocean and, in winter, migrating whales, take the marked road off Highway 1 to this 115-foot lighthouse, completed in 1908. If the structure is open, climb the 145 steps, and a 360-degree panorama unfolds. The ground-level museum displays the original Fresnel lens and other maritime artifacts. Six cottages with full kitchens can be booked for overnight stays. ⊠ *45500 Lighthouse Rd., Point Arena* ✛ *Off Hwy. 1, 19 miles south of Elk* ☎ *707/882–2809, 877/725–4448* ⊕ *www.pointarenalighthouse.com* ✍ *Tour $8 ($5 if no tour).*

Restaurants

★ Harbor House Inn Restaurant

$$$$ | **MODERN AMERICAN** | The chef at this ocean-bluff inn's redwood-paneled dining room describes the Mendocino Coast's most intricate meal—an 8- to 12-course, prix-fixe extravaganza—as "hyperlocal" seasonal cuisine revolving around seafood and vegetables (many of the latter grown on-site). The artistry displayed in every dish lives up to the raves the restaurant has received from local and national food writers. **Known for:** breathtaking views; swoonworthy cuisine; astute wine pairings. ⑤ *Average main: $220* ⊠ *5600 S. Hwy. 1* ☎ *707/877–3203* ⊕ *theharborhouseinn.com/dine* ⊘ *Closed Tues. and Wed.* ☞ *Reservations essential.*

Queenie's Roadhouse Cafe

$ | AMERICAN | If the day's sunny, grab one of the picnic tables in front of this beloved hangout for big breakfasts (served until closing, at 3) and lunches that include blue-cheese burgers topped with onions browned in bourbon and butter. The café's deck and wide windows provide Pacific views to enjoy with your meal. **Known for:** omelets, huevos rancheros, waffles, and pancakes; burgers, salads, and sandwiches; local wines and microbrews. ⑤ *Average main: $15 ⊠ 6061 S. Hwy. 1 ☎ 707/877–3285 ⊕ www.queeniesroadhousecafe.com ⊘ Closed Tues. and Wed. and late Dec.– mid-Feb. No dinner.*

Hotels

Elk Cove Inn & Spa

$$ | B&B/INN | Perched on a bluff above pounding surf and a driftwood-strewn beach, this property has stunning views from most of its accommodations, which include seven rooms, five suites, and four cottages. **Pros:** gorgeous views; filling breakfast; steps to the beach. **Cons:** rooms in main house are smallish; not suitable for young children; spa's massage calendar often full. ⑤ *Rooms from: $199 ⊠ 6300 S. Hwy. 1 ☎ 707/877–3321, 800/275–2967 ⊕ www.elkcoveinn.com ➪ 16 units ⃢⃝⃢ Free breakfast.*

★ Harbor House Inn

$$$$ | B&B/INN | Prepare to be bowled over by every aspect of this showcase property with a rugged Pacific-cliff setting, destination restaurant, sterling hospitality, and luxurious accommodations in a 1916 redwood Craftsman-style house and a few newer cottages. **Pros:** romantic, ocean-view setting; luxurious base for wine tasting and outdoor activities; destination restaurant. **Cons:** not ideal for kids; 16 miles from Mendocino; best accommodations expensive for the area. ⑤ *Rooms from: $399 ⊠ 5600 S. Hwy. 1 ☎ 707/877–3203, 800/720–7474 ⊕ www.theharborhouseinn. com ➪ 11 rooms ⃢⃝⃢ Free breakfast.*

Little River

13½ miles north of Elk.

The town of Little River is not much more than a post office and a convenience store; Albion, its neighbor to the south, is even smaller. Along this winding portion of Highway 1 you'll find numerous inns and restaurants, all situated to take advantage of the breathtaking ocean views.

GETTING HERE AND AROUND

Little River is along Highway 1, 7 miles north of Highway 128. Mendocino Transit Authority buses serve the area.

Sights

Van Damme State Park

NATIONAL/STATE PARK | Best known for its quiet beach, a prime diving spot, this park is also popular with day hikers. A ¼-mile stroll on a boardwalk leads to the bizarre **Pygmy Forest,** where acidic soil and poor drainage have produced mature cypress and pine trees that are no taller than a person. For more of a challenge, hike the moderate 4¼-mile Pygmy Forest and Fern Canyon Loop past the forest and sword ferns that grow as tall as 4 feet. The visitor center has displays on ocean life and the historical significance of the redwood lumber industry along the coast. ⊠ *Little River Park Rd., off Hwy. 1 ☎ 707/937–5804 ⊕ www.parks. ca.gov ➪ $8 per vehicle, walk-ins free (park at beach).*

Restaurants

Ledford House

$$ | FRENCH | The only thing separating this bluff-top wood-and-glass restaurant from the Pacific Ocean is a great view. Entrées evoke the flavors of southern France and include hearty bistro dishes—stews, cassoulet, and pastas—and large portions of grilled meats and freshly caught fish (though the restaurant also is vegetarian

friendly). **Known for:** outdoor deck; Mendocino-centric wine list; three-course bistro special. $ *Average main: $26* ⊠ *3000 N. Hwy. 1, Albion* ☎ *707/937–0282* ⊕ *www.ledfordhouse.com* ⊗ *Closed Mon. and Tues. and late-Feb.–early Mar. and mid-Oct.–early Nov. No lunch.*

Little River Inn
$$$ | **AMERICAN** | Straightforward seafood preparations and seasonal cocktails (best sipped from the ocean-view Whale Watch Bar) rank high among the pleasures of a visit to the Little River Inn resort, opened in 1939 and still run by members of the same family. Start with clam chowder, fried calamari, or Dungeness crab cakes before settling into cioppino, the day's catch, a 12-ounce rib eye, or red-wine-braised short ribs. **Known for:** step-back-in-time feel; alfresco dining in garden courtyard; olallieberry cobbler from founder's wife's recipe. $ *Average main: $32* ⊠ *7901 N. Hwy. 1* ☎ *707/937–5942* ⊕ *littleriverinn.com* ⊗ *No lunch.*

 Hotels

Albion River Inn
$$ | **B&B/INN** | Contemporary, New England–style cottages at this inn overlook the dramatic bridge and seascape where the Albion River empties into the Pacific. **Pros:** ocean views; great bathtubs; romantic glassed-in restaurant. **Cons:** often foggy in summer; no TV in rooms; 2-night weekend minimum. $ *Rooms from: $195* ⊠ *3790 N. Hwy. 1, Albion* ☎ *707/937–1919, 800/479–7944* ⊕ *albionriverinn.com* ⇌ *22 rooms* ❍❘ *Free breakfast.*

★ Glendeven Inn & Lodge
$$$ | **B&B/INN** | If Mendocino is the New England village of the West Coast, then Glendeven—an 1867 farmhouse and several other buildings—is the local country manor, with sea views and 8 acres of gardens, complete with llamas and chickens that provide eggs for three-course breakfasts served in-room. **Pros:** romantic

setting with acres of gardens; owners' attention to detail; ocean views. **Cons:** no TVs in two buildings; per website no guests under age 18; weekend minimum-stay requirement. $ *Rooms from: $255* ⊠ *8205 N. Hwy. 1* ☎ *707/937–0083, 800/822–4536* ⊕ *glendeven.com* ⇌ *21 rooms* ❍❘ *Free breakfast.*

Mendocino

3 miles north of Little River.

A flourishing logging town in the late-19th century, Mendocino seduces 21st-century travelers with windswept cliffs, phenomenal Pacific Ocean views, and boomtown-era New England–style architecture. Following the timber industry's mid-20th-century decline, artists and craftspeople began flocking here, and so did Hollywood: Mendocino served as a backdrop for *East of Eden* (1955), starring James Dean, and the town stood in for fictional Cabot Cove, Maine, in the TV series *Murder, She Wrote*. Today, shops, galleries, inns, and cafés predominate in the small downtown area.

GETTING HERE AND AROUND
Main Street is off Highway 1 about 10 miles north of Highway 128. Mendocino Transit Authority buses serve the area.

 Sights

★ Mendocino Headlands State Park
NATIONAL/STATE PARK | A 3-mile easy-to-walk trail leads across the spectacular seaside cliffs bordering Mendocino. The restored Ford House, built in 1854, serves as the visitor center for the park and the town. The house has a scale model of Mendocino as it looked in 1890, when it had 34 water towers and a 12-seat public outhouse. ⊠ *45035 Main St.* ☎ *707/937–5397* ⊕ *mendoparks.org/ mendocino-headlands* 🎟 *Park and visitor center free, museum $2.*

Point Cabrillo Light Station

LIGHTHOUSE | Completed in 1909 and noteworthy for its original, third-order, Fresnel lens that glows like a jewel day or night, the still-active station inhabits a breezy plateau 3 miles north of Mendocino village. Dirt and paved paths lead downhill from the parking lot to the station. ■**TIP**➜ **The lighthouse museum and other historic buildings are worth a peek if open, but the park merits a visit for its views alone.** ⊠ *45300 Lighthouse Rd.* ✛ *Point Cabrillo Dr. off Hwy. 1* ☎ *707/937–6123* ⊕ *pointcabrillo.org* 🎟 *Park free, museum $5.*

Restaurants

Cafe Beaujolais

$$$ | **AMERICAN** | A garden of heirloom and exotic plantings surrounds this popular restaurant inside a yellow Victorian cottage. Local ingredients find their way into dishes that might include Oaxacan-style ceviche, smash burgers, pizzas from a wood-fired brick oven, fish and prawn tacos, beef bourguignon, and oven-roasted cauliflower with house-made mole verde. **Known for:** garden dining in fine weather; bowls and other vegan and vegetarian selections; "Waiting Room" for morning pastries and other grab-and-go fare. ⑤ *Average main: $28* ⊠ *961 Ukiah St.* ☎ *707/937–5614* ⊕ *www.cafebeaujolais.com* ⊘ *Closed Mon. and Tues.*

Fog Eater Cafe

$$ | **VEGETARIAN** | The culinary influences are Deep South and Californian at this vegetarian (mostly vegan) restaurant with salmon-colored walls, teal tables, and white trim. The chefs' flair for the dramatic might exhibit itself in carrot-cake waffles at Sunday brunch; hush-puppies and beet-dyed deviled eggs as happy-hour nibbles; and dinnertime fried-green-tomato biscuit sliders and Mississippi Delta–style hot tamales. **Known for:** all-organic Mendocino and Sonoma produce; outdoor dining; natural wines and local beers. ⑤ *Average main: $20* ⊠ *45104 Main St.* ✛ *At Albion St.* ☎ *707/397–1806* ⊕ *fogeatercafe.com* ⊘ *Closed Mon. and Tues. No lunch Wed.–Sat. No dinner Sun.*

Trillium Cafe

$$$ | **AMERICAN** | The term "light rustic" applies equally well to this comely café's decor—plank flooring, wood-top tables, gas fireplace with brick hearth—and its cuisine, which emphasizes local produce and seafood. The menu changes seasonally, with the grilled flatbread, albacore appetizer, Point Reyes blue cheese salad, and grilled organic pork chop among the year-round crowd-pleasers. **Known for:** outdoor patio area with garden and ocean views; wine list favoring Northern California wines, particularly Mendocino; organic grass-fed meats. ⑤ *Average main: $33* ⊠ *10390 Kasten St.* ☎ *707/937–3200* ⊕ *www.trilliummendocino.com* ⊘ *Closed Wed. and Thurs. (but check).*

🛏 Hotels

Blue Door Inns

$$ | **B&B/INN** | Each of the three Victorian properties operated by California-based Four Sisters Inns has its appeal—Blue Door for its garden, Packard House for its serene setting, JD House for its ocean views—with all three worth consideration for their proximity to restaurants, shops, and the Mendocino Headlands. **Pros:** historic properties with modern decor; service-oriented staff; range of prices and room types. **Cons:** some rooms are on the small side; lacks personal touch of on-site owner-innkeeper; best rooms are pricey. ⑤ *Rooms from: $175* ⊠ *10481 Howard St.* ☎ *707/937–4892, 800/234–1425* ⊕ *www.bluedoorgroup.com* ⇆ *19 rooms* �’⊙❘ *Free breakfast.*

★ Brewery Gulch Inn

$$$$ | **B&B/INN** | The feel is modern yet tasteful at this inn with stained-wood and leather furnishings and plush beds; two rooms have whirlpool tubs with views. **Pros:** luxury in tune with nature; peaceful ocean views; complimentary wine hour and light dinner buffet. **Cons:** a mile from Mendocino village; expensive in-season; 2-night minimum on weekends. Ⓢ *Rooms from: $425* ✉ *9401 N. Hwy. 1* ☎ *707/937–4752, 800/578–4454* ⊕ *www.brewerygulchinn.com* ⌐ *11 rooms* ❍| *Free breakfast.*

Stanford Inn by the Sea

$$$$ | **HOTEL** | This woodsy yet luxurious family-run property a few minutes south of town feels like the Northern California version of an old-time summer resort, with an ecologically friendly twist. **Pros:** lovely grounds; on-site bike and kayak rentals; on-site vegetarian restaurant. **Cons:** New Age feel won't appeal to everyone; carnivores may find menus challenging; least expensive rooms lack ocean views. Ⓢ *Rooms from: $351* ✉ *44850 Comptche Ukiah Rd.* ☎ *707/937–5615, 800/331–8884* ⊕ *www.stanfordinn.com* ⌐ *41 rooms* ❍| *Free breakfast.*

Fort Bragg

10 miles north of Mendocino.

Fort Bragg is a working-class town that many feel is the most authentic place on the coast. The city maintains a local vibe since most people who work at the area hotels and restaurants also live here, as do many artists and commercial anglers. The pleasures of a visit are mainly outdoors, a stroll through the botanical gardens or along the town's coastal trail, touring by train or boat, tidepooling or fishing at the state park, or tasting wine within steps of the ocean.

GETTING HERE AND AROUND

Highway 20 winds west 33 miles from Willits to Highway 1 just south of Fort Bragg. Mendocino Transit Authority buses serve the town.

 Sights

Fort Bragg Coastal Trail

TRAIL | A multiuse path, much of it flat and steps from rocky and highly photogenic shoreline, stretches the length of Fort Bragg. A particularly pleasant section, lined with benches created by local artists, follows the coast north about 2 miles between Noyo Headlands Park in southern Fort Bragg and Glass Beach. From the beach you can continue well into MacKerricher State Park. ■**TIP**→ **There's free parking at both Noyo Headlands Park and Glass Beach.** ✉ *Fort Bragg* ✛ *Noyo Headlands Park, W. Cypress St. off S. Main St. (Hwy. 1); Glass Beach, W. Elm St. off N. Main St.*

★ Mendocino Coast Botanical Gardens

GARDEN | Something beautiful is always abloom in these marvelous gardens. Along 4 miles of trails, including pathways with ocean views and observation points for whale-watching, lie a profusion of flowers. The rhododendrons are at their peak from April through June; the dahlias begin their spectacular show in July and last through September. In winter the heather and camellias add more than a splash of color. The main trails are wheelchair accessible. ✉ *18220 N. Hwy. 1, 2 miles south of Fort Bragg* ☎ *707/964–4352* ⊕ *www.gardenbythesea.org* ⊟ *$15.*

★ Noyo Harbor Tours with Captain Dan

TOUR—SIGHT | The genial Captain Dan has piloted commercial fishing boats on the high seas, but, for his gentle tours of Noyo Harbor from the river up to (but not into) the ocean, he ordered a custom-built, 18-foot, eco-friendly Duffy electric boat. Having been in Fort Bragg for decades he knows everyone and everyone's story, including those of the harbor seals, sea lions, birds, and other wildlife you'll see on his excursion. ✉ *32399 Basin St.* ✛ *From S. Main St. (Hwy. 1), take Hwy. 20 east ¼ mile, S. Harbor Dr. north ¼ mile, and Basin St. northeast 1* mile ☎ 707/734–0044 ⊕ www.noyohar-bortours.com ⊠ From $35.

Pacific Star Winery

WINERY/DISTILLERY | When the sun's out and you're sipping wine while viewing whales or other sea creatures swimming offshore, this bluff-top winery's outdoor tasting spaces feel mystical and magical. Equally beguiling on a brooding stormy day, Pacific Star has still more aces up its sleeve: its engaging owner-wine-maker, Sally Ottoson, whose cheery staffers pour a lineup of varietals that includes Charbono and Sangiovese. The wines, among them a vibrant blend of Mendocino County Zinfandel, Barbera, Charbono, and Petite Sirah, are good, and they're reasonably priced. ⊠ 33000 N. Hwy. 1 ⊹ 12 miles north of downtown ☎ 707/964-1155 ⊕ www.pacificstarwin-ery.com ⊠ Tasting $10 ⊗ Closed Dec. and Mon.–Wed.

Skunk Train and Rail Bikes

TOUR—SIGHT | **FAMILY** | A reproduction train travels a few miles of the route of its 1920s predecessor, a fume-spewing gas-powered motorcar that shuttled passengers along a rail line dating from the 1880s logging days. Nicknamed the Skunk Train, the original traversed redwood forests inaccessible to auto-mobiles. There are also excursions from the town of Willits as well as seasonal and holiday-themed tours. ■**TIP→ For a separate fee you can pedal the same rails as the Skunk Train on two-person, side-by-side, reclining bikes outfitted for the track, an experience many patrons find more diverting (albeit pricier) than the train trip.** ⊠ 100 W. Laurel St. ⊹ At Main St. ☎ 707/964–6371 ⊕ www.skunktrain.com ⊠ Train rides from $42; rail bikes from $195 for 2 people (no single-rider fee) ⊗ Days, hrs vary; call or check website.

Beaches

MacKerricher State Park

NATIONAL/STATE PARK | This park begins at **Glass Beach,** its draw an unfortunately dwindling supply of sea glass (remnants from the city dump once in this area), and stretches north for 9 miles, begin-ning with rocky headlands that taper into dunes and sandy beaches. The headlands are a good place for whale-watching from November through April. Fishing, canoeing, hiking, tidepooling, jogging, bicycling, beachcombing, camping, and harbor seal watching at Laguna Point are among the popular activities, many accessible to the mobility-impaired. ⚠ **Be vigilant for rogue waves—don't turn your back on the sea. Amenities:** park-ing; toilets. **Best for:** solitude; sunset; walking. ⊠ 24100 MacKerricher Park Rd. ⊹ Off Hwy. 1, 3 miles north of town ☎ 707/937–5804 ⊕ www.parks.ca.gov ⊠ Free.

Restaurants

North Coast Brewing

$$ | **AMERICAN** | Clam chowder, pork chili, and nachos are among the beer-friendly starters at the brewing company's expan-sive restaurant, whose headlining entrées include burgers, pulled-pork sandwiches, shrimp po'boys, and beer-batter fish-and-chips. The beers, award-winners world-wide, run the gamut from pilsners and the flagship Red Seal amber ale to the heavier Russian-style Rasputin stout and Old Stock Ale. **Known for:** seasonal beers; sampler flights; beer-wise staffers. ⑤ Average main: $18 ⊠ 444 N. Main St. ☎ 707/964–3400 ⊕ northcoastbrewing.com/brewery-tap-room ⊗ Closed Tues. and Wed. (but check).

Noyo River Grill

$$ | **SEAFOOD** | The Noyo River Bridge looms high above this family-owned har-borside restaurant whose outdoor tables have views of the river emptying (via Noyo Bay) into the Pacific. No surprises with the straightforward, beer-friendly, seafood-oriented cuisine—fried calamari, fish-and-chips, prawns scampi, and the like—but it's executed well, especially the grilled local salmon. **Known for:** harbor-watching from outdoor tables; po'boys and homemade tacos at lunch; shellfish apps at lunch and dinner. $ *Average main: $24* ⊠ *32150 N. Harbor Dr. ⊕ Off S. Main St. (Hwy. 1) almost 1 mile* ☎ *707/962–9050* ⊗ *Closed Thurs.*

★ Princess Seafood Market & Deli

$ | SEAFOOD | Captain Heather Sears leads her all-woman crew of "girls gone wild for wild-caught seafood" that heads oceanward on the *Princess* troller, returning with some of the seafood served at this shanty astride the vessel's Noyo Harbor dock. Order chowder (might be clam, crab, or salmon), crab rolls and shrimp po'boys, raw or barbecued oysters, or other sturdy fare at the counter, dining under the all-weather tent kept toasty by heaters and a firepit when the wind's ablowin'. **Known for:** fresh, sustainable seafood; canned wines and beer; crew members who clearly love their jobs. $ *Average main: $16* ⊠ *32410 N. Harbor Dr. ⊕ Off S. Main St. (Hwy. 1) about ½ mile* ☎ *707/962–3123* ⊕ *fvprincess. com/p/fish-market* ⊗ *Closed Tues.–Thurs. (but check). No dinner.*

Hotels

★ Inn at Newport Ranch

$$$$ | B&B/INN | Attention to detail in design and hospitality makes for an incomparable stay at this 2,000-acre working cattle ranch with 1½ miles of private coastline. **Pros:** over-the-top design; mesmerizing Pacific views; UTV ranch tour, horseback riding, ocean-side cocktails by a firepit, and other diversions. **Cons:** all this design and glamour comes at a price; lengthy drive back from Mendocino and Fort Bragg restaurants at night; coast can be foggy in summer. $ *Rooms from: $475* ⊠ *31502 N. Hwy.*

1 ☎ *707/962–4818* ⊕ *theinnatnewportranch.com* ⌁ *11 rooms* ⦿| *Free breakfast.*

★ Noyo Harbor Inn

$$$ | HOTEL | Craftsman touches abound in this luxury inn's lavishly restored, 1868 main structure, which overlooks Noyo Harbor, and a nearby newer wing with Pacific Ocean views. **Pros:** landscaped grounds; warm service; brunch or dinner on harbor-view deck. **Cons:** barking of sea lions in harbor at certain times of year; expensive during high season; some rooms lack water views. $ *Rooms from: $255* ⊠ *500 Casa del Noyo Dr.* ☎ *707/961–4200* ⊕ *noyoharborinn.com* ⌁ *15 rooms* ⦿| *No meals.*

Surf and Sand Lodge

$$ | HOTEL | As its name implies, this five-building, two-story property, whose owners run two similar lodgings nearby, sits practically on the beach; pathways lead from the accommodations down to the rock-strewn shore. **Pros:** beach location; gorgeous sunsets from decks and patios of ocean-side rooms; very affordable in the off-season. **Cons:** motel style; no restaurants close by; least expensive rooms lack view. $ *Rooms from: $159* ⊠ *1131 N. Main St.* ☎ *707/964–9383* ⊕ *www.surfsandlodge.com* ⌁ *30 rooms* ⦿| *No meals.*

Activities

All Aboard Adventures

FISHING | Captain Tim of All Aboard operates whale-watching trips from late December through April. He also heads out to sea for salmon, crab, rock cod, and other excursions. ⊠ *Noyo Harbor, 32410 N. Harbor Dr.* ☎ *707/964–1881* ⊕ *www. allaboardadventures.com* ⌁ *From $50.*

Philo

34 miles southeast of Mendocino, 5 miles west of Boonville.

Many wineries straddle Highway 128 in Philo, where the tasting rooms are more low-key than their counterparts in Napa. The wineries here, however, produce world-class Pinot Noirs, Chardonnays, Rieslings, and Gewürztraminers, whose grapes thrive in the moderate coastal climate.

GETTING HERE AND AROUND

Highway 128 travels east from coastal Highway 1 south of Mendocino and west from Boonville to Philo. Mendocino Transit Authority buses serve the area.

 Sights

Goldeneye Winery

WINERY/DISTILLERY | Established in 1996 by the founders of the Napa Valley's well-respected Duckhorn Wine Company, Goldeneye makes Pinot Noirs from estate and other local grapes, along with a Brut Rosé sparkling wine, Gewürztraminer, Pinot Gris, Chardonnay, and a blush Vin Gris of Pinot Noir. Leisurely tastings, some by appointment only, take place in either a restored farmhouse or on a patio with vineyard views. ⊠ *9200 Hwy. 128, Philo* ☎ *800/208–0438, 707/895–3202* ⊕ *www.goldeneyewinery.com* 🍷 *Tastings from $15* ⊘ *Closed Wed.*

Handley Cellars

WINERY/DISTILLERY | International folk art collected by founding winemaker the late Milla Handley adorns the tasting room at this Anderson Valley pioneer whose lightly oaked Chardonnays and Pinot Noirs earn high praise from wine critics. The winery, which has an arbored outdoor patio picnic area, also makes Gewürztraminer, Pinot Gris, Riesling, Zinfandel, sparklers, and several other wines. Reservations are recommended, but walk-ins are accommodated

when possible. ⊠ *3151 Hwy. 128, Philo* ☎ *707/895–3876, 800/733–3151* ⊕ *www. handleycellars.com* 🍷 *Tasting $15* ⊘ *Closed Tues. and Wed. Dec.–Mar.*

Hendy Woods State Park

NATIONAL/STATE PARK | Two groves of ancient redwoods accessible via short trails from the parking lot are the main attractions at this park that's also perfect for a picnic or a summer swim. ⊠ *18599 Philo Greenwood Rd., Philo* ✥ *Entrance ½ mile southwest of Hwy. 128* ☎ *707/937–5804* ⊕ *www.parks.ca.gov* 🍷 *$8 per vehicle.*

Husch Vineyards

WINERY/DISTILLERY | A century-old former pony barn houses the tasting room of the Anderson Valley's oldest winery, founded in 1971. Wines of note include Gewürztraminer, Chardonnay, Pinot Noir, and old-vine Zinfandel. You can picnic on the deck or at tables under grape arbors. ⊠ *4400 Hwy. 128, Philo* ☎ *800/554–8724* ⊕ *www.huschvineyards.com* 🍷 *Tasting free.*

★ Lula Cellars

WINERY/DISTILLERY | Seventeen miles inland from Highway 1, the fun, relaxing, and pet-friendly Lula is among the Anderson Valley wineries closest to the coast. Lula produces Sauvignon Blanc, Gewürztraminer, Zinfandel, and a rosé of Pinot Noir, but the several Pinot Noirs, each flavorful and with its own personality, are the highlights. ⊠ *2800 Guntly Rd., Philo* ✥ *At Hwy. 128* ☎ *707/895–3737* ⊕ *www.lulacellars.com* 🍷 *Tastings from $10.*

★ The Madrones Tasting Rooms

WINERY/DISTILLERY | Expand your palate at this 2-acre complex's trio of tasting rooms pouring wines from a dozen varietals. Chardonnay and Pinot Noir are the focus at **Long Meadow Ranch,** where you can also order well-brewed espresso or tea. Next door, **Drew Family Wines** specializes in Pinot Noir and Syrah beloved by sommeliers. Nearby **Smith Story** makes Anderson Valley Pinots plus wines from Sonoma County grapes.

Across from Smith Story, the own-er-chefs at Wickson bake bread and roast meat and vegetables in a wood-fired oven. ■TIP→ **The Bohemian Chemist bills itself as a "curated cannabis apothecary" and spa for sun-grown marijuana products and CBD skin-care treatments and facials.** ⊠ *9000 Hwy. 128, Philo* ☎ *707/895–2955* ⊕ *www.themadrones.com/tasting-rooms* ▦ *Tastings from $15* ⏱ *Days closed vary.*

Navarro Vineyards

WINERY/DISTILLERY | A visit to this fami-ly-run winery, opened in 1974, is a classic Anderson Valley experience, with tastings in fine weather on several perches over-looking sustainably farmed vineyards. Best known for Alsatian varietals such as Gewürztraminer and Riesling, Navarro also makes Chardonnay, Pinot Noir, and other wines. ⊠ *5601 Hwy. 128, Philo* ☎ *707/895–3686, 800/537–9463* ⊕ *www. navarrowine.com* ▦ *Tasting $10.*

★ Phillips Hill Winery

WINERY/DISTILLERY | You're apt to meet owner-winemaker Toby Hill on a visit to this winery whose tasting room occupies the upper floor of a weatherworn former apple dryer barn. The grapes for the Pinot Noirs here come from the Anderson Valley's floor and hillsides. Hill also makes whites that include Gewürztraminer and Riesling. ■TIP→ **Picnic tables on the willow-shaded lawn below the tasting room invite lingering.** ⊠ *5101 Hwy. 128, Philo* ☎ *707/895–2209* ⊕ *www.phillipshill.com* ▦ *Tastings $12* ⏱ *Closed Tues. and Wed.*

Roederer Estate

WINERY/DISTILLERY | The Anderson Valley is particularly hospitable to Pinot Noir and Chardonnay grapes, the two varietals used to create Roederer's sparkling wines. The view of vineyards and rolling hills from the patio is splendid. ⊠ *4501 Hwy. 128, Philo* ☎ *707/895–2288* ⊕ *www.roedererestate.com* ▦ *Tasting $10.*

Toulouse Vineyards & Winery

WINERY/DISTILLERY | The view west across the Anderson Valley from this winery's tasting room and deck is captivating enough to warrant a visit, but the wines don't disappoint either. Tastings begin with whites that might include Pinot Gris, Riesling, or Gewürztraminer—there's also a rosé of Pinot Noir that sells out quickly each spring—followed by Pinot Noir from estate and sourced fruit and perhaps another red. ⊠ *8001 Hwy. 128, Philo* ☎ *707/895–2828* ⊕ *www.toulouse-vineyards.com* ▦ *Tasting $15.*

🍴 Restaurants

★ The Bewildered Pig

$$$$ | **MODERN AMERICAN** | Chef Janelle Weaver cooked for seven years at a pres-tigious appointment-only Napa Valley win-ery, perfecting skills that serve her well at this low-key yet polished roadside res-taurant. Her prix-fixe menu, which varies with the season, might include smoked trout or extraordinary Peking duck breast from a local provider, with miso deviled eggs (all the better with sparkling wine) among the tantalizing starters. **Known for:** garden dining area; phenomenally fresh salads; inspired wine pairings. ⑤ *Aver-age main: $105* ⊠ *1810 Hwy. 128, Philo* ☎ *707/895–2088* ⊕ *www.bewilderedpig. com* ⏱ *Closed Sun.–Thurs. (but check). No lunch.*

Wickson Restaurant

$$$ | **MODERN AMERICAN** | A wood-fired oven anchors the small kitchen of this contempo-rustic restaurant whose chefs' deeply held views about environmentally sensitive food sourcing influence their seasonally oriented menu. Small plates might include marinated olives, a citrus and avocado salad, or smoked trout with crème fraîche and pickled onions, with spinach lasagna and quail with roasted carrots and chimichurri sauce typical of the entrées. **Known for:** wood-fired bread and focaccia; pizza Mondays; alfresco dining, especially at lunch. ⑤ *Average*

*main: $27 ✉ 9000 Hwy. 128, Philo
☎ 707/895–2955 ⊕ wicksonrestaurant.
com ⊙ Closed Tues. and Wed. (occasionally other days).*

Hotels

★ The Madrones Guest Quarters
$$$ | B&B/INN | The centerpiece of a 2-acre
spread that includes tasting rooms, a gift
shop, an apothecary-style cannabis dis-
pensary, and a restaurant, this property
has nine eclectically decorated accommodations that range from apartment-like
studios to duplex cottages, some with
patios or balconies facing landscaped
gardens. **Pros:** location near wineries and
Hendy Woods State Park; on-site Wickson Restaurant; nearby sister property
The Brambles set among redwoods for a
more casual experience. **Cons:** weekend minimum-stay requirement; pricey
on summer weekends; yogurt, cereal,
and coffee/tea provided in-room but no
breakfast served. ⑤ *Rooms from: $255*
⊠ *9000 Hwy. 128, Philo* ☎ *707/895–2955*
⊕ *www.themadrones.com* ⌁ *9 rooms*
†⊙| *No meals.*

Boonville

*6 miles east of Philo, 28 miles northwest
of Hopland.*

At first glance Boonville, population a little
more than 1,000, looks pretty much as
it has for decades, with the 19th-century
Boonville Hotel anchoring the few blocks
downtown and sheep farms and fruit
orchards fanning out on either side of
Highway 128, albeit with more grapevines
these days. The founding of the Anderson Valley Brewing Company in the late
1980s and the revitalization of the hotel
by its current owners, the Schmitt family,
jump-started the transformation of Boonville into a haven of artisanal food, wine,
and beer. Despite this, the town retains
its old-school character—listen carefully and you may hear fragments of the
academically recognized Boontling argot,
which dates to the time when this stretch
of the valley was even more isolated.

GETTING HERE AND AROUND
Boonville lies along Highway 128 at its
junction with Highway 253. Mendocino
Transit Authority buses serve the area.

Sights

Anderson Valley Brewing Company
WINERY/DISTILLERY | Brewery tours, tast-
ings, and cornhole, bocce, and disc golf
provide an entertaining and diversified,
mainly outdoor experience at the home
of Boont Amber Ale, double and triple
Belgian style ales, and other brews. Local
winemakers clear their palates with the
Bourbon Barrel Stout, aged in Tennessee
whiskey barrels. ⊠ *17700 Hwy. 253,
Boonville* ✛ *At Hwy. 128* ☎ *707/895–2337*
⊕ *www.avbc.com* ⌁ *Tastings from $15.*

Bee Hunter Wine
WINERY/DISTILLERY | Winemaker Andy
DuVigneaud of Bee Hunter Wine prefers
vineyards close to the ocean because
the cool climate requires that grapes stay
longer on the vine, preventing them from
ripening before their flavors have fully
developed. His restrained yet delicious
wines, which he pours with enthusiasm
in a former car repair shop in Boonville,
include Sauvignon Blanc, Chardonnay,
dry Riesling, a dry and light rosé of Pinot
Noir, several Pinot Noirs, and a few
other reds. ⊠ *14251 Hwy. 128, Boonville*
☎ *707/895–3995* ⊕ *www.beehunterwine.
com* ⌁ *Tasting free.*

★ Foursight Wines
WINERY/DISTILLERY | Four generations of
the Charles family have farmed the land
that produces this winery's vegan-friend-
ly all-estate lineup of Sauvignon Blanc,
Semillon, Vin Gris of Pinot Noir (aka rosé),
and Pinot Noir. With the Pinots, winemaker Joe Webb employs various techniques
to produce four very different wines,
from the light Zero, aged solely in used
oak barrels, to the "richer, riper" Paraboll,

its flavors heightened by new French oak. ■TIP→ **After a tasting, you can picnic outside the casual wood-frame tasting room, enjoying a glass or bottle.** ⊠ *14475 Hwy. 128, Boonville* ☎ *707/895–2889* ⊕ *www. foursightwines.com* ⬚ *Tastings $25* ⊘ *Closed Tues. and 3rd wk of June.*

★ Pennyroyal Farm

WINERY/DISTILLERY | FAMILY | At this ranch with a contemporary-barn tasting room and vineyard-view patio you can sample Sauvignon Blanc, velvety Pinot Noirs, and other wines from estate and sourced grapes, along with cheeses made on the premises from goat and sheep milk. Engaging tours of the farmstead should have resumed by the time you read this. The wines, cheeses, pastoral setting, and adorable animals win most guests' hearts. All visits require a reservation. ⊠ *14930 Hwy. 128, Boonville* ☎ *707/895–2410* ⊕ *www.pennyroyalfarm.com* ⬚ *Tastings from $25* ⊘ *Closed Tues. and Wed. (check for updates).*

🍴 Restaurants

Disco Ranch Wine Bar + Specialty Market

$ | WINE BAR | In a rough-hewn structure that for years housed a beloved coffee haunt called the Horn of Zeese—the local "Boontling" lingo for a cup (horn) of coffee (zeese)—international wine expert Wendy Lamer operates this combination wine bar and gourmet mini-mart. Well versed in the local wine scene and generous with advice, she pours wines by the glass or bottle and serves up sliders and other "disco snacks." **Known for:** wines by Anderson Valley producers without tasting rooms; European and other wines complementing local selection; good stop for light lunch. ⑤ *Average main: $8* ⊠ *14025 Hwy. 128, Boonville* ☎ *707/901–5002* ⊕ *discoranch.com* ⊘ *Closed Tues. and Wed. No dinner.*

Lauren's

$ | AMERICAN | Boonville locals and frequent visitors love Lauren's for its down-home vibe and healthful comfort food—vegetarian and ground-beef burgers, pizzas, chicken tostadas, meat loaf, and curry noodle bowls. Chocolate brownie sundaes and (seasonally) apple tarts and honey-baked pears are among the desserts worth a trip on their own. **Known for:** "made-from-scratch American-International cooking"; many ingredients grown or produced nearby; Taco Tuesdays. ⑤ *Average main: $16* ⊠ *14081 Hwy. 128, Boonville* ☎ *707/895–3869* ⊕ *laurensgoodfood.com* ⊘ *Closed Wed. No lunch Tues.*

★ Restaurant at The Boonville Hotel

$$$$ | AMERICAN | This stylishly funky restaurant's chef, Perry Hoffman, got his start (at age five) working in the kitchen of Napa Valley's The French Laundry, which his grandmother founded and later sold to Thomas Keller. As an adult, Hoffman made a name for himself at three highly praised Napa and Sonoma spots before returning to Boonville in 2019 to prepare prix-fixe, California farm-to-table cuisine (including a few original French Laundry dishes) at his extended family's hotel. **Known for:** many ingredients grown on-site or nearby; superior protein sources; alfresco patio dining. ⑤ *Average main: $75* ⊠ *Boonville Hotel, 14050 Hwy. 128, Boonville* ☎ *707/895–2210* ⊕ *www. boonvillehotel.com/eats* ⊘ *Closed Mon.–Thurs. Nov.–Apr., closed Tues. and Wed. May–Oct. No lunch.*

Hotels

★ The Boonville Hotel

$$ | HOTEL | From the street, this looks like a standard small-town hotel with nine freestanding cottages and a two-room, two-story building in the back garden, but once you cross the threshold you begin to sense the laid-back sophistication that makes the entire Anderson Valley so

You'll find excellent wines and great places to taste them in the laid-back Anderson Valley.

appealing. **Pros:** stylish yet homey; beautiful gardens and grounds; restaurant's excellent prix-fixe meals. **Cons:** minimum-stay requirement most weekends; no TVs or phones, no a/c in some rooms; lacks big-hotel amenities. ⑤ *Rooms from: $185* ✉ *14050 Hwy. 128, Boonville* ☎ */0//895–2210* ⊕ *www.boonvillehotel. com* 🛏 *17 rooms* ⦿ *Free breakfast.*

Hopland

28 miles east of Boonville, 14 miles south of Ukiah, 32 miles north of Healdsburg.

U.S. 101 briefly narrows to one lane in each direction to become this small town's main drag. For many years a center for the cultivation and drying of beer hops—the source of its name—Hopland these days is a center of grape growing and wine making and a pleasant stop for tastings and a meal.

GETTING HERE AND AROUND

Car travelers from Sonoma and Humboldt counties arrive in Hopland via U.S. 101. Highway 253 will get you here from Boonville. Mendocino Transit Authority buses serve the area.

ESSENTIALS

VISITOR INFORMATION Destination Hopland. ☎ *707/564-2582* ⊕ *destination-hopland.com.*

 Sights

Campovida

WINERY/DISTILLERY | Wines from Italian and Rhône varietals grown in Mendocino County organic, biodynamic, and sustainable vineyards are the focus of Campovida, on a historic 56-acre property whose previous owners include local railroad magnate A.W. Foster and the Fetzer wine-making clan. The Rhônes are the strong suit, especially the estate organic Viognier and the Grenache and rosé of Grenache from the biodynamically farmed Dark Horse Vineyard. All visits are by appointment only. ■TIP→ Sister property Stock Farm in downtown Hopland provides prepared foods for a picnic amid the landscaped gardens (no outside food). ✉ 13601 Old River Rd., Hopland ✢ Head east ¾ mile from U.S. 101 on Hwy. 175 ☎ 707/744–8797 ⊕ www.campovida.com ⊒ Tastings from $25.

Graziano Family of Wines

WINERY/DISTILLERY | A winemaker who never met a grape he didn't want to transform in the cellar, Gregory Graziano creates wines for four separate labels, one devoted to Burgundian grapes like Pinot Noir, two to Italian varietals, and the last to Zinfandel, Rhône, and a few other types. The winery's oldest Mendocino County vineyard was planted just before Prohibition by Gregory's grandfather. The lineup poured in the downtown Hopland tasting space might include Pinot Gris and Arneis whites and Dolcetto and Nebbiolo reds. ✉ 13275 U.S. 101, Hopland ☎ 707/744–8466 ⊕ grazianofamilyofwines.com ⊒ Tasting free.

★ Saracina Vineyards

WINERY/DISTILLERY | Guests at this boutique winery's contemporary, stone-and-glass hospitality center enjoy views of landscaped outdoor picnic and tasting areas and the olive grove and vineyards beyond. Tastings sometimes begin with a Sauvignon Blanc that helped establish Saracina. Some of the wine's organic grapes come from California's oldest Sauvignon Blanc vines (1945). The standout reds include Zinfandel, Cabernet Sauvignon, and Malbec. ■TIP→ Wine caves are rare in Mendocino, but there's one here, and it's sometimes open by appointment for free tours. ✉ 11684 U.S. 101, Hopland ☎ 707/670–0199 ⊕ www.saracina.com ⊒ Tastings from $15.

🍴 Restaurants

★ Golden Pig

$$ | AMERICAN | Grass-fed burgers, pulled-pork and pork-schnitzel sandwiches, and cod ceviche are among the popular items this hip-casual restaurant serves all day, with bone-in pork chops, rotisserie chicken, and similar plates appearing for dinner. Well-selected breads and buns, crispy fries with the burgers, perfect pickles with the sandwiches, and slivers of fresh ginger in the ceviche elevate the farm-to-table comfort fare, much of it showcasing ingredients from local purveyors. **Known for:** Northern California beers, Mendocino County wines; everything on menu made gluten-free if desired; tastings at affiliated wine shop 200 feet south. ⑤ Average main: $24 ✉ 13380 U.S. 101, Hopland ☎ 707/670–6055 ⊕ www.thegoldenpig.com.

Hopland Tap and Grill

$ | AMERICAN | A plaque out front hints at the layers of history that have unfolded in this hangout's redbrick 1880s structure. The mood's invariably upbeat in the bar, even more so in the courtyard beer garden, where patrons chow down on burgers, sandwiches (including four griddled-cheese options), chicken wings, and other pub grub. **Known for:** California brews on tap; down-home atmosphere; live rock on Saturday night. ⑤ Average main: $11 ✉ 13351 U.S. 101, Hopland ☎ 707/510–9000 ⊕ hoplandtap.com ⊗ Closed Mon. and Tues. (but check).

Stock Farm

$$ | MODERN AMERICAN | Gourmet wood-fired pizzas, many with ingredients grown a mile away at Campovida winery, are the main attraction at this country-casual restaurant and bar whose owners also operate the seven-room Stock Farm Inn upstairs and the Thatcher Hotel next door. Menu staples include burgers; grilled vegetables; pasta dishes; and seasonal soups, stews, and salads. **Known for:**

rustic-chic bar's specialty cocktails; street-side patio dining; well-made coffee drinks. ⑤ *Average main: $20* ✉ *13441 U.S. 101, Hopland* ☎ *707/744–1977* ⊕ *www.stockfarmhopland.com* ☾ *Closed Mon.–Wed.*

 Hotels

Stock Farm Inn

$$$$ | B&B/INN | Atop the same-named pizzeria and bar, this inn—whose owners also operate Campovida winery less than a mile away and the boutique 1890s Thatcher Hotel next door—sits along Hopland's main drag near shops, tasting rooms, and other restaurants. **Pros:** plush furnishings; two rooms with pullout couches sleep four; fireplaces, wet bars, whirlpool tubs, refrigerators, and balconies in all rooms. **Cons:** single-person whirlpool tubs in two rooms; more self-serve than pampering; weekend minimum-stay requirement. ⑤ *Rooms from: $370* ✉ *13441 U.S. 101, Hopland* ☎ *707/744–1977* ⊕ *www.stockfarmhopland.com/inn* ⤴ */ rooms* ⋔ *No meals.*

Ukiah

14 miles north of Hopland, 21 miles northeast of Boonville.

About 16,000 people live in Ukiah, the Mendocino County seat and largest town. Logging and beer hops were two prominent industries starting in the late-19th century and continuing well into the 20th. Grape plantings date from the late 1800s, though many of the head-trained (no trellising) old vines were planted in the early 1900s and during and just after Prohibition. Warmer than the Anderson Valley, the Ukiah area is known for Zinfandel, Cabernet Sauvignon, and other varietals that thrive in high heat. Should you need to cool off, you can repair to the redwoods of Montgomery Woods State Natural Reserve.

GETTING HERE AND AROUND

Ukiah is off U.S. 101; if coming from Boonville, take Highway 253 northeast to U.S. 101 and head north. Mendocino Transit Authority buses serve the area.

ESSENTIALS

VISITOR INFORMATION Ukiah Visitor Center. ✉ *200 S. School St.* ☎ *707/467–5766* ⊕ *www.visitukiah.com.*

 Sights

Montgomery Woods State Natural Reserve

NATIONAL/STATE PARK | Narrow Orr Springs Road winds 13 miles west from Ukiah to this secluded park whose 2-mile loop trail leads to serene old-growth redwood groves. Only the intermittent breezes, rustling of small wildlife, and calls of resident birds punctuate the prehistoric quiet of the most remote one. The reserve (no dogs allowed) is a place like few others in all of California. ■ TIP→ **From the town of Mendocino you can access the park by taking the Comptche Ukiah Road to Orr Springs Road.** ✉ *15825 Orr Springs Rd., Ukiah* ⊕ *13 miles west of N. State St.* ☎ *707/937–5804* ⊕ *www.parks.ca.gov* ⛿ *Free.*

Nelson Family Vineyards

WINERY/DISTILLERY | The grandparents of the current winemaker moved to Mendocino County in the early 1950s, establishing a ranch just north of Hopland that now encompasses 2,000 acres. About 10% of the land is devoted to grapes (Chardonnay and Cabernet Sauvignon are two strong suits), with olives and pears among the other plantings. Tastings take place inside the former family home or in an outdoor area with views of grapevines and a redwood grove. ✉ *550 Nelson Ranch Rd., Ukiah* ☎ *707/462–3755* ⊕ *www.nelsonfamilyvineyards.com* ⛿ *Tastings from $10.*

Rivino Winery

WINERY/DISTILLERY | The open-air tasting room and outdoor spaces at Rivino are oriented to maximize the views of the 215-acre estate's vineyard and pond. As with the architecture, owner-winemaker Jason McConnell takes a minimalist approach with his wines, all from grapes grown on-site. The Sangiovese and Sedulous blend of Merlot, Cabernet Sauvignon, and a touch of Viognier stand out, as does the Amber Eve rosé, a brisk seller. All visits are by appointment. ■TIP➔ **Talented local musicians perform some days from April through October.** ⊠ 4101 Cox Schrader Rd., Ukiah ✛ Exit 545 off U.S. 101 ☎ 707/293–4262 ⊕ www.rivino.com ⊠ Tastings from $10.

★ Testa Vineyards

WINERY/DISTILLERY | This family-owned winery sells most of its grapes—some from vines planted in the 1930s and 1940s—to notable Napa, Sonoma, and Mendocino brands but withholds some of its certified organic and biodynamic output for its small label. Winemaker Maria Testa Martinson, whose great-grandparents established Testa Ranch in 1912, makes Charbono, Carignane, Petite Sirah, old-vine Zinfandel, Cabernet Sauvignon, and other reds from grapes grown on the estate, with a few whites from outside sources. Tastings, preferably by appointment (though walk-ins might be possible), take place in or just outside in a spiffed-up former chicken coop with views of a pond and rolling vineyards. ⊠ 6400 N. State St., Calpella ✛ From Ukiah take U.S. 101 north to Exit 555A, turning right on Moore St. and left on N. State ☎ 707/485–7051 ⊕ testaranch.com ⊠ Tastings from $15 ⊘ Closed Sun.

 Restaurants

Cultivo

$$ | AMERICAN | An oasis of low-key sophistication in downtown Ukiah, Cultivo is known for inventive wood-fired pizzas (try the braised-pork or wild-boar-sausage pie or go meatless with one starring trumpet mushrooms) but also plates up oysters on the half shell, fish tacos, a kale Caesar salad (sourdough croutons make it work), and a heritage pork chop. Meals are served on thick wooden tables in the downstairs bar area and in the mezzanine; there's also sidewalk dining out front. **Known for:** something for everyone; California beers on tap; gluten-free options. ⑤ Average main: $21 ⊠ 108 W. Standley St., Ukiah ☎ 707/462–7007 ⊕ cultivorestaurant.com ⊘ Closed Sun. No lunch Mon.–Wed.

 Hotels

Vichy Springs Resort

$$$ | RESORT | The cottages and multiunit one-story buildings of this historic hot-springs resort—luminaries from Ulysses S. Grant to Nancy Pelosi have unwound here—surround a broad lawn shaded by mature manzanitas and oaks. **Pros:** rural solitude; naturally carbonated hot springs; some accommodations have full kitchens. **Cons:** pool is only heated part of the year; not a pampering-type spa; noise from nearby gun range. ⑤ Rooms from: $275 ⊠ 2605 Vichy Springs Rd., Ukiah ☎ 707/462–9515 ⊕ www.vichysprings.com ⇆ 26 rooms ⊀⊘⊦ Free breakfast.

Avenue of the Giants

74 miles northeast of Fort Bragg, 98 miles north of Ukiah.

Conservationists banded together a century ago as the Save the Redwoods League and scored a crucial victory when a memorial grove was dedicated in 1921. That grove is now part of Humboldt Redwoods State Park. About a third of the park's more than 53,000 acres contain untouched old-growth coast redwoods most easily viewed while driving the 32-mile Avenue of the Giants.

GETTING HERE AND AROUND

The Avenue of the Giants is off U.S. 101 between Exits 645 and 674. Southern Humboldt Intercity (hta.org) buses serve the area.

👁 Sights

★ Avenue of the Giants

NATIONAL/STATE PARK | FAMILY | Some of the tallest trees on Earth tower over this magnificent 32-mile stretch of two-lane blacktop, also known as Highway 254, that follows the south fork of the Eel River through Humboldt Redwoods State Park. The highway runs more or less parallel to U.S. 101 from Phillipsville in the south to the town of Pepperwood in the north. A brochure available at either end of the highway or the visitor center, 2 miles south of Weott, contains a self-guided tour, with short and long hikes through various redwood groves. A trail at **Founders Grove** passes by several impressive trees, among them the fallen 362-foot-long Dyerville Giant, whose root base points skyward 35 feet. The tree can be reached via a short trail that begins 4 miles north of the visitor center. About 6 miles north of the center lies Rockefeller Forest. The largest remaining old-growth coast redwood forest, it contains more than a third of the 100 tallest trees in the world. ✉ *Humboldt Redwoods State Park Visitor Center, 17119 Ave. of the Giants, Weott* ☎ *707/946–2263* ⊕ *www.parks.ca.gov/humboldtredwoods* 🎟 *Free; $8 day-use fee for Williams Grove.*

Briceland Vineyards

WINERY/DISTILLERY | Lean yet flavorful Humboldt County Pinot Noirs are the specialty of this winery set amid the trees. In good weather, the low-key tastings take place in front of the weathered original winery building. Guests sip Chardonnay, Sauvignon Blanc, or other whites before sampling Pinots and perhaps Syrah or Zinfandel. ■ **TIP→** From late May through August, drop-ins are welcome 3–6 on weekends; otherwise tastings are by appointment. ✉ *5959 Briceland Rd., 10½ miles southwest of Ave. of the Giants southern entrance* ✛ *Take Briceland Rd. 5½ miles west from Redwood Dr. in Redway (from north, U.S. 101 Exit 642; from south, Exit 639B)* ☎ *707/923–2429* ⊕ *bricelandvineyards.com* 🎟 *Tastings $20.*

🛏 Hotels

Scotia Lodge

$$ | HOTEL | Eureka-based entrepreneurs passionate about providing safe legal places for patrons to enjoy cannabis products renovated a century-old logging hotel near the northern Avenue of the Giants entrance into a hip, stylish hub welcoming all travelers. **Pros:** snappy reboot of historic property; some adjoining rooms; restaurant's comfort food includes vegan- and gluten-free items. **Cons:** some rooms a little dark; pot vibe may not work for all travelers; a tad pricey for the area. ⑤ *Rooms from: $185* ✉ *100 Main St.* ☎ *707/783–3059* ⊕ *www.scotia-lodge.com* ⤴ *22 rooms* ⦿ *No meals.*

Eureka

33 miles north of Avenue of the Giants north entrance.

An excellent place to fuel up, buy groceries, and learn a little about the region's mining, timber, and fishing pasts, historic Eureka was named after a gold miner's hearty exclamation. The county visitor center has maps of self-guided walking tours of the town's nearly 100 Victorians. Art galleries and antiques stores liven up the Old Town district from C to N Street between the waterfront and 4th Street, and a walking pier extends into the harbor.

GETTING HERE AND AROUND

Eureka is set along the North Coast's main north–south highway, U.S. 101. Give yourself about 45 minutes to drive to Kuchel Visitor Center, at the park's south end.

ESSENTIALS

VISITOR INFORMATION Humboldt County Visitors Bureau. ✉ *322 1st St.* ☎ *707/443–5097, 800/346–3482* ⊕ *www.visitredwoods.com.*

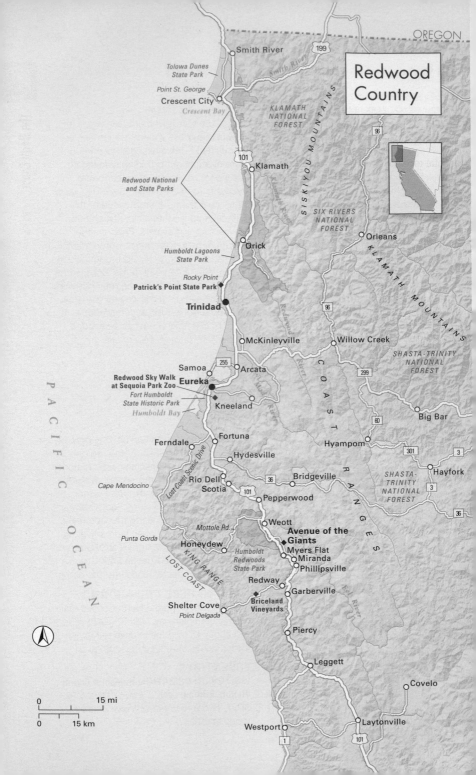

Sights

Blue Ox Millworks

FACTORY | This woodshop is among a handful in the country specializing in Victorian-era architecture, but what makes it truly unique is that its craftspeople use antique tools to do the work. Visitors can watch artisans use printing presses, lathes, and other equipment to create gingerbread trim, fence pickets, and other signature Victorian embellishments. The shop is less interesting on Saturday, when most craftspeople take the day off. ⊠ *1 X St.* ☎ *707/444–3437* ⊕ *www.blueoxmill.com* 🖃 *$12* ⊗ *Closed Sun. and Dec.–Mar., Sat.*

Lost Coast Scenic Drive

SCENIC DRIVE | A loop drive counterclockwise from the town of Ferndale, 20 miles south of Eureka, yields astounding ocean views and winds through forests and small towns before heading into Humboldt Redwoods State Park and then back up U.S. 101 toward the starting point. The road has numerous curves and some rugged stretches are in need of repair, but driving this 100-or-so-mile route is exhilarating. ■ **TIP→ Allot four hours for this excursion.** ✛ *From Ferndale, head southwest on Wildcat Ave., which soon becomes Mattole Rd. Follow Mattole west to the coast, south to Petrolia, and east to Honeydew and the park. At U.S. 101 return north to Ferndale or Eureka.* ⊕ *visitredwoods.com/listing/lost-coast-scenic-drive/148.*

★ Redwood Sky Walk at Sequoia Park Zoo

ZOO | FAMILY | Stroll as high as 100 feet above the forest floor on the elevated walkway, an instant hit following its 2021 debut at California's oldest zoo. Although relatively small, Sequoia Park, which opened in 1907, is conservation-focused and fully accredited. Favorite areas for wildlife viewing include the red panda exhibit, a barnyard petting zoo, and a walk-in aviary with local and exotic birds. ⊠ *3414 W St.* ☎ *707/441–4263* ⊕ *redwoodskywalk.com* 🖃 *$25* ⊗ *Closed Mon.*

Restaurants

★ Brick & Fire Bistro

$$ | MODERN AMERICAN | Nearly every seat in this urbane downtown bistro has a view of its most important feature—a wood-fired brick oven used to prepare everything from local Kumamoto oysters and creatively topped pizzas to wild-mushroom cobbler. Even the "fries," char-roasted potatoes tossed in olive oil and spices, come out of the oven, with grilled meats and seafood rounding out the menu. **Known for:** house-made sausage pizzas; polenta lasagna and (lunch only) vegetarian eggplant "blt"; affiliated 2 Doors Down wine bar is just steps away. ⑤ *Average main: $23* ⊠ *1630 F St.* ☎ *707/268–8959* ⊕ *www.brickandfirebistro.com* ⊗ *Closed Tues. No lunch weekends.*

Café Waterfront

$$ | SEAFOOD | Amid Old Town's vibrant dining district, this rollicking spot in what served as a saloon and brothel in the 1950s turns out consistently fresh locally caught seafood. Steamed clams, grilled snapper, oyster burgers, and chowders are all on the menu—one of the West Coast's top oyster beds, in the bay across the street, supplies the oysters on the half shell. **Known for:** historic vibe and Old Town setting; excellent locally sourced oysters (raw and grilled); homemade clam chowder. ⑤ *Average main: $21* ⊠ *102 F St.* ☎ *707/443–9190* ⊕ *www.cafewaterfronteureka.com.*

Hotels

★ Carter House Inns

$$ | HOTEL | Richly painted and aglow with wood detailing, the rooms, in two main Victorian buildings and several historic cottages, contain a mix of modern and antique furnishings; some have whirlpool tubs and separate sitting areas. **Pros:** elegant ambience; attention to detail; superb on-site Restaurant 301. **Cons:** not suitable for children; restaurant is a bit pricey; two-night minimum on weekends. $ *Rooms from: $195* ⊠ *301 L St.* ☎ *707/444–8062, 800/404–1390* ⊕ *www.carterhouse.com* ➯ *33 rooms* ⦿ *Free breakfast.*

Trinidad

23 miles north of Eureka.

A mellow base for exploring the southern portion of Redwood National and State Parks, coastal Trinidad got its name from the Spanish mariners who entered the bay on Trinity Sunday, June 9, 1775. Formerly the principal trading post for mining camps along the Klamath and Trinity rivers, these days Trinidad is a quiet and genuinely charming community with several beaches and a small but impressive selection of restaurants and romantic inns.

GETTING HERE AND AROUND

Trinidad sits right off U.S. 101, about 10 miles north of Highway 299.

Sights

Patrick's Point State Park

BEACH—SIGHT | This park on a forested plateau almost 200 feet above the surf offers stunning views of the Pacific, great whale- and sea lion–watching spots, campgrounds, picnic areas, bike paths, and hiking trails through old-growth spruce forest. There are also tidal pools at Agate Beach, a re-created Yurok Indian village, and a small visitor center with exhibits. It's uncrowded and sublimely quiet here. Dogs are not allowed on trails or the beach. ⊠ *4150 Patricks Point Dr.* ✛ *Off U.S. 101, 5 miles north of town* ☎ *707/677–3570* ⊕ *www.parks.ca.gov* ⊠ *$8 parking.*

Restaurants

★ Larrupin' Cafe

$$$$ | AMERICAN | Set in a two-story house on a quiet country road north of town, this casually sophisticated restaurant— one of the North Coast's best places

to eat—is often packed with people enjoying mesquite-grilled fresh seafood, beef brisket, St. Louis–style ribs, and vegetarian dishes. The garden setting and candlelight stir thoughts of romance. **Known for:** refined but friendly service; rosemary-crusted garlic, Cambozola cheese, and toast points appetizer; superb wine list. $ *Average main: $37* ⊠ *1658 Patricks Point Dr.* ☎ *707/677– 0230* ⊕ *www.larrupin.com* ⊗ *No lunch.*

Trinidad Bay Eatery & Gallery

$$ | SEAFOOD | A short stroll from Trinidad's bayfront, this unpretentious combination gallery and seafood-oriented restaurant cooks up tasty meals, starting with breakfast's buttermilk pancakes and Dungeness crab Benedict. Burgers, crab Louie salads, and clam chowder star at lunch; for dinner, consider the starter of ahi poke with crème fraîche, followed by lemon-caper calamari steak, red-coconut-curry scallops, or cioppino in chipotle broth. **Known for:** well-curated wine list; cioppino in chipotle broth; blackberry cobbler. $ *Average main: $21* ⊠ *607 Parker St.* ☎ *707/677–3777* ⊕ *www. trinidadeatery.com.*

🛏 Hotels

Lost Whale Inn

$$$ | B&B/INN | For a romantic, special-occasion getaway, look to this intimate, luxurious inn perched on a seaside bluff near Patrick's Point State Park. **Pros:** stunning ocean views; elaborate and delicious breakfast spread; spa services, in-room or out on the lawn, are offered. **Cons:** no pets allowed (but you'll find a few adorable pets residing at the inn); 2-night minimum on summer weekends; sometimes books up fully for weddings. $ *Rooms from: $300* ⊠ *3452 Patricks Point Dr.* ☎ *707/677–3425* ⊕ *www.lostwhaleinn. com* ➯ *8 rooms* ⦿ *Free breakfast.*

Chapter 14

REDWOOD NATIONAL AND STATE PARKS

Updated by
Andrew Collins

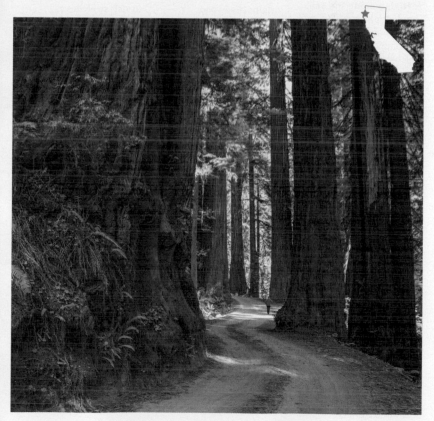

🏕 Camping	🛏 Hotels	🏃 Activities	👁 Scenery	👥 Crowds
★★★☆☆	★★★★☆	★★★★☆	★★★★★	★★★★☆

WELCOME TO REDWOOD NATIONAL AND STATE PARKS

TOP REASONS TO GO

★ **Giant trees:** These mature coastal redwoods, which you can hike beneath in numerous groves throughout the park, are the tallest trees in the world.

★ **Hiking along the sea:** The park offers many miles of ocean access, including the Coastal Trail, which runs along the western edge of the park.

★ **Rare wildlife:** Mighty Roosevelt elk favor the park's flat prairie and open lands; seldom-seen black bears roam the backcountry; trout and salmon leap through streams; and Pacific gray whales swim along the coast during their spring and fall migrations.

★ **Stepping back in time:** Hike mossy and mysterious Fern Canyon Trail and explore a prehistoric scene of lush vegetation and giant ferns—a memorable scene in *Jurassic Park 2* was shot here.

★ **Getting off-the-grid:** Amid the majestic redwoods you're usually out of cell phone range and often free from crowds, offering a rare opportunity to disconnect.

1 South. The highlights of the parks' southern section are the hikes and scenic driving along Bald Hills Road, including the Lady Bird Johnson Grove, and the beautiful coastal scenery at Thomas H. Kuchel Visitor Center and the estuarial lagoons to the south. This section encompasses much of the original Redwood National Park and is where you'll find the small village of Orick, which has a gas station and a few other basic services.

2 Middle. Here in the span of park that extends from north of Orick to the Yurok tribal community of Klamath, you'll find some of the most magnificent and accessible stands of old-growth redwoods. Start your adventures at Prairie Creek Redwoods State Park's visitor center, from which several trails emanate. Also set aside time to explore the meadows inhabited by Roosevelt elk, the trail to Fern Canyon from Gold Bluffs Beach, and the gorgeous drives along Newton B. Drury Scenic Parkway and Klamath's Coastal Drive Loop

3 North. Anchored by the region's largest community, Crescent City, the park's northern third encompasses the rugged, pristine forests of Jedediah Smith Redwoods State Park, which is slightly inland, and Del Norte Coast Redwoods State Park, which also offers visitors the chance to visit stretches of windswept beaches, steep sea cliffs, and forested ridges. On a clear day it's postcard-perfect; with fog, it's mysterious and mesmerizing.

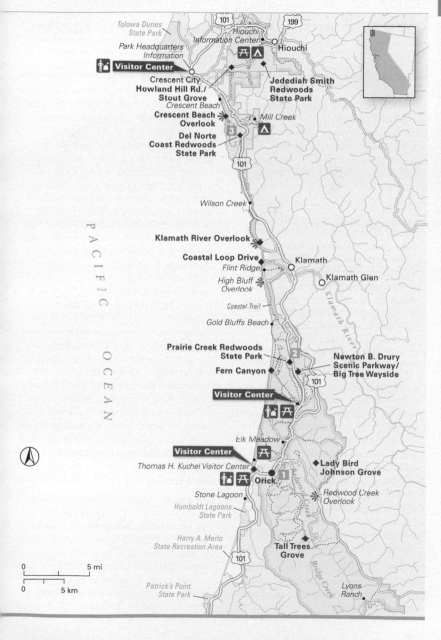

Soaring more than 375 feet high, California's coastal redwoods are miracles of efficiency—some have survived hundreds of years, a few more than two millennia.

These massive trees glean nutrients from the rich alluvial flats at their feet and from the moisture and nitrogen trapped in their uneven canopy. Their thick bark can hold thousands of gallons of water, which has helped them withstand centuries of fires.

Redwood differs from other national parks, in that it's administered by a joint partnership between the National Park Service and the California Department of Parks and Recreation. This sprawling 139,000-acre park system has a footprint that extends nearly 50 miles up the coast, encompasses three state parks, and snakes in and around a handful of towns and small cities, including Orick, Klamath, and Crescent City.

Indigenous people have been stewards of this special ecosystem for millennia—hunting, fishing, and foraging the land early on, and in more recent centuries harvesting timber from downed redwoods to build homes. Despite the cruel efforts of gold prospectors and loggers who in the 1850s arrived and swiftly began trying to eradicate them, the region's native communities survived and continue to this day to thrive here. Both the Yurok and Tolowa tribes have large land holdings within the borders of the Redwood National and State Parks (RNSP) system.

Northern California's gold rush immediately transformed the natural landscape. Large-scale logging, aided by rapid technological advances, reduced the region's

2 million acres of old-growth redwoods by nearly 90% in a little over a century—only about 5% of the old-growth forest remains today. Fortunately, by the 1910s, a small but determined conservation-minded minority began lobbying to protect these special trees, beginning with the formation of the Save-the-Redwoods League, whose efforts helped to establish Del Norte Coast Redwoods and Prairie Creek Redwoods state parks in 1925, and Jedediah Smith Redwoods State Park in 1939 (these successes came on the heels of the 1921 designation of Humboldt Redwoods State Park, which is about 30 miles southeast of Eureka and not part of RNSP). A huge demand for lumber, particularly following World War II, continued to deplete the unprotected tracts of forest, which led the federal government to establish Redwood National Park in 1968. Finally, in 1994, federal and state agencies officially joined forces to manage the newly designated Redwood National and State Parks, whose mission is both to preserve uncut old-growth redwood forest and to restore and replant some significant sections that have already been logged.

The easiest way to approach exploring the rather vast and complex RNSP system is to divide it geographically into North, Middle, and South sections, each of which contains at least one visitor center. Crescent City is in the North, as are two of the three state parks—Jedediah Smith Redwoods and Del Norte Coast Redwoods. The town of Klamath is

AVERAGE HIGH/LOW TEMPERATURES					
JAN.	FEB.	MAR.	APR.	MAY	JUNE
54/39	56/41	57/41	59/42	62/45	65/48
JULY	AUG.	SEPT.	OCT.	NOV.	DEC.
67/51	67/51	68/49	64/46	58/43	55/40

in the Middle section, as is Prairie Creek Redwoods State Park. And the village of Orick is in the South, which also contains much of the original national park, although you'll find other sections of it in the Middle and North sections, too. Additionally, there are four coastal parks just south of RNSP: Humboldt Lagoons State Park, Harry A. Merlo State Recreation Area, Big Lagoon Beach and County Park, and Patrick's Point State Park. U.S. 101 is the main north–south route through the park, but the northern section is also bisected by a short stretch of U.S. 199 east of Crescent City.

Some park attractions, scenic drives, and trails are in the national park, and others are in state parks, but as you explore, it's difficult—and not particularly important—to know which section you're in. Just adhere to the excellent map in the free park brochure and visitor guide newspaper, and you'll easily figure out where you're going and how to get around this magnificent preserve that aims to protect one of the world's oldest and largest living things.

Planning

When to Go

Campers and hikers flock to the park from mid-June to early September. The crowds disappear in winter, but you'll have to contend with frequent rains and nasty potholes and even occasional closures on side roads. Temperatures fluctuate widely: the foggy coastal lowland is much cooler than the higher-altitude interior.

The average annual rainfall is between 60 and 80 inches, most of it falling between November and April. During the dry summer, thick fog rolling in from the Pacific can veil the forests, providing the redwoods a large portion of their moisture intake.

Getting Here and Around

AIR

United Airlines flies a few times daily between San Francisco and the most practical gateway, California Redwood Coast–Humboldt County Airport, between Trinidad and Arcata, about 16 miles north of Eureka. The regional carrier Contour offers daily service from Oakland to Del Norte County Regional Airport in Crescent City. Another option is Oregon's Rogue Valley International Medford Airport, which is served by Alaska, Allegiant, American, Delta, and United, and is about a two-hour drive from the northern end of the park in Crescent City.

CAR

U.S. 101 runs north–south nearly the entire length of the park. You can access all the main park roads via U.S. 101 and U.S. 199, which runs east–west through the park's northern portion. Many roads within the park aren't paved, and winter rains can turn them into obstacle courses; sometimes they're closed completely. Motor homes/RVs and trailers aren't permitted on some routes. The drive from San Francisco to the park's southern end takes about six hours via U.S. 101. From Portland it takes roughly the same

Redwood in One Day

From Crescent City head south on U.S. 101, pausing for a stroll overlooking the ocean either at **Crescent Beach** or a little farther south with a short stroll along the **Yurok Loop Trail.** A mile south of Klamath, detour onto the 9-mile-long, narrow, and mostly unpaved **Coastal Drive** loop. Along the way, you'll pass the old **Douglas Memorial Bridge**, destroyed in the 1964 flood. Coastal Drive turns south above Flint Ridge. In less than a mile you'll reach the **World War II B-71 Radar Station**, which looks like a farmhouse, its disguise in the 1940s. Continue south to the intersection with Alder Camp Road, stopping at the **High Bluff Overlook**—keep an eye out for whales during the winter and spring migrations.

Back on U.S. 101, head south to reach **Newton B. Drury Scenic Parkway**, a 10-mile drive through one of the park's best and most accessible expanses of old-growth redwood forest. Stop at **Prairie Creek Visitor Center**, housed in a small redwood lodge. Enjoy a picnic lunch and an engaging tactile walk in a grove behind the lodge on the Revelation Trail, which was designed for vision-impaired visitors, or if you have an hour or two, hike the stunning 3½-mile **Prairie Creek–Big Tree–Cathedral Trees Loop.** Return to U.S. 101, and turn west on mostly

unpaved **Davison Road**, checking out **Elk Meadow** on your left, where you'll sometimes see a portion of the park's Roosevelt elk herd roaming about. In about 30 minutes you'll curve right to **Gold Bluffs Beach**. Continue north a short way and make the hike into lush and spectacular **Fern Canyon**. Return to U.S. 101, and drive south to the turnoff onto **Bald Hills Road**, and follow it for 2 miles to the **Lady Bird Johnson Grove Nature Loop Trail**. Take the footbridge to the easy 1.4-mile loop, which follows an old logging road through a mature redwood forest. If you have an extra hour, continue south on Bald Hills Road to **Redwood Creek Overlook** or even all the way to 3,097-foot **Schoolhouse Peak**, before backtracking to U.S. 101 and driving south through Orick to the **Thomas H. Kuchel Visitor Center**. This is a beautiful spot late in the day to watch the sunset over the ocean. Note that if you're approaching the park from Trinidad or Eureka, it's easy to undertake this itinerary in reverse. ■TIP→ **Motor homes/RVs and trailers are not allowed on Coastal Drive or Davison Road and are not advised on Bald Hills Road. Conditions on these roads can sometimes lead to closures or the requirement of high-clearance vehicles—check with the visitor centers before you set out.**

amount of time to reach the park's northern section via Interstate 5 to U.S. 199. ■TIP→ **Don't rely solely on GPS, which is inaccurate in parts of the park; closely consult official park maps.**

Park Essentials

PARK FEES AND PERMITS

Admission to Redwood National Park is free; a few areas in the state parks collect day-use fees of $8, including the Gold Bluffs Beach and Fern Canyon sections of Prairie Creek Redwoods State Park, and the day-use areas accessed via the campground entrances in Jedediah Smith and Del Norte Coast state parks (the fee for camping overnight is $35). To visit the popular Tall Trees Grove, you must get a free permit at the Kuchel Visitor Center in Orick. Free permits, available at the Kuchel, Crescent City, and (summer only) Hiouchi visitor centers, are needed to stay at all designated backcountry camps.

PARK HOURS
The park is open year-round, 24 hours a day.

CELL PHONE RECEPTION
It's difficult to pick up a signal in much of the park, especially in the camping areas and on many hiking trails. The Prairie Creek and Jedediah Smith visitor centers have pay phones.

Hotels

The only lodgings within park grounds are the Elk Meadow Cabins, near Prairie Creek Redwoods Visitor Center. Orick, to the south of Elk Meadow, and Klamath, to the north, have basic motels, and in Klamath there's also the charming and historic Requa Inn. Elegant Victorian inns, seaside motels, and fully equipped vacation rentals are among the options in Crescent City to the north, and Eureka and to a more limited extent Trinidad and Arcata to the south. In summer, try to book at least a week ahead at lodgings near the park.

Restaurants

The park has no restaurants, but Eureka and Arcata have diverse dining establishments—everything from hip oyster bars to some surprisingly good ethnic restaurants. The dining options are more limited, though decent, in Crescent City and Trinidad, and there are just a couple of very basic options in Klamath and tiny

Orick. Most small-town restaurants close early, around 7:30 or 8 pm.

Hotel and restaurant reviews have been shortened. For full information visit Fodors.com. Hotel prices are the lowest cost of a standard double room in high season. Restaurant prices are the average cost of a main course at dinner, or if dinner is not served, at lunch

What It Costs			
$	$$	$$$	$$$$
RESTAURANTS			
under $17	$17–$26	$27–$36	over $36
HOTELS			
under $150	$150–$250	$251–$350	over $350

Visitor Information

CONTACTS Redwood National and State Parks Headquarters. ⊠ *1111 2nd St., Crescent City* ☎ *707/465–7306* ⊕ *www.nps.gov/redw.*

South

19 miles north of Trinidad, 8 miles south of Prairie Creek Visitor Center, 44 miles south of Crescent City.

This is the section of the park system that you'll reach if driving up the coast from Eureka and Trinidad, and it's home to one of the largest visitor information resources, the beachfront Thomas H. Kuchel Visitor Center, which is on U.S. 101 shortly after you enter the park. For the purposes of this chapter, this section includes the town of Orick and everything else south of the turnoff onto Bald Hills Road, which leads to some of the largest stands of redwoods in the park, including the Lady Bird Johnson and Tall Trees groves.

Sights

SCENIC DRIVES
Bald Hills Road

SCENIC DRIVE | A winding, steep, and dramatic road that stretches into the park's southernmost section and highest elevations, Bald Hills Road accesses some great hikes—Lady Bird Johnson Grove and Lyons Ranch among them—as well as the access road to the Tall Trees Grove. But it's also wondrously scenic route all on its own, passing through sometimes misty patch of redwoods before entering a stretch of open meadows with wildflowers in spring and the chance to see Roosevelt elk and bears any time of year. Do stop at Redwood Creek Overlook, a 2,100-foot elevation pullout at mile 6.6. Bald Hills Road is paved for the first 13 miles. It continues another 4 miles unpaved to the park's southern boundary, and it's then possible to continue another 20 miles or so to the small village of Weitchpec and then onward inland toward Redding or Yreka. ⊠ *Off U.S. 101, Orick.*

TRAILS
★ Lady Bird Johnson Grove Trail

TRAIL | One of the park's most accessible spots to view big trees, this impressive grove just a short drive northeast of Orick was dedicated by, and named for, the former first lady. A level 1.4-mile nature loop crosses a neat old wooden footbridge and follows an old logging road through this often mist-shrouded forest of redwoods. *Easy.* ⊠ *Orick* ✛ *Trailhead: Bald Hills Rd., 2 miles east of U.S. 101.*

Lyons Ranch Trail

TRAIL | You won't see redwoods on this open upper-elevation 3.7-mile round-trip trail, but on summer days when the coast is socked in with rain or fog, an adventure to this typically sunny prairie at the park's southeastern boundary is highly rewarding, as is the steep—but slow—17-mile drive on Bald Hills Road. The trail leads hikers to a former sheep and cattle ranch with a few interesting old outbuildings that date to the turn-of-the-20th-century. *Moderate.* ⊠ *Redwood National Park* ✛ *Trailhead: Off Bald Hills Rd., 17 miles south of U.S. 101.*

Tall Trees Trail

TRAIL | Although every bit as beautiful as the other stands of old-growth redwood in the park, getting to this roughly 30-acre grove requires a steep and windy 14-mile drive, followed by a somewhat rigorous 4-mile round-trip hike that involves an 800-foot descent into the Redwood Creek flood plain. Additionally, you must obtain a free permit at the Kuchel Visitor Center to access the unpaved road off of Bald Hills Road. Rangers dispense a limited number per day, first come, first served. No trailers or RVs. Given the effort required, if you don't have a lot of time, it's best to save this one for your second or third visit. *Moderate.* ⊠ *Orick* ✛ *Trailhead: Tall Trees Access Rd., off Bald Hills Rd., 7 miles from U.S. 101, then 6½ miles to trailhead.*

VISITOR CENTER
★ Thomas H. Kuchel Visitor Center

INFO CENTER | **FAMILY** | The park's southern section contains this largest and best of the Redwoods visitor centers. Rangers here dispense brochures, advice, and free permits to drive up the access road to Tall Trees Grove. Whale-watchers find the center's deck an excellent observation point, and bird-watchers enjoy the nearby Freshwater Lagoon, a popular layover for migrating waterfowl. Many of the center's exhibits are hands-on and kid-friendly. ⊠ *U.S. 101, Orick* ✛ *Redwood Creek Beach County Park* ☎ *707/465–7765* ⊕ *www.nps.gov/redw.*

Middle

8 miles north of Thomas H. Kuchel Visitor Center, 34 miles south of Crescent City.

Encompassing a relatively narrow band of coastal forest that extends north of Orick (starting around Elk Meadow) to north of Klamath (up to Requa Road), the park's middle section is home to one of the most magical places to stroll through a redwood forest, Prairie Creek State Park, which is laced with both easy and challenging trails and traversed by the stunning Newton B. Drury Scenic Parkway. Near the visitor center and in nearby Elk Meadow, you can often view herds of Roosevelt elk. The state park extends west to famously spectacular Gold Bluffs Beach and Fern Canyon on the coast. The middle section's other highlight are the sections of the park along both sides of the Klamath River, including Coastal Drive and Klamath River Overlook.

 ## Sights

SCENIC DRIVES
★ Coastal Drive Loop
SCENIC DRIVE | The 9-mile, narrow, and partially unpaved Coastal Drive Loop takes about 45 minutes to traverse. Weaving through stands of redwoods, the road yields close-up views of the Klamath River and expansive panoramas of the Pacific. Recurring landslides have closed sections of the original road; this loop, closed to trailers and RVs, is all that remains. Hikers access the Flint Ridge section of the Coastal Trail off the drive. ⊠ *Klamath* ⊕ *Off Klamath Beach Rd. exit from U.S. 101.*

★ Newton B. Drury Scenic Parkway
SCENIC DRIVE | This paved 10-mile route threads through Prairie Creek Redwoods State Park and old-growth redwoods. It's open to all noncommercial vehicles. Great stops along the route include the 0.8-mile walk to Big Tree Wayside and observing Roosevelt elk in the

prairie—both of these are near the Prairie Creek Visitor Center. ⊠ *Orick* ⊕ *Entrances off U.S. 101 about 5 miles south of Klamath and 5 miles north of Orick.*

SCENIC STOPS
★ Fern Canyon
CANYON | Enter another world and be surrounded by 50-foot canyon walls covered with sword, deer, and five-finger ferns. Allow an hour to explore the ¼-mile-long vertical garden along a 0.7-mile loop. From the northern end of Gold Bluffs Beach it's an easy walk, although you'll have to wade across or scamper along planks that traverse a small stream several times (in addition to driving across a couple of streams on the way to the parking area). But the lush, otherworldly surroundings, which appeared in *Jurassic Park 2,* are a must-see when creeks aren't running too high. Motor homes/RVs and all trailers are prohibited. You can also hike to the canyon from Prairie Creek Visitor Center along the challenging West Ridge–Friendship Ridge–James Irvine Loop, 12½ miles round-trip. ⊠ *Orick* ⊕ *2¾ miles north of Orick, take Davison Rd. northwest off U.S. 101 and follow signs to Gold Bluffs Beach.*

Klamath River Overlook
VIEWPOINT | This grassy, windswept bluff rises 650 feet above the confluence of the Klamath River and the Pacific. It's one of the best spots in the park for spying migratory whales in early winter and late spring, and it accesses a section of the Coastal Trail. Warm days are ideal for picnicking at one of the tables. ⊠ *End of Requa Rd., Klamath* ⊕ *2¼ miles west of U.S. 101.*

TRAILS
★ Coastal Trail
TRAIL | This gorgeous 70-mile trail, much of it along dramatic bluffs high above the crashing surf, can be tackled in both short, relatively easy sections and longer, strenuous spans that entail backcountry overnight camping. Here are some of the most alluring smaller sections, listed in order from north to south, which are

accessible at well-marked trailheads. The moderate-to-difficult **DeMartin section** (accessed from mile marker 15.6 on U.S. 101) leads south past 6 miles of old-growth redwoods and through sweeping prairie. It connects with the moderate 5½-mile-long **Klamath section,** which proceeds south from Wilson Creek Picnic Area to Klamath River Overlook, with a short detour to Hidden Beach and its tide pools, providing coastal views and whale-watching opportunities. If you're up for a real workout, hike the brutally difficult but stunning **Flint Ridge section** (accessed from the Old Douglas Memorial Bridge Site on Klamath Beach Rd.), with its 4½ miles of steep grades and numerous switchbacks past Marshall Pond and through stands of old-growth redwoods. There are additional spans at the northern and southern ends of the park. *Moderate.* ⊠ *Klamath.*

★ Prairie Creek–Big Tree–Cathedral Trees Loop

TRAIL | FAMILY | This flat, well-maintained 3½-mile loop starts and ends at the Prairie Creek Visitor Center and passes beneath some of the most awe-inspiring redwoods in the park. The 1-mile section along the Prairie Creek Trail fringes a babbling brook; you then cross Newton B. Drury Scenic Parkway, turn south onto the Cathedral Trees Trail and make a short detour along the 0.3-mile Big Tree Loop before meandering south and west through yet more gorgeous old-growth forest. Options for extending your hike include walking 1½ miles up Cal-Barrel Road (an old, unpaved logging route), and then looping back 2 miles on the Rhododendron Trail to rejoin Cathedral Trees. *Easy–Moderate.* ⊠ *Orick* ✛ *Trailhead: Prairie Creek Visitor Center.*

Trillium Falls Trail

TRAIL | FAMILY | On this lush trek through a mix of old-growth redwoods, ferns, smaller deciduous trees, and some clusters of trillium flowers, you'll encounter the pretty cascades that give the hike

its name after the first ½ mile. It's worth continuing on, though, and making the full 2.8-mile loop, as the southern end of the hike offers the best views of soaring redwoods. Herds of elk sometimes roam in the meadow by the trailhead. *Easy–Moderate.* ⊠ *Orick* ✛ *Trailhead: Elk Meadow parking lot, Davison Rd., just west of U.S. 101.*

VISITOR CENTER

★ Prairie Creek Visitor Center

INFO CENTER | FAMILY | A massive stone fireplace anchors this small redwood lodge with wildlife displays that include a section of a tree a young elk died beside. Because of the peculiar way the redwood grew around the elk's skull, the tree appears to have antlers. The center has information about interpretive programs as well as a gift shop, a picnic area, restrooms, and exhibits on flora and fauna. Roosevelt elk often roam the vast field adjacent to the center, and several trailheads begin nearby. Stretch your legs with an easy stroll along **Revelation Trail,** a short loop that starts behind the lodge. ⊠ *Prairie Creek Rd., Orick* ✛ *Off southern end of Newton B. Drury Scenic Pkwy.* ☎ *707/488–2039* ⊕ *www.nps.gov/redw.*

Hotels

★ Elk Meadow Cabins

$$$ | B&B/INN | FAMILY | From the porches of these beautifully restored 1,200-square-foot former mill workers' cottages, guests often see Roosevelt elk meandering in the meadows—or even their backyards. **Pros:** elks frequently congregate on the grounds; perfect for groups or families; adjacent to stunning Prairie Creek State Park. **Cons:** a bit of a drive from most area restaurants; expensive for just two occupants, though reasonable for families or groups; furnishings are comfortable but plain. ⑤ *Rooms from: $314* ⊠ *7 Valley Green Camp Rd., off U.S. 101 north of Davison Rd., Orick* ☎ *707/488–2222, 866/733–9637* ⊕ *www.elkmeadowcabins. com* ➬ *9 cabins* ❢◎❢ *No meals.*

Redwood trees, and the moss that often coats them, grow best in damp, shady environments.

North

34 miles north of Prairie Creek Redwoods State Park, 84 miles north of Eureka, 73 miles south of Grants Pass, OR, 133 miles south of Coos Bay, OR.

Home to the small city of Crescent City, which is also where you'll find the Redwood National and State Parks headquarters, the North is home to two state parks: Del Norte Redwoods and Jedediah Smith Redwoods. Del Norte lies 5 miles south of Crescent City on U.S. 101 and contains 15 memorial redwood groves and 8 miles of pristine coastline, which you can most easily access at Crescent Beach and Wilson Beach. Jedediah Smith is 5 miles east of Crescent City on U.S. 199 and is home to the legendary Stout Memorial Grove, along with some 20 miles of hiking and nature trails. The park is named after a trapper who in 1826 became the first white man to explore Northern California's interior. If coming from interior Oregon, this is your first chance to drive and hike among stands of soaring redwoods.

Sights

SCENIC DRIVES

★ Howland Hill Road through Stout Grove

SCENIC DRIVE | Take your time as you drive this 10-mile route along Mill Creek, which meanders within inches of the hulking trunks of old-growth redwoods and past the Smith River. Trailers and RVs are prohibited on this route, which is unpaved but well maintained for the roughly 7 miles that pass through Jedediah Smith Redwoods State Park. There are several pull-outs along the route, including the trailheads for the Stout Grove and Boy Scout Tree trails. You can enter either from downtown Crescent Road or off U.S. 199, via South Fork and Douglas Park Roads. ⊕ *Western access from Elk Valley Rd. in Crescent City.*

Plants and Wildlife in Redwood

Coast redwoods, the world's tallest trees, grow in the moist, temperate climate of California's North Coast. The current record holder, named Hyperion, tops out at 380 feet and was found in the Redwood Creek watershed in 2006. These ancient giants thrive in an environment that exists in only a few hundred coastal miles along the Pacific Ocean. They commonly live 600 years—though some have been around for more than 2,000 years.

Diverse, Complex

A healthy redwood forest is diverse and includes Douglas firs, western hemlocks, tan oaks, and madrone trees. The complex soils of the forest floor support a profusion of ferns, mosses, and fungi, along with numerous shrubs and berry bushes. In spring, California rhododendron bloom all over, providing a dazzling purple and pink contrast to the dense greenery.

Old-Growth Forests

Redwood National and State parks hold nearly 50% of California's old-growth redwood forests, but only about a third of the forests in the park are old-growth. Of the original 3,125 square miles (2 million acres) in the Redwoods Historic Range, only 4% survived logging that began in 1850. A quarter of these trees are privately owned and on managed land. The rest are on public tracts.

Wildlife Species

In the park's backcountry, you might spot mountain lions, black bears, black-tailed deer, river otters, beavers, and minks. Roosevelt elk roam the flatlands, and the rivers and streams teem with salmon and trout. Gray whales, seals, and sea lions cavort near the coastline. More than 280 species of birds have been recorded in the park, which is located along the Pacific Flyway. A plan is also underway to reintroduce California condors to the park by 2022.

SCENIC STOPS

Crescent Beach Overlook

VIEWPOINT | The scenery here includes views of the ocean and, in the distance, Crescent City and its working harbor. In balmy weather this is a great place for a picnic. You may spot migrating gray whales between November and April. ⊠ *Enderts Beach Rd.* ✛ *4½ miles south of Crescent City.*

TRAILS

★ Boy Scout Tree Trail

TRAIL | This is the most challenging but also the most rewarding of the hikes along Howland Hill Road. Give yourself about three hours to complete this 5.6-mile round-trip trek to verdant Fern Falls, as the old-growth redwoods along this tranquil trek are absolutely magnificent.

If you don't have as much time, the easy ½-mile-loop Stout Grove Trail is a good alternative along this route. *Moderate.* ⊠ *Crescent City* ✛ *Trailhead: Howland Hill Rd., 3.7 miles east of Elk Valley Rd.*

Simpson-Reed Trail

TRAIL | FAMILY | Of the redwood hikes in Jedediah Smith Redwoods State Park, this flat and easy 1-mile loop through an incredibly dense forest is the best fit if you have only an hour or so. The trailhead is a short hop off U.S. 199 between Crescent City and Hiouchi, and interpretative signs tell a bit about the diverse flora— you'll encounter hemlocks, huckleberries, and lots and lots of ferns along this route. *Easy.* ⊠ *Crescent City* ✛ *Trailhead: Walker Rd., off U.S. 199, 2.5 miles east of U.S. 101.*

KEY

- 🏚 Ranger Station
- ⛺ Campground
- ⛱ Picnic Area
- 🍴 Restaurant
- ⚹ Scenic Viewpoint
- State Parklands
- National Parklands

Lake Earl State Wildlife Area Headquarters

Lake Earl

Tolowa/Dunes State Park

POINT ST. GEORGE

Old Mill Rd.

Lake Earl Dr.

Simpson-Reed Grove

197

199

199

Hiouchi Information Center

Hiouchi

Elk Valley Rd.

⛱ ⛺ Information

Jedediah Smith Redwoods State Park

Stout Grove

101

Northcrest Dr.

Crescent City

Howland Hill Rd.

Little Bald Hills ⛺

Castle Rock

Park Headquarters Information

Battery Point Lighthouse

Humboldt Rd.

⛱ Crescent Beach

Enderts Beach Rd.

⛱ Crescent Beach Overlook ⚹

⛺ Nickel Creek

Enderts Beach

Mill Creek ⛺

101

P A C I F I C

Del Norte Coast Redwoods State Park

SISTER ROCKS

C O A S T

Overlook ⚹ ⛱ DeMartin ⛺

FOOTSTEPS ROCKS

R

Wilson Creek

False Klamath Cove

⛱ Lagoon Creek

A

O C E A N

N

G

101

E

Klamath River Overlook ⚹ Requa

Requa Rd.

Coastal Drive

⛺ Flint Ridge

Klamath

169

Alder Camp Rd.

⛱ High Bluff Overlook ⚹

Klamath Glen

Klamath River

Coastal Trail

0 — 3 mi

0 — 3 km

Redwood NP
Northern Areas

Yurok Loop Trail

BEACH—SIGHT | FAMILY | Providing a lovely opportunity to stretch your legs and breathe in the fresh sea air, this 1.2-mile loop starts at the Lagoon Creek Picnic Area on U.S. 101, at the very southern end of Del Norte Coast Redwoods State Park, and follows a short stretch of the California Coastal Trail. It then forks off toward False Klamath Cove, providing sweeping views of the ocean—keep an eye out for shore birds and migrating whales. Just to the north of False Klamath Cove, there's great beachcombing to be had along Wilson Creek Beach. *Easy.* ⊠ *Klamath* ✛ *Trailhead: Lagoon Creek Picnic Area on U.S. 101, 6.5 miles north of Klamath.*

VISITOR CENTERS

Crescent City Information Center

INFO CENTER | At the park's headquarters, this downtown Redding visitor center with a gift shop and picnic area is the main information stop if you're approaching the Redwoods from the north. ⊠ *1111 2nd St., Crescent City* ☎ *707/465–7335* ⊕ *www.nps.gov/redw* ⊘ *Closed Tues. and Wed. in Nov.–Mar.*

Hiouchi Information Center

INFO CENTER | This small center at Jedediah Smith Redwoods State Park has exhibits about the area flora and fauna and screens a 12-minute park film. A starting point for ranger programs, the center has restrooms and a picnic area. ⊠ *U.S. 199* ✛ *Opposite Jedediah Smith Campground, 9 miles east of Crescent City* ☎ *707/458–3294* ⊕ *www.nps.gov/ redw.*

Jedediah Smith Visitor Center

INFO CENTER | Adjacent to the Jedediah Smith Redwoods State Park main campground, this seasonal center has information about ranger-led walks and evening campfire programs. Also here are nature and history exhibits, a gift shop, and a picnic area. ⊠ *U.S. 199, Hiouchi* ✛ *At Jedediah Smith Campground* ☎ *707/458–3496* ⊕ *www.nps.gov/redw* ⊘ *Closed Oct.–May.*

Activities

BIKING

Besides the roadways, you can bike on several trails, many of them along former logging roads. Best bets include the 11-mile Lost Man Creek Trail, which begins 3 miles north of Orick; the 12-mile round-trip Coastal Trail (Last Chance Section), which starts at the southern end of Enderts Beach Road and becomes steep and narrow as it travels through dense slopes of foggy redwood forests; and the 19-mile, single-track Ossagon Trail Loop in Prairie Creek Redwoods State Park, on which you're likely to see elk as you cruise through redwoods before coasting ocean side toward the end. ■ **TIP→ You can rent electric bikes, which are especially nice for riding the hilly Lost Man Creek Trail, from Redwood Adventures (see Hiking).**

BIRD-WATCHING

Many rare and striking winged specimens inhabit the area, including chestnut-backed chickadees, brown pelicans, great blue herons, pileated woodpeckers, northern spotted owls, and marbled murrelets. By 2022, California condors are planned to be reintroduced to the park.

CAMPING

Within a 30-minute drive of Redwood National and State parks, you'll find roughly 60 public and private camping facilities. None of the primitive or backcountry areas in Redwood—DeMartin, Elam Creek, Flint Ridge, 44 Camp, Little Bald Hills, or Redwood Creek—is a drive-in site, although Flint Ridge is just a ¼-mile from the road. You must obtain a free permit from the Kuchel or Hiouchi visitor centers before camping in these areas; all are first come, first served. Bring your own drinking water—there are no sources at the sites.

Redwood has four developed, drive-in campgrounds—Elk Prairie, Gold Bluffs Beach, Jedediah Smith, and Mill

Creek, all of them within the state-park boundaries. None has RV hookups, but Jedediah Smith and Mill Creek have dump stations. Fees are $35 nightly. For reservations, contact ☎ 800/444–7275 or ⊕ www.reserveamerica.com.

DEVELOPED CAMPGROUNDS

Elk Prairie Campground. Roosevelt elk frequent this popular campground adjacent to a prairie and old-growth redwoods. ⊠ Newton B. Drury Scenic Pkwy., Prairie Creek Redwoods State Park.

Gold Bluffs Beach Campground. You can camp in tents right on the beach at this Prairie Creek Redwoods State Park campground near Fern Canyon. ⊠ End of Davison Rd., off U.S. 101.

Jedediah Smith Campground. This is one of the few places to camp—in tents or RVs—within groves of old-growth redwood forest. ⊠ 9 miles east of Crescent City on U.S. 199.

Mill Creek Campground. Redwoods tower over large Mill Creek, in the remote and quiet interior of Del Norte Coast Redwoods State Park. Open mid-May–September. ⊠ U.S. 101, 7 miles southeast of Crescent City.

EDUCATIONAL PROGRAMS
RANGER PROGRAMS

All summer long, ranger-led programs explore the mysteries of both the redwoods and the sea. Topics include how the trees grow from fleck-size seeds to towering giants, what causes those weird fungi on old stumps, why the ocean fog is so important to redwoods, and exactly what those green-tentacled creatures are that float in tide pools. Campfire programs can include slide shows, storytelling, music, and games. Check with visitor centers for offerings and times.

Junior Ranger Program

LOCAL SPORTS | FAMILY | Kids earn a badge by completing activity books, which are available from visitor centers.

Additionally, rangers lead programs for kids throughout the summer, including nature walks and lessons in bird identification and outdoor survival.

Ranger Talks

LOCAL SPORTS | From mid-May through mid-September, state park rangers regularly lead discussions on the redwoods, tide pools, geology, and Native American culture. Check schedules at the visitor centers.

Redwood EdVentures

TOUR—SIGHT | FAMILY | Fun and engaging Redwood EdVentures nature scavenger hunts for kids, called Quests, include ones in the park. Visit the website for "treasure map" PDFs detailing the Quests, which typically take no more than an hour. Participants receive a patch upon completion. ⊕ www.redwood-edventures.org.

FISHING

Deep-sea and freshwater fishing are popular here. Anglers often stake out sections of the Klamath and Smith rivers seeking salmon and trout. A single state license (⊕ www.wildlife.ca.gov/licensing/fishing) covers both ocean and river fishing. A two-day license costs about $27. You can go crabbing and clamming on the coast, but check the tides carefully: rip currents and sneaker waves can be deadly. No license is needed to fish from the long B Street Pier in Crescent City.

HIKING

The park has miles of trails, including quite a few short, level treks just off the main roads and easily managed even if you have limited experience. Avid hikers will find plenty of fantastic rambles with serious elevation gains and thrilling flora and fauna. Note that some of the park's most delightful treks don't actually pass any big trees but rather hug Northern California's pristine and wild shoreline. Most famous is the Coastal Trail, which runs for about 70 miles from the northern to southern ends of the park.

★ **Redwood Adventures**

HIKING/WALKING | Operated by and run out of the office of Elk Meadow Cabins, this small agency with a highly knowledge-able, passionate staff offers half- and full-day hikes through some of the park's most stunning stands of redwoods, as well as adventures exploring coastal tidepools and Fern Canyon. Backpacking with overnight camping options are also available, as are electric-bike rentals, which are great for touring around the park, especially the Lost Man Creek Trail. ⊠ *7 Valley Green Camp Rd., Orick* ☎ *866/733–9637* ⊕ *www.redwoodadventures.com.*

KAYAKING

With many miles of often shallow rivers, streams, and estuarial lagoons, kay-aking is a popular pastime in the park, especially in the southern end of the park near Kuchel Visitor Center, on Arcata and Humboldt bays near Eureka, up north along the Klamath and Smith rivers, and on the ocean in Crescent City.

Humboats Kayak Adventures

KAYAKING | You can rent kayaks and book kayaking tours that from December to June include whale-watching trips. Half-day river kayaking trips pass beneath massive redwoods; the whale-watching outings get you close enough for good photos. ⊠ *Woodley Island Marina, 601 Startare Dr., Dock A, Eureka* ☎ *707/443–5157* ⊕ *www.humboats.com* 🖃 *From $30 rentals, $55 tours.*

★ **Kayak Trinidad**

KAYAKING | This respected outfitter rents kayaks and stand-up paddleboards, good for touring the beautiful estuarial and freshwater lagoons of Humboldt Lagoons State Park or sea kayaking out at sea. You can also book guided half-day paddles around Big Lagoon and Stone Lagoon, and along Trinidad Bay. The lagoons are stunning. Herds of Roosevelt elk sometimes traipse along the shoreline of Big Lagoon; raptors, herons, and waterfowl abound in both lagoons; and

you can paddle across Stone Lagoon to a spectacular secluded Pacific-view beach. ⊠ *Trinidad* ☎ *707/329–0085* ⊕ *www.kayaktrinidad.com.*

WHALE-WATCHING

Good vantage points for whale-watching include Crescent Beach Overlook, the Kuchel Visitor Center in Orick, points along the Coastal Trail, Klamath Beach Road, and Klamath River Overlook. From late November through January is the best time to see their southward migrations; from February through April the whales return, usually passing closer to shore.

What's Nearby

Arcata

8 miles north of Eureka, 33 miles south of Kuchel Visitor Center.

Begun in 1850 as a base camp for miners and lumberjacks, Arcata is today an artsy, progressive college town. Activity centers on the grassy Arcata Plaza, which is surrounded by restored buildings containing funky bars, cafés, and indie shops.

GETTING HERE AND AROUND

Set along U.S. 101, Arcata also lies just south of the junction with the main road, Highway 299, that connects the region to the east with Redding and Interstate 5. Highway 299 is a windy, hilly route—allow about two hours and 45 minutes to make the 135-mile drive to Redding.

ESSENTIALS

VISITOR INFORMATION **Arcata Humboldt Visitor Center.** ⊠ *1635 Heindon Rd., Arcata* ☎ *707/822–3619* ⊕ *www.arcatachamber.com.*

🍴 Restaurants

Cafe Brio
$ | AMERICAN | With an inviting indoor dining room and outside seating overlooking bustling Arcata Plaza, this artisan bakery and restaurant is known for its savory and sweet breads. Notable noshes include ham-and-cheese breakfast croissants, focaccia sandwiches with avocado and Humboldt Fog goat cheese from Arcata's Cypress Grove creamery, and farm-to-table dinner fare. **Known for:** lemon cream tarts and other pastries available all day; small but terrific wine selection; Blue Bottle coffees. ⑤ *Average main: $14* ✉ *791 G St., Arcata* ☎ *707/822–5922* ⊕ *www.cafebrioarcata. com* ☾ *No dinner.*

★ Salt Fish House
$$ | SEAFOOD | Just a couple of blocks from Arcata's festive Plaza, this hip seafood restaurant inside a beautifully converted old machine shop offers seating in both an airy dining room and on a large side patio. Specialties include classic panko-crusted cod and chips and seared-rare steelhead with polenta cakes, but you could also make a meal of small plates from the raw bar—octopus ceviche, scallop crudo, and grilled Pacific oysters with *nuoc cham* (dipping sauce) among them. **Known for:** sharable raw-seafood trays and towers; superb wine and cocktail list; housemade ice cream in seasonal flavors. ⑤ *Average main: $25* ✉ *935 I St., Arcata* ☎ *707/630–5300* ⊕ *www.saltfishhouse. com* ☾ *Closed Mon. No lunch.*

☕ Coffee and Quick Bites

Wildberries Marketplace
$ | DELI | This market with juice and salad bars and a small café carries a great selection of deli items, cheeses, and picnic provisions, many of them produced regionally. There's a good selection of local wine and beer, too. **Known for:** burgers and jerk chicken sandwiches; organic produce; excellent pizzas, tarts, pies, and other baked goods. ⑤ *Average main: $8* ✉ *747 13th St., Arcata* ☎ *707/822–0095* ⊕ *www.wildberries.com* ▭ *No credit cards.*

Klamath

13 miles north of Prairie Creek Redwoods Visitor Center, 22 miles south of Crescent City, 64 miles north of Eureka.

A low-key, unincorporated community surrounded by Redwood parkland on all sides, Klamath is a hub of the Yurok indigenous tribe, which makes up nearly 50% of the town's population and operates a casino resort in its center. There are a few mostly inexpensive, no-frills motels and eateries in town and nearby along with the inviting and historic Requa Inn.

ESSENTIALS
VISITOR INFORMATION Yurok Country Visitor Center. ✉ *101 Klamath Blvd., Klamath* ☎ *707/482–1555* ⊕ *www.visityurokcountry.com.*

👁 Sights

Trees of Mystery
FOREST | FAMILY | Since opening in 1946, this unabashedly goofy but endearing roadside attraction has been doling out family fun. From the moment you pull your car up to the 49-foot-tall talking statue of Paul Bunyan (alongside Babe the Blue Ox), the kitschy thrills begin. You can then explore a genuinely informative museum of Native American artifacts, admire intricately carved redwood figures, and browse tacky souvenirs. For a fee you can ride a six-passenger gondola over the redwood treetops for a majestic view of the forest canopy, and stroll along several mostly easy trails through the adjacent forest of redwoods, Sitka spruce, and Douglas firs. ✉ *15500 U.S. 101 N, between Klamath and Del Norte Coast Redwoods State Park, Klamath*

☏ 800/638–3389 ⊕ www.treesofmystery. net ⊠ Museum free, trails and gondola $20.

🍴 Restaurants

Woodland Villa Restaurant

$ | **AMERICAN** | This homey diner-style café just north of Klamath serves the sort of hearty American fare that'll fuel you up before a big day of hiking. There's breakfast sandwiches, Belgian waffles, and chicken-fried steaks in the morning, and deli sandwiches, salads, and pizzas offered throughout the rest of the day. **Known for:** big portions; good selection of craft beer and cider; local smoked-salmon in the adjacent market. ⑤ Average main: $9 ⊠ 15870 U.S. 101, Klamath ☏ 707/482–2081 ⊕ www.woodlandvillacabins.com ⊘ Closed Mon.

🛏 Hotels

★ Historic Requa Inn

$ | **B&B/INN** | This serene 1914 inn overlooks the Klamath River a mile east of where it meets the ocean. **Pros:** serene; relaxing yet central location with river views; excellent restaurant. **Cons:** least expensive rooms are quite small; not a good choice for families with kids; not many dining options in the area. ⑤ Rooms from: $132 ⊠ 451 Requa Rd., Klamath ☏ 707/482–1425 ⊕ www. requainn.com ⟿ 16 rooms ⦿ Free breakfast.

Motel Trees

$ | **HOTEL** | Operated by and adjacent to the joyfully kitschy Trees of Mystery roadside attraction, this casual mid century motel has simply furnished rooms brightened with paintings and in some cases wall-length photographic murals of local redwoods and coastal scenes. **Pros:** very affordable; close to park beaches and trails; fun retro-'50s vibe. **Cons:** not a lot of frills; on-site restaurant is just so-so;

some highway noise from U.S. 101. ⑤ Rooms from: $89 ⊠ 15495 U.S. 101, Klamath ☏ 707/482–3152, 800/848–2982 ⊕ www.moteltrees.com ⟿ 23 rooms ⦿ No meals.

Crescent City

5 miles north of Del Norte Coast Redwoods State Park, 5 miles west of Jedediah Smith Redwoods State Park, 25 miles south of Brookings, OR, 82 miles southwest of Grants Pass, OR.

The northern gateway to and headquarters of Redwood National and State Parks, this small oceanfront city just below the Oregon border offers close access to many of the park's key features, from the redwoods of Stout and Simpson-Reed groves in Jedediah Smith park to the sweeping, boulder-strewn beaches of Del Norte Coast park. The town itself enjoys a remarkable scenic setting overlooking the Pacific and contains several mostly mid-priced places to eat and stay, although it's often socked in by fog in summer or pelted by big storms in winter.

ESSENTIALS

VISITOR INFORMATION Visit Del Norte County. ⊠ 1001 Front St., Crescent City ☏ 707/464–3174 ⊕ www.visitdelnortecounty.com.

👁 Sights

Battery Point Lighthouse

LIGHTHOUSE | Only during low tide, you can walk from the pier across the ocean floor to this working lighthouse, which was built in 1856. It houses a museum with nautical artifacts and photographs of shipwrecks. There's even a resident ghost. ⊠ Lighthouse parking, 235 Lighthouse Way, Crescent City ☏ 707/464–3089 ⊕ www.delnortehistory.org ⊠ $5 ⊘ Closed weekdays Oct.–Mar.

Northcoast Marine Mammal Center

ZOO | The nonprofit center rescues and rehabilitates stranded, sick, and injured seals, sea lions, dolphins, and porpoises. Its facility isn't a museum or an aquarium, but placards and kiosks provide information about marine mammals and coastal ecosystems, and even when the place is closed you can observe the rescued animals through a fence enclosing individual pools. The gallery and gift shop is open on most weekends and some weekdays, especially in summer, and volunteers are often on hand to answer questions. It's worth calling the day of your visit to find out when feedings will take place. ✉ *424 Howe Dr., Crescent City* ☎ *707/465–6265* ⊕ *www.northcoastmmc.org* ✐ *Free.*

Restaurants

Good Harvest Cafe

$$ | **AMERICAN** | **FAMILY** | This cheerful café, which serves great breakfasts and espresso drinks, lives up to its name with ample use of locally grown and organic ingredients. For lunch and dinner there are salads, burgers, sandwiches, vegetarian specialties, and several fish entrées, plus a nice range of local beers and West Coast wines. **Known for:** fish-and-chips and other local seafood; hearty, delicious breakfasts; plenty of vegetarian items. ⑤ *Average main: $17* ✉ *575 U.S. 101 S, Crescent City* ☎ *707/465–6028* ⊕ *www. goodharvest-cafe.com.*

★ SeaQuake Brewing

$ | **PIZZA** | Water from the cool and clean Smith River goes into the dozen or so beers poured at this microbrewery with a spacious modern-industrial interior. They pair well with wood-fired thin-crust pizzas that include one with grilled chicken, bacon, artichoke hearts, garlic cream sauce, and cheeses from the local Rumiano Cheese Company. **Known for:** attractive patio with heat lamps; well-crafted beers on tap; the caramel stout sundae. ⑤ *Average main: $15* ✉ *400 Front St., Crescent City* ☎ *707/465–4444* ⊕ *seaquakebrewing. com* ◷ *Closed Sun. and Mon.*

Hotels

Curly Redwood Lodge

$ | **HOTEL** | A single redwood tree produced the 57,000 board feet of lumber used to build this budget 1957 motor lodge. **Pros:** large rooms; several restaurants within walking distance; cool retro furnishings. **Cons:** road noise can be bothersome; very basic amenities; no breakfast. ⑤ *Rooms from: $75* ✉ *701 U.S. 101 S, Crescent City* ☎ *707/464–2137* ⊕ *www.curlyredwoodlodge.com* ⇋ *36 rooms* ⏦ *No meals.*

Ocean View Inn & Suites

$ | **HOTEL** | This clean, comfortable, and reasonably priced hotel doesn't have a lot of bells and whistles, but it does enjoy a great location on the edge of downtown Crescent City very close to the water. **Pros:** views of the water; many restaurants nearby; good value. **Cons:** on a busy road; cookie-cutter furnishings; nearby foghorn can be a little noisy. ⑤ *Rooms from: $125* ✉ *270 U.S. 101, Crescent City* ☎ *707/465–1111, 855/623–2611* ⊕ *www. oceanviewinncrescentcity.com* ⇋ *65 rooms* ⏦ *Free breakfast.*

Chapter 15

THE FAR NORTH

WITH LAKE SHASTA, MT. SHASTA, AND LASSEN VOLCANIC NATIONAL PARK

Updated by
Daniel Mangin

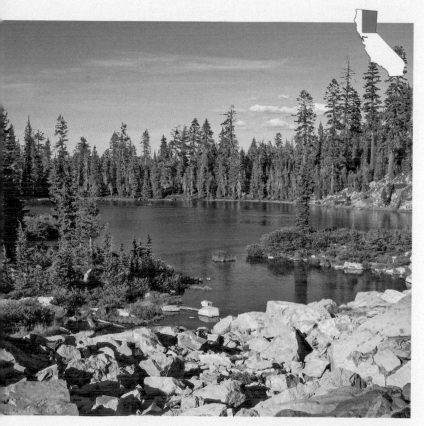

◉ Sights
★★★★☆

🍴 Restaurants
★★★☆☆

🛏 Hotels
★★★☆☆

💼 Shopping
★★★☆☆

🍸 Nightlife
★★★☆☆

WELCOME TO THE FAR NORTH

TOP REASONS TO GO

★ **Mother Nature's wonders:** California's Far North has more rivers, streams, lakes, forests, and mountains than you'll ever have time to explore.

★ **Volcanoes:** With two volcanoes to view—Lassen and Shasta—you can learn firsthand what happens when a mountain blows its top.

★ **Fantastic fishing:** Whether you like casting from a riverbank or letting your line bob beside a boat, you'll find fabulous fishing in all the northern counties.

★ **Cool hops:** On a hot day there's nothing quite as inviting as a visit to Chico's world-famous Sierra Nevada Brewery. Take the tour, and then savor a chilled glass on tap at the adjacent brewpub.

★ **Shasta:** Wonderful in all its forms: lake, dam, river, mountain, forest, and town.

1 Chico. A state university and a famous brewery help set the mood in this city also known for its artisans and farmers.

2 Corning. Olive-oil tasting rooms make this small town a fun stop for travelers along I–5.

3 Redding. This northern gateway to Lassen Volcanic National Park, has several points of interest within city limits, and day trips to Weaverville, Shasta Dam, and Lake Shasta Caverns National Natural Landmark are easily undertaken from here.

4 Weaverville. A 19th-century temple erected by Chinese miners is the centerpiece of this laid-back town's historic district.

5 Shasta Lake. Caverns, Shasta Dam, and vacation houseboats count among this quiet town's draws.

6 Dunsmuir. The upper Sacramento River near Dunsmuir consistently ranks among the country's best fishing spots. Most of the accommodations at a popular resort here were formerly cabooses.

7 Mt. Shasta. The town named for the peak that towers above it lures outdoorsy types year-round—hikers and golfers in summer, skiers in winter.

8 Chester. The southern gateway to Lassen Volcanic National Park sits on the forested edge of Lake Almanor.

9 Mineral. Lassen's official address is this town within the 165-square-mile national treasure.

10 Burney. President Theodore Roosevelt was among the fans of two magnificent waterfalls here.

11 Tulelake. Hundreds of underground lava tube caves make this town's Lava Beds National Monument well worth the remote drive.

OREGON

Dorris
Tulelake **11**

Yreka
Montague

Fort
Jones

Weed
Mt. Shasta
14,179 ft.
Mount Shasta **7**

Lava Beds
National
Monument

Clear
Lake

Goose
Lake

97

Canby
Alturas

299

Dunsmuir
Castle Crags
State Park **6**
McCloud

89

Adin

395

McArthur-Burney Falls
Memorial State Park

139

Trinity
Lake
Lake
Shasta

Burney **10**

299
89

Volcanic Legacy
Scenic Byway

Weaverville
299
Shasta
Dam

Old Station

44

395

iskeytown
Lake

Redding **3**

44/89
Shingletown

44

Lassen Volcano
National Park

Anderson
Cottonwood

Mt. Lassen
Mineral **9**
Chester **8**

Susanville

Red Bluff

36

Westwood

36

Honey
Lake
(Dry)

Los Molinos

Lake
Almanor

Greenville

395

Corning **2**
Vina
New Clairvaux Vineyard

32

Quincy

Orland

99

70

Chico **1**

Portola

Willows

45

70
Loyalton

Oroville
Gridley
Live Oak

99

Nevada
City

Reno

Williams
Colusa

70
20

Grass Valley

Truckee **80**

Yuba
City
Olivehurst
Wheatland

49

70
65

Colfax

Lake
Tahoe

Auburn

30 mi

30 km

505

Esparto
Sacramento

Woodland

Rocklin
Citrus Heights

50

NEVADA

SIERRA NEVADA

The Far North's soaring mountain peaks, trail-filled national forests, alpine lakes, and wild rivers teeming with trout make it the perfect destination for outdoor enthusiasts, including hikers, cyclists, kayakers, and bird-watchers.

You won't find many hot nightspots or cultural enclaves in this region, but you will discover crowd-free national and state parks, crystal-clear mountain streams, superlative hiking and fishing, plus small towns worth exploring. And the spectacular landscapes of Lassen Volcanic National Park and Mt. Shasta are sure to impress.

The wondrous landscape of California's northeastern corner is the product of volcanic activity. At the southern end of the Cascade Range, Lassen Volcanic National Park is the best place to witness the Far North's fascinating geology. Beyond the sulfur vents and bubbling mud pots, the park owes much of its beauty to 10,457-foot Mt. Lassen and 50 wilderness lakes. Mt. Lassen and another volcano, Mt. Shasta, draw amateur geologists, weekend hikers, and avid mountain climbers to their rugged terrain. An intricate network of high-mountain watersheds feeds lakes large and small, plus streams and rivers that course through several forests.

The most enduring image of the region, though, is Mt. Shasta, whose 14,179-foot snowcapped peak beckons outdoor adventurers of all kinds. There are many versions of Shasta to enjoy—the mountain, the lake, the river, the town, the dam, and the forest—all named after the Native Americans known as the Shatasla, or Sastise, who once inhabited the region.

MAJOR REGIONS

From Chico to Mt. Shasta. The Far North is bisected, south to north, by I–5, which passes through several historic towns and state parks, as well as miles of mountainous terrain. Halfway to the Oregon border is Lake Shasta, a favorite recreation destination, and farther north stands the spectacular snowy peak of Mt. Shasta.

The Backcountry. East of I–5, the Far North's main corridor, dozens of scenic two-lane roads crisscross the wilderness, leading to dramatic mountain peaks and fascinating natural wonders. Small towns settled in the second half of the 19th century seem frozen in time, except that they are well equipped with tourist amenities.

Planning

When to Go

Heat scorches the valley in summer. Temperatures above 110°F are common, but the mountains provide cool respite. Fall throughout the Far North is beautiful, rivaled only by spring, when wildflowers bloom and mountain creeks fed by the snowmelt splash through the forests. Winter is usually temperate in the valley, but cold and snowy in the high country. As a result, some tourist attractions are closed in winter or have sharply curtailed hours.

Getting Here and Around

AIR

For the cheapest fares, fly into Sacramento, rent a car (you'll need one anyway), and drive north. United Express and Avelo serve Redding's small airport, which has no shuttle service. Ride-sharing (starting at about $15 to downtown) is the best option.

AIR CONTACTS Redding Municipal Airport. ✉ *6751 Woodrum Circle, off Airport Rd., Redding* ☎ *530/224–4320* ⊕ *www.cityofredding.org/departments/airports.*

BUS

Greyhound buses stop in Chico and Redding. STAGE buses serve Dunsmuir and Mt. Shasta. Various other agencies provide local public transit.

BUS CONTACTS STAGE. ☎ *530/842–8220* ⊕ *www.co.siskiyou.ca.us/generalservices/page/stage-schedule.*

CAR

Interstate 5 runs up the center of California through Redding and Mt. Shasta. Chico is east of I–5 where Highways 32 and 99 intersect. Lassen Volcanic National Park can be reached off I–5 by Highway 36 from Red Bluff or (except in winter) Highway 44 from Redding. Highway 299 connects Weaverville and Redding. Check weather reports and carry detailed maps, warm clothing, and tire chains if you head into mountainous terrain in winter.

TRAIN

Amtrak serves Chico, Redding, and Dunsmuir.

Restaurants

Redding and Chico have the most varied restaurant options. Cafés and simple eateries are the norm in smaller towns. Dress is always informal.

Hotels

Chain properties predominate in this region, with the occasional inn or restored hotel. Wilderness resorts close in fall and reopen in mid-spring after snow season ends. Book well ahead for summer visits to Mt. Shasta, Dunsmuir, Mineral, and Chester and to ensure state or national park campsite availability.

Restaurant and hotel reviews have been shortened. For full information, visit Fodors.com. Restaurant prices are the average cost of a main course at dinner, or if dinner is not served, at lunch. Hotel prices are the lowest cost of a standard double room in high season.

What It Costs			
$	$$	$$$	$$$$
RESTAURANTS			
under $17	$17–$26	$27–$36	over $36
HOTELS			
under $150	$150–$250	$251–$350	over $350

Visitor Information

CONTACTS Shasta Cascade Wonderland Association. ✉ *Shasta Outlets, 1699 Hwy. 273, off I–5, Exit 667, Anderson* ☎ *530/365–7500* ⊕ *www.shastacascade.com.* **Visit Trinity County.** ✉ *509 Main St., Weaverville* ☎ *530/623–6101* ⊕ *www.visittrinity.com.*

15

The Far North PLANNING

Chico

86 miles north of Sacramento.

Its name is Spanish for "small," but with a 40% increase in population between censuses, Chico outpaced Redding as the Far North's largest city. Chico State University, the scores of local artisans, and area agriculture all influence life here, but the Sacramento Valley city's main claim to fame—and the premier tourist attraction—is the nationally renowned Sierra Nevada Brewery.

GETTING HERE AND AROUND

Highway 99, off I–5 from the north or south, and Highway 32 east off the interstate, intersect Chico. Amtrak and Greyhound stop here, and Butte Regional Transit's B-Line buses serve the area. Chico's downtown neighborhoods are walkable.

BUS CONTACT B-Line. ☎ 530/342–0221 ⊕ www.blinetransit.com.

ESSENTIALS

VISITOR INFORMATION Chico Chamber of Commerce. ⊠ 180 E. 4th St., Suite 120 ☎ 530/891–5556, 800/852–8570 ⊕ www.chicochamber.com.

 Sights

Bidwell Mansion State Historic Park

HOUSE | Built between 1865 and 1868 by General John Bidwell, the founder of Chico, this mansion was designed by Henry W. Cleaveland, a San Francisco architect. Bidwell and his wife, Annie, welcomed many distinguished guests to their pink Italianate home, including President Rutherford B. Hayes, naturalist John Muir, suffragist Susan B. Anthony, and General William T. Sherman. When offered, a one-hour tour takes you through most of the three-story mansion's 26 rooms. ⊠ 525 Esplanade, at Memorial Way ☎ 530/895–6144 ⊕ bidwellmansionpark.com ☜ $6 ⊙ Closed Tues.–Fri.

Bidwell Park

CITY PARK | The sprawling 3,670-acre Bidwell Park is a community green space straddling Big Chico Creek, where scenes from *Gone With the Wind* and the 1938 version of *Robin Hood* (starring Errol Flynn) were filmed. The region's recreational hub, it includes a golf course, swimming areas, and biking, hiking, horseback riding, and skating trails. Chico Creek Nature Center serves as the official information site for Bidwell Park. ⊠ 1968 E. 8th St., off Hwy. 99 ☎ 530/891–4671 ⊕ chicorec.com/chico-creek-nature-center ☜ Park free, nature center $4 ⊙ Nature center closed Sun.–Tues.

Chico Museum

MUSEUM | Immerse yourself in all things Chico at this small but engaging museum near Chico State University. Past exhibits have surveyed the city's Native American legacy, its former Chinatowns and agricultural past, and area movers and shakers. ⊠ 141 Salem St., at 2nd St. ☎ 530/891–4336 ⊕ www.chicohistorymuseum.org ☜ $5 ⊙ Closed Mon.–Wed.

Museum of Northern California Art

MUSEUM | After several years of successful pop-up exhibitions around town, this engaging museum found a permanent home in the Veterans Memorial Building, a handsome 1927 Classical Revival structure designed by the local architecture firm of Cole & Brouchaud. The focus is contemporary art produced from San Jose north to Oregon, some of it by area artists. ⊠ 900 Esplanade, at E. Washington Ave. ☎ 530/487–7272 ⊕ www.monca.org ☜ $5 ⊙ Closed Mon.–Wed.

National Yo-Yo Museum

MUSEUM | Cast aside images of a grand edifice and curators of renown: this yo-yo collection spanning multiple decades occupies the back of a downtown toy and novelty shop, itself a throwback to some era or another. If you've ever aspired to Walk the Dog or venture Around the World, you'll find this a diverting 15-minute stop. Highlights include the 256-pound No-Jive 3-in-1 yo-yo and comedian Tom Smothers's collection. ■TIP→ **In the shop, don't miss the posters for years of Chico events.** ⊠ *Bird in Hand, 320 Broadway, near W. 3rd St.* ☎ *530/893–0545* ⊕ *nationalyoyo.org* ⊠ *Free.*

★ Sierra Nevada Brewing Company

WINERY/DISTILLERY | This pioneer of the microbrewery movement still has a hands-on approach to beer making. Take the free Brewery Tour and see how the beer is produced—from sorting hops through fermentation and bottling, and concluding with a tasting. Other tours, for which there is a fee, focus on topics like hops, the brewery's history, and sustainability initiatives. ■TIP→ **When offered, tours fill up fast; reserve by phone or online before you visit.** ⊠ *1075 E. 20th St., at Sierra Nevada St.* ☎ *530/345–2739 taproom, 530/899–4776 tours* ⊕ *www. sierranevada.com* ⊠ *Tours free–$50 (includes tasting).*

🍴 Restaurants

★ Bidwell Perk

$ | AMERICAN | A clean and tidy, many-windowed chain alternative for coffee (several different roasts daily) and pastries, Bidwell Perk also serves full breakfasts and light lunches. Bagels, French toast, quiche, and croissant sandwiches in the morning give way to small plates, salads, panini, and sliders as the day moves along. **Known for:** mostly small-batch beers and wines; outdoor patio; well-crafted espresso drinks. ⑤ *Average main: $9* ⊠ *664 E. 1st Ave., at Mangrove Ave.* ☎ *530/899–1500* ⊕ *bidwellperk.com* ⊙ *No dinner.*

★ 5th Street Steakhouse

$$$$ | STEAKHOUSE | Hand-cut steak is the star in this refurbished early 1900s building, the place to come when you're craving red meat, a huge baked potato, or some fresh seafood. Exposed redbrick walls warm the dining rooms, and a

long mahogany bar catches the overflow crowds that jam the place on weekends. **Known for:** alfresco dining on outdoor patio; weekend crowds; prime cuts of beef with white-tablecloth service. ⑤ *Average main: $37* ⊠ *345 W. 5th St., at Normal Ave.* ☎ *530/891–6328* ⊕ *www. 5thstreetsteakhouse.com* ⊙ *Closed Mon. No lunch Sat.–Thurs.*

Red Tavern

$$$ | MEDITERRANEAN | With its burgundy carpet, white linen tablecloths, and mellow lighting, this is one of Chico's coziest restaurants. The Mediterranean-influenced menu, inspired by fresh local produce, with vegetarian and pescatarian fare in addition to meat and poultry dishes, changes seasonally—fettuccine with beef short-rib ragout and seared salmon with citrus beurre blanc are among recent offerings. **Known for:** California wine list; nightly specials; patio seating. ⑤ *Average main: $29* ⊠ *1250 Esplanade, at E. 3rd Ave.* ☎ *530/894–3463* ⊕ *www. redtavern.com* ⊙ *Closed Mon. No lunch Tues.–Sat.*

Sierra Nevada Brewery Taproom

$$ | AMERICAN | An easy choice, especially if you've just done a tour and are steeped in company lore, the famous brewery's high-ceilinged, heavy-on-the-wood taproom bustles day and night with patrons washing down well-conceived gastropub grub with the best-selling Pale Ale and smaller-batch offerings, some of which are only available here. The open kitchen turns out burgers, wood-oven pizzas, and fish-and-chips (the fish's batter made with Pale Ale) with remarkable speed. **Known for:** beer cheese and pretzels with mustard; soups and salads; beer flights on patio. ⑤ *Average main: $17* ⊠ *1075 E. 20th St.* ✛ *½ mile west of Hwy. 99, Exit 384* ☎ *530/345–2739* ⊕ *www.sierranevada.com/brewery/california/taproom.*

Hotels

Hotel Diamond

$$ | HOTEL | Crystal chandeliers and gleaming century-old wood floors and banisters welcome guests into the foyer of this restored 1904 gem near Chico State University. **Pros:** downtown location; refined rooms, some with bay windows and fireplaces; Diamond Steakhouse. **Cons:** street scene can be noisy on weekends; some rooms are small; some rooms lack tubs. ⑤ *Rooms from: $151* ✉ *220 W. 4th St., near Broadway* ☎ *530/893–3100, 866/993–3100* ⊕ *www.hoteldiamond-chico.com* ⊷ *43 rooms* ⦶ *No meals.*

Corning

29 miles northwest of Chico, 50 miles south of Redding.

Signs along Highway 99 and I–5 beckon travelers to Corning, whose favorable soil and plentiful sunshine have made the town a center of olive cultivation and olive-oil manufacturing. At several tasting rooms you can sample olives, olive oil, and other products.

GETTING HERE AND AROUND

Corning lies just off I–5 at Exit 631. From Chico take Highway 99 for 17½ miles and follow signs west to Corning. TRAX provides weekday bus service.

CONTACTS TRAX. ☎ *530/385–2877* ⊕ *www.taketrax.com.*

 Sights

New Clairvaux Vineyard

WINERY/DISTILLERY | History converges in fascinating ways at this winery and vineyard whose tale involves pioneer-rancher Peter Lassen (Mt. Lassen is named for him), railroad baron Leland Stanford, newspaper magnate William Randolph Hearst, the Napa Valley's five-generation Nichelini wine-making family, and current owners the Trappist-Cistercian monks. In the 1890s the rambling redbrick tasting room, erected by Stanford, stored 2 million gallons of wine. These days the hosts pour Albariño, Tempranillo, Barbera, and other small-lot bottlings from grapes mostly grown nearby. The Syrah and Cabernet stand out, but everything's well made. The on-site chapel (the Hearst connection) has a convoluted story all its own. ✉ *26240 7th St., Vina* ⊹ *10 miles from Corning, South Ave. east off I–5 or Hwy. 99 to Rowles Rd. north to 7th St. west* ☎ *530/839–2434* ⊕ *www.newclairvauxvineyard.com* ✸ *Tastings $10.*

Olive Pit

LOCAL INTEREST | Three generations of the Craig family run this combination café, store, and tasting room where you can learn all about California olive production and sample olive products, craft beers and small-lot wines, and artisanal foods. Sandwich selections at the café include muffulettas and olive burgers. Wash your choice down with a balsamic shake in flavors that include peach, coconut, strawberry, and chocolate. ✉ *2156 Solano St., Corning* ⊹ *Off I–5, Exit 631 (Corning Rd.)* ☎ *530/824–4667* ⊕ *www.olivepit.com* ✸ *Tastings free for olive oil, fee (varies) for beer and wine.*

Redding

50 miles north of Corning.

A handy gateway to Lassen Volcanic National Park, Redding, population about 95,000, sits along the busy I–5 corridor, with attractions that include the photogenic Sundial Bridge in Turtle Bay Exploration Park. The city makes a good base for visiting Shasta Lake and Lake Shasta Caverns to the north. It's also a good stopover if you're traveling between Lassen and Redwood National and State Parks on the coast.

GETTING HERE AND AROUND

Interstate 5 is the major north–south route through Redding. Highway 299 bisects the city east–west, and Highway 44 connects Redding and Lassen Park's northwest entrance.

ESSENTIALS

VISITOR INFORMATION Visit Redding.
✉ *1448 Pine St.* ☎ *530/225–4100* ⊕ *www.visitredding.com.*

Sights

Moseley Family Cellars

WINERY/DISTILLERY | Although its street name conjures up pastoral images, this appointment-only winery whose grapes come from vineyards as far afield as Napa, Sonoma, Lodi, and Oregon's Rogue Valley is actually in an industrial park. Despite the location, it's worth a visit for its Chardonnay and Viognier whites and Syrah, Mourvèdre, old-vine Zinfandel, and other reds. ✉ *4712 Mountain Lakes Blvd., Suite 300* ☎ *530/229–9463* ⊕ *www.moseleyfamilycellars.com* ⚲ *Tastings $10* ⊙ *Closed Mon.–Wed. (sometimes Thurs.) except by appointment.*

Shasta State Historic Park

HISTORIC SITE | Six miles west of downtown and straddling Highway 299 lies the former town of Shasta City, which thrived in the mid- to late 1800s. The park's 19 acres of half-ruined brick buildings, accessed via trails, are a reminder of the glory days of the California gold rush. The former county courthouse building (whose exhibits include rare California landscape paintings), jail, and gallows have been restored to their 1860s appearance. The Litsch General Store (1850–1950), now a museum, displays items once sold here. ■TIP➜ **Next to the store in a wooden shack, family-run Shorty's Eatery serves up good sandwiches and Filipino dishes.** ✉ *15312 Hwy. 299* ☎ *530/243–8194* ⊕ *www.parks.ca.gov/shastashp* ⚲ *Free to park, $3 Courthouse Museum* ⊙ *Courthouse Museum closed Mon.–Wed.*

★ **Turtle Bay Exploration Park**

CITY PARK | FAMILY | This peaceful downtown park has 300 acres of walking trails, an aquarium, an arboretum and botanical gardens, and many interactive exhibits for kids. The main draw is the stunning Santiago Calatrava–designed **Sundial Bridge,** a metal and translucent glass pedestrian walkway, suspended by cables from a single tower, spanning a broad bend in the Sacramento River. On sunny days the 217-foot tower lives up to the bridge's name, casting a shadow on the ground below to mark time. Access to the bridge and arboretum is free, but there's a fee for the museum and gardens. ✉ *844 Sundial Bridge Dr.* ☎ *530/243–8850* ⊕ *www.turtlebay.org* ⚲ *Museum $18* ⊙ *Museum closed Mon. and Tues. early Sept.–mid-Mar.*

🍴 Restaurants

From the Hearth Artisan Bakery & Café

$ | AMERICAN | A homegrown variation on the Panera theme, this extremely popular operation (as in expect a wait at peak dining hours) serves pastries, eggs and other hot dishes, and good coffee drinks, juices, and smoothies for breakfast. The chefs whip up a diverse selection of wraps, panini, sandwiches, burgers, rice bowls, and soups the rest of the day. **Known for:** baked goods; pork breakfast tacos; two other Redding locations (one downtown) plus a Shasta Lake drive-through. ⑤ *Average main: $11* ✉ *2650 Churn Creek Rd.* ☎ *530/424–2233* ⊕ *www.fthcafe.com.*

Jack's Grill

$$$ | STEAKHOUSE | The original Jack opened his grill (and an upstairs brothel) in 1938. Tamer these days, this place is famous for its 16-ounce steaks and deep-fried shrimp and chicken dishes. **Known for:** 1930s atmosphere; great martinis; thick slabs of beef. ⑤ *Average main: $29*

✉ *1743 California St.* ☎ *530/241–9705*
⊕ *www.jacksgrillredding.com* ⊘ *Closed Sun. No lunch.*

View 202

$$$ | **MODERN AMERICAN** | The view at this glass-walled hilltop restaurant is of the Sacramento River below the wide outdoor patio and well beyond the waterway to snowcapped mountains. It's best to stick with the least complicated preparations on the New American menu, which emphasizes grilled meats and fish from noted California purveyors but also includes Asian-tinged appetizers and house-made ravioli. **Known for:** Friday and Saturday prime rib; specialty cocktails; wine list. ⑤ *Average main: $29* ✉ *202 Hemsted Dr., off E. Cypress Ave.* ☎ *530/226–8439* ⊕ *www.view202redding.com.*

Vintage Public House

$$ | **AMERICAN** | Patrons of this comfort-food haven across from downtown's 1935 Cascade movie palace wash down elevated pub grub with classic and craft cocktails and an international selection of wines and beers. The fare includes homemade soups, a few salads, rice bowls, jalapeño wonton nachos, a locally revered mac and cheese, plenty of burgers (one grilled with a whiskey glaze and topped with candied bacon), and heartier entrées like lasagna and chicken marsala. **Known for:** patio dining; weekly appetizer special; artisanal spirits. ⑤ *Average main: $22* ✉ *1790 Market St., at Sacramento St.* ☎ *530/229–9449* ⊕ *vintageredding.com* ⊘ *Closed Sun. and Mon. No lunch Sat.*

 Hotels

★ **Bridgehouse Bed & Breakfast**

$ | **B&B/INN** | In a residential area a block from the Sacramento River and a ½-mile from downtown Redding, this inn contains six rooms in two side-by-side homes. **Pros:** easygoing hospitality; proximity to downtown and Turtle Bay; freshly baked scones at full breakfast.

Cons: lacks pool, fitness center, and other standard hotel amenities; the two least expensive rooms are small; books up well ahead in summer. ⑤ *Rooms from: $119* ✉ *1455 Riverside Dr.* ☎ *530/247–7177* ⊕ *www.bridgehousebb.com* ➹ *6 rooms* ⦿ *Free breakfast.*

★ **Sheraton Redding Hotel at Sundial Bridge**

$$ | **HOTEL** | **FAMILY** | Stylish and modern, this hotel at the entrance to Sundial Bridge and Turtle Bay Exploration Park makes a great, family-friendly base for visiting Lassen, Whiskeytown and Shasta lakes, and other area attractions. **Pros:** pool and gym; excellent restaurant; patio dining. **Cons:** parking fee; neighborhood not very walkable; nearly an hour's drive to Lassen Volcanic NP. ⑤ *Rooms from: $209* ✉ *820 Sundial Bridge Dr.* ☎ *530/364–2800* ⊕ *www.marriott.com* ➹ *130 rooms* ⦿ *No meals.*

 Nightlife

Final Draft Brewing Company

BREWPUBS/BEER GARDENS | This spacious brick-walled brewpub receives high acclaim for its accessible ales and above-average pub grub. Try the beer-battered Sidewinder Fries instead of regular ones. While they're cooking, order a sampler flight to decide which of the brews to wash them down with. ✉ *1600 California St., at Placer St.* ☎ *530/338–1198* ⊕ *www.finaldraftbrewingcompany.com.*

Woody's Brewing Company

BREWPUBS/BEER GARDENS | A fun downtown hangout with a party vibe, Woody's has built a loyal following for its Polish nachos (kettle chips, beer cheese, smoked sausage, and sauerkraut), special-recipe tater tots, and range of beers from fruited wheat ales to an unfiltered dry-hopped IPA and the Pray for Powder porter. ✉ *1257 Oregon St., at Shasta St.* ☎ *530/768–1034* ⊕ *www.woodysbrewing.com.*

Activities

The Fly Shop

FISHING | This store that bills itself as "Northern California's fly-fishing headquarters" sells gear and other products and has information about guides, conditions, and fishing trips. ✉ *4140 Churn Creek Rd., at Denton Way* ☎ *530/222–3555, 800/669–3474* ⊕ *www.theflyshop.com.*

Weaverville

46 miles west of Redding on Hwy. 299.

Chinese miners erected the 1874 Joss House that anchors Weaverville's downtown historic district. The town, population about 3,200, is a popular headquarters for family vacations and hiking, fishing, and gold-panning excursions.

GETTING HERE AND AROUND

Highway 299, east from the Pacific Coast or west from Redding, becomes Main Street in central Weaverville. Trinity Transit provides bus service.

ESSENTIALS

VISITOR INFORMATION Trinity County Visitors Bureau. ✉ *509 Main St.* ☎ *530/623–6101* ⊕ *www.visittrinity.com.*

👁 Sights

Hal Goodyear Historical Park

HISTORIC SITE | For a vivid sense of Weaverville's past, visit this outdoor park of old mining equipment, and step inside the adjacent **Jake Jackson Memorial Museum.** A blacksmith shop and a stamp mill (where ore is crushed) from the 1890s are still in use during certain community events. ✉ *780 Main St.* ☎ *530/623–5211* ⊕ *www.trinitymuseum.org* ⊗ *Museum closed various days Jan.–Apr. and Oct.–Dec.*

★ Weaverville Joss House State Historic Park

HISTORIC SITE | Weaverville's main attraction is the Joss House, a Taoist temple built in 1874 and called Won Lim Miao ("the temple of the forest beneath the clouds") by Chinese miners. The oldest continuously used Chinese temple in California, it attracts worshippers from around the world. With its golden altar, antique weaponry, and carved wooden canopies, the Joss House is a piece of California history best appreciated on a guided 30-minute tour. ✉ *630 Main St., at Oregon St.* ☎ *530/623–5284* ⊕ *www.parks.ca.gov* ✉ *Museum free; guided tour $4* ⊗ *Closed Mon.–Wed.*

🍴 Restaurants

Mamma Llama Eatery & Café

$ | **AMERICAN** | Tap into the spirit of 21st-century Weaverville at this mellow café that serves breakfast (all day) and lunch and in winter specializes in hot soups to warm body and soul. Expect all the usual suspects at breakfast along with Country Cheesy Potatoes (topped with green chili) and sausage between two biscuits topped with homemade sausage gravy; a spicy club wrap and several vegetarian sandwiches are among the lunch offerings. **Known for:** mellow vibe; good soups; espresso drinks. ⑤ *Average main: $9* ✉ *490 Main St.* ☎ *530/623–6363* ⊕ *www.mammallama.com* ⊗ *Closed weekends. No dinner.*

Trinity County Brewing Company

$ | **AMERICAN** | Craft brews, from pale ales to stout, and pub grub a cut above the expected made this 2020 newcomer with a cavernous industrial interior an instant hit despite opening during difficult times. The cheese-curd and chicken-wing starters and burger and grilled-chicken sandwich are the best sellers. **Known for:** community feel; mellow outside patio; garlic fries with secret sauce. ⑤ *Average main: $11* ✉ *301 Main St.* ☎ *530/423–4114*

⊕ *trinitycountybrewery.com* ⊘ *Closed Mon. and Tues. (but check).*

Hotels

Weaverville Hotel

$ | HOTEL | Originally built during the gold rush, this beautifully restored hotel is filled with antiques and period furniture. **Pros:** gracious on-site owners; in heart of town's historic district; beautifully restored. **Cons:** no breakfast on-site; children under 12 not permitted; only one room has a TV. $ *Rooms from: $140* ✉ *481 Main St., near Court St.* ☎ *530/623–2222, 800/750–8853* ⊕ *www. weavervillehotel.com* ⇨ *7 rooms* ⅋ *No meals.*

Activities

Weaverville Ranger Station

HIKING/WALKING | Check here for maps, free wilderness and campfire permits, and information about local fishing and the 600 miles of hiking trails in the 500,000-acre Trinity Alps Wilderness. ✉ *360 Main St.* ☎ *530/623–2121.*

Shasta Lake

10 miles north of Redding.

The city of Shasta Lake, population about 10,000, is a portal to water, wilderness, and dazzling stalagmites, with the monolithic Shasta Dam in the midst of it all.

GETTING HERE AND AROUND

Shasta Lake lies at the intersection of I–5 and Highway 151. There is no local bus service.

Sights

Lake Shasta

BODY OF WATER | Created when Shasta Dam corraled the Sacramento River in the 1940s, Lake Shasta evolved into a habitat for numerous types of fish, including rainbow trout, salmon, bass, brown trout, and catfish. The lake region also supports a large nesting population of bald eagles. You can rent fishing boats, ski boats, sailboats, canoes, paddleboats, Jet Skis, and windsurfing boards at marinas and resorts along the 370-mile shoreline. ✉ *Shasta Lake* ⊕ *www.shasta-cascade.com.*

★ Lake Shasta Caverns National Natural Landmark

NATURE SITE | FAMILY | Stalagmites, stalactites, flowstone deposits, and crystals entice visitors to the Lake Shasta Caverns. To see this impressive spectacle, you must take the two-hour tour, which includes a catamaran ride across the McCloud arm of Lake Shasta and a bus ride up North Grey Rocks Mountain to the cavern entrance. The temperature in the caverns is 58°F year-round, making them a cool retreat on a hot summer day. The most awe-inspiring of the limestone rock formations is the glistening Cathedral Room, which appears to be gilded. ■TIP→ **In summer it's wise to purchase tickets online a day or more ahead of your visit.** ✉ *20359 Shasta Caverns Rd., Lakehead* ✛ *20 miles north of Redding (take I–5 Exit 695 and follow signs)* ☎ *530/238–2341, 800/795–2283* ⊕ *www. lakeshastacaverns.com* ✆ *$32.*

Shasta Dam

DAM | Road-trippers traveling along I–5 often stop at the second-largest concrete dam in the United States—only Grand Coulee in Washington is bigger. Shasta Dam was completed in 1945 by a crew that included many women because potential male workers were fighting World War II. Exhibits at the visitor center explain the engineering and construction, but even if the facility isn't open, the photogenic view north to snowcapped Mt. Shasta makes the landmark worth the detour. Hour-long guided tours, suspended in 2020, may resume by 2022, but you can tour the top of the dam on your own. ✉ *16349 Shasta Dam Blvd.,*

Shasta Lake ✛ From I–5 Exit 685, take Hwy. 151/Shasta Dam Blvd. west to Lake Blvd. north ☎ 530/247–8555 ⊕ www. usbr.gov/mp/ncao/dam-tours.html ✉ Free ⊙ Closed Tues. and Wed. (but check).

🏃 Activities

Shasta Marina at Packers Bay
BOATING | FAMILY | Trips aboard this highly regarded operator's amenities-packed houseboats, which sleep up to 20 people, qualify as waterborne glamping. Some boats even have a hot tub on board. The outfit conducts pre-trip lessons in the basics for first-time houseboaters. ✉ *16814 Packers Bay Rd., Lakehead ✛ West from I–5, Exit 693 (see directions on website) ☎ 800/959–3359 ⊕ shastalake.net ✉ From $350 per night (more in summer), 3-night minimum.*

Dunsmuir

10 miles south of Mt. Shasta.

Surrounded by towering forests and boasting world-class upper Sacramento River fly-fishing, Dunsmuir acquired its current moniker when a Scottish coal baron built a fountain in exchange for the town renaming itself in his honor. An upscale restaurant and a boutique hotel do business downtown. Farther out lie the restored-caboose lodgings of the fun Railroad Park Resort.

GETTING HERE AND AROUND
Reach Dunsmuir via exits off I–5 at the north and south ends of town. Amtrak stops here. On weekdays, STAGE buses serve Dunsmuir.

ESSENTIALS
VISITOR INFORMATION Dunsmuir Chamber of Commerce. ✉ *5915 Dunsmuir Ave., Suite 100 ☎ 530/235–2177 ⊕ dunsmuir. com.*

Fine Fishing

The upper Sacramento River near Dunsmuir is consistently rated one of the best fishing spots in the country. Check with the chamber of commerce for local fishing guides.

👁 Sights

★ Castle Crags State Park
NATIONAL/STATE PARK | Named for its 2,000–6,500-foot glacier-polished crags, formed by volcanic activity centuries ago, this park offers fishing on the upper Sacramento River, hiking in the backcountry, and a view of Mt. Shasta. The 4,350-acre park has 28 miles of hiking trails, including a 2¾-mile access trail to **Castle Crags Wilderness,** part of the **Shasta-Trinity National Forest.** The excellent trails at lower altitudes include the ¼-mile Vista Point Trail (near the entrance), which leads to views of Castle Crags and Mt. Shasta. ✉ *20022 Castle Creek Rd., Castella ✛ I–5, Exit 724, 6 miles south of Dunsmuir ☎ 530/235–2684 ⊕ www. castlecragspark.org ✉ $10 per vehicle, day-use.*

🍴 Restaurants

Café Maddalena
$$$ | MEDITERRANEAN | The chef here gained experience working in top San Francisco restaurants before moving north to prepare adventurous Mediterranean fare with a French influence. Appetizers like a recent menu's crispy quail and pea-and-mint croquettes hint at the level of refinement on display, as do entrées that might include sea bass served with Meyer lemon risotto or rabbit-and-porcini ragout atop pappardelle. **Known for:** elevated cuisine; artisanal small-lot wines; outdoor dining under an arbor. $ *Average main: $29* ✉ *5801 Sacramento Ave.* ☎ *530/235–2725* ⊕ *www.*

cafemaddalena.com ⊘ *Closed Mon.–Wed. and Jan.–mid-Feb. No lunch.*

Dunsmuir Brewery Works

$$ | **AMERICAN** | Travelers mingle with locals at this downtown spot for microbrews and pub fare that includes vegetarian-nut, elk, and ½-pound Angus-beef burgers, along with pesto-cream mussels, baby back ribs, and bratwurst in a brioche bun with kraut and cheese sauce. The house brews range from pale ale to a porter, with growlers available to go. **Known for:** outdoor patio; house-made beer cheese bread; clam chowder Fridays. $ *Average main: $19* ⊠ *5701 Dunsmuir Ave.* ☎ *530/235–1900* ⊕ *www.dunsmuirbreweryworks.com* ⊘ *Closed Mon. early Sept.–late May.*

Yaks on the 5

$$ | **AMERICAN** | Beloved on social media for its sticky buns, addictive two-cheese tater tots, and bacon-jalapeño and other 100% grass-fed burgers, this festive, brightly painted joint wins most diners' hearts with its house-made ingredients, dozens of beers, and upbeat staff. You'll pay more than expected but will likely leave feeling you got your money's worth. **Known for:** murals and artworks; smoked wings and ribs with house barbecue sauce; Yaks Shack in Mt. Shasta. $ *Average main: $19* ⊠ *4917 Dunsmuir Ave.* ☎ *530/678–3517* ⊕ *www.yaks.com* ⊘ *Closed Wed.*

 Hotels

★ Mossbrae Hotel

$$ | **HOTEL** | Patrons of this urbane, two-story, boutique hotel bask in au courant comfort in guest rooms with kitchenettes and either queen or California king beds. **Pros:** luxury feel; queen rooms, though small, are a good value; easy walk to Dunsmuir Brewing, Cafe Maddalena, art venues. **Cons:** costs a bit more than town's other properties (but outshines them); no elevator (one ground-floor ADA suite); some rooms have no tubs.

$ *Rooms from: $159* ⊠ *5734 Dunsmuir Ave.* ☎ *530/235–7019* ⊕ *mossbraehotel.com* ⇌ *7 rooms* ⊙ *No meals.*

Railroad Park Resort

$ | **HOTEL** | **FAMILY** | The antique cabooses here were collected over more than three decades and converted into 23 cozy motel rooms in honor of Dunsmuir's railroad legacy; there are also four cabins. **Pros:** gorgeous setting; unique accommodations; kitschy fun. **Cons:** cabooses can feel cramped; must drive to Dunsmuir restaurants; some guests find location too remote. $ *Rooms from: $135* ⊠ *100 Railroad Park Rd.* ☎ *530/235–4440* ⊕ *www.rrpark.com* ⇌ *27 rooms* ⊙ *No meals.*

Mt. Shasta

34 miles north of Lake Shasta.

While a snow-covered dormant volcano is the area's dazzling draw, the town of Mt. Shasta charms visitors with its small shops, friendly residents, and beautiful scenery in all seasons.

GETTING HERE AND AROUND

Three exits off I–5 lead to the town of Mt. Shasta. When snow hasn't closed Highway 89, you can take it northwest from the Lassen Park area to Mt. Shasta. Greyhound stops at Weed, 10 miles north; Amtrak stops at Dunsmuir, 10 miles south. STAGE provides bus service.

ESSENTIALS

VISITOR INFORMATION Visit Mt. Shasta. ⊠ *Visitor Center, 300 Pine St., at W. Lake St.* ☎ *530/926–4865* ⊕ *visitmtshasta.com.*

 Sights

★ Mt. Shasta

VOLCANO | The crown jewel of the 2.5-million-acre Shasta-Trinity National Forest, Mt. Shasta, a 14,179-foot-high dormant volcano, is a mecca for day hikers. It's especially enticing in spring, when fragrant Shasta lilies and other flowers adorn the rocky slopes. A paved road, the Everitt Memorial Highway, reaches only as far as the timberline; the final 6,000 feet are a tough climb of rubble, ice, and snow (the summit is perpetually ice-packed). Hiking enthusiasts include this trek with those to the peaks of Kilimanjaro and Mt. Fuji in lists of iconic must-do mountain hikes. ■TIP➜ **Always check weather predictions; sudden storms—with snow and freezing temperatures—have trapped climbers.** ⊠ *Mt. Shasta ⊕ visitmtshasta.com/activities/mountaineering.*

Restaurants

Lilys

$$ | ECLECTIC | This restaurant in a white-clapboard home, framed by a picket fence and arched trellis, offers an eclectic menu, starting with bananas Foster French toast for breakfast. The varied lunch and dinner selections might include a Brussels sprout salad, herb-stuffed fresh trout, pad Thai, filet mignon, and always several burgers. **Known for:** patio dining; Wednesday sushi night; weekend brunch. ⑤ *Average main: $24* ⊠ *1013 S. Mt. Shasta Blvd., at Holly St.* ☎ *530/926–3372* ⊕ *www.lilysrestaurant.com* ⊙ *Per website, hrs "subject to change".*

Poncho & Lefkowitz

$ | MEXICAN | The cuisine is Mexican and American at this small stand popular for its quesadillas, fish tacos, tamales, sausages, Seattle dogs (bratwurst with cream cheese, cabbage, and jalapeños), and filling Big Nasty burritos. Order at the window, and enjoy your meal at outdoor picnic tables with Mt. Shasta views. **Known for:** fish tacos; strawberry lemonade; vegetarian offerings. ⑤ *Average main: $9* ⊠ *401 S. Mt. Shasta Blvd.* ☎ *530/926–1505* ⊙ *Closed Sun. No dinner.*

Seven Suns Coffee and Cafe

$ | CAFÉ | A favorite gathering spot for locals, this small coffee shop in a stone building serves specialty wraps and burritos for breakfast and lunch (both served all day), plus soups and salads. Pastries, made daily, include muffins, cookies, and scones (great blackberry ones in season). **Known for:** coffee, tea, chai, spiced cider, Italian sodas; outside patio; vegetarian offerings. ⑤ *Average main: $11* ⊠ *1011 S. Mt. Shasta Blvd., at Holly St.* ☎ *530/926–9701* ⊙ *No dinner.*

Hotels

Best Western Tree House Motor Inn

$$ | HOTEL | The clean, standard rooms at this motel less than a mile from downtown Mt. Shasta are decorated with natural-wood furnishings. **Pros:** close to ski park; heated indoor pool; lobby's roaring fireplace is a big plus on winter days. **Cons:** not all lodging buildings have elevators; pricier than other chain properties (though it delivers more); doesn't offer free breakfast like much of BW chain. ⑤ *Rooms from: $175* ⊠ *111 Morgan Way* ☎ *530/926–3101, 800/545–7164* ⊕ *www.bestwesterncalifornia.com/hotels/bestwestern-plus-tree-house* ⤶ *98 rooms* ⦿l *No meals.*

Inn at Mount Shasta

$$ | HOTEL | This two-story, motel-style property on Mt. Shasta's main drag wins points for its cleanliness, comfortable beds, and spacious (325 square feet minimum) rooms with Wi-Fi, microwaves, refrigerators, hair dryers, and flat-screen TVs with satellite HDTV. **Pros:** solicitous hosts; 500-square-foot family suite with three beds; convenient location. **Cons:** minimal style; some street and room-to-room noise; no elevator to second-floor rooms. ⑤ *Rooms from: $169* ⊠ *710 S. Mt. Shasta Blvd.* ☎ *530/918–9292* ⊕ *innatmountshasta.com* ⤶ *30 rooms* ⦿l *No meals.*

Mount Shasta Resort

$$ | RENTAL | The private chalets, all with gas-log fireplaces, are nestled among tall pine trees along the shore of Lake Siskiyou. **Pros:** romantic woodsy setting

with incredible views; full kitchens in many lodgings; largest chalets sleep up to six people. **Cons:** kids may get bored; must drive to Mt. Shasta restaurants; some hospitality lapses. $ *Rooms from: $189* ⊠ *1000 Siskiyou Lake Blvd.* ☎ *530/926–3030, 800/958–3363* ⊕ *www. mountshastaresort.com* ↝ *65 rooms* ⦵ *No meals.*

 ## Activities

Fifth Season Mountaineering Shop
CLIMBING/MOUNTAINEERING | This shop rents bicycles and skiing and climbing equipment, and operates a recorded 24-hour climber-skier report. ⊠ *300 N. Mt. Shasta Blvd.* ☎ *530/926–3606, 530/926–5555 mountain report* ⊕ *www. thefifthseason.com.*

Jack Trout Fly Fishing
FISHING | The upper Sacramento River is a world-class fly-fishing destination, and few anglers have as much experience fishing it as Jack Trout. He and his guides also book trips to several other Northern California rivers. ⊠ *Mt. Shasta* ☎ *530/926–4540* ⊕ *www.jacktrout.com* ⊞ *Rates vary depending on trip, number of guests.*

Mt. Shasta Board & Ski Park
SKIING/SNOWBOARDING | **FAMILY** | Three-quarters of the trails at this ski park on Mt. Shasta's southeast flank are for beginning or intermediate skiers. A package for children, available through the ski school, includes a lift ticket, ski rental, and a lesson. There's twilight skiing on some nights for those who want to see the moon rise as they schuss. The base lodge has a bar, a few dining options, a ski shop, and a ski-snowboard rental shop. **Facilities:** 32 trails; 425 skiable acres; 1,435-foot vertical drop; 5 lifts. ⊠ *4500 Ski Park Hwy.* ⊹ *Hwy. 89 exit east from I–5, south of Mt. Shasta City* ☎ *530/926–8610 winter only, 530/926– 8686 snow phone* ⊕ *www.skipark.com* ⊞ *Lift ticket $74.*

Mt. Shasta Forest Service Ranger Station
HIKING/WALKING | Check here for current trail conditions and avalanche reports. ⊠ *204 W. Alma St., at Pine St.* ☎ *530/926–4511, 530/926–9613 avalanche conditions* ⊕ *www.fs.usda.gov/ main/stnf.*

Mt. Shasta Nordic Center
SKIING/SNOWBOARDING | This center, run by a nonprofit, maintains 15 miles of groomed cross-country ski trails, plus a short snowshoeing trail. ⊠ *Ski Park Hwy.* ⊹ *North off Hwy. 89, 7 miles southeast of Mt. Shasta City* ☎ *530/925–3495, 530/925–3494 grooming report* ⊕ *mt- shastanordic.org.*

Chester

30 miles southeast of Lassen's southwest entrance, 71 miles east of Red Bluff.

A gateway to Lassen Volcanic National Park on Lake Almanor's north shore, Chester, population 2,200, supports locals and tourists with modest restaurants, hotels, and shops. The Dixie Fire of 2021, the second-largest wildfire in California's history, consumed much of the lake's western shore, but firefighters saved Chester. Expect to see evidence of the conflagration and recovery efforts when traveling in the area, though.

GETTING HERE AND AROUND
Chester is on Highway 36, the main route east from I–5 at Red Bluff, at the junction of Highway 89, which leads northwest to Lassen.

ESSENTIALS
VISITOR INFORMATION Lake Almanor Area Chamber of Commerce. ⊠ *278 Main St.* ☎ *530/258–2426* ⊕ *www.lakealmanorarea.com.*

👁 Sights

★ Volcanic Legacy Scenic Byway

SCENIC DRIVE | A 500-mile scenic drive, the byway connects Lassen with Oregon's Crater Lake National Park. The route's **southern loop** begins in Chester and winds for about 185 miles through the forests, volcanic peaks, hydrothermal springs, and lava fields of Lassen National Forest and Lassen Volcanic National Park. The all-day excursion into dramatic wilderness includes a detour north to 129-foot-tall Burney Falls. The Dixie Fire of 2021 scorched the forested areas along Highway 36 and Lassen National Park Highway near Chester. Damage is likely to remain visible for a few years at least. ✛ *From Chester, take Hwy. 36 west to Hwy. 89 (Lassen Nat'l Park Hwy. within the park) north to Burney Falls. Backtrack south on Hwy. 89, turning southeast on Hwy. 44. At Hwy. 36 head west past Lake Almanor back to Chester* ⊕ *www.volcaniclegacybyway.org* ⊗ *In most yrs, snow closes parts of the byway from mid-fall to mid-spring.*

🍴 Restaurants

★ Cravings Cafe Espresso Bar & Bakery

$ | CAFÉ | This casual breakfast and lunch place inside a white clapboard house satisfies diners' cravings with dishes like homemade slow-cooked corned-beef hash topped with two eggs and accompanied by a slice of sourdough or gluten free bread. You can get breakfast and excellent pastries all day, with soups, salads, sandwiches, and burgers on the menu for lunch. **Known for:** waffles with applewood-smoked bacon in the batter; attached bookstore's hiking and nature titles; outdoor patio. ⑤ *Average main: $10* ⊠ *278 Main St.* ☎ *530/258–2229* ⊗ *Closed Tues. and Wed. No dinner.*

The Ranch House

$$ | AMERICAN | FAMILY | This convivial neighborhood pub stands out because of its abundance of shaded patio seating—and full horseshoes pit—set in the restaurant's landscaped backyard. It's a reliable bet for filling up on hearty comfort fare after a long day of hiking and exploring—consider the decadent "loaded" fries with cheese, bacon, and pulled pork. **Known for:** substantial kids' menu; garlic and sweet potato fries; molten lava chocolate cake. ⑤ *Average main: $17* ⊠ *669 Main St.* ☎ *530/258–4226* ⊗ *Closed Mon. and Tues. No dinner Sun.*

🛏 Hotels

Antlers Motel

$ | HOTEL | A spotlessly clean, simple, and affordable option in downtown Chester, this homey, two-story motel is a handy base for exploring Warner Valley and the southern end of Lassen Park Highway. **Pros:** reasonable rates; coffeemakers and refrigerators in every room; short walk to restaurants and bars. **Cons:** no breakfast; basic decor; parking tight when motel is fully booked. ⑤ *Rooms from: $90* ⊠ *268 Main St.* ☎ *530/258–2722* ⊕ *www.antlersmotel.com* ⊃ *20 rooms* ⊘ *No meals.*

Mineral

58 miles east of Redding, 42 miles east of Red Bluff.

Fewer than 200 people live in Mineral, which serves as Lassen Volcanic National Park's official address.

GETTING HERE AND AROUND

Reach the park's southern entrance by turning north off Highway 36 onto Highway 89. Access the northwest entrance via Highway 44 from Redding. No buses serve the area.

Lassen Volcanic National Park

👁 Sights

★ Lassen Volcanic National Park

NATIONAL/STATE PARK | A plug dome, Lassen Peak is the main focus of Lassen Volcanic National Park, but this 166-square-mile tract of coniferous forests and alpine meadows also abounds with memorable opportunities for hiking, camping, and wildlife photography. The famed peak began erupting in May 1914, sending pumice, rock, and snow thundering down the mountain and gas and hot ash billowing into the atmosphere. Lassen's most spectacular outburst occurred in 1915, when it blew a cloud of ash almost 6 miles high. The resulting mudflow destroyed vegetation for miles, and the evidence is still visible today. The volcano finally came to rest in 1921 but is not considered dormant: frothy mud pots, steamy fumaroles, and boiling springs create a fascinating if dangerous landscape that can be viewed throughout the park, especially via a hiked descent into Bumpass Hell. Because of its significance as a volcanic landscape, Lassen became a national park in 1916. Several volcanoes—the largest of which is now Lassen Peak—have been active in the area for roughly 600,000 years. Lassen Park Road (the continuation of Highway 89 within the park) and numerous hiking trails provide access to many of these wonders. The café at the main Kohm Yah-mah-nee Visitor Center, in the park's southern section, serves pizza, salads, sandwiches, burgers, and the like, along with coffee, hot cocoa, beer (some of it from local producer Lassen Ale Works), and wine. Although the Dixie Fire of 2021 ravaged more than half the park, the visitor center, Bumpass Trail, and other popular spots survived. ⚠ **Heed signs warning visitors to stay on the trails and railed boardwalks to avoid falling into boiling water or through thin-crusted areas.** ✉ *Mineral* ☎ *530/595–4480* ⊕ *www.nps.gov/lavo* 🚗 *$30 car, $25 motorcycle, $15 person not in motor vehicle (fees good for 7 days)* 🕐 *Visitor center closed Mon. and Tues. Nov.–Apr. except Mon. nat'l holidays.*

Sulphur Works Thermal Area

NATURE SITE | **FAMILY** | Proof of Lassen Peak's volatility becomes evident shortly after you enter the park at the southwest entrance. Sidewalks skirt boiling springs and sulfur-emitting steam vents. This area is usually the last site to close in winter, but even when the road is closed, you can access the area via a 2-mile round-trip hike through the snow. ✉ *Lassen Park Hwy., Lassen Volcanic National Park* ⊹ *1 mile from southwest entrance.*

🍴 Restaurants

★ Highlands Ranch Restaurant and Bar

$$$ | **AMERICAN** | Dining at the Highlands Ranch Resort's contemporary roadhouse restaurant is in a stained-wood, high-ceilinged indoor space or out on the deck, which has views of a serene meadow and the hillside beyond. Among the few sophisticated eating options within Lassen Volcanic National Park's orbit, the restaurant serves updated classics like rib-eye steak (up to 24 ounces), balsamic-marinated Muscovy duck, and blackened ahi. **Known for:** striking views inside and out; small plates and burgers in the bar; inventive sauces and preparations. 💲*Average main: $32* ✉ *41515 Hwy. 36, Mill Creek* ☎ *530/595–3388* ⊕ *www.highlandsranchresort.com/restaurant* 🕐 *Closed Mon. Wed. Nov.–late May.*

🛏 Hotels

★ Highlands Ranch Resort

$$$ | **B&B/INN** | On a gorgeous 175-acre alpine meadow 10 miles from Lassen's southwest entrance, this cluster of smartly designed upscale bungalows is peaceful and luxurious. **Pros:** stunning views; most luxurious accommodations near the park; friendly and helpful staff. **Cons:** pricey for the area; remote location; books up months ahead for summer stays. $ Rooms from: $299 ✉ 41515 Hwy. 36, Mill Creek ☎ 530/595–3388 ⊕ www.highlandsranchresort.com ☽ Closed Mon.–Wed. Nov.–late May ⇆ 7 cottages ⦿ Free breakfast.

Mill Creek Resort

$ | RESORT | FAMILY | Set amid towering evergreens in a tranquil patch of Lassen National Forest, this delightfully unfussy 1930s cabin and camping resort feels as though it could be inside the national park, although it's actually about 10 miles south, on a scenic country road. **Pros:** utterly peaceful, wooded setting; one of the closest lodging options to Lassen's southwest entrance; old-fashioned, family-friendly summer-camp vibe. **Cons:** remote location is a bit of a drive from other restaurants and services; bedrooms and bathrooms in each cabin are quite cozy; there's no cell reception or Wi-Fi (although cell phones work 2 miles away). $ Rooms from: $120 ✉ 40271 Hwy. 172, Mill Creek ☎ 530/595–4449 ⊕ www.millcreekresort.net ☽ Closed mid-Oct.–Apr. ⇆ 9 cabins ⦿ No meals.

Activities

★ Bumpass Hell Trail

TRAIL | FAMILY | This 3-mile round-trip hike leads to arguably the park's most mesmerizing feature, a wondrous landscape of hydrothermal activity characterized by boiling springs, hissing steam vents, and roiling gray mud pots. Allow two hours to complete the loop, which involves a gradual 300-foot descent into the Bumpass Hell basin, and be sure to venture to the basin's several upper viewpoints, which provide amazing views of the entire scene. Stay on trails and boardwalks near the thermal areas, as what appears to be firm ground may be only a thin crust over scalding mud. From the basin, you have the option of continuing another 1.9 miles along a scenic ridge to Cold Boiling Lake, from which you can trek farther to Kings Creek Picnic Area or Crumbaugh Lake. *Moderate.* ✉ *Lassen Park Hwy., Lassen*

Volcanic National Park ✛ Trailhead: 6 miles from southwest entrance.

★ Lassen Peak Trail

TRAIL | This trail winds 2½ miles to the mountaintop. It's a tough climb—2,000 feet uphill on a steady, steep grade—but the reward is a spectacular view. At the peak you can see into the rim and view the entire park (and much of California's Far North). Give yourself about five hours to complete this climb, and bring sunscreen, water, snacks, a first-aid kit, and a jacket—it can be windy and cold at the summit. *Difficult.* ✉ *Lassen Park Hwy., Lassen Volcanic National Park* ✛ *Trailhead: 7 miles north of southwest entrance.*

Burney

62 miles southeast of Mt. Shasta, 41 miles north of Lassen Volcanic National Park.

One of the most spectacular sights in the Far North is Burney Falls, where countless ribbon-like streams pour from moss-covered crevices. The park's beauty is well worth the trek along two forested highways.

GETTING HERE AND AROUND

To get to the falls, head east off I–5 on Highway 89 at Mt. Shasta. From Redding, head east on Highway 299 to Highway 89; follow signs 6 miles to the park.

Sights

★ McArthur–Burney Falls Memorial State Park

NATIONAL/STATE PARK | FAMILY | Just inside this park's southern boundary, Burney Creek wells up from the ground and divides into two falls that cascade over a 129-foot cliff into a pool below. Countless ribbon-like streams pour from hidden moss-covered crevices; resident bald eagles are frequently

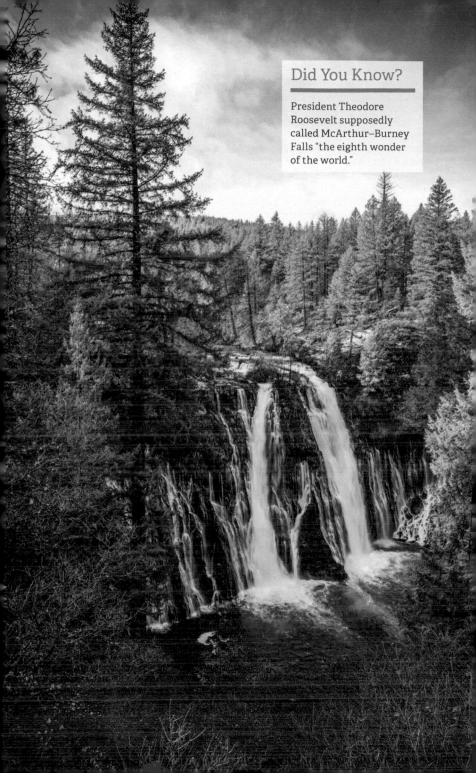

seen soaring overhead. You can walk a self-guided nature trail that descends to the foot of the falls, which Theodore Roosevelt—according to legend—called "the eighth wonder of the world." On warm days, swim at Lake Britton; lounge on the beach; rent motorboats, paddleboats, and canoes; or relax at one of the campsites or picnic areas. ⊠ *24898 Hwy. 89, 6 miles north of Hwy. 299, Burney* ☎ *530/335–2777* ⊕ *www.burneyfallspark. org* ⊠ *$10 per vehicle, day-use.*

Tulelake

89 miles from Burney, 85 miles from Mt. Shasta City.

Lava Beds National Monument, the chief attraction of Tulelake, is so far north that one of the two main routes to it briefly passes into Oregon before looping back south into California. Stunning underground lava tube caves make the trip to this off-the-beaten-path geological site well worth the detour.

GETTING HERE AND AROUND

From McArthur-Burney state park, take Highway 89 south to Highway 299 east to Bieber-Lookout Road and Highway 139 north. At Forest Service Rte. 97 turn left (west) and follow signs. From Mt. Shasta City, take Highway 89 to Forest Service Routes 97 and 10. There's no public transportation.

Sights

★ Lava Beds National Monument

NATURE SITE | FAMILY | Thousands of years of volcanic activity created this rugged landscape, distinguished by cinder cones, lava flows, spatter cones, pit craters, and more than 400 underground lava tube caves. During the Modoc War (1872–73), Modoc Indians under the leadership of their chief "Captain Jack" Kintpuash took refuge in a natural lava fortress now known as Captain Jack's Stronghold. They managed to hold off U.S. Army forces, which outnumbered them 20 to 1, for five months. When exploring this area, be sure to wear hard-soled boots and a bump hat. Bring a flashlight with you, although some are available for borrowing at the Indian Well Visitor Center, at the park's southern end. This is the departure point for summer activities such as guided walks, cave tours, and campfire programs. As you drive through Lava Beds you may see the effects of a 2020 wildfire that destroyed more than half the monument, though not its main attractions. ■ **TIP➜ Lava Beds is extremely remote; visit the website for detailed driving instructions.** ⊠ *1 Indian Well, Tulelake* ⊹ *Take Forest Rte. 97 to Forest Rte. 10* ☎ *530/667–8113* ⊕ *www.nps.gov/labe* ⊠ *$25 per vehicle, good for 7 days.*

Index

508

510

Photo Credits

Fodor's NORTHERN CALIFORNIA

Publisher: Stephen Horowitz, *General Manager*

Editorial: Douglas Stallings, *Editorial Director*; Jill Fergus, Amanda Sadlowski, Caroline Trefler, *Senior Editors*; Kayla Becker, Alexis Kelly, *Editors;* Angelique Kennedy-Chavannes, *Assistant Editor*

Design: Tina Malaney, *Director of Design and Production*; Jessica Gonzalez, *Graphic Designer*

Production: Jennifer DePrima, *Editorial Production Manager*; Elyse Rozelle, *Senior Production Editor;* Monica White, *Production Editor*

Maps: Rebecca Baer, *Senior Map Editor*; Mark Stroud (Moon Street Cartography), David Lindroth, *Cartographers*

Photography: Viviane Teles, *Senior Photo Editor;* Namrata Aggarwal, Payal Gupta, Ashok Kumar, *Photo Editors;* Rebecca Rimmer, *Photo Production Associate;* Eddie Aldrete, *Photo Production Intern*

Business & Operations: Chuck Hoover, *Chief Marketing Officer*; Robert Ames, *Group General Manager*; Devin Duckworth, *Director of Print Publishing*

Public Relations and Marketing: Joe Ewaskiw, *Senior Director of Communications & Public Relations*

Fodors.com: Jeremy Tarr, *Editorial Director;* Rachael Levitt, *Managing Editor*

Technology: Jon Atkinson, *Director of Technology;* Rudresh Teotia, *Lead Developer*; Jacob Ashpis, *Content Operations Manager*

Writers: Andrew Collins, Cheryl Crabtree, Trevor Felch, Daniel Mangin, Monique Peterson, Coral Sisk, Ava Liang Zhao

Editor: Laura M. Kidder

Production Editor: Elyse Rozelle

16th Edition

ISBN 978-1-64097-417-3

ISSN 1543–1045

All details in this book are based on information supplied to us at press time. Always confirm information when it matters, especially if you're making a detour to visit a specific place. Fodor's expressly disclaims any liability, loss, or risk, personal or otherwise, that is incurred as a consequence of the use of any of the contents of this book.

SPECIAL SALES

This book is available at special discounts for bulk purchases for sales promotions or premiums. For more information, e-mail SpecialMarkets@fodors.com.

PRINTED IN THE UNITED STATES OF AMERICA

10 9 8 7 6 5 4 3 2 1

About Our Writers

 Native Californian **Cheryl Crabtree** has worked as a freelance writer since 1987 and regularly travels up, down, and around the state for work and fun. She has contributed to *Fodor's California* since 2003, and she also contributes regularly to the *Fodor's Oahu* and *National Parks* guides. Cheryl is editor of *Montecito Magazine* and co-author of *The California Directory of Fine Wineries* hardcover book series (Napa-Sonoma and Central Coast editions). Her articles have appeared in many regional and national magazines, and she has also authored travel apps for mobile devices and content for travel websites. For this edition, Cheryl updated the Monterey Bay Area, Sequoia and Kings Canyon National Parks, Yosemite National Park, Eastern Sierra, and Lake Tahoe chapters.

 Daniel Mangin has been a Fodor's Travel writer and editor for more than a quarter century. The author of all four editions of *Fodor's Napa and Sonoma,* he has also written about wine and wineries for *The California Directory of Fine Wineries, Napa Valley Life,* and other print and online outlets. For this edition, Daniel updated the Travel Smart, Northern California's Best Road Trips, Napa and Sonoma, Sacramento and the Gold Country, North Coast, and Far North chapters.

Our San Francisco chapter was updated by a team of Fodor's San Francisco writers: **Trevor Felch, Monique Peterson, Coral Sisk,** and **Ava Liang Zhao.**

The Redwood National and State Parks chapter was updated by **Andrew Collins.**